World Cultures

AND

GEOGRAPHY

McDOUGAL LITTELL

World Cultures
AND
GEOGRAPHY

Sarah Witham Bednarz

Inés M. Miyares

Mark C. Schug

Charles S. White

McDougal Littell

Evanston, Illinois • Boston • Dallas

Senior Consultants

Sarah Witham Bednarz is associate professor of geography at Texas A&M University, where she has taught since 1988. She earned a Ph.D. in educational curriculum and instruction in 1992 from Texas A&M University and has written extensively about geography literacy and education. Dr. Bednarz was an author of *Geography for Life: National Geography Standards,* 1994. In 1997 she received the International Excellence Award from the Texas A&M University International Programs Office.

Inés M. Miyares is associate professor of geography at Hunter College–City University of New York. Born in Havana, Cuba, and fluent in Spanish, Dr. Miyares has focused much of her scholarship on Latin America, immigration and refugee policy, and urban ethnic geography. She holds a Ph.D. in geography from Arizona State University. In 1999 Dr. Miyares was the recipient of the Hunter College Performance Excellence Award for excellence in teaching, research, scholarly writing, and service.

Mark C. Schug is director of the University of Wisconsin–Milwaukee Center for Economic Education. A 30-year veteran of middle school, high school, and university classrooms, Dr. Schug has been cited for excellence in teaching by the University of Wisconsin–Milwaukee and the Minnesota Council on Economic Education. In addition to coauthoring eight national economics curriculum programs, Dr. Schug has spoken on economic issues to audiences throughout the world. Dr. Schug edited *The Senior Economist* for the National Council for Economics Education from 1986 to 1996.

Charles S. White is associate professor in the School of Education at Boston University, where he teaches methods of instruction in social studies. Dr. White has written and spoken extensively on the role of technology in social studies education. He has received numerous awards for his scholarship, including the 1995 Federal Design Achievement Award from the National Endowment for the Arts, for the Teaching with Historic Places project. In 1997, Dr. White taught his Models of Teaching doctoral course at the Universidad San Francisco de Quito, Ecuador.

Acknowledgments begin on page R50.

ISBN 0-618-16841-9

Printed in the United States of America
4 5 6 7 8 9 – VJM – 07 06 05 04 03

Consultants and Reviewers

Content Consultants

Charmarie Blaisdell
Department of History
Northeastern University
Boston, Massachusetts

David Buck, Ph.D.
Department of History
University of Wisconsin–Milwaukee
Milwaukee, Wisconsin

Erich Gruen, Ph.D.
Departments of Classics and History
University of California, Berkeley
Berkeley, California

Charles Haynes, Ph.D.
Senior Scholar for Religious Freedom
The Freedom Forum First
    Amendment Center
Arlington, Virginia

Alusine Jalloh, Ph.D.
The Africa Program
University of Texas at Arlington
Arlington, Texas

Shabbir Mansuri
Council on Islamic Education
Fountain Valley, California

Michelle Maskiell, Ph.D.
Department of History
Montana State University
Bozeman, Montana

Vasudha Narayanan, Ph.D.
Department of Religion
University of Florida
Gainesville, Florida

Amanda Porterfield, Ph.D.
Department of Religious Studies
University of Wyoming
Laramie, Wyoming

Mark Wasserman, Ph.D.
Department of History
Rutgers University
New Brunswick, New Jersey

Multicultural Advisory Board

Dr. Munir Bashshur
Education Department
American University of Beirut
Beirut, Lebanon

Stephen Fugita
Ethnic Studies Program
Santa Clara University
Santa Clara, California

Sharon Harley
Afro-American Studies Program
University of Maryland at
    College Park
College Park, Maryland

Doug Monroy
Department of Southwest Studies
Colorado College
Colorado Springs, Colorado

Cliff Trafzer
Departments of History and
    Ethnic Studies
University of California, Riverside
Riverside, California

UNIT 1 Introduction to World Cultures and Geography

Chapter 1   Welcome to the World

Chapter 2   The Geographer's World

UNIT 2

The United States and Canada

UNIT 4 — Europe, Russia, and the Independent Republics

 *continued from page ix*

UNIT 5 North Africa and Southwest Asia

UNIT 6 Africa South of the Sahara

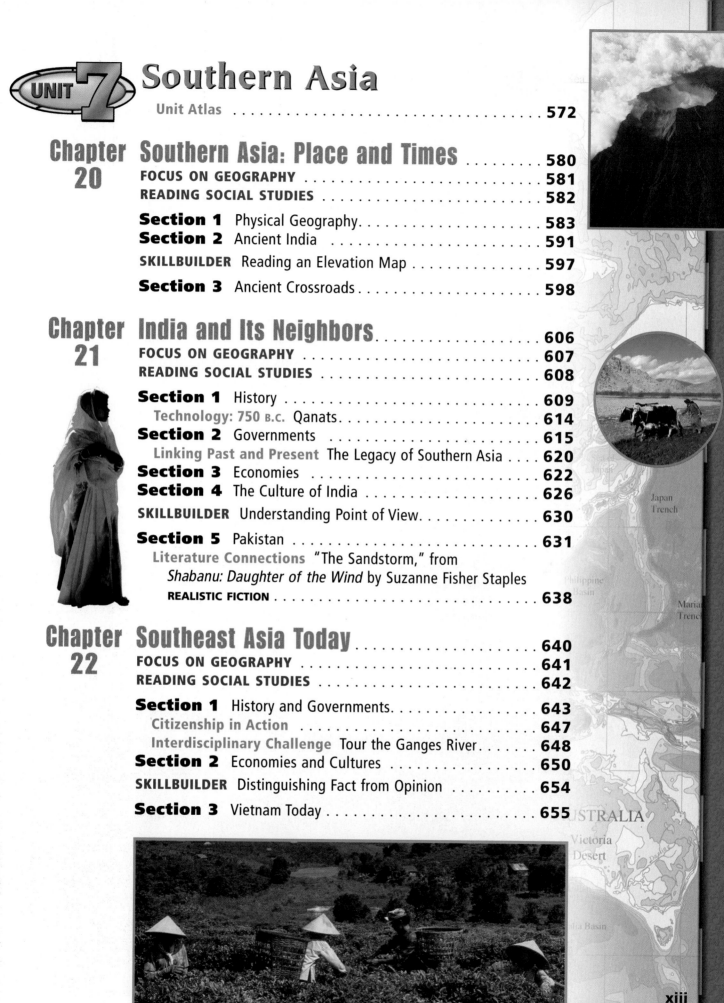

UNIT 8 East Asia, Australia, and the Pacific Islands

Features

Interdisciplinary Challenge

Infographics, Time Lines, and Cartoons

Literature Connections

Linking Past and Present

DATELINE

SKILLBUILDER

Citizenship IN ACTION

Strange but TRUE

Connections To...

Spotlight on CULTURE

Biography

FOCUS ON GEOGRAPHY

The WORLD'S HERITAGE

VOICES FROM . . .

MAPS

CHARTS, DIAGRAMS, AND GRAPHS

This section will help you develop and practice the skills you need to study social studies and to take standardized tests. Part 1, **Strategies for Studying Social Studies,** shows you the features of this book. It also shows you how to improve your reading and study skills.

Part 2, **Test-Taking Strategies and Practice,** gives you strategies to help you answer the different kinds of questions that appear on standardized tests. Each strategy is followed by a set of questions you can use for practice.

CONTENTS

Part 1: Strategies for Studying Social Studies

Reading is important in the study of social studies or any other subject. You can improve your reading skills by practicing certain strategies. Good reading skills help you remember more when you read. The next four pages show how some of the features of *World Cultures and Geography* can help you learn and understand social studies.

Preview Chapters Before You Read

Each chapter begins with a two-page chapter opener. Study these pages to help you get ready to read.

1 Read the chapter title. Read the section titles. These tell what topics will be covered in the chapter.

2 Look at the art and photographs. Use the illustrations to help you identify themes or messages of the chapter.

3 Study the **Focus on Geography** feature. Use the questions to help you think about the information you might find in the chapter.

CHAPTER 7

Mexico Today

SECTION 1   The Roots of Modern Mexico
SECTION 2   Government in Mexico: Revolution and Reform
SECTION 3   Mexico's Changing Economy
SECTION 4   Mexico's Culture Today

MEXICO
Mexico City

Place Mexico City's main plaza, the Zócalo, is the center of one of the world's largest cities.

FOCUS ON GEOGRAPHY

How has Mexico's lack of farmable land shaped how people live?

Human-Environment Interaction • Only 12 percent of Mexico's land is arable—that is, farmable. The rest is too steep and rocky or too dry. Even the land that people can farm is not always very productive. For example, flooding and lack of drainage can pose serious challenges. Also, some people do farm in mountainous regions, but planting and harvesting crops there can be very difficult.

What do you think?

- How do countries benefit economically from having a great deal of arable land?
- What challenges does Mexico face—in its economy and daily life—by having little arable land?

162 CHAPTER 7

Mexico Today 163

Preview Sections Before You Read

Each chapter has three, four, or five sections. These sections cover shorter time periods or certain themes.

1 Study the sentences under the headings **Main Idea** and **Why It Matters Now.** These headings tell what's important in the material you're about to read.

2 Look at the **Terms & Names** list. This list tells you what people and issues will be covered in the section.

3 Read the feature titled **Dateline.** It tells about a historical event as if it were happening today.

4 Skim the pages to see how the section is organized. Red headings are major topics. Blue headings are smaller topics or subtopics. The headings provide an outline of the section.

5 Skim the pages of the section to find key words. These words will often be in **boldface** type. Use the **Vocabulary** notes in the margin to help you with unfamiliar terms.

TERMS & NAMES
peninsulares
criollos
mestizo
encomienda
Father Miguel Hidalgo
Treaty of Guadalupe Hidalgo
Gadsden Purchase

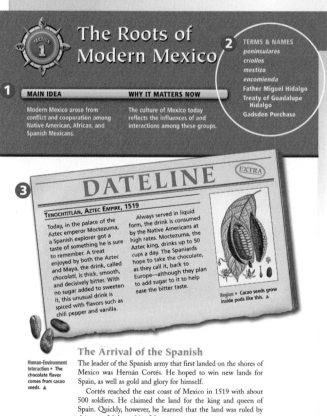

The Roots of Modern Mexico

SECTION 1

2 TERMS & NAMES
péninsulares
criollos
mestizo
encomienda
Father Miguel Hidalgo
Treaty of Guadalupe Hidalgo
Gadsden Purchase

1 MAIN IDEA

Modern Mexico arose from conflict and cooperation among Native American, African, and Spanish Mexicans.

WHY IT MATTERS NOW

The culture of Mexico today reflects the influences of and interactions among these groups.

3 DATELINE (EXTRA)

TENOCHTITLÁN, AZTEC EMPIRE, 1519

Today, in the palace of the Aztec emperor Moctezuma, a Spanish explorer got a taste of something he is sure to remember. A treat enjoyed by both the Aztec and Maya, the drink, called *chocolatl*, is thick, smooth, and decisively bitter. With no sugar added to sweeten it, this unusual drink is spiced with flavors such as chili pepper and vanilla.

Always served in liquid form, the drink is consumed by the Native Americans at high rates. Moctezuma, the Aztec king, drinks up to 50 cups a day. The Spaniards hope to take the chocolate, as they call it, back to Europe—although they plan to add sugar to it to help ease the bitter taste.

Region • Cacao seeds grow inside pods like this. ▲

Human-Environment Interaction • The chocolate flavor comes from cacao seeds. ▲

The Arrival of the Spanish

The leader of the Spanish army that first landed on the shores of Mexico was Hernán Cortés. He hoped to win new lands for Spain, as well as gold and glory for himself.

Cortés reached the east coast of Mexico in 1519 with about 500 soldiers. He claimed the land for the king and queen of Spain. Quickly, however, he learned that the land was ruled by the powerful Aztec king Moctezuma.

Mexico Today **165**

4 A Clash of Cultures

Moctezuma ruled an empire of between 10 million and 25 million people. However, many of his Native American subjects wanted to be free. They helped the Spanish conquer the Aztec king. They did not expect that the Spanish would become their new rulers.

The First Encounter When Moctezuma heard about the arrival of the Spanish, he welcomed Cortés with gifts. He even allowed Cortés to stay in a royal palace in the Aztec capital, Tenochtitlán. Within a week, Cortés took Moctezuma prisoner—and took control of the Aztec Empire.

The Spanish Takeover Other Aztec leaders drove the Spanish from Tenochtitlán. However, during the fighting that followed, Moctezuma was killed. The Spanish then retook the city, greatly aided by their Native American allies. The Spanish also had an essential advantage over the Aztec: their weapons. The Aztec had only war clubs, spears, and arrows. The Spanish soldiers had steel swords, armor, guns, and cannons, as well as horses. The invading army destroyed Tenochtitlán street by street.

Culture • Aztec feather shields offered less protection than Spanish metal helmets and armor. ▲

Reading **Social Studies**
A. Analyzing Motives Why did some Native Americans help the Spanish fight the Aztec?

The Founding of New Spain

The fall of Tenochtitlán in 1521 marked the end of the Aztec empire and the beginning of Spanish rule in Mexico. The Spanish called their empire "New Spain," just as the English called their territory in North America "New England." Where Tenochtitlán had stood, the Spanish established Mexico City as their capital. Spain ruled Mexico for the next 300 years.

A New Way of Life The Spanish victory caused more than a change of rulers in Mexico. The Spanish introduced a different way of life into the region. They brought new animals, such as horses, cattle, sheep, and pigs. They also brought new trades, such as ironsmithing and shipbuilding. They brought a new religion as well—Christianity.

Connections to Science

Invisible Weapons Smallpox and other diseases from Europe killed millions of Native Americans between 1500 and 1900. Smallpox (germ cell shown below) had long been widespread in Europe, and most Europeans were at least partly immune. Native Americans, however, had no immunity to it because it had never before existed in the Americas.

Within months of the Spanish soldiers' arrival in Mexico, many thousands of Native Americans got sick with smallpox (shown below) and died from it—including Moctezuma's successor. Smallpox proved far more deadly to Native Americans than Spanish swords and cannons.

Vocabulary **5**
ironsmithing: making items out of iron

166 CHAPTER 7

Use Active Reading Strategies As You Read

Now you're ready to read the chapter. Read one section at a time, from beginning to end.

1 Begin by looking at the **Reading Social Studies** page. Consider the questions under the **Before You Read** heading. Think about what you know already about the chapter topic and what you'd like to learn.

2 Review the suggestions in the **Read and Take Notes** section. These will help you understand and remember the information in the chapter.

3 Ask and answer questions as you read. Look for the **Reading Social Studies** questions in the margin. Answering these questions will show whether you understand what you've just read.

4 Study the **Background** notes in the margin for additional information on people, places, events, or ideas discussed in the chapter.

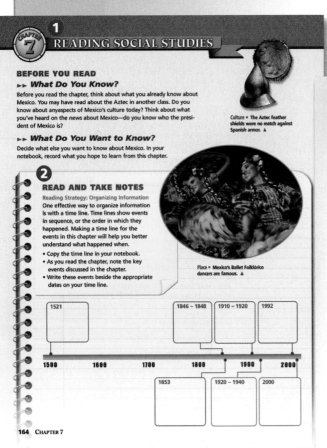

CHAPTER 7 — READING SOCIAL STUDIES

BEFORE YOU READ

▶▶ **What Do You Know?**

Before you read the chapter, think about what you already know about Mexico. You may have read about the Aztec in another class. Do you know about any aspects of Mexico's culture today? Think about what you've heard on the news about Mexico—do you know who the president of Mexico is?

▶▶ **What Do You Want to Know?**

Decide what else you want to know about Mexico. In your notebook, record what you hope to learn from this chapter.

Culture • The Aztec feather shields were no match against Spanish armor. ▲

2
READ AND TAKE NOTES

Reading Strategy: Organizing Information
One effective way to organize information is with a time line. Time lines show events in sequence, or the order in which they happened. Making a time line for the events in this chapter will help you better understand what happened when.

• Copy the time line in your notebook.
• As you read the chapter, note the key events discussed in the chapter.
• Write these events beside the appropriate dates on your time line.

Place • Mexico's Ballet Folklórico dancers are famous. ▲

| 1521 | | 1846 – 1848 | 1910 – 1920 | 1992 |

| 1500 | 1600 | 1700 | 1800 | 1900 | 2000 |

| 1853 | 1920 – 1940 | 2000 |

164 CHAPTER 7

Reading Social Studies

B. Clarifying
What ideas from other parts of the world did Mexicans agree with?

Population of Mexico in 1810

- Native American
- Criollo
- Mestizo
- Peninsular
- African

0.3%
0.2%
12.8%
19.8%
66.9%

SKILLBUILDER: Reading a Graph
1. What percentage of the Mexican population in 1810 was Native American?
2. Were there more *peninsulares* or *criollos* in Mexico in 1810?

A fourth group of people arrived in Mexico unwillingly—the enslaved Africans brought by European slave ships. African farming techniques, musical traditions, and crafts soon blended into the Mexican culture.

Encomienda New Spain's largest group were Native Americans. They made up the bottom layer of society. The rulers of Spain established in Mexico a system called **encomienda** (en-coh-mee-AYN-duh). Under this system, Spanish men were each given a Native American village to oversee. The villagers had to pay tribute—in goods, money, or labor—to this Spaniard. They were essentially enslaved. The results of their labor helped to make Spain rich. However, the villagers lived in poverty and hardship.

Vocabulary
tribute:
a forced payment

The War of Independence

By 1800, political writers in Europe and the United States were saying that people should be free to choose their own governments. Many Mexican religious and political leaders agreed. They argued that Mexico should be independent from Spain. The demand for Mexican independence grew stronger after 1808, when France conquered Spain.

Reading Social Studies **3**
B. Clarifying
What ideas from other parts of the world did Mexicans agree with?

A Cry for Freedom Then, before dawn on September 16, 1810, the farmers in the mountain village of Dolores heard their church bells ringing. At the church their priest, **Father Miguel Hidalgo**, gave a fiery speech urging them to throw off Spanish rule. No one knows the exact text of the speech, but it is known as the *Grito de Dolores* (Cry of Dolores). Urged on by his words, a small army of Native Americans and *mestizos* marched with Father Hidalgo toward Mexico City. Along the way, thousands more joined them.

BACKGROUND **4**
Although *dolores* means "sorrow" in Spanish, here it is a reference to the town of Dolores.

A Difficult Challenge Father Hidalgo's army had few weapons. Mostly, his men carried clubs and farm tools, such as sickles and axes. When they faced the government soldiers, the farmers were soon defeated. Father Hidalgo was captured and executed. But the revolution he had sparked did not die.

Vocabulary
sickle:
a blade used for cutting tall grass or grain

168 CHAPTER 7

BACKGROUND

Although *dolores* means "sorrow" in Spanish, here it is a reference to the town of Dolores.

Review and Summarize What You Have Read

When you finish reading a section, review and summarize the information you have learned. Reread any information that is still unclear.

1 Look again at the red and blue headings for a quick summary of the section.

2 Study the photographs, maps, charts, graphs, and illustrated features in the section. Think about how these visuals relate to the information you've learned.

3 Answer the questions in the **Assessment** section. This will help you think critically about what you've just read.

1 **The Influence of the Church**

Because the Catholic Church was powerful in Spain, it soon became powerful in New Spain. Catholic priests set up churches, schools, and hospitals. Sometimes Native Americans accepted Christianity willingly. Sometimes, though, they were forced to become Christian against their will.

A Cultural Blend Even though the Native Americans had to accept many new ways of life, the old ways were not lost. For instance, an essential element of Native American cooking was the *tortilla*, a flat, round bread made from corn or flour. *Tortillas* are still made daily all over Mexico. As with food, many other aspects of the two cultures blended in the new Mexican culture.

Life in New Spain

A new multilayered society developed in Mexico. The ruling class were Spanish officials who were born in Spain. They were called *peninsulares* (pen·in·soo·LAR·ays) because they were from the Iberian Peninsula in Europe.

BACKGROUND
The Iberian Peninsula consists of two countries—Portugal and Spain. (See the map of Europe on page 252.)

A second class were *criollos* (cree·OH·yohs), people who were born in Mexico but whose parents were born in Spain. *Criollos* were often wealthy and powerful, but they were not in the same social class as the *peninsulares.*

A *mestizo* (mess·TEE·zoe) is a person who is of mixed European and Native American ancestry. *Mestizos* formed the third layer of New Spain's society.

Movement • Mexicans today celebrate Catholic holy days that the Spanish established. This festival honors Our Lady of Guadalupe. ▼

Mexico Today **167**

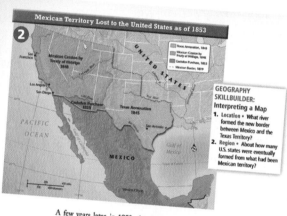

Mexican Territory Lost to the United States as of 1853

Texas Annexation, 1845
Mexican Cession by Treaty of Hidalgo, 1848
Gadsden Purchase, 1853
Mexican Border, 1819

GEOGRAPHY SKILLBUILDER: Interpreting a Map
1. **Location •** What river formed the new border between Mexico and the Texas Territory?
2. **Region •** About how many U.S. states were eventually formed from what had been Mexican territory?

A few years later, in 1853, the **Gadsden Purchase** gave the United States more of Mexico's northern land. The two countries have since made slight adjustments to the border, but they have not fought a war again.

SECTION 1 ASSESSMENT

Terms & Names
1. Identify:
(a) peninsulares
(b) criollos
(c) mestizo
(d) encomienda
(e) Father Miguel Hidalgo
(f) Treaty of Guadalupe Hidalgo
(g) Gadsden Purchase

Taking Notes
2. Use a chart like this one to list the five social groups that made up New Spain and their characteristics.

Social Group	Characteristics

Main Ideas
3. (a) What advantages allowed Cortés's small army to conquer Mexico?
(b) In what ways did Spanish rule change life in Mexico?
(c) What were the results of the war between Mexico and the United States?

Critical Thinking
4. **Analyzing Causes**
Why did Mexicans decide to fight for independence from Spain?

Think About
• influential events around the world
• reasons for discontent among the criollos, mestizos, and Native Americans

ACTIVITY -OPTION- Reread the information about the first meeting of the Spanish and Aztec. Write a short story describing the event from either the Spanish or Aztec viewpoint.

170 CHAPTER 7

Part 2: Test-Taking Strategies and Practice

Use the strategies in this section to improve your test-taking skills. First read the tips on the left page. Then use them to help you with the practice items on the right page.

Multiple Choice

A multiple-choice question is a question or incomplete sentence and a set of choices. One of the choices correctly answers the question or completes the sentence.

1 Read the question or incomplete sentence carefully. Try to answer the question before looking at the choices.

2 Look for key words in the question. They may help you figure out the correct answer.

3 Read each choice with the question. Don't decide on your final answer until you have read all the choices.

4 Rule out any choices that you know are wrong.

5 Watch answers with words like *all, never,* and *only.* These answers are often incorrect.

6 Sometimes the last choice is *All of the above.* Make sure that the other choices are all correct if you pick this answer.

7 Be careful with questions that include the word *not.*

1 **1** The Sahara is (mostly)

  A sand, rocks, and gravel.
  B boulders and sand.
  3 choices
  C cliffs and gulleys.
  D grasses and bushes. **4**

> **2** Words like *mostly* or *partly* are key words in multiple choice. Look for answers that are mostly true or partly true about the subject.

> **4** You know that if the Sahara is a desert, **D** is incorrect. A desert cannot be mostly covered with grass and bushes.

2 Over hundreds of years, Bantu people migrated from West Africa to

  A South and Southwest Asia.
  B (every) continent on earth.
  C East and South Africa.
  D (all) of North Africa and Arabia.

> **5** Watch for answers that have words like *all, never, always, every,* and *only.* These answers are often incorrect.

3 The people of West Africa passed on their history by

  A painting pictures.
  B telling stories.
  C creating dances.
  6 **D** All of the above

4 Which of the following is (not) one of the nations in southern Africa?

  A Zimbabwe
  B Nigeria
  C Mozambique
  D Namibia

> **7** First rule out all the answers that name southern African countries. The answer that remains is the correct choice.

answers: 1 (A); 2 (C); 3 (D); 4 (B)

Directions: Read each question carefully. Choose the *best* answer from the four choices.

1   Which of the following was *not* a result of the Black Death?

   A Cities worked together during the plague.

   B Europe lost one-third of its population.

   C The Church lost its prestige among the people.

   D The economies of many countries were ruined.

2   Martin Luther started a reform movement when he

   A published the New Testament in German.

   B criticized some of the Church's practices.

   C wrote his 95 Theses and made them public.

   D All of the above

3   The Ottoman Empire reached its greatest size and glory under the rule of

   A Mehmet II.

   B Selim the Grim.

   C Suleiman the Lawgiver.

   D Timur the Lame.

4   During the 1700s, England controlled which of the following?

   A the sugar trade

   B the Atlantic slave trade

   C the cotton trade

   D the coconut trade

Primary Sources

Sometimes you will need to look at a document to answer a question. Some documents are primary sources. Primary sources are written or made by people who either saw an event or were actually part of the event. A primary source can be a photograph, letter, diary, speech, or autobiography.

1 Look at the source line to learn about the document and its author. If the author is well known and has been quoted a lot, the information is probably true.

2 Skim the article to get an idea of what it is about.

3 Note any special punctuation. For example, ellipses (. . .) indicate that words and sentences have been left out.

4 Ask yourself questions about the document as you read.

5 Review the questions. This will give your reading a purpose and also help you find the answers more easily. Then reread the document.

Good Government

Chap 2.20 Lord Ji Kang asked, "What should I do in order to make the people respectful, loyal, and zealous [hard-working]?" The Master said: "Approach them with dignity and they will be respectful. Be yourself a good son and kind father, and they will be loyal. Raise the good and train the incompetent, and they will be zealous."

Chap. 13.2 Ran Yong (. . .) asked about government. The Master said: "Guide the officials. Forgive small mistakes. Promote [people] of talent." "How does one recognize that a [person] has talent and deserves to be promoted?" The Master said: "Promote those you know. Those whom you do not know will hardly remain ignored."

—The Analects of Confucius

> The *Analects* is a book of thoughts and ideas by Confucius. He was a scholar and teacher in ancient China.

1 Confucius is giving advice on

   A how to be a gentleman.

   B how to be a good ruler.

   C how to become wealthy.

   D how to raise a good family.

2 Which sentence *best* expresses the idea of these paragraphs?

   A The wise ruler governs people through fear.

   B People should obey their rulers no matter what.

   C A good ruler gives a lot of orders to people.

   D If rulers do things well, people will follow them.

answers: 1 (B); 2 (D)

For more test practice online . . .

TEST PRACTICE
CLASSZONE.COM

Directions: Read this passage from Magna Carta. Use the passage and your knowledge of social studies to answer the questions.

No constable or other bailiff [officer] . . . shall take anyone's grain or other chattels [property] without immediately paying for them in money. . . .

No sheriff or bailiff, or any one else, shall take horses or wagons of any free man . . . except on the permission of that free man.

Neither we nor our bailiffs will take the wood of another man for castles, or for anything else . . . except by the permission of him to whom the wood belongs. . . .

—Magna Carta (1215)

1 These paragraphs place limits on the

   A rights of the king.

   B powers of officials to take property.

   C rights of nobles to tax people.

   D power of Parliament.

2 The rights guaranteed by the Magna Carta are similar to those listed in the Bill of Rights of

   A France.

   B the Netherlands.

   C the United States.

   D Germany.

Secondary Sources

A secondary source is an account of events by a person who did not actually experience them. The author often uses information from several primary sources to write about a person or event. Biographies, many newspaper articles, and history books are examples of secondary sources.

1 Read the title to get an idea of what the passage is about. (The title here indicates that the passage is about a person named Malinche about whom people have different opinions.)

2 Skim the paragraphs to find the main idea of the passage.

3 Look for words that help you understand the order in which events happen.

4 Ask yourself questions as you read. (You might ask yourself: Why did people's opinions about Malinche change over time?)

5 Review the questions to see what information you will need to find. Then reread the passage.

1 **Malinche—Heroine or Traitor?**

No one knows much about Malinche's early life. People do know that in 1519 she met Hernán Cortés. The Spanish conquistador had landed in Mexico earlier that year. Malinche was only 15 years old. Even though she was very **2** young, Malinche helped Cortés conquer the Aztecs. She spoke the languages of the Aztec and the Maya. Over time, she learned Spanish. She translated for Cortés and advised him on Native American politics.

The Spanish conquistadors admired Malinche, calling **3** her Doña Marina. For many centuries, the Spanish people regarded her as a heroine. In the 1800s, however, Mexico won its independence from Spain. People rejected their Spanish rulers. Writers and artists started calling Malinche a traitor to her people. Today, however, she is seen as a heroine again. **4**

1 Which of the following statements about Malinche is an opinion?

> Remember that an opinion is a statement that cannot be proved. A fact is a statement that can be proved.

A She was very young when she met Cortés.

B She became a translator for Cortés.

C She was a traitor to her own people.

D She understood Native American politics.

2 Based on this source, which person or group would view Malinche as a heroine?

A a fighter for Mexican independence from Spain

B the soldiers and officers in Cortés's army

C the Aztec ruler and his court in Mexico

D an historian writing about Mexico in the 1800s

answers: 1 (C); 2 (B)

Directions: Read this passage. Use the passage and your knowledge of social studies to answer the questions.

Before World War I

In 1892, France and Russia had become military allies. Later, Germany signed an agreement to protect Austria. If any nation attacked Austria, Germany would fight on her side. France and Russia had to support each other as well. For instance, if France got into a war with Germany, Russia had to fight Germany, too. This meant that in any war, Germany would have to fight on two fronts: France on the west and Russia on the east.

If a war broke out, what part would England play? No one knew. She might remain neutral, like Belgium. She might, if given a reason, fight against Germany.

1 If Russia and Germany went to war, which country had to help Russia?

A England

B Belgium

C Austria

D France

2 When World War I broke out, what part did England play?

A She remained neutral, like Belgium.

B She sided with Germany and Austria.

C She joined France in fighting Germany.

D She fought Russia after its revolution.

Political Cartoons

Cartoonists who draw political cartoons use both words and art to express opinions about political issues.

1 Try to figure out what the cartoon is about. Titles and captions may give clues.

2 Use labels to help identify the people, places, and events represented in the cartoon.

3 Note when and where the cartoon was published.

4 Look for symbols—that is, people, places, or objects that stand for something else.

5 The cartoonist often exaggerates the physical features of people and objects. This technique will give you clues as to how the cartoonist feels about the subject.

6 Try to figure out the cartoonist's message and summarize it in a sentence.

1 NEXT!

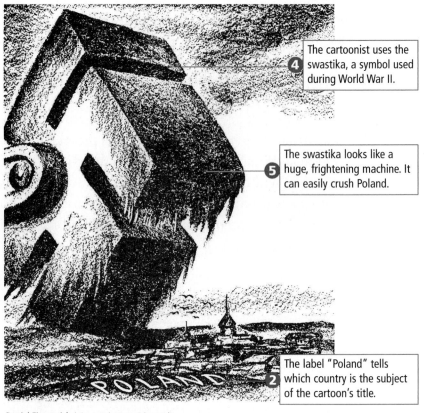

4 The cartoonist uses the swastika, a symbol used during World War II.

5 The swastika looks like a huge, frightening machine. It can easily crush Poland.

2 The label "Poland" tells which country is the subject of the cartoon's title.

Daniel Fitzpatrick / *St. Louis Post-Dispatch,* August 24, 1939.

3 The date is a clue that the cartoon refers to the beginning of World War II.

1 What does the swastika in the cartoon stand for?

A the Soviet Union

B Nazi Germany

C the Polish army

D the Austrian military

6 2 Which sentence *best* summarizes the cartoonist's message?

A Germany will attack Poland next.

B Poland should stop Germany.

C Germany will lose this battle.

D Poland will fight a civil war.

answers: 1 (B); 2 (A)

Directions: Study this cartoon. Use the cartoon and your knowledge of social studies to answer the questions.

Steve Sack, *Minneapolis Star-Tribune,* January 1, 1992.

1   How has the cartoonist drawn this leader?

   A As Count Dracula
   B As Darth Vader
   C As Frankenstein's monster
   D As a military leader

2   Notice all the "MADE IN" labels on the leader. The *best* title for the cartoon would be

   A "A Monster Never Sleeps."
   B "The Monster of Iraq."
   C "They've Made a Mistake."
   D "They've Created a Monster."

Charts

Charts present facts in a visual form. History textbooks use several different types of charts. The chart that is most often found on standardized tests is the table. A table organizes information in columns and rows.

❶ Read the title of the chart to find out what information is represented.

❷ Read the headings at the top of each column. Then read the headings at the left of each row.

❸ Notice how the information in the chart is organized.

❹ Compare the information from column to column and row to row.

❺ Try to draw conclusions from the information in the chart.

❻ Read the questions and then study the chart again.

❶ This chart is about the number of people who immigrated to different countries.

❹ Notice that different years are used for different countries.

Immigration to Selected Countries		
❷ Country	Years	Number of Immigrants
Argentina	1856-1932	6,405,000
Australia	1861-1932	2,913,000
Brazil	1821-1932	4,431,000
British West Indies	1836-1932	1,587,000
Canada	1821-1932	5,206,000
Cuba	1901-1932	857,000
Mexico	1911-1931	226,000
New Zealand	1851-1932	594,000
South Africa	1881-1932	852,000
United States	1821-1932	34,244,000
Uruguay	1836-1932	713,000

Source: Alfred W. Crosby, Jr. *The Columbian Exchange: Biological and Cultural Consequences of 1492*

❸ This chart lists countries in alphabetical order. Other charts organize information by years or by numbers.

❺ Of all the countries listed, six received the most immigrants. Think about what these countries have in common.

1 The country that received the most immigrants was
A Canada.
B the British West Indies.
❻ C the United States.
D Brazil.

2 Different countries received immigrants in different years. Which countries received immigrants the earliest?
A Argentina, New Zealand, and Canada
B Canada, Brazil, and United States
C Mexico, United States, and British West Indies
D Brazil, South Africa, and Cuba

answers: 1 (C); 2 (B)

For more test practice online . . .
TEST PRACTICE
CLASSZONE.COM

Directions: Read the chart carefully. Use the chart and your knowledge of social studies to answer the questions.

Ancient Civilizations				
Feature	China	Egypt	Indus Valley	Mesopotamia
Location	River valley	River valley	River valley	River valley
Period	2000 B.C.-400 B.C.	3200 B.C.-600 B.C.	2500 B.C.-1500 B.C.	3500 B.C.-2000 B.C.
Specialized workers	Priests; government workers, soldiers; craft workers in bronze and silk; farmers	Priests; government workers, scribes, soldiers; workers in pottery, stone; farmers	Government officials; priests; workers in pottery, bricks; farmers	Priests; government officials, scribes, and soldiers; workers in pottery, textiles; farmers
Institutions	Walled cities; oracle-bone reading	Ruling class of priests, nobles; education system	Strong central government	Ruling class of priests and nobles; education for scribes
Record keeping	Pictographic writing	Hieroglyphic writing	Pictographic writing	Cuneiform writing
Advanced technology and artifacts	Writing; making bronze and silk; irrigation systems	Papyrus; mathematics; astronomy, engineering; pyramids; mummification; medicine	Irrigation systems; indoor plumbing; seals	Wheel; plow; sailboat; bronze weapons

1 Which civilization appeared first?

A China

B Egypt

C Indus Valley

D Mesopotamia

2 The Indus Valley civilization did *not* have

A an irrigation system.

B walled cities.

C government officials.

D indoor plumbing.

Line and Bar Graphs

Graphs are often used to show numbers. Line graphs often show changes over time. Bar graphs make it easy to compare numbers.

1 Read the title of the graph to find out what information is represented.

2 Study the labels on the graph.

3 Look at the source line that tells where the graph is from. Decide whether you can depend on the source to provide reliable information.

4 See if you can make any generalizations about the information in the graph. Note whether the numbers change over time.

5 Read the questions carefully and then study the graph again.

1 **Exports of English Manufactured Goods, 1699–1774**

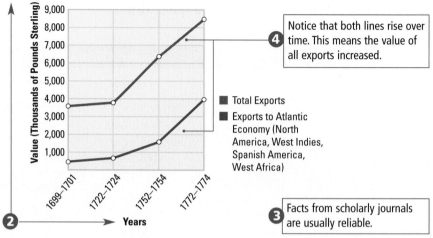

Notice that both lines rise over time. This means the value of all exports increased. **4**

Facts from scholarly journals are usually reliable. **3**

Source: R. Davis, "English Foreign Trade, 1700–1774," *Economic History Review* (1962)

5 **1** Which of the following is a true statement?

A Exports to the New World declined over time.

B Total exports stayed the same over time.

C Total exports rose sharply after 1724.

D Exports to the New World fell sharply after 1754.

1 **Nations with High Foreign Debt, 1998**

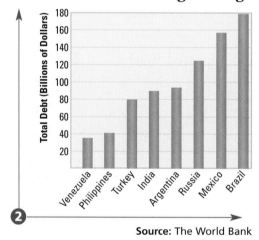

Source: The World Bank

Facts from major organizations, such as the World Bank, usually are reliable. **3**

5 **2** The nation with the second largest foreign debt is

A Brazil.

B Argentina.

C Russia.

D Mexico.

answers: 1 (C); 2 (A)

Directions: Read the graphs carefully. Use the graphs and your knowledge of social studies to answer the questions.

Japan: Gross Domestic Product, 1983–1999

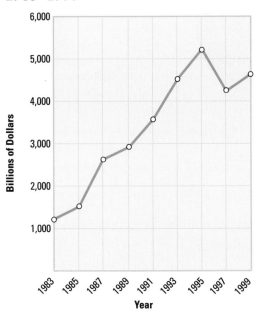

Source: *Annual Report on National Accounts 2001,* Cabinet Office of the Government of Japan

Unemployment Rates for Selected Countries, 2000

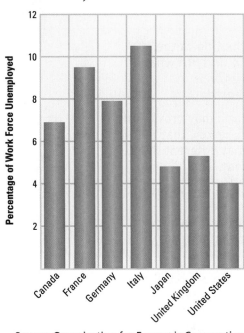

Source: Organization for Economic Cooperation and Development

1 Japan's gross domestic product grew in every period except

   A 1983 to 1985.

   B 1987 to 1989.

   C 1995 to 1997.

   D 1997 to 1999.

2 Which country had the highest unemployment rate in 2000?

   A Italy

   B France

   C Germany

   D Canada

Pie Graphs

A pie, or circle, graph shows the relationship among parts of a whole. These parts look like slices of a pie. Each slice is shown as a percentage of the whole pie.

1 Read the title of the chart to find out what information is represented.

2 The graph may provide a legend, or key, that tells you what different slices represent.

3 The size of the slice is related to the percentage. The larger the percentage, the larger the slice.

4 Look at the source line that tells where the graph is from. Ask yourself if you can depend on this source to provide reliable information.

5 Read the questions carefully, and study the graph again.

1 **World Population by Region, 2000**

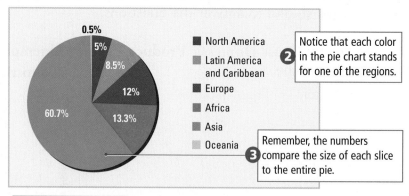

2 Notice that each color in the pie chart stands for one of the regions.

3 Remember, the numbers compare the size of each slice to the entire pie.

The Population Reference Bureau studies population data for the United States and other countries.

4 **Source:** Population Reference Bureau

1 Which region accounts for nearly two-thirds of the world's population?

A Africa

B North America

C Europe

D Asia

2 Two regions have nearly the same percentage of the world's population. They are

To answer this question, find the two percentages in the pie graph that are almost the same.

A Africa; Latin America and Caribbean.

B Europe; Africa.

C Latin America and Caribbean; Europe.

D North America; Europe.

answers: 1 (D); 2 (B)

Directions: Read the pie graph. Use the graph and your knowledge of social studies to answer the questions.

World Energy Consumption by Region

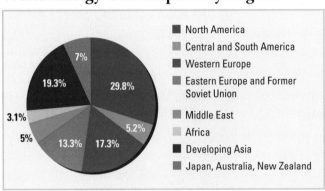

■ North America
■ Central and South America
■ Western Europe
■ Eastern Europe and Former Soviet Union
■ Middle East
■ Africa
■ Developing Asia
■ Japan, Australia, New Zealand

Source: "Earth Pulse," *National Geographic* (March 2001)

1 Which region uses the most energy?

A Western Europe

B Developing Asia

C North America

D Eastern Europe and Former Soviet Union

2 Japan, Australia, and New Zealand are grouped together because they

A are in the same part of the world.

B have about the same number of people.

C are roughly the same size.

D use the same power sources.

Political Maps

Political maps show the divisions within countries. A country may be divided into states, provinces, etc. The maps also show where major cities are. They may also show mountains, oceans, seas, lakes, and rivers.

1 Read the title of the map. This will give you the subject and purpose of the map.

2 Read the labels on the map. They also give information about the map's subject and purpose.

3 Study the key or legend to help you understand the symbols in the map.

4 Use the scale to estimate distances between places shown on the map. Maps usually show the distance in both miles and kilometers.

5 Use the North arrow to figure out the direction of places on the map.

6 Read the questions. Carefully study the map to find the answers.

1 Canada and Its Provinces

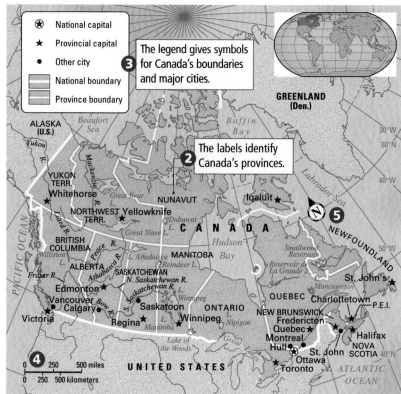

The legend gives symbols for Canada's boundaries and major cities.

The labels identify Canada's provinces.

1 Which province or territory is the furthest west?

A Northwest Territories

B Yukon Territory

C British Columbia

D Alberta

2 About how many miles is the United States-Canada border from the Great Lakes to the Pacific Ocean?

A 1,000

B 1,500

C 2,000

D 2,500

answers: 1 (B); 2 (B)

S20

Directions: Study the map carefully. Use the map and your knowledge of social studies to answer the questions.

The Roman Empire, A.D. 400

1 Which area was part of the Eastern Roman Empire?

   A Spain

   B Gaul

   C Anatolia

   D All of the above

2 The most northern country in the Western Roman Empire was

   A Syria.

   B Gaul.

   C Spain.

   D Britain.

Thematic Maps

Thematic maps focus on special topics. For example, a thematic map might show a country's natural resources or major battles in a war.

1 Read the title of the map. This will give you the subject and purpose of the map.

2 Read the labels on the map. They give information about the map's subject and purpose.

3 Study the key or legend to help you understand the symbols on the map. (The arrows show where Buddhism started and where it spread.)

4 Ask yourself whether the symbols show a pattern.

5 Read the questions. Carefully study the map to find the answers.

❶ The Spread of Buddhism

❷ The labels name the major areas of South and East Asia. The dates show when Buddhism first came to each area.

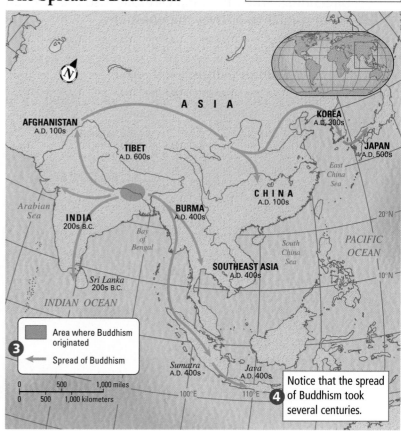

❹ Notice that the spread of Buddhism took several centuries.

Legend:
- Area where Buddhism originated
- ← Spread of Buddhism

1 Where did Buddhism start?

A Japan
B India
C Borneo
D Afghanistan

2 Buddhism spread from China to

A Japan and Tibet.
B Tibet and Korea.
C Korea and Japan.
D All of the above

answers: 1 (B); 2 (C)

S22

For more test practice online . . .

TEST PRACTICE
CLASSZONE.COM

Directions: Read the map carefully. Use the map and your knowledge of social studies to answer the questions.

The Christian Conquest of Muslim Spain

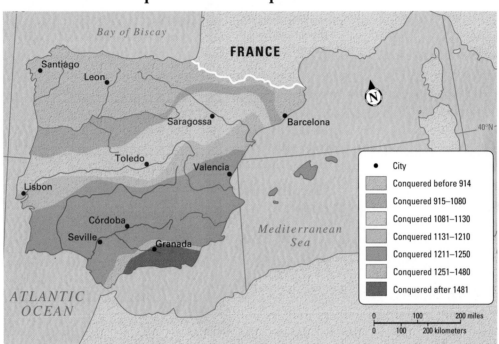

•	City
	Conquered before 914
	Conquered 915–1080
	Conquered 1081–1130
	Conquered 1131–1210
	Conquered 1211–1250
	Conquered 1251–1480
	Conquered after 1481

1 By A.D. 1250, how much of Spain did Christians control?

  A Only a small portion

  B About one third

  C About one half

  D Almost all the land

2 When did Spain recover Granada?

  A 1000

  B 1150

  C 1450

  D 1492

Time Lines

A time line is a chart that lists events in the order in which they occurred. Time lines can be vertical or horizontal.

1 Read the title to learn what period of time the time line covers.

2 Note the dates when the time line begins and ends.

3 Read the events in the order they occurred.

4 Think about what else was going on in the world on these dates. Try to make connections.

5 Read the questions. Then carefully study the time line to find the answers.

1 **The End of Colonialism in Africa**

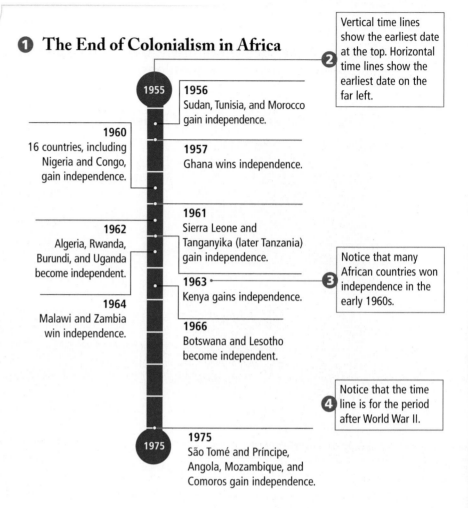

2 Vertical time lines show the earliest date at the top. Horizontal time lines show the earliest date on the far left.

1955

1956
Sudan, Tunisia, and Morocco gain independence.

1960
16 countries, including Nigeria and Congo, gain independence.

1957
Ghana wins independence.

1961
Sierra Leone and Tanganyika (later Tanzania) gain independence.

1962
Algeria, Rwanda, Burundi, and Uganda become independent.

3 Notice that many African countries won independence in the early 1960s.

1963
Kenya gains independence.

1964
Malawi and Zambia win independence.

1966
Botswana and Lesotho become independent.

4 Notice that the time line is for the period after World War II.

1975

1975
São Tomé and Príncipe, Angola, Mozambique, and Comoros gain independence.

1 How many countries became independent from 1961 to 1966?

A 7

B 9

C 11

D 13

5

2 Why do you think so many countries won their independence after World War II?

A European nations were weaker after the war.

B All Europeans in Africa moved back to Europe.

C Europe no longer wanted to own colonies.

D Europe gave each colony its own army after the war.

answers: 1 (C); 2 (A)

Directions: Read the time line. Use the information shown and your knowledge of social studies to answer the questions.

The Breakup of the Soviet Union

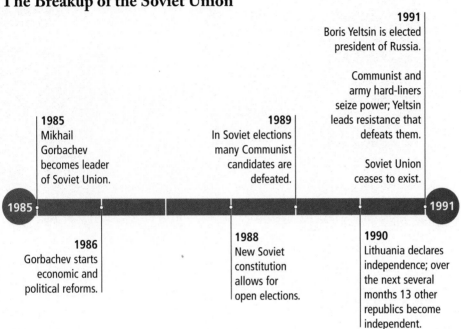

1991
Boris Yeltsin is elected president of Russia.

Communist and army hard-liners seize power; Yeltsin leads resistance that defeats them.

Soviet Union ceases to exist.

1985
Mikhail Gorbachev becomes leader of Soviet Union.

1989
In Soviet elections many Communist candidates are defeated.

1985

1991

1986
Gorbachev starts economic and political reforms.

1988
New Soviet constitution allows for open elections.

1990
Lithuania declares independence; over the next several months 13 other republics become independent.

1   What happened after Lithuania became independent?

A Gorbachev started economic and political reforms.

B Many other republics became independent.

C A new constitution allowed for open elections.

D Gorbachev defeated Yeltsin in a new election.

2   In which year did Communist and army hard-liners try to seize power?

A 1985

B 1988

C 1990

D 1991

Constructed Response

Constructed-response questions focus on a document, such as a photograph, cartoon, chart, graph, or time line. Instead of picking one answer from a set of choices, you write a short response. Sometimes, you can find the answer in the document. Other times, you will use what you already know about a subject to answer the question.

1 Read the title of the document to get an idea of what it is about.

2 Study the document.

3 Read the questions carefully. Study the document again to find the answers.

4 Write your answers. You don't need to use complete sentences unless the directions say so.

1 The Salt March

2 This document is a photograph showing Mohandas K. Gandhi leading a demonstration.

Copyright © Hulton Archive

Mohandas Gandhi and poet Sarojini Naidu lead Indians in a march down the west coast of India. They are protesting the Salt Acts of 1930.

1 Mohandas Gandhi was an important leader in what country?

4 *India*

2 Read the title of the photograph. What was the Salt March?

It was a protest against the Salt Acts. These acts said that Indians could buy salt only from the British. They also had to pay sales taxes when they bought salt.

3 The question uses the plural "ways." Your answer must include more than one way.

3 What principle did Gandhi follow to win independence for India? Describe the (ways) he put this principle into action.

passive resistance, civil disobedience, or nonviolence. He led peaceful marches against unjust laws. He organized boycotts of British goods. He also told people not to cooperate with the British government.

Directions: Read the following passage from *Zlata's Diary.* Use the passage and your knowledge of social studies to answer the questions.
You do not need to use complete sentences

> *Saturday, May 2, 1992*
>
> Dear Mimmy,
>
> Today was truly, absolutely the worst day ever in Sarajevo. The shooting started around noon. Mommy and I moved into the hall. Daddy was in his office, under our apartment, at the time. We told him on the intercom to run quickly to the downstairs lobby where we'd meet him. . . . The gunfire was getting worse, and we couldn't get over the wall to the Bobars', so we ran down to our own cellar.
>
> The cellar is ugly, dark, smelly. Mommy, who's terrified of mice, had two fears to cope with. The three of us were in the same corner as the other day. We listened to the pounding shells, the shooting, the thundering noise overhead. We even heard planes. At one moment I realized that this awful cellar was the only place that could save our lives. Suddenly, it started to look almost warm and nice. It was the only way we could defend ourselves against all this terrible shooting. We heard glass shattering in our street. Horrible. I put my fingers in my ears to block out the terrible sounds. I was worried about Cicko. We had left him behind in the lobby. Would he catch cold there? Would something hit him? I was terribly hungry and thirsty. We had left our half-cooked lunch in the kitchen.
>
> —Zlata Filipovic, *Zlata's Diary: A Child's Life in Sarajevo* (1994)

1 In the early 1990s, war broke out in the Balkans. Why were people fighting in Bosnia and Herzegovina?

2 What does Zlata say is happening in the city of Sarajevo?

3 How does the war affect Zlata and her family?

Extended Response

Extended-response questions, like constructed-response questions, focus on a document of some kind. However, they are more complicated and require more time to complete. Some extended-response questions ask you to present the information in the document in a different form. You might be asked to present the information in a chart in graph form, for example. Other questions ask you to complete a document such as a chart or graph. Still others require you to apply your knowledge to information in the document to write an essay.

1 Read the title of the document to get an idea of what it is about.

2 Carefully read directions and questions.

3 Study the document.

4 Sometimes the question may give you part of the answer. (The answer given tells how inventions were used and what effects they had on society. Your answers should have the same kind of information.)

5 The question may require you to write an essay. Write down some ideas to use in an outline. Then use your outline to write the essay. (A good essay will contain the ideas shown in the rubric to the right.)

3 Read the column heads carefully. They offer important clues about the subject of the chart. For instance, the column head "Impact" is a clue about why these inventions were so important.

1 Inventions of the Industrial Revolution

Invention	Impact
Flying shuttle, spinning jenny, water frame, spinning mule, power loom	Spun thread and wove cloth faster; more factories were built and more people were hired **4**
Cotton gin	Cleaned seeds faster from cotton; companies produced more cotton
Macadam road, steamboat, locomotive	Made travel over land and water faster; could carry larger, heavier loads; railroads needed more coal and iron
Mechanical reaper	Made harvesting easier; increased wheat production

2 1   Read the list of inventions in the left-hand column. Then in the right-hand column briefly state what the inventions meant to industry. The first item has been filled in for you.

2   The chart shows how some inventions helped create the Industrial Revolution. Write a short essay describing how the Industrial Revolution changed people's lives.

5   **Essay Rubric** The best essays will point out that progress in agriculture meant that fewer people were needed to work the farms. As a result, many farm workers went to the city looking for work in factories. As cities grew, poor sanitation and poor housing made them unhealthy and dangerous places to live. Life for factory workers was hard. They worked long hours under very bad conditions. At first, the Industrial Revolution produced three classes of people: an upper class of landowners and aristocrats; a middle class of merchants and factory owners; and a large lower class of poor people. Over the long term, though, working and living conditions improved even for the lower class. This was partly because factory goods could be sold at a lower cost. In time, even lower classes could afford to buy many goods and services.

Directions: Use the drawing and passage below and your knowledge of social studies to answer the following question.

Smallpox Spreads Among the Aztecs

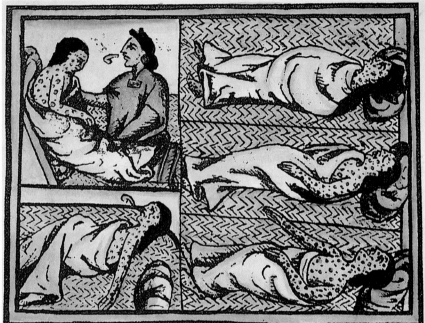

The Granger Collection, New York.

European diseases were like a second "army" of conquerors. Native people had no way to treat diseases like smallpox, typhoid fever, or measles. This "army" was more deadly than swords or guns.
— Based on P. M. Ashburn, *The Ranks of Death* (1947)

1 What role did disease play in the Spanish conquest of the Aztecs and Inca?

Document-Based Questions

To answer a document-based question, you have to study more than one document. First you answer questions about each document. Then you use those answers and information from the documents as well as your own knowledge of history to write an essay.

1 Read the "Historical Context" section. It will give you an idea of the topic that will be covered in the question.

2 Read the "Task" section carefully. It tells you what you will need to write about in your essay.

3 Study each document. Think about the connection the documents have to the topic in the "Task" section.

4 Read and answer the questions about each document. Think about how your answers connect to the "Task" section.

Introduction

1 **Historical Context:** For hundreds of years, Mongol nomads lived in different tribes. They sometimes fought among themselves. In the late 1100s, a new leader—Genghis Khan—united these tribes. He turned the Mongols into a powerful fighting army.

2 **Task:** Discuss how the Mongols conquered Central and East Asia and how their rule affected Europeans' lives.

Part 1: Short Answer

Study each document carefully. Answer the questions that follow.

3 **Document 1: Mongol Warrior**

Victoria & Albert Museum, London/Art Resource, New York.

4 **What were the characteristics of a Mongol warrior?**

The Mongols were great horsemen who could ride a long way without rest. They attacked without warning and showed no mercy. They used clever tricks to frighten their enemies. Also, they borrowed or invented new weapons of war.

Document 2: The Mongol Empire

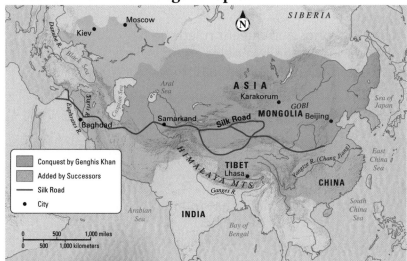

What route linked the Mongol Empire to Europe? What was the main purpose of this route?

Silk Road; as a trade route between Asia and Europe

Document 3: The Great Khan's Wealth

. . . All those who have gems and pearls and gold and silver must bring them to the Great Khan's mint. . . . By this means the Great Khan acquires all the gold and silver and pearls and precious stones of all his territories [lands]. . . .

. . . The Great Khan must have, as indeed he has, more treasure than anyone else in the world. . . . All the world's great [rulers] put together have not such riches as belong to the Great Khan alone.

—Marco Polo, *The Travels of Marco Polo* (c. 1300)

Why do you think Marco Polo's travels made Europeans want to see East Asia?

Europeans were interested in the treasure of the Great Khan and East Asia.

Part 2: Essay

❺ Write an essay discussing how the Mongols conquered Central and East Asia and how their rule affected Europeans' lives. Use information from the documents, your short answers, and your knowledge of social studies. ❻

❺ Read the essay question carefully. Then write a brief outline for your essay.

❻ Write your essay. The first paragraph should introduce your topic. The middle paragraphs should explain it. The closing paragraph should restate the topic and your conclusion. Support your ideas with quotations or details from the documents. Add other supporting facts or details from your knowledge of world history.

❼ A good essay will contain the ideas in the rubric below.

❼ **Essay Rubric** The best essays will describe how the Mongols' tactics, fierce will, and strong military organization enabled them to conquer Central and East Asia. (Documents 1 and 2). The essays will also state that Mongol rule brought a period of peace and unity to regions that had been divided. This peace allowed trade to start again along the Silk Road (Document 2). This trade brought new ideas and products to Europe. Stories of the immense wealth in Mongol lands made Europeans want to tap into those riches (Document 3).

Introduction

Historical Context: For many centuries, kings and queens ruled the countries of Europe. Their power was supported by nobles and armies. European society began to change. In the late 1700s, those changes produced a violent revolution in France.

Task: Discuss how social conflict and new ideas contributed to the French Revolution and why the Revolution turned radical.

Part 1: Short Answer

Study each document carefully. Answer the questions that follow.

Document 1: Social Classes in Pre-Revolutionary France

LE GRAND ABUS

This cartoon shows a peasant woman carrying women of nobility and the Church. What does the cartoon say about the lives of the poor before the revolution?

Engraving: *Le Grand Abus.* Engraving of a cartoon held in the collection of M. de baron de Vinck d'Orp of Brussels/Mary Evans Picture Library, London.

Document 2: A Declaration of Rights

1.   Men are born and remain free and equal in rights. . . .

2.   The aim of all political association is the preservation of the natural and [unlimited] rights of man. These rights are liberty, property, security, and resistance to oppression. . . .

— *Declaration of the Rights of Man and of the Citizen* (1789)

According to this document, which rights belong to all people?

Document 3: The French Revolution — Major Events

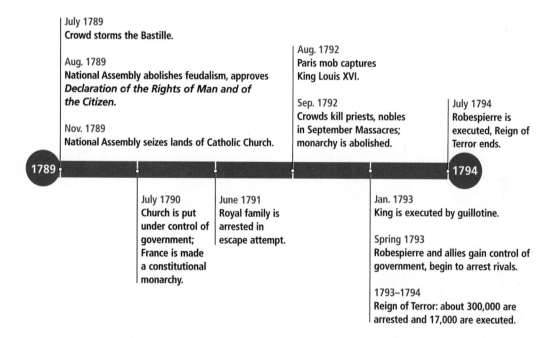

July 1789
Crowd storms the Bastille.

Aug. 1789
National Assembly abolishes feudalism, approves *Declaration of the Rights of Man and of the Citizen.*

Nov. 1789
National Assembly seizes lands of Catholic Church.

Aug. 1792
Paris mob captures King Louis XVI.

Sep. 1792
Crowds kill priests, nobles in September Massacres; monarchy is abolished.

July 1794
Robespierre is executed, Reign of Terror ends.

1789

1794

July 1790
Church is put under control of government; France is made a constitutional monarchy.

June 1791
Royal family is arrested in escape attempt.

Jan. 1793
King is executed by guillotine.

Spring 1793
Robespierre and allies gain control of government, begin to arrest rivals.

1793–1794
Reign of Terror: about 300,000 are arrested and 17,000 are executed.

Over time, the revolution became more violent. How does the information in the time line show this?

Part 2: Essay

Write an essay discussing how social conflict and new ideas led to the French Revolution and why it became so violent. Use information from the documents, your short answers, and your knowledge of social studies to write your essay.

RAND McNALLY
World Atlas

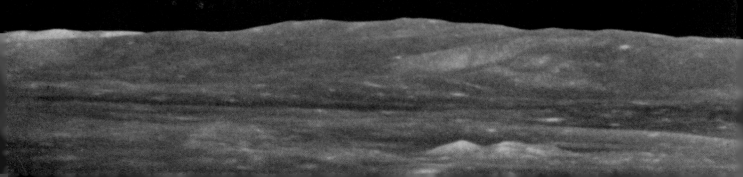

Contents

Complete Legend for Physical and Political Maps

Symbols

 Lake

 Salt Lake

 Seasonal Lake

 River

\ Waterfall

— Canal

△ Mountain Peak

▲ Highest Mountain Peak

Cities

■ Los Angeles — City over 1,000,000 population

▣ Calgary — City of 250,000 to 1,000,000 population

• Haifa — City under 250,000 population

✪ *Paris* — National Capital

★ Vancouver — Secondary Capital (State, Province, or Territory)

Type Styles Used to Name Features

CHINA — Country

O N T A R I O — State, Province, or Territory

PUERTO RICO (U.S.) — Possession

A T L A N T I C O C E A N — Ocean or Sea

A l p s — Physical Feature

Borneo — Island

Boundaries

 International Boundary

Secondary Boundary

Land Elevation and Water Depths

Land Elevation

Meters		Feet
3,000 and over --		-- 9,840 and over
2,000 - 3,000 --		-- 6,560 - 9,840
500 - 2,000 --		-- 1,640 - 6,560
200 - 500 --		-- 656 - 1,640
0 - 200 --		-- 0 - 656

Water Depth

Less than 200 --		-- Less than 656
200 - 2,000 --		-- 656 - 6,560
Over 2,000 --		-- Over 6,560

ARCTIC OCEAN

Greenland

Jan Mayen

Baffin Island

Baffin Bay

Iceland

Arctic Circle

Yukon

Mackenzie

Canadian Shield

Faroe Is.

Mt. McKinley
20,320 Ft.
6,194m

NORTH

Hudson Bay

British Isles

Aleutian Islands

Rocky Mountains

Great Plains

AMERICA

St. Lawrence

Newfoundland

London

Vancouver

Appalachian Mts.

Washington D.C.

Iberian Peninsula

Azores

Los Angeles

Colorado

Mississippi

Cape Hatteras

ATLANTIC

Atlas Mts.

Midway Is.

Baja California

Gulf of Mexico

Canary Islands

Tropic of Cancer

Yucatan Peninsula

Cuba

Hispaniola

Cape Verde Islands

Hawaiian Islands

Jamaica

Puerto Rico

Cape Verde

PACIFIC

Caribbean Sea

Trinidad

OCEAN

Niger

Palmyra

Orinoco

Galapagos Islands

Amazon

OCEAN

Equator

Amazon

SOUTH

Kiribati

Basin

Marquesas Is.

Andes

AMERICA

Samoa Islands

Mato Grosso Plateau

St. Helena

Tonga Is.

Cook Islands

Tahiti

Tropic of Capricorn

Rio de Janeiro

Easter Island

Andes

Paraná

Archipiélago Juan Fernández

Mt. Aconcagua
22,831 Ft.
6,959m

Buenos Aires

N

Patagonia

Chatham Is.

Falkland Is.

South Georgia

0   1000   2000 Miles

South Sandwich Is.

0   1000   2000   3000 Kilometers

Tierra del Fuego

South Orkney Is.

Copyright by Rand McNally & Co.
Robinson Projection

Cape Horn

South Shetland Is.

Antarctic Circle

Antarctic Peninsula

Weddell Sea

Ross Sea

Marie Byrd Land

Vinson Massif
16,066 Ft.
4,897m

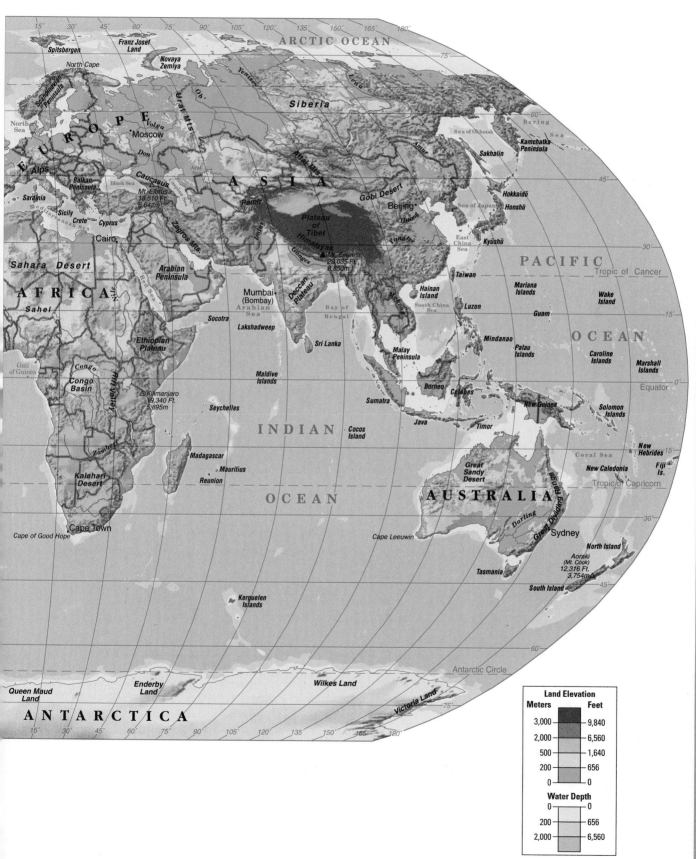

ARCTIC OCEAN

Spitsbergen

Franz Josef Land

North Cape

Novaya Zemlya

Scandinavian Peninsula

EUROPE

North Sea

Moscow

Volga

Don

Ural Mts.

Ob'

Yenisey

Lena

Siberia

Bering Sea

Sea of Okhotsk

Kamchatka Peninsula

Sakhalin

Alps

Balkan Peninsula

Sardinia

Sicily

Crete

Black Sea

Caspian Sea

Caucasus

Mt. Elbrus 18,510 Ft. 5,642m

Aral Sea

Altai Mts.

ASIA

Gobi Desert

Beijing

Huang

Amur

Hokkaidō

Honshū

Sea of Japan

Mediterranean Sea

Cairo

Cyprus

Zagros Mts.

Pamir

Plateau of Tibet

Himalayas

Mt. Everest 29,035 Ft. 8,850m

Yangtze

Mekong

East China Sea

Kyūshū

PACIFIC

Tropic of Cancer

Sahara Desert

AFRICA

Sahel

Arabian Peninsula

Red Sea

Nile

Mumbai (Bombay)

Arabian Sea

Deccan Plateau

Ganges

Bay of Bengal

Taiwan

Hainan Island

South China Sea

Luzon

Mariana Islands

Guam

Wake Island

OCEAN

Socotra

Lakshadweep

Sri Lanka

Mindanao

Palau Islands

Caroline Islands

Marshall Islands

Ethiopian Plateau

Congo

Gulf of Guinea

Congo Basin

Kilimanjaro 19,340 Ft. 5,895m

Rift Valley

Seychelles

Maldive Islands

Malay Peninsula

Borneo

Celebes

Sumatra

Java

Timor

New Guinea

Solomon Islands

Equator

INDIAN

Cocos Island

Zambezi

Madagascar

Mauritius

Reunion

Coral Sea

New Hebrides

New Caledonia

Fiji Is.

Tropic of Capricorn

Kalahari Desert

OCEAN

Great Sandy Desert

AUSTRALIA

Darling

Great Dividing Range

Sydney

Cape Town

Cape of Good Hope

Cape Leeuwin

North Island

Aoraki (Mt. Cook) 12,316 Ft. 3,754m

Tasmania

South Island

Kerguelen Islands

Queen Maud Land

Enderby Land

Wilkes Land

Victoria Land

Antarctic Circle

ANTARCTICA

Land Elevation

Meters		Feet
3,000		9,840
2,000		6,560
500		1,640
200		656
0		0

Water Depth

0		0
200		656
2,000		6,560

RAND McNALLY

A3

ARCTIC OCEAN

GREENLAND
(Den.)

Arctic Circle

ICELAND

FAROE IS.
(Den.)

Baffin
Bay

RUSSIA   ALASKA
Yukon (U.S.)

Anchorage

UNITED
KINGDOM

IRELAND

London

FRANCE

C A N A D A

Hudson
Bay

Newfoundland

Aleutian Islands

Vancouver

Missouri

Montréal

Ottawa

PORTUGAL   Madrid

SPAIN

Azores
(Port.)

Chicago

New York

Washington D.C.

UNITED STATES

Colorado

Casablanca

MOROCCO

Los Angeles

Mississippi

Canary
Islands
(Sp.)

ATLANTIC

MIDWAY IS.
(U.S.)

Houston

Tropic of Cancer

MEXICO

Gulf of Mexico

BAHAMAS

W. SAHARA

Hawaiian
Islands
(U.S)

Mexico City

CUBA

CAPE
VERDE

MAURITANIA   MALI

DOM. REP.

HAITI

PUERTO RICO (U.S.)

SENEGAL

PACIFIC

BELIZE

JAMAICA

GAMBIA

Niger

BURK.
FASO

GUINEA-BISSAU   GUINEA

GUAT.   HOND.

Caribbean
Sea

EL. SAL.   NIC.

SIERRA LEONE

COTE
D'IVOIRE

Caracas

TRINIDAD AND TOBAGO

LIBERIA

COSTA
RICA

VENEZUELA   GUYANA

PANAMA

SURINAME

FRENCH GUIANA

COLOMBIA

OCEAN

Galapagos Islands
(Ecuador)

ECUADOR

Amazon

Equator

KIRIBATI

BRAZIL

OCEAN

PERU

Lima

O C E A N

St. HELENA
(U.K.)

SAMOA

AMERICAN
SAMOA

BOLIVIA

COOK
ISLANDS (N.Z.)

TONGA

PARAGUAY

Rio de Janeiro

FRENCH POLYNESIA

Tropic of Capricorn

ARGENTINA

Easter Island
(Chile)

URUGUAY

CHILE

Santiago

Buenos
Aires

N

FALKLAND IS.
(U.K.)

South
Georgia
(U.K.)

0		1000		2000 Miles

0	1000	2000	3000 Kilometers

Copyright by Rand McNally & Co.
Robinson Projection

South
Orkney Is.
(U.K.)

Antarctic Circle

South
Shetland Is.
(U.K.)

W e d d e l l
S e a

ARCTIC OCEAN

Spitsbergen
(Nor.)

Franz Josef
Land

Novaya
Zemlya

NORWAY
FINLAND
North
Sea
SWEDEN
EST.
LAT.
LITH.
DEN.
GERMANY
BEL.
NETH.
POLAND
BELARUS
SWITZ.
AUS.
CZECH
SLVK.
HUNG.
UKRAINE
ITALY
CRO.
BOS.
ROM.
MOLD.
Rome
ALB.
MA.
BUL.
GREECE
Black Sea
TURKEY
GEO.
ARM.
AZER.
Mediterranean Sea
Crete
CYPRUS
LEB.
SYRIA
TUNISIA
ISRAEL
IRAQ
JORDAN
ALGERIA
LIBYA
EGYPT
Cairo
KUWAIT
NIGER
CHAD
SUDAN
NIGERIA
Lagos
CAMEROON
CENTRAL
AFRICAN
REPUBLIC
EQUATORIAL
GUINEA
GABON
REP. OF
CONGO
DEM. REP.
OF CONGO
RWANDA
BURUNDI
UGANDA
KENYA
TANZANIA
ANGOLA
ZAMBIA
ZIMBABWE
NAMIBIA
BOTSWANA
MOZAMBIQUE
SWAZILAND
SOUTH
AFRICA
LESOTHO
Cape Town

RUSSIA
Moscow
Volga
Novosibirsk
KAZAKHSTAN
UZBEKISTAN
TURKMENISTAN
AFGHANISTAN
IRAN
PAKISTAN
SAUDI
ARABIA
QATAR
U.A.E.
OMAN
YEMEN
DJIBOUTI
ETHIOPIA
SOMALIA
Addis
Ababa
Red Sea
Nile
Congo
SEYCHELLES
COMOROS
MADAGASCAR
REUNION
(Fr.)
MAURITIUS

MONGOLIA
CHINA
Beijing
KYRG.
TAJIK.
NEPAL
Ganges
INDIA
Mumbai
(Bombay)
Arabian
Sea
MALDIVES
SRI LANKA
Bay of
Bengal
BNGL.
Kolkata
(Calcutta)
MYANMAR
LAOS
THAILAND
Bangkok
CAMBODIA
VIETNAM
Chang Jiang
Yangtze
Shanghai
Guangzhou
TAIWAN
South China
Sea
PHILIPPINES
BRUNEI
MALAYSIA
SINGAPORE
Borneo
Sumatra
Jakarta
Java
INDONESIA
EAST TIMOR

NORTH
KOREA
Sea of Japan
SOUTH
KOREA
JAPAN
Tokyo
PACIFIC
Tropic of Cancer
NORTHERN
MARIANA ISLANDS
(U.S.)
WAKE ISLAND
(U.S.)
GUAM (U.S.)
OCEAN
PALAU
FED. STATES OF
MICRONESIA
MARSHALL
ISLANDS
New Guinea
PAPUA
NEW GUINEA
Equator
SOLOMON
ISLANDS
Darwin
Coral Sea
NEW CALEDONIA
(Fr.)
VANUATU
FIJI
Tropic of Capricorn
AUSTRALIA
Perth
Darling
Sydney
Melbourne
NEW ZEALAND
Tasmania
Wellington

Sea of Okhotsk
Bering
Sea

INDIAN
OCEAN

Kerguelen
Islands
(Fr.)

Antarctic Circle

ANTARCTICA

GINEA

GINEA

★ National Capital

• Major Cities

RAND McNALLY

A5

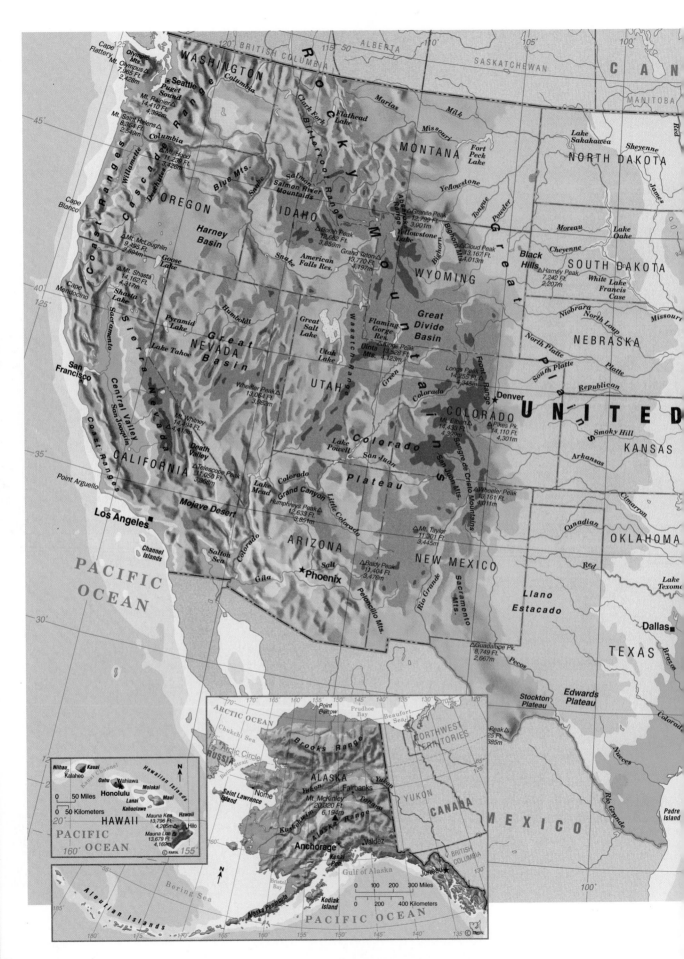

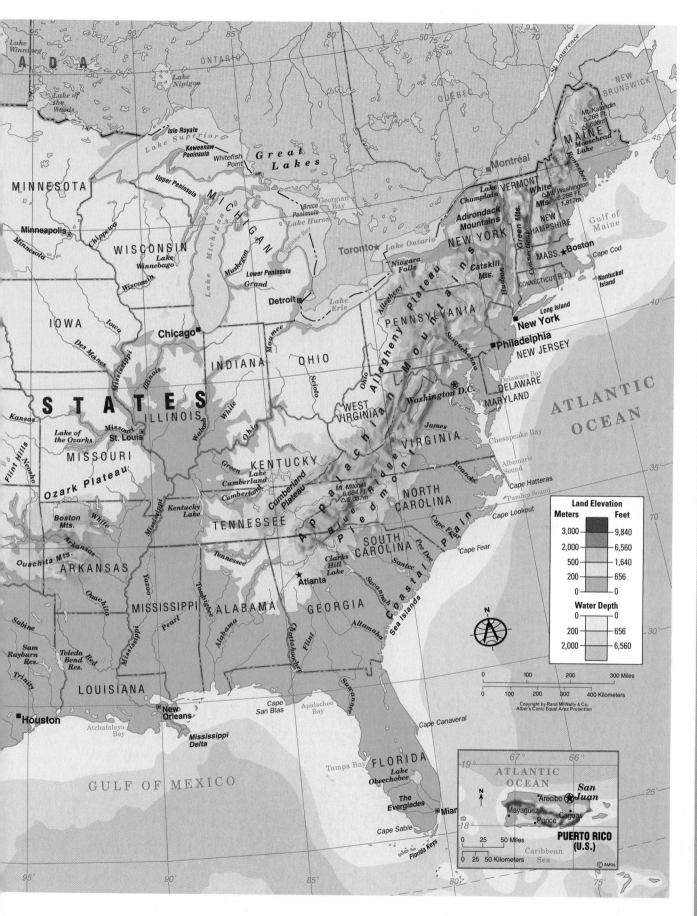

CANADA

ONTARIO

QUEBEC

NEW BRUNSWICK

Lake Winnibeg

Lake of the Woods

Lake Nipigon

Isle Royale

Lake Superior

Keweenaw Peninsula

Whitefish Point

Great Lakes

Mt. Katahdin 5,268 Ft. 1,606m

MAINE

Moosehead Lake

MINNESOTA

Upper Peninsula

MICHIGAN

Bruce Peninsula

Georgian Bay

Lake Huron

Lake VERMONT Champlain

White Mts.

Mt. Washington 6,288 Ft. 1,917m

Kennebec

Gulf of Maine

Minneapolis

Minnesota

Chippewa

WISCONSIN

Lake Winnebago

Wisconsin

Muskegon

Lower Peninsula

Grand

Saginaw Bay

Green Bay

Lake Michigan

Adirondack Mountains

Green Mts.

NEW HAMPSHIRE

Montréal

NEW YORK

MASS. ★ Boston

Cape Cod

Detroit

Lake Erie

Toronto ★

Lake Ontario

Niagara Falls

Allegheny Plateau

Catskill Mts.

Hudson

CONNECTICUT R.I.

Nantucket Island

IOWA

Iowa

Des Moines

Chicago ■

Maumee

OHIO

INDIANA

Scioto

Ohio

Allegheny

PENNSYLVANIA

Appalachian Mountains

Susquehanna

Long Island

New York ■

Philadelphia ■

NEW JERSEY

Delaware Bay

DELAWARE

MARYLAND

Mississippi

Illinois

ILLINOIS

White

Wabash

Ohio

WEST VIRGINIA

Washington D.C. ⊛

VIRGINIA

ATLANTIC OCEAN

STATES

Kansas

Lake of the Ozarks

Missouri

St. Louis

MISSOURI

Ozark Plateau

Flint Hills

Neosho

Boston Mts.

White

Arkansas

Green

Lake Cumberland

Cumberland

KENTUCKY

Kentucky Lake

TENNESSEE

Cumberland Plateau

Mt. Mitchell 6,684 Ft. 2,037m

James

Chesapeake Bay

Roanoke

Albemarle Sound

Cape Hatteras

Pamlico Sound

Blue Ridge Mountains

Piedmont

NORTH CAROLINA

Cape Lookout

Ouachita Mts.

Ouachita

ARKANSAS

Tennessee

Mississippi

Yazoo

Tombigbee

Kentucky

Tennessee

Clarks Hill Lake

SOUTH CAROLINA

Santee

Pee Dee

Cape Fear

Cape Fear

Sabine

MISSISSIPPI

ALABAMA

Pearl

Alabama

Atlanta ★

GEORGIA

Chattahoochee

Flint

Savannah

Altamaha

Coastal Plain

Sea Islands

Sam Rayburn Res.

Toledo Bend Res.

Red

Trinity

LOUISIANA

■ Houston

Atchafalaya Bay

New Orleans ■

Mississippi Delta

Cape San Blas

Apalachee Bay

Suwannee

Cape Canaveral

GULF OF MEXICO

Tampa Bay

FLORIDA

Lake Okeechobee

The Everglades

Miami ■

Cape Sable

Florida Keys

Land Elevation		
Meters		Feet
3,000		9,840
2,000		6,560
500		1,640
200		656
0		0

Water Depth		
0		0
200		656
2,000		6,560

N

0   100   200   300 Miles
0   100   200   300   400 Kilometers

Copyright by Rand McNally & Co.
Alber's Conic Equal Area Projection

ATLANTIC OCEAN

Arecibo

San Juan ⊛

Mayagüez

Ponce

Caguas

PUERTO RICO (U.S.)

0   25   50 Miles
0   25   50 Kilometers

Caribbean Sea

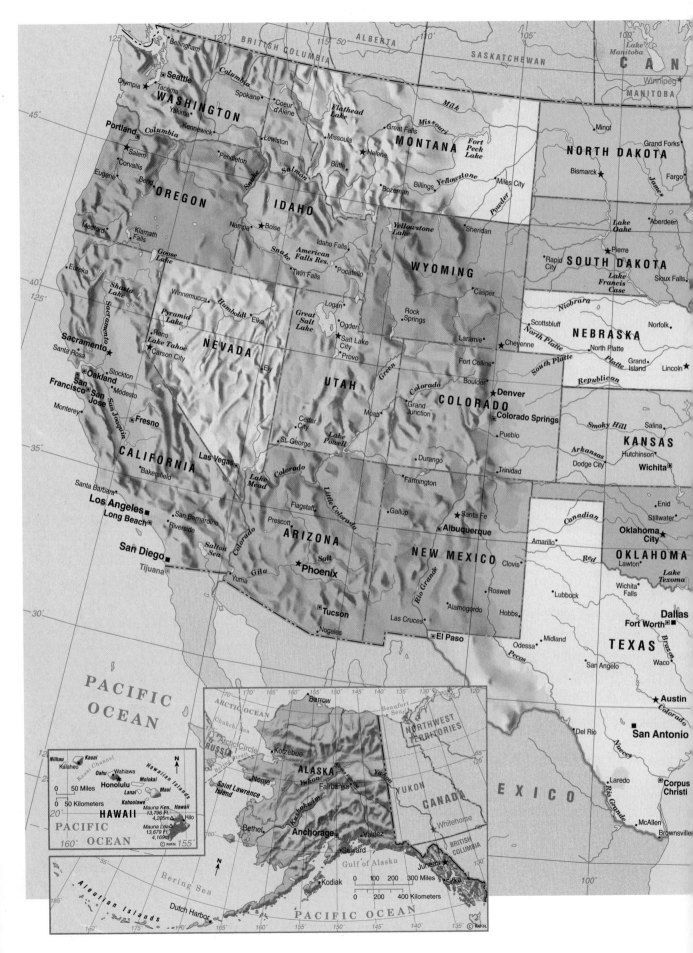

RAND McNALLY

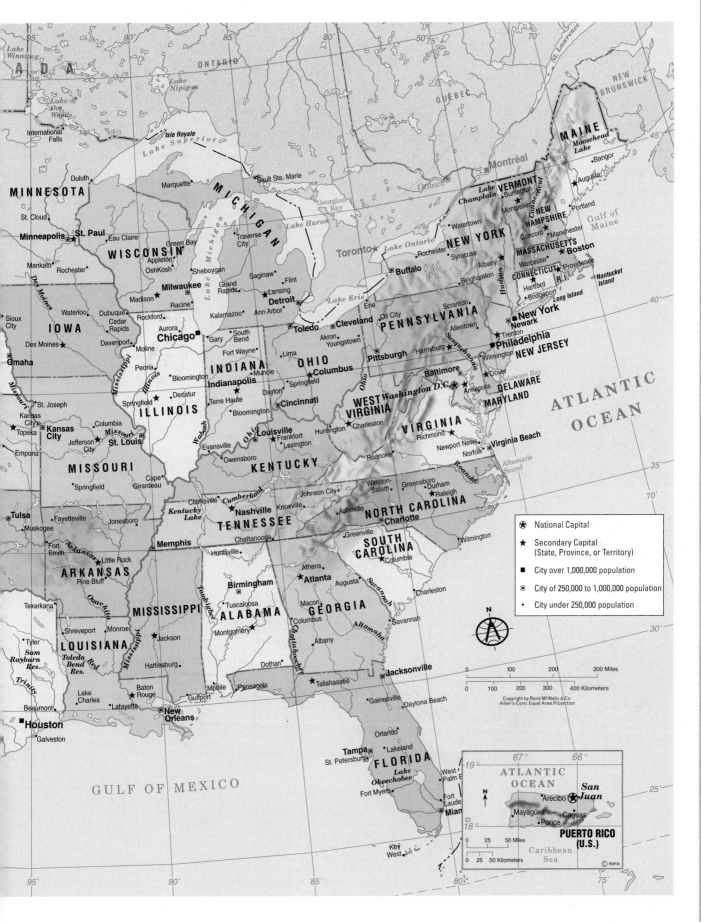

CANADA

ONTARIO

QUÉBEC

NEW BRUNSWICK

Lake Winnipeg

Lake of the Woods

International Falls

Lake Superior

Isle Royale

St. Lawrence

Montréal

Ottawa

MAINE

Moosehead Lake

Bangor

Augusta

MINNESOTA

Duluth

Marquette

Sault Ste. Marie

MICHIGAN

Georgian Bay

Lake Huron

Lake Champlain

VERMONT

Montpelier

Burlington

NEW HAMPSHIRE

Concord

Manchester

Portland

Gulf of Maine

St. Cloud

Eau Claire

Traverse City

Toronto

Lake Ontario

Watertown

NEW YORK

Rochester

Syracuse

Albany

MASSACHUSETTS

Worcester

Boston

Providence

Nantucket Island

Minneapolis

St. Paul

WISCONSIN

Green Bay

Appleton

OshKosh

Sheboygan

Saginaw

Flint

Lansing

Grand Rapids

Buffalo

Binghamton

CONNECTICUT

Hartford

Bridgeport

R.I.

Long Island

Mankato

Rochester

Madison

Milwaukee

Racine

Kalamazoo

Detroit

Ann Arbor

Lake Erie

Erie

Cleveland

Oil City

Scranton

PENNSYLVANIA

Allentown

Trenton

New York

Newark

IOWA

Waterloo

Dubuque

Cedar Rapids

Rockford

Aurora

Chicago

Gary

South Bend

Fort Wayne

Toledo

Akron

Youngstown

Pittsburgh

Harrisburg

Susquehanna

Philadelphia

NEW JERSEY

Wilmington

Sioux City

Davenport

Moline

Peoria

Lima

OHIO

Columbus

Dayton

Springfield

Baltimore

Dover

Delaware Bay

DELAWARE

Des Moines

Omaha

Bloomington

INDIANA

Muncie

Indianapolis

Cincinnati

Washington D.C.

Annapolis

MARYLAND

ATLANTIC OCEAN

St. Joseph

Springfield

Decatur

Terre Haute

Bloomington

ILLINOIS

WEST VIRGINIA

Charleston

VIRGINIA

Kansas City

Topeka

Columbia

Jefferson City

St. Louis

Louisville

Frankfort

Lexington

Huntington

Richmond

Newport News

Norfolk

Virginia Beach

Emporia

MISSOURI

Evansville

Owensboro

KENTUCKY

Roanoke

Albemarle Sound

Springfield

Cape Girardeau

Clarksville

Cumberland

Kentucky Lake

Nashville

Knoxville

Johnson City

Winston-Salem

Greensboro

Durham

Raleigh

Tulsa

Fayetteville

Jonesboro

Asheville

NORTH CAROLINA

Muskogee

Memphis

Chattanooga

Charlotte

Wilmington

Fort Smith

Little Rock

Huntsville

Greenville

SOUTH CAROLINA

Columbia

ARKANSAS

Pine Bluff

Birmingham

Athens

Atlanta

Augusta

Charleston

Texarkana

Tuscaloosa

Macon

Savannah

MISSISSIPPI

ALABAMA

GEORGIA

Tyler

Sam Rayburn Res.

Toledo Bend Res.

Shreveport

Monroe

Jackson

Montgomery

Columbus

Albany

Trinity

LOUISIANA

Hattiesburg

Dothan

Tallahassee

Beaumont

Lake Charles

Baton Rouge

Lafayette

Gulfport

Mobile

Pensacola

Jacksonville

Houston

Galveston

New Orleans

GULF OF MEXICO

Gainesville

Daytona Beach

Orlando

FLORIDA

Tampa

Lakeland

St. Petersburg

Lake Okeechobee

West Palm Beach

Fort Myers

Fort Lauderdale

Miami

Key West

✪	National Capital
★	Secondary Capital (State, Province, or Territory)
■	City over 1,000,000 population
▣	City of 250,000 to 1,000,000 population
•	City under 250,000 population

N

100   200   300 Miles

100   200   300   400 Kilometers

Copyright by Rand McNally & Co.
Alber's Conic Equal Area Projection

ATLANTIC OCEAN

San Juan

Arecibo

Mayagüez

Caguas

Ponce

PUERTO RICO (U.S.)

N

0   25   50 Miles

0   25   50 Kilometers

Caribbean Sea

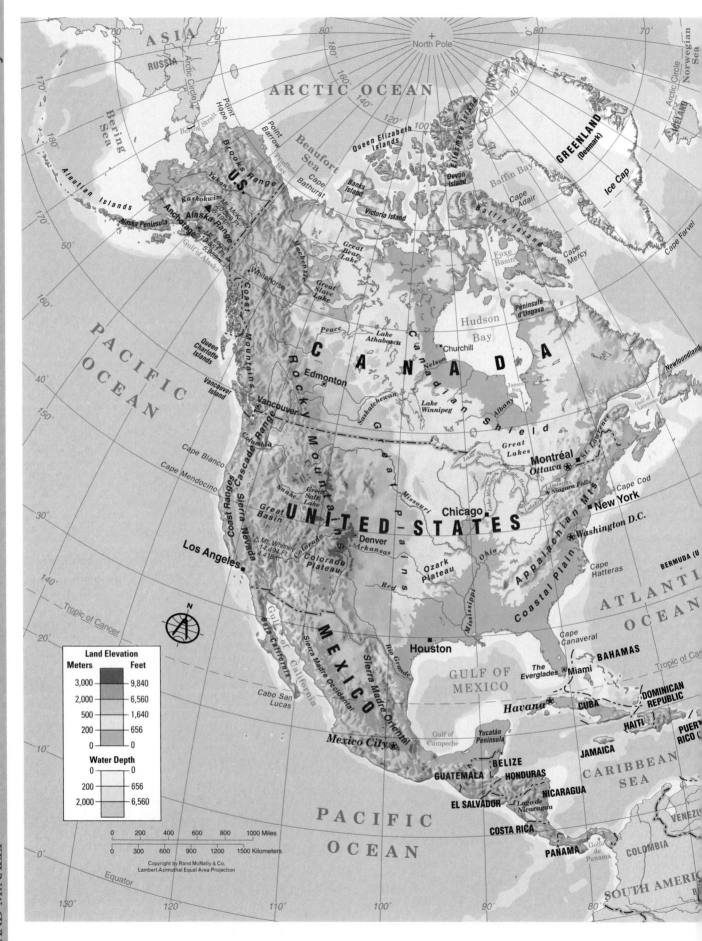

ASIA
RUSSIA
Arctic Circle

ARCTIC OCEAN
North Pole

Bering Sea

Point Hope
Point Barrow
Prudhoe Bay
Bering Strait
Brooks Range
U.S.
Yukon
Kuskokwim
Mt. McKinley 20,320 Ft. 6,198 m
Alaska Range
Anchorage
Mt. Logan 19,551 Ft. 5,959 m
Gulf of Alaska

Beaufort Sea
Cape Bathurst
Banks Island
Victoria Island

Queen Elizabeth Islands
Ellesmere Island
Devon Island
Baffin Bay
Cape Adair
Baffin Island
Cape Mercy
Foxe Basin

GREENLAND (Denmark)
Ice Cap

Arctic Circle
ICELAND
Norwegian Sea
Cape Farvel

Aleutian Islands
Alaska Peninsula

PACIFIC OCEAN

Whitehorse
Coast Mountains
Queen Charlotte Islands
Vancouver Island
Vancouver

Mackenzie
Great Bear Lake
Great Slave Lake

Peace
Lake Athabasca
Saskatchewan
Edmonton

CANADA
Churchill
Nelson
Hudson Bay
Péninsule d'Ungava

James Bay
Newfoundland
Gulf of St. Lawrence

Cape Blanco
Cape Mendocino

Rocky Mountains
Columbia
Cascade Range
Coast Ranges
Sierra Nevada
Snake
Great Salt Lake
Great Basin
Mt. Whitney 14,494 Ft. 4,418 m
Colorado
Colorado Plateau

Lake Winnipeg

Great Plains

Canadian Shield

Great Lakes
Lake Superior
Lake Michigan
Lake Huron
Lake Ontario
Lake Erie

Montréal
Ottawa
St. Lawrence
Niagara Falls
New York
Cape Cod
Washington D.C.

UNITED STATES
Denver
Arkansas
Missouri
Chicago
Ozark Plateau
Ohio
Appalachian Mts.
Coastal Plain
Cape Hatteras

ATLANTIC OCEAN
BERMUDA (U

Los Angeles

Red
Mississippi

Tropic of Cancer

N

Gulf of California
Baja California
Sierra Madre Occidental
MEXICO
Sierra Madre Oriental
Rio Grande

Houston
Cape Canaveral
The Everglades
Miami
BAHAMAS
Tropic of Ca

Cabo San Lucas

Havana
GULF OF MEXICO
CUBA
HAITI
DOMINICAN REPUBLIC
PUERTO RICO (U

Mexico City
Gulf of Campeche
Yucatán Peninsula
BELIZE
GUATEMALA
HONDURAS
EL SALVADOR
NICARAGUA
Lago de Nicaragua
COSTA RICA
PANAMA
Golfo de Panamá

JAMAICA
CARIBBEAN SEA

VENEZU

Land Elevation

Meters		Feet
3,000		9,840
2,000		6,560
500		1,640
200		656
0		0

Water Depth

0		0
200		656
2,000		6,560

0   200   400   600   800   1000 Miles
0   300   600   900   1200   1500 Kilometers

Copyright by Rand McNally & Co.
Lambert Azimuthal Equal Area Projection

PACIFIC OCEAN

COLOMBIA
SOUTH AMERIC

Equator

ATLAS

ASIA
RUSSIA
Arctic Circle
Bering
Strait

ARCTIC OCEAN

North Pole

ICELAND
Reykjavik
Arctic Circle

Aleutian Islands

Bering
Sea

Queen Elizabeth
Islands

Beaufort
Sea

Banks
Island

Devon
Island

Ellesmere Island

GREENLAND
(Denmark)

U.S.

Anchorage
Fairbanks
Valdez
Gulf of Alaska
Whitehorse
Juneau

Yukon
Prudhoe
Bay

Mackenzie

Victoria Island

Great
Bear
Lake

Yellowknife
Great
Slave
Lake

Baffin Island

Baffin Bay

Godthåb

PACIFIC

OCEAN

Edmonton

Calgary
Victoria
Vancouver
Seattle
Columbia
Spokane
Portland

Saskatoon

Peace

CANADA

Nelson

Saskatchewan
Regina

Lake
Winnipeg

Winnipeg

Hudson
Bay

Nelson

Newfoundland
St. John's

Gulf of
St. Lawrence

Halifax
Saint John

Thunder Bay

Quebec
St. Lawrence

Montréal
Ottawa
Toronto

Boston

Billings

Great
Salt
Lake

Minneapolis

Milwaukee
Chicago
Lake Michigan
Lake Superior
Lake Huron
Lake Erie
Lake Ontario

Detroit
Cleveland

New York
Philadelphia
Washington D.C.

Sacramento
San Francisco

UNITED STATES

Omaha

Missouri

Denver
Colorado
Las Vegas
Arkansas

Kansas City

Indianapolis
St. Louis
Ohio

Cincinnati
Nashville

Norfolk

Los Angeles
San Diego
Tijuana

Phoenix
Albuquerque

Red

Oklahoma
City

Memphis

Charlotte

Atlanta

BERMUDA (U.K.)

ATLANTIC

Ciudad
Juárez
Hermosillo

Dallas

MEXICO

Houston

Rio Grande

San Antonio

New Orleans

Jacksonville

Tampa

OCEAN

30

Tropic of Cancer

Chihuahua

Culiacán

Torreón

Monterrey

Gulf of California

GULF OF
MEXICO

Miami

Nassau

BAHAMAS

Tropic of Cancer

San Luis Potosí

Guadalajara

León

Mérida

Cancún

Havana

CUBA

Kingston

JAMAICA

HAITI
Port-au-
Prince

DOMINICAN
REPUBLIC

Santo
Domingo

PUERTO
RICO
(U.S.)

Mexico City
Puebla

Veracruz

Acapulco

BELIZE
Belmopan

GUATEMALA

Guatemala City

HONDURAS
Tegucigalpa

San Salvador
EL SALVADOR

Managua

Lago de
Nicaragua

NICARAGUA

CARIBBEAN

SEA

Caracas

VENEZUELA

Panama
City

PACIFIC

OCEAN

COSTA RICA
San José

PANAMA

Golfo
de
Panamá

COLOMBIA

Bogotá

SOUTH AMERICA

BRAZIL

Equator

Legend:

- ✺ National Capital
- ★ Secondary Capital
  (State, Province, or Territory)
- ■ City over 1,000,000 population
- ▣ City of 250,000 to 1,000,000 population
- • City under 250,000 population

Scale:
0 200 400 600 800 1000 Miles
0 300 600 900 1200 1500 Kilometers

Copyright by Rand McNally & Co.
Lambert Azimuthal Equal Area Projection

RAND M℠NALLY

A11

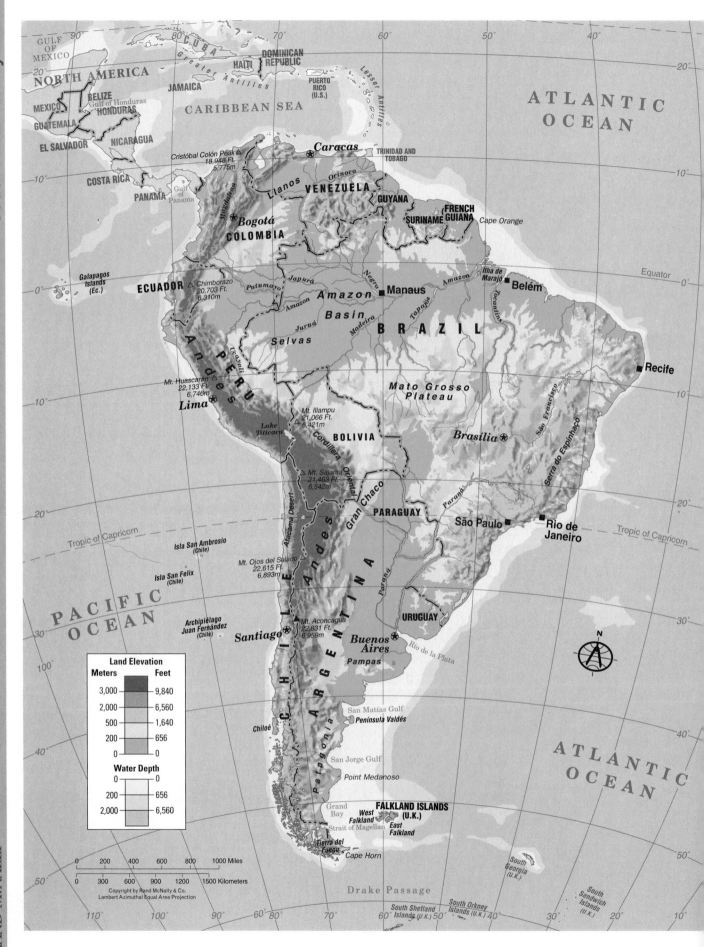

GULF OF MEXICO
90°
80°
CUBA
70°
60°
NORTH AMERICA
20°
MEXICO
BELIZE
Gulf of Honduras
HONDURAS
GUATEMALA
EL SALVADOR
NICARAGUA
COSTA RICA
PANAMA
Gulf of Panama
HAITI
DOMINICAN REPUBLIC
JAMAICA
Greater Antilles
CARIBBEAN SEA
PUERTO RICO (U.S.)
Lesser Antilles
ATLANTIC OCEAN
20°

Cristóbal Colón Peak
18,948 Ft.
5,775m
Caracas
TRINIDAD AND TOBAGO
10°
Llanos
Orinoco
VENEZUELA
GUYANA
FRENCH GUIANA
SURINAME
Cape Orange
Bogotá
COLOMBIA
Magdalena
10°

Galapagos Islands (Ec.)
ECUADOR
Chimborazo
20,703 Ft.
6,310m
Putumayo
Japurá
Negro
Amazon
Manaus
Ilha de Marajó
Belém
Equator
0°
Amazon
Amazon
Tapajós
Tocantins
Juruá
Basin
Madeira
BRAZIL
0°

Andes
Selvas
Ucayali
Mt. Huascarán
22,133 Ft.
6,746m
PERU
Mato Grosso Plateau
Recife
São Francisco
Serra do Espinhaço
10°
Lima
Mt. Illampu
21,066 Ft.
6,421m
Lake Titicaca
Cordillera Oriental
BOLIVIA
Brasília
10°

Mt. Sajama
21,463 Ft.
6,542m
Gran Chaco
PARAGUAY
Paraná
20°
Atacama Desert
São Paulo
Rio de Janeiro
Tropic of Capricorn
Tropic of Capricorn
Isla San Ambrosio (Chile)

PACIFIC OCEAN
Isla San Felix (Chile)
Mt. Ojos del Salado
22,615 Ft.
6,893m
Andes
Paraná
ARGENTINA
N

Archipiélago Juan Fernández (Chile)
Mt. Aconcagua
22,831 Ft.
6,959m
URUGUAY
30°
Santiago
CHILE
Buenos Aires
Pampas
Río de la Plata
30°

Land Elevation

Meters		Feet
3,000		9,840
2,000		6,560
500		1,640
200		656
0		0

Water Depth

0		0
200		656
2,000		6,560

San Matías Gulf
Península Valdés
Chiloé
Patagonia
San Jorge Gulf
Point Medanoso
40°
ATLANTIC OCEAN
40°

100°

0 200 400 600 800 1000 Miles
0 300 600 900 1200 1500 Kilometers

Grand Bay
West Falkland
FALKLAND ISLANDS (U.K.)
East Falkland
Strait of Magellan
Tierra del Fuego
Cape Horn
South Georgia (U.K.)
50°
South Sandwich Islands (U.K.)
50°

Drake Passage
South Orkney Islands (U.K.)
South Shetland Islands (U.K.)
60°
50°
40°
30°
20°
10°

110°
100°
90°
80°
70°
60°

ATLAS

GULF OF MEXICO
Havana
90°
CUBA
80°
70°
HAITI
DOMINICAN REPUBLIC
60°
50°
40°
20°
NORTH AMERICA
JAMAICA
PUERTO RICO (U.S.)
Lesser Antilles
ATLANTIC OCEAN
MEXICO
BELIZE
HONDURAS
GUATEMALA
EL SALVADOR
NICARAGUA
COSTA RICA
PANAMA
CARIBBEAN SEA

Barranquilla
Cartagena
Maracaibo
Barquisimeto
Valencia
Caracas
TRINIDAD AND TOBAGO

Cúcuta
Medellín
Bucaramanga
VENEZUELA
Orinoco
Ciudad Guayana
Georgetown
GUYANA
Paramaribo
SURINAME
Cayenne
FRENCH GUIANA
-10°

Bogotá
COLOMBIA
Cali
Macapá

Galapagos Islands (Ec.)
Quito
ECUADOR
Putumayo
Japurá
Negro
Equator
0°

Guayaquil
Amazon
Manaus
Santarém
Belém
São Luís
Fortaleza
0°

Iquitos
Juruá
Madeira
Tapajós
B R A Z I L
Imperatriz
Teresina
Natal

Chiclayo
PERU
Ucayali
Amazon
Pôrto Velho
Recife
Maceió

Trujillo
Feira de Santana
Aracaju
Salvador
-10°

Lima
Cusco
Lake Titicaca
BOLIVIA
La Paz
Cochabamba
Santa Cruz
Cuiabá
Goiânia
Brasília
Montes Claros
-10°

Arequipa
Sucre
Uberlândia
Belo Horizonte
Vitória

Antofagasta
Campo Grande
PARAGUAY
Campinas
Rio de Janeiro
-20°

Tropic of Capricorn
Isla San Ambrosio (Chile)
Salta
San Miguel de Tucumán
Asunción
São Paulo
Curitiba

Isla San Felix (Chile)
Caxias do Sul
Pôrto Alegre

Archipiélago Juan Fernández (Chile)
Córdoba
A R G E N T I N A
Rosario
Santa Fe
URUGUAY

Valparaíso
Santiago
Mendoza
Buenos Aires
La Plata
Río de la Plata
Montevideo
-30°

Concepción
C H I L E
Bahía Blanca
Mar del Plata

PACIFIC OCEAN
ATLANTIC OCEAN

Chiloé
Archipiélago de los Chonos
Comodoro Rivadavia
-40°

National Capital

Secondary Capital (State, Province, or Territory)

City over 1,000,000 population

City of 250,000 to 1,000,000 population

City under 250,000 population

FALKLAND ISLANDS (U.K.)
West Falkland
East Falkland
Strait of Magellan

Punta Arenas
Tierra del Fuego

South Georgia (U.K.)

0   200   400   600   800   1000 Miles
0   300   600   900   1200   1500 Kilometers
Copyright by Rand McNally & Co.
Lambert Azimuthal Equal Area Projection

Drake Passage
South Shetland Islands (U.K.)
South Orkney Islands (U.K.)
South Sandwich Islands (U.K.)
-50°

RAND McNALLY

A13

RAND M℠NALLY

A14

Land Elevation

Meters		Feet
3,000		9,840
2,000		6,560
500		1,640
200		656
0		0

Water Depth

0		0
200		656
2,000		6,560

0	100	200	300	400 Miles
0	200	400	600 Kilometers	

Copyright by Rand M℠Nally & Co.
Lambert Conformal Conic Projection

Horn

Fontur

ICELAND

Surtsey

Arctic Circle

NORWEGIAN SEA

Lofoten Islands

Tornedtraven

Kebnekaise
6,926 Ft.
2,111m

Lap

ATLANTIC OCEAN

Scandinavian Peninsula

NORWAY   SWEDEN

Galdhøpiggen △
8,100 Ft.
2,469m

Umeälven

Klarälven

Dalälven

Gulf of Bothnia

FAROE ISLANDS
(Den.)

Hebrides

Orkney Islands

Grampian Mts.

UNITED

NORTH SEA

Stockholm ✪

Vänern

Vättern

Skagerrak

DENMARK

Öland

BALTIC SEA

Cheviot Hills

KINGDOM

Irish Sea

IRELAND

St. George's Channel

Great Britain

Bornholm (Den.)

RUSSIA

NETHERLANDS

Elbe

Northern Europ

Thames

London ✪

Berlin ✪

Oder

POLAND

English Channel

Strait of Dover

BELGIUM

GERMANY

Wisla

Rhine

LUX.

CZECH REPUBLIC

SLOVAKIA

Paris ✪
Paris Basin

Seine

Bohemian Forest

Loire

Black Forest

Danube

AUSTRIA

HUNGARY

FRANCE

Saône

Jura

SWITZERLAND   LIECH.

Mt. Blanc
15,771 Ft.
4,808m

A l p s

SLOVENIA

Drava

Great Hungarian Plain

Bay of Biscay

Cantabrian Mts.

Pyrenees

Massif Central

Rhône

Po

CROATIA

Apennines

Dinaric Alps

BOSNIA AND HERZEGOVINA

Balkan

Douro

Dordogne

MONACO

SAN MARINO

ADRIATIC SEA

YUGOSLAVIA

Iberian Mts.

Ebro

ANDORRA

Corsica (Fr.)

ALBANIA

MACE-DONIA

Duero

Iberian Peninsula

Rome ✪

ITALY

Pindus Mts.

Lisbon ✪

PORTUGAL

SPAIN

Tagus

Sierra Morena

Balearic Islands

Minorca

Sardinia (It.)

Vesuvius △
4,190 Ft.
1,277m

Strait of Gibraltar

Ibiza

Majorca

TYRRHENIAN SEA

IONIAN SEA

GIBRALTAR
(U.K.)

Mt. Etna
10,902 Ft.
3,323m △

Sicily

Algiers

MEDITERRANE

MOROCCO

AFRICA

ALGERIA

TUNISIA

MALTA

Murmansk

Kola
Peninsula
Ponoy

WHITE SEA

FINLAND

Mezen

Timan Ridge

Pechora

Ural Mountains

Ob'

Irtysh

Northern Dvina

Onega

Lake
Onega

Sukhona

Northern Uvals
(Uplands)

Kama

ASIA

Lake
Ladoga

Helsinki

Gulf of Finland

Rybinsk
Res.

RUSSIA

50°

ESTONIA

Lake
Peipus

Moscow

Oka

LATVIA

Valdai
Hills

LITHUANIA

e a n
Plain

Central
Russian
Upland

Khoper

Don

Ural

KAZAKHSTAN

Caspian Depression

Syr Darya

Neman

BELARUS

Aral Sea

Pripyat

Dnieper

Lowland

Donets Basin

Volga

UZBEKISTAN

Amu Darya

Kiev

UKRAINE

Dnieper

Dniester

CASPIAN

TURKMENISTAN

40°

MOLDOVA

Sea of Azov

Carpathian Mts.

Crimean
Peninsula

Caucasus

Baku

SEA

ROMANIA

Transylvanian Alps

Mt. Elbrus
18,510 Ft.
5,642m

GEORGIA

ARMENIA

AZERBAIJAN

60°

Danube

BLACK   SEA

AZER.

Peninsula

BULGARIA

Tehran

Istanbul

TURKEY

IRAN

Mt. Olympus
9,570 Ft.
2,917m

GREECE

AEGEAN SEA

IRAQ

SYRIA

Euphrates

Tigris

N

Rhodes

SEA

NORTH
CYPRUS

30°

CYPRUS

LEBANON

50°

30°

Crete

40°

Legend

- ✪ National Capital
- ★ Secondary Capital (State, Province, or Territory)
- ■ City over 1,000,000 population
- ▣ City of 250,000 to 1,000,000 population
- • City under 250,000 population

Scale:
0 — 100 — 200 — 300 — 400 Miles
0 — 200 — 400 — 600 Kilometers

Copyright by Rand McNally & Co.
Lambert Conformal Conic Projection

ICELAND — Reykjavík

ATLANTIC OCEAN

Arctic Circle

NORWEGIAN SEA

Hammerfest

FAROE ISLANDS (Den.)

NORWAY — Trondheim, Bergen, Oslo

SWEDEN — Umeå, Tampere, Stockholm, Vänern, Vättern, Göteborg

Gulf of Bothnia

Skagerrak

NORTH SEA

DENMARK — Copenhagen

BALTIC SEA

LITHUANIA

Kaliningrad **RUSSIA**

Gdańsk

Szczecin **POLAND** — Warsaw, Wisła

SCOTLAND — Aberdeen, Glasgow, Edinburgh

UNITED KINGDOM

NORTHERN IRELAND — Belfast

IRELAND — Dublin, Cork

Irish Sea

Liverpool, Manchester

WALES — Cardiff, Birmingham

ENGLAND — London

St. George's Channel

Plymouth, Le Havre

English Channel

Strait of Dover

NETHERLANDS — Amsterdam, The Hague

Hamburg, Elbe

Berlin, Oder

GERMANY — Cologne, Bonn, Frankfurt, Dresden, Wrocław

BELGIUM — Brussels

LUX. — Luxembourg

Rhine

Stuttgart, Munich

Nantes, Loire, Seine, Strasbourg

Paris

FRANCE — Lyon, Bordeaux, Toulouse, Marseille, Nice

Rhône

Prague CZECH REPUBLIC — Kraków

SLOVAKIA — Bratislava

Vienna AUSTRIA

Budapest HUNGARY

Danube

Zürich, Bern, Geneva

SWITZERLAND

LIECH.

SLOVENIA — Ljubljana

Zagreb

CROATIA

Turin, Milan, Genoa, Venice, Po

SAN MARINO

Belgrade

BOSNIA AND HERZEGOVINA — Sarajevo

ADRIATIC SEA

Florence, **Rome**, **VATICAN CITY**

ITALY — Naples, Bari

YUGOSLAVIA

Skopje MACEDONIA

ALBANIA — Tiranë

MONACO

ANDORRA

Ebro, Zaragoza, **Barcelona**

SPAIN — Madrid, Valladolid, Bilbao, Córdoba, Seville, Valencia, Palma, Málaga

PORTUGAL — Lisbon, Porto, Gijón, A Coruña

Tagus

Bay of Biscay

Corsica (Fr.)

Sardinia (It.)

Cagliari

Palermo, Sicily, Catania

IONIAN SEA

TYRRHENIAN SEA

Strait of Gibraltar

GIBRALTAR (U.K.)

Rabat, **MOROCCO**

Algiers, **ALGERIA**

Tunis, **TUNISIA**

AFRICA

Valletta **MALTA**

MEDITERRANEAN SEA

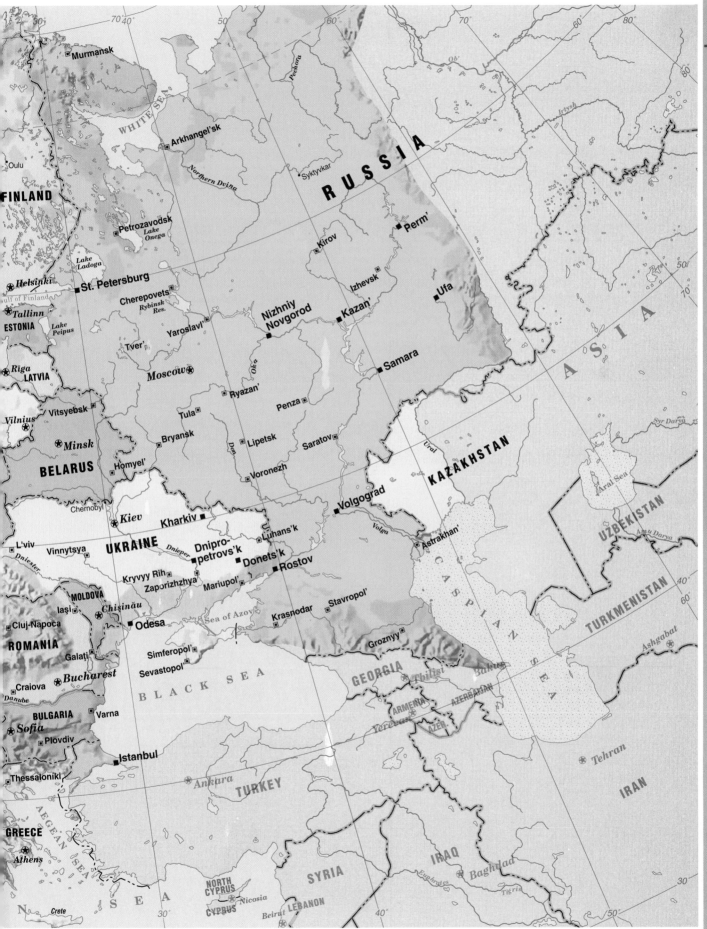

ATLAS

Murmansk

Oulu

FINLAND

WHITE SEA

Arkhangel'sk

Northern Dvina

Pechora

Ob'

RUSSIA

Syktyvkar

ASIA

Perm'

Petrozavodsk
Lake
Onega

Kirov

Izhevsk

Ufa

Helsinki

St. Petersburg

Cherepovets

Rybinsk
Res.

Nizhniy
Novgorod

Kazan'

Lake
Ladoga

Gulf of Finland

Tallinn

ESTONIA

Yaroslavl'

Lake
Peipus

Tver'

Oka

Samara

Riga

LATVIA

Moscow

Ryazan'

Penza

Saratov

Syr Darya

Vilnius

Vitsyebsk

Tula

Don

Lipetsk

Ural

KAZAKHSTAN

Aral Sea

Minsk

Bryansk

Voronezh

UZBEKISTAN

BELARUS

Homyel'

Volgograd

Volga

Amu Darya

Chernobyl

Kiev

Kharkiv

Astrakhan'

L'viv

UKRAINE

Luhans'k

Vinnytsya

Dnieper

Dnipro-
petrovs'k

Donets'k

Rostov

CASPIAN

TURKMENISTAN

Dniester

Kryvyy Rih

Zaporizhzhya

Mariupol'

Ashgabat

MOLDOVA

Iaşi

Chişinău

Krasnodar

Stavropol'

SEA

Cluj-Napoca

Odesa

Sea of Azov

Groznyy

ROMANIA

Simferopol'

GEORGIA

Tbilisi

Baku

Tehran

Galaţi

Sevastopol'

Yerevan

AZERBAIJAN

Bucharest

BLACK SEA

ARMENIA

AZER.

Craiova

Danube

BULGARIA

Varna

IRAN

Sofia

Plovdiv

Istanbul

Thessaloniki

Ankara

TURKEY

SYRIA

IRAQ

Euphrates

Baghdad

GREECE

AEGEAN SEA

Tigris

Athens

N

Crete

NORTH
CYPRUS

Nicosia

CYPRUS

Beirut

LEBANON

SEA

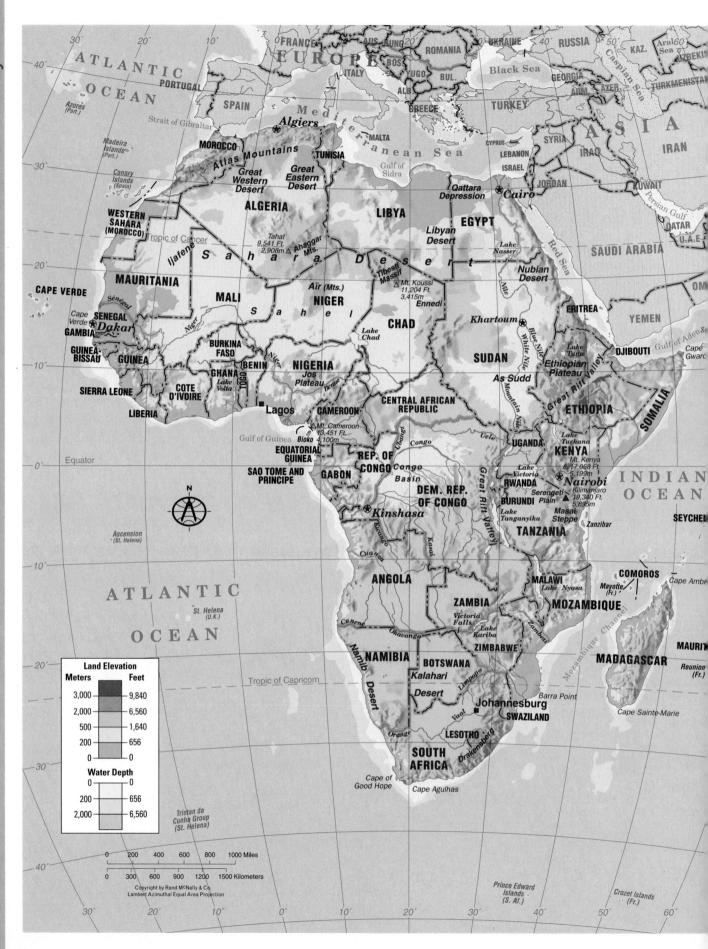

ATLANTIC OCEAN

PORTUGAL

Azores
(Port.)

Strait of Gibraltar

SPAIN

Madeira
Islands
(Port.)

Canary
Islands
(Spain)

MOROCCO

Atlas Mountains

Great
Western
Desert

WESTERN
SAHARA
(MOROCCO)

Tropic of Cancer

Ijafene

ALGERIA

Great
Eastern
Desert

TUNISIA

Tahat
9,541 Ft.
2,908m △ Ahaggar
Mts.

S a h a r a   D e s e r t

LIBYA

Mediterranean Sea

Gulf of
Sidra

MALTA

EUROPE

FRANCE

ITALY

YUGO.

ALB.

GREECE

BOS.

ROMANIA

BUL.

Black Sea

TURKEY

CYPRUS

SYRIA

LEBANON

ISRAEL

JORDAN

Qattara
Depression

Cairo

EGYPT

Libyan
Desert

Lake
Nasser

Nubian
Desert

Red Sea

GEORGIA

ARM.

AZER.

Caspian Sea

KAZ.

Aral
Sea

UZBEK.

TURKMENISTAN

ASIA

IRAQ

KUWAIT

Persian Gulf

SAUDI ARABIA

QATAR

U.A.E.

IRAN

OM

CAPE VERDE

MAURITANIA

MALI

S a h e l

Aïr (Mts.)

NIGER

Tibesti
Massif

△ Mt. Koussi
11,204 Ft.
3,415m

Ennedi

CHAD

Lake
Chad

Khartoum

White Nile

Blue Nile

ERITREA

Lake
Tana

Ethiopian
Plateau

DJIBOUTI

YEMEN

Gulf of Aden

Cape
Gward

Cape
Verde

SENEGAL

Dakar

GAMBIA

Sénégal

Niger

GUINEA-
BISSAU

GUINEA

BURKINA
FASO

Niger

BENIN

NIGERIA

Jos
Plateau

Benue

CENTRAL AFRICAN
REPUBLIC

As Sudd

SUDAN

Mountain Nile

Great Rift Valley

ETHIOPIA

SOMALIA

SIERRA LEONE

LIBERIA

GHANA

TOGO

Lake
Volta

COTE
D'IVOIRE

Gulf of Guinea

Lagos

CAMEROON

△ Mt. Cameroon
13,451 Ft.
4,100m

Bioko

EQUATORIAL
GUINEA

SAO TOME AND
PRINCIPE

GABON

Ubangi

Congo

Uele

REP. OF
CONGO

Congo
Basin

Kinshasa

DEM. REP.
OF CONGO

Kasai

Lake
Victoria

UGANDA

RWANDA

BURUNDI

Lake
Tanganyika

Serengeti
Plain

TANZANIA

Masai
Steppe

Zanzibar

Lake
Turkana

KENYA

△ Mt. Kenya
17,058 Ft.
5,199m

Nairobi

Kilimanjaro
19,340 Ft.
5,895m

INDIAN
OCEAN

SEYCHE

Equator

N

Ascension
(St. Helena)

ATLANTIC

OCEAN

St. Helena
(U.K.)

Cuanza

Cunene

Kwango

ANGOLA

ZAMBIA

Victoria
Falls

Lake
Kariba

Zambezi

MALAWI

Lake Nyasa

COMOROS

Mayotte
(Fr.)

Cape Amb

MOZAMBIQUE

MAURIT

Reunion
(Fr.)

MADAGASCAR

Mozambique Channel

Okavango

Cubango

ZIMBABWE

Tropic of Capricorn

Namib
Desert

NAMIBIA

Kalahari
Desert

BOTSWANA

Limpopo

Cape Sainte-Marie

Barra Point

Johannesburg

SWAZILAND

Orange

Vaal

LESOTHO

Drakensberg

SOUTH
AFRICA

Cape of
Good Hope

Cape Agulhas

Tristan da
Cunha Group
(St. Helena)

Land Elevation

Meters		Feet
3,000		9,840
2,000		6,560
500		1,640
200		656
0		0

Water Depth

0		0
200		656
2,000		6,560

0   200   400   600   800   1000 Miles

0   300   600   900   1200   1500 Kilometers

Copyright by Rand McNally & Co.
Lambert Azimuthal Equal Area Projection

Prince Edward
Islands
(S. Af.)

Crozet Islands
(Fr.)

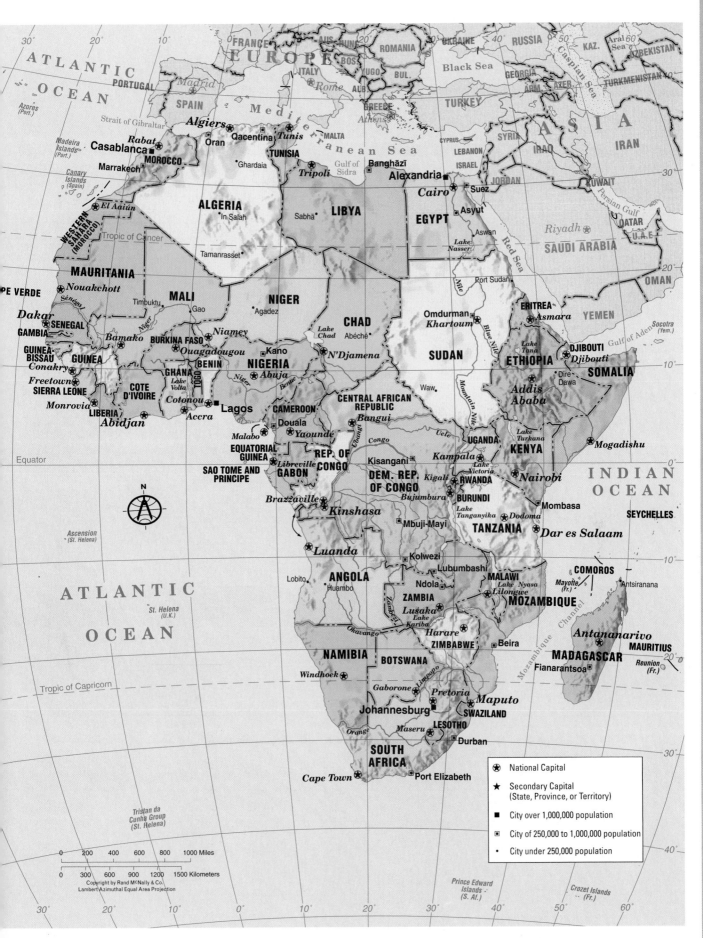

ATLAS

RAND McNALLY

ATLANTIC
OCEAN

ATLANTIC

OCEAN

EUROPE

FRANCE
ITALY
Rome
Madrid
SPAIN
PORTUGAL
Azores
(Port.)
Madeira
Islands
(Port.)
Canary
Islands (Spain)

AUS. HUN.
BOS.
YUGO
BUL.
ROMANIA

UKRAINE
RUSSIA
KAZ.
Aral
Sea
UZBEKISTAN
TURKMENISTAN
Caspian Sea
GEORGIA
ARM. AZER.
Black Sea
TURKEY
GREECE
Athens
ALB.
CYPRUS
SYRIA
LEBANON
ISRAEL
JORDAN
IRAQ
IRAN
KUWAIT
Persian Gulf
QATAR
U.A.E.
Riyadh
SAUDI ARABIA
OMAN
Red Sea
YEMEN
Gulf of Aden (Yem.)
Socotra (Yem.)

Mediterranean Sea
Strait of Gibraltar
Algiers
Oran
Qacentina
Tunis
TUNISIA
MALTA
Gulf of Sidra
Tripoli
Banghāzī
Rabat
Casablanca
MOROCCO
Marrakech
Ghardaia
Alexandria
Cairo
Suez
Asyut
Aswan
Lake Nasser

WESTERN SAHARA (MOROCCO)
El Aaiún
Tropic of Cancer
ALGERIA
In Salah
Sabhā
LIBYA
EGYPT
Tamanrasset
Port Sudan

MAURITANIA
Nouakchott
MALI
Timbuktu
Gao
NIGER
Agadez
CHAD
Lake Chad
Abéché
N'Djamena
SUDAN
Khartoum
Omdurman
Blue Nile
ERITREA
Asmara
Nile
PE VERDE
Dakar
SENEGAL
GAMBIA
GUINEA-BISSAU
Conakry
GUINEA
Freetown
SIERRA LEONE
Monrovia
LIBERIA
Abidjan
Bamako
BURKINA FASO
Niamey
Ouagadougou
BENIN
GHANA
Lake Volta
TOGO
Kano
NIGERIA
Abuja
Niger
Benue
Accra
Cotonou
Lagos
CAMEROON
Douala
Yaoundé
Malabo
EQUATORIAL GUINEA
SAO TOME AND PRINCIPE
Libreville
GABON
CENTRAL AFRICAN REPUBLIC
Bangui
Ubangi
Congo
Uele
Waw
Mountain Nile
ETHIOPIA
Lake Tana
Addis Ababa
Dire Dawa
DJIBOUTI
Djibouti
SOMALIA
Mogadishu
UGANDA
Kampala
Lake Turkana
KENYA
Nairobi
Mombasa
Kisangani
DEM. REP. OF CONGO
Kigali
RWANDA
BURUNDI
Bujumbura
Lake Victoria
INDIAN
OCEAN
SEYCHELLES

Equator
Ascension (St. Helena)

REP. OF CONGO
Brazzaville
Kinshasa
Luanda
Mbuji-Mayi
Lake Tanganyika
Dodoma
TANZANIA
Dar es Salaam
Kolwezi
Lubumbashi
Ndola
COMOROS
Mayotte (Fr.)
Antsiranana

St. Helena (U.K.)

Lobito
ANGOLA
Huambo
ZAMBIA
Lusaka
Lake Kariba
MALAWI
Lake Nyasa
Lilongwe
MOZAMBIQUE
Antananarivo
MAURITIUS
Reunion (Fr.)
Zambezi
Okavango
Harare
ZIMBABWE
Beira
MADAGASCAR
Fianarantsoa
Mozambique Channel

Tropic of Capricorn
NAMIBIA
BOTSWANA
Windhoek
Gaborone
Limpopo
Pretoria
Maputo
SWAZILAND
Johannesburg
Orange
Maseru
LESOTHO
Durban
SOUTH AFRICA
Cape Town
Port Elizabeth

Tristan da Cunha Group (St. Helena)

0 200 400 600 800 1000 Miles
0 300 600 900 1200 1500 Kilometers
Copyright by Rand McNally & Co.
Lambert Azimuthal Equal Area Projection

Prince Edward Islands (S. Af.)
Crozet Islands (Fr.)

National Capital
Secondary Capital (State, Province, or Territory)
City over 1,000,000 population
City of 250,000 to 1,000,000 population
City under 250,000 population

ATLANTIC OCEAN

ARCTIC OCEAN

ICELAND

Arctic Circle

Barents Sea

Severnaya Zemlya

Novaya Zemlya

Kara Sea

Yamal Pen.

UNITED KINGDOM

IRELAND

PORTUGAL

SPAIN

MOROCCO

ALGERIA

TUNISIA

ITALY

FRANCE

NORWAY

SWEDEN

FINLAND

DENMARK

North Sea

London

GERMANY

POLAND

UKRAINE

Moscow

Volga

Ural Mountains

Ob

West Siberian Lowland

Novosibirsk

Irtysh

Ishim

Ob

Astana

KAZAKHSTAN

Aral Sea

Ust-Urt Plateau

Caspian Depression

Caspian Sea

Lake Balkhash

Tian Shan

Syr Darya

UZBEKISTAN

Amu Darya

KYRGYZSTAN

Tarim Basin

Altun Shan

Kunlun Mts.

HIMALAYA MTS.

ROMANIA

BULGARIA

GREECE

Black Sea

Ankara

TURKEY

GEORGIA

Caucasus

Mount Ararat 16,940 Ft. 5,165m

ARM. AZER.

Tigris

Euphrates

Zagros Mts.

Tehran

Dasht-e Kavir

IRAN

Kara Kum (Desert)

TURKMENISTAN

TAJIKISTAN

Pamirs

Hindu Kush

K2 (Qogir Feng) 28,250 Ft. 8,611m

N. CYPRUS

CYPRUS

LEBANON

SYRIA

ISRAEL

JORDAN

IRAQ

KUWAIT

Persian Gulf

BAHRAIN

QATAR

U.A.E.

Gulf of Oman

AFGHANISTAN

PAKISTAN

Indus

Great Indian Desert

New Delhi

Ganges

NEPAL

Mt. Everest 29,035 Ft. 8,850m

Cairo

Nile

Sinai Pen.

EGYPT

Red Sea

An-Nafud

SAUDI ARABIA

Arabian Peninsula

Rub Al-Khali

YEMEN

OMAN

LIBYA

CHAD

SUDAN

ERITREA

DJIBOUTI

ETHIOPIA

Gulf of Aden

Socotra (Yem.)

Arabian Sea

INDIA

Godavari

Mumbai (Bombay)

Deccan Plateau

Western Ghats

Eastern Ghats

Bay of Bengal

Lakshadweep (India)

SRI LANKA

MALDIVES

DEM. REP. OF THE CONGO (ZAIRE)

UGANDA

RWANDA

BURUNDI

KENYA

SOMALIA

TANZANIA

ZAMBIA

MALAWI

MOZAMBIQUE

N

INDIAN OCEAN

0   200   400   600   800 Miles

0   200 400 600 800 1000 Kilometers

Copyright by Rand McNally & Co.
Lambert Azimuthal Equal Area Projection

Mediterranean Sea

Land Elevation

Meters	Feet
3,000	9,840
2,000	6,560
500	1,640
200	656
0	0

Water Depth

0	0
200	656
2,000	6,560

Taymyr
Peninsula

Central
Siberian
Uplands

New Siberian
Islands

Laptev Sea

East Siberian
Sea

Arctic Circle

Kolyma

Indigirka

Bering
Sea

Aleutian Islands
(U.S.)

RUSSIA

Angara

Siberia

Verkhoyansk Mts.

Lena

Sea of
Okhotsk

Kamchatka
Peninsula

Lake
Baikal

Stanovoy Range

Amur

Greater Khingan Range

Sikhote-Alin Mts.

Sakhalin

Kuril Islands

Sayan Mountains

MONGOLIA

Altai Mts.

Gobi Desert

Tartar Strait

Sea of
Japan

Hokkaido

Honshu

Tokyo

JAPAN

Mt. Fuji
12,388 ft.
3,776m

NORTH
KOREA

Beijing

SOUTH
KOREA

Shikoku

Kyushu

Qilian Shan

Yellow
Sea

PACIFIC

OCEAN

Tropic of Cancer

CHINA

Qinling Shandi

Huang

Chang (Yangtze)

Shanghai

East
China
Sea

NORTHERN MARIANA
ISLANDS
(U.S.)

GUAM (U.S.)

FEDERATED STATES OF
MICRONESIA

BHUTAN

Brahmaputra

Xi

TAIWAN

Philippine
Sea

Luzon Strait

Luzon

Hainan Island

PHILIPPINES

BNGL

Irrawaddy

Salween

Red

Gulf of
Tonkin

MYANMAR

LAOS

Mekong

South
China
Sea

Manila

Mindanao

PALAU

Equator

THAILAND

VIETNAM

Bangkok

CAMBODIA

Sulu Sea

Andaman
Islands
(India)

Andaman
Sea

Gulf of
Thailand

Celebes
Sea

Moluccas

New
Guinea

PAPUA NEW
GUINEA

Nicobar
Islands
(India)

MALAY
PENINSULA

BRUNEI

MALAYSIA

Ceram

MALAYSIA

Str. of Malacca

Celebes

Banda Sea

Arafura Sea

Coral
Sea

Singapore

Borneo

Gulf
of
Carpentaria

Sumatra

Greater Sunda
Islands

INDONESIA

EAST TIMOR

AUSTRALIA

Jakarta

Java

Java Sea

Timor

Timor Sea

RAND McNALLY

ATLANTIC OCEAN

ARCTIC OCEAN

ICELAND

Arctic Circle

Norwegian Sea

FAROE ISLANDS (Den.)

IRELAND

UNITED KINGDOM

London

North Sea

NORWAY

SWEDEN

DENMARK

FINLAND

ESTONIA

LATVIA

LITH.

Svalbard (Nor.)

Franz Josef Land

Severnaya Zemlya

Barents Sea

Novaya Zemlya

Kara Sea

Noril'sk

Yenisey

R U S

Yekaterinburg

Chelyabinsk

Novosibirsk

Omsk

Barnaul

Ob'

Semipalatinsk

Öskemen

Irtysh

Ishim

Astana

Karaganda

K A Z A K H S T A N

Aral Sea

Lake Balkhash

Almaty

Ürümqi

PORTUGAL

SPAIN

FRANCE

Paris

GERMANY

POLAND

BELARUS

Kiev

UKRAINE

Moscow

Volga

Ob'

GIBRALTAR (U.K.)

MOROCCO

ANDORRA

MONACO

Rhine

SWITZ.

AUSTRIA

LIECH.

SLOV.

HUNGARY

CROATIA

BOS.

MONT.

SERBIA

ROMANIA

BULGARIA

Danube

Adriatic Sea

ITALY

MAC.

ALB.

GREECE

ALGERIA

TUNISIA

Mediterranean Sea

LIBYA

CAIRO

Black Sea

Istanbul

Izmir

Ankara

TURKEY

GEORGIA

Tbilisi

ARM.

Yerevan

AZER.

Baku

Caspian Sea

UZBEKISTAN

Tashkent

Bishkek

KYRGYZSTAN

TURKMENISTAN

Ashgabat

Syr Darya

CYPRUS

N. CYPRUS

LEBANON

Damascus

SYRIA

ISRAEL

Amman

JORDAN

IRAQ

Baghdad

Euphrates

Tigris

Tabriz

Tehran

Mashhad

IRAN

Esfahan

Dushanbe

TAJIKISTAN

Kabul

AFGHANISTAN

Islamabad

PAKISTAN

Lahore

Amritsar

Indus

Delhi

New Delhi

Kanpur

NEPAL

Kathmandu

Brahmaputra

Ganges

EGYPT

Nile

CHAD

SUDAN

Red Sea

Jiddah

SAUDI ARABIA

Riyadh

Kuwait

KUWAIT

BAHRAIN

QATAR

Abu Dhabi

U.A.E.

Persian Gulf

Muscat

OMAN

Gulf of Oman

Karachi

Hyderabad

Ahmadābād

Nāgpur

INDIA

Godāvari

Hyderābād

Kolkata (Calcutta)

Ganges

Mumbai (Bombay)

ERITREA

Blue Nile

DJIBOUTI

ETHIOPIA

Gulf of Aden

Socotra (Yem.)

YEMEN

Sanaa

Arabian Sea

Bangalore

Lakshadweep (India)

Chennai (Madras)

DEM. REP. OF THE CONGO (ZAIRE)

UGANDA

RWANDA

BURUNDI

KENYA

SOMALIA

TANZANIA

ZAMBIA

MALAWI

MOZAMBIQUE

Colombo

SRI LANKA

MALDIVES

INDIAN OCEAN

N

0   200   400   600   800 Miles

0   200   400 600 800 1000 Kilometers

Copyright by Rand McNally & Co.
Lambert Azimuthal Equal Area Projection

National Capital

Secondary Capital
(State, Province, or Territory)

City over 1,000,000 population

City of 250,000 to 1,000,000 population

City under 250,000 population

New Siberian
Islands

Laptev Sea

East Siberian Sea

Bering Sea

ALEUTIAN ISLANDS
(U.S.)

Palana

Kamchatka
Peninsula

Petropavlovsk-
Kamchatskiy

Sea of
Okhotsk

Anadyr

Magadan

Lena

Yakutsk

Yana

A S I A

Angara

Kraynoyarsk

Lake
Baikal

Chita

Irkutsk

Yenisei

Amur

Khabarovsk

Sakhalin

Kuril Islands

PACIFIC

OCEAN

Tropic of Cancer

Ulaanbaatar

MONGOLIA

Qiqihar

Harbin

Vladivostok

Sapporo

Hokkaido

Changchun

Shenyang

NORTH
KOREA

Sea of
Japan

Honshu

Tokyo

Beijing

Seoul

Nagoya

JAPAN

Tianjin

SOUTH
KOREA

Osaka

Taiyuan

Jinan

Yellow
Sea

Pusan

Shikoku

Kyushu

Lanzhou

Huang

C H I N A

Nanjing

Shanghai

East
China
Sea

Xi'an

Wuhan

Hangzhou

Chengdu

Chang (Yangtze)

Chongqing

Lhasa

Guiyang

Fuzhou

Taipei

TAIWAN

BHUTAN

Kunming

Guangzhou

Kaohsiung

Brahmaputra

Nanning

Hong
Kong

Luzon Strait

BNGL.

Dhaka

Hanoi

Hainan Island

Luzon

Chittagong

Gulf of
Tonkin

PHILIPPINES

Samar

MYANMAR

LAOS

South
China
Sea

Manila

Cebu

Vientiane

Da Nang

Mindanao

Yangon

THAILAND

Mekong

Davao

Bangkok

VIETNAM

Andaman
Islands
(India)

Andaman
Sea

CAMBODIA

Phnom Penh

Ho Chi Minh City

Sulu Sea

Celebes Sea

Manado

Gulf of
Thailand

New Guinea

PAPUA NEW
GUINEA

Nicobar
Islands
(India)

Bandar Seri
Begawan

BRUNEI

Ceram

MALAYSIA

MALAYSIA

Borneo

Celebes

Medan

Kuala
Lumpur

I N D O N E S I A

Arafura Sea

Coral
Sea

Sumatra

Singapore

Banda Sea

Gulf
of
Carpentaria

Palembang

Jakarta

Bandung

Java

Surabaya

Java Sea

Banjarmasin

EAST TIMOR

Timor

Timor
Sea

AUSTRALIA

Equator

NORTHERN MARIANA
ISLANDS
(U.S.)

GUAM (U.S.)

FEDERATED STATES OF
MICRONESIA

Philippine Sea

PALAU

Land Elevation

Meters	Feet
3,000	9,840
2,000	6,560
500	1,640
200	656
0	0

Water Depth

0	0
200	656
2,000	6,560

National Capital

★ Secondary Capital (State, Province, or Territory)

■ City over 1,000,000 population

▣ City of 250,000 to 1,000,000 population

· City under 250,000 population

PACIFIC OCEAN

POLYNESIA

MICRONESIA

MELANESIA

Tropic of Cancer

Equator

Tropic of Capricorn

International Date Line

Hawaiian Islands

Hawaii

Kiritimati

Line Islands

Marquesas Is.

FRENCH POLYNESIA

Tuamotu Archipelago

Tahiti

Society Islands

Austral Is.

Northern Cook Islands

COOK ISLANDS (N.Z.)

Southern Cook Islands

NIUE (N.Z.)

TOKELAU (N.Z.)

SAMOA

AMERICAN SAMOA

TONGA

WALLIS AND FUTUNA (FR.)

KIRIBATI

TUVALU

FIJI

Koro Sea

Kermadec Islands (N.Z.)

NAURU

VANUATU

NEW CALEDONIA (FR.)

New Caledonia

NORFOLK ISLAND (Aust.)

MARSHALL ISLANDS

SOLOMON ISLANDS

Coral Sea

Auckland

North Island

Wellington

NEW ZEALAND

Mt. Cook 12,316 ft. 3,754m

South Island

Tasman Sea

Chatham Islands

PITCAIRN (U.K.)

NORTHERN MARIANA ISLANDS (U.S.)

FEDERATED STATES OF MICRONESIA

GUAM (U.S.)

PALAU

Mount Wilhelm 14,793 ft. 4,509m

PAPUA NEW GUINEA

Port Moresby

New Guinea

Bismarck Sea

Solomon Sea

Cape York Peninsula

Great Barrier Reef

Torres Strait

Gulf of Carpentaria

Brisbane

Sydney

Canberra

Melbourne

Mount Kosciuszko 7,310 ft. 2,229m

GREAT DIVIDING RANGE

Darling

Murray

Bass Strait

Tasmania

AUSTRALIA

GREAT VICTORIA DESERT

Gibson Desert

Great Sandy Desert

Kimberley Plateau

Great Australian Bight

Arafura Sea

Timor Sea

Timor

EAST TIMOR

Banda Sea

Moluccas

Ceram

Halmahera

Celebes

Celebes Sea

INDONESIA

Mindanao

Sulu Sea

Mindoro

Luzon

PHILIPPINES

Manila

South China Sea

Luzon Strait

Taipei

TAIWAN

CHINA

Philippine Sea

Puncak Jaya 16,503 ft. 5,030m

Palau

N

RAND McNALLY

Copyright by Rand McNally & Co.
Lambert Azimuthal Equal Area Projection

| 0 | 200 | 400 | 600 | 800 Miles |

| 0 | 200 | 400 | 600 | 800 | 1000 Kilometers |

A24

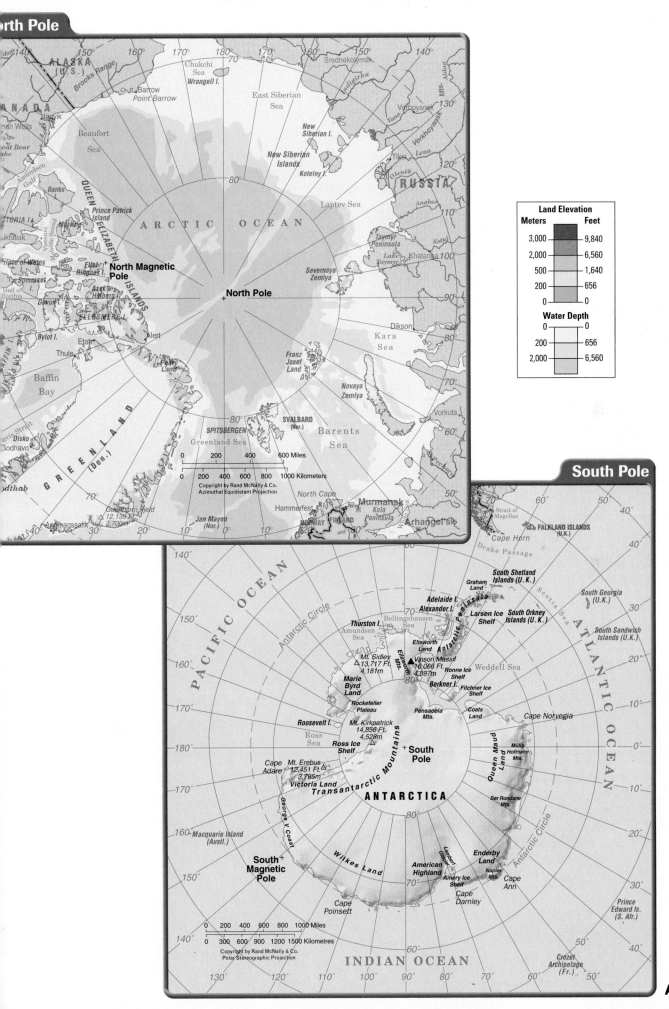

ALASKA
(U.S.)
CANADA
Brooks Range
Barrow
Point Barrow
Chukchi
Sea
Wrangell I.
East Siberian
Sea
Srednekolymsk
Indigirka
Verkhoyansk
Yana
Aldan
130°
Great Bear
Lake
Beaufort
Sea
New
Siberian I.
New Siberian
Islands
Kotelny I.
Tiksi
Olenek
Lena
RUSSIA
Verkhoyansk
Mts.
120°
Amundsen
Gulf
Banks
ARCTIC OCEAN
Laptev Sea
Anabar
110°
VICTORIA I.
Prince Patrick
Island
Melville I.
QUEEN ELIZABETH ISLANDS
North Magnetic
Pole
North Pole
Taymyr
Peninsula
Khatanga
Lake
Taymyr
100°
Viscount
Melville Sound
Prince of Wales
Eglinton I.
Ellef
Ringnes I.
Axel
Heiberg I.
Severnaya
Zemlya
Dikson
90°
Gulf of
Boothia
Devon I.
ELLESMERE I.
Kara
Sea
Somerset
Alert
80°
Bylot I.
Etah
Peary
Land
Franz
Josef
Land
70°
Thule
Novaya
Zemlya
BAFFIN
Baffin
Bay
GREENLAND
(Den.)
80°
SVALBARD
(Nor.)
SPITSBERGEN
Barents
Sea
60°
Vorkuta
Davis Strait
Disko
Godhavn
Greenland Sea
0   200   400   600 Miles
0 200 400 600 800 1000 Kilometers
Copyright by Rand McNally & Co.
Azimuthal Equidistant Projection
50°
Godthåb
70°
North Cape
Hammerfest
Kola
Peninsula
Murmansk
Pechora
Angmagssalik
12,139 ft.
3,700m
Gunnbjörn Field
40°
Jan Mayen
(Nor.)
NORWAY
FINLAND
Arhangel'sk

Land Elevation

Meters		Feet
3,000		9,840
2,000		6,560
500		1,640
200		656
0		0

Water Depth

0		0
200		656
2,000		6,560

South Pole

Strait of
Magellan
60°
50°
40°
Cape Horn
FALKLAND ISLANDS
(U.K.)
40°
Drake Passage
South Shetland
Islands (U.K.)
Scotia
Sea
South Georgia
(U.K.)
30°
PACIFIC OCEAN
140°
Antarctic Circle
Graham
Land
Adelaide I.
Alexander I.
Antarctic Peninsula
Larsen Ice
Shelf
South Orkney
Islands (U.K.)
South Sandwich
Islands (U.K.)
30°
150°
70°
Thurston I.
Bellingshausen
Sea
ATLANTIC OCEAN
20°
Amundsen
Sea
Ellsworth
Land
Ellsworth
Mts.
Vinson Massif
16,066 Ft.
4,897m
Ronne Ice
Shelf
Weddell Sea
Mt. Sidley
13,717 Ft.
4,181m
160°
Marie
Byrd
Land
Berkner I.
Filchner Ice
Shelf
10°
170°
Rockefeller
Plateau
Pensacola
Mts.
Coats
Land
Cape Norvegia
Roosevelt I.
Mt. Kirkpatrick
14,856 Ft.
4,528m
South
Pole
Queen Maud
Land
Mülig
Hofmann
Mts.
0°
180°
Ross
Sea
Ross Ice
Shelf
Transantarctic Mountains
10°
Cape
Adare
Mt. Erebus
12,451 Ft.
3,795m
ANTARCTICA
Ser Rondane
Mts.
170°
Victoria Land
Antarctic Circle
20°
George V Coast
Wilkes Land
160°
Macquarie Island
(Austl.)
South
Magnetic
Pole
Lambert Glacier
American
Highland
Enderby
Land
Napier
Mts.
Cape
Ann
Prince
Edward Is.
(S. Afr.)
30°
150°
Amery Ice
Shelf
Cape
Darnley
30°
Cape
Poinsett
0   200   400   600   800   1000 Miles
0   300   600   900   1200 1500 Kilometres
Copyright by Rand McNally & Co.
Polar Stereographic Projection
140°
130°   120°   110°   100°   90°   80°   70°   60°
INDIAN OCEAN
Crozet
Archipelago
(Fr.)
50°

A25

An orbiting satellite took these photographs of Earth after dark. They have been combined into one image. The glow of electric lights shows the locations of cities and towns.

INTRODUCTION TO WORLD CULTURES AND GEOGRAPHY

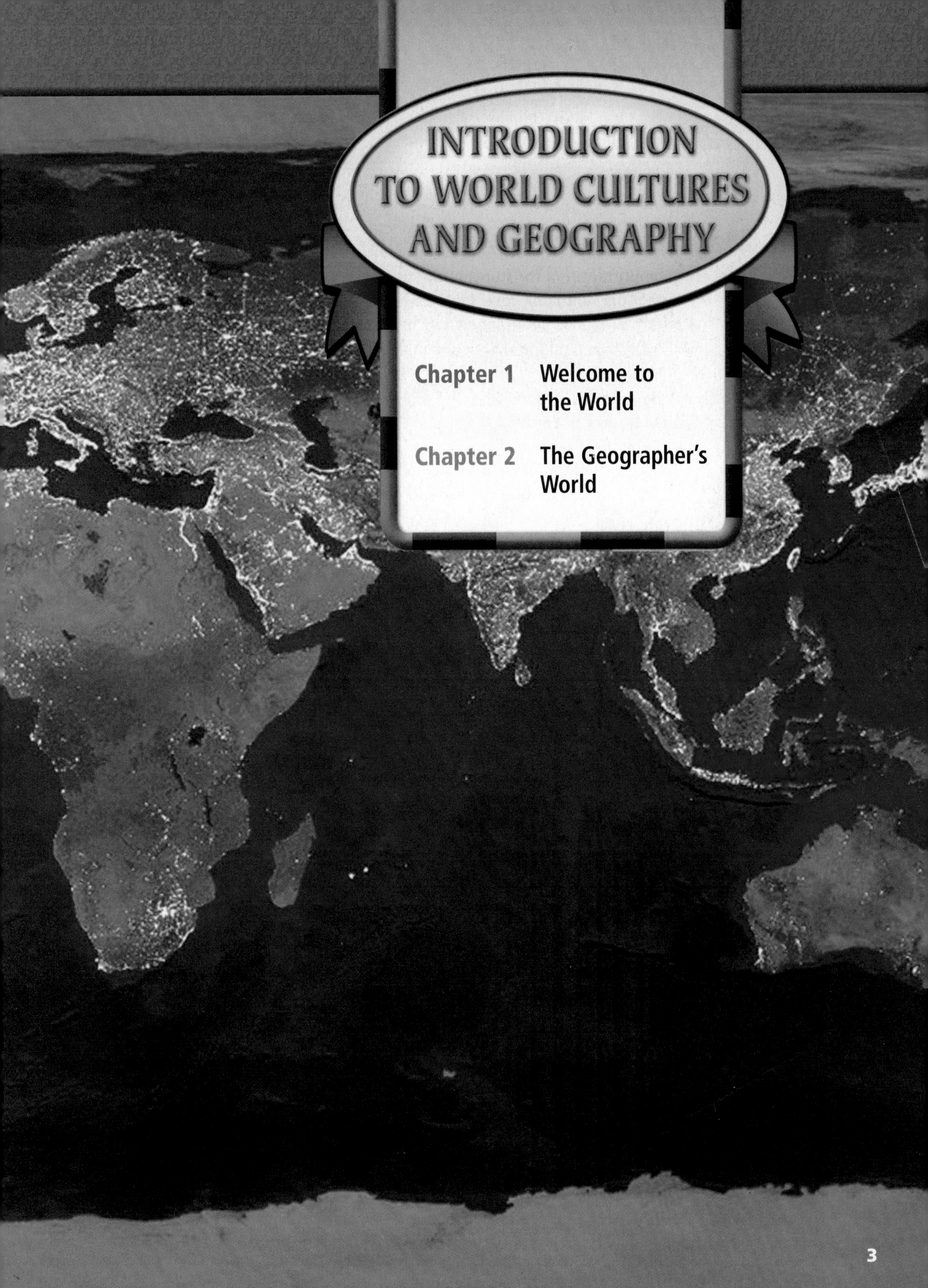

Map Basics

Maps are an important tool for studying the use of space on Earth. This handbook covers the basic map skills and information that geographers rely on as they investigate the world—and the skills you will need as you study geography.

Mapmaking depends on surveying, or measuring and recording the features of Earth's surface. Until recently, this could be undertaken only on land or sea. Today, aerial photography and satellite imaging are the most popular ways to gather data.

Location • Magnetic compasses, introduced by the Chinese in the 1100s, help people accurately determine directions. ▲

Location • Determining a ship's location at sea was the purpose of this 1750 instrument, called a sextant. ▶

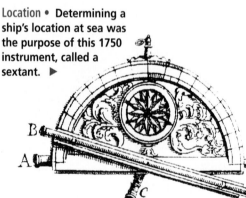

Location • An early example of a three-dimensional geographic grid. ▼

Human-Environment Interaction • Nigerian surveyors use a theodolite, which measures angles and distances on Earth. ▲

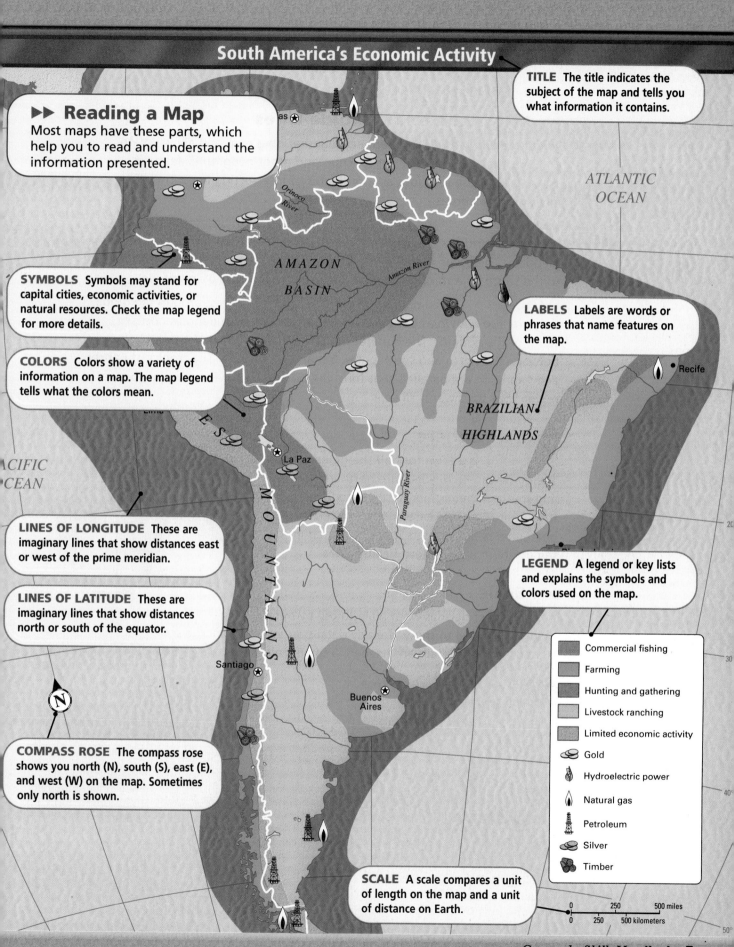

South America's Economic Activity

▶▶ Reading a Map
Most maps have these parts, which help you to read and understand the information presented.

TITLE The title indicates the subject of the map and tells you what information it contains.

ATLANTIC OCEAN

Orinoco River

AMAZON BASIN

Amazon River

SYMBOLS Symbols may stand for capital cities, economic activities, or natural resources. Check the map legend for more details.

LABELS Labels are words or phrases that name features on the map.

COLORS Colors show a variety of information on a map. The map legend tells what the colors mean.

Lima

Recife

BRAZILIAN HIGHLANDS

La Paz

PACIFIC OCEAN

LINES OF LONGITUDE These are imaginary lines that show distances east or west of the prime meridian.

Paraguay River

LINES OF LATITUDE These are imaginary lines that show distances north or south of the equator.

M O U N T A I N S

LEGEND A legend or key lists and explains the symbols and colors used on the map.

Santiago

Buenos Aires

N

COMPASS ROSE The compass rose shows you north (N), south (S), east (E), and west (W) on the map. Sometimes only north is shown.

	Commercial fishing
	Farming
	Hunting and gathering
	Livestock ranching
	Limited economic activity
	Gold
	Hydroelectric power
	Natural gas
	Petroleum
	Silver
	Timber

SCALE A scale compares a unit of length on the map and a unit of distance on Earth.

0   250   500 miles
0   250   500 kilometers

Map Basics, cont.

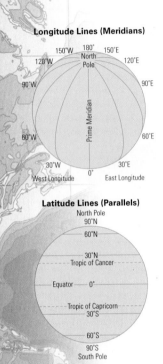

Longitude Lines (Meridians)

Latitude Lines (Parallels)

▶▶ Longitude and Latitude Lines

Longitude and latitude lines appear together on a map and allow you to pinpoint the absolute locations of cities and other geographic features. You express these locations as coordinates of intersecting lines. These are measured in degrees.

Longitude lines are imaginary lines that run north and south; they are also known as meridians. They show distances in degrees east or west of the prime meridian. The prime meridian is a longitude line that runs from the North Pole to the South Pole through Greenwich, England. It marks 0° longitude.

Latitude lines are imaginary lines that run east to west around the globe; they are also known as parallels. They show distances in degrees north or south of the equator. The equator is a latitude line that circles Earth halfway between the north and south poles. It marks 0° latitude. The tropics of Cancer and Capricorn are parallels that form the boundaries of the tropical zone, a region that stays warm all year.

▶▶ Hemisphere

Hemisphere is a term for half the globe. The globe can be divided into northern and southern hemispheres (separated by the equator) or into eastern and western hemispheres. The United States is located in the northern and western hemispheres.

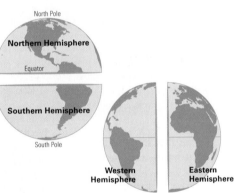

▶▶ Scale

A geographer decides what scale to use by determining how much detail to show. If many details are needed, a large scale is used. If fewer details are needed, a small scale is used.

Small scale used, without a lot of detail. ▼

WASHINGTON, D.C., METRO AREA
Scale: 1:4,500,000
1 inch = 70 miles

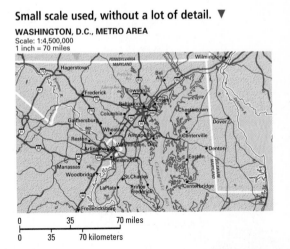

Larger scale used, with a lot of detail. ▼

WASHINGTON, D.C.
Scale: 1:88,700
1 inch = 1.4 miles

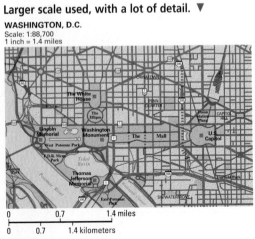

▶▶ Projections

A projection is a way of showing the curved surface of Earth on a flat map. Flat maps cannot show sizes, shapes, and directions with total accuracy. As a result, all projections distort some aspect of Earth's surface. Below are four projections.

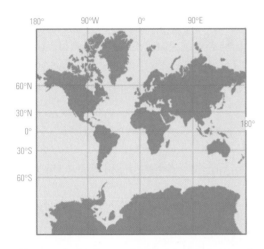

Mercator Projection • The Mercator projection shows most of the continents as they look on a globe. However, the projection stretches out the lands near the north and south poles. The Mercator projection is used for all kinds of navigation. ▲

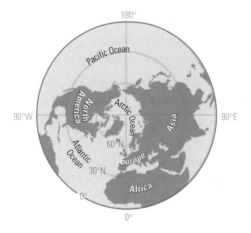

Azimuthal Projection • An azimuthal projection shows Earth so that a straight line from the central point to any other point on the map corresponds to the shortest distance between the two points. Sizes and shapes of the continents are distorted. ▲

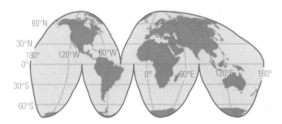

Homolosine Projection • This projection shows landmasses' shapes and sizes accurately, but distances are not correct. ▲

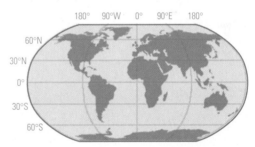

Robinson Projection • For textbook maps, the Robinson projection is commonly used. It shows the entire Earth, with continents and oceans having nearly their true sizes and shapes. However, the landmasses near the poles appear flattened. ▲

MAP PRACTICE

MAIN IDEAS

1. (a) What are the longitude and latitude of your city or town?

    (b) What information is provided by the legend in the map on page 5?

    (c) What is a projection? Compare and contrast the depictions of Antarctica in the Mercator and Robinson projections.

CRITICAL THINKING

2. **Making Inferences** Why do you think latitude and longitude are important to sailors?

Think About

- the landmarks you use to find your way around
- the landmarks available to sailors on the ocean

Different Types of Maps

▶▶ Physical Maps

Physical maps help you see the landforms and bodies of water in specific areas. By studying a physical map, you can learn the relative locations and characteristics of places in a region.

On a physical map, color, shading, or contour lines are used to show elevations or altitudes, also called relief.

Ask these questions about the physical features shown on a physical map:

- ♦ Where on Earth's surface is this area located?
- ♦ What is its relative location?
- ♦ What is the shape of the region?
- ♦ In which directions do the rivers flow? How might the directions of flow affect travel and transportation in the region?
- ♦ Are there mountains or deserts? How might they affect the people living in the area?

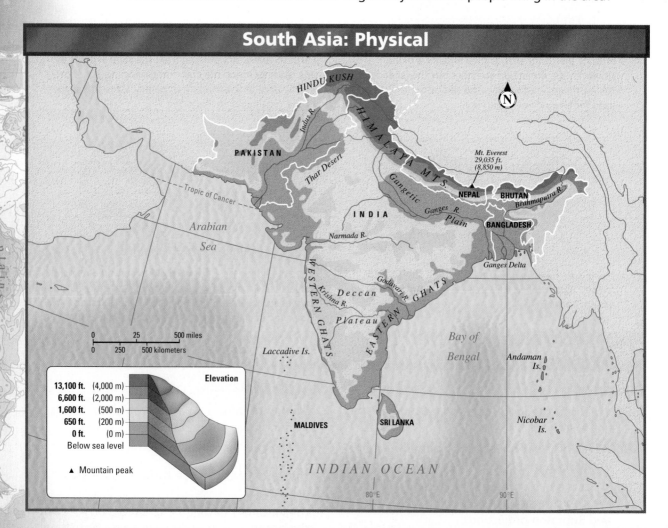

South Asia: Physical

►► Political Maps

Political maps show features that humans have created on Earth's surface. Included on a political map may be cities, states, provinces, territories, and countries.

Ask these questions about the political features shown on a political map:

♦ Where on Earth's surface is this area located?

♦ What is its relative location? How might a country's location affect its economy and its relationships with other countries?

♦ What is the shape and size of the country? How might its shape and size affect the people living in the country?

♦ Who are the region's, country's, state's, or city's neighbors?

♦ How populated does the area seem to be? How might that affect activities there?

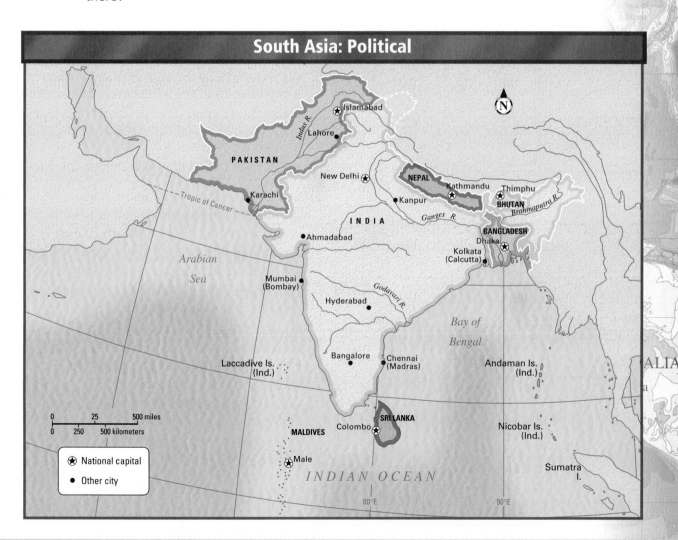

South Asia: Political

Different Types of Maps, cont.

▶▶ Thematic Maps

Geographers also rely on thematic maps, which focus on specific ideas. For example, in this textbook you will see thematic maps that show climates, types of vegetation, natural resources, population densities, and economic activities. Some thematic maps show historical trends; others may focus on movements of people or ideas. Thematic maps may be presented in a variety of ways.

Cultural Legacy of the Roman Empire

Christian areas around A.D. 500

Romance language spoken, present day

Boundary of Roman Empire, A.D. 395

North Sea · Rhine · ATLANTIC OCEAN · Rome · Danube R. · Black Sea · 40°N · Mediterranean Sea · 30°N · Red Sea · 20°N

0   500   1,000 miles
0   500   1,000 kilometers
Azimuthal Equidistant Projection

Qualitative Maps On a qualitative map, colors, symbols, dots, or lines are used to help you see patterns related to a specific idea. The map shown here depicts the influence of the Roman Empire on Europe, North Africa, and Southwest Asia.

Use the suggestions below to help you interpret the map.

◆ Check the title to identify the theme and the data being presented.

◆ Carefully study the legend to understand the theme and the information presented.

◆ Look at the physical or political features of the area. How might the theme of the map affect them?

◆ What are the relationships among the data?

Cartograms A cartogram presents information about countries other than their shapes and sizes. The size of each country is determined by the data being presented, and not by its actual land size. On the cartogram shown here, the countries' sizes show the amounts of their oil reserves.

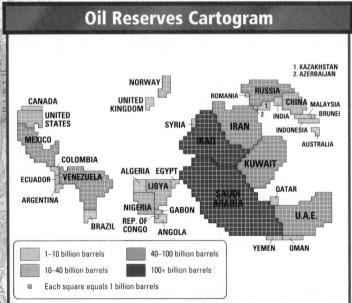

Oil Reserves Cartogram

1. KAZAKHSTAN
2. AZERBAIJAN

NORWAY · CANADA · UNITED KINGDOM · ROMANIA · RUSSIA · CHINA · MALAYSIA · UNITED STATES · SYRIA · IRAN · INDIA · BRUNEI · MEXICO · IRAQ · INDONESIA · AUSTRALIA · COLOMBIA · KUWAIT · ECUADOR · VENEZUELA · ALGERIA · EGYPT · LIBYA · QATAR · ARGENTINA · NIGERIA · GABON · SAUDI ARABIA · U.A.E. · BRAZIL · REP. OF CONGO · ANGOLA · YEMEN · OMAN

1–10 billion barrels   40–100 billion barrels
10–40 billion barrels   100+ billion barrels
■ Each square equals 1 billion barrels

Use the suggestions below to help you interpret the map.

◆ Check the title and the legend to identify the data being presented.

◆ Look at the relative sizes of the countries shown. Which is the largest?

◆ Which countries are smallest?

◆ How do the sizes of these countries on a physical map differ from their sizes in the cartogram?

◆ What are the relationships among the data?

Flow-Line Maps

Flow-line maps illustrate movements of people, goods, or ideas. The movements are usually shown by a series of arrows. Locations, directions, and scopes of movement can be seen. The width of an arrow may show how extensive a flow is. Often the information is related to a period of time. The map shown here portrays the movement of the Bantu peoples in Africa.

Use the suggestions below to help you interpret the map.

♦ Check the title and the legend to identify the data being presented.

♦ Over what period of time did the movement occur?

♦ In what directions did the movement occur?

♦ How extensive was the movement?

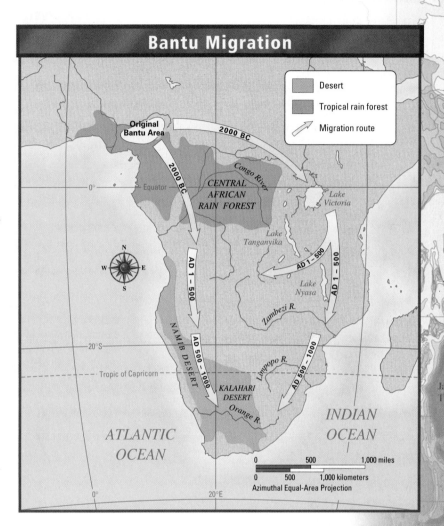

Bantu Migration

Legend:
- Desert
- Tropical rain forest
- Migration route

Original Bantu Area
2000 BC
CENTRAL AFRICAN RAIN FOREST
Congo River
Lake Victoria
Lake Tanganyika
Lake Nyasa
Zambezi R.
NAMIB DESERT
KALAHARI DESERT
Orange R.
Limpopo R.
AD 1–500
AD 500–1000
ATLANTIC OCEAN
INDIAN OCEAN
Equator
Tropic of Capricorn

0   500   1,000 miles
0   500   1,000 kilometers
Azimuthal Equal-Area Projection

MAP PRACTICE

Use pages 8–11 to help you answer these questions. Use the maps on pages 8–9 to answer questions 1–3.

1. In what direction does the Ganges River flow?

2. Kathmandu is the capital of which South Asian nation?

3. Which city is closer to the Thar Desert— Lahore, Pakistan, or New Delhi, India?

4. Why are only a few nations shown in the cartogram?

5. Which kind of thematic map would be best for showing the locations of climate zones?

GeoActivity

Exploring Local Geography Obtain a physical-political map of your state. Use the data on it to create **two separate maps.** One should show physical features only, and the other should show political features only.

Geographic Dictionary

SEA LEVEL
the level of the ocean's surface, used as a reference point when measuring heights and depths on Earth's surface

VOLCANO
an opening in Earth's surface through which gases and lava escape from Earth's interior

BAY
part of an ocean or a lake partially enclosed by land

(RIVER) MOUTH
the place where a river flows into a lake or an ocean

CAPE
a pointed piece of land extending into an ocean or a lake

HARBOR
a sheltered area of water, deep enough for docking ships

STRAIT
a narrow strip of water connecting two large bodies of water

MARSH
a soft, wet, low-lying, grassy area located between water and dry land

ISLAND
a body of land surrounded by water

DELTA
a triangular area of land formed from deposits at the mouth of a river

FLOOD PLAIN
flat land alongside a river, formed by mud and silt deposited by floods

SWAMP
an area of land that is saturated by water

DESERT
a dry area where few plants grow

OASIS
a spot of fertile land in a desert, supplied with water by a well or spring

BUTTE
a raised, flat area of land with steep sides, smaller than a mesa

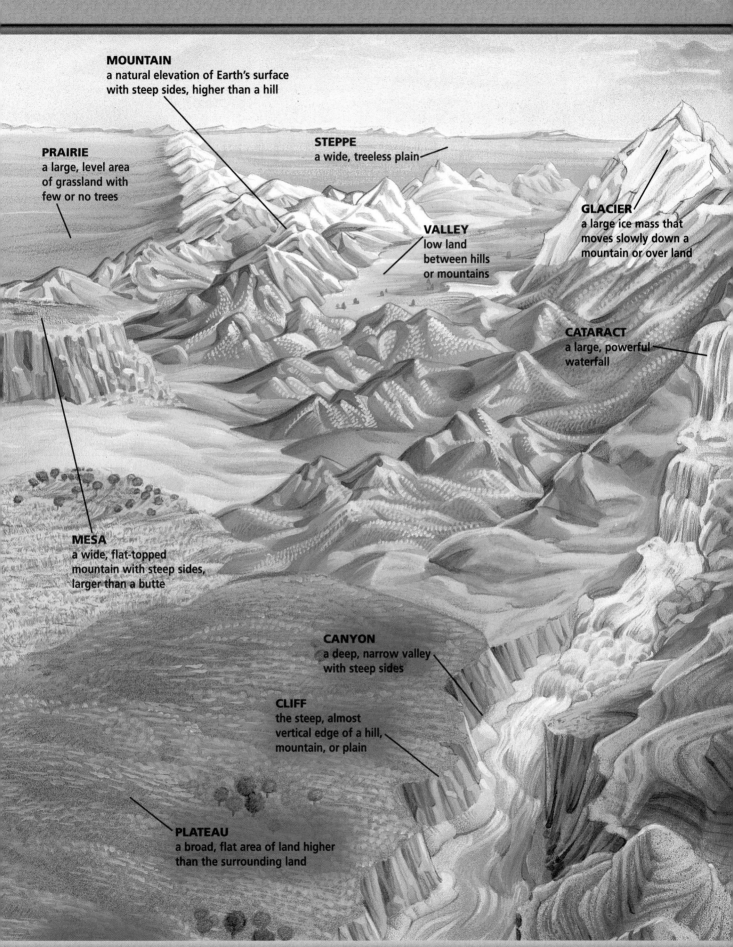

MOUNTAIN
a natural elevation of Earth's surface with steep sides, higher than a hill

PRAIRIE
a large, level area of grassland with few or no trees

STEPPE
a wide, treeless plain

VALLEY
low land between hills or mountains

GLACIER
a large ice mass that moves slowly down a mountain or over land

CATARACT
a large, powerful waterfall

MESA
a wide, flat-topped mountain with steep sides, larger than a butte

CANYON
a deep, narrow valley with steep sides

CLIFF
the steep, almost vertical edge of a hill, mountain, or plain

PLATEAU
a broad, flat area of land higher than the surrounding land

CHAPTER 1

Welcome to the World

SECTION 1 The World at Your Fingertips

SECTION 2 Many Regions, Many Cultures

Region The peoples of the world live in an astonishing variety of ways.

How have geographic features influenced settlement patterns?

Movement • People settle where they can most easily and comfortably meet their needs for clean water, food, work, communication, trade, and transportation. Before there were good roads, boats were the easiest way to travel or send and receive goods. As a result, people often settled near rivers, lakes, and oceans. They also often settled where the land was suitable for cultivation and the climate was comfortable. You will not find many cities in the frozen wastelands of Siberia.

What do you think?

♦ Why are there few settlements in the desert?

♦ Why is there often a city where two rivers meet?

BEFORE YOU READ

▶▶ *What Do You Know?*

You live in the world, but how much do you know about it? The best way to find out is through social studies. *Social studies* is an umbrella term. It covers history, geography, economics, government, and culture. History, as you probably know, is the study of the past. How clearly can you define the other terms? How do you think they can help you to learn about the world?

▶▶ *What Do You Want to Know?*

Think about what else you need to know before you can come up with clear, complete, and accurate definitions. Record any questions you have in a notebook before you read this chapter.

Region • Citizens have more rights under some governments than others. ▼

READ AND TAKE NOTES

Reading Strategy: Categorizing One way to make sense of information is to organize it in a chart. Writing your notes in a chart with categories can help you remember the most important parts of what you have read.

- Copy the chart below into your notebook.
- As you read the chapter, note the definition of each term listed on the chart.
- Write these definitions next to the appropriate heading.

Region •
Prepared for a flood,
this house was built to suit its environment. ▲

Term	Definition
history	
geography	
economics	
government	
culture	

The World at Your Fingertips

TERMS & NAMES
history
geography
government
citizen
economics
scarcity
culture
culture trait

MAIN IDEA

Social studies includes information from five fields of learning to provide a well-rounded picture of the world and its peoples.

WHY IT MATTERS NOW

Understanding your world is essential if you are to be an informed citizen of a global society.

DATELINE

EXTRA

SAN FRANCISCO, USA, JUNE 26, 1945

Fifty nations signed a charter today to establish a new organization called the United Nations. The organization will go into effect October 24.

The United Nations is a successor to the old League of Nations, founded after World War I to prevent another world war, which it failed to do.

The purpose of the new organization is to maintain peace and develop friendly relations among nations.

The member nations hope to cooperate to solve economic, social, cultural, and humanitarian problems and to promote respect for human rights and freedom.

Region • Flags of member countries fly in front of the United Nations headquarters in New York City. ▲

The Peoples of the World

For centuries, people in different parts of the world have been trying to get along with one another, not always with success. Part of the problem is a lack of understanding of other people's ways of life. Certain advances in communication and transportation, such as the Internet and high-speed planes, have brought people closer together. So have increased international trade and immigration. Knowledge of other societies can be a key to understanding them.

Learning About the World

Social studies is a way to learn about the world. It draws on information from five fields of learning—geography, history, economics, government, and culture. Each field looks at the world from a different angle. Consider the approaches you might use if you were starting at a new school. Figuring out how to get around would be learning your school's geography. Asking other students where they come from is learning their history. Making choices about which school supplies you can afford to buy is economics. Learning the school rules is learning about its government. Clubs, teams, styles of clothing, holidays, and even ways of saying things are part of the school's culture.

Place • The five fields of learning in social studies are well represented in daily life. ▲

History and Geography

Knowing history and geography helps orient you in time and space. **History** is a record of the past. The people and events of the past shaped the world as it is today. Historians search for primary sources, such as newspapers, letters, journals, and other documents, to find out about past events.

Vocabulary

orient: to become familiar with a situation

> **A VOICE FROM TODAY**
>
> How can we know who we are and where we are going if we don't know anything about where we have come from and what we have been through, the courage shown, the costs paid, to be where we are?
>
> *David McCullough, Historian*

The Five Themes of Geography **Geography** is the study of people, places, and the environment. Geography deals with the world in spatial terms. The study of geography focuses on five themes: location, region, place, movement, and human-environment interaction.

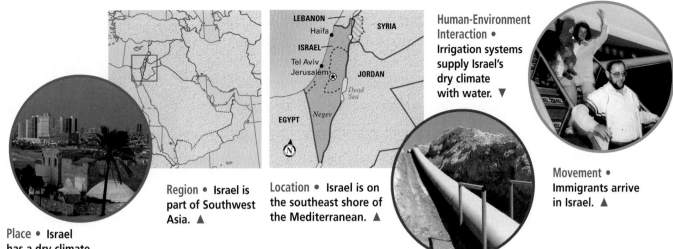

Region • **Israel is part of Southwest Asia.** ▲

Location • **Israel is on the southeast shore of the Mediterranean.** ▲

Human-Environment Interaction • **Irrigation systems supply Israel's dry climate with water.** ▼

Movement • **Immigrants arrive in Israel.** ▲

Place • **Israel has a dry climate in the south, and a wetter climate in the north, with prosperous farms and thriving cities.** ▲

Location tells where a place is. Several countries that have features in common form a region. Place considers an area's distinguishing characteristics. Movement is a study of the migrations of people, animals, and even plants. Human-environment interaction considers how people change and are changed by the natural features of Earth.

Government

Every country has laws and a way to govern itself. Laws are the rules by which people live. **Government** is the people and groups within a society that have the authority to make laws, to make sure they are carried out, and to settle disagreements about them. The kind of government determines who has the authority to make the laws and see that they are carried out.

Limited and Unlimited Governments In a limited government, everyone, including those in charge, must obey the laws. Some of the laws tell the government what it cannot do. Democracies and republics are two forms of limited government. In a democracy, the people have the authority to make laws directly. In a republic, the people make laws through elected representatives. The governments of the United States, Mexico, and India are examples of republics.

Rulers in an unlimited government can do whatever they want without regard to the law. Totalitarianism is a form of unlimited government. In a totalitarian government the people have no say. Rulers have total control.

BACKGROUND

Local, state, and national governments provide needed services, such as schools, parks, electricity, and roads.

Vocabulary

totalitarian government: a government in which the rulers have total control

Citizenship A **citizen** is a legal member of a country. Citizens have rights, such as the right to vote in elections, and duties, such as paying taxes. Being born in a country can make you a citizen. Another way is to move to a country, complete certain requirements, and take part in a naturalization ceremony.

Economics

Looking at the long list of flavors at the ice cream store, you have a decision to make. You have only enough money for one cone. Will it be mint chip or bubble gum flavor? You will have to choose. **Economics** is the study of how people manage their resources by producing, exchanging, and using goods and services. Economics is about choice.

Some economists claim that people's desires are unlimited. Resources to satisfy these desires, however, are limited. These economists refer to the conflict between people's desires and their limited resources as **scarcity**.

Resources Economists identify three types of resources: natural, human, and capital. Natural resources are gifts of nature, such as forests, fertile soil, and water. Human resources are skills people have to produce goods and services. Capital resources are the things people make, such as machines and equipment, to produce goods and services.

Kinds of Economies

Blue jeans are a product. Who decides whether to make them and how many to make and what price to charge? In a command economy, the government decides. In a market economy, individual businesses decide, based on what they think consumers want.

Levels of Development Different countries and regions have different levels of economic development. In a country with a high level of development, most people are well educated, have good health, and earn decent salaries. Services such as clean running water, electricity, and transportation are plentiful. Technology is advanced, and businesses flourish.

Movement •
One way people become American citizens is by participating in a naturalization ceremony. ▲

Biography

Amartya Sen (b. 1933)
Amartya Sen (ah•MART•yah sen) was born in India. As a professor at Trinity College in Cambridge, England, he taught and studied economics. An important part of his research was to look at catastrophes, such as famine, that happen to the world's poorest people. By showing governments that food shortages are often caused by social and economic conditions, he hoped to prevent famines in the future. In 1998, Sen won the Nobel Prize in Economic Sciences for his research in welfare economics.

Reading
Social Studies

A. Contrasting How does a market economy differ from a command economy?

Vocabulary

literacy:
ability to read and write

life expectancy:
average number of years people live

A country with a low level of development is marked by few jobs in industry, poor services, and low literacy rates. Life expectancy is low. These countries are often called developing countries.

Culture

Some people wear saris. Others wear T-shirts. Some people eat cereal and milk for breakfast. Others eat pickled fish. Some people go to church on Sunday morning. Others kneel and pray to Allah five times a day. All these differences are expressions of **culture.** Culture consists of the beliefs, customs, laws, art, and ways of living that a group of people share.

Reading
Social Studies

B. Recognizing Important Details
What are three characteristics that can define a culture?

Religion is part of most cultures; so is a shared language. The ways people express themselves through music, dance, literature, and the visual arts are important parts of every culture; so are the technology and tools they use to accomplish various tasks. Each kind of food, clothing, or technology, each belief, language, or tool shared by a culture is called a **culture trait.** Taken together, the culture traits of a people shape their way of life.

High Tech for the Developing World Mae Jemison, below, is a former astronaut and the first African-American woman to orbit Earth. In 1993, she left the space program and set up the Jemison Institute for Advancing Technology in Developing Countries. This organization uses space program technology to help developing countries.

One project uses a satellite-based telecommunication system to improve health care in West Africa. Another project is an international science camp for students aged 12 to 16.

SECTION ① ASSESSMENT

Terms & Names

1. Identify: (a) history   (b) geography   (c) government   (d) citizen
         (e) economics   (f) scarcity   (g) culture   (h) culture trait

Taking Notes

2. Use a chart like this one to list the five themes of geography and their characteristics.

Theme	Characteristics

Main Ideas

3. (a) What five areas of learning does social studies include?

(b) What are the three main kinds of resources, and how is each one defined?

(c) What is the difference between limited and unlimited government?

Critical Thinking

4. **Making Inferences**

Does the United States have a shared, or common, culture?

Think About

• what you eat and wear, where you live, how you spend your free time

• who else shares these activities with you

-OPTION-

Reread the section on citizenship. Make a **poster** showing the rights and responsibilities of a citizen.

Investigate Your World

Suppose that someone has given you a globe as a gift. What a great present! Unlike a flat map, your globe gives you a more accurate view of the world. Best of all, this new globe is programmable. You can input new information about different features and places on Earth. In fact, the manufacturer has set up a contest—the Global Game—giving prizes for the best and most creative approaches to programming the globe. Good luck!

COOPERATIVE LEARNING On these pages are challenges you will meet in trying to win the Global Game. Working with a small group, choose which one you want to solve. Divide the work among group members. Look for helpful information in the Data File. Keep in mind that you will present your solution to the class.

STATE CAPITOL

Austin

HISTORY/ECONOMICS CHALLENGE

". . . you want to know more about the world closer to home."

Now that your globe has shown you the worldwide picture, you want to know more about the world closer to home. How has geography influenced the history of your community? What features or resources brought settlers there? Choose one of these options. Look in the Data File for information.

ACTIVITIES

1. Make a time line of major events in the growth of your community. If possible, begin with the Native Americans who originally inhabited the area. Include the arrival of immigrants from various places.
2. Draw or trace an outline of your state. Then make a thematic map of its major products and industries. Use words or symbols (such as a cow, a factory, a computer) and create a map key to identify each product.

Ft. Worth ● ● Dallas

T E X A S

★ Austin

Rio Grande

● San Antonio

Gulf of Mexico

WORLD STATISTICS

- **Circumference** at Equator: 24,902 mi.
- **Earth's speed** of orbit: 18.5 mi./sec.
- **Total area:** 197,000,000 sq. mi.; land area: 57,900,000 sq. mi.
- **Highest point:** 29,035 ft.— Mt. Everest.
- **Lowest point:** 35,800 ft. below sea level—Marianas Trench, Pacific Ocean.
- **Lowest point on land:** 1,312 ft. below sea level, Dead Sea, Israel, and Jordan.

HIGHEST ELEVATIONS BY CONTINENT

- **Asia:** Mt. Everest, Nepal–Tibet, 29,035 ft.
- **South America:** Mt. Aconcagua, Argentina–Chile, 22,834 ft.
- **North America:** Mt. McKinley (Denali), Alaska, 20,320 ft.
- **Africa:** Mt. Kilimanjaro, Tanzania, 19,340 ft.
- **Europe:** Mt. Elbrus, Russia, 18,510 ft.
- **Antarctica:** Vinson Massif, 16,066 ft.
- **Western Europe:** Mont Blanc, France, 15,771 ft.
- **Australia:** Mt. Kosciusko, 7,310 ft.

SOME MAJOR RIVER SYSTEMS

- **Nile,** Africa: 4,160 mi.
- **Amazon,** South America: 4,080 mi.
- **Mississippi**–Missouri, North America (U.S.): 3,740 mi.
- **Chang Jiang** (Yangtze), China: 3,915 mi.
- **Yenisey,** Russia: 2,566 mi.
- **Plata,** South America: 3,030 mi.
- **Huang He** (Yellow), China: 3,010 mi.
- **Congo** (Zaire), Africa: 2,880 mi.

To learn more about Earth's geography, go to

RESEARCH LINKS
CLASSZONE.COM

LANGUAGE ARTS CHALLENGE

". . . you are taken on an audio journey to new places."

Your new globe has built-in sensors activated by a laser wand. When you point the wand at a spot on the globe, you are taken on an audio journey to new places. The sound clip introduces you to a place's culture—the things that make it unique.

As part of the Global Game, the manufacturer is looking for new ways to present this information. What will you include in your approach? How can you add to the globe's popular appeal? Choose one of these options. Look in the Data File for help.

ACTIVITIES

1. Choose one continent and write a script about it for a seven-minute "audio journey." Remember to include information about geographic features as well as aspects of culture.
2. Design another geography game that the manufacturer can use to market its globe. The game should appeal to students of your age. Write a brief description of the game and its rules.

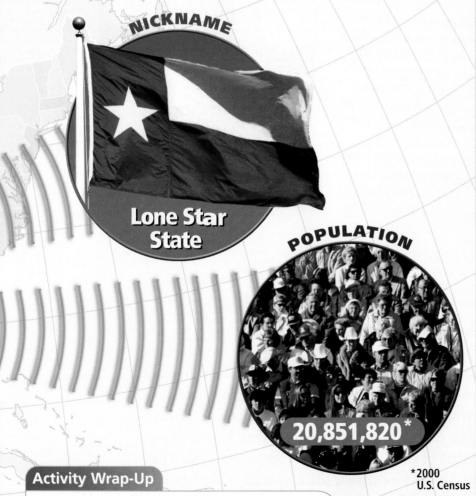

NICKNAME

Lone Star
State

POPULATION

20,851,820*

*2000
U.S. Census

Activity Wrap-Up

As a group, review your solution to the challenge you selected. Then present your solution to the class.

Many Regions, Many Cultures

MAIN IDEA

The world can be divided into regions according to culture.

WHY IT MATTERS NOW

Understanding other cultures can help you understand how people in other regions live and think.

DATELINE

MEERUT, INDIA, MAY 10, 1857— Indian troops serving in the army of the British East India Company rebelled today. Reasons given for the revolt include anger at the way the company has been taking over Indian lands and a lack of respect for Indian customs. The immediate cause was the new Enfield rifles issued to the troops. To load them, soldiers have to bite off the ends of the cartridges.

Word quickly spread that the cartridges were greased with cow and pig fat. This was an insult to both Hindu and Muslim soldiers.

Hindus hold cows sacred and never kill them. Muslims believe the meat of pigs is unclean.

Place • The rebellion in Meerut spread to the city of Lucknow and left the Chutter Munzil Palace in ruins. ▲

Different Places, Different Cultures

Indian soldiers and British officials belonged to cultures with different beliefs. The British came from a region of the world where most people ate the meat of pigs and cows. The Indians lived in a region where most people did not. A **culture region** is an area of the world in which many people share similar beliefs, history, and languages. The people in a culture region may have religion, technology, and ways of earning a living in common as well. They may grow and eat similar foods, wear similar kinds of clothes, and build houses in similar styles.

Culture • Cows are sacred to Hindus in India. ▲

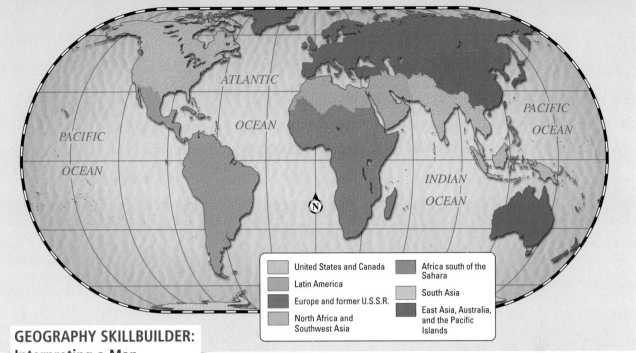

GEOGRAPHY SKILLBUILDER:
Interpreting a Map

1. Region • How many culture regions are shown on this map?

2. Location • Name three culture regions in the Eastern Hemisphere.

The World's Culture Regions

The map above shows the major culture regions of the world. Latin America is one culture region. The Spanish and Portuguese languages help to tie its people together. So does its common history. Southwest Asia and North Africa is another culture region. Most countries in this region share a common desert climate and landscape. People have adapted to the desert in similar ways, thus creating a common culture. Islam, which is the major religion in this region, also helps shape a common culture.

Usually, not every person in a region belongs to the dominant, or mainstream, culture. Some regions are multicultural. For example, the United States and Canada contain other cultures besides the dominant one. Although most people in this region speak English, many people in eastern Canada speak French. Many people in the United States speak Spanish, especially in the Southwest. In both countries, Catholics, Protestants, Jews, Muslims, Buddhists, and members of other religions are free to worship.

Reading
Social Studies

A. Recognizing Important Details Name two characteristics that make the United States multicultural.

Children Invent Language In the late 1700s, most people in Hawaii spoke English or native Hawaiian. As people began immigrating to Hawaii to work on the sugar cane plantations, they brought their native languages with them: Japanese, Chinese, Korean, Spanish, and Portuguese.

At school, the children of these immigrants began speaking a form of English that was a blend of native Hawaiian, Pidgin English, Pidgin Hawaiian, and their native languages, especially Portuguese. Eventually, children began to learn this form of English as their native language. This was the beginning of Hawaii Creole English, and it soon became the language of the majority of Hawaiians.

Da kaet ste in da haus.

Culture Regions Change For thousands of years, culture regions have changed and evolved as they have borrowed culture traits from one another. They have also come to depend upon each other economically. Decisions and events in one part of the world affect other parts. Advances in transportation and communication have increased this **interdependence**. When oil-producing nations in the Middle East raise the price of oil, for example, the price of gasoline at the neighborhood gas station is likely to rise. If there is an especially abundant banana crop in parts of Latin America, the price of bananas may drop at the local grocery store. More and more, people of different countries are becoming part of one world.

SECTION 2 ASSESSMENT

Terms & Names

1. Identify: (a) culture region   (b) interdependence

Taking Notes

2. Use a chart to list the major culture regions of the world.

Major Culture Regions of the World
1.
2.
3.
4.
5.
6.
7.

Main Ideas

3. (a) List at least three things people in a culture region may have in common.

(b) Which continents have more than one culture region?

(c) What is one cause of cultural change?

Critical Thinking

4. **Clarifying**

Why might Brazilian coffee at your local supermarket suddenly cost more?

Think About

• price setting
• coffee supplies

ACTIVITY -OPTION-   Write a **dialogue** between you and a visitor from another country in which you explain what makes the culture in your region different from others.

Reading a Time Zone Map

▶▶ Defining the Skill

A time zone map shows the 24 time zones of the world. The prime meridian runs through Greenwich (GREHN•ich), England. Each zone east of Greenwich is one hour later than the zone before. Each zone west of Greenwich is one hour earlier. The International Date Line runs through the Pacific Ocean. It is the location where each day begins. If it is Saturday to the east of the International Date Line, then it is Sunday to the west of it.

▶▶ Applying the Skill

Use the strategies listed below to help you find times and time differences on a time zone map.

How to Read a Time Zone Map

Strategy ❶ Read the title. It tells you what the map is intended to show.

Strategy ❷ Read the labels at the top of the map. They show the hours across the world when it is noon in Greenwich. The labels at the bottom show the number of hours earlier or later than the time in Greenwich.

Strategy ❸ Locate a place whose time you know. Locate the place where you want to know the time. Count the number of time zones between them. Then add or subtract that number of hours.

For example, if it is noon time on the west coast of Africa, you can see that it is 7:00 A.M. on the east coast of the United States. That is a difference of five hours.

❶ **WORLD TIME ZONES**

▶▶ Practicing the Skill

Practice determining the difference in hours between various time zones. For example, if you select the yellow zone in western Asia and you live in Texas, you will have a time difference of 11 hours. Now select one time zone in Africa, one in Europe, and one in Australia. For each location, determine the number of hours' difference with the time zone in which you live.

The Giant Kuafu Chases the Sun

FROM THE EARLIEST TIMES, people have created myths and legends to explain the natural world. Some stories explain why earthquakes occur or lightning strikes. Others tell how rivers, deserts, canyons, and other landforms came to be. This ancient Chinese myth, dating back at least 2,500 years, comes from the area of northern China where Chinese civilization first began. The myth explains how the province of Shaanxi got its mountains.

Shaanxi, also known as Shensi, is in northern China. The southern part of the province contains the high and rugged Qinling Range, also called the Tsinling Mountains, where the average peak is 8,000 feet high and some are over 12,000 feet high.

Long ago, soon after time began, giants roamed the flat and fertile Earth. One of the largest, bravest, and fastest of them all was named Kuafu—and his strength knew no bounds.

Every day, Kuafu watched the sun rise in the east and set in the west. When night came, he became greatly saddened. He thought, "I do not like the darkness. All life falls into a silent slumber. If I could catch the sun, then I could keep night as bright as day. The plants could grow forever, and it would always be warm. I would never have to sleep again."

The next day, Kuafu stretched his legs and started to race after the sun. He ran like the wind over several thousand miles without rest. Finally, he chased the sun to the Yu Valley where it came to rest every day but Kuafu was thirsty and very, very tired. His thirst grew, and soon it became overwhelming. He had never known a thirst like this, and his body seemed to be drying up like mud bricks in an oven.

Kuafu found the nearest stream and drank it dry. It was not enough. With a giant's stride, he quickly reached the mighty Yellow River. He drank it dry, but again, it was not enough. He continued toward the Great Sea—surely it held water enough to quench his thirst.

On his journey, he drank dry every well and every stream and every lake he came across. His thirst became overpowering, and Kuafu fell to the ground before he reached the Sea. In a fit of anger, with a branch of a peach tree, he made a final swing at the sun. But before the branch reached the sun, Kuafu died of thirst.

The sun set in the Yu Valley, and night came. When the sun rose again, Kuafu's body had been transformed into a mountain range. The peach tree branch extended from his side and formed a peach tree grove. To this day, the peaches in this grove are sweet and moist, always ready to relieve the thirst of those who would choose to chase the sun.

Reading
THE LITERATURE

Before you read, examine the title. Why might the title character want to chase the sun? What abilities will he or she need to catch it?

Thinking About
THE LITERATURE

Contests involving the sun, as well as efforts to reach the sun, are common in the myths and legends of many societies. Why do you think stories about the sun are told in so many cultures?

Writing About
THE LITERATURE

Although Kuafu was not a real person, his myth has survived for thousands of years. Why? What does it teach about human behavior?

Further Reading

Legends of Landforms by Carole G. Vogel explores Native American legends about the origins of many places in the United States.

Why Snails Have Shells by Carolyn Han retells the folk tales of the Han people and other Chinese ethnic groups.

TERMS & NAMES

Explain the significance of each of the following:

1. history
2. geography
3. government
4. citizen
5. economics
6. scarcity
7. culture
8. culture trait
9. culture region
10. interdependence

REVIEW QUESTIONS

The World at Your Fingertips *(pages 17–21)*

1. What are the five themes of geography?
2. What are the main differences between a limited and an unlimited government?
3. How can someone become a citizen of a country?
4. What is the difference between a command economy and a market economy?
5. What are some characteristics of a culture?

Many Regions, Many Cultures *(pages 24–26)*

6. How can decisions made in one part of the world affect people in another part of the world?
7. What aspects of daily life might people in the same culture region share?
8. What makes the United States and Canada a multicultural region?

CRITICAL THINKING

Remembering Definitions

1. Using your completed chart from Reading Social Studies, p. 16, tell how understanding the culture could help you make friends in a new country.

Making Inferences

2. Why might someone's life expectancy be low in a region with a low level of development?

Identifying Problems

3. If countries in the Middle East stopped producing oil, how might that affect the economy of the United States?

Visual Summary

1

The World at Your Fingertips

- History, geography, government, economics, and culture are five ways to understand Earth and its peoples.

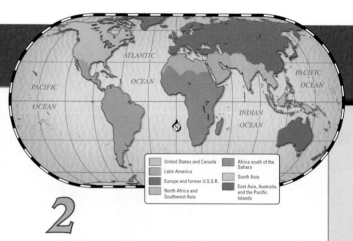

2

Many Regions, Many Cultures

- People live, dress, and think differently in each of the world's culture regions.

SOCIAL STUDIES SKILLBUILDER

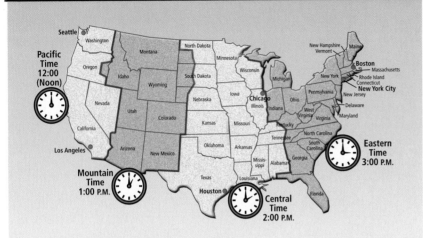

SKILLBUILDER: Reading a Time Zone Map

1. If it is 2 P.M. in Houston, what time is it in Chicago?
2. What is the time difference between Los Angeles and New York City?

FOCUS ON GEOGRAPHY

1. **Human-Environment Interaction** • What needs determine where people settle?
2. **Place** • What geographic features made the location of this town a good place to settle?

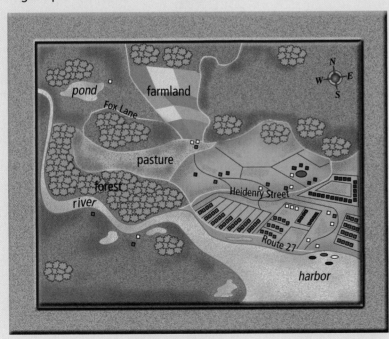

CHAPTER PROJECTS

Interdisciplinary Activity: Art
Making a Poster Research what kinds of clothing people wear in other parts of the world. Create a poster that shows the clothing, both modern and traditional, that different groups of people wear. Use photographs or drawings with captions that illustrate the types of clothes.

Cooperative Learning Activity
Setting Up a Peace Conference With a group of three to five students, set up a peace conference to help two warring groups make peace. Choose two specific groups and a specific issue that caused the hostility, such as harming a cow in a Hindu society.
• Take on the roles of intermediary and spokesperson for each group.
• See how understanding the other group's perspective helps you agree.
• Present your conference to the class as a skit.

INTERNET ACTIVITY

Use the Internet to research a culture, such as the people of Lebanon or Hong Kong. Find out what most people value, what jobs they have, what foods they eat, what governments they live under, and what difficulties they face.

Writing About Geography Write a report of your findings. List the Web sites you used to prepare your report.

For Internet links to support this activity, go to

CLASSZONE.COM

CHAPTER 2

The Geographer's World

SECTION 1   The Five Themes of Geography

SECTION 2   The Geographer's Tools

Place "Viewed from the distance of the moon," said scientist and writer Lewis Thomas, "the astonishing thing about the Earth . . . is that it is alive."

How has new technology increased our knowledge of Earth?

Human-Environment Interaction • *Terra*, the Earth Observing System (EOS) satellite launched in 1999, helps scientists understand how Earth's lands, oceans, air, ice, and plant and animal life work together as a system. Scientists at the National Aeronautics and Space Administration (NASA) use sensors mounted on satellites to study Earth's air, land, and water.

Terra helps to answer such questions as: Which environmental changes result from natural causes? Which are caused by humans? Satellites like *Terra* also help scientists study natural disasters such as hurricanes, volcanic eruptions, and floods. Today, several countries are working together in the Earth Observing System program to gather information about climate and environmental change on Earth.

What do you think?

♦ How can *Terra* benefit people?

♦ Why do countries work together to study climate and environmental change?

READING SOCIAL STUDIES

BEFORE YOU READ

▶▶ *What Do You Know?*

Do you know how to find important places in your town? Have you visited cities, towns, or rural areas and noticed what made these places special? Do you ever use terms like "up north" or "back east"? Have you ever moved from one neighborhood, town, or country to another? Do you know about the harmful effects of pollution on wildlife habitats? If you answered yes, then you know something about each of geography's five big themes—location, place, region, movement, and human-environment interaction.

▶▶ *What Do You Want to Know?*

Decide what more you want to learn about geography's five themes. Write your ideas, and any questions you may have, in your notebook before you read this chapter.

Place • Physical and human characteristics reveal patterns in places. ▲

READ AND TAKE NOTES

Reading Strategy: Identifying Main Ideas One way to make sense of what you read is to look for main ideas and supporting details. Each paragraph, topic heading, and section in a chapter usually has a main idea. Supporting details help to explain the main idea. Use this spider map to write a main idea and its supporting details from this chapter.

- Copy the spider map in your notebook.
- As you read, look for information about the five themes of geography.
- Write a main idea in the center circle.
- Write details supporting the main idea in the other circles.

The Five Themes of Geography

The Five Themes of Geography

TERMS & NAMES
continent
absolute location
latitude
longitude
relative location
migrate

MAIN IDEA

The five themes of geography are location, place, region, movement, and human-environment interaction.

WHY IT MATTERS NOW

The five themes enable you to discuss and explain people, places, and environments of the past and present.

DATELINE

EXTRA

FRANKFURT, GERMANY, JANUARY 6, 1912

Scientist Alfred Wegener sent out shock waves today when he proposed a radical new hypothesis. The continents were once joined together as one huge landmass. In time, he suggests, pieces of this landmass broke away and drifted apart.

Wegener calls this supercontinent *Pangaea*. To support his theory, Wegener points out that the continents seem to fit together.

He notes, for example, that the east coast of South America fits snugly against the west coast of Africa. Mountain ranges continue across both continents as smoothly as the lines of print across torn pieces of a newspaper.

Other scientists reject Wegener's claim. They say that they know of no force strong enough to cause continents to move.

Movement • Seven continents were once one continent. A <u>continent</u> is a landmass above water on earth. ▲

Region • Alfred Wegener was born in Germany in 1880. ▲

The Five Themes

Eventually, the scientific community accepted Alfred Wegener's theory. Scientists discovered that giant slabs of Earth's surface, called tectonic plates, move, causing the continents to drift. This creates earthquakes, volcanoes, and mountains. Geographers study the processes that cause changes like these. To help you understand how geographers think about the world, consider geography's five themes—location, place, region, movement, and human-environment interaction.

Vocabulary

tectonic plates: huge slabs of Earth's surface

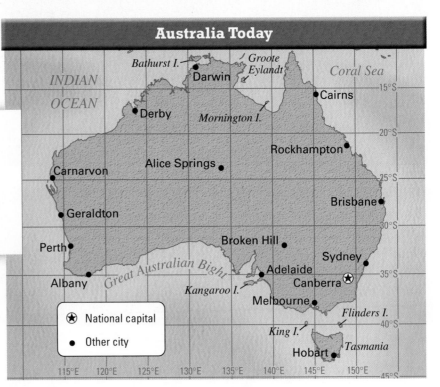

Australia Today

GEOGRAPHY SKILLBUILDER:
Interpreting a Map

1. **Location** • What is the latitude of Adelaide?
2. **Location** • What island is almost entirely enclosed by the lines 40° and 45° south latitude and 145° and 150° east longitude?

The WORLD'S HERITAGE

The Galápagos Islands The Galápagos Islands are an archipelago, or group of islands, 600 miles off the coast of South America. These islands, which contain many forms of plant and animal life found nowhere else in the world, are a unique "living museum."

Scientists and tourists are fascinated by the islands' creatures, such as Galápagos hawks, land iguanas, waved albatrosses, and blue-footed boobies. The islands are also home to giant tortoises, which can weigh up to 650 pounds and can live to be 200 years old. One of the 11 subspecies of giant tortoises has only one member left. Lonesome George, shown below, is about 80 years old.

Location

Often, the first thing you want to know about a place is where it is located in space. Geography helps you think about things spatially—where they are located and how they got there. Location allows you to discuss places in the world in terms everyone can understand.

Absolute Location If someone asks you where your school is, you might say, "At the corner of Fifth Street and Second Avenue." Ask a geographer where Melbourne, Australia, is located, and you may get the answer "38° south latitude, 145° east longitude." This is the absolute location of the city of Melbourne. **Absolute location** is the exact spot on Earth where a place can be found.

Using a system of imaginary lines drawn on its surface, geographers can locate any place on Earth. Lines that run parallel to the equator are called **latitude** lines. They show distance north and south of the equator. Lines that run between the North and South Poles are called **longitude** lines. They show distance east and west of the prime meridian.

Relative Location Another way to define the location of a place is to describe its relation to other places. You might say your school is "near the fire station" or "two blocks west of the pet store." If someone asks you where Canada is, you might say, "North of the United States." The location of one place in relation to other places is called its **relative location**.

Reading
Social Studies

A. Contrasting
Contrast absolute location with relative location.

Place • **Thousands of years ago, this part of Southwest Asia, then called Mesopotamia, was green and fertile. Today, as you can see, this area is mostly desert. ▲**

Place

Another useful theme of geography is place. If you go to a new place, the first thing you want to know is what it is like. Is it crowded or is there a lot of open space? How is the climate? What language do people speak? Every place on Earth has a distinct group of physical features, such as its climate, landforms and bodies of water, and plant and animal life. Places can also have human characteristics, or features that human beings have created, such as cities and towns, governments, and cultural traditions.

Places Change If you could go back to the days when dinosaurs roamed Earth, you would see a world much different from the one you know. Much of Earth had a moist, warm climate, and the continents were not located where they are today. Rivers, forests, wetlands, glaciers, oceans—the physical features of Earth—continue to change. Some changes are dramatic, caused by erupting volcanoes, earthquakes, and hurricanes. Others happen slowly, such as the movement of glaciers or the formation of a delta.

Place • **This satellite photo shows the Ganges River delta. It was formed from sediment and mud carried by the river to its mouth. ▼**

Region

Geographers group places into regions. A region is a group of places that have physical features or human characteristics, or both, in common. A geographer interested in languages, for example, might divide the world into language regions. All the countries where Spanish is the major language would form one Spanish-speaking language region. Geographers compare regions to understand the differences and similarities among them.

Natural Regions of the World		
Region	**Climate**	**Plant Life**
Tropical Rain Forest	Hot and wet all year	Thick trees, broad leaves Trees stay green all year
Tropical Grassland	Hot all year Wet and dry seasons	Tall grasses Some trees
Mediterranean	Hot, dry summers Cool-to-mild winters	Open forests Some clumps of trees Many shrubs, herbs, grasses
Temperate Forest	Warm summers Cold-to-cool winters	Mixed forests; some trees lose leaves in winter, others stay green all year
Cool Forest	Cool-to-mild summers Long, cold winters	Mostly trees with needles; stay green all year; some trees lose leaves in winter
Cool Grassland	Warm summers Cool winters Drier than forest regions	Prairies: Tall, thick grass Higher lands: Shorter grass
Desert	Hot all year Very little rain	Sand or bare soil, few plants May have cactus, some grass and bushes
Tundra	Short, cool summers Long, cold winters Little rain or snow	Rolling plains: No trees Some patches of moss, short grass, flowering plants
Arctic	Very cold Covered in ice all year	None
High Mountain	Varies, depending on altitude	Varies, depending on altitude

SKILLBUILDER: Interpreting a Chart

1. **Region** • How are desert regions and tropical grasslands alike and how are they different?
2. **Region** • In which type of climate are trees most likely to stay green all year?

Region • The tundra is one of the ten natural regions of the world. ▲

Natural Regions The world can be divided into ten natural regions. A natural region has its own unique combination of plant and animal life and climate. Tropical rain forest regions are in Central and South America, Africa south of the Sahara, Southeast Asia, Australia, and the Pacific Islands. Where are desert regions located?

Movement

People, goods, and ideas move from one place to another. So do animals, plants, and other physical features of Earth. Movement is the fourth geographic theme. The Internet is a good tool for the movement of ideas. Sometimes people move within a country. For example, vast numbers of people have migrated from farms to cities. **Migrate** means to move from one area to settle in another. You may have ancestors who immigrated to the United States—perhaps from Africa, Europe, Latin America, or Asia. When people emigrate, they take their ideas and customs with them. They may also adopt new ideas from their new home.

Reasons for Moving Migration is a result of push and pull factors. Problems in one place push people out. Advantages in another place pull people in. Poverty, overcrowding, lack of jobs and schooling, prejudice, war, and political oppression are push factors. Pull factors include a higher standard of living, employment and educational opportunities, rights, freedom, peace, and safety.

Vocabulary

immigrate: to move to an area

emigrate: to move away from an area

Reading
Social Studies

B. Synthesizing How do push and pull factors work together?

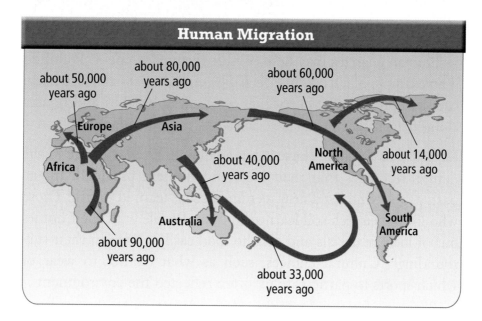

Human Migration

about 50,000 years ago

about 80,000 years ago

about 60,000 years ago

Europe

Asia

Africa

North America

about 40,000 years ago

about 14,000 years ago

Australia

about 90,000 years ago

South America

about 33,000 years ago

Movement • As you can see, people have been on the move for at least 90,000 years. ◄

Barriers to Movement Natural barriers, such as mountain ranges, canyons, and raging rivers, can make migration difficult. Oceans, lakes, navigable rivers, and flat land can make it easier. Modern forms of transportation have made it easier than ever for people to move back and forth between countries.

Vocabulary

navigable: deep and wide enough for boats to travel on

Human-Environment Interaction

Interaction between human beings and their environment is the fifth theme of geography. Human-environment interaction occurs because humans depend on, adapt to, and modify the world around them. Human society and the environment cannot be separated. Each shapes and is shaped by the other. Earth is a unified system.

Some places are the way they are because people have changed them. For example, if an area has a lot of open meadows, this may be because early settlers cleared the land for farming.

Citizenship IN ACTION

Saving Special Places Many of the most wonderful and special places on Earth may be destroyed or ruined over time unless they are protected. To prevent this, UNESCO (the United Nations Educational, Scientific, and Cultural Organization) set up the World Heritage Committee in 1972. This group identifies human-made and natural wonders all over the world and looks for ways to protect them for the benefit of the world community. So far, the list of World Heritage Sites numbers more than 690. The Grand Canyon (see photograph at right), the Galápagos Islands, the Roman Colosseum, and the Pyramids of Giza are just a few of the places protected for future generations.

Human changes may help or hurt the environment. Pollution is an example of a harmful effect. The environment can also harm people. For example, hurricanes wash away beaches and houses along the shore; earthquakes cause fire and destruction.

Adaptation Humans have often adapted their way of life to the natural resources that their local environment provided. In the past, people who lived near teeming oceans learned to fish. Those who lived near rich soil learned to farm. People built their homes out of local materials and ate the food easily grown in their surroundings. Cultural choices, such as what clothes to wear or which sports to participate in, often reflected the environment.

Because of technology, this close adaptation to the environment is not as common as it once was. Airplanes, for example, can quickly fly frozen fish from the coast to towns far inland. Even so, there are many more ice skaters in Canada and surfers in California than the other way around.

Interaction People and the environment continually interact. For example, when thousands of people in a city choose to use public transportation or ride bicycles rather than drive, less gasoline is burned. When less gasoline is burned, there is less air pollution. In other words, when the environment is healthy, the people who live in it are able to lead healthier lives.

SECTION 1 ASSESSMENT

Terms & Names

1. Identify: (a) continent   (b) absolute location   (c) latitude   (d) longitude   (e) relative location   (f) migrate

Taking Notes

2. Use a chart like this one to list and explain the five themes of geography.

Theme	Explanation

Main Ideas

3. (a) What physical processes can cause places to change over time?

   (b) How do push and pull factors cause migration?

   (c) What are some ways people have adapted to their environment?

Critical Thinking

4. **Making Inferences**

   What factors make your part of the United States a region?

   Think About
   - similar human geography
   - similar physical geography

ACTIVITY -OPTION-   Write and illustrate a **magazine advertisement** to persuade people to move to a new place. Include several pull factors for the place you are advertising.

Reading Latitude and Longitude

▶▶ Defining the Skill

To locate places, geographers use a global grid system (see the chart directly below). Imaginary lines of latitude, called parallels, circle the globe. The equator circles the middle of the globe at 0°. Parallels measure distance in degrees north and south of the equator.

Lines of longitude, called meridians, circle the globe from pole to pole. Meridians measure distance in degrees east and west of the prime meridian. The prime meridian is at 0°. It passes through Greenwich, England.

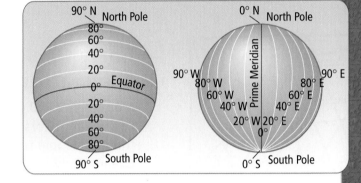

▶▶ Applying the Skill

The world map below shows lines of latitude and longitude. Use the strategies listed directly below to help you locate places on Earth.

How to Read Latitude and Longitude

Strategy ❶ Place a finger on the place you want to locate. With a finger from your other hand, find the nearest parallel. Write down its number. Be sure to include north or south. (You may have to guesstimate the actual number.)

Strategy ❷ Keep your finger on the place you want to locate. Now find the nearest meridian. Write down its number. Be sure to include east or west. (You may have to guesstimate the actual number.)

Strategy ❸ If you know the longitude and latitude of a place and want to find it on a map, put one finger on the line of longitude and another on the line of latitude. Bring your fingers together until they meet.

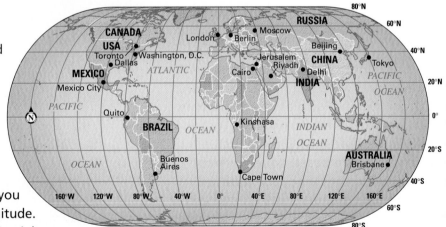

Write a Summary

Writing a summary will help you understand latitude and longitude. The paragraph below and to the right summarizes the information you have learned.

▶▶ Practicing the Skill

Turn to page 36 in Chapter 2, Section 1, "The Five Themes of Geography." Look at the map of Australia and write a paragraph summarizing how you located the city of Adelaide.

Use latitude and longitude to locate a place on a globe or map. Lines of latitude circle Earth. Lines of longitude run through the poles. The numbers of the lines at the place where two lines cross is the location of that place.

Linking Past and Present

The Legacy of World Exploration

Early Pacific Navigation

More than 2,000 years ago, Polynesian sailors were among the first people to sail the Pacific Ocean. Without charts or instruments to help them find their way, these ancient navigators made sea charts from palm sticks tied together with coconut threads, using small shells to represent islands.

Magnetic Compass

In the 1100s, mariners of China and Europe independently discovered the magnetic compass. They discovered that an iron or steel needle touched by a lodestone, or piece of magnetic ore, tends to point roughly in a north-south direction. Today, surveyors and navigators consider the magnetic compass an essential tool for determining direction.

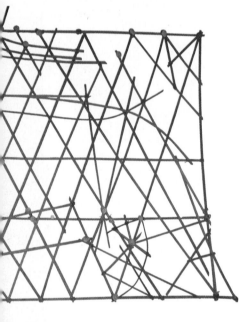

Portolan Charts

Portolan charts were first made in the 1300s in Italy and Spain. *Portolan* comes from an Italian word meaning "navigation instructions." These charts, which were actually rough maps, were based on accounts of medieval Europeans who sailed the Mediterranean and Black seas. Drawn on sheepskin, portolan charts show coastal features and main ports. The straight lines crisscrossing the charts represent the 32 directions of the mariner's compass.

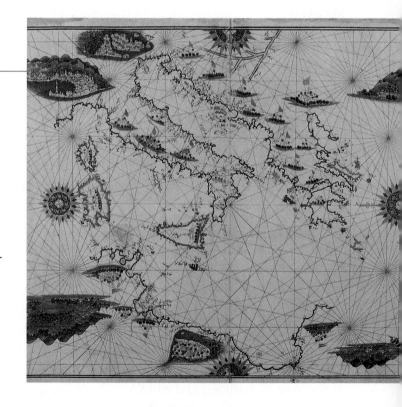

Modern Electronic Navigation

In the 1970s, the U.S. Department of Defense developed the Global Positioning System (GPS). GPS allows people on land, at sea, or in the air to pinpoint their location or to track moving objects in any weather. A network of 24 satellites that orbit Earth beam down data to palm-sized receivers, aiding the military in maneuvers. Civilians use them for hiking or finding shorter travel routes.

Chronometer

John Harrison worked for nearly half a century before he perfected, in 1762, a ship's clock that would revolutionize navigation. This tool, called a chronometer, enabled sailors for the first time to determine accurately a ship's longitude, or east-west position. The modern chronometer, which looks like a large, heavy watch, continues to help sailors find their ships' longitude.

Sextant

In the 1730s, the sextant replaced the astrolabe. This device measures the angle between the horizon and the sun, the moon, or a star and is used to calculate latitude, or north-south position. The sextant continues to be a basic navigational tool today.

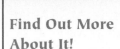

Astrolabe

The astrolabe was first used in the 1400s in Europe and the Islamic world. It is a flat, circular piece of either metal or wood. The edge of the circle is marked to show 360 degrees. Sailors used the astrolabe to measure the sun's and stars' angles above the horizon in order to determine their ships' positions at sea.

Find Out More About It!

Study the text and photos on these pages to learn about world exploration. Then choose the item that interests you the most and research it in the library or on the Internet to learn more about it. Use the information you gather to write a short play that you and your classmates can perform.

RESEARCH LINKS
CLASSZONE.COM

A Map of Earth in 3-D

On February 11, 2000, the space shuttle *Endeavour* was launched into space on an 11-day mission to complete the most in-depth mapping project in history. The Shuttle Radar Topography Mission (SRTM) collected data on 80 percent of Earth's surface. This information was gathered by beaming radar waves at Earth and converting the echoes into images through a process known as interferometry (ɪʜɴ•tuhr•fuh•RAHM•ih•tree).

With the aid of computers, the resulting information can be used to produce almost limitless numbers of three-dimensional (3-D) maps. These maps show the topography—rivers, forests, mountains, and valleys—of Earth's surface. It took one year to process the data into 3-D maps. These maps, the most accurate topographical maps ever, will help scientists to better study Earth's surface. The data will also be useful to the general public; for example, it can be used to find new locations for cellular-phone towers and to create maps for hikers.

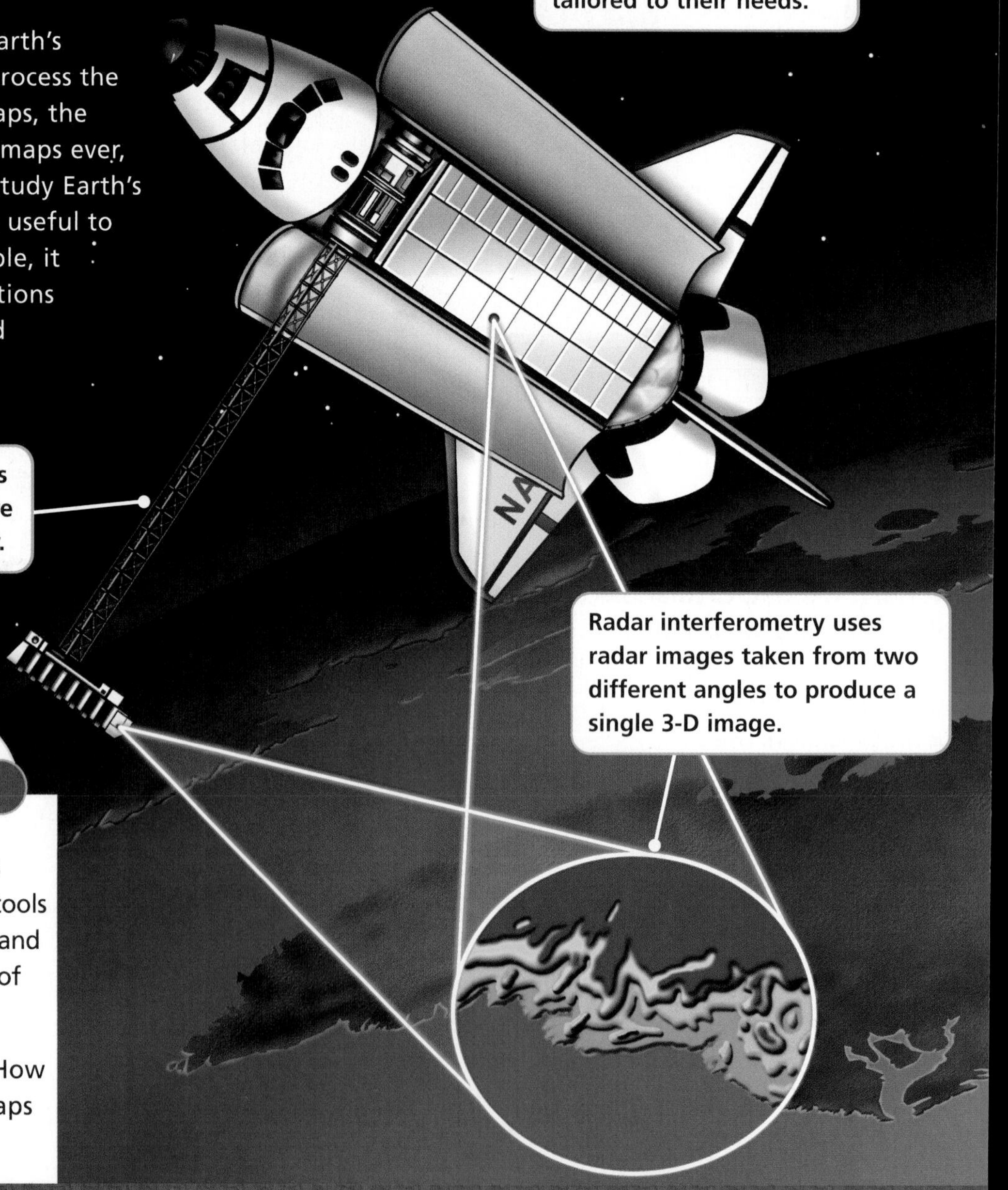

The data collected on the 11-day SRTM mission can be used by many people— such as the military, the science community, and civic groups—and can be tailored to their needs.

The 200-foot mast is the longest structure used in space today.

Radar interferometry uses radar images taken from two different angles to produce a single 3-D image.

THINKING Critically

1. Drawing Conclusions
How will new, sophisticated tools such as radar interferometry and computers change the study of Earth and the environment?

2. Making Predictions
How will these topographical maps help the world?

The Geographer's Tools

TERMS & NAMES
cartographer
thematic map
map projection

MAIN IDEA

Geographers use maps, globes, charts, graphs, and new technology to learn about and display the features of Earth.

WHY IT MATTERS NOW

Knowing how to use the tools of geography adds to your ability to understand the world.

DATELINE

BABYLONIA, ABOUT 600 B.C.— Palace officials today released the first map of the world seen in this area. As suspected, Babylon lies at the center of the world. The star-shaped map is drawn on a clay tablet disk about four inches high.

It shows the world surrounded by the Earthly Ocean, which we call the Bitter River. Seven outer regions are also shown as equal triangles rising up out of the oceans. One side of the tablet gives the names of the countries and cities in cuneiform. The other side describes the seven islands. Officials say the map will enable viewers to see the relation of these foreign places to Babylon.

Location • The Babylonian world map was drawn on a clay tablet. ▲

Location • This diagram shows the Babylonian world map translated into English. ▲

Maps and Globes

People have been drawing maps of their world for thousands of years. Geographers today have many tools, such as remote sensing and the Global Positioning System, to help them represent Earth. Increased knowledge and technology allows a **cartographer,** or mapmaker, to construct maps that give a much more detailed and accurate picture of the world. The "Linking Past and Present" and "Technology: 2000" features on pages 42–44 provide more information on modern mapmaking technology.

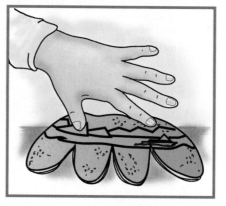

Location • Draw a picture on the entire surface of an orange and then peel the orange in one continuous piece. After you lay the peel flat, your image will be distorted. ◄

Differences Between Maps and Globes Both maps and globes represent Earth and its features. A globe is an accurate model of the world because it has three dimensions and can show its actual shape. Globes are difficult to carry around, however. Maps are more practical. They can be folded, carried, hung on a wall, or printed in a book or magazine. However, because maps show the world in only two dimensions, they are not perfectly accurate. Look at the pictures above to see why. When the orange peel is flattened out, the picture on the orange is distorted, or twisted out of shape. Cartographers have the same problem with maps.

Three Kinds of Maps General reference maps, which show natural and human-made features, are used to locate a place. **Thematic maps** focus on one specific idea or theme. The population map on page 48 is an example of a thematic map. Pilots and sailors use nautical maps to find their way through air and over water. A nautical map is sometimes called a chart.

Reading
Social Studies

A. Clarifying
Why does a globe represent Earth better than a map?

Location • A road map is a reference map that shows how to get from one place to another. ▼

Connections to Math

Measuring Earth In 230 B.C., the Greek scientist Eratosthenes used basic geometry to measure the circumference of Earth. Eratosthenes knew that at noon on June 21, the sun cast no shadow in the Egyptian city of Syene (now Aswan). (See the diagram below.) At the same time, the sun cast a shadow of 7°12′ in Alexandria, about 500 miles from Syene.

The circumference of a circle is 360°; 7°12′ is about 2 percent, or 1/50, of 360°. Therefore, he concluded, 500 miles must be about 2 percent of the distance around Earth, which at the equator would be about 25,000 miles.

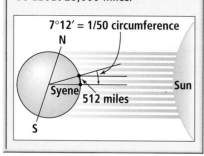

7°12′ = 1/50 circumference

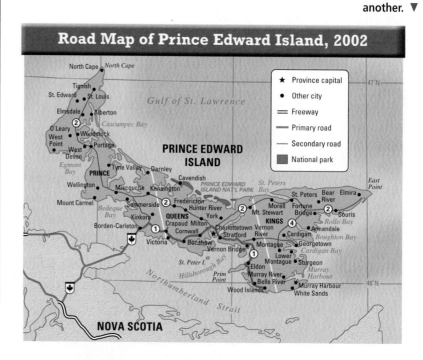

Road Map of Prince Edward Island, 2002

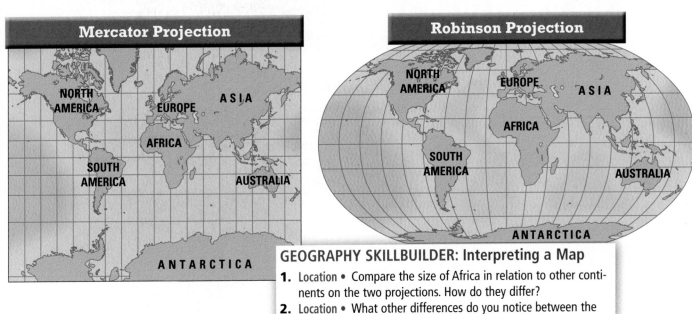

Mercator Projection

NORTH
AMERICA

EUROPE

ASIA

AFRICA

SOUTH
AMERICA

AUSTRALIA

ANTARCTICA

Robinson Projection

NORTH
AMERICA

EUROPE

ASIA

AFRICA

SOUTH
AMERICA

AUSTRALIA

ANTARCTICA

GEOGRAPHY SKILLBUILDER: Interpreting a Map

1. Location • Compare the size of Africa in relation to other continents on the two projections. How do they differ?
2. Location • What other differences do you notice between the Mercator projection and the Robinson projection?

Reading
Social Studies

B. Identifying Problems What are the main problems faced by cartographers?

Map Projections The different ways of showing Earth's curved surface on a flat map are called **map projections**. All projections distort Earth, but different projections distort it in different ways. Some make places look bigger or smaller than they really are in relation to other places. Other projections distort shapes. For more than 400 years, the Mercator projection was most often shown on maps of the world. Recently, the Robinson projection has come into common use because it gives a fairer and more accurate picture of the world.

Spotlight on CULTURE

Mercator Map This map of the Arctic was drawn in 1595 by Gerardus Mercator (1512–1594), the famous mapmaker for whom the map projection was named. It is one of many old maps that are rare, beautiful, and important historical artifacts.

THINKING CRITICALLY

1. **Recognizing Important Details** Does Mercator's map show more land or more water?

2. **Identifying Problems** What types of problems might Mercator have faced when he created this map?

World Population and Life Expectancy, 2000

Population

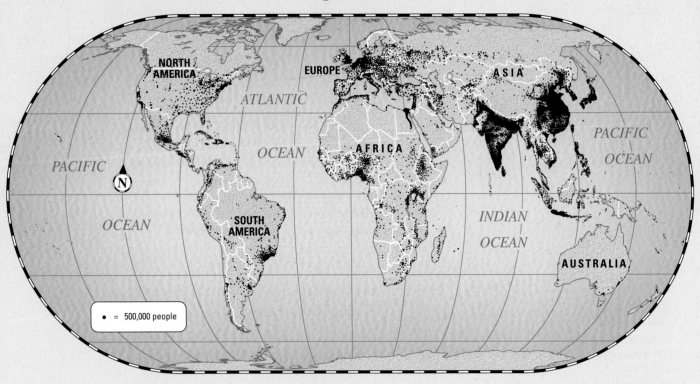

• = 500,000 people

Life Expectancy

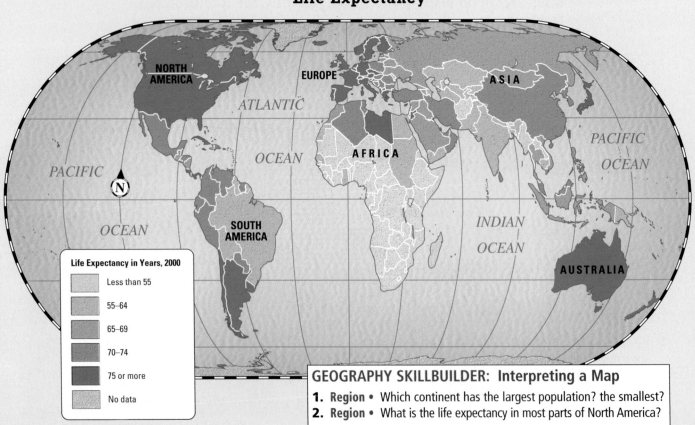

Life Expectancy in Years, 2000

- Less than 55
- 55–64
- 65–69
- 70–74
- 75 or more
- No data

GEOGRAPHY SKILLBUILDER: Interpreting a Map

1. **Region** • Which continent has the largest population? the smallest?
2. **Region** • What is the life expectancy in most parts of North America?

Comparing Maps, Charts, and Graphs

Along with maps, geographers use charts and graphs to display and compare information. The graphs on this page and the maps on page 48 contain related information about the world's population. Notice how each quickly and clearly presents facts that would otherwise take up many paragraphs of text.

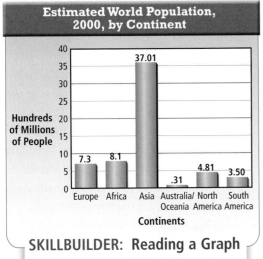

Estimated World Population, 2000, by Continent

SKILLBUILDER: Reading a Graph

1. How many people live in Europe?
2. Which continent has the smallest population?

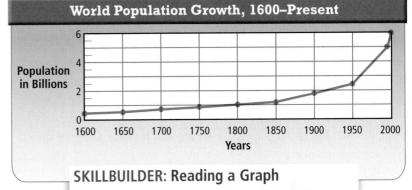

World Population Growth, 1600–Present

SKILLBUILDER: Reading a Graph

1. How many people lived in the world in 1900?
2. How much did the world's population increase between 1600 and 1900? between 1900 and 2000?

SECTION 2 ASSESSMENT

Terms & Names

1. **Identify:** (a) cartographer (b) thematic map (c) map projection

Taking Notes

2. Use a chart like the one below to compare the advantages and disadvantages of maps and globes.

	Maps	Globes
Advantages		
Disadvantages		

Main Ideas

3. (a) What are the differences among the three main kinds of maps?

   (b) How have new tools and knowledge helped cartographers?

   (c) What kinds of information can be displayed in maps and graphs?

Critical Thinking

4. **Using Maps**

   What kind of map would show how many students are in each school in your district?

   Think About

   • the three kinds of maps

   • what information different kinds of population maps show

---

ACTIVITY -OPTION- Draw a **map** of the route you take to and from school or some other familiar destination. Include the names of streets, landmarks such as shops and other buildings, and any other useful information.

TERMS & NAMES

Explain the significance of each of the following:

1. absolute location
2. latitude
3. longitude
4. relative location
5. cartographer
6. thematic map
7. map projection
8. migrate
9. continent

REVIEW QUESTIONS

The Five Themes of Geography *(pages 35–40)*

1. What system do geographers use to determine absolute location?
2. How is relative location different from absolute location?
3. What are some of the natural barriers that made migration difficult in the past?
4. How has technology changed the way humans adapt to their environment?

The Geographer's Tools *(pages 45–49)*

5. Why is a globe an accurate representation of the world?
6. Why would a pilot use a nautical map?
7. How has modern technology helped cartography?
8. Why do most modern cartographers prefer the Robinson projection to the Mercator projection?

CRITICAL THINKING

Drawing Conclusions

1. Using your completed spider map from Reading Social Studies, p. 34, draw a conclusion about which theme of geography is most useful in familiarizing you with an area of the world. Which details in your chart help you understand a country or region?

Contrasting

2. Maps and globes both represent Earth and its features. Contrast the advantages of a map with the advantages of a globe.

Clarifying

3. Why would the leaders of a country find a population density map of their country useful?

Visual Summary

The Five Themes of Geography 1

- The five themes of geography are location, place, region, movement, and human-environment interaction.
- These themes are the keys to understanding the geography of the world.

The Geographer's Tools 2

- Maps, globes, charts, graphs, and other tools are available to geographers to help them understand the features of Earth.
- Geographers use these tools to organize and explain Earth's features.

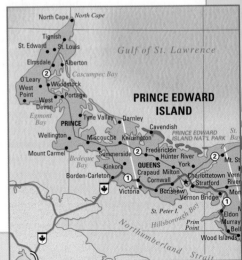

SOCIAL STUDIES SKILLBUILDER

SKILLBUILDER: Reading Longitude and Latitude

A hurricane is expected to touch land briefly at latitude 34°N and longitude 79°W. It will move over the water and touch land again at latitude 30°N and longitude 82°W. Then it will move out over the sea.

1. Which state will feel the effects of the hurricane first?
2. Which state will be touched by the hurricane next?

FOCUS ON GEOGRAPHY

1. Location • What is special about a satellite view of Earth?
2. Location • How might scientists use satellite images such as this to help people?

CHAPTER PROJECTS

Interdisciplinary Activity: Language Arts

Writing a Description Most people use relative location when they are giving directions. Write a paragraph describing the relative location of your home.

Cooperative Learning Activity

Describing Geography In a group of three to five students, choose a country and use the five themes of geography to describe it. Assign the themes to members of the group:

• Where is your country located?
• What are the physical and human characteristics of the place?
• How can you classify the region?
• What movement has occurred in the country?
• How have the people who live there adapted to the environment?

Gather your findings and present them to the class in the form of a book or on a poster board.

INTERNET ACTIVITY

Use the Internet to research how technology can be used to study natural events. Focus on one natural event, like tropical rainfall or global warming, and look into how technology is helping us understand it.

Writing About Geography Write a report of your findings. Include information about the technology and how it is used. Make a prediction about the future uses of technology.

For Internet links to support this activity, go to

RESEARCH LINKS
CLASSZONE.COM

Place Mount Rushmore is a monument located in the Black Hills of South Dakota. The 60-foot likenesses of (from left to right) George Washington, Thomas Jefferson, Theodore Roosevelt, and Abraham Lincoln took 14 years to carve into the granite cliff.

THE UNITED STATES AND CANADA

X

MOUNT RUSHMORE

THE UNITED STATES AND CANADA

N

PACIFIC OCEAN

ATLANTIC OCEAN

INDIAN OCEAN

PACIFIC OCEAN

PACIFIC OCEAN

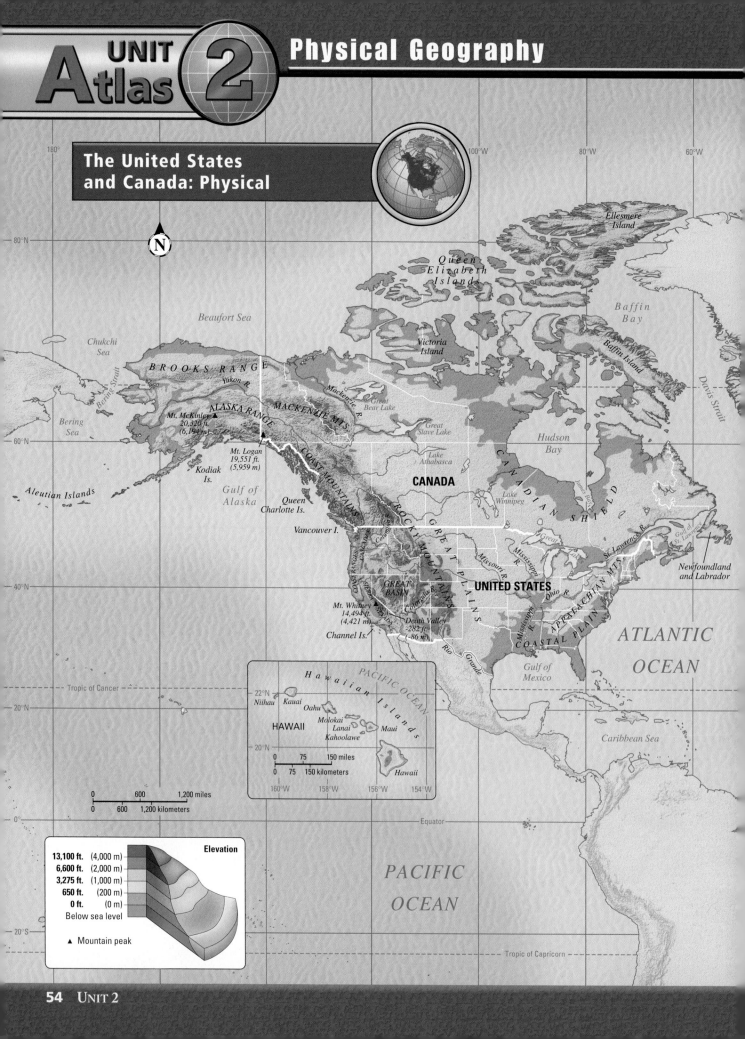

The United States and Canada: Physical

N

Ellesmere Island

Beaufort Sea

Chukchi Sea

Queen Elizabeth Islands

Baffin Bay

Victoria Island

Baffin Island

Davis Strait

B R O O K S   R A N G E

Yukon R.

Bering Strait

ALASKA RANGE

MACKENZIE MTS.

Mackenzie R.

Great Bear Lake

Mt. McKinley 20,320 ft. (6,194 m)

Bering Sea

Mt. Logan 19,551 ft. (5,959 m)

COAST MOUNTAINS

Great Slave Lake

Hudson Bay

C A N A D I A N   S H I E L D

Kodiak Is.

Gulf of Alaska

Lake Athabasca

Aleutian Islands

Queen Charlotte Is.

CANADA

Lake Winnipeg

James Bay

Gulf of St. Lawrence

Vancouver I.

COAST RANGES

CASCADES

Columbia R.

R O C K Y   M O U N T A I N S

G R E A T   P L A I N S

Great Lakes

St. Lawrence R.

Newfoundland and Labrador

GREAT BASIN

SIERRA NEVADA

Colorado R.

Missouri R.

Mississippi R.

Ohio R.

APPALACHIAN MTS.

ATLANTIC OCEAN

Mt. Whitney 14,494 ft. (4,421 m)

Death Valley -282 ft. (-86 m)

UNITED STATES

Channel Is.

Mississippi R.

C O A S T A L   P L A I N

Tropic of Cancer

PACIFIC OCEAN

Rio Grande

Gulf of Mexico

Hawaiian Islands

22°N

Niihau   Kauai   Oahu

HAWAII

Molokai
Lanai
Kahoolawe

Maui

Caribbean Sea

20°N

0   75   150 miles

0   75   150 kilometers

Hawaii

160°W   158°W   156°W   154°W

0   600   1,200 miles

0   600   1,200 kilometers

Equator

Elevation

13,100 ft.   (4,000 m)
6,600 ft.   (2,000 m)
3,275 ft.   (1,000 m)
650 ft.   (200 m)
0 ft.   (0 m)
Below sea level

▲ Mountain peak

PACIFIC OCEAN

Tropic of Capricorn

Natural Hazards of the United States and Canada

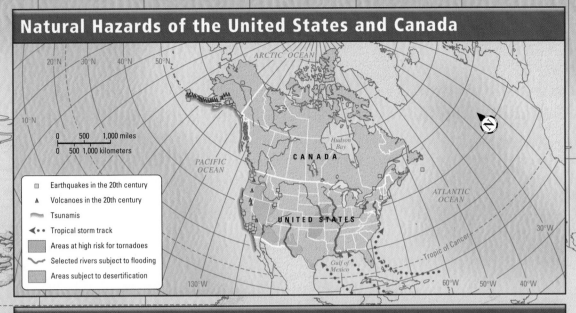

Legend:
- Earthquakes in the 20th century
- Volcanoes in the 20th century
- Tsunamis
- Tropical storm track
- Areas at high risk for tornadoes
- Selected rivers subject to flooding
- Areas subject to desertification

Canada–United States: Landmass and Population

Canada

United States

LANDMASS

Canada
3,851,809 square miles

Continental United States
3,165,630 square miles

POPULATION

Canada
30,750,100

United States
281,421,906

= 50,000,000

FAST FACTS

HIGHEST TIDE:
The Bay of Fundy, between New Brunswick and Nova Scotia in Canada, has the highest tides in the world, sometimes running as high as 70 feet.

HIGHEST MOUNTAIN:
Mt. McKinley, 20,320 ft.

LONGEST RIVER:
Mississippi River, 2,357 mi.

HIGHEST RECORDED TEMPERATURE:
134°F, Death Valley, California, July 10, 1913

LOWEST RECORDED TEMPERATURE:
–81.4°F, Snag, Yukon, February 3, 1947

GEOGRAPHY SKILLBUILDER: Interpreting Maps and Visuals
1. **Location** • What is the elevation of the land along the Gulf of Mexico and Hudson Bay?
2. **Place** • Where are most of the volcanoes in the United States and Canada?

The United States
and Canada: Political

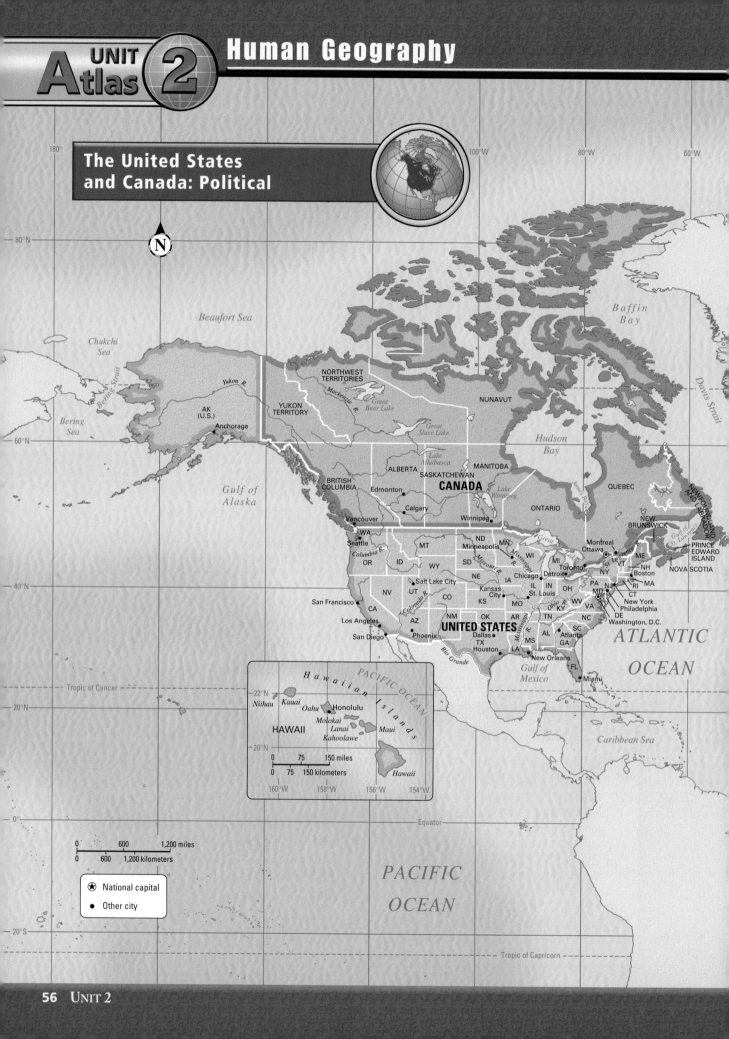

National capital
Other city

Population Density of the United States and Canada, 2001

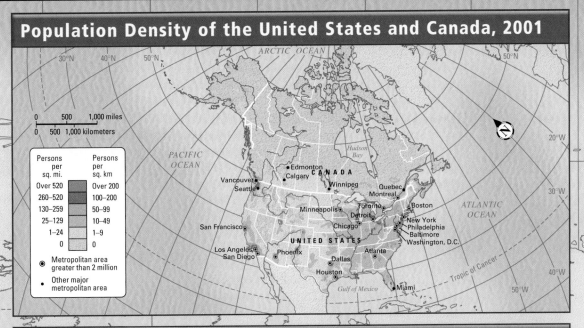

The United States and Canada: Selected Native Peoples, c. 1600

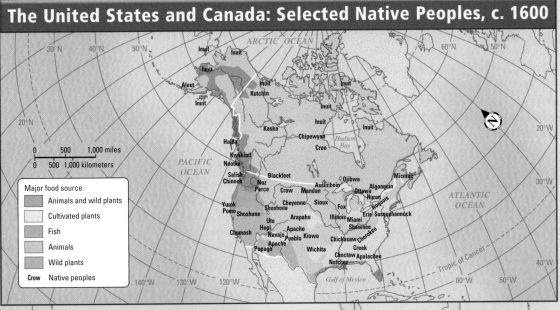

FAST FACTS

✔ **WORLD'S HIGHEST IMMIGRATION RATE:** Canada, with about 240,000 immigrants per year.

✔ **LOWEST POPULATION DENSITY:** Canada has only about 3.4 people per square kilometer. Nearly 90 percent of Canada's population lives within about 100 miles of the Canada–U.S. border.

✔ **LARGEST CITY:** New York City, 16,640,000 (2000)

GEOGRAPHY SKILLBUILDER: Interpreting Maps and Visuals

1. **Location** · Name the Canadian provinces and the U.S. states that lie along the border between the two countries.
2. **Location** · Which native peoples lived along the Pacific Coast circa 1600?

State Flag	State/ Capital	Population (2000)	Population Rank (2000)	Infant Mortality (per 1,000 live births) (1998)	Doctors (per 100,000 pop.) (1998–1999)
	Alabama (AL) Montgomery	4,447,100	23	10.2	198
	Alaska (AK) Juneau	626,900	48	5.9	167
	Arizona (AZ) Phoenix	5,130,600	20	7.5	202
	Arkansas (AR) Little Rock	2,673,400	33	8.9	190
	California (CA) Sacramento	33,871,600	1	5.8	247
	Colorado (CO) Denver	4,301,300	24	6.7	238
	Connecticut (CT) Hartford	3,405,600	29	7.0	354
	Delaware (DE) Dover	783,600	45	9.6	234
	*District of Columbia (DC)	572,100	—	12.5	737
	Florida (FL) Tallahassee	15,982,400	4	7.2	238
	Georgia (GA) Atlanta	8,186,500	10	8.5	211
	Hawaii (HI) Honolulu	1,211,500	42	6.9	265
	Idaho (ID) Boise	1,294,000	39	7.2	154
	Illinois (IL) Springfield	12,419,300	5	8.4	260
	Indiana (IN) Indianapolis	6,080,500	14	7.6	195
	Iowa (IA) Des Moines	2,926,300	30	6.6	173
	Kansas (KS) Topeka	2,688,400	32	7.0	203

*The federal district of Washington, D.C., is the capital city of the United States.

DATA FILE

Population Density (per square mile)	Per Capita Income ($) (1999)	High School Graduates (%) (1998)	Area Rank (2000)	Total Area (square miles)	Map (not to scale)
85.1	21,941	78.8	30	52,237	
1.0	27,274	90.6	1	615,230	
45.0	24,199	81.9	6	114,006	
50.3	21,146	76.8	28	53,182	
213.2	28,513	80.1	3	158,869	
41.3	30,291	89.6	8	104,100	
614.3	37,452	83.7	48	5,544	
327.0	29,341	85.2	49	2,396	
8,412.6	36,554	83.8	51	68	
266.7	26,796	81.9	23	59,928	
138.8	26,007	80.0	24	58,977	
187.6	26,623	84.6	47	6,459	
15.5	22,418	82.7	14	83,574	
214.4	29,908	84.2	25	57,918	
167.0	24,949	83.5	38	36,420	
51.9	24,600	87.7	26	56,276	
32.7	25,467	89.2	15	82,282	

State Flag	State/ Capital	Population (2000)	Population Rank (2000)	Infant Mortality (per 1,000 live births) (1998)	Doctors (per 100,000 pop.) (1998–1999)
	Kentucky (KY) Frankfort	4,041,800	25	7.5	209
	Louisiana (LA) Baton Rouge	4,469,000	22	9.1	246
	Maine (ME) Augusta	1,274,900	40	6.3	223
	Maryland (MD) Annapolis	5,296,500	19	8.6	374
	Massachusetts (MA) Boston	6,349,100	13	5.1	412
	Michigan (MI) Lansing	9,938,400	8	8.2	224
	Minnesota (MN) St. Paul	4,919,500	21	5.9	249
	Mississippi (MS) Jackson	2,844,700	31	10.1	163
	Missouri (MO) Jefferson City	5,595,200	17	7.7	230
	Montana (MT) Helena	902,200	44	7.4	190
	Nebraska (NE) Lincoln	1,711,300	38	7.3	218
	Nevada (NV) Carson City	1,998,300	35	7.0	173
	New Hampshire (NH) Concord	1,235,800	41	4.4	237
	New Jersey (NJ) Trenton	8,414,400	9	6.4	295
	New Mexico (NM) Santa Fe	1,819,000	36	7.2	212
	New York (NY) Albany	18,976,500	3	6.3	387
	North Carolina (NC) Raleigh	8,049,300	11	9.3	232

DATA FILE

Population Density (per square mile)	Per Capita Income ($) (1999)	High School Graduates (%) (1998)	Area Rank (2000)	Total Area (square miles)	Map (not to scale)
100.0	22,147	77.9	37	40,411	
90.0	21,794	78.6	31	49,651	
37.8	23,867	86.7	39	33,741	
430.7	30,757	84.7	42	12,297	
687.1	34,168	85.6	45	9,241	
102.8	26,625	85.4	11	96,705	
56.6	29,281	89.4	12	86,943	
58.9	19,608	77.3	32	48,286	
80.3	25,040	82.9	21	69,709	
6.1	21,337	89.1	4	147,046	
22.1	26,235	87.7	16	77,358	
18.1	29,022	89.1	7	110,567	
133.1	29,552	84.0	44	9,283	
1,024.3	34,525	86.5	46	8,215	
15.0	21,097	79.6	5	121,598	
351.5	32,459	81.5	27	53,989	
153.0	25,072	81.4	29	52,672	

State Flag	State/Capital	Population (2000)	Population Rank (2000)	Infant Mortality (per 1,000 live births) (1998)	Doctors (per 100,000 pop.) (1998–1999)
	North Dakota (ND) Bismarck	642,200	47	8.6	222
	Ohio (OH) Columbus	11,353,100	7	8.0	235
	Oklahoma (OK) Oklahoma City	3,450,700	27	8.5	169
	Oregon (OR) Salem	3,421,400	28	5.4	225
	Pennsylvania (PA) Harrisburg	12,281,100	6	7.1	291
	Rhode Island (RI) Providence	1,048,300	43	7.0	338
	South Carolina (SC) Columbia	4,012,000	26	9.6	207
	South Dakota (SD) Pierre	754,800	46	9.1	184
	Tennessee (TN) Nashville	5,689,300	16	8.2	246
	Texas (TX) Austin	20,851,800	2	6.4	203
	Utah (UT) Salt Lake City	2,233,200	34	5.6	200
	Vermont (VT) Montpelier	608,800	49	7.0	305
	Virginia (VA) Richmond	7,078,500	12	7.7	241
	Washington (WA) Olympia	5,894,100	15	5.7	235
	West Virginia (WV) Charleston	1,808,300	37	8.0	215
	Wisconsin (WI) Madison	5,363,700	18	7.2	227
	Wyoming (WY) Cheyenne	493,800	50	7.2	171
	United States Washington, D.C.	281,422,000	3	7.0	251

DATA FILE

Population Density (per square mile)	Per Capita Income ($) (1999)	High School Graduates (%) (1998)	Area Rank (2000)	Total Area (square miles)	Map (not to scale)
9.1	22,488	84.3	18	70,704	
253.3	25,895	86.2	34	44,828	
49.4	21,802	84.6	20	69,903	
35.2	25,947	85.5	10	97,132	
266.6	27,420	84.1	33	46,058	
851.6	24,418	80.7	50	1,231	
128.6	22,467	78.6	40	31,189	
9.8	24,007	86.3	17	77,121	
135.0	24,461	76.9	36	42,146	
78.0	25,363	78.3	2	267,277	
26.3	22,333	89.3	13	84,904	
63.3	24,758	86.7	43	9,615	
167.2	28,193	82.6	35	42,326	
83.4	28,968	92.0	19	70,637	
74.6	19,973	76.4	41	24,231	
82.0	26,212	88.0	22	65,499	
5.0	24,864	90.0	9	97,818	
74.3	33,900	83.0	4	3,787,319	

Data File

Province or Territory Flag	Province or Territory/ Capital	Population (2000)	Population Rank (2000)	Infant Mortality (per 1,000 live births) (1998)	Doctors (per 100,000 pop.) (1998–1999)
	Alberta (AB) Edmonton	2,997,200	4	4.8	162
	British Columbia (BC) Victoria	4,063,800	3	4.7	193
	Manitoba (MB) Winnipeg	1,147,900	5	7.5	177
	New Brunswick (NB) Fredericton	756,600	8	5.7	153
	Newfoundland and Labrador (NF) St. John's	538,800	9	5.2	171
	Northwest Territories (NT) Yellowknife	42,100	11	10.9	92
	Nova Scotia (NS) Halifax	941,000	7	4.4	196
	Nunavut (NU) Iqaluit	27,700	13	N/A	N/A
	Ontario (ON) Toronto	11,669,300	1	5.5	178
	Prince Edward Island (PE) Charlottetown	138,900	10	4.4	128
	Quebec (QC) Quebec City	7,372,400	2	5.6	211
	Saskatchewan (SK) Regina	1,023,600	6	8.9	149
	Yukon Territory (YT) Whitehorse	30,700	12	8.4	149
	Canada Ottawa, Ontario	30,750,000	36	5.5	185

DATA FILE

Population Density (per square mile)	Per Capita Income ($) (1999)	High School Graduates (%) (1998)	Area Rank (2000)	Total Area (square miles)	Map (not to scale)
11.7	30,038	86	6	255,285	
11.1	31,592	87	5	366,255	
4.6	26,829	79	8	250,934	
26.7	26,607	78	11	28,345	
3.4	27,692	71	10	156,649	
0.08	33,738 (1994)	64 (1996)	3	503,951	
44.0	25,712	78	12	21,425	
0.03	27,421 (1994)	N/A	1	818,959	
28.3	32,537	84	4	412,582	
49.4	25,534	74	13	2,814	
12.4	28,826	78	2	594,860	
4.1	26,463	82	7	251,700	
0.2	36,130	67 (1996)	9	186,661	
8.0	23,000	82	3	3,850,420	

GEOGRAPHY SKILLBUILDER: Interpreting a Chart

1. **Place** • Which province or territory in Canada has the fewest people? How is it ranked in area? How do these two facts explain the population density?
2. **Place** • What is the highest percentage of high school graduates in a state? What is the lowest percentage?

Atlas **65**

CHAPTER 3

The Physical Geography of the United States and Canada

SECTION 1 From Coast to Coast

SECTION 2 A Rich Diversity in Climate and Resources

THE UNITED STATES AND CANADA

Place The aurora borealis, or northern lights, is a natural phenomenon most commonly seen in the winter skies over Alaska and northern Canada.

How do Canada and the U.S. benefit from the variety of natural features?

Place • North America is a vast area with varied physical features and climates. A mountain range runs parallel to each coastline. Grasslands cover much of the land between the mountain ranges. One of the world's longest rivers runs from north to south through the east central portion of the United States. Oceans and seas almost completely surround the continent. In northern Canada, the ground is always frozen. In the southeastern United States, plants grow year round.

What do you think?

♦ How does the variety of types of land benefit the people of North America?

♦ How are some places in North America better to live in than others?

♦ Describe the landforms, climate, and vegetation where you live.

BEFORE YOU READ

▶▶ *What Do You Know?*

Before you read the chapter, reflect on what you already know about the United States and Canada. On which continent will you find these countries? Remember what you have read, seen, or learned in other classes about their physical features and natural resources. They are two of the wealthiest and most powerful countries in the modern world. What makes nations powerful in today's world?

▶▶ *What Do You Want to Know?*

Decide what you want to know about the United States and Canada. In your notebook, record what you hope to learn from this chapter.

Region • Water resources, such as the Mississippi River, contribute to the wealth of the United States and Canada and to their positions of leadership in the world. ▲

READ AND TAKE NOTES

Reading Strategy: Drawing Conclusions
As you read Chapter 3, think about how geographic factors support the strong economies of the United States and Canada. Use this chart to show how natural features have assisted in creating a strong economy. Notice that several geographic features may contribute to the same economic strength.

- Copy the chart into your notebook.
- On the chart, read the characteristics of the strong economies of the United States and Canada.
- As you read the chapter, identify the geographic features that contribute to each group of economic strengths. Note them on the chart.

Human-Environment Interaction • Rich soil and a moderate climate support a productive agricultural industry. ▲

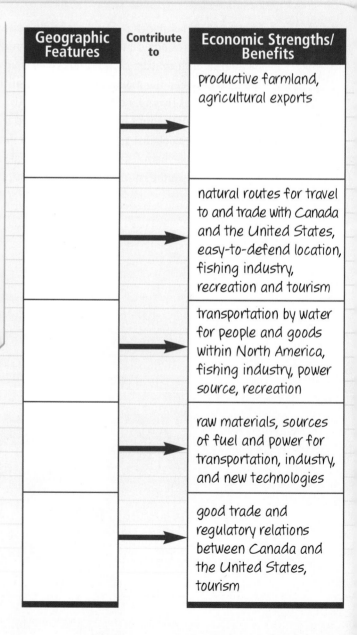

Geographic Features	Contribute to	Economic Strengths/ Benefits
	→	productive farmland, agricultural exports
	→	natural routes for travel to and trade with Canada and the United States, easy-to-defend location, fishing industry, recreation and tourism
	→	transportation by water for people and goods within North America, fishing industry, power source, recreation
	→	raw materials, sources of fuel and power for transportation, industry, and new technologies
	→	good trade and regulatory relations between Canada and the United States, tourism

From Coast to Coast

TERMS & NAMES
Sacagawea
landform
glacier
erosion
river system

MAIN IDEA

North America has varied regions and landforms.

WHY IT MATTERS NOW

North America's geography contributes to the prosperity of the people who live there.

DATELINE

EXTRA

MOUNT ST. HELENS, WASHINGTON, MAY 18, 1980

Mount St. Helens, an ancient volcano in Washington's Cascade Mountains, erupted this morning, killing 60 people and thousands of animals. An earthquake caused the mountain's north face to fall away. The debris from this landslide filled Spirit Lake. Hot air blasts traveling at 300 miles per hour threw both gas and volcanic ash 12 miles high and destroyed 10 million trees.

The avalanche and the mudslide that followed buried parts of the Toutle River Valley to a depth of almost 500 feet. The hot ash and rock started forest fires, ruined crops, and covered cities. Fortunately, the land around the volcano has begun to recover from the eruptions.

Place • Gas and volcanic ash from the eruption of Mount St. Helens vaporized trees and caused widespread devastation as far as 19 miles from the volcano. ▲

Region •
More than 200 square miles of forest were destroyed by the eruption and its aftermath. ▲

North America

Earth's geography changes continually. Sometimes change happens violently, as in the eruption of a volcano such as Mount St. Helens, or the jolt of an earthquake. At other times, change occurs very slowly, as when rain washes away soil, or weather wears down a mountain. All these natural processes affect the physical geography of North America.

The Middle Latitudes

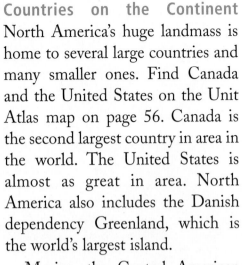

GEOGRAPHY SKILLBUILDER:
Interpreting a Map

1. **Region** • Do you think Canada or the United States has the colder climate? Why?
2. **Location** • Where in Canada would you expect to find the most people living? Explain.

Countries on the Continent North America's huge landmass is home to several large countries and many smaller ones. Find Canada and the United States on the Unit Atlas map on page 56. Canada is the second largest country in area in the world. The United States is almost as great in area. North America also includes the Danish dependency Greenland, which is the world's largest island.

Mexico, the Central American countries, and the Caribbean island nations, such as Cuba, the Dominican Republic, and Haiti, are part of the continent of North America. These countries, along with the South American nations, make up what is considered Latin America. Find these countries on the Unit 3 Atlas map on page 144. Their heritage differs from that of the United States and Canada. Historically, Latin America owes much of its culture to Spain and Portugal. The United States and Canada were greatly influenced by the British and French. Because of these different cultural heritages, geographers study the United States and Canada separately from Latin America.

Middle Latitudes Most of the United States and Canada is located in the middle latitudes of the northern hemisphere of Earth. This area between the Arctic Circle and the Tropic of Cancer has a temperate climate. It is not as hot as land closer to the Equator. It is not as cold as regions near the North or South Poles. Many plants and animals thrive in this climate. Productive farming enables countries in the middle latitudes to feed large populations.

Human-Environment Interaction • **Crops raised in the United States and Canada feed the people of these countries and are exported to other countries all over the world.** ▼

Reading
Social Studies

A. Analyzing Effects Why do the middle latitudes have a moderate climate?

An Isolated Continent

North America is almost completely surrounded by water. Its landmass stretches from the Arctic Ocean to the Gulf of Mexico and from the Pacific Ocean to the Atlantic Ocean. Find these bodies of water on page 54 of the Unit Atlas.

At one time, these waters isolated North America, or kept it separate from the rest of the world. Unique plants, such as the giant sequoia and the saguaro cactus, and animals, such as the bald eagle and the American alligator, developed in North America.

Region • The bald eagle has been the national bird of the United States since 1782. ▲

The oceans and seas were also a barrier to people. The earliest settlers arrived 12,000 to 35,000 years ago. No other people reached this continent until thousands of years later.

Crossing the Barriers

As people learned more about shipbuilding and navigation, the oceans became a hazardous but passable travel route. Settlers arrived in North America with plants and animals from their home countries. Many of these plants and animals were new to the continent. In some places, these replaced the native plants and animals.

In the 20th century, the distance from other countries helped protect Canada and the United States mainland from attack during the two World Wars. Today, satellites, the Internet, modern transportation, and other technologies link people everywhere.

Place • Sailors have used the sextant to navigate their ships since its invention in 1731. ▲

Sacagawea <u>Sacagawea</u> (SAK•uh•guh•WEE•uh) was a Shoshone woman who had a vital role in the exploration of what is now the northwestern United States. She guided explorers Meriwether Lewis and William Clark from what is now North Dakota into the Pacific Northwest. They had been sent to explore the newly purchased Louisiana Territory. Sacagawea's husband, French Canadian trapper Toussaint Charbonneau, and their baby son were also on the journey, which lasted from 1804 to 1806.

Sacagawea identified fruits and vegetables for the group to eat and helped the explorers communicate with the Native Americans whom they met along the trail. Historians believe that she was born around 1786 and probably died in 1812.

Regions of the United States and Canada

The United States and Canada share many geographic regions. Find these regions on the Unit Atlas map on page 54.

Atlantic Coastal Plain This region runs along the Gulf of Mexico and the east coast of North America. The region has much rich farmland and some swamps and wetlands.

Appalachian Mountains This 400-million-year-old mountain range lies west of the Atlantic Coastal Plain. These forest-covered mountains have weathered, or worn down, over time.

Central Lowlands West of the Appalachians are the Central Lowlands. They extend west to the Great Plains and are generally flat. The soil is rich, and many farms are located here.

Great Plains The Great Plains have grasslands and few trees. The land gradually rises from the Central Lowlands to the Rocky Mountains. Farmers grow crops and ranchers raise cattle in some areas.

The Rocky Mountains and Coastal Ranges North America's highest mountain ranges lie in the west. They include the Rocky Mountains, the Sierra Nevada and the Cascade ranges of the United States, and the Coast Mountains of Canada. These high, rugged, and heavily forested mountain ranges run along the western part of the continent from Mexico to Alaska.

Region • The Canadian Rocky Mountains are part of the rugged range that reaches from Mexico to Alaska in western North America. ▼

Intermountain Region Located between the Rocky Mountains and the western coastal mountains, this region is dry and contains plateaus, basins, and deserts. Ranchers raise cattle and sheep in some areas. The Grand Canyon is found here.

Region • The Grand Canyon in Arizona is one of the natural wonders of the world. ▼

Reading
Social Studies

B. Clarifying
Which regions of Canada and the United States have productive farmland?

Canadian Shield or Laurentian Plateau The Canadian Shield covers most of Greenland, curves around the Hudson Bay, and reaches into the United States along the Great Lakes. The central and northwestern part of this huge rocky region has flat plains with hills and lakes. The northeast has high mountains and the south is covered with forests. The shield is rich in minerals, such as iron, gold, copper, and uranium. Most of the land is not farmable and is sparsely populated.

Physical Processes That Shaped the Land

Natural processes have shaped North America. Some of the continent's most dramatic landforms were created by the action of wind, water, ice, and moving slabs of Earth's crust. **Landforms** are features of Earth's surface, such as mountains, valleys, and plateaus.

A **glacier** is a thick sheet of ice that moves slowly across land. Thousands of years ago, when Earth was much colder, glaciers covered much of North America. As they flowed across the land, they smoothed out rough surfaces, carved depressions and deep trenches, and piled up rock and dirt. When the ice melted, North America had new valleys, lakes, and hills.

Quakes Shake Central U.S. Lands Usually, earthquakes shake up California and other parts of the western United States. But from December 1811 to February 1812, Mississippi River Valley residents were shocked by several powerful quakes.

The earthquakes changed the Mississippi River's path. Islands disappeared, riverbanks collapsed, and waves capsized boats and drowned people. Farmland was flooded, new lakes appeared, and forests were destroyed. Trees such as this one were uprooted.

Eyewitnesses saw "houses, gardens, and fields . . . swallowed up" in New Madrid, Missouri, in the final quake.

Formation of the Rocky Mountains

Plates collide over millions of years

Main Ranges

Collision causes uplifting of rock layers

Front Ranges

Movement of plate under Pacific Ocean

Movement of North American plate

Region •
The Rocky Mountains were formed 40 to 70 million years ago as a result of a collision between the tectonic plate under the Pacific Ocean and the North American plate. ◄

The St. Lawrence Seaway This seaway, completed in 1959 by Canada and the United States, is one of the largest civil engineering projects ever built. It enables ships to travel 2,340 miles inland from the Atlantic Ocean through locks such as this one, to the Great Lakes. As a result, trade between the United States and Canada and between North America and other continents has improved. Grain, iron ore, and coal are three vital goods shipped on the seaway.

Wind, rivers, and rain wear away soil and stone in a process called **erosion.** Erosion can create magnificent landforms. The Grand Canyon is at least partly the result of millions of years of erosion by the Colorado River. Volcanoes, such as Mount St. Helens, and earthquakes are other natural forces that change the land. All these mighty forces have created landforms across North America.

Waterways

North America has an extensive **river system**, or network of major rivers and their tributaries. The longest rivers are the Mississippi and Missouri rivers in the United States and the Mackenzie River in Canada. Find these rivers on the Unit Atlas map on page 54. When snow melts and rain falls, the water runs down into creeks that collect more water, becoming rivers. North America's rivers empty into bays, oceans, seas, gulfs, lakes, and other rivers.

Vocabulary
gulf: large area of a sea or ocean partially enclosed by land

---

SECTION 1 ASSESSMENT

Terms & Names
1. Identify: (a) Sacagawea   (b) landform   (c) glacier
   (d) erosion   (e) river system

Taking Notes
2. Use a Venn diagram like the one shown, to compare two geographic regions of North America.

Region 1   Both   Region 2

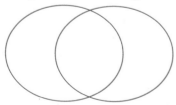

Main Ideas
3. (a) Describe North America's location on Earth and tell how this affects its climate and plant and animal life.
   (b) What barriers prevented plants, animals, and people from reaching North America? How were the barriers overcome?
   (c) What processes of nature help to shape the land?

Critical Thinking
4. **Making Inferences**
   What natural features of North America attracted people from other lands? Support your conclusion with details from the text.

   Think About
   • the natural resources
   • the climate

ACTIVITY -OPTION- **List** two regions of North America. Describe in a few words the kinds of plants, animals, and jobs that are found in each.

A Rich Diversity in Climate and Resources

SECTION 2

TERMS & NAMES
weather
precipitation
climate
vegetation
economy

MAIN IDEA

A region's climate, vegetation, and natural resources are contributing factors to economic activities.

WHY IT MATTERS NOW

The prosperity of people living in the United States and Canada affects the prosperity of the modern global economy.

DATELINE

ST. LOUIS, MISSOURI, U.S.A., OCTOBER 7, 1993—The worst flood in United States history is finally over. Heavy, almost continuous rain fell on much of the upper Midwest. In St. Louis, where the Mississippi and Missouri rivers meet, the flooding began in April and continued for six months.

The disaster affected nine states. Tens of thousands of people had to leave their homes. More than 10,000 homes were destroyed, and 50 people lost their lives.

Human-Environment Interaction • At least 75 towns are under water as a result of the flooding. ▲

Climate and Vegetation

The flood of 1993 was caused by unusual **weather**. Weather is the state of the atmosphere near Earth at a given time and place. It includes temperature, wind, and **precipitation**, or moisture such as rain or snow that falls to Earth. **Climate** is the typical weather in a region over a long period of time. A region's climate helps determine what types of **vegetation**—trees, shrubs, grasses, and other plants—will grow there.

The Dust Bowl Disaster From 1931 to 1939, the southern Great Plains suffered one of the worst droughts in U.S. history. In the 1920s, farmers used up the soil's natural nutrients, and cattle and sheep ranchers destroyed native grasses by over-grazing. When the drought began, crops died, and there were no plant root systems to hold the soil.

The southern Great Plains became known as the Dust Bowl. By 1934, dust storms of topsoil were causing serious damage in 27 states. Ships 300 miles off the Atlantic Coast were covered by blowing dirt. Thousands of people, like this boy, had to leave their farms.

Vegetation Zones

North America's vegetation zones are determined by the climate and physical geography of each area. It is usually warmer in the south and colder in the north, but physical features such as mountains and oceans also affect the climate. Find these vegetation zones on the map on page 77.

Polar and Tundra Northern Canada and Alaska have cool summers and very cold winters. It is usually above freezing (32°F/0°C) there for only two months each year. Precipitation varies from 4 to 20 inches a year. Much of the ground is frozen all year except for the surface, which thaws in summer.

Forest Forests of conifer (evergreen) and broadleaf trees cover much of Canada and the northwest, northeast, and southeast United States. Precipitation averages between 10 and 80 inches annually. Temperatures vary from mild to cold in different forested areas.

Rain Forest Along the Pacific Coast, precipitation can reach 167 inches each year. Rain forests with trees 300 feet tall grow in these areas. The ground is covered in bushes, small trees, and other plants. Moss and lichen are the smallest vegetation. One acre of rain forest might have 6,000 pounds of these tiny plants. The temperature is moderate even in the north, seldom falling below 32°F in winter.

Vocabulary
lichen (LY•kuhn): organism that grows with algae on rocks or tree trunks

Grassland The center of North America is covered by grasslands. The prairie in the Mississippi Valley may get 30 inches or more of precipitation each year. Grasses are tall and thick. Farther west, the land gets less rainfall—as little as 15 inches in Alberta, Canada—and the grass is shorter. People grow grain and raise cattle in these areas.

Reading Social Studies

A. Recognizing Effects How do climate and geography influence the attraction of people to an area?

Desert The deserts of the American Southwest get less than 10 inches of precipitation a year. Plants in the deserts must be able to endure harsh sun, high temperatures, and little rain. Only the hardiest bushes, shrubs, a few small trees, and cacti survive there.

Vegetation Zones of Canada and the United States

ARCTIC OCEAN

ALASKA (U.S.)

Baffin Bay

80°W

60°N

60°W

40°W

Hudson Bay

50°N

CANADA

PACIFIC OCEAN

40°N

UNITED STATES

ATLANTIC OCEAN

30°N

HAWAII (U.S.)

PACIFIC OCEAN

22°N

20°N

160°W   158°W   156°W   154°W

0   50   150 miles
0   50   150 kilometers

MEXICO

Gulf of Mexico

Tropic of Cancer

20°N

Caribbean Sea

120°W

100°W

Legend:
- Temperate rain forest
- Tropical rain forest
- Tropical grassland
- Desert and dry shrub
- Temperate grassland
- Mediterranean shrub
- Deciduous and mixed forest
- Coniferous forest
- Tundra
- Icecap

0   250   500 miles
0   250   500 kilometers

GEOGRAPHY SKILLBUILDER: Interpreting a Map

1. **Region** • What kind of vegetation zone covers most of Canada?
2. **Region** • What part of the United States is covered by temperate grassland?

Natural Wealth

The United States and Canada are rich in natural resources. This wealth has influenced their economic development.

Land and Power Resources The farmlands of the midwestern United States and the prairies in the central provinces of Canada have rich soil. Forests are found in western Canada and the northwestern, northeastern, and southeastern United States. There are oil fields in Alberta, Canada; in Texas, California, Louisiana, Oklahoma, and Alaska; and in the Gulf of Mexico. Coal is in Canada's western provinces; in the Appalachian Mountains; and in Illinois, Indiana, and Wyoming.

Water Resources Water routes affect where people and industry are located. Settlers in North America followed rivers to areas where fresh water and good soil permitted farming and raising cattle. Businesses grew in new communities. People still use rivers to ship natural resources, such as timber and coal, and as trade and travel routes. Fishing is a food source and an industry. Rivers and lakes supply water and power, and offer recreational activities.

Region • The Mississippi River has been an important commercial shipping route for more than a century. ▼

BACKGROUND

The Mississippi River is the largest river in North America. From its source, Lake Itasca in Minnesota, to its mouth in the Gulf of Mexico, it flows for 2,350 miles. The name *Mississippi* is from the Native American Algonquian language and means "Big River."

Spotlight on CULTURE

The Cajuns: Americans with Canadian Roots The French settled in Acadia, which is now Nova Scotia, Canada, in 1604. The British gained control of much of Nova Scotia, and in 1755, they expelled most French Acadians. Many of the displaced settlers relocated to southern Louisiana, which was under the rule of France at that time.

Known as Cajuns, the descendants of those French Canadians share a special cultural heritage. Their language has French, English, Spanish, German, and Native American influences. Their music is played with fiddles, accordions, and guitars and has a unique sound. The man shown at left plays the accordion at a Cajun music festival in Louisiana.

THINKING CRITICALLY

1. **Recognizing Effects** What effect did Britain's rule over Nova Scotia have on the French in Acadia?

2. **Recognizing Important Details** What are some features of the Cajun culture?

Neighbors and Leaders

More than 200 million people cross the U.S.-Canadian border every year. Trade between the two countries exceeds $1 billion a day. They cooperate on issues as diverse as national security and defense, the environment, air traffic, and fishing regulations. A United States president described the relationship between these countries.

Citizenship IN ACTION

The Nature Conservancy The Conservancy works with communities to protect natural areas, plants, and animals. It has safeguarded 12 million acres and 1,400 land preserves, such as this one, in the United States. In its Great Lakes Program, and in Minnesota, the Conservancy is working with Canadian and U.S. groups to protect wildlife and 10,000 acres of the last tallgrass prairie on the U.S.-Canadian border.

A VOICE FROM THE UNITED STATES

Geography has made us neighbors, history has made us friends, economics has made us partners, and necessity has made us allies.

John F. Kennedy

Reading
Social Studies

B. Finding Causes
What common interests make the United States and Canada allies and partners?

Both countries have strong economies and are leaders in world trade. An **economy** is the way that business owners use resources to provide the goods and services that people want.

SECTION **2** ASSESSMENT

Terms & Names

1. Identify:
   (a) weather
   (b) precipitation
   (c) climate
   (d) vegetation
   (e) economy

Taking Notes

2. Make a chart such as this one to list details about vegetation zones of the United States and Canada.

Polar and Tundra	Forest	Rain Forest	Grassland	Desert

Main Ideas

3. (a) How do climate and geography affect vegetation?

   (b) What natural resources are found in North America?

   (c) How have waterways affected settlement and development in the United States and Canada?

Critical Thinking

4. **Drawing Conclusions**

   How does the variety of vegetation zones affect the economies of the United States and Canada?

   Think About

   • crops and resources found in each vegetation zone

   • world economy

ACTIVITY
-OPTION-

Choose one of the vegetation zones discussed in the section. Draw a **picture** showing what the land looks like.

Reading a Physical Map

▶▶ Defining the Skill

Physical maps show the natural features of Earth's surface. These include landforms such as mountains, hills, and plains; and bodies of water such as rivers, lakes, bays, and oceans. Land elevation may be shown in a map key. National boundaries and major cities may also be included.

▶▶ Applying the Skill

The physical map below shows the natural features of Canada. Use these strategies to identify the information shown on the map.

How to Read a Physical Map

Strategy ❶ Read the title. It tells you which region's physical features are being represented.

Strategy ❷ Read the key. It tells you the elevation of land each color represents. A map key may also show boundaries between nations, national capitals, and other cities.

Strategy ❸ Read the scale. It tells you how many miles or kilometers each inch on the map represents.

Make a Chart

A chart can help you organize information given on maps. The chart below organizes information from the map on this page.

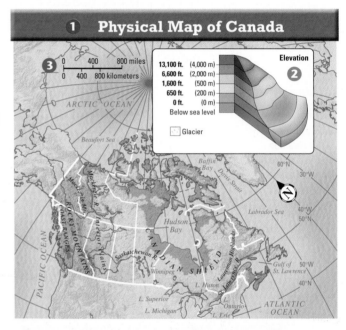

Canada	
Bodies of Water	Atlantic Ocean, Pacific Ocean, Arctic Ocean, Hudson Bay, Davis Strait, Baffin Bay, Labrador Sea, Beaufort Sea, Mackenzie River, Lake Winnipeg, Saskatchewan River, Lake Superior, Lake Huron, Lake Erie, Lake Ontario, St. Lawrence River, Gulf of St. Lawrence
Landforms	Rocky Mountains, Coast Ranges, Mackenzie Mountains, Canadian Shield, Interior Plains, Laurentian Highlands

▶▶ Practicing the Skill

Turn to page 54 in the Unit 2 Atlas. Study the physical map of North America. Make a chart listing major physical landforms of North America that you see on the map. You may also include a section in your chart labeled "Countries."

Technology: 1971

IMAX

Although the IMAX system was first successfully demonstrated during Expo '70 (a world's fair) in Osaka, Japan, it has its roots in Expo '67 in Montreal, Canada. There people flocked to special motion-picture theaters, where they stood in the middle of circular auditoriums to watch images projected on the surrounding walls. What they saw was incredible. Hockey players seemed to skate right through them, and cars seemed to drive over them!

The first permanent IMAX theater was built in Toronto in 1971. Two years later, the first IMAX Dome (also called OMNIMAX) was built in San Diego. Since then, IMAX has developed three-dimensional and high-definition systems and incorporated the technology into amusement-park rides. Because of the size of its frames, an IMAX movie generally has a shorter running time than a standard movie. However, IMAX movies require more film. A typical 45-minute IMAX feature requires nearly 16,000 feet of film!

① Dome Early IMAX theaters had flat screens up to eight stories high, but most are now domes up to 100 feet in diameter. When large images are projected, they extend beyond normal peripheral vision—what a person can see without moving his or her eyes—and create the sensation of being in the middle of the action.

② Film IMAX movies use what is called the 15/70 format, in which the film has 15 perforations—little holes along the side—per frame and is 70 millimeters wide. This makes each frame ten times larger than conventional 35-millimeter film and accounts for the exceptional size and sharpness of IMAX images.

③ Projector Because of its size, IMAX film is fed through the projector horizontally in a wavelike motion, or "rolling loop" movement. The newest IMAX systems project film at 48 frames per second, twice the rate of standard movie film, which results in even sharper images.

THINKING Critically

1. Recognizing Effects
How does IMAX make images appear three-dimensional?

2. Drawing Conclusions
Despite the system's technical advantages, IMAX theaters have not been as financially successful as standard movie theaters. Why do you think this is so?

TERMS & NAMES

Explain the significance of each of the following:

1. Sacagawea
2. landform
3. glacier
4. erosion
5. river system
6. weather
7. precipitation
8. climate
9. vegetation
10. economy

REVIEW QUESTIONS

From Coast to Coast (pages 69–74)

1. Describe the location of North America.
2. What effect did the oceans have on the settlement of North America?
3. What regions are best for farming and ranching? for mining? for lumber?
4. What natural processes have changed the geography of North America?

A Rich Diversity in Climate and Resources (pages 75–79)

5. Why are there different vegetation zones?
6. Which vegetation zones permit farming and ranching?
7. How do natural resources affect the economies of the United States and Canada?
8. How have waterways helped people in the past, and how do they help people today?

CRITICAL THINKING

Synthesizing

1. Using your completed chart from Reading Social Studies p. 68, list the geographic features that contribute to productive farmland and agricultural exports.

Drawing Conclusions

2. Choose one of the regions of the United States and Canada. Think about what you know about the region's natural resources and economics. What do you think are the economic advantages and disadvantages of the region?

Making Inferences

3. What industries that depend on natural resources might flourish in the United States and Canada? Why?

Visual Summary

From Coast to Coast

- North America is located in the middle latitudes and is surrounded on most sides by oceans.
- Various regions, each with its own characteristics, make up the United States and Canada.

A Rich Diversity in Climate and Resources

- The vegetation of North America is affected by both climate and geography.
- Natural resources contribute to the prosperous economies of the United States and Canada.

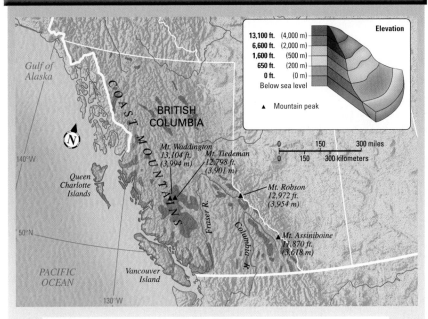

SKILLBUILDER: Reading a Physical Map

1. **Place** • What is the highest mountain in British Columbia? How tall is it?
2. **Place** • Near what island does the Fraser River empty into the Pacific Ocean?

FOCUS ON GEOGRAPHY

1. **Region** • Name four major tributaries of the Mississippi River.
2. **Region** • Into what body of water does the Mississippi River flow?

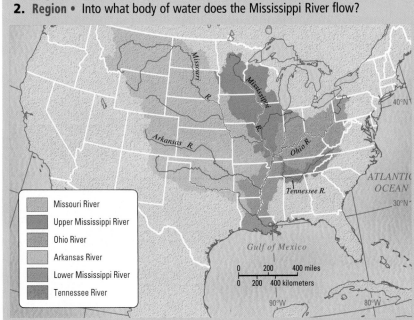

Interdisciplinary Activity: Art

Drawing a Map Research fur traders, such as Jedediah Smith, John Jacob Astor, Alexander Mackenzie, or James McGill, who first traveled across the United States and Canada. Draw a map that one of them might have created to illustrate one of the major trade routes. Show important landmarks along the way.

Cooperative Learning Activity

Presenting a Television News Report In a group of two or three classmates, prepare and present a television news report on the Lewis and Clark Expedition.

- One of you should be the news anchor. Others will be reporters, Lewis, Clark, Sacagawea, Native Americans, or other members of the group.
- Make a list of interview questions.
- Do research to learn answers to the questions.
- Present your news broadcast to your class.

INTERNET ACTIVITY

Use the Internet to learn more about the climate and vegetation of one region of North America. Focus on how climate and vegetation affect people's lives, the economy, or history in the region.

Writing About Geography Write a report of your findings. If possible, include photographs that you find on the Internet. Create a map or chart to present information. Include a list of the Web sites you used.

For Internet links to support this activity, go to

RESEARCH LINKS
CLASSZONE.COM

The United States Today

Movement Between 1892 and 1943, 17 million immigrants arrived in the United States through Ellis Island in New York Harbor. Today, ferries bring tourists to the Ellis Island Immigration Museum, which commemorates the stories of these immigrants.

How do immigrants contribute to a country's culture?

Hakeem Olajuwon

Itzhak Perlman

Midori

Andy Garcia

Isabel Allende

I. M. Pei

Madeleine Albright

FOCUS ON **GEOGRAPHY**

Movement • In 1998, about 675,000 people immigrated to the United States from around the world. Of these immigrants, 33 percent came from Asia and 20 percent came from Mexico.

This country has been a land of immigrants from its earliest days. People have contributed customs, art, music, languages, foods, and ideas from their homelands to enrich U.S. culture. Violinist Itzhak Perlman, writer Isabel Allende, violinist Midori, actor Andy Garcia, architect I. M. Pei, basketball player Hakeem Olajuwon, and former Secretary of State Madeleine Albright are just a few famous U.S. immigrants.

What do you think?

♦ How do immigrants change and benefit the United States?

♦ What contributions by immigrants have influenced your life?

BEFORE YOU READ

▶▶ *What Do You Know?*

Before you read the chapter, think about how you would describe the United States to a person from another country. What do you and your classmates do for fun? What information could you give about U.S. history, government, economy, and culture? Reflect on your experience and what you have already read or learned about these aspects of the United States. How accurate and complete do you think your knowledge is?

▶▶ *What Do You Want to Know?*

Decide what you want to know about the characteristics of history, government, economy, and culture that make the United States unique. In your notebook, record what you hope to learn from this chapter.

Place • **After years of campaigning, women won the right to vote in 1920 when the 19th Amendment to the Constitution was adopted.** ▲

READ AND TAKE NOTES

Reading Strategy: Identifying Main Ideas Look for main ideas as you read to help you identify and remember important information. Record the main ideas of this chapter in the chart below.

- Copy the chart into your notebook.

- Notice that each section of Chapter 4 covers a different topic: history, government, economy, and culture.

- As you read each section, look for the main ideas. Use section titles and headings, and find the main idea of each paragraph.

- After you read each section, record what you think are the main ideas about aspects of the United States.

Place • **Firefighters and rescue personnel rushed to the scene of the terrorist attacks on New York City's World Trade Center, on September 11, 2001.** ▲

The United States Today	
History	
Government	
Economy	
Culture	

We the People

TERMS & NAMES
immigrant
Anasazi
equal opportunity
citizenship
democracy
political process
patriotism
republic

MAIN IDEA

Citizens of the United States come from many cultures and share the same rights and responsibilities.

WHY IT MATTERS NOW

The ideas and values of U.S. immigrants have helped shape the success of the country in the world today.

DATELINE

EXTRA

NEW YORK CITY, 1849

Ships docked today, bringing more people from their Irish home-land to live in the United States. These immigrants have suffered through four years of a deadly potato famine. A blight, or disease, has almost completely destroyed the potato crop every year since 1845. The Irish, especially those who are poor, depend on this crop to survive.

The failure of the potato crop has resulted in the deaths of more than 1 million people—12% of the population of Ireland—from starvation and disease. Today's arrivals join more than 1 million Irish people who are already in the United States.

Movement • Irish immigrants wait to board a ship that will bring them to the United States. ▲

One Country, Many Cultures

Immigrants, such as the Irish, have brought unique contributions to the United States from their homelands all over the world. The United States is sometimes called a "melting pot," a "salad bowl," or a "patchwork quilt" to illustrate how U.S. society combines aspects of many cultures. Some features may blend into the culture of the United States, while others retain their original characteristics.

For example, settlers from Great Britain brought English, the most widely spoken language in the United States. Spanish is often spoken in the Southeast and the Southwest, where people from Spain and Mexico settled. French is heard in Louisiana, which was once held by France. People in the United States enjoy the influence of different groups on their foods, music, sports, and other areas of their lives.

Why People Immigrate An **immigrant** is someone who chooses to move to a new country. They come to the United States for different reasons. Some are escaping from discrimination, persecution, or war. Others leave their homelands because of drought, earthquake, or other natural disasters. Often, people come hoping to improve their economic or educational opportunities.

Reading
Social Studies

A. Summarizing Why have people immigrated to the United States?

People from Many Lands

Over the past 500 years, millions of immigrants have come to the land that is now the United States and Canada. However, this land was inhabited long before they arrived. In fact, people have lived in North America for thousands of years.

The First Americans Native Americans were the first people to inhabit the Western Hemisphere. They came to North America from Eastern Asia, 12,000 to 35,000 years ago. Some groups, such as the Mississippians and **Anasazi** (Navajo for "Ancient Ones"), developed complex civilizations.

The Anasazi civilization developed around A.D. 100 and reached its height in the 11th to 13th centuries. The Anasazi were experts at irrigation. They built homes called cliff dwellings that had from 20 to 1,000 rooms. Remains of these structures survive in the Mesa Verde National Park in Colorado and in other places in the Southwestern United States.

Human-Environment Interaction • **The remains of Anasazi cliff dwellings, such as Cliff Palace in Mesa Verde National Park, are found in the Southwestern United States.** ◄

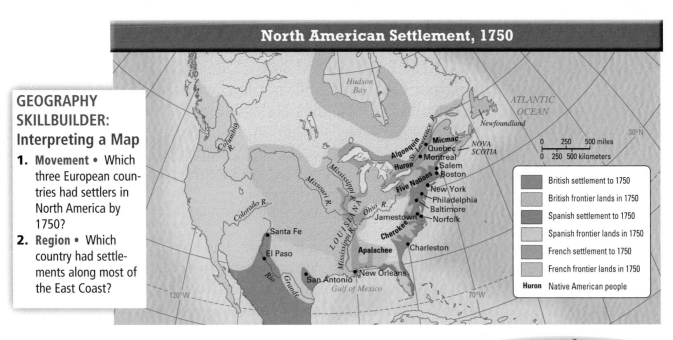

North American Settlement, 1750

GEOGRAPHY SKILLBUILDER:

Interpreting a Map

1. **Movement** • Which three European countries had settlers in North America by 1750?
2. **Region** • Which country had settlements along most of the East Coast?

Map labels: Hudson Bay, ATLANTIC OCEAN, Newfoundland, Columbia R., St. Lawrence R., Algonquin, Micmac, Quebec, NOVA SCOTIA, Montreal, Huron, Salem, Boston, Five Nations, New York, Philadelphia, Baltimore, Norfolk, Jamestown, Missouri R., Ohio R., Mississippi R., LOUISIANA, Colorado R., Cherokee, Santa Fe, Apalachee, Charleston, El Paso, New Orleans, Rio Grande, San Antonio, Gulf of Mexico, 120°W, 70°W, 30°N

Legend:
- British settlement to 1750
- British frontier lands in 1750
- Spanish settlement to 1750
- Spanish frontier lands in 1750
- French settlement to 1750
- French frontier lands in 1750
- **Huron** Native American people

Scale: 0 250 500 miles / 0 250 500 kilometers

The Europeans Arrive European exploration of the Americas began in the late 1400s. Colonists soon followed the explorers. The British settled along the Atlantic coast, in what is now southeastern Canada and the Northeastern United States. Spaniards settled in Florida and came north from Mexico to build towns in the Southwest. Often, the settlers' ways of life and needs for resources conflicted with those of the Native Americans. As the European population grew, competition for land intensified. Europeans often took land from Native Americans. Cultural differences and land disputes led to distrust and war.

Slaves in the Colonies European settlers began to plant and harvest crops and started businesses and towns. This created a demand for cheap labor, so Europeans forced some people to migrate to America.

They had been buying people from slave traders in Africa since the 1500s. Beginning in 1619, enslaved Africans were shipped to the American colonies under such harsh conditions that many died during the journey. Those who survived were bought and sold as property and forced to work for free all their lives. Their children were born into slavery. Although these Africans did not arrive by choice, their labor helped build the country, and their influence is seen in our culture today.

Connections to History

Indentured Servants Indentured servants were immigrants who agreed to work in the colonies for a certain number of years in exchange for passage to America. Their indentures, or contracts, could be bought and sold by employers.

Indentured servants were often forced to work long hours and were sometimes treated very badly. Many did not live long enough to gain their freedom. Most, however, settled in the colonies after completing their contracts.

From Far and Near In the second half of the 1800s, many Chinese immigrants entered the United States. Some worked in mines, while others helped build the transcontinental railroad. In the 1880s and the 1920s, new laws limited the number of U.S. immigrants from various countries. In 1952, legislation again allowed immigrants of all nationalities to become citizens.

Rights of Citizens

Although the United States is among the world's leaders in protecting individual freedom, many U.S. citizens have struggled for their rights. Even after African Americans were freed from slavery in 1865 by the 13th Amendment to the Constitution, they were denied their rights. Women could not vote in the United States until 1920. Native Americans, as well as Hispanics, Asians, the Irish, and other immigrants, have fought against discrimination.

The guarantee of **equal opportunity** in education, employment, and other areas of life has expanded over the years. Today, it is illegal for the government or private institutions to discriminate because of race, gender, religion, age, or disability.

Responsibilities of Citizenship

U.S. citizens' rights come with responsibilities. Citizens should help decide who will run their government and what actions it will take.

Reading
Social Studies

B. Making Inferences Do you think citizens of a democracy have greater responsibilities because they have more rights? Explain.

Americans Join Together On September 11, 2001, terrorists hijacked four U.S. planes. They flew two into the twin towers of the World Trade Center in New York City and one into the Pentagon in Washington, D.C. Both towers collapsed, and one wing of the Pentagon was damaged. Thousands of people were killed, and hundreds more were injured or trapped under debris. The fourth plane crashed in Pennsylvania after passengers struggled with the hijackers.

During the crisis, Americans like these rescue workers showed their patriotism and heroism. Hundreds of firefighters, police officers, and medical personnel worked tirelessly, risking their own lives to save others. Citizens and companies across the country donated time, blood, supplies, and millions of dollars to the victims and their families through organizations such as the Red Cross and the United Way. Americans came together in response to the attack on their nation.

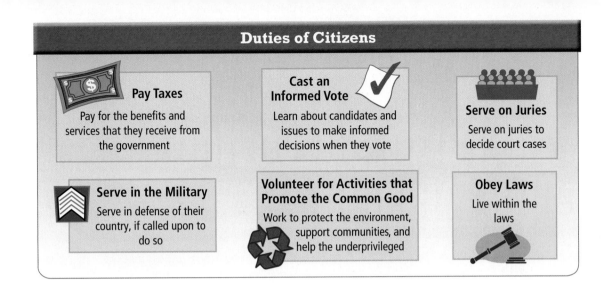

Duties of Citizens

Pay Taxes
Pay for the benefits and services that they receive from the government

Cast an Informed Vote
Learn about candidates and issues to make informed decisions when they vote

Serve on Juries
Serve on juries to decide court cases

Serve in the Military
Serve in defense of their country, if called upon to do so

Volunteer for Activities that Promote the Common Good
Work to protect the environment, support communities, and help the underprivileged

Obey Laws
Live within the laws

Citizenship is a combination of the duties and rights of a citizen. Good citizenship means doing more than the minimum required by law to secure the good of the people.

The Political Process in a Democracy and a Republic In a democracy, government receives its power from the people. **Democracy** is a Greek word that means "rule of the people." In a **republic,** the people also hold power, but they rule through elected representatives. The United States is a republic. The citizens of a democracy or a republic have the responsibility to take part in the political process. The **political process** refers to those legal activities through which citizens can change public policy. By becoming involved, citizens demonstrate their **patriotism,** or love for their country.

Vocabulary

public policy:
Actions that a government takes to carry out its responsibilities, such as making laws and creating rules and regulations.

SECTION 1 ASSESSMENT

Terms & Names

1. **Identify:**
   (a) immigrant
   (b) Anasazi
   (c) equal opportunity
   (d) citizenship
   (e) democracy
   (f) political process
   (g) patriotism
   (h) republic

Taking Notes

2. Use a chart like this one to list five groups that immigrated to America. List the approximate date they began arriving.

Group	First Arrived

Main Ideas

3. (a) Why do people immigrate to the United States?

   (b) What are some of the rights guaranteed to U.S. citizens by the Constitution?

   (c) What are some responsibilities of U.S. citizens?

Critical Thinking

4. **Draw Conclusions**

   In what ways do the rights and duties of U.S. citizens reflect the ideas of the writers of the Constitution?

   Think About

   • reasons people immigrated to the colonies
   • the way a democracy works

ACTIVITY -OPTION- Think about one of the immigrant populations described. Write and illustrate a **magazine article** about the contributions this group has made to the culture of the United States.

Plan an Earth-Surveying Satellite Mission

You and your team of scientists are getting ready to launch a new satellite. Satellites supply scientists with a great deal of information, such as data on Earth's surface, the atmosphere, and even the ocean floor. They carry sensitive instruments to analyze weather conditions and survey the ozone layer. They relay phone conversations and TV programs. Satellites measure heat radiation, plant growth, ocean conditions, tropical rainfall, and other features of our environment. Your job is to plan a new Earth-surveying satellite mission.

COOPERATIVE LEARNING On these pages are challenges you will encounter as you plan a satellite mission. Working with a small group, choose one of these challenges to meet. Divide the work among group members. You will find helpful information in the Data File. Keep in mind that you will present your solution to the class.

LANGUAGE ARTS CHALLENGE

"How can you find these talented people?"

As your planning continues, you find that you need new team members for a variety of jobs. You need computer scientists and software engineers. Other engineers will design instruments to measure data. Experts in forestry, geology, weather, and other fields will help interpret the satellite data. How can you find these talented people? Use one of these options to present information. Look in the Data File for help.

ACTIVITIES

1. As part of the satellite team, you give recruitment speeches to science students. Write and deliver a speech explaining what you do, what background and education you needed, and why your job is interesting.

2. Write help-wanted ads for three different positions on the satellite team. Describe the education, technical background, and personality traits needed for each position.

Engineers working on the satellite. ▲

GEOGRAPHY CHALLENGE

The satellite "swoops around Earth from the North Pole to the South Pole."

An Earth-observation satellite usually follows a sun-synchronous polar orbit. That is, it swoops around Earth from the North Pole to the South Pole, then from the South Pole to the North Pole. How can you make the best use of this satellite path? How can you schedule your work? Choose one of these options. Look for information in the Data File.

ACTIVITIES

1. Your sun-synchronous satellite passes over the equator twice a day—at 10:00 A.M. traveling north to south, at 10:00 P.M. traveling south to north. At what time will the satellite pass over the South Pole? At about what time will the satellite pass over North America? Make a diagram to illustrate the satellite's movement.

2. Suppose you decide instead to put the satellite in orbit above the equator. Plot its course and list the countries and bodies of water it will fly over.

Integral satellite in orbit. ◄

SATELLITE ORBITS

- **High-altitude geosynchronous orbit:** The satellite travels above the equator at a height of about 22,300 miles. It moves at the same speed and in the same direction as Earth is turning. Because the satellite's orbit coordinates with Earth's movement, to an observer on the ground it seems to hover overhead at the same place in the sky.

- **Sun-synchronous polar orbit:** The satellite passes over the north and south poles, circling the globe north to south and south to north in a 24-hour day. As a result, the satellite always crosses the equator at the same local times—say, 2:00 A.M. and 2:00 P.M. As it circles Earth, it makes observations of lands at every latitude.

- **Low-altitude orbit:** The satellite travels within Earth's atmosphere, but in the highest layer, where friction is less because the air is thin.

TYPES OF ARTIFICIAL SATELLITES

- **Earth observation:** map and monitor physical changes on Earth.

- **Scientific research:** gather data for scientists to analyze.

- **Weather:** make local or worldwide observations, depending on orbit; measure cloud patterns, air pressure, air pollution, and air chemistry.

- **Communications:** relay radio, TV, and telephone signals.

- **Navigation:** provide location information.

- **Military:** gather information for military use.

To learn more about Earth-surveying satellites, go to

RESEARCH LINKS
CLASSZONE.COM

Activity Wrap-Up

As a group, review your solution to the challenge you selected. Then present your solution to the class.

A Constitutional Democracy

TERMS & NAMES

United States Constitution

limited government

unlimited government

constitutional amendment

Bill of Rights

federal government

MAIN IDEA

The founders of the United States drafted a constitution that protected the rights of citizens.

WHY IT MATTERS NOW

After more than 200 years, the Constitution continues to protect the freedoms of U.S. citizens.

DATELINE

U.S. SUPREME COURT, MAY 17, 1954—Oliver Brown, an African American, wanted his daughter to attend a nearby all-white school. When the Board of Education in Topeka, Kansas, refused to admit her, Brown went to court. Today, the U.S. Supreme Court ruled that separate schools for different races violate the equal protection guaranteed by the 14th Amendment to the U.S. Constitution.

In 1896, the Supreme Court had allowed states to provide "separate but equal" facilities for blacks and whites. The words in the Constitution remain the same, but changes in society have led to a new interpretation of those words.

Place • Soldiers and police escort students into a formerly all-white school following this Supreme Court ruling. ▲

The Law of the Land

The basis for U.S. law is the **United States Constitution,** written by the country's first leaders. Amazingly, this document remains the foundation for all laws and the framework for the U.S. government more than 200 years after its creation. The Supreme Court decides whether the actions of states, businesses, and individuals are in accordance with the ideas in the Constitution, as it did in this 1954 case.

Forming a New Government American colonists living under British rule did not have the rights and the protections they wanted. After gaining independence from Great Britain in 1783, they established a nation called the United States of America. The writers of the Constitution designed a government that received its power from the people.

Reading
Social Studies

Making Inferences
What were two goals that the writers of the Constitution wanted to achieve?

The founders, or early American leaders, wanted to protect people's individual rights and freedoms from government interference. They also knew that a society needs strong laws and a stable government to ensure the common good. They wrote a constitution that achieved both goals. The U.S. Constitution describes and limits the power of the government and its leaders. It also defines the rights of citizens and their role in governing their country. In 1902, President Theodore Roosevelt explained the relationship between U.S. citizens and their government.

A VOICE FROM THE UNITED STATES

The government is us; we are the government, you and I.

Theodore Roosevelt

Limited and Unlimited Governments

The constitutional republic of the United States is one example of a **limited government**. In other types of government, called **unlimited governments**, the leaders have almost total power. For instance, dictators control their countries' laws and people.

The United States Constitution The U.S. Constitution is the oldest national constitution still in use. It was written in 1787 at the Constitutional Convention in Philadelphia and ratified in 1789. Ideas that shaped the U.S. Constitution came from many places and times, including Great Britain, France, and ancient Rome. Native American nations, such as the Iroquois Confederacy, may also have influenced political ideas at the time that the Constitution was drafted. This painting, *Scene at the Signing of the Constitution of the United States* by H. C. Christy, hangs in the Capitol in Washington, D.C.

Place • Women began the fight for suffrage, or the right to vote, in the early 1800s and continued until they succeeded in 1920. ▲

The Constitution Grows and Changes

The Constitution went into effect in 1789. A condition of ratifying, or approving, it in many states was the promise of a bill of rights. In 1791, the states adopted ten constitutional amendments proposed by Congress. A **constitutional amendment** is a change or addition to the Constitution. This **Bill of Rights** lists specific freedoms guaranteed to every U.S. citizen. Among them are freedom of speech and religion, the right to a fair trial, and the right to gather peaceably. In all, 27 amendments have adapted the Constitution to the country's changing needs. Some amendments passed after the Bill of Rights include ones that ended slavery, gave women the right to vote, and limited a president's terms to two.

Limiting Powers of Government

Leaders of the new country wanted to limit government power and to preserve each state's right to govern itself. To accomplish these goals, they created a federal system in which power is divided between the **federal government,** or national government, and the state governments. The federal government is a republic headed by the President.

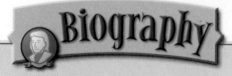

Martin Luther King, Jr. (1929–1968) Reverend King was a civil rights leader in the 1950s and 1960s. A gifted speaker, he argued for voting rights, equal opportunities in education and jobs, and justice not based on the color of people's skin. He expressed these hopes in a famous 1963 speech in Washington, D.C., shown at right.

Influenced by his study of Christianity and his admiration for India's civil rights leader Mahatma Gandhi, Reverend King used nonviolent protest. He received the Nobel Peace Prize in 1964.

On April 4, 1968, he was assassinated. Since 1986, a U.S. holiday has been observed in January to honor him, and he is remembered around the country for his leadership in the civil rights movement.

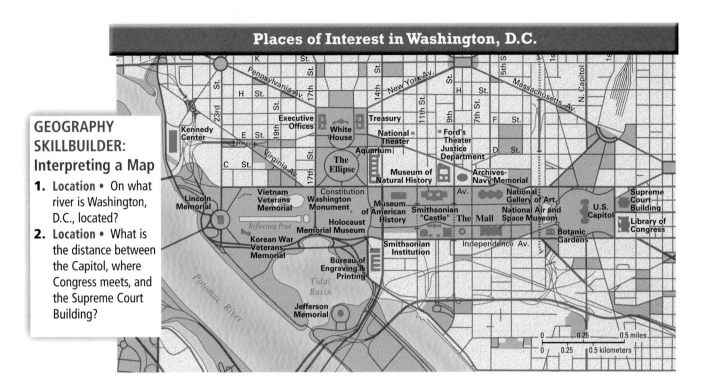

Places of Interest in Washington, D.C.

GEOGRAPHY SKILLBUILDER:
Interpreting a Map

1. **Location** • On what river is Washington, D.C., located?
2. **Location** • What is the distance between the Capitol, where Congress meets, and the Supreme Court Building?

Federal and State Government The Constitution gives the federal government specific powers, including establishing an army, waging war, raising money through taxes, and making laws to carry out its duties. All other powers are held by the states. The Constitution does not refer to local government, so each state determines the form of town or county rule.

Checks and Balances Three branches share the powers of the U.S. government. Each branch checks the power of the other branches. The process by which a bill, or a proposal for a new law, becomes a law shows how this balance of power works.

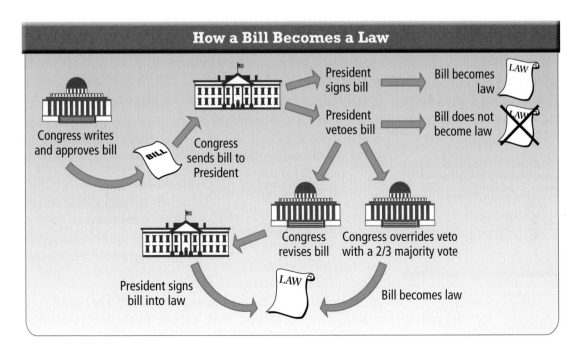

How a Bill Becomes a Law

Three Branches of Government

The Constitution separates powers of government into the executive, legislative, and judicial branches. Each branch has its own job. All are located in the U.S. capital, Washington, D.C.

Executive Branch
Enforces the laws

The Executive Branch The President is elected to head the executive branch. He enforces the laws, serves as commander in chief of the armed forces, and conducts foreign affairs. The Vice-President is elected with the President. The President's cabinet includes the secretaries of the 14 executive departments and other key members of the executive branch.

Legislative Branch
Makes the laws and controls taxes and spending

The Legislative Branch Congress is made up of two houses—the Senate and the House of Representatives—and makes national laws. Two senators are elected from each of the 50 states. The House of Representatives has 435 members, elected from each state according to its population. The two houses have some shared responsibilities and some separate ones.

Judicial Branch
Decides if laws agree with the U.S. Constitution

The Judicial Branch The judicial branch is the system of federal courts that makes sure all laws and treaties are constitutional, or agree with the U.S. Constitution. The highest federal court, the Supreme Court, has nine justices, or judges, nominated by the President and approved by the Senate.

SECTION 2 ASSESSMENT

Terms & Names

1. **Identify:**
   (a) United States Constitution
   (b) limited government
   (c) unlimited government
   (d) constitutional amendment
   (e) Bill of Rights
   (f) federal government

Taking Notes

2. Use a diagram like this one to record the organization of the government.

Branches of Government		
Executive	Legislative	Judicial

Main Ideas

3. (a) What two goals did the writers of the U.S. Constitution try to achieve?

   (b) Why did people think it was important to add the Bill of Rights to the Constitution?

   (c) Why does the Constitution create a balance of powers among the three branches of government?

Critical Thinking

4. **Drawing Inferences**

   Why do you think Congress is made up of two parts, the Senate and the House of Representatives?

   Think About

   • the wish to limit the power of government
   • the number of senators and representatives from each state

---

ACTIVITY -OPTION-

If you were going to add an amendment to the Constitution, what would it be? Write a **proposal** for it. Tell what the law would do, whom it would affect, and why people should support it.

Sequencing Events

▶▶ Defining the Skill

Sequence is the order in which events follow one another. If you learn to follow the sequence of events through history, you can better understand how events relate to each other.

▶▶ Applying the Skill

This passage at the right describes the sequence of events that improved the transportation of natural resources and goods in the United States. Use the strategies listed below to understand how transportation has improved.

How to Sequence Events

Strategy ❶ Look for time periods of events or discoveries. Some dates may be exact, and others may be indicated only by decades or centuries. Words such as *day, month, year,* or *century* may help you to sequence the events or discoveries.

Strategy ❷ Look for clues about time that allow you to order events according to sequence. Words such as *first, next, later,* and *finally* may help you order events that are not dated.

Make a Time Line

Making a time line can help you sequence events. This time line shows the sequence of events in the passage you just read.

RESOURCES, GOODS, AND PEOPLE

The United States could not have developed without new ways of transporting natural resources and goods. ❶ In the early 19th century, water provided the fastest way to transport goods. Canals linked some lakes and rivers, so places became more accessible. ❷ A little later, steamboats allowed river traffic to go upstream and downstream easily.

❶ By the middle of the century, steam-powered railroads had replaced steamboats because they could reach more places and carry larger loads. At the ❶ beginning of the 20th century, people and goods in many cities and towns were linked by railroad.

❶ In the early 1900s, automobiles and trucks began to move raw materials and goods. Airplanes ❶ began to transport goods in the 1930s. By the ❶ 1950s, paved roads connected much of the country. ❷ Today, fast jets also bring goods and people to many parts of the United States.

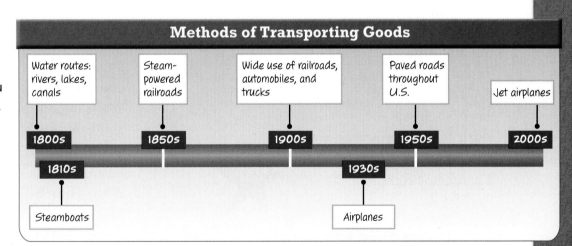

Methods of Transporting Goods

Water routes: rivers, lakes, canals	Steam-powered railroads	Wide use of railroads, automobiles, and trucks	Paved roads throughout U.S.	Jet airplanes
1800s	**1850s**	**1900s**	**1950s**	**2000s**

1810s — Steamboats

1930s — Airplanes

▶▶ Practicing the Skill

Turn to Chapter 4, Section 1, "We the People." Read about the different groups of people who settled the land that became the United States. Make a list showing the sequence of the arrival of different immigrant groups.

LITERATURE CONNECTIONS

WITH A LAND AREA of over 3.7 million square miles and a population of more than 285 million, the United States is an amazingly varied country. From small towns, forests, and farmland to big cities like San Francisco and New York, the United States has a wealth of both human-made and natural features. The poems here celebrate this variety.

CONEY

By Virginia Schonborg

There's hot corn
And franks.
There's the boardwalk
With lots of games,
With chances
To win or lose.
There's the sun.
Underneath the boardwalk
It's cool,
And the sand is salty.
The beach is
Like a fruitstand of people,
Big and little,
Red and white,
Brown and yellow.
There's the sea
With high green waves.
And after,
There's hot corn
And franks.

KNOXVILLE, TENNESSEE

By Nikki Giovanni

I always like summer
best
you can eat fresh corn
from daddy's garden
and okra
and greens
and cabbage
and lots of
barbecue
and buttermilk
and homemade ice-cream
at the church picnic
and listen to
gospel music
outside
at the church
homecoming
and go to the mountains with
your grandmother
and go barefooted
and be warm
all the time
not only when you go to bed
and sleep

SCENIC ★

By John Updike

O when in San Francisco do
As natives do: they sit and stare
And smile and stare again. The view
Is visible from anywhere.

Here hills are white with houses whence,
Across a multitude of sills,
The owners, lucky residents,
See other houses, other hills.

The meanest[1] San Franciscan knows,
No matter what his past has been,
There are a thousand patios
Whose view he is included in.

The Golden Gate, the cable cars,
Twin Peaks, the Spreckles habitat,[2]
The local ocean, sun, and stars—
When fog falls, one admires *that*.

Here homes are stacked in such a way
That every picture window has
An unmarred prospect of the Bay
And, in its center, Alcatraz.[3]

1. Poorest.

2. In the late 1950s, Twin Peaks was a well-to-do residential neighborhood where a very wealthy family, the Spreckles, lived.

3. An island in San Francisco Bay, site of a former federal prison.

Reading THE LITERATURE

Pick out the words each poet uses to give a sense of place. How can you tell that some places are rural, some urban? What aspects of geography has each poet highlighted?

Thinking About THE LITERATURE

Imagine that you live in one of these places. What kinds of jobs might people have there? What might they do for fun? How does the place where you live influence your daily activities?

Writing About THE LITERATURE

Which of the poems creates the strongest image in your mind? Using examples from that poem, write a short paragraph explaining why.

About the Authors

Virginia Schonborg (b. 1913) was born in Rhode Island and is the author of *The Salt Marsh* and *Subway Swinger.*

Nikki Giovanni (b. 1943) was born in Tennessee and became well-known as a poet in the 1960s.

John Updike (b. 1932), born in Shillington, Pennsylvania, is the author of many short stories, novels, and poems.

Further Reading For more outstanding poems about the United States, read *My America: A Poetry Atlas of the United States*, edited by Lee Bennett Hopkins.

The United States Economy

TERMS & NAMES

factors of production

GDP

free enterprise/ market economy

consumer

profit

competition

MAIN IDEA

The United States has an economy based on free enterprise. Consumers and business owners decide what goods and services to produce.

WHY IT MATTERS NOW

This economic system has made it possible for the United States to become a leader in the worldwide economy.

Back Forward Stop Refresh Home

Address: ▶ go

DATELINE

JUNE 2001, THE UNITED STATES—The collapse of many dot-coms has shaken consumer confidence. Internet-based companies, nicknamed "dot-coms" for the last part of their Web addresses, have been failing by the hundreds.

In the mid-1990s, investors backed dot-com companies in hopes of making a huge return on their investments. This ready money encouraged people with limited management experience, untested technologies, and experimental Web sales strategies to start companies. In 1999, more than 1,700 Internet start-ups were born.

When investors realized that many start-ups were losing money, they began to withdraw their support. Between January 2000 and May 2001, 435 Internet companies shut down. Over 31,000 people have lost their jobs.

Place • When companies fail, employees are often left without jobs and office equipment is sold. ▲

The Study of Economics

Business start-ups and shutdowns, the rise and fall of investor and consumer confidence, the increase and decrease in the number of people without jobs—all of these changes are part of the market economy of the United States. Investors, service providers, manufacturers, and consumers make choices each day, and these choices affect the state of the economy.

Vocabulary

investor: one who commits money or capital in order to earn a financial return

Goods and Services Suppose you want a CD recording just released by your favorite music group. To earn the money to pay for it, you might rake your neighbor's leaves or care for his or her child for a few hours. The CD is a good. A good is any object you can buy to satisfy a want. Raking leaves or baby-sitting is a service you provide. A service is an action that meets a want. Your neighbor buys your service to meet his or her want.

What to Buy People constantly decide which goods and services to buy. They usually satisfy basic needs such as food, clothing, housing, transportation, childcare, and medical treatment first. If there is money left over, they might choose to spend it on music CDs, in-line skates, a computer game, or a vacation.

A government must also make decisions. Tax dollars must be set aside to pay for police and fire protection, schools, roads, and military forces. Once these expenses have been determined, other choices can be made.

Reading Social Studies

A. Synthesizing After a government has set aside money for basic wants, what additional goods or services might it pay for?

A Growing Economy

A nation must produce goods and provide services to support a growing economy. In an expanding economy, citizens have better-paying jobs, so the government collects more tax money. Then people and the government can satisfy more wants.

To sustain a growing economy, business owners must keep production at a high level. Production is the making of goods and services. The four **factors of production** are the ingredients, or elements, needed for production to occur.

Culture • Christina Aguilera's critical contribution in the production of a CD is as one of the labor resources. ▼

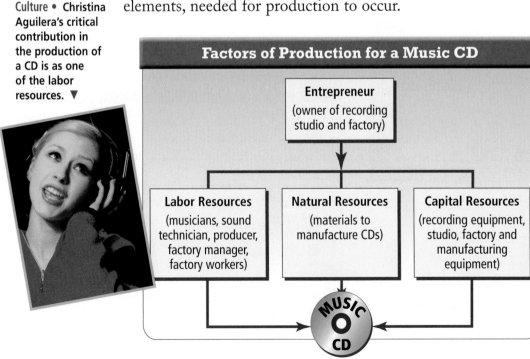

Factors of Production for a Music CD

Entrepreneur
(owner of recording studio and factory)

Labor Resources
(musicians, sound technician, producer, factory manager, factory workers)

Natural Resources
(materials to manufacture CDs)

Capital Resources
(recording equipment, studio, factory and manufacturing equipment)

MUSIC O CD

Natural Resources Raw materials are used to make goods. Examples include land, water, forests, minerals, soil, and climate.

Labor Resources Workers are needed with the appropriate knowledge, skills, and experience to make goods or provide services.

Capital Resources Machines, factories, and supplies are needed.

Entrepreneurs These are the people who bring natural resources, labor resources, and capital resources together to produce goods and services.

Strange but TRUE

The Value of Money The U.S. Department of the Treasury first issued paper money in 1861. During the Civil War, people hoarded coins. This caused a severe shortage of coins in circulation.

The Bureau of Engraving and Printing printed "fractional currency" bills of 3 cents, 5 cents, 10 cents, 25 cents, and 50 cents. These were the smallest bills ever printed in this country. The largest note was the $100,000 Gold Certificate printed in 1934 and 1935. These notes were used for bank transactions and were not available for the public to use.

The United States Economy

The U.S. economy is one of the wealthiest in the world. One way to measure a country's economy is to look at its **GDP**, or gross domestic product. This tells the total value of the goods and services that a country produces each year. The GDP is also a way to compare the economies of different countries.

U.S. industries include services, such as health care and legal services; communications, such as publishing, television and radio, telephone, and mail delivery; finance, such as banks and stock markets; manufacturing, such as food products, automobiles, and clothing; and electronics, such as televisions, computers, and sound equipment. The success of these industries helps make many Americans wealthier than people in other parts of the world.

BACKGROUND

In 2000, 2.8 billion of the world's 6 billion people lived on less than $2 a day.

Estimated 2000 Per Capita* GDP

Country	U.S. Dollars
United States	36,200
China	3,600
India	2,200
Saudi Arabia	10,500
France	24,400
Zimbabwe	2,500

*Per capita means for each person.
Source: CIA World Factbook

The Free Enterprise or Market Economy U.S. citizens and businesses make most economic decisions. Business owners control the factors of production. The government plays a limited role. It does not decide which or how many goods are produced. It does not set prices or tell people where to work. These are the qualities of a **free enterprise/market economy**. A market is a setting for exchanging goods and services. In a free enterprise economy, business owners compete in the market with little government interference. Other nations, such as Canada, many countries in Western Europe, Japan, and some Latin American countries, also have market economies.

Culture • The machines that make CDs are a capital resource, one of the four factors of production. ▲

Supply and Demand In a free enterprise or market economy, **consumers**—the people who use goods and services—help decide what will be produced. Prices affect how products are distributed to consumers. For example, suppose a music company produces 1,000 CDs priced at $16.95 each, but 1,100 people want to buy them. There are not enough CDs to satisfy the wants of these consumers. Because demand for the good is greater than the supply, the seller can increase the price to $17.95. He or she sells all the CDs and makes an extra $1.00 profit on each. The seller, like all entrepreneurs, wants to increase profit. **Profit** is the money that remains after all the costs of producing a product have been paid.

Now suppose the seller offers 1,000 more CDs at the original $16.95 price. One hundred sell right away, leaving 900 CDs that no one wants at this price. The seller then reduces the price to $15.95. Consumers who didn't want the CD at $16.95 may want it at this lower price. Because the supply of the good is greater than the demand, the seller must reduce the price.

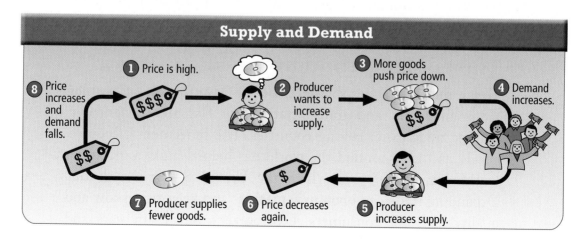

Supply and Demand

8 Price increases and demand falls.

1 Price is high.

2 Producer wants to increase supply.

3 More goods push price down.

4 Demand increases.

5 Producer increases supply.

6 Price decreases again.

7 Producer supplies fewer goods.

Supply and demand explain how price and availability are affected by how much consumers are willing to pay for an item and how much the seller decides to charge for it. The number of CDs offered at each price is the supply. The number of CDs that people will buy at each price is the demand.

Competition In a free enterprise or market economy, many businesses produce similar goods or services. There is competition to attract consumers. **Competition** is the rivalry among businesses to sell goods to consumers and make the greatest profit. To achieve these goals, a company may offer an improved product, manufacture it more cheaply, or sell it at a better price.

Culture • Stores compete in malls and online to attract consumers. They use advertising and appealing store displays to catch the attention of potential customers. ▲

Other Economic Systems

Most countries combine features from three types of economic systems: market, command, and traditional economies.

Command Economy In this system, the government decides how many of which goods are produced and sets the prices. Countries, such as North Korea and Cuba with Communist governments, have command economies. China has elements of market and command economies.

Traditional Economy In this system, social roles and culture determine how goods and services are produced, what prices and individual incomes are, and which consumers are allowed to buy certain goods. For instance, a family's status may determine whether they can own a tractor. Farmers may give much of their produce to community leaders. India has features of both market and traditional economies.

Reading
Social Studies

B. Making Inferences Why might countries combine features of different economic systems?

The Global Economy

Today, more countries than ever before have market economies. Communication and transportation are fast and dependable, making trade easier among countries. The movement of people, goods, and ideas around the world has helped build a global, or worldwide, economy in which the United States is a leader. Expanding trade can open new markets and keep prices low and quality high for consumers. U.S. citizens buy many cars and clothes from other countries that take part in the global economy.

World Trade Partners of the United States, 2000

NAFTA – 32.9%

East Asia NICs* – 19.8%

European Union – 19.3%

Japan – 10.6%

Latin America – 7.8%

Middle East – 2.9%

Africa – 1.9%

East Europe and
Former Soviet Union – 1.1%

India – 0.4%

* Newly industrialized countries:
China, Hong Kong, Indonesia,
Malaysia, Singapore, South Korea,
Taiwan, Thailand

Source: U.S. Dept. of Commerce,
International Trade Summary, 1998–2001

0   3,000 miles
0   3,000 kilometers

ATLANTIC OCEAN

PACIFIC OCEAN

PACIFIC OCEAN

INDIAN OCEAN

GEOGRAPHY SKILLBUILDER: Interpreting a Map

1. **Movement** • Who are the largest U.S. trade partners?
2. **Movement** • With which countries or regions does the United States trade least?

Trade Barriers Sometimes countries establish barriers to restrict trade because they prefer to produce their own goods or services. Tariffs, or taxes on imported goods, raise the price to the consumer and make it more difficult for other countries to compete.

In 1994, NAFTA, the North American Free Trade Agreement, reduced trade barriers among the United States, Canada, and Mexico. There was concern that companies would move factories to Mexico, where workers earn less, and U.S. workers would lose jobs. However, many economists believe free trade benefits all three countries.

SECTION 3 ASSESSMENT

Terms & Names

1. **Identify:** (a) factors of production (b) GDP (c) free enterprise/market economy
(d) consumer (e) profit (f) competition

Taking Notes

2. Use a chart like this one to take notes on the characteristics of free enterprise/market, command, and traditional economies.

Free Enterprise/ Market Economy	Command Economy	Traditional Economy

Main Ideas

3. (a) How is the price of goods decided in the U.S. economic system?

(b) What are the four factors of production?

(c) What role does government have in the U.S. market economy?

Critical Thinking

4. **Making Inferences**

What effect will reducing trade barriers between countries have on the price of goods? Explain.

Think About

• the characteristics of a free enterprise/market economy

• competition

ACTIVITY -OPTION-

Write an **advertisement** for a new business showing the goods or services it will produce. Make a chart showing the type of materials, labor, and capital you will need to produce the product.

The Legacy of North America

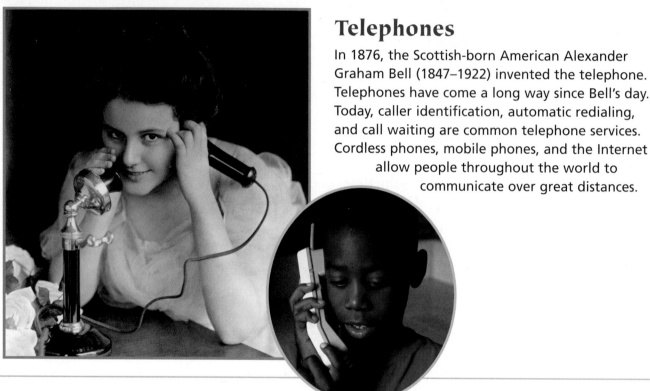

Telephones

In 1876, the Scottish-born American Alexander Graham Bell (1847–1922) invented the telephone. Telephones have come a long way since Bell's day. Today, caller identification, automatic redialing, and call waiting are common telephone services. Cordless phones, mobile phones, and the Internet allow people throughout the world to communicate over great distances.

Lacrosse

Native peoples of North America played an early version of lacrosse long before Columbus landed. Players used a racket, now known as a crosse, to throw a hard ball down the field and into the opposing team's goal. Today, lacrosse is a popular sport not only in North America but also in Ireland, Australia, and South Africa. Men's teams play for the ILF World Championship, and women's teams compete for the World Cup.

Airplanes

In 1903, Wilbur (1867–1912) and Orville (1871–1948) Wright achieved the first powered, sustained flight near Kitty Hawk, N.C. The flight lasted 12 seconds and reached a height of 120 feet. By the 1920s, aviation had become a booming industry. Today, jumbo and supersonic jets allow people to travel around the world in just a day or two. More than 1.5 billion passengers land and take off at the world's 50 busiest airports every year.

Find Out More About It!

Study the text and photos on these pages to learn about inventions, creations, and contributions that have come from North America. Then choose the item that interests you the most and do research in the library or on the Internet to learn more about it. Use the information you gather to construct a model of the item you choose.

RESEARCH LINKS
CLASSZONE.COM

Skyscrapers

In the late 1800s, U.S. architects and engineers worked together to build the first skyscrapers in Chicago and New York City. Today, these enormous structures rise in cities all over the world. The tallest skyscrapers in the world are the Petronas Towers in Kuala Lumpur, Malaysia, which reach a height of 1,483 feet.

Snowmobiles

In the winter of 1922, 15-year-old Joseph-Armand Bombardier of Canada invented the first crude snowmobile by attaching a car engine to sleigh runners and adding a wooden propeller to the back. In 1935, he refined his invention after his young son died from appendicitis because they couldn't make it through the snow to the hospital in time. Today, people around the world use snowmobiles for winter fun, and people in the remote north depend on them for transportation when the snows are deep.

United States Culture: Crossing Borders

MAIN IDEA

The American way of life reflects the cultures of people from many countries around the world.

WHY IT MATTERS NOW

People around the world are more closely connected than ever before.

DATELINE

NEW YORK CITY, 1905—Visit Gennaro Lombardi's pizzeria—the first in the United States—to try a pizza. This baked, flat pie has a bread crust covered with cheese, tomato sauce, and seasonings.

Lombardi's pizzas are not exactly like the pizzas made in Naples, Italy, because different seasonings, flour, and cheese are available here. Also, instead of using sliced tomatoes like those put on Italian pizzas, Lombardi adds a spicy homemade tomato sauce. Customers say this pizza is as good as any from Naples. Judging by the warm reception it has received so far, pizza may become a popular U.S. food.

Place • Pizza, brought here by Italian immigrants, is becoming a popular food. ▲

American Way of Life

People in the United States have brought diverse customs, traditions, and foods, like pizza, from their homelands, but they share many of the same values. **Values** are the principles and ideals by which people live. U.S. citizens care about individual freedoms; equal opportunities for jobs and education; fair treatment of people regardless of race, religion, or gender; and private ownership of property. Many of these values are part of the U.S. Constitution and help define American culture.

Education U.S. citizens believe they can improve their lives through education. In 1647, Massachusetts established the first colonial public school system. Today, state laws require that all children attend school or be taught at home until they are at least 16. More than 99 percent of U.S. children finish elementary school, and more than 85 percent complete high school.

U.S. Religions About 70 percent of all U.S. citizens are members of religious groups. Many colonists, such as British Protestants and Catholics, settled in America so that they could worship as they wished. Since then, people with many different religious beliefs have come to the United States. Most Spanish, French, and Italian immigrants were Catholic. In the 1900s, many European Jews settled in the United States. Asian immigrants practice Buddhism and Hinduism. North Africans and Southwest Asians brought Islam. Many Native Americans continue to practice their ancestors' religions.

Reading
Social Studies
Drawing Conclusions
Why do you think values such as freedom of religion were written into the U.S. Constitution?

The Arts and Entertainment

Leisure activities in the United States reflect the influence of other cultures. For example, sports such as tennis, golf, soccer, and even baseball originated in other countries. Tennis came from France, golf from Scotland, and soccer from England. Baseball is probably based on rounders, a game played in Great Britain in the late 1700s. Basketball was invented in the United States by a Canadian and later spread to other countries. Football is played chiefly in the United States and Canada.

Culture • Baseball, often called America's national pastime, was probably adapted from a British game played in the 1700s. ▲

Place •
Americans eat foods from the traditions of many countries, such as Japanese sushi and sashimi. ▼

The movie and television industries and certain musical forms, such as rock 'n' roll, developed in the United States, although they were affected by other cultures. Jazz was greatly influenced by the blues, which is rooted in spirituals once sung by enslaved Africans. Today, artists and audiences around the world enjoy these American musical styles.

Globalization of Culture The international popularity of U.S. music is an example of the globalization of culture. **Globalization** means spreading around the world. Today, cultural influences often cross national boundaries. People around the world enjoy blue jeans, sodas, and fast food from the United States. McDonald's serves about 45 million people a day in 121 countries.

U.S. citizens eat Japanese sushi, listen to Italian operas, and drive South Korean cars. Literature from many nations is translated into different languages. Print and electronic communication, television, movies, and the Internet provide speedy ways to share the products and creations of different cultures.

U.S. Science and Technology

U.S. scientists are mapping DNA, discovering treatments and cures for diseases, and finding new energy sources for industry and homes. Once discoveries are made, inventors create **technology,** such as tools or equipment, to apply the new knowledge in practical ways. Modern technology enables U.S. scientists to work with other scientists from around the world.

Science and Technology Change the World Discoveries by U.S. scientists help people throughout the world. Polio, a disease that usually affects children, was widespread in the 1940s and 1950s.

BACKGROUND

DNA is the molecule that carries the information that determines the characteristics of every living thing. It was first identified by Francis Crick, James Watson, and others in 1953.

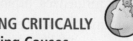

CULTURE

Skyscrapers The skyscraper originated in the United States in the 1870s and has caught on in other countries. Limited space in cities, plus materials and technology, such as steel and elevators, have inspired architects to design taller buildings.

The height of each building is measured from the ground-level main entrance to the structural top, including spires but not antennas or flagpoles. Today, many of the tallest buildings are located outside the United States in places such as Kuala Lumpur, Malaysia, and Hong Kong and Shanghai in China.

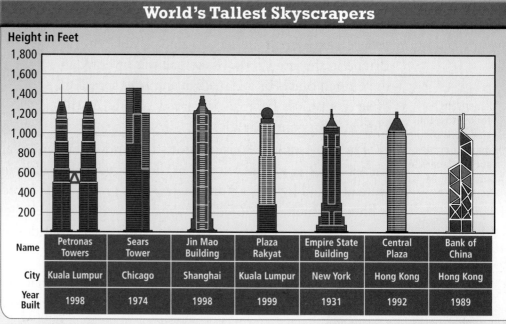

World's Tallest Skyscrapers

Height in Feet

Name	Petronas Towers	Sears Tower	Jin Mao Building	Plaza Rakyat	Empire State Building	Central Plaza	Bank of China
City	Kuala Lumpur	Chicago	Shanghai	Kuala Lumpur	New York	Hong Kong	Hong Kong
Year Built	1998	1974	1998	1999	1931	1992	1989

THINKING CRITICALLY
1. **Finding Causes**
   What were two factors that led architects to design skyscrapers?
2. **Recognizing Important Details**
   How is building height measured?

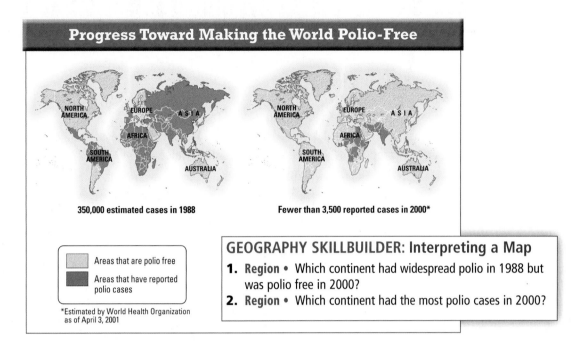

Progress Toward Making the World Polio-Free

350,000 estimated cases in 1988

Fewer than 3,500 reported cases in 2000*

Areas that are polio free

Areas that have reported polio cases

*Estimated by World Health Organization as of April 3, 2001

GEOGRAPHY SKILLBUILDER: Interpreting a Map

1. **Region** • Which continent had widespread polio in 1988 but was polio free in 2000?
2. **Region** • Which continent had the most polio cases in 2000?

Then, U.S. doctors Jonas Salk and Albert Sabin each developed a different vaccine. As a result, great progress has been made toward making the world free of polio.

Negative effects of technology include increased pollution of the environment and the loss of unique cultural features as countries share languages, foods, and customs. Poorer nations may lack the money and skilled labor needed to benefit from new applications of science.

SECTION 4 ASSESSMENT

Terms & Names

1. Identify: (a) value   (b) globalization   (c) technology

Taking Notes

2. Make a chart like the one below to show features of U.S. culture and science that have spread to other parts of the world.

U.S. Culture and Science Around the World	
Culture	Science and Technology

Main Ideas

3. (a) What are some values shared by people in the United States?

(b) What are some examples of contributions from other cultures to the American way of life?

(c) In what ways does American culture influence people in other countries?

Critical Thinking

4. **Forming and Supporting Opinions**

Do you think globalization has a positive or a negative effect on the world? Support your opinion.

Think About

- the effects of globalization
- the changes caused by international trade and communication
- the effects of scientific discoveries worldwide

Reread "The Arts and Entertainment" on page 111. Think about the sports, music, and movies you enjoy. Write an **essay** describing how the cultures of other countries influence your activities.

TERMS & NAMES

Explain the significance of each of the following:

1. immigrant
2. citizenship
3. democracy
4. political process
5. United States Constitution
6. Bill of Rights
7. factors of production
8. free enterprise/ market economy
9. value
10. globalization

REVIEW QUESTIONS

We the People *(pages 87–91)*

1. What are some reasons that people have immigrated to the United States?
2. What are some responsibilities of citizens of the United States?

A Constitutional Democracy *(pages 94–98)*

3. What were the goals of the early leaders when they wrote the United States Constitution?
4. What were the leaders attempting to do when they set up a system of checks and balances within the federal government?

The United States Economy *(pages 102–107)*

5. What are examples of wants that a government must fund?
6. How does each factor of production contribute to the making of a product?

United States Culture: Crossing Borders *(pages 110–113)*

7. What can you conclude from the fact that cultural values were directly stated in the U.S. Constitution?
8. If globalization continues, how will it affect the cultures of the world?

CRITICAL THINKING

Synthesizing

1. Using your completed chart from Reading Social Studies, p. 86, explain why the economy, form of government, and cultural values of the United States continue to attract so many immigrants each year.

Forming and Supporting Opinions

2. Martin Luther King, Jr., fought against laws he thought were unjust. How was this good citizenship? Explain.

Making Inferences

3. What were the major concerns of the leaders who wrote the U.S. Constitution and how did they address them?

Visual Summary

1 We the People

- The United States is made up of immigrants from many countries.
- U.S. citizens share many rights and responsibilities.

2 A Constitutional Democracy

- After the American colonists gained independence, they wrote a Constitution that created a limited government and protected their rights and freedoms.

3 The United States Economy

- The United States has a free enterprise/market economy.
- Because more countries have market economies, a global economy is developing with expanded trade among nations.

4 United States Culture: Crossing Borders

- Americans believe in strong values, many of which are protected by the U.S. Constitution.
- American culture has been shaped by many groups and now influences the cultures of other nations.

SOCIAL STUDIES SKILLBUILDER

Civil Rights Movement in the U.S.

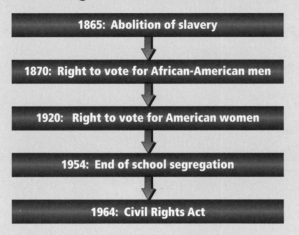

1865: Abolition of slavery

1870: Right to vote for African-American men

1920: Right to vote for American women

1954: End of school segregation

1964: Civil Rights Act

SKILLBUILDER: Sequencing Events

1. What information does this sequence chart show?
2. When did segregation in schools end?
3. Did school segregation end before or after women received the right to vote?

FOCUS ON GEOGRAPHY

1. **Place** • Which states have the highest percentage of foreign-born people?
2. **Place** • Name three states where less than 5 percent of the population is foreign-born.
3. **Region** • Why do you think most states with a high percentage of foreign-born people are on the coasts or borders of the United States?

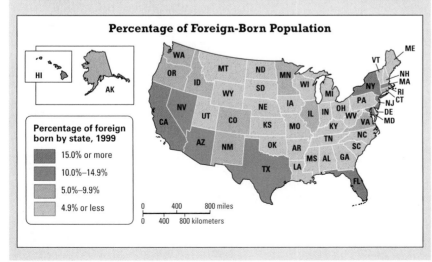

Percentage of Foreign-Born Population

Percentage of foreign born by state, 1999

- 15.0% or more
- 10.0%–14.9%
- 5.0%–9.9%
- 4.9% or less

0   400   800 miles
0   400   800 kilometers

CHAPTER PROJECTS

Interdisciplinary Activity: Music
Writing a Magazine Article Research a favorite musician of today or from the past. Learn what musical influences shaped this performer's work. Were some of the influences from other cultures or times? Include illustrations with captions for your article.

Cooperative Learning Activity
Creating a Display In a group of four to six classmates, think of a natural event, such as a flood, drought, or storm, that affected your community or your region of the country. Working in pairs, research the event in the library or interview people. Together with your group, create a display about the event, explaining its causes and exploring how it affected the area.

- Create drawings or models. Prepare labels to identify and explain them.
- Consider using audio recordings of eyewitness accounts or interviews.
- Use before-and-after photographs or diagrams, if appropriate.

 INTERNET ACTIVITY

Use the Internet to learn about the Constitutional Convention. What were the concerns of the large and small states? Explore how a compromise was reached that allowed the Convention to draft the Constitution.

Writing About Government Write a report of your findings. If possible, use a chart or graph to present information about the different proposals and the final compromise. In your report, include a list of the Internet sites you used to gather information.

For Internet links to support this activity, go to

RESEARCH LINKS
CLASSZONE.COM

CHAPTER 5

Canada Today

CANADA

ATLANTIC

PACIFIC
OCEAN

PACIFIC

OCEAN

INDIAN
OCEAN

OCEAN

How does a country's geography influence its culture?

Region • In 1989, the Canadian Museum of Civilization opened in Hull, Quebec, on the banks of the Ottawa River. The museum celebrates the geographic and cultural diversity of Canada. Douglas Cardinal, an architect from Calgary, Alberta, and a descendant of the Canadian Blackfoot people, designed the two distinct buildings. He wanted them to reflect Canada's landforms.

The structures evoke the glaciers and rocky formations of the western Canadian Shield. The limestone from which the walls are made comes from the province of Manitoba. Totem poles carved from red cedar trees by First Nations people of British Columbia line the museum entrance.

What do you think?

♦ How are the varied landforms and resources of Canada represented in the museum?

♦ Describe some geographic features in the area where you live. Explain how they affect the traditions and activities of people in your community.

Region Hudson Bay, a huge body of water in northeast Canada, is home to ice floes nine months of the year. Nevertheless, the bay is open to shipping throughout the year.

BEFORE YOU READ

▶▶ *What Do You Know?*

Before you read this chapter, consider what you know about Canada. Have you ever read that Canada has the world's longest coastline? Did you know that Canada is an independent democracy with a constitution, yet it pledges loyalty to the British monarch? Perhaps you know that 60 percent of the National Hockey League's players are Canadian? Recall what you have learned about Canada from personal experience, television, and other classes. Think about how Canada is similar to the United States and how it is different.

▶▶ *What Do You Want to Know?*

Decide what you would like to know about Canada's history, government, economy, and culture. In your notebook, record what you hope to learn from this chapter.

Culture • The art of totem pole carving almost disappeared in the mid-1800s. Museums began to preserve totem poles in the 1850s. ▼

READ AND TAKE NOTES

Reading Strategy: Analyzing Causes and Effects To help you understand how geographic, historical, and cultural factors have influenced Canada's development, pay attention to causes and effects as you read Chapter 5. Notice that several factors may cause the same effect. Use the chart below to make connections between statements about geography, history, and culture and statements describing Canada today.

- Copy the chart into your notebook.
- On the chart, read statements describing issues and conditions in Canada today (effects).
- As you read the chapter, identify the effects of the listed causes and note them on the chart.

Culture • The 1893 Montreal Amateur Athletic Association was the first hockey team to win the Stanley Cup. ▲

Causes		Effects
Early settlers were from France and Britain, two nations that had conflicts.		
French-speaking Canadians have kept their own language and culture separate from the rest of the nation.	→	
The people of First Nations and other culture groups want to preserve their traditions.		
Cold climate, geographic barriers, and poor soil exist in northern parts of Canada.	→	
The Arctic Ocean and Hudson Bay are frozen for most of the year.		
Landforms such as the Rocky Mountains create transportation barriers.	→	

O Canada! Immigrant Roots

MAIN IDEA

Canada's population includes many groups of people from different lands who retain their cultural identities.

WHY IT MATTERS NOW

Knowing the history of the people of Canada helps in understanding Canada's policy of multiculturalism.

DATELINE

EXTRA

QUEBEC, NEW FRANCE, JUNE 1609

New colonists have just arrived to join the first settlers of Quebec. Only French explorer Samuel de Champlain and 8 of the 32 men he led here survived their first winter in the new colony. Champlain chose this location that the Algonquins call Quebec, or the Narrows, after much searching.

After arriving last July, he and his men built houses, planted grain, and worked to encourage fur trading and friendly relations with the native people. Champlain has spent years traveling around New France and mapping and recording information about the seacoast and rivers.

Place • Champlain has great hopes for the future of Quebec. ▲

Champlain used an astrolabe, such as this one, to navigate during his travels. ▲

Who Are the Canadians?

The people of Canada come from many countries—not just France. More than 50 ethnic groups make up the population. More than two-thirds of Canadians have European ancestry. About 40 percent have British roots and 27 percent share a French heritage. Other Canadians trace their families back to Germany, Italy, and Ukraine, as well as to nations in Africa and Asia. Less than 5 percent of all Canadians are people of the First Nations.

The First Nations

People have lived in North America for at least 12,000 years. At times in the past, the levels of the oceans were as much as 300 feet lower than they are today. Then the narrow water passage between Asia and North America—the Bering Strait—became dry land. Small bands of people crossed this land bridge into North America and settled throughout North America and South America.

The Canadians of the **First Nations** are descendants of those first settlers from Asia. In the Arctic north, Inuit and other native people make up more than half the population. Large numbers of First Nations people, including Cree, Micmac, Abenaki, and Ojibwa, live in southern Canada near the United States border.

European Immigrants

The first major wave of European settlement began in the 1600s. Both Britain and France established colonies in what is now Canada. These two countries had a long history of conflict, and they continued their rivalry on the North American continent. Between 1754 and 1763, they fought the French and Indian War for control of North America.

Totem Poles—Carving History The Haida people in Canada's Queen Charlotte Islands and the Kwakiutl in central British Columbia have been skilled totem carvers for centuries. Early craftspeople believed that red cedar was a gift from the Great Spirit. They used simple tools to carve beautiful, detailed totem poles from these trees.

Totem poles, such as these in Stanley Park, Vancouver, display brightly painted animal figures, or totems. These include eagles, whales, grizzly bears, wolves, ravens, frogs, and halibut. Totems are symbols that tell stories, celebrate important events, and preserve the history of native clans. Totem poles have also been used as grave markers and monuments.

THINKING CRITICALLY

1. **Making Inferences**
   What do the totem poles tell you about the First Nations people's relationship with nature?

2. **Drawing Conclusions**
   What roles do totem poles play in native culture?

France lost the war and surrendered most of its Canadian territory to Great Britain. However, many French settlers remained, and disputes continued between them and the fast-growing population of British settlers.

Canada and the United Kingdom
In 1791, the British government established itself in two areas in Canada. Upper Canada, now Ontario, had mostly British settlers. Lower Canada, now Quebec, remained largely French. Although hostilities continued between the two populations, in 1867 they were united as the Dominion of Canada, along with Nova Scotia and New Brunswick. Canada became a self-governing nation, although the British monarch remained its head of state.

In 1869, the Hudson's Bay Company sold land to Canada that later became the provinces of Manitoba, Alberta, and Saskatchewan. In 1871, British Columbia joined the Dominion, and Canada now reached to the Pacific Ocean. In 1931, with the enactment of the Statute of Westminster, Canada gained equal status with the United Kingdom and joined the Commonwealth of Nations. In 1982, the last legal connection between Canada and the British Parliament ended, although Canada remains a member of the Commonwealth.

Later Immigrants Most of Canada's early immigrants were English, Scottish, Irish, and French. After World War I, other Europeans arrived from countries such as Italy, Poland, and Ukraine. Most Italian immigrants settled in Toronto and Montreal. Most Ukrainians moved to the prairies of central Canada. After World War II, Germans and Dutch entered the country, settling primarily in Ontario and British Columbia. In the 1960s, new immigration laws allowed people to migrate from Africa, Latin America, Asia, and the Pacific Islands.

Culture • British General James Wolfe's troops defeated the French and captured Quebec in 1759 during the French and Indian War. Benjamin West's painting *The Death of General Wolfe* shows Wolfe's death at the end of the battle. ▲

Canadian Citizens and Citizenship

As Canadian citizens, those of English or French descent have retained their separate languages and identities. Other groups have also kept the traditions of their homelands after settling in Canada. To support these citizen groups, Canada has adopted an official policy of **multiculturalism**—an acceptance of many cultures instead of just one.

Reading
Social Studies

A. Drawing Inferences How might Canada's policy of multiculturalism lead to increased immigration?

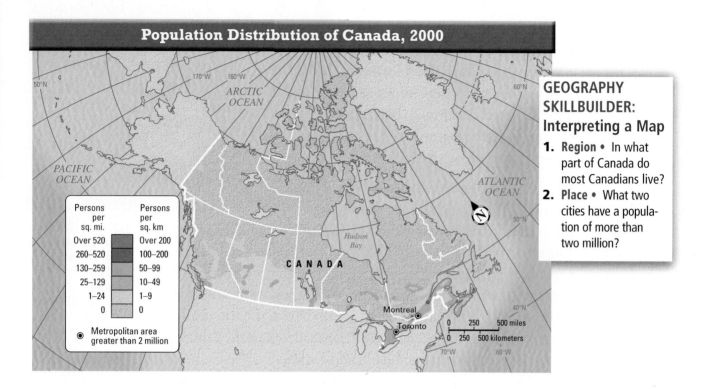

Population Distribution of Canada, 2000

Persons per sq. mi.		Persons per sq. km
Over 520		Over 200
260–520		100–200
130–259		50–99
25–129		10–49
1–24		1–9
0		0

⊙ Metropolitan area greater than 2 million

GEOGRAPHY SKILLBUILDER: Interpreting a Map

1. **Region** • In what part of Canada do most Canadians live?
2. **Place** • What two cities have a population of more than two million?

Canadian citizens have many of the same rights and responsibilities as U.S. citizens. They must obey Canada's laws. They have the option of voting and participating in the political system. They are guaranteed freedom of religion, speech, and assembly, as well as equal protection and treatment for all under Canadian law.

Where Do Most Canadians Live?

While Canada's land area is second only to Russia's, its population is a relatively small 31 million people. Canadians often live where they find a favorable combination of geographic features and economic opportunities. Three-fourths of the population live in the cities and towns of southern Canada. In this region, the Great Lakes, the St. Lawrence Seaway, numerous rivers, and an excellent railway system provide convenient transportation for people and goods. Some Canadians live on farms in the central prairies and in port cities along the coasts. The northern regions of Canada are rugged and very cold. Few people live in those remote areas.

Vancouver, Gateway to the Pacific Vancouver, British Columbia, is called Canada's "Gateway to the Pacific." As Canada's largest port, it trades heavily with Asian countries.

Thousands of Chinese from Hong Kong and many Japanese arrived in Canada at the end of the 20th century. Recent refugees have come from Vietnam, Laos, and Cambodia. **Refugees** are people who flee a country because of war, disaster, or persecution.

Reading
Social Studies

B. Analyzing Motives What geographic and economic features attract people to settle in some parts of Canada?

Toronto, City of Immigrants Toronto, Ontario's capital, is home to one-twelfth of Canada's population but contains one-fourth of its immigrants. More than 70,000 immigrants arrive each year from more than 100 countries in Asia, Europe, the West Indies, and North America. More than 40 percent of Toronto's population is foreign-born, and 10 percent arrived after 1991. Toronto's location, with access to the Atlantic Ocean and the United States, has helped it become a center of industry and international trade.

Place • Toronto is on the shore of Lake Ontario, the easternmost Great Lake. Toronto's skyline is highlighted by the CN Tower. ▲

SECTION 1 ASSESSMENT

Terms & Names
1. Identify: (a) First Nation   (b) multiculturalism   (c) refugee

Taking Notes
2. Make a spider map like this one to record details about the people who settled in Canada.

Canadian People — First Nations — **Canadians** — European Immigration — Recent Immigration

Main Ideas
3. (a) How did the first people reach North America? Who are their descendants?

(b) Describe the relationship between the British and Canada in the 1700s and the 1800s.

(c) What are some of the rights and responsibilities of Canadian citizens?

Critical Thinking
4. **Synthesizing**

How has the policy of multiculturalism benefited recent immigrants to Canada?

Think About

- the historic relations between the French and the English
- the many groups of immigrants and refugees in Canada

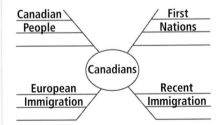

ACTIVITY -OPTION-   Choose one place in Canada where you might like to live. Look at the information in the Unit Atlas and in this section. Write and illustrate a **magazine article** about this location.

A Constitutional Monarchy

TERMS & NAMES
constitutional monarchy
Parliament
prime minister
Pierre Trudeau
separatist

MAIN IDEA

Canada is a democracy that protects the rights of individuals and of different cultures.

WHY IT MATTERS NOW

Canada's form of government has enabled the country to remain united despite conflicts among different groups of citizens.

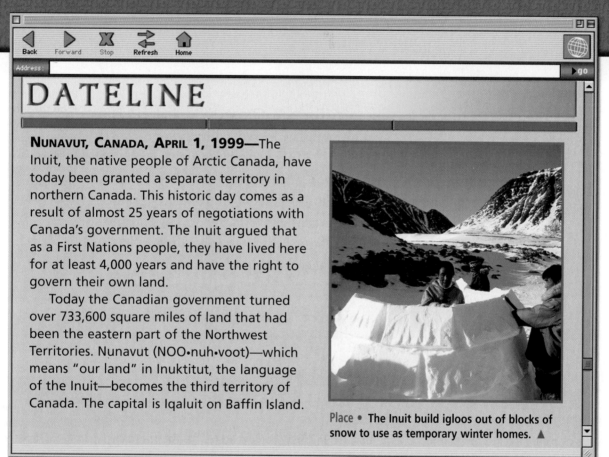

| Back | Forward | Stop | Refresh | Home |

Address: ▶ go

DATELINE

NUNAVUT, CANADA, APRIL 1, 1999—The Inuit, the native people of Arctic Canada, have today been granted a separate territory in northern Canada. This historic day comes as a result of almost 25 years of negotiations with Canada's government. The Inuit argued that as a First Nations people, they have lived here for at least 4,000 years and have the right to govern their own land.

Today the Canadian government turned over 733,600 square miles of land that had been the eastern part of the Northwest Territories. Nunavut (NOO•nuh•voot)—which means "our land" in Inuktitut, the language of the Inuit—becomes the third territory of Canada. The capital is Iqaluit on Baffin Island.

Place • The Inuit build igloos out of blocks of snow to use as temporary winter homes. ▲

A Nation of Provinces and Territories

Other First Nations people also seek the self-government that the Inuit won. At this time, Canada remains a nation of ten provinces and three territories. The responsibilities of the central government include national defense, trade and banking, immigration, criminal law, and postal service. The provincial governments administer education, property rights, local government, hospitals, and provincial taxes. Territorial governments have fewer responsibilities but still enjoy limited self-government.

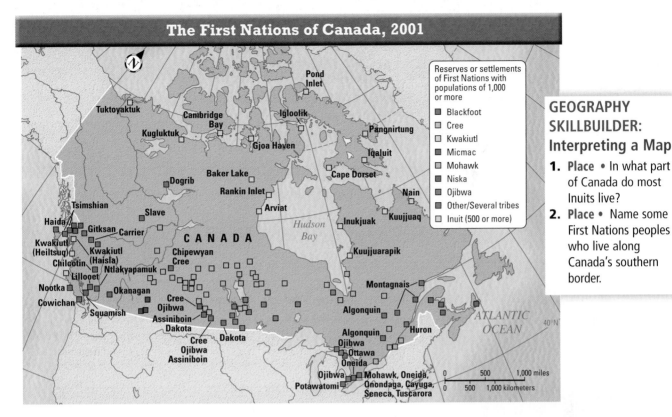

The First Nations of Canada, 2001

Reserves or settlements of First Nations with populations of 1,000 or more

- Blackfoot
- Cree
- Kwakiutl
- Micmac
- Mohawk
- Niska
- Ojibwa
- Other/Several tribes
- Inuit (500 or more)

GEOGRAPHY SKILLBUILDER: Interpreting a Map

1. Place • In what part of Canada do most Inuits live?

2. Place • Name some First Nations peoples who live along Canada's southern border.

Organization of Canada's Government

BACKGROUND

The prime minister and his cabinet are accountable to the members of the House of Commons. If they lose the support of the majority of members, they must resign, or ask the governor-general to dissolve Parliament and call an election.

Canada is a **constitutional monarchy**. It has a constitution to explain the powers of the government and owes allegiance to a monarch, a king or a queen. The Canadian government consists of the legislative and the judicial branches. Executive duties are within the legislature.

Head of State The British monarch is Canada's head of state. Since the queen or king does not live in Canada, she or he selects a governor-general as a representative. The monarch and the governor-general have little genuine power in Canadian government. They represent the historical traditions of Canada.

Legislature Canada's legislature, called **Parliament,** has two bodies, the House of Commons and the Senate. Together they determine Canadian laws and policies. Citizens elect members of the House of Commons. The leader of the party with the most members becomes the head of government, or **prime minister,** who runs the executive branch within the legislature. Senators are chosen by the prime minister from each of the ten provinces and three territories.

Reading Social Studies

A. Comparing What are some of the powers of the prime minister, and how do these differ from those of the U.S. president?

Location • The Parliament Buildings in Ottawa, Canada's capital, house the legislature of the central government. ▼

Comparing the Canadian and U.S. Governments

SKILLBUILDER:
Reading a Chart

1. **Place** • Name three ways in which the government of Canada differs from that of the United States.
2. **Place** • How are the governments of Canada and the United States alike?

Aspects of Government	Canada	United States
Type	Constitutional Monarchy (limited power)	Constitutional Republic (limited power)
Head of State	Monarch	President
Head of Government	Prime Minister	President
Legislature	Parliament	Congress
System	Federal (central and provinces)	Federal (central and states)

Judiciary Canada has both federal and provincial courts. The highest court is the federal Supreme Court. It is made up of the chief justice of Canada and eight other judges.

Vocabulary

judiciary: the judicial branch of government, the court system

Equality and Justice

Canada is a democracy. Its government is responsible for protecting people's rights.

Civil Rights Prime Minister **Pierre Trudeau** led an effort to add a Charter of Rights and Freedoms to the Canadian Constitution in 1982. The Charter is similar to the U.S. Constitution's Bill of Rights. Among other rights, the Charter guarantees freedom of speech and freedom of religion. It protects every citizen's right to vote and to be assisted by a lawyer if arrested. It says that Canadians are free to live and work anywhere in Canada. The Charter also says that people have equal rights regardless of their race, religion, gender, age, or national origin.

Reading
Social Studies

B. Analyzing Motives Why did Prime Minister Trudeau want a special document stating the rights of all Canadians?

Biography

Pierre Elliott Trudeau (1919–2000) From 1968 to 1979 and from 1980 to 1984, Pierre Trudeau was Canada's prime minister. Born in Montreal, Quebec, of French and Scottish ancestry, he grew up speaking both French and English. Despite his French-Canadian background, Trudeau successfully opposed Quebec's attempts to separate from Canada. He considered keeping Quebec a part of Canada one of his great achievements.

In 1982, Trudeau also helped enact a new Canadian constitution. At right, British Queen Elizabeth II signs a proclamation in 1982, making the new Canadian Constitution law, while Trudeau, seated, looks on. He worked to establish diplomatic relations with China and achieved Canada's complete independence from the British Parliament.

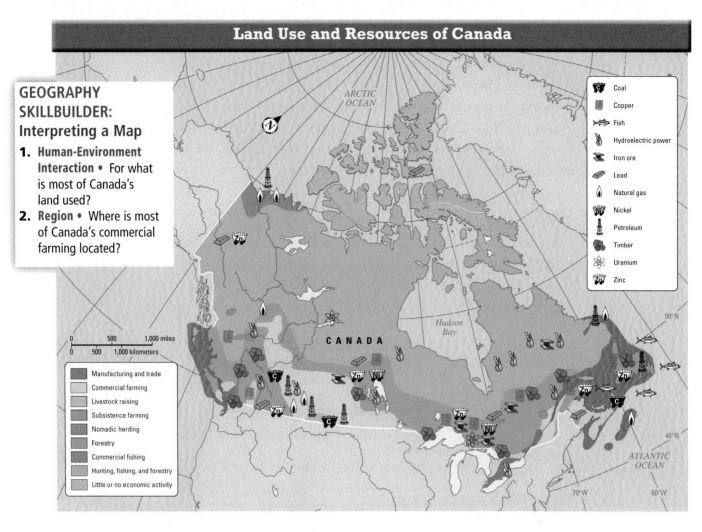

GEOGRAPHY
SKILLBUILDER:
Interpreting a Map

1. **Human-Environment Interaction** • For what is most of Canada's land used?
2. **Region** • Where is most of Canada's commercial farming located?

Legend (map key):

Coal
Copper
Fish
Hydroelectric power
Iron ore
Lead
Natural gas
Nickel
Petroleum
Timber
Uranium
Zinc

0   500   1,000 miles
0   500   1,000 kilometers

Manufacturing and trade
Commercial farming
Livestock raising
Subsistence farming
Nomadic herding
Forestry
Commercial fishing
Hunting, fishing, and forestry
Little or no economic activity

ARCTIC OCEAN

CANADA

Hudson Bay

50°N
40°N

ATLANTIC OCEAN

70°W   60°W

Industry Based on Natural Resources A nation's resources are a source of wealth. The prairie provinces of central Canada have extensive grasslands and good soil, making this area an ideal place to raise beef cattle and grow wheat. On the rich farmlands along the St. Lawrence River, farmers harvest grains, vegetables, and fruit. People plant potatoes and raise dairy cattle on the east coast. The Grand Banks, located off the coast of Newfoundland, is one of the world's most abundant fisheries. The salmon caught off Canada's Pacific coast enrich that area's economy.

Much of Canada is covered in forests, making the timber industry important, especially in British Columbia. **Industry** refers to any area of economic activity. Mining in the northern territories yields iron ore, gold, silver, copper, and other metals.

Trade Canada's openness to trade has contributed to the growth of its economy. Today almost 80 percent of Canada's raw materials are shipped as exports. **Exports** are goods traded to other countries. Canada's main exports are wood and paper products, fuel, minerals, aluminum, wheat, and oil. These and manufactured goods are sold around the world.

BACKGROUND

The Grand Banks, first noted by explorer John Cabot in 1498, extends 350 miles north to south and 420 miles east to west.

Reading
Social Studies

A. **Recognizing Important Details** What are Canada's main exports?

Canada and the United States share a valuable trade partnership. Most of Canada's exports go to the United States. Most of its **imports**, or goods brought into the country, are from the United States. In 1994, Canada, the United States, and Mexico signed the North American Free Trade Agreement, or NAFTA, which lowered trade barriers among the three countries.

Industry and the Economy

Canada's well-educated work force is important to its economy. Canadians work in all four types of industry seen in the chart shown below. Since World War II, Canada has shifted from a mostly rural economy to a major industrial and urban economy.

Types of Industry	
Primary Industries	Prepare and process raw materials, such as timber, wheat, and iron ore, so other companies or consumers can use them *Examples:* **farms; mining companies; logging companies**
Secondary Industries	Manufacturing—turn raw materials into products that consumers or other businesses can use *Examples:* **bakeries; car manufacturers; furniture makers**
Tertiary Industries	Service industries—do not make goods or consume goods; distributors—move goods from the manufacturer to another business or to consumers *Examples:* **wholesalers; transportation companies (truck, train, airplane, or ship); retailers of food, clothing, and other goods; health care; education; recreation; banking**
Quaternary Industries	Pass on information *Examples:* **communication companies, such as Internet service providers and cable companies; financial, research, and other companies that gather and pass on information**

Tertiary, or service, industries, such as health care, recreation, education, transportation, banking, and the government, occupy about two-thirds of Canada's work force. About 30 percent of Canadians work in secondary, or manufacturing, industries. One of Canada's main products is transportation equipment, including automobiles, trucks, subway cars, and airplanes. Food processing, especially meat and poultry processing, is an important industry in Canada as well. Canada also makes chemicals, medicines, machinery, metal products, steel, and paper.

Transportation

Transportation is a major Canadian industry. The ability to import and export goods and move them from place to place across Canada's vast land area affects many consumers and businesses.

Reading
Social Studies

**B. Analyzing
Effects** Why are
transportation
corridors
important to the
development of
industry?

Vocabulary

transcontinental:
spanning or crossing
a continent

Canada's geography both helps and hinders transportation. Canada has natural **transportation corridors**, or paths that make transportation easier. Rivers and coastal waters, sometimes combined with human-made canals and locks, provide convenient travel routes. The St. Lawrence Seaway, for example, allows oceangoing ships to travel between the Atlantic Ocean and the Great Lakes. Another important route is Canada's transcontinental railway system, which crosses the continent from coast to coast.

Canada also has **transportation barriers**, or geographic features that prevent or slow down transportation. In much of the north, snow and ice block travel by land or water. The Rocky Mountains in the west are another major obstacle. Industry develops slowly in regions where transportation is difficult.

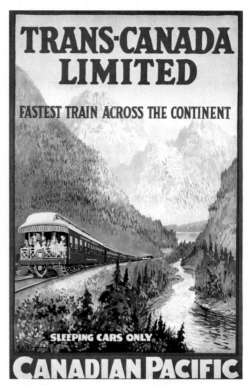

Region • The Canadian Pacific Railway Company completed a transcontinental line from Montreal to a Vancouver suburb in 1885. ▲

SECTION 3 ASSESSMENT

Terms & Names

1. Identify: (a) industry   (b) export   (c) import
              (d) transportation corridor   (e) transportation barrier

Taking Notes

2. Make a chart like the one shown below to list goods that might be produced in each area.

Prairie Provinces	St. Lawrence River Valley	East Coast	British Columbia	Northern Territories

Main Ideas

3. (a) What important factors have helped build Canada's economy?

   (b) Give an example of a primary, a secondary, a tertiary, and a quaternary industry.

   (c) What are some transportation corridors and barriers in Canada?

Critical Thinking

4. **Drawing Conclusions**

   Why do you think Canada and the United States have become such good trade partners?

   Think About
   - geographic location
   - their languages
   - their governments

**ACTIVITY
-OPTION-**   Imagine that you are prospecting for gold in Dawson during the Klondike Gold Rush. Write a **newspaper article** describing what you have brought with you, how you traveled there, and what the town is like.

A Multicultural Society

MAIN IDEA

Many immigrant groups have contributed to Canadian culture while preserving their own identities.

WHY IT MATTERS NOW

Canada's desire to safeguard its cultural diversity is one of its most serious challenges.

DATELINE

MONTREAL, CANADA, 1893—Score! The Montreal Amateur Athletic Association team is the best hockey team in Canada, and it has a silver trophy cup to prove it. Canada's governor-general, Sir Frederick Arthur, Lord Stanley of Preston, presented the award to "the championship hockey club of the Dominion of Canada."

Many Canadians love this sport. First played by the Micmac, a First Nations people in Nova Scotia, ice hockey has spread across Canada and south to the United States. Competition for Stanley's Cup will make the sport even more exciting.

Culture • The winning team poses with Lord Stanley's Cup, which was purchased for about $50. ▲

Canadian Identity

Hockey is one of many good things about living in Canada. From 1994 to 2000, the United Nations rated Canada the best of 175 countries in a survey that examines the health, education, and wealth of each country's citizens. Yet, Canadians still seek a **national identity,** or sense of belonging to a nation, to unite its many immigrant cultures.

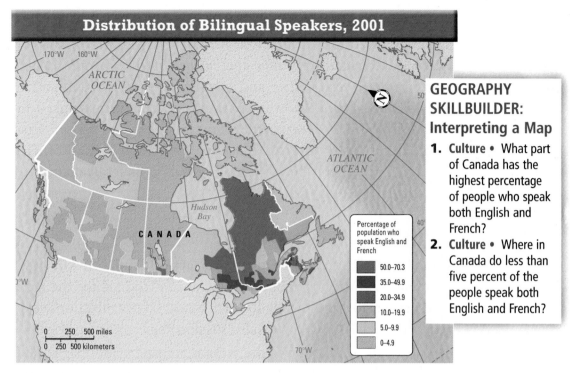

Distribution of Bilingual Speakers, 2001

170°W 160°W

ARCTIC
OCEAN

ATLANTIC
OCEAN

Hudson
Bay

CANADA

**Percentage of
population who
speak English and
French**

■	50.0–70.3
■	35.0–49.9
■	20.0–34.9
	10.0–19.9
	5.0–9.9
	0–4.9

0   250   500 miles
0   250   500 kilometers

70°W

GEOGRAPHY SKILLBUILDER: Interpreting a Map

1. **Culture** • What part of Canada has the highest percentage of people who speak both English and French?
2. **Culture** • Where in Canada do less than five percent of the people speak both English and French?

Languages Many Canadians are **bilingual,** which means they speak two languages. Look at this map to see where bilingual Canadians live. Canada has two official languages, English and French. Literature, official documents, road signs, newspapers, and television broadcasts are in both languages. The two languages are not exactly like those spoken in England, the United States, and France. **Francophones** are French-speaking people. Canadian French, based on the French of the 1800s, is pronounced differently from the French spoken in modern France.

Culture •
Business signs on a street in Quebec City reflect the strong influence of French culture. ▶

Canadian English uses some words, pronunciations, and spellings that differ from those used in the United States. For example, Canadians say *taps* and *serviettes* when people in the United States say *faucets* and *napkins*. For *about* and *house*, Canadians might say *aboot* and *hoos*. Many Canadians write *colour* for *color*, *theatre* for *theater*, and *cheque* for *check*. The nation's first prime minister, Sir John A. Macdonald, ordered that all official Canadian documents be written using standards set by dictionaries written in England.

Reading
Social Studies

A. **Synthesizing** Why does Canada have two official languages?

Arts and Entertainment

Canada has rich traditions in the arts, actively supported by government funding. For example, the Canada Council for the Arts gives money to more than 8,400 artists and art organizations each year. Provincial governments also support regional arts programs.

Canadians read many of the same newspapers and magazines, and watch many of the same television shows and movies as do people in the United States. Canadian musicians, such as Neil Young, Joni Mitchell, Buffy Ste. Marie, Céline Dion, and Shania Twain, are popular in both countries. Comedian-actors Dan Aykroyd and Jim Carrey are also from Canada.

Vocabulary

provincial: of, or relating to, a province

Culture • **The National Gallery of Canada in Ottawa is a visual arts museum that exhibits works by both Canadian and international artists.** ◀

Culture • Notre-Dame was built in Montreal between 1824 and 1829. The architecture of the church—as well as the paintings, sculptures, and stained-glass windows inside—attracts many thousands of visitors each year. ◀

Religion

Christianity is widely practiced in Canada, but many other religions are followed as well, including Buddhism, Hinduism, Islam, and Judaism. Some religions are grounded in a spirituality based on respect for Earth and all forms of life. People of every cultural group are free to worship as they choose.

Culture Regions

Most Canadian immigrants during the 1600s, 1700s, and 1800s were European. Recently, more people have arrived from Asia and South America. People who share the same language and background often settle in the same area. As a result, Canada has various culture regions, or areas where many people belonging to one cultural group live together.

Culture regions exist in different parts of Canada. Quebec is home to many French-speaking Canadians. In Nunavut more than 50 percent of the people are Inuit. Almost 16 percent of the population of Vancouver are Chinese, mostly from Hong Kong.

Connections to History

Raising the Maple Leaf A country's flag is an important national symbol. After 1763, when the United Kingdom won the French and Indian War, the British Royal Union Flag, or Union Jack, became Canada's flag. Efforts to design a new flag for Canada began in 1925. The Red Ensign, which had the Union Jack in its upper left corner and the Canadian coat of arms on its right side, was raised 20 years later.

In 1965, the Houses of Parliament adopted the Maple Leaf, which remains the flag of Canada today. The red background is a connection to the Red Ensign, and the maple leaf is Canada's national symbol.

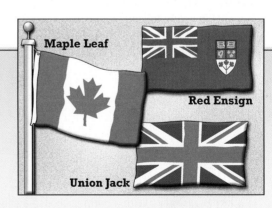

Maple Leaf

Red Ensign

Union Jack

Getting different culture regions to agree on national issues is sometimes difficult. The adoption of the Maple Leaf as Canada's flag in 1965 was one successful effort to unite all Canadians.

A VOICE FROM CANADA

The flag is the symbol of the nation's unity, for it, beyond any doubt, represents all the citizens of Canada without distinction of race, language, belief or opinion.

—*Speaker of the Senate Maurice Bourget*

Conflict and Cooperation Languages, customs, and lifestyles differ among the cultural groups of Canada. Sometimes these differences lead to conflict. For example, in the second half of the 20th century, some Canadians thought that the thousands of Chinese immigrants settling in the Vancouver area would change Canadian culture through their language and customs.

In 1975, the government began reviewing immigration policy. Chinese groups in Vancouver organized a Chinese-Canadian conference. They asked for continued support of multiculturalism and that immigration laws remain open for all people. The concerned groups solved the problem through human rights laws.

Reading
Social Studies

B. Analyzing Causes How do cultural differences cause conflicts among people?

SECTION 4 ASSESSMENT

Terms & Names
1. Identify: (a) national identity (b) bilingual (c) Francophone

Taking Notes

2. Make a spider map like the one shown below to illustrate how various groups contribute to making a unique Canadian culture.

Main Ideas

3. (a) What are the two main languages spoken in Canada?

(b) How does Canada support its own arts and entertainment?

(c) What do people living in culture regions have in common?

Critical Thinking

4. **Forming and Supporting Opinions**

Do culture regions create more benefits or more disadvantages for Canada as a whole?

Think About

- existing and future conflicts
- how different groups contribute to Canadian culture

ACTIVITY -OPTION- With a partner, choose a culture region of Canada. Create a **mural** or **collage** to show characteristics of the culture.

Identifying Cause and Effect

▶▶ Defining the Skill

A cause is an event, a person, or an idea that brings about a result, or an effect. An effect is something that results from a cause. Understanding the relationship between cause and effect is key to understanding the world and its cultures.

▶▶ Applying the Skill

The following paragraph describes where most Canadians live. Use the strategies listed below to help you identify why Canadians live there.

How to Identify a Cause-and-Effect Relationship

Strategy ❶ Look for the cause of, or reason for, the cause-and-effect relationship. It might be suggested in the title and topic sentence. Ask yourself what happened and why it happened. Writers may indicate a cause-and-effect relationship by using words such as *thus, therefore, so,* and *as a result.* Use those words as clues.

Strategy ❷ Look for the results of the event or action. Ask yourself what happened as a result of the action. You have found the effect.

Strategy ❸ Remember that several causes can combine to create one event. Also remember that one cause can have several effects. Ask yourself if anything else helped to bring about the event. Ask yourself if there are any other results.

> ❶ WHERE CANADIANS LIVE
> ❷ Most of Canada's people live within 100 miles of the United States border. This heavily populated area covers only about 10 percent of the country. ❶ The mild climate in that part of the country makes living there more pleasant than living in the colder northern regions. ❸ People can find jobs more easily in the large cities located near the border. ❸ Many Americans who live in Canada can cross the border easily to visit family and friends.

Make a Diagram

Using a diagram can help you understand causes and effects. The diagram to the right shows what causes people in Canada to live close to the U.S. border and what effect is created.

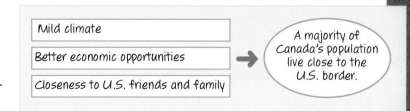

Mild climate

Better economic opportunities

Closeness to U.S. friends and family

→ A majority of Canada's population live close to the U.S. border.

▶▶ Practicing the Skill

Turn to Chapter 5, "Canada Today," Section 3, "Canada's Economy," and make a diagram of the causes that have resulted in Canada's strong economy.

TERMS & NAMES

Explain the significance of each of the following:

1. multiculturalism
2. refugee
3. Parliament
4. prime minister
5. export
6. import
7. transportation corridor
8. transportation barrier
9. bilingual
10. Francophone

REVIEW QUESTIONS

O Canada! Immigrant Roots (pages 119–123)

1. How did the United Kingdom gain control of Canada?
2. What effects does the policy of multiculturalism have on Canada?

A Constitutional Monarchy (pages 124–127)

3. How is Canada's federal government organized?
4. How has Canada tried to satisfy the needs of its many culture groups?

Canada's Economy (pages 128–131)

5. How does Canada's wealth of natural resources contribute to its economy?
6. What are Canada's chief transportation corridors and barriers?

A Multicultural Society (pages 132–136)

7. How have the native languages of England and France changed in Canada?
8. What are some major culture groups of Canada?

CRITICAL THINKING

Analyzing Causes and Effects

1. Using your completed chart from Reading Social Studies, p. 118, describe some factors that influence where people settle in Canada.

Drawing Conclusions

2. Many people in Quebec wanted the province to separate from the rest of Canada. What in Prime Minister Pierre Trudeau's background made him effective in keeping Quebec part of Canada?

Making Inferences

3. How do you think the policy of multiculturalism affects the way Canadians of different cultures respond to one another?

Visual Summary

1 O Canada! Immigrant Roots

- The Canadian people have come from many countries.
- Canada is a very large country with a small population; most people settled in the southern part of the country.

2 A Constitutional Monarchy

- The Canadian government is a constitutional monarchy that is made up of two main branches: a legislative branch and a judicial branch.
- Canada has passed laws to protect the civil rights of its people and to support multiculturalism.

3 Canada's Economy

- Canada has many natural resources that contribute to its economy.
- Canada's most important trade partner is the United States.

4 A Multicultural Society

- Many cultural groups have helped to build the unique Canadian culture of today.

- The diverse cultures of the population create challenges in unifying Canada.

SOCIAL STUDIES SKILLBUILDER

First Migration to North America

Climate became colder.

↓ CAUSE

EFFECT
More of Earth's water froze.

↓ CAUSE

EFFECT
Ocean water level was as much as 125 feet below its current level.

↓ CAUSE

EFFECT
Land between Asia and North America became dry.

↓ CAUSE

EFFECT
People could walk from Asia to North America.

SKILLBUILDER: Identifying Cause and Effect

1. What information does this cause-and-effect chart show?
2. What happened because the ocean level fell to 125 feet below its current level?

FOCUS ON GEOGRAPHY

1. **Movement** • About how many miles would you have to travel to transport limestone from Manitoba to Quebec?
2. **Region** • Which provinces are along the Atlantic Coast? the Pacific Coast?
3. **Place** • In which province is Canada's capital city, Ottawa, located?

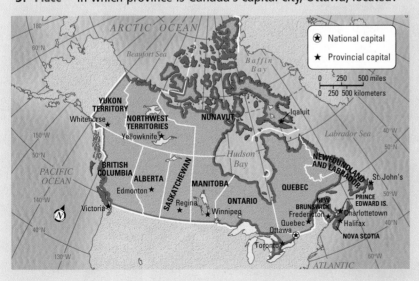

CHAPTER PROJECTS

Interdisciplinary Activity: Art
Writing an Editorial Research the Canadian government's support of the arts. Decide whether government support is necessary. Should it be increased or decreased? Write an editorial stating your views.

Cooperative Learning Activity
Presenting a Television-News Interview In a group of four or five classmates, prepare an interview for a public television broadcast. Your topic will be self-government for cultural groups.
- One of you should take the role of news moderator. Each of the others will represent a cultural group.
- Brainstorm a list of cultural groups. Then prepare questions.
- Do research to learn what your group thinks about self-government.
- Present your discussion to the class.

INTERNET ACTIVITY

Use the Internet to learn more about the geography of Canada. Choose a region, such as the Yukon Territory or the Maritime Provinces. Research what it is like to live there. What kind of weather and plants are there? What kinds of jobs do residents have? How would you travel around the area?

Writing About Geography Write a report of your findings. If possible, include photographs or your own illustrations. Include a list of Internet sites you used.

For Internet links to support this activity, go to

RESEARCH LINKS
CLASSZONE.COM

LATIN AMERICA

ATLANTIC

PACIFIC

OCEAN

PACIFIC

OCEAN

OCEAN

INDIAN
OCEAN

X

MACHU PICCHU   LATIN
                       AMERICA

Place Machu Picchu is a
complex of Inca ruins perched
high in the Andes Mountains
of Peru. The remains of the
impressive granite structures
were designated a UNESCO
World Heritage Site in 1983.

Latin America: Physical

MEXICO

Baja California

Gulf of California

Sierra Madre Occidental

Sierra Madre Oriental

Rio Grande

Gulf of Mexico

Tropic of Cancer

20°N

BAHAMAS

CUBA

Orizaba 18,854 ft. (5,747 m)

Yucatán Peninsula

Greater Antilles

DOMINICAN REPUBLIC

HAITI

WEST

INDIES

ATLANTIC OCEAN

Popocatépetl 17,930 ft. (5,465 m)

CENTRAL AMERICA

BELIZE

HONDURAS

JAMAICA

Tajumulco 13,844 ft. (4,220 m)

NICARAGUA

Caribbean Sea

Netherlands Antilles

Lesser Antilles

GUATEMALA

EL SALVADOR

COSTA RICA

Isthmus of Panama

Panama Canal

PANAMA

VENEZUELA

GUYANA

SURINAME

French Guiana (Fr.)

Barú 11,400 ft. (3,475 m)

Orinoco R.

Llanos

Guiana Highlands

COLOMBIA

0° Equator

ECUADOR

Negro R.

Amazon R.

AMAZON BASIN

SOUTH AMERICA

PERU

Madeira R.

BRAZIL

Xingu R.

Araguaia R.

São Francisco R.

PACIFIC OCEAN

ANDES

Lake Titicaca

Mato Grosso Plateau

BOLIVIA

PARAGUAY

BRAZILIAN HIGHLANDS

Paraná R.

20°S

Atacama Desert

Gran Chaco

Paraguay R.

Tropic of Capricorn

Mt. Aconcagua 22,831 ft. (6,959 m)

ARGENTINA

Uruguay R.

URUGUAY

Pampas

Plata R.

CHILE

40°S

Patagonia

ATLANTIC OCEAN

Elevation

13,100 ft.	(4,000 m)
6,600 ft.	(2,000 m)
3,275 ft.	(1,000 m)
650 ft.	(200 m)
0 ft.	(0 m)
Below sea level	

▲ Mountain peak

0   500   1,000 miles

0   500   1,000 kilometers

Tierra del Fuego

Falkland Is.

South Georgia I.

Cape Horn

100°W   80°W   60°W   40°W

Elevation Profile: South America

21,000 ft.
18,000 ft.
15,000 ft.
12,000 ft.
9,000 ft.
6,000 ft.
3,000 ft.
1,200 ft.
sea level
–12,000 ft.
–24,000 ft.

ANDES MOUNTAINS

COASTAL LOWLANDS OF BRAZIL

BRAZILIAN PLATEAU

AMAZON RIVER BASIN

PACIFIC OCEAN

PERU-CHILE TRENCH

ATLANTIC OCEAN

Latin America–United States Landmass and Population

Latin America

United States

LANDMASS

Latin America

7,981,950 square miles

Continental United States

3,165,630 square miles

POPULATION

Latin America
514,662,785

United States
281,421,906

= 50,000,000

FAST FACTS

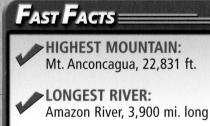

HIGHEST MOUNTAIN:
Mt. Anconcagua, 22,831 ft.

LONGEST RIVER:
Amazon River, 3,900 mi. long

HIGHEST RECORDED TEMPERATURE:
120°F, Rivadavia, Argentina,
December 11, 1905

LOWEST RECORDED TEMPERATURE:
-27°F, Sarmiento, Argentina,
June 1, 1907

HIGHEST AVERAGE ANNUAL PRECIPITATION IN THE WORLD:
Lloro, Colombia, 523.6 in.

LOWEST AVERAGE ANNUAL PRECIPITATION IN THE WORLD:
Arica, Chile, 0.03 in.

GEOGRAPHY SKILLBUILDER: Interpreting Maps and Visuals

1. **Location** • The Isthmus of Panama separates what two bodies of water?
2. **Place** • What is the depth of the Peru-Chile Trench?

Tijuana
Ciudad Juárez
Chihuahua
Monterrey
MEXICO
Tropic of Cancer
Gulf of Mexico
Gulf of California
Guadalajara
México City
Puebla
Córdoba
Acapulco
GUATEMALA
Guatemala City
San Salvador
EL SALVADOR
BELIZE
Belmopan
HONDURAS
Tegucigalpa
NICARAGUA
Managua
San José
COSTA RICA
Panama City
PANAMA

Havana
CUBA
Cayman Is. (U.K.)
JAMAICA
Kingston
HAITI
Port-au-Prince

BAHAMAS

Latin America: Political

Turks & Caicos (U.K.)
DOMINICAN REPUBLIC
Santo Domingo
San Juan
Puerto Rico (U.S.)
Virgin Is. (U.S. & U.K.)
Anguilla (U.K.)
ST. KITTS & NEVIS
ANTIGUA & BARBUDA
Guadeloupe (Fr.)
Montserrat (U.K.)
DOMINICA
Martinique (Fr.)
ST. LUCIA
BARBADOS
GRENADA
ST. VINCENT & THE GRENADINES
TRINIDAD & TOBAGO

ATLANTIC OCEAN

Caribbean Sea

Netherlands Antilles (Neth.)
Aruba (Neth.)
Maracaibo
Mérida
Caracas
VENEZUELA
GUYANA
Georgetown
SURINAME
Paramaribo
Cayenne
French Guiana (Fr.)

Medellín
Bogotá
Cali
COLOMBIA

Quito
ECUADOR
Guayaquil

Equator

Galápagos Is. (Ec.)

PACIFIC OCEAN

Manaus
Belém
Fortaleza
Recife

PERU
Lima

BRAZIL

Salvador

BOLIVIA
La Paz
Santa Cruz
Sucre

Brasília
Goiânia
Belo Horizonte
Rio de Janeiro
São Paulo
Curitiba

PARAGUAY
Asunción

Pôrto Alegre

Juan Fernández Is. (Chile)

Santiago

ARGENTINA
Rosario
Buenos Aires

URUGUAY
Montevideo

CHILE

ATLANTIC OCEAN

Falkland Is. (U.K.)

South Georgia I. (U.K.)

National boundary
National capital
Other city

0   500   1,000 miles
0   500   1,000 kilometers

100°W   80°W   60°W   40°W

City Populations of Latin America

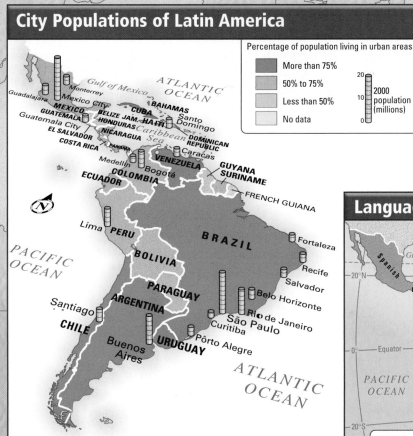

Percentage of population living in urban areas
- More than 75%
- 50% to 75%
- Less than 50%
- No data

2000 population (millions)

Languages of Latin America

- Indo-European
- Other languages
- **French** Spoken language

0   500   1,000 miles
0   500 1,000 kilometers

FAST FACTS

✓ **LARGEST COUNTRY (in land area):** Brazil, 3,300,171 sq. mi.

✓ **SMALLEST COUNTRY (in land area):** Grenada, 120 sq. mi.

✓ **LARGEST CITY (population):** Mexico City, 18,131,000 (2000)

✓ **HIGHEST POPULATION DENSITY:** Barbados, 1,612 people per sq. mi.

✓ **LOWEST POPULATION DENSITY:** French Guiana, 5 people per sq. mi.

GEOGRAPHY SKILLBUILDER: Interpreting Maps and Visuals

1. **Location** • Which countries have no coastline?
2. **Region** • What language do most people in Brazil speak?

Country Flag	Country/Capital	Currency	Population (2001 estimate)	Life Expectancy (years)	Birthrate (per 1,000 pop.) (2000)
	Antigua and Barbuda St. John's	East Caribbean Dollar	67,000	70	20
	Argentina Buenos Aires	Peso	37,385,000	75	19
	Bahamas Nassau	Bahamian Dollar	298,000	71	20
	Barbados Bridgetown	Barbadian Dollar	275,000	73	14
	Belize Belmopan	Belizean Dollar	256,000	71	32
	Bolivia La Paz, Sucre	Boliviano	8,300,000	64	28
	Brazil Brasília	Real	174,469,000	63	19
	Chile Santiago	Chilean Peso	15,328,000	76	17
	Colombia Bogotá	Colombian Peso	40,349,000	70	23
	Costa Rica San José	Costa Rican Colon	3,773,000	76	21
	Cuba Havana	Peso	11,184,000	76	13
	Dominica Roseau	East Caribbean Dollar	71,000	73	18
	Dominican Republic Santo Domingo	Dominican Peso	8,581,000	73	25
	Ecuador Quito	U.S. Dollar and Sucre	13,184,000	71	27
	El Salvador San Salvador	Salvadoran Colon	6,238,000	70	29
	Grenada St. George's	East Caribbean Dollar	89,000	65	23
	Guatemala Guatemala City	Quetzal	12,974,000	66	35
	Guyana Georgetown	Guyanese Dollar	697,000	64	18

DATA FILE

Infant Mortality (per 1,000 live births) (2000)	Doctors (per 100,000 pop.) (1997–1998)	Literacy Rate (percentage) (1996–1998)	Passenger Cars (per 1,000 pop.) (1991–1998)	Total Area (square miles)	Map (not to scale)
20.0	114	90	207	171	
17.8	268	96	136	1,073,399	
17.8	152	98	245	5,386	
16.2	125	97	167	166	
30.8	55	93	10	8,867	
60.2	130	83	26	424,164	
33.8	127	85	84	3,300,171	
9.6	110	95	62	292,135	
23.2	116	91	31	440,831	
12.7	141	95	14	19,730	
7.7	530	96	2	42,804	
8.5	49	90	104	290	
40.8	216	82	14	18,704	
29.3	170	90	22	103,930	
27.2	107	71	6	8,124	
10.9	50	96	94	120	
45.0	93	56	9	42,042	
48.6	18	98	34	83,000	

Country Flag	Country/Capital	Currency	Population (2000 estimate)	Life Expectancy (years)	Birthrate (per 1,000 pop.) (2000)
	**Haiti** Port-au-Prince	Gourde	6,965,000	49	32
	**Honduras** Tegucigalpa	Lempira	6,406,000	70	33
	**Jamaica** Kingston	Jamaican Dollar	2,666,000	75	19
	**Mexico** Mexico City	New Peso	101,879,000	71	23
	**Nicaragua** Managua	Gold Cordoba	4,918,000	69	28
	**Panama** Panama City	Balboa	2,846,000	75	20
	**Paraguay** Asunción	Guarani	5,734,000	74	31
	**Peru** Lima	New Sol	27,484,000	70	24
	**St. Kitts and Nevis** Basseterre	East Caribbean Dollar	39,000	71	19
	**St. Lucia** Castries	East Caribbean Dollar	158,000	72	22
	**St. Vincent and the Grenadines** Kingstown	East Caribbean Dollar	116,000	72	18
	**Suriname** Paramaribo	Surinamese Guilder	434,000	71	21
	**Trinidad and Tobago** Port of Spain	Trinidad and Tobago Dollar	1,170,000	68	14
	**Uruguay** Montevideo	Uruguayan Peso	3,360,000	75	17
	**Venezuela** Caracas	Bolivar	23,917,000	73	21
	**United States** Washington, D.C.	Dollar	281,422,000	77	15

DATA FILE

Infant Mortality (per 1,000 live births) (2000)	Doctors (per 100,000 pop.) (1997–1998)	Literacy Rate (percentage) (1996–1998)	Passenger Cars (per 1,000 pop.) (1991–1998)	Total Area (square miles)	Map (not to scale)
96.3	8	45	5	10,714	
39.8	83	73	14	43,277	
13.4	140	85	17	4,244	
23.4	186	90	87	756,066	
38.7	86	66	16	50,464	
22.7	167	91	54	29,157	
35.3	110	92	14	157,048	
37.1	93	89	20	496,225	
16.9	117	90	130	104	
16.2	47	80	68	238	
14.6	88	82	44	150	
25.6	25	93	111	63,251	
18.3	79	98	107	1,978	
12.9	370	97	147	68,498	
25.5	236	91	68	352,144	
7.0	251	97	489	3,787,319	

GEOGRAPHY SKILLBUILDER: Interpreting a Chart
(Do not give United States as an answer.)
1. **Place** • Which countries have the highest life expectancy?
2. **Place** • Which country has the most cars per person?

CHAPTER 6

Latin America: Its Land and History

SECTION 1 Physical Geography

SECTION 2 Ancient Latin America

FOCUS ON GEOGRAPHY

What conflicts arise when there is competition for a natural resource?

Human-Environment Interaction • About 50 percent of the world's rain forests are in Latin America, with 30 percent in Brazil alone. In Latin America, the rain forest is a natural resource that plays many different roles. It serves as a habitat for exotic plants and animals and a home to Native Americans. It is a moderator of the world climate and a destination for tourists. It also acts as a source of land that can be cleared and put to other uses, such as cattle ranching or logging.

What do you think?

♦ How might different groups want to use a rain forest as a resource? Think about the rain forest's inhabitants, tourists, environmentalists, and businesses.

♦ How might these different uses conflict with one another?

Culture Between A.D. 900 and 1200, this Maya city, called Chichén Itzá (chee•CHEN ee•TSAH), was the leading center of Maya life on Mexico's Yucatán Peninsula. ▲

151

READING SOCIAL STUDIES

BEFORE YOU READ

▶▶ *What Do You Know?*

Before you read the chapter, consider what you already know about the history and geography of Latin America. What countries make up Latin America? Does the region have well-known geographic features, such as mountains or rivers? You may have read folk tales from the ancient Maya, Aztec, and Inca civilizations. Think about what happened to these cultures and their people. Have you heard of the Aztec ruler Montezuma II?

Culture • The Maya carved many stone monuments. ▼

▶▶ *What Do You Want to Know?*

Decide what else you want to know about Latin America. In your notebook, record what you hope to learn from this chapter.

Culture • Montezuma II became the Aztec ruler in 1502. ▼

READ AND TAKE NOTES

Reading Strategy: Comparing and Contrasting Comparing and contrasting can be a useful strategy for studying cultures. When you compare, you look for similarities. When you contrast, you look for differences. Use the chart shown here to compare and contrast the ancient civilizations of Latin America.

- Copy the chart into your notebook.
- As you read Section 2, take notes on the Maya, Aztec, and Inca.
- Write your notes under the appropriate headings.

	Maya	Aztec	Inca
Location			
Dates			
Achievements			
Reasons for Decline			

Latin America: Physical Geography

TERMS & NAMES
tributary
deforestation
Tropical Zone
El Niño

MAIN IDEA

Latin America's landforms, bodies of water, and climate offer a wide range of environments and resources.

WHY IT MATTERS NOW

Physical geography influences Latin America's cultures, offering them both resources and obstacles.

DATELINE

EXTRA

PUEBLA, MEXICO, DECEMBER 19, 2000

Yesterday, Mount Popocatépetl erupted, spewing out glowing five-foot-long rocks for miles in one of its largest eruptions in a thousand years. More than 30 million people live within sight of the volcano, and tens of thousands live close enough to be at risk when it erupts.

Government trucks drove through villages sounding warnings on speakers while church bells rang out the danger. In spite of the resulting damage, no one has been killed. However, authorities warn, a larger eruption could occur at any time.

Place • The Aztec named the volcano Popocatépetl, which means "smoking mountain." ▲

Defining Latin America

Latin America includes Mexico, Central America, the Caribbean, and South America. Because the languages of most of its colonizers—Spanish and Portuguese—are derived from Latin, Europeans later referred to the region's colonies as *Latin America*. Because the region is defined by a cultural connection, in this case language, it is called a culture region.

Mexico

Look at the map on page 155. Mexico is the farthest north of the Latin American countries. You can see that Mexico's major physical features include mountains, plateaus, and plains.

A Varied Landscape Mexico's two major mountain ranges share the name Sierra Madre (see·EHR·uh MAH·dray). Notice that in between the two ranges—the Sierra Madre Occidental and the Sierra Madre Oriental—sits Mexico's large central plateau. The vast northern stretches of the central plateau are desert.

Now look just south of the central plateau. There you will see Mexico's two highest mountain peaks, Orizaba (or·ih·ZAH·buh) and Popocatépetl (POH·puh·KAT·uh·PEHT·uhl). Both are volcanoes. Volcanic activity and earthquakes frequently plague Mexico—and many other parts of Latin America too. They are caused by the movement of five tectonic plates.

A Problem of Place At the southern end of the central plateau sits Mexico City, the world's second most populated city. Air pollution is severe there, and the city's location has contributed to this problem. The mountains surrounding the city to the east, south, and west trap automobile exhaust and other pollutants that the city's huge population generates.

An added problem of location for Mexico City is the ground on which it was built—a drained lakebed. The vibrations that earthquakes send through Earth grow much stronger and more damaging when they pass through the soft, loose soils of a lakebed, thus making Mexico City highly vulnerable to the effects of earthquakes.

Vocabulary
occidental: western
oriental: eastern

Eruption Disruption On February 20, 1943, something very strange happened in a cornfield in west-central Mexico. Before the eyes of a startled farmer, the land violently split open. Within 24 hours, a small, smoking cone had appeared—the tiny beginning of a mighty volcano called Paricutín (pah·REE·koo·TEEN). Scientists rushed to the area to watch the volcano being born. Within a year, a mountain stood in place of what had been farmland and a village.

While it was active, Paricutín rose to 10,400 feet above sea level. It poured lava over about a 10-square-mile area, burying streets and buildings, such as this nearby church. In 1952, it stopped erupting completely and became dormant. But the volcano that sprouted in a cornfield had given scientists a rare opportunity to study the life cycle of one of nature's most dramatic and dangerous features.

GEOGRAPHY SKILLBUILDER:
Interpreting a Map

1. **Location** • What is the tallest mountain in Central America?
2. **Region** • Which area of Mexico is almost entirely at sea level?

UNITED STATES

ATLANTIC OCEAN

Gulf of California

Sierra Madre Occidental

Central Plateau

Sierra Madre Oriental

Gulf Coastal Plain

Gulf of Mexico

Popocatépetl
17,802 ft.
(5,426 m.)

Havana

Tropic of Cancer

Pico Duarte
10,417 ft.
(3,175 m.)

Paricutín
9,210 ft.
(2,808 m.)

Mexico City

Pico de Orizaba
18,854 ft.
(5,747 m.)

Yucatán Peninsula

Pico Turquino
6,561 ft.
(2,000 m.)

Sierra Madre del Sur

Belmopan

Port-au-Prince

Santo Domingo

Tacaná
13,428 ft.
(4,093 m.)

Tegucigalpa

Caribbean Sea

Tajumulco
13,845 ft.
(4,220 m.)

Guatemala City

San Salvador

Managua

San José

Chirripó Grande
12,530 ft.
(3,819 m.)

Barú
11,400 ft.
(3,475 m.)

Panama City

Elevation	
13,100 ft.	(4,000 m)
6,600 ft.	(2,000 m)
1,600 ft.	(500 m)
650 ft.	(200 m)
0 ft.	(0 m)

Below sea level

▲ Mountain peak

✪ National capital

0   250   500 miles
0   250   500 kilometers

Equator

SOUTH AMERICA

PACIFIC OCEAN

110°W   100°W   90°W   80°W

20°N

10°N

0°

10°S

155

Place • Seven islands make up the Caribbean island group that is called Guadeloupe (GWAHD•uhl•OOP). ▲

Central America and the Caribbean

Look at the physical map in the Unit Atlas. Central America is the mountainous landmass that forms a bridge between Mexico and South America. Now look to the east, and you will see island nations scattered throughout the Caribbean Sea.

Central America About 80 percent of Central America is hilly or mountainous, and most of it is covered with forests. Rain forests cover much of the lowlands. In the higher regions, deciduous trees cloak many of the slopes.

A string of more than 40 volcanoes lines 900 miles of Central America's Pacific coast, where two tectonic plates crash against each other. This is the most active group of volcanoes in North or South America. Earthquakes also occur frequently. They can completely destroy buildings, towns, and cities. They can also set landslides and mudslides in motion, sending land, houses, and people hurtling down the slopes.

The Caribbean Islands As you can see on the map (page 155), the Caribbean Islands lie to the east of Central America. Some of these islands, such as St. Kitts and Grenada, are actually the peaks of volcanic mountains rising from the ocean floor. Over thousands of years, the volcanoes erupted, spewing lava that cooled, hardened, and added to the mountains' height.

Other islands, such as the Bahamas, began as coral reefs. Coral is made of organisms that shed hard skeletons when they die. The skeletons pile up, and a reef, or ridge, develops. A coral reef that becomes an island usually encircles a volcanic island and then grows over it.

Place • Coral reefs form in lots of different colors. ▼

Vocabulary

deciduous:
a tree that loses its leaves each year

Reading
Social Studies

A. Clarifying
What causes so many volcanoes and earthquakes in this region?

South America

Look at the map on page 142 of the Unit Atlas. You can see that the equator runs through Ecuador, Colombia, and Brazil. You can also see that only the Isthmus of Panama links South America to North America.

Vocabulary

isthmus:
a narrow strip of land that connects two landmasses

The Andes On the map, you can see the Andes mountain range, which stretches over 5,000 miles along South America's west coast. It is the longest continuous mountain range on Earth's surface. Mount Aconcagua (AK·uhn·KAH·gwuh) in Argentina is the highest peak in the Western Hemisphere.

Beyond the Andes Notice the central plains east of the Andes. The plains in southern South America are called the *Pampas*. South America's largest rivers begin in the Andes, drain the central plains, and then flow into the Atlantic Ocean. They include the Orinoco (AWR·uh·NOH·koh), the Paraná-Paraguay-Plata (PAR·uh· NAH-PAR·uh·gwy-PLAH·tuh), and the Amazon.

BACKGROUND

The word *pampa*, meaning "flat surface," comes from the language of an Andean group of Native Americans called the Quechua (KEHCH·wuh).

The Amazon In 2000, 22 people explored the Andes's rivers to confirm the source of the Amazon River, which had been discovered in 1971. The mighty river begins in the Peruvian Andes as a trickle of water. It then flows for nearly 4,000 miles to the Atlantic Ocean. No other river carries as much water to the sea. Along with more than 1,000 **tributaries,** which are rivers or streams that flow into a larger body of water, the Amazon drains water from Peru, Ecuador, Colombia, Bolivia, Venezuela, and Brazil.

The Amazon at Risk **Deforestation,** or the process of cutting and clearing away trees from a forest, has greatly affected the Amazon rain forest. In recent years, Amazon deforestation has provided timber and cleared land for cattle ranches.

Vocabulary

timber:
wood used as building material

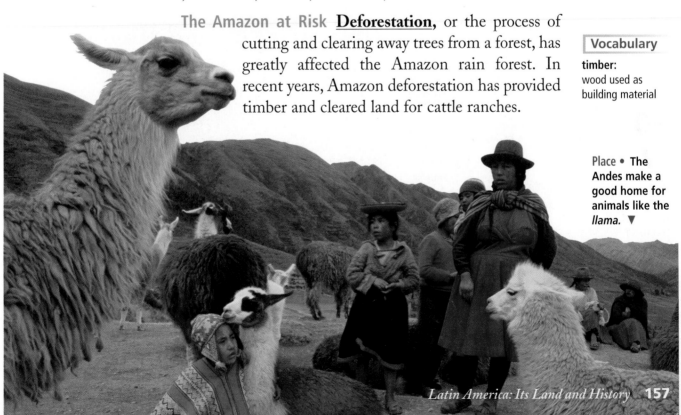

Place • The Andes make a good home for animals like the *llama*. ▼

Most plants release oxygen into the air and absorb carbon dioxide. By reducing the number of trees and plants, deforestation increases the amount of carbon dioxide in the air. Some scientists think the increase in carbon dioxide contributes to global warming because carbon dioxide traps warm air at Earth's surface.

Others worry that animals who find food in the rain forest may need to move—or may die out—when large areas of forest are cut down. The Native American tribes that inhabit the rain forest are also at risk of being squeezed out of the land they live on.

Climate

Latin America's climate varies greatly from area to area. It is influenced by elevation, location, wind patterns, and ocean currents.

The Tropical Zone A large portion of Latin America lies in the **Tropical Zone,** which, as you can see on the map below, is between the latitudes 23°27' north and 23°27' south. The Tropical Zone may be rainy or dry, but it is typically hot. Also, temperature is always lower at higher elevations, but in the Tropical Zone, all elevations are warmer than they are elsewhere.

Wind and Water The waters in the Caribbean Sea stay warm most of the year and heat the air over them. A warm wind then blows across the islands, keeping the climate warm even in the winter.

Reading
Social Studies

B. Drawing Conclusions
What aspect of the Tropical Zone's location on Earth causes it to be warmer than the other areas?

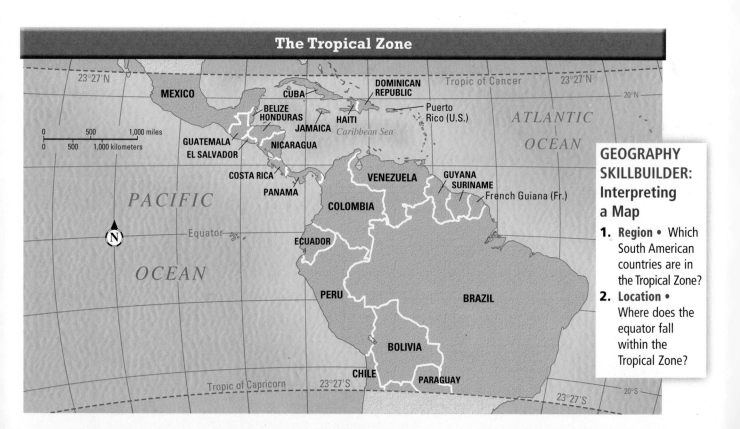

The Tropical Zone

GEOGRAPHY SKILLBUILDER: Interpreting a Map

1. **Region** • Which South American countries are in the Tropical Zone?
2. **Location** • Where does the equator fall within the Tropical Zone?

Normal Year

Westerly trade winds

Warm surface water

El Niño Year

Westerly trade winds die out

Warm surface water, warm air, and storms

SKILLBUILDER:
Interpreting a Diagram

1. What effect does the increased air pressure of *El Niño* have on the warm surface water of the Pacific?
2. What are the patterns of wind and water in a normal year?

El Niño At times, unusually high air pressure in the south Pacific causes certain winds over the ocean, called trade winds, to die out. Without the trade winds, the ocean's sun-warmed surface water flows eastward, toward North and South America. Because this typically occurs around Christmastime, people call the current **El Niño** (ehl NEE·nyaw). This term is Spanish for "the Christ child" because Christmas celebrates the birth of Jesus.

The warmer water of *El Niño* warms the air. Warmer air holds more water and so releases more rain when it cools. This added precipitation often causes heavy rains and flooding in Latin America and other parts of the eastern Pacific. At the same time, areas in the western Pacific, such as Indonesia, may have less rain than usual.

SECTION 1 ASSESSMENT

Terms & Names

1. **Identify:** (a) tributary (b) deforestation (c) Tropical Zone (d) *El Niño*

Taking Notes

2. Use a chart like the one below to list the key physical features of each country or region.

Key Physical Features			
Mexico	Central America	The Caribbean Islands	South America

Main Ideas

3. (a) Name two types of natural disasters that occur frequently in Latin America.

(b) Describe two ways in which the Caribbean Islands formed.

(c) What happens when increased air pressure causes trade winds to lessen?

Critical Thinking

4. **Forming and Supporting Opinions**
Do you favor limiting the deforestation of the Amazon rain forest? Why? Why not?

Think About

♦ the economic benefits of timber production and cattle ranching

♦ the destruction of habitats

♦ the effects on the global environment

Look at the map on page 158 that shows the Tropical Zone. Make a **list** of all the Latin American countries that are wholly or partly in the Tropical Zone.

Ancient Latin America

TERMS & NAMES
hieroglyph
chinampa
Machu Picchu
Hernán Cortés
Montezuma II
Francisco Pizarro
Atahualpa
Columbian Exchange

MAIN IDEA

The ancient cultures of Latin America established civilizations in challenging geographic settings.

WHY IT MATTERS NOW

These cultures serve as models for how successful civilizations develop.

DATELINE

EL MIRADOR, GUATEMALA, 200 B.C.—In El Mirador today, a council of the city's leaders made a major announcement. Next month, construction will begin on a massive building complex for the city's center.

The plans include an enormous pyramid made of three smaller pyramids sitting atop a large stepped platform. The council expects to employ thousands of people to cut and carry the stone slabs that will be used to build the structure. The project is expected to take many months to complete.

Place • An artist made this drawing to show what El Mirador's three-part pyramid will look like. ▼

Place •
The building complex will be made of cut slabs of limestone. ▲

Ancient Civilizations of Latin America

Many ancient civilizations, such as the Egyptian, developed in river valleys and thrived there. The rivers provided water for both irrigation and transportation. In Latin America, however, some ancient civilizations flourished far from rivers. For example, the Maya of Mexico and Central America built cities in dense jungles. The Aztec of Mexico constructed their capital on a swampy island. The Inca of South America built cities high up in the Andes.

The Maya

In the areas that are today southern and eastern Mexico, western Honduras, Guatemala, El Salvador, and Belize, the ancient Maya built a widespread civilization. Small Maya communities existed as early as 1600 B.C. From A.D. 250 to A.D. 900, the Maya established one of Latin America's most important civilizations.

Maya Intellectual Advances The ancient Maya studied math and astronomy extensively. The Maya were among the first civilizations in the world known to understand the advanced mathematical concept of zero. They also had an intricate calendar system that included a 260-day calendar of sacred days, a 365-day calendar based on the sun's movement, and a calendar that measured the number of days that had passed since a fixed starting point.

The Maya established the best-developed written language in ancient Latin America. The basic units of the writing system were symbols called **hieroglyphs,** or glyphs. Each glyph represented a word or a syllable. The U.S. lawyer John Lloyd Stephens, while traveling through the Maya area in the 1800s, described his awe at seeing the glyphs and not being able to read them because no one had yet deciphered them.

Culture • The Maya often carved hieroglyphs on stone monuments. ▲

A VOICE FROM LATIN AMERICA

These structures . . . these stones . . . standing as they do in the depths of a tropical forest, silent and solemn, strange in design, excellent in sculpture, rich in ornament . . . their whole history so entirely unknown, with hieroglyphics explaining all, but perfectly unintelligible.

John Lloyd Stephens

Reading
Social Studies

A. Drawing Conclusions How does having a system of writing help a civilization survive?

Maya Agriculture Farming was essential to Maya life. Using a method called slash-and-burn agriculture, the Maya cut down and burned trees, planting crops in their place. After a few years, they let the forest grow back, so the soil could regain its nutrients. Later the area could again be cut, burned, and farmed. The Maya also built up ridges of farming land on floodplains. The floodplains were rich with nutrients, and the ridges kept the crops from getting too wet.

Colossal Olmec Heads Mexico's oldest known civilization is called the Olmec, which flourished from about 1200 to 600 B.C. The Olmec are famous for the colossal heads (like the one shown below) that they carved from a type of stone called basalt.

Thought to be portraits of Olmec rulers, some of these heads stand over nine feet tall. Each weighs thousands of pounds. All of Mexico's later Native American cultures were influenced by the Olmec. However, only the Olmec produced these giant stone monuments.

Decline of Maya Civilization Around A.D. 900, the Maya way of life began to change. For unknown reasons, the construction of massive temples and stone monuments stopped. Cities were abandoned. However, the Maya people did not disappear—they just spread out. More than 6 million Maya people still live in Guatemala, Belize, and southern Mexico and speak dialects based on the languages of their Maya ancestors.

The Aztec

Where modern Mexico City now stands, the waters of Lake Texcoco once lapped the shores of an island city called Tenochtitlán (teh·NOHCH·tee·TLAHN). With as many as 200,000 inhabitants, Tenochtitlán served as the capital of the Aztec Empire.

Aztec Origins The Aztec were composed of a number of tribes of wandering warriors. Of these, the Mexica (MEH·hee·KAH) were dominant. Mexico took its name from the Mexica. During the 1200s, the Aztec gradually grew in numbers and military strength until they controlled the region. They dominated until the early 1500s, when the Spanish conquered them.

Aztec Warfare and Religion The Aztec Empire centered on warfare. All able men, including priests, were expected to join the Aztec army, for two reasons. The first was to maintain a powerful empire, but the second was religious. The Aztec believed that anyone who died in battle had the great honor of dying for Huitzilopochtli (WEE·tsuh·loh·POHCH·tlee), the Aztec god of war.

Culture • This stone carving honors the Aztec sun god, whose face is shown in the center. ▼

Aztec Agriculture The Aztec held great power over their empire. One reason for their success was that the island location of their capital protected them from attack. However, much of the island was marsh, posing a major challenge to farming. The resourceful Aztec built floating gardens, called **_chinampas_** (chee·NAHM·pahs), on which they grew crops. First, they piled up plants from the water. Then they anchored these rafts between trunks of willow trees.

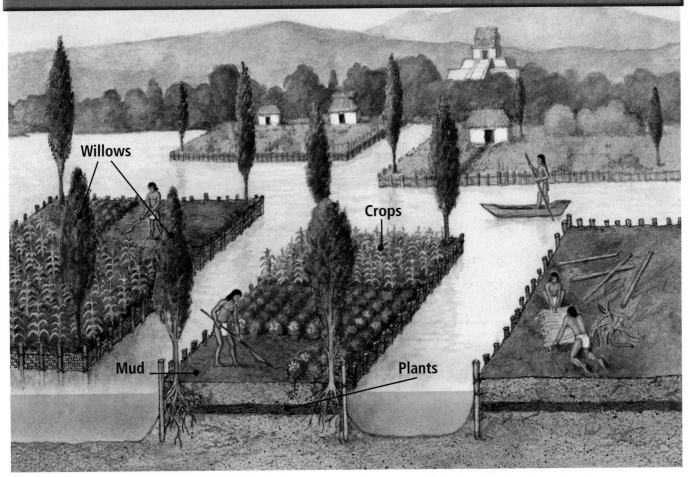

Willows

Crops

Mud

Plants

Finally, they heaped the lake's fertile mud on the piles to create plots for farming. The Aztec grew many crops, such as maize, beans, squash, avocados, tomatoes, peppers, and flowers. They also raised turkeys, ducks, geese, and dogs for food.

The Inca

Around 1400, high in the Andes of Peru, a group of people called the Inca rose up to conquer the people of the surrounding areas. From their capital, Cuzco, the Inca soon ruled a huge empire that included parts of what are now Colombia, Ecuador, Bolivia, northern Chile, and northwestern Argentina.

Inca Agriculture To farm on the steep mountainsides, the Inca built stone terraces. These gave the Inca large areas of flat land to farm. The terraces also helped prevent erosion of the soil. In the desert lands to the west, the Inca built irrigation canals to water their crops. Some of these canals spanned entire valleys. Because of terracing and irrigation, Inca farmers were able to grow crops such as potatoes, maize, and a grain called *quinoa*.

Andean Agriculture

Long before the rise of the Inca Empire, people living in the Andes had learned to farm the steep valley walls by building terraces into the sides of the mountains. They had also learned to build canals, many of them lined with stone, to carry water to their crops. The Inca improved and expanded the existing terraces and canals until they could feed 15 million people, with enough food left over to put away stores for three to seven years.

In the Andes, valley walls rise as high as 10,000 feet and temperatures can span a 55-degree range.

Inca canals stretched for miles. They were often lined and covered with stones. Some were cut through solid rock.

The Inca grew maize, hundreds of kinds of potatoes, and many other crops. Farmers had to plant crops adapted to many different climates because of the great variations in altitude and temperature.

The Inca had few farm tools. The most widely used was the *taclla*, or digging stick. It consisted of a pointed hardwood pole with a footrest for pushing the tool into the ground. Some *tacllas* had metal tips. The other main tools were hoes and clubs.

THINKING Critically

1. Analyzing Motives
Why did people living in the Andes need to build terraces and canals?

2. Recognizing Effects
What role did agriculture play in the building and maintenance of the Inca Empire?

Workers directed by royal architects built stone retaining walls. Inside the walls, they placed layers of stone, clay, gravel, and topsoil. This combination allowed water to slowly work its way to lower terraces.

Communicating Across the Inca Empire Stone roads were a major technological feat of the Inca. These roads are still in use today. Having no written language or knowledge of the wheel, Inca rulers ordered roads built on which runners carried verbal messages to distant places. The runners worked in relay teams stationed along the roads. One runner told the message to the next. Messages could travel 150 miles a day along the stone roads. This system of communication was important to the Inca because their empire spread out over thousands of miles.

Culture •
The Inca kept records by tying knots in a series of strings called *quipu* (KEE•poo). ◄

Reading
Social Studies

B. Recognizing Effects How did building stone roads improve the ability of the Inca rulers to control a large region?

Inca Stonework The Inca are known for their stonework. They erected many massive buildings, some with stones weighing as much as 200 tons. Wooden rollers were used to move these heavy stone blocks. The most remarkable of Inca stonework is the city of **Machu Picchu** (MAH•choo PEEK•choo), which still stands almost 8,000 feet above sea level. The walls of Machu Picchu were constructed so that they appear to emerge from the mountainsides. Around them, terraces connected by stairways run down the steep slopes. (See photograph on pages 140–141.)

Spotlight on CULTURE

Inca Weaving The Inca had no formal written language, but they used weaving as a means of representing ideas. Using wool sheared from llamas and alpacas, as well as many colorful plant dyes, the Inca wove images into the fabrics they wore and traded. Concepts related to the passing of seasons, agricultural practices, and history were all represented in the weavings. In Peru today, Edwin Sulca Lagos is famous for his Inca-inspired weavings. This one is covered in designs from the Inca calendar.

THINKING CRITICALLY

1. **Hypothesizing**
   What sorts of images might the Inca have used to convey concepts such as time or seasons?

2. **Identifying Problems**
   What risks did the Inca face by recording ideas only on fabric?

The Spanish in Latin America

Until about 500 years ago, Latin America was populated solely by Native Americans. In the 1500s, the Spanish arrived in the region. One famous Spanish soldier, **Hernán Cortés** (ehr·NAHN kawr·TEHS), captured the Aztec ruler, **Montezuma II** (MAHN·tih·ZOO·muh), in 1519. He claimed the Aztec Empire for Spain in 1521 and renamed it New Spain. A decade later, another Spanish soldier, **Francisco Pizarro,** defeated the Inca ruler, **Atahualpa** (AH·tuh·WAHL·puh), and claimed Atahualpa's empire for Spain.

Culture •
Montezuma II was a great warrior who was feared throughout the Aztec Empire. ▲

Time of Change Once in control of Latin America, the Spanish enslaved many Native Americans and forced them to do labor, such as mining silver. The Spanish also worked hard to convert the Native Americans to Christianity.

Latin America and Spain also exchanged culture. Ships carrying Latin American goods sailed to Spain. The Spanish soon began growing corn, peppers, and tomatoes—crops they had never seen before. Manufactured products from Spain, especially textiles, were also shipped to Latin America. So were foods and animals, such as peaches and pigs. This trade was part of the **Columbian Exchange,** or the exchange of goods and ideas between European countries and their colonies in North and South America.

SECTION 2 ASSESSMENT

Terms & Names

1. Identify:
   (a) hieroglyph
   (b) *chinampa*
   (c) Machu Picchu
   (d) Hernán Cortés
   (e) Montezuma II
   (f) Francisco Pizarro
   (g) Atahualpa
   (h) Columbian Exchange

Taking Notes

2. Use a chart like the one below to list effects of the Spanish arriving in Latin America.

Effects of Spanish Arrival in Latin America	
1.	
2.	
3.	
4.	

Main Ideas

3. (a) Describe the writing system that the Maya developed.
   (b) How did the Inca pass important messages across great distances?
   (c) What was the Columbian Exchange and how did it work?

Critical Thinking

4. **Recognizing Effects**
   How did the Maya, Aztec, and Inca develop agricultural methods that responded to the environments in which they each lived?

   Think About
   ◆ physical surroundings
   ◆ available resources

ACTIVITY -OPTION-   Imagine you live in Tenochtitlán and have spent the day constructing *chinampas.* Write a **letter** to a friend describing the process.

Finding and Summarizing the Main Idea

▶▶ Defining the Skill

When you find and summarize the main idea, you restate the subject of a written passage in fewer words. You include only the main idea and the most important details. It is important to use your own words when summarizing.

▶▶ Applying the Skill

The passage to the right tells about the climate in Latin America. Use the strategies listed below to help you find the main idea and summarize a passage.

How to Summarize

Strategy ❶ Look for a topic sentence stating the main idea. This is often at the beginning of a section or paragraph. Briefly restate the main idea in your own words.

Strategy ❷ Include key facts, numbers, dates, amounts, or percentages from the text.

Strategy ❸ After writing your summary, review it to see that you have included the main idea and the most important details.

The Tropical Zone

❶ A large portion of Latin America lies within the Tropical Zone, ❷ which is the region between the latitudes 23°27' north and 23°27' south. ❷ The Tropical Zone may be rainy or dry, but it is typically hot. ❷ Also, temperature is always lower at higher elevations, but in the Tropical Zone, all elevations are warmer than they are elsewhere.

Write a Summary

You can write your summary in a paragraph. The paragraph below summarizes the passage you just read.

> ❸ Much of Latin America is in the Tropical Zone. This zone is between latitudes 23°27' north and 23°27' south. Usually, the Tropical Zone is hot. Also, the elevations in the Tropical Zone are warmer than the same elevations in other places.

▶▶ Practicing the Skill

Turn to page 161 in Chapter 6, Section 2, "Ancient Latin America." Read "Maya Agriculture," find the main idea, and write a paragraph summarizing the passage.

TERMS & NAMES

Explain the significance of each of the following:

1. tributary
2. deforestation
3. Tropical Zone
4. *El Niño*
5. hieroglyph
6. *chinampa*
7. Machu Picchu
8. Hernán Cortés
9. Montezuma II
10. Columbian Exchange

REVIEW QUESTIONS

Physical Geography *(pages 153–159)*

1. Describe two problems that Mexico City faces because of its location.
2. What two types of islands are found in the Caribbean?
3. Describe the climate in the Tropical Zone.
4. How have tectonic plates affected Latin America's physical geography? Give two examples.

Ancient Latin America *(pages 160–166)*

5. Explain the use of each of the three Maya calendars.
6. Why was warfare so important to the Aztec?
7. Describe two means of communication used by the Inca.
8. What types of changes took place in Latin America once the Spanish took control?

CRITICAL THINKING

Comparing

1. Using your completed chart from Reading Social Studies, p. 152, compare two ancient Latin American civilizations. List the similarities in the locations, dates, characteristics, achievements, and declines of the two civilizations.

Synthesizing

2. How are the farming methods of the Maya, the Aztec, and the Inca examples of people adapting to their environment?

Hypothesizing

3. Around A.D. 900, the Maya civilization—though not the people—began to disappear. What might have contributed to this decline?

Visual Summary

1 Physical Geography

- A variety of physical features, such as mountains and rivers, have impacted life in Latin America. Also, natural disasters, such as earthquakes and volcanic eruptions, occur frequently because of the region's location on five tectonic plates.
- The variations in Latin America's climate are caused by factors such as elevation, location, wind, and water.

2 Ancient Latin America

- The Maya, the Aztec, and the Inca all built major civilizations in Latin America.
- Each civilization developed creative solutions to problems presented by the physical geography around them.

SOCIAL STUDIES SKILLBUILDER

Inca Stone Roads Stone roads were a major technological feat of the Inca. These roads are still in use today. Having no written language or knowledge of the wheel, Inca rulers ordered roads built on which runners carried verbal messages to distant places. The runners worked in relay teams stationed along the roads. One runner told the message to the next. Messages could travel 150 miles a day along the stone roads. This system of communication was important to the Inca because their empire spread out over thousands of miles.

SKILLBUILDER: Finding and Summarizing the Main Idea

1. What is the main idea of the paragraph?
2. What details support the main idea?

FOCUS ON GEOGRAPHY

1. **Region** • In 2000, was South America's rain forest larger or smaller than the original forest?
2. **Region** • Was there any rain forest in the southern parts of South America in 2000?
3. **Location** • In what region of South America did the largest area of rain forest still exist in 2000?

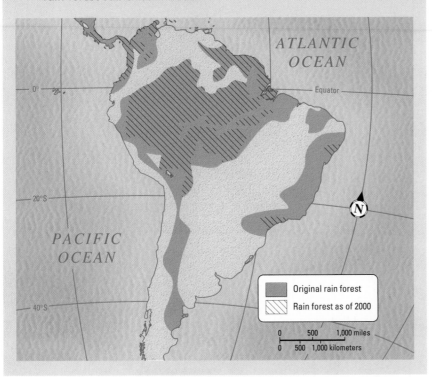

ATLANTIC OCEAN

Equator

PACIFIC OCEAN

0°

20°S

40°S

	Original rain forest
	Rain forest as of 2000

0   500   1,000 miles
0 500 1,000 kilometers

CHAPTER PROJECTS

Interdisciplinary Activity: Language Arts

Writing a Magazine Article Research the Columbian Exchange. Find out what crops, goods, and animals were sent in each direction across the Atlantic Ocean. Write a magazine article that explains which trade items came from Latin America and which came from Europe. Also include information about how the new items were used in each region.

Cooperative Learning Activity

Creating a Calendar Like the Maya, the Aztec used both a calendar with 260 days and a calendar with 365 days. Working in a small group, research one of the Maya or Aztec calendars. Find out how many months were in a year and how many days were in a month. Also find out the names of months or days. Then create a calendar that shows what your group found, and display it in your classroom.

INTERNET ACTIVITY

Use the Internet to do research about daily life in the Aztec, Maya, or Inca culture. Focus on one part of daily life, such as religion, trade, or warfare.

Writing About Culture Write a report of your findings. Include any illustrations you found or make your own drawings. List the Web sites you used to prepare your report. Then create a calendar that shows what your group found, and display it in your classroom.

For Internet links to support this activity, go to

RESEARCH LINKS
CLASSZONE.COM

Mexico Today

Place Mexico City's main plaza, the Zócalo, is the center of one of the world's largest cities.

How has Mexico's lack of farmable land shaped how people live?

Human-Environment Interaction • Only 12 percent of Mexico's land is arable—that is, farmable. The rest is too steep and rocky or too dry. Even the land that people can farm is not always very productive. Inconsistent rainfall, erosion, and pollution problems can pose serious challenges to farming. Also, some people do farm in mountainous regions, but planting and harvesting crops there can be very difficult.

What do you think?

♦ How do countries benefit economically from having a great deal of arable land?

♦ What challenges does Mexico face—in its economy and daily life—as a result of having little arable land?

BEFORE YOU READ

▶▶ *What Do You Know?*

Before you read the chapter, think about what you already know about Mexico. You may have read about the Aztec in another class. Do you know about any aspects of Mexico's culture today? Think about what you've heard on the news about Mexico—do you know who the president of Mexico is?

Culture • **The Aztec feather shields were no match for Spanish armor.** ▲

▶▶ *What Do You Want to Know?*

Decide what else you want to know about Mexico. In your notebook, record what you hope to learn from this chapter.

READ AND TAKE NOTES

Reading Strategy: Organizing Information
One effective way to organize information is with a time line. Time lines show events in sequence, or the order in which they happened. Making a time line for the events in this chapter will help you better understand what happened when.

- Copy the time line in your notebook.
- As you read the chapter, note the key events discussed in it.
- Write these events beside the appropriate dates on your time line.

Place • **At the Ballet Folklórico, the culture of Mexico takes center stage.** ▲

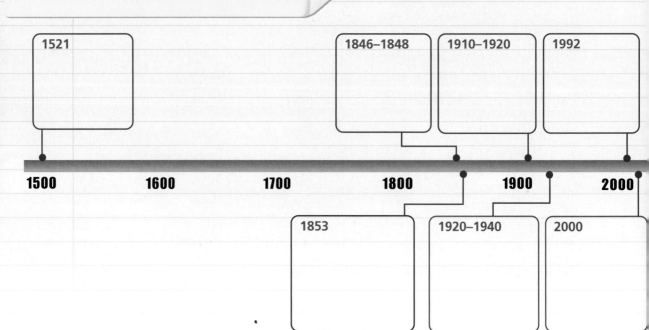

| 1521 | | | 1846–1848 | 1910–1920 | 1992 |

| **1500** | **1600** | **1700** | **1800** | **1900** | **2000** |

| | | 1853 | | 1920–1940 | 2000 |

The Roots of Modern Mexico

TERMS & NAMES

peninsular

criollo

mestizo

encomienda

Father Miguel Hidalgo

Treaty of Guadalupe Hidalgo

Gadsden Purchase

MAIN IDEA

Modern Mexico arose from conflict and cooperation among Native American, African, and Spanish Mexicans.

WHY IT MATTERS NOW

The culture of Mexico today reflects the influences of and interactions among these groups.

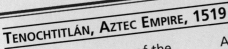

DATELINE

EXTRA

TENOCHTITLÁN, AZTEC EMPIRE, 1519

Today, in the palace of the Aztec emperor Montezuma II, a Spanish explorer got a taste of something he is sure to remember. A treat enjoyed by both the Aztec and Maya, the drink, called *chocolatl*, is thick, smooth, and decidedly bitter. With no sugar added to sweeten it, this unusual drink is spiced with flavors such as chili pepper and vanilla.

Always served in liquid form, the drink is consumed by the Native Americans at a high rate. Emperor Montezuma II drinks up to 50 cups a day. The Spaniards hope to take the chocolate, as they call it, back to Europe—although they plan to find some way to help ease the bitter taste.

Region • Cacao seeds grow inside pods like this. ▲

The Arrival of the Spanish

Human-Environment Interaction • The chocolate flavor comes from cacao seeds. ▲

The leader of the Spanish army that first landed on the shores of Mexico was Hernán Cortés. He hoped to win new lands for Spain, as well as gold and glory for himself.

Cortés reached the east coast of Mexico in 1519 with about 500 soldiers. He claimed the land for the king and queen of Spain. Quickly, however, he learned that the land was ruled by the powerful Aztec emperor Montezuma II.

A Clash of Cultures

Montezuma II ruled an empire of between 5 and 6 million people. However, many of his Native American subjects wanted to be free. They helped the Spanish conquer the Aztec king. They did not expect that the Spanish would become their new rulers.

The First Encounter Montezuma II heard about the arrival of the Spanish, and soon he welcomed Cortés with gifts. He even allowed Cortés to stay in a royal palace in the Aztec capital, Tenochtitlán. Within a week, Cortés took Montezuma II prisoner—and took control of the Aztec Empire.

The Spanish Takeover Other Aztec leaders drove the Spanish from Tenochtitlán. However, during the fighting that followed, Montezuma II was killed. The Spanish then retook the city, greatly aided by their Native American allies. The Spanish also had an essential advantage over the Aztec: their weapons. The Aztec had only war clubs, spears, and arrows. The Spanish soldiers had steel swords, armor, guns, and cannons, as well as horses. The invading army destroyed Tenochtitlán street by street.

Culture • Aztec feather shields offered less protection than Spanish metal helmets and armor. ▲

The Founding of New Spain

The fall of Tenochtitlán in 1521 marked the end of the Aztec Empire and the beginning of Spanish rule in Mexico. The Spanish called their empire "New Spain," just as the English called their territory in North America "New England." Where Tenochtitlán had stood, the Spanish established Mexico City as their capital. Spain ruled Mexico for the next 300 years.

A New Way of Life The Spanish victory caused more than a change of rulers in Mexico. The Spanish introduced a different way of life to the region. They brought new animals, such as horses, cattle, sheep, and pigs. They also brought new trades, such as ironsmithing and shipbuilding. They brought a new religion as well—Christianity.

Connections to Science

Invisible Weapons Smallpox and other diseases from Europe killed millions of Native Americans between 1500 and 1900. Smallpox (germ cell shown below right) had long been widespread in Europe, and most Europeans were at least partly immune. Native Americans, however, had no immunity to it because it had never before existed in the Americas.

Within months of the Spanish soldiers' arrival in Mexico, many thousands of Native Americans got sick with smallpox (shown below) and died from it—including Montezuma II's successor. Smallpox proved far more deadly to Native Americans than Spanish swords and cannons.

Reading Social Studies

A. Analyzing Motives Why did some Native Americans help the Spanish fight the Aztec?

Vocabulary

ironsmithing: making items out of iron

The Influence of the Church

Because the Catholic Church was powerful in Spain, it soon became powerful in New Spain. Catholic priests set up churches, schools, and hospitals. Sometimes Native Americans accepted Christianity willingly. Sometimes, though, they were forced to become Christian against their will.

A Cultural Blend Even though the Native Americans had to accept many new ways of life, the old ways were not lost entirely. For instance, an essential element of Native American cooking was the tortilla, a flat, round bread made from corn or flour. Tortillas are still made daily all over Mexico. As with food, many other aspects of the two cultures blended in the new Mexican culture.

Life in New Spain

A new multilayered society developed in Mexico. The ruling class were Spanish officials who were born in Spain. They were called **_peninsulares_** (peh·neen·soo·LAH·rehs) because they were from the Iberian Peninsula in Europe.

A second class were **_criollos_** (kree·AW·yaws), people who were born in Mexico but whose parents were born in Spain. _Criollos_ were often wealthy and powerful, but they were not in as high a social class as the _peninsulares_.

A **_mestizo_** (mehs·TEE·saw) is a person who is of Spanish and Native American ancestry. _Mestizos_ formed the third layer of New Spain's society.

BACKGROUND

The Iberian Peninsula consists of two countries—Portugal and Spain. (See the map of Europe on page 262.)

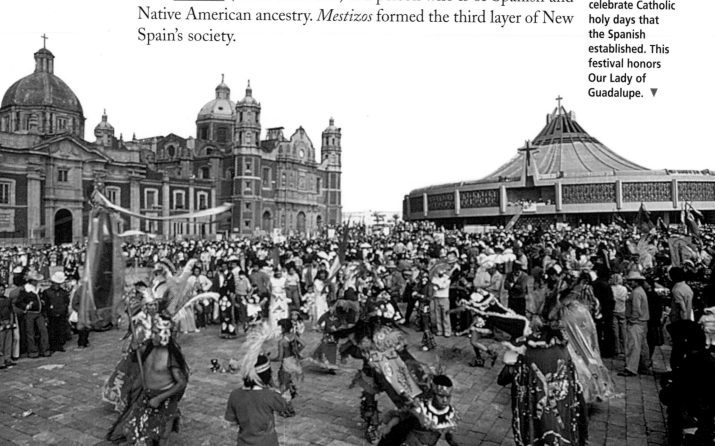

Movement • Mexicans today celebrate Catholic holy days that the Spanish established. This festival honors Our Lady of Guadalupe. ▼

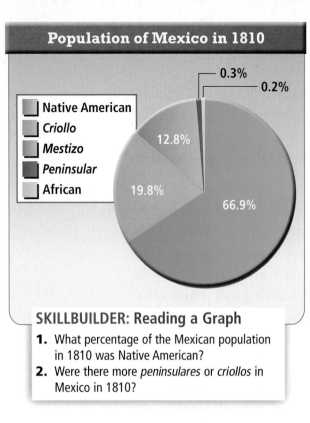

Population of Mexico in 1810

- Native American
- Criollo
- Mestizo
- Peninsular
- African

0.3%
0.2%
12.8%
19.8%
66.9%

SKILLBUILDER: Reading a Graph

1. What percentage of the Mexican population in 1810 was Native American?
2. Were there more *peninsulares* or *criollos* in Mexico in 1810?

A fourth group of people arrived in Mexico unwillingly—the enslaved Africans brought by European slave ships. African farming techniques, musical traditions, and crafts soon blended into the Mexican culture.

Encomienda New Spain's largest group was the Native Americans. They made up the bottom layer of society. The rulers of Spain set up in Mexico a system called **_encomienda_** (ehn·kaw·MYEHN·dah). Under this system, Spanish men were each given a Native American village to oversee. The villagers had to pay tribute—in goods, money, or labor—to this Spaniard. They were essentially enslaved. The results of their labor helped to make Spain rich. However, the villagers lived in poverty and hardship.

Vocabulary

tribute:
a forced payment

The War of Independence

Based on earlier European and American political writers, many Mexican religious and political leaders in the early 1800s were saying that Mexicans should be free to choose their own government. They argued that Mexico should be independent from Spain. The demand for Mexican independence grew stronger after 1808, when France conquered Spain.

A Cry for Freedom Then, before dawn on September 16, 1810, the farmers in the mountain village of Dolores heard their church bells ringing. At the church, their priest, **Father Miguel Hidalgo,** gave a fiery speech urging them to throw off Spanish rule. No one knows the exact text of the speech, but it is known as the *Grito de Dolores* (Cry of Dolores). Urged on by his words, a small army of Native Americans and *mestizos* marched with Father Hidalgo toward Mexico City. Along the way, thousands more joined them.

A Difficult Challenge Father Hidalgo's army had few weapons. Mostly, his men carried clubs and farm tools, such as sickles and axes. When they faced the government soldiers, the farmers were soon defeated. Father Hidalgo was captured and executed, but the revolution he had sparked did not die.

Reading
Social Studies

B. Clarifying
What ideas from other parts of the world did Mexicans agree with?

Vocabulary

sickle:
a blade used for cutting tall grass or grain

BACKGROUND

Mexico's independence was based on "three guarantees": that it would be independent from Spain, that it would be Catholic, and that *criollos* and *peninsulares* would be equal.

Independence at Last New leaders took Father Hidalgo's place. A few wealthy Spanish nobles and many *criollos* joined the fight for independence. The struggle lasted for 11 years. In 1821, the rebels finally overthrew the Spanish government, and Mexico became independent. However, the *peninsulares* and *criollos* still ruled the country. Native Americans and *mestizos* benefited little from independence from Spain.

War with the United States

In 1821, the new nation of Mexico was far larger than it is today. You can see on the map on page 178 that northern Mexico included much of what is now the Southwestern United States. Spanish explorers claimed this entire region in the 1500s and 1600s. Spanish and Mexican priests built missions there in the 1600s.

Desert and Distance Much of this land was desert. Travel was slow and communication difficult. Mexico was at war with Native Americans in this region, such as the Apache and the Comanche tribes. For all these reasons, few Mexicans settled there.

To encourage settlement, the Mexican government invited foreigners to move into these northern lands. Most of the newcomers were from the United States and still felt some loyalty to that country. By the 1830s, settlers in Texas from the United States greatly outnumbered those from Mexico.

Texas Independence In 1835, many settlers in Texas decided to break away from Mexico and rose in revolt. After several fierce battles, the Texans won their independence. They set up the Republic of Texas in 1836.

Most Texans wanted to become part of the United States. In 1845, the United States agreed, but Mexico and the United States could not agree where the boundary between Texas and Mexico should be. Each side claimed land that the other wanted.

The Mexican War In 1846, the dispute grew into a war. During the next two years, U.S. forces won control of northern Mexico; it was made official when Mexico was forced to sign the **Treaty of Guadalupe Hidalgo.**

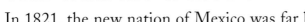

Place • **You can still see this mission, built in 1700, in Arizona today.** ▼

Biography

Father Hidalgo Father Miguel Hidalgo y Costilla, shown in the center of the illustration above, was born in 1753. He was a *criollo* who felt great sympathy for the Native Americans and *mestizos*. As a priest in the small village of Dolores, Father Hidalgo joined a secret group that fought for Mexico's independence.

Father Hidalgo is known as the Father of Mexican Independence. Every September 16, Mexicans shout slogans from the *Grito de Dolores* in celebration of their independence and Father Hidalgo.

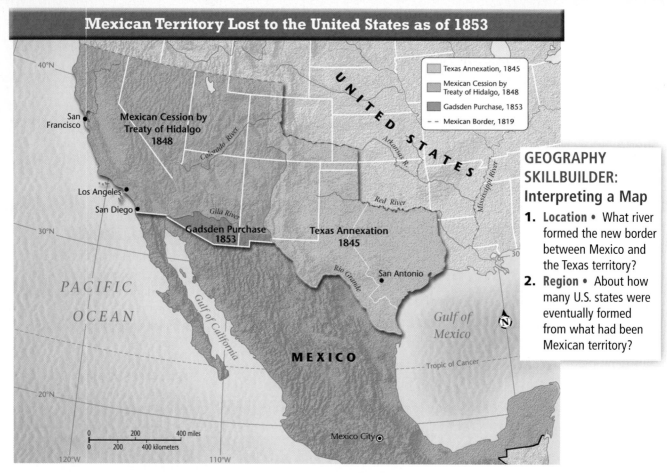

Mexican Territory Lost to the United States as of 1853

Texas Annexation, 1845
Mexican Cession by Treaty of Hidalgo, 1848
Gadsden Purchase, 1853
– – Mexican Border, 1819

GEOGRAPHY SKILLBUILDER: Interpreting a Map

1. **Location** • What river formed the new border between Mexico and the Texas territory?
2. **Region** • About how many U.S. states were eventually formed from what had been Mexican territory?

A few years later, in 1853, the **Gadsden Purchase** gave the United States more of Mexico's northern land. The two countries have since made slight adjustments to the border, but they have not fought a war again.

SECTION 1 ASSESSMENT

Terms & Names

1. **Identify:**
   (a) *peninsular*   (b) *criollo*   (c) *mestizo*   (d) *encomienda*
   (e) Father Miguel Hidalgo   (f) Treaty of Guadalupe Hidalgo   (g) Gadsden Purchase

Taking Notes

2. Use a chart like this one to list the five social groups that made up New Spain and their characteristics.

Social Group	Characteristics

Main Ideas

3. (a) What advantages allowed Cortés's small army to conquer Mexico?

   (b) In what ways did Spanish rule change life in Mexico?

   (c) What were the results of the war between Mexico and the United States?

Critical Thinking

4. **Analyzing Causes**

   Why did Mexicans decide to fight for independence from Spain?

   Think About

   ◆ influential events around the world

   ◆ reasons for discontent among the *criollos, mestizos,* and Native Americans

---

Reread the information about the first meeting of the Spanish and the Aztec. Write a **short story** describing the event from either the Spanish or Aztec viewpoint.

Government in Mexico: Revolution and Reform

TERMS & NAMES
Benito Juárez
Francisco Madero
hacienda
Emiliano Zapata
ejido
Institutional Revolutionary Party
Vicente Fox

MAIN IDEA

Through periods of reform and revolution, Mexico struggled to establish a strong democratic national government.

WHY IT MATTERS NOW

Other countries, such as the United States, are more willing to work as partners with Mexico because its government is democratic.

DATELINE

QUERÉTARO, MEXICO, 1917—Amid the battles of the Mexican Revolution, politicians today took a step toward reforming the nation. After many weeks of discussion and debate, they produced a new constitution for Mexico. The document presents new approaches to issues such as education, landownership, and religion.

Perhaps this constitution will become a basis for a new and stable Mexican government. For now, though, the constant fighting among sides continues. The potential power of the constitution will be revealed only in time, as the government puts the document into action.

Location • President Venustiano Carranza organized the meetings that resulted in the 1917 constitution. ▲

A Struggle for Power

The constitution of 1917 was written as a response to the struggles of the previous century. During that time, Mexico spent many years fighting wars. In 1821, Mexico won its war for independence from Spain. Two decades later, Mexicans entered into and then lost a war with the United States over Texas, California, and other lands. During all these years, still another struggle was going on—a struggle for power within Mexico.

In the years after independence, army leaders often took over Mexico's government. In some parts of the country, bandits attacked travelers. Elsewhere, Mexicans fought with Spanish landowners. Everywhere, a few people enjoyed great wealth, while many suffered in poverty.

Benito Juárez Brings Reform

By the 1850s, many Mexicans were eager for reform. They found a leader in **Benito Juárez,** a man who rose from poverty to become president of Mexico and a hero to his people. He became minister of justice in 1855, and he later became chief justice of the Supreme Court. In 1858, he gained the presidency, giving control of the Mexican government to the reformers.

Response to Reform The reformers wrote a new constitution for Mexico in 1857. For the first time, Mexicans had a bill of rights, promising them freedom of speech and equality under the law. The constitution of 1857 also ended slavery and forced labor. However, the new constitution did not promise freedom of religion. Nor did it make Catholicism Mexico's official religion, as many church leaders had hoped it would. The reformers also cut back the army's power in the government.

These reforms stirred up a storm of controversy. Church leaders, army leaders, and wealthy landowners were outraged. From 1858 to 1860, the War of Reform raged between the reformers and their opponents.

Foreign Intervention in Mexico The War of Reform left Mexico so weak—because of death, debt, and unemployment—that the country was an easy target for foreign takeover. Spain, Britain, and France sent troops into Mexico. In 1863, after more than a year of fighting, the French marched into Mexico City and established themselves in control of the country. They made a European nobleman named Maximilian emperor. Maximilian did not reign long. The Mexicans overthrew Maximilian and executed him in 1867.

Culture • Benito Juárez was a Zapotec, one of the many Native American groups in Mexico. He grew up in a mountain village, studied law, and then went into politics. ▲

Culture • Mexican forces fight their way to victory in an early battle against the French in 1862. ▼

An End to Reform That same year, Benito Juárez and the reformers returned to power. Juárez remained president until his death in 1872. Unfortunately, his successors cared about reform less than he had. Poverty and lack of education remained problems. A few rich families held most of the political and economic power. Not until the 20th century did a new wave of reform begin.

The Mexican Revolution

By 1910, the divisions between rich and poor in Mexico were huge. Just 800 families owned more than 90 percent of the farmland. Of Mexico's 15 million people, 10 million owned no land at all.

A Decade of War Once again, many Mexicans decided to fight for reforms. And once again, the struggle turned bloody. From 1910 to 1920, Mexico endured the Mexican Revolution.

The Revolution was a fight among many armies. Almost every part of Mexico had an army of rebels and reformers with particular goals. One of the first revolutionary leaders was a wealthy rancher named **Francisco Madero,** who became president in 1911. For Madero and his supporters, the key issue was free, honest elections. For others, however, the most important problem was landownership.

Reading
Social Studies

A. Analyzing Issues What sorts of concerns led Mexicans to fight in the Mexican Revolution?

The Problem of Land Poor farmers wanted land of their own. They believed the government should give each farm family a few acres by breaking up the giant *haciendas*. A **hacienda** is a big farm or ranch, often as large as 40,000 or 50,000 acres. Much of the *hacienda* land had once belonged to village farmers. But a law passed in 1883 allowed some of the wealthiest ranch owners to easily take away land from the village farmers. During the 1880s and 1890s, the ranch owners took over millions of acres of land owned by village farmers, and that land became part of their *haciendas*.

Region • During the Revolution, Francisco "Pancho" Villa was a famous leader in the north of Mexico. ▼

Region • Like this one, many of Mexico's *haciendas* were situated on huge pieces of land. ▶

Emiliano Zapata was a legendary fighter for farmers' rights. With his famous motto—"Land and Liberty!"—Zapata gathered an army in the south of Mexico and urged farmers to join him.

Connections to Citizenship

The Mexican Flag In the middle of Mexico's flag sits an eagle holding a snake in its mouth— a symbol from an Aztec legend about the founding of their capital, Tenochtitlán. The legend says that in the 1100s, the Aztec sun god told the Aztec to build a city on the spot where they saw an eagle with a snake in its mouth. When they saw just such an eagle in the middle of Lake Texcoco, they knew where to build their capital.

Each of the flag's red, white, and green stripes represents one of the "three guarantees" of the Mexican War of Independence. By flying a flag that combines a symbol from Aztec times with one from the period of independence, Mexico shows how important its roots are to its modern identity.

A Continuing Revolution

Over the course of a decade, dozens of large and small armies fought with one another. In 1913, Madero was murdered. The same fate befell Zapata in 1919. Between 1910 and 1920, more than 1 million Mexicans died in the battles of the Revolution. In 1920, a new government managed to make peace among the many armies. The fighting was over, but the Revolution—the effort to reform Mexico's government and economy— went on.

Answering Demands for Land In 1917, a new constitution was written, and one of its promises was to distribute land more equally among the people. Between 1920 and 1940, the government broke up many of the giant *haciendas*. Millions of acres were divided among small farmers or given to *ejidos*. An **ejido** (eh·HEE·daw) is a community farm owned by all the villagers together. Farmers were proud and happy to have their own land once again.

Reading **Social Studies**

B. Summarizing How did the 1917 constitution respond to concerns about landownership?

The Revolution in Politics The idea of the Revolution was so important and popular among new Mexicans that the most powerful political party called itself the party of the Revolution. Its name changed several times, but the word *revolution* was always part of it. Today, it is called the **Institutional Revolutionary Party** (Partido Revolucionario Institucional, or PRI). This party won every presidential election in Mexico from 1929 until 2000, with power passing peacefully from one president to the next.

Mexico's Government Today

December 1, 2000, was a historic occasion in Mexico. On that day, **Vicente Fox** became Mexico's new president. Fox was the first president in more than 70 years who did not belong to the PRI. Instead, he belonged to the National Action Party (Partido Acción Nacional, or PAN). The election of a president from a party other than the PRI confirmed that Mexico was entering a time of new political possibilities.

National Government Mexico's official name is Estados Unidos Mexicanos, or the United Mexican States. Thirty-one states make up the nation. Mexico is a democracy and a republic. All Mexicans who are 18 or older have the right to vote. The Mexican government has three branches. As in the United States, these branches are the executive, legislative, and judicial.

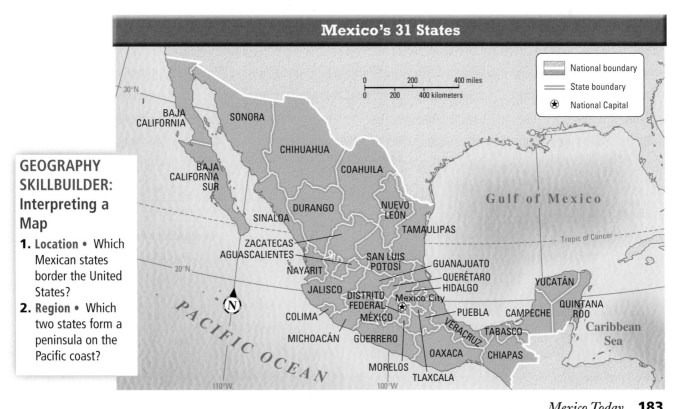

Mexico's 31 States

**GEOGRAPHY SKILLBUILDER:
Interpreting a Map**

1. **Location** • Which Mexican states border the United States?
2. **Region** • Which two states form a peninsula on the Pacific coast?

State Government Like the United States, Mexico has a federal system of government, in which power is shared between the national government and state governments. Voters in each state elect a governor. Each state also has its own legislature that makes laws. However, the national government has some control over the state governments. For example, the president and the national Senate together can remove a state governor from office.

Local Government Most towns and villages depend on money from the national government. Therefore, a local government has less say in its town's affairs than the national government does. However, local governments do provide essential public services, such as maintaining sewer systems and public safety.

Region •
The Mexican government issues stamps that celebrate its people and achievements. ▶

SECTION 2 ASSESSMENT

Terms & Names

1. **Identify:**
   (a) Benito Juárez
   (b) Francisco Madero
   (c) *hacienda*
   (d) Emiliano Zapata
   (e) *ejido*
   (f) Institutional Revolutionary Party
   (g) Vicente Fox

Taking Notes

2. Use a chart like this one to record details about each level of Mexico's government.

National	State	Local

Main Ideas

3. (a) What changes did reformers such as Benito Juárez help bring about in Mexico?

   (b) Why was the Mexican Revolution fought among many armies?

   (c) How did the Mexican government help farmers gain land of their own?

Critical Thinking

4. **Analyzing Points of View**

   How did different groups view the need for reform and change in Mexico during the years from 1850 to 1940?

   Think About

   • Juárez and the reformers
   • Madero and his supporters
   • the owners of the *haciendas*
   • Zapata and the small farmers

ACTIVITY -OPTION- Think about a constitution's bill of rights. Write a **speech** explaining why a bill of rights is important to citizens.

Mexico's Changing Economy

SECTION 3

TERMS & NAMES
Carlos Salinas
   de Gortari
privatization
distribution
maquiladora
nationalize
PEMEX
tourism

MAIN IDEA

In the mid-1900s, the basis of Mexico's economy changed from farming to industry and tourism.

WHY IT MATTERS NOW

Mexico's successful expansion of its economy has helped the nation to prosper.

DATELINE

EXTRA

MEXICO CITY, MEXICO, MARCH 18, 1938

President Lázaro Cárdenas's radio address today established a new course for Mexico's economy. Speaking to the nation, the president announced that foreigners will no longer be allowed to control petroleum companies in Mexico.

The oil industry will now be run by the Mexican government itself. It is hoped that this change will boost both Mexico's economy and its national identity.

Human-Environment Interaction • The Mexican government will now own all oil-producing equipment, such as these oil wells in Veracruz. ▶

Farming in a Time of Change

The 1938 decision that the government would own Mexico's oil industry was made in an effort to expand Mexico's economy. The expansion was necessary because, from ancient times until the mid-1900s, most Mexicans worked in just one industry—farming. Since the 1950s, great numbers of Mexicans have left farming for other kinds of work. However, farming is still important to Mexico's economy.

The Problems of Farming About one-fourth of Mexican workers are farmers. Many small farmers still work on the *ejidos*, or community farms, that were set up after the Revolution.

Although the *ejido* system gave land to many poor villagers, it did not lift them out of poverty. Farmers could not use the land as security for a bank loan because they did not really own their land—the *ejido* did. Without much money, they could not buy tractors, plows, or fertilizer. They had to continue to farm in the old ways, with hand tools on worn-out soil.

A New System In 1991, Mexican president **Carlos Salinas de Gortari** decided it was time to change the *ejido* system. Under Salinas's new laws, farmers could vote to divide their *ejido* into individual farms. Each farm family would have its own piece of land. The family could sell, rent, or trade its land. This process of replacing community ownership with individual, or private, ownership is called **privatization.**

The supporters of privatization hope that private farms will be able to grow more crops. Many of these farms are run like big businesses. Banks lend them money so they can afford to buy and use modern machinery. They can then grow the crops that Mexico sells to other countries, such as cotton, coffee, sugar cane, and strawberries.

Ejidos still make up about half the farmland in Mexico. This is partly because some farmers do not want to divide their *ejidos* into private farms. They worry that privatization might once again put most of the country's land into the hands of a few wealthy people.

Reading Social Studies

A. Clarifying How does using land on an *ejido* differ from owning one's own land?

Region • In this Mexican factory, workers make car parts. ▲

The Growth of Business and Industry

During the mid-1900s, industry became a larger part of Mexico's economy because the Mexican government took steps to encourage its growth. For example, the government built new power plants to supply energy for factories. It also constructed homes for factory workers.

The Mexican government also helped new companies get started by lending them money from the national bank. Sometimes the government lowered taxes on businesses or helped companies pay back money they had borrowed.

Effects of Government Aid The new policies encouraged production. As a result, new factories sprang up that made products such as steel, chemicals, paper, soft drinks, and textiles. The Mexican government also promoted the building of highways, railroads, and airports to aid manufacturers in the distribution of goods. **Distribution** is the process of moving products to their markets.

Privatization of Business In the same way that it was privatizing farms, the Mexican government during the 1990s began to privatize businesses. It raised millions of dollars by selling businesses, such as banks, mines, and steel mills, to private companies. By 2000, only a few key industries—such as the oil industry—were still in government hands.

Foreign-Owned Businesses in Mexico During the 1990s, many of Mexico's fastest-growing factories were situated along its border with the United States. These factories are called *maquiladoras*. In Mexico, a ***maquiladora*** (mah·kee·lah·DAW·rah) is a factory that imports duty-free parts from the United States to make products that it then exports back across the border. The lack of a tax on the parts helps keep operating costs low. Also, most of Mexico's *maquiladoras* are owned by foreigners, who save money because wages are lower in Mexico than in countries such as the United States. Although the wages are not great, *maquiladoras* have provided hundreds of thousands of jobs in Mexico.

Vocabulary

duty-free: free of government-imposed taxes

Citizenship IN ACTION

Na Bolom Since 1951, an organization called Na Bolom (headquarters shown below) has tried to help maintain Mexico's national heritage. Na Bolom works with the Maya living in the southeastern part of Mexico to uphold their traditional ways of life while also developing their economic opportunities. The group also tries to protect the often-threatened resources of the surrounding environment, such as the rain forest.

NAFTA Giving tax breaks on trade items is also a goal of the North American Free Trade Agreement (NAFTA). NAFTA has reduced taxes on items traded among Mexico, the United States, and Canada. However, some Mexicans are not sure NAFTA is a good idea—they worry that having such close ties to the United States and Canada gives those countries too much influence over Mexico. Despite these concerns, Mexico has nearly doubled its trade with the United States and with Canada since NAFTA was approved in 1992.

Mexico's Rich Resources

Just as gold and silver drew the Spanish to Mexico in the 1500s, other minerals that are found there attract worldwide interest today. While Mexico produces more silver than any other country in the world, it also mines lead, zinc, graphite, sulfur, and copper.

The Booming Oil Industry By far the most important of Mexico's natural resources is petroleum, or oil. In 1938, the Mexican government decided to **nationalize,** or establish government control of, the oil industry. Today, when many other businesses have been privatized, the oil industry is still government owned. An agency called **PEMEX** (which stands for Petróleos Mexicanos, or Mexican Petroleum) runs the industry. PEMEX is Mexico's largest and most important company. Oil is Mexico's biggest export, and the United States is its largest buyer.

Reading
Social Studies

B. Contrasting
How does nationalization differ from privatization?

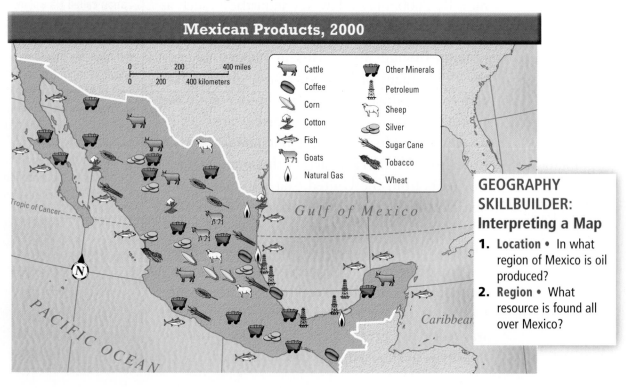

Mexican Products, 2000

Cattle · Coffee · Corn · Cotton · Fish · Goats · Natural Gas · Other Minerals · Petroleum · Sheep · Silver · Sugar Cane · Tobacco · Wheat

0 200 400 miles
0 200 400 kilometers

Tropic of Cancer

Gulf of Mexico

PACIFIC OCEAN

Caribbean

GEOGRAPHY SKILLBUILDER: Interpreting a Map

1. **Location** • In what region of Mexico is oil produced?
2. **Region** • What resource is found all over Mexico?

Tourism Is Big Business

Mexico's second-largest business is tourism. **Tourism** is the business of helping people travel on vacations. Tourists come to Mexico to enjoy its warm weather and its sunny beaches. Many people also visit the ancient Native American ruins. Visitors admire art in Mexico City's spectacular museums. They also shop for fine silver jewelry, weavings, wood carvings, and other handicrafts.

Place •
Tourists who travel to Santa Catalina Island, off western Mexico, can see rattleless rattlesnakes, which live nowhere else on Earth. ▲

Economic Effects of Tourism A popular tourist place in Mexico is Cancún, on the country's southeastern coast. The story of Cancún shows the effect tourism has had on Mexico's economy.

Until 1970, Cancún was a small Maya village of about 100 people. Its shoreline had white sand beaches and palm trees. The weather was sunny almost every day. In 1970, the Mexican government decided Cancún was an ideal place for a holiday resort. Working together, the government and private businesses built an airport, new roads, and skyscraper hotels.

Today, more than 2.5 million people from all over the world visit Cancún's resorts each year. Because of the tourism boom, the once tiny village has become a city with about 500,000 people.

SECTION 3 ASSESSMENT

Terms & Names

1. Identify:
   (a) Carlos Salinas de Gortari   (b) privatization   (c) distribution   (d) *maquiladora*
   (e) nationalize   (f) PEMEX   (g) tourism

Taking Notes

2. Use a chart like this one to take notes on four important parts of Mexico's economy.

Mexico's Economy	
Farming	
Industry	
Mining	
Tourism	

Main Ideas

3. (a) How has privatization changed the *ejido* system?

   (b) What part has Mexico's government played in the growth of industry?

   (c) How does tourism contribute to Mexico's economy?

Critical Thinking

4. **Forming and Supporting Opinions**

   Do you think the privatization of farmland in Mexico has been a positive step for Mexico's farmers? Why or why not?

   Think About

   • the concerns of some *ejido* farmers
   • farmers' need to modernize
   • Mexico's history of land reform

Draw a **flow chart** that shows the process by which goods are produced and distributed by a *maquiladora*.

Mexico's Culture Today

TERMS & NAMES
Diego Rivera
Frida Kahlo
Octavio Paz
rural
urban
Day of the Dead
fiesta

MAIN IDEA	WHY IT MATTERS NOW
Modern Mexican culture reflects a blending of Native American and Spanish heritages, as well as many new elements.	Cultures change over time, but understanding their histories can help you better understand their characteristics today.

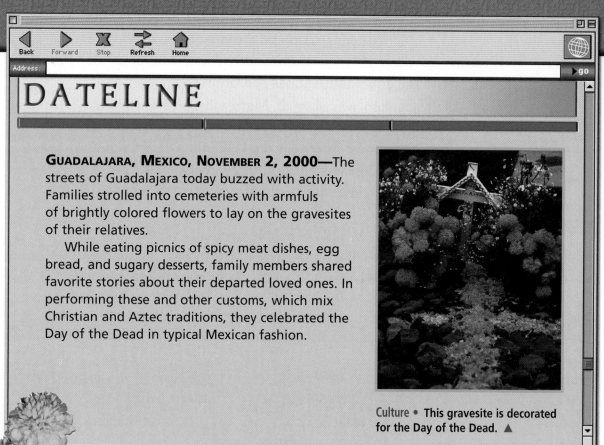

Back **Forward** **Stop** **Refresh** **Home**

Address: ▶go

DATELINE

GUADALAJARA, MEXICO, NOVEMBER 2, 2000—The streets of Guadalajara today buzzed with activity. Families strolled into cemeteries with armfuls of brightly colored flowers to lay on the gravesites of their relatives.

While eating picnics of spicy meat dishes, egg bread, and sugary desserts, family members shared favorite stories about their departed loved ones. In performing these and other customs, which mix Christian and Aztec traditions, they celebrated the Day of the Dead in typical Mexican fashion.

Culture • **This gravesite is decorated for the Day of the Dead.** ▲

Mexico's Blend of Cultures

Culture • **Marigolds are the most popular flowers left on graves on the Day of the Dead.** ▲

Mexican culture today reflects the same pattern seen in the Day of the Dead celebrations—a mixing of traditions. This mix includes three main cultures. The first two, Native American and Spanish, have long histories. The third, modern Mexican, results from the natural changes Mexicans have gone through over time.

Culture in Architecture A plaza near the center of Mexico City symbolizes the traditions that have come together in Mexico. At the center of this Plaza of Three Cultures stand the stone ruins of the Aztec marketplace. Nearby, a Spanish Catholic church borders the plaza. Beyond the plaza, skyscrapers rise against the sky and stand as landmarks of modern Mexico.

Culture in Other Forms of Art Just as Mexico's architecture reveals the multiple layers of its culture, so do other art forms. A series of historical murals decorates the walkways of the National Palace in Mexico City. Painted by **Diego Rivera,** one of Mexico's most celebrated 20th-century artists, these murals depict scenes from the Aztec Empire, New Spain, and the Mexican Revolution. Rivera's wife, **Frida Kahlo** (FREE·duh KAH·loh), is another favorite Mexican painter. After being injured badly in a bus accident, Kahlo painted many famous self-portraits from her bed.

BACKGROUND

Each year, a foundation in Sweden gives a Nobel Prize to a world leader in a particular field, such as literature.

Mexican literature also echoes the country's three cultural traditions. **Octavio Paz,** who won the Nobel Prize in literature in 1990, often writes about the connections between elements of Mexico's past.

Life in the City

About one of every five Mexicans lives in Mexico City. Thousands of people move there each year, hoping to work in factories or attend one of the city's universities or colleges. While Mexico City is by far the largest city in the country, many other cities and towns are growing quickly. Like Mexico City, they offer a blend of opportunities and problems.

Place • Aztec ruins, Spanish colonial architecture, and modern high-rises share space in the Plaza of Three Cultures. ▼

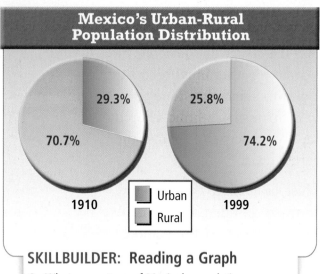

Mexico's Urban-Rural Population Distribution

29.3%

70.7%

1910

25.8%

74.2%

1999

Urban
Random

Rural

SKILLBUILDER: Reading a Graph

1. What percentage of Mexico's population was urban in 1910? in 1999?
2. What does this tell you about changes that have taken place in Mexican society?

A Lively Capital With more than 18 million inhabitants, Mexico City is the second-largest city in the world, after Tokyo, Japan. It is also the cultural center of Mexico. The great marble Palace of Fine Arts houses the national opera, theater, and symphony. It is also home to the famous Ballet Folklórico, a group that performs spectacular dances based on Mexican traditions.

The Cost of Growth Growth has, however, created problems. Streets are jammed with traffic. Car exhaust creates a blanket of smog over the city. The government has responded to the pollution problem in a number of ways. One solution was to free taxi drivers from paying taxes on their vehicles if they drive cars that pollute less.

Spotlight on CULTURE

Culture • The dancers in Ballet Folklórico wear detailed, bright costumes. ▶

As is true in most large cities, a noticeable gap exists between the lives of Mexico City's rich and poor citizens. While luxurious homes and fine shopping centers line some streets, many people also live in poverty.

Life in the Countryside

In the smaller villages and farming towns, much of Mexico's older way of life still goes on. At the center of each village is a plaza, where people gather to talk and visit with neighbors. Most people speak Spanish, but many also speak Native American languages, such as those of the Aztec and Maya.

Each village sets aside one day a week as market day. People gather in the plaza to buy, sell, or trade food, clothing, and other goods. Farmers come in from surrounding areas, bringing vegetables and handicrafts. The scent of freshly baked *tortillas* and *frijoles*, or beans, fills the air.

Poverty in the Countryside Mexico's **rural** areas—those in the countryside—face the serious problem of poverty. Some homes have only one room and a dirt floor. Farmhouses may lack electricity and running water. These hardships have driven many rural Mexicans to seek jobs in **urban,** or city, settings.

Education is also more limited in the rural areas than in the urban ones. Without education, it is especially hard for people to escape poverty.

Mexican Muralist After the Mexican Revolution, artist Diego Rivera (1886–1957) painted a series of famous murals on the walls of the National Palace in Mexico City. Rivera wanted to use his art to remind Mexicans of the important events in their country's past. This mural shows a typical day in the Aztec capital, Tenochtitlán—now Mexico City.

THINKING CRITICALLY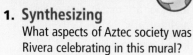

1. **Synthesizing**
   What aspects of Aztec society was Rivera celebrating in this mural?

2. **Recognizing Details**
   Identify three activities depicted in the mural.

Our Lady of Guadalupe In 1531, many Mexicans believe, Mary, the mother of Jesus, appeared to Juan Diego, a Native American man, in the Villa de Guadalupe Hidalgo. Mary asked Juan Diego to carry some roses in his cloak to the local bishop. Amazingly, Juan Diego found that roses were blooming even in winter on a harsh, rocky hillside. More astonishingly, when he opened his cloak, Juan Diego saw on it an image of Mary.

Many Mexicans saw these events as miraculous. They began calling Mary "Our Lady of Guadalupe" (shown at right). She was so loved that Father Hidalgo carried a banner with her image to rally support for independence. Mexicans still regard her as their protector.

Holidays

September 16 is Mexico's Independence Day. To celebrate, Mexicans reenact Father Hidalgo's call in 1810 to rise up against Spanish rule. Then people watch fireworks, dance, and play music in the streets late into the night.

Another major holiday has a somber name— the **Day of the Dead.** Nevertheless, Mexicans see it as a joyful time. They set aside November 1 and 2 to remember and honor their loved ones who have died. They decorate the graves with candles and flowers. Bakeries sell loaves of bread shaped like bones, and many stores sell small candy skulls. Relatives gather for meals at the cemeteries.

At least once a year, each village or town celebrates a **fiesta.** A fiesta is a holiday with parades, games, and feasts. It usually takes place on a saint's day—a day set aside by the Catholic Church to honor the memory of a holy person. While these days have religious origins, they are also celebrated as big neighborhood parties.

SECTION 4 ASSESSMENT

Terms & Names

1. Identify:
(a) Diego Rivera
(b) Frida Kahlo
(c) Octavio Paz
(d) rural
(e) urban
(f) Day of the Dead
(g) fiesta

Taking Notes

2. Use a chart like this one to list the positive and negative features of living in urban or in rural Mexico.

	Positive Features	Negative Features
Rural Mexico		
Urban Mexico		

Main Ideas

3. (a) What three traditions mix in Mexico's culture today?

(b) Why is Mexico City growing so rapidly? What are the effects of that growth?

(c) Describe some of Mexico's holidays.

Critical Thinking

4. Comparing

Do you see any similarities between the mix of cultural traditions in Mexico and the mix in the United States? What are they?

Think About

• forms of art, music, dance, and architecture

• languages spoken

• holidays celebrated

ACTIVITY -OPTION- Imagine that you are traveling through Mexico. Write a **journal entry** describing what you saw and did in its cities and towns.

Reading a Graph

▶▶ Defining the Skill

Graphs use pictures and symbols, along with words, to show information. There are many different kinds of graphs. Bar graphs, line graphs, and pie graphs are the most common. Bar graphs compare numbers or sets of numbers. The length or height of each bar shows a quantity. It is easy to compare different categories using a bar graph.

▶▶ Applying the Skill

The bar graph to the right shows the number of Mexican state governors who belong to each political party. Use the strategies listed below to help you interpret the graph.

How to Read a Graph

Strategy ❶ Read the title to identify the main idea of the graph.

Strategy ❷ Read the vertical axis (the one that goes up and down) on the left side of the graph. This one shows the number of state governors. Each bar represents the number of Mexican state governors who were members of a particular political party.

Strategy ❸ Read the horizontal axis (the one that runs across the bottom of the graph). This one shows the three political parties of Mexico's governors in 2000.

Strategy ❹ Summarize the information given in each part of the graph. Use the title to help you focus on what information the graph is presenting.

Write a Summary

Writing a summary will help you understand the information in the graph. The paragraph to the right summarizes the information from the bar graph.

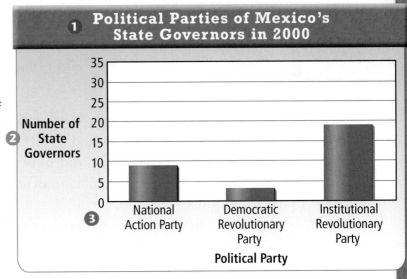

❶ **Political Parties of Mexico's State Governors in 2000**

❷ Number of State Governors

❸ National Action Party — Democratic Revolutionary Party — Institutional Revolutionary Party

Political Party

❹ In the year 2000, the state governors in Mexico belonged to three different political parties. The majority belonged to the Institutional Revolutionary Party. The next largest group was the National Action Party, and the smallest number of governors belonged to the Democratic Revolutionary Party. This shows that the Institutional Revolutionary Party was probably the most powerful party in Mexico.

▶▶ Practicing the Skill

Turn to page 176 in Chapter 7, Section 1, "The Roots of Modern Mexico." Look at the graph entitled "Population of Mexico in 1810," and write a paragraph summarizing what you learned from it.

How Quetzalcoatl Brought Music to the World

THIS MEXICAN FOLK TALE was first written down as a poem in Nahuatl (NAH•WAHT•uhl), the language of the Aztec, in the 1500s. The myth on which it is based may be a thousand years older. It was passed by word of mouth from one storyteller to another for centuries.

When time began, Earth had no music. Brooks did not babble, and birds did not sing. This, however, does not mean that music did not exist. High in the heavens in the Palace of the Sun, musicians of every sort filled the air with dazzling notes.

The god Smoking Mirror[1] envied this music, and he knew that the Sun would never share his prized possession with Earth. Therefore, Smoking Mirror lifted his voice to the air and shouted in every valley and cave for his friend Quetzalcoatl,[2] the feathered serpent who was also Lord of the Winds.

At a distance just beyond the horizon, Quetzalcoatl slumbered in silence. At the sound of Smoking Mirror's call, Quetzalcoatl slowly opened one eye and muttered with a sigh, "What does Smoking Mirror want now? Just as I find a dream, he finds a problem." With that being said, he whirled his serpent body 'round and stormed toward Smoking Mirror's ringing voice.

When Quetzalcoatl reached Smoking Mirror, he asked, "What is the matter now?" Smoking Mirror replied, "This morning, as I walked upon the bright and brilliant Earth that the two of us created, I realized that it is incomplete."

1. A name of Tezcatlipoca (tehs•KAH•tlee•POH•kah), a powerful Aztec god.

2. The quetzal is a bird that lives in the rain forests of southern Mexico and Central America. *Coatl* means "serpent" in Nahuatl.

Quetzalcoatl responded doubtfully, "That is not so! There are beautiful creeks and colorful birds in the world! Don't you smell the fragrance of the rose or feel the soft grass beneath your feet?"

"I do," responded Smoking Mirror, "but there is no music! Earth cannot sing its joy when there is no music. That is why I must ask you to go to the Palace of the Sun and return with musicians who are able to spread music across Earth."

"The musicians are faithful servants of the Sun," replied Quetzalcoatl. "They will never leave him." Smoking Mirror remained silent. After a while, the silence began to bother Quetzalcoatl, and he realized the importance of music. So up he went, through the blue smoke of the sky, to the Palace of the Sun.

The Sun saw the Lord of the Winds coming and told his musicians that they must be very quiet, or the feathered serpent would carry them away to the dark and silent Earth. As Quetzalcoatl reached the palace, the glorious music stopped, and the musicians turned their instruments away from the feathered serpent.

But with his command over the wind, Quetzalcoatl brought forth fierce storm clouds that blocked the radiance of the Sun. He then produced his own light as a guide for the frightened musicians. Mistaking the serpent's light for the light of the Sun, the musicians stepped into Quetzalcoatl's embrace. The feathered serpent gently floated the musicians to Earth.

When the musicians saw Smoking Mirror, they knew instantly that they had been tricked. What they saw, however, was not the horrible place described by the Sun. Instead, Earth was full of wondrous colors and activity. It was still within reach of the Sun's warming rays. The musicians then embarked on journeys throughout the world. On their way, they taught the birds to sing, the brooks to babble, the leaves to rustle, and the people to make music of their very own.

Reading
THE LITERATURE

What words and phrases give the reader a sense of Quetzalcoatl's personality? How does the author convey Quetzalcoatl's attitude toward the task Smoking Mirror gives him?

Thinking About
THE LITERATURE

What does this folk tale suggest about the role of music in Aztec society? Why might this folk tale be popular in Mexico today?

Writing About
THE LITERATURE

Write a dialogue involving the musicians, Quetzalcoatl, and the Sun, in which Quetzalcoatl tries to persuade the musicians to come with him to Earth and the Sun urges them to stay. As a class, compare and contrast the arguments each side makes.

Further Reading To learn about more Mexican stories, read *The Tree Is Older Than You Are*, edited by Naomi Shihab Nye.

TERMS & NAMES

Explain the significance of each of the following:

1. *criollo*   **2.** *mestizo*   **3.** Father Miguel Hidalgo   **4.** Treaty of Guadalupe Hidalgo   **5.** Benito Juárez

6. *hacienda*   **7.** *maquiladora*   **8.** PEMEX   **9.** Diego Rivera   **10.** fiesta

REVIEW QUESTIONS

The Roots of Modern Mexico *(pages 173–178)*

1. Why did Cortés need the help of some Native Americans to defeat Montezuma II?

2. How was Mexico's War of Independence connected to events elsewhere in the world at that time?

Government in Mexico: Revolution and Reform
(pages 179–184)

3. What concerns did Mexicans in the 1800s and 1900s have about land ownership?

4. What was unique about Mexico's presidential election in 2000?

Mexico's Changing Economy *(pages 185–189)*

5. Why has the *ejido* system been unsuccessful at ending poverty for many villagers?

6. What is the role of oil in Mexico's economy?

Mexico's Culture Today *(pages 190–194)*

7. What are some of the problems caused by Mexico City's rapid growth?

8. What event do Mexicans celebrate every September 16?

CRITICAL THINKING

Sequencing Events

1. Using your completed time line from Reading Social Studies, p. 172, list the points in Mexico's history when the nation's government changed drastically.

Forming and Supporting Opinions

2. Do you think the Mexican government's decision in the 1990s to privatize farming and business was a good one? Explain.

Hypothesizing

3. Modern artists, such as Diego Rivera and Octavio Paz, have used images from both Mexico's past and its present in their works. What do you think this says about the way Mexicans today view their nation's history?

Visual Summary

The Roots of Modern Mexico

• From 1810 to 1821, Mexico fought for and gained independence from Spain.

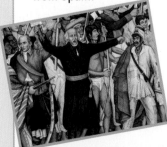

Government in Mexico: Revolution and Reform

• The Mexican Revolution (1910–1920) established a new government.

• Today, the government of Mexico is a federal republic.

Mexico's Changing Economy

• Farming is still an important part of Mexico's economy, but today its top businesses are oil production and tourism.

Mexico's Culture Today

• Mexico's culture combines its Native American and Spanish pasts with new elements.

• Mexico's holidays and arts show the influence of its history.

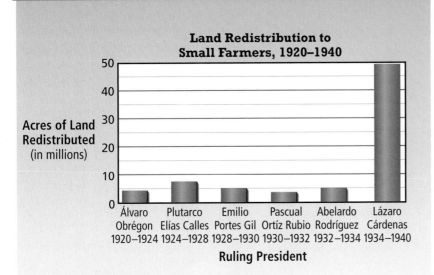

Land Redistribution to Small Farmers, 1920–1940

Acres of Land Redistributed (in millions)

President	Years
Álvaro Obrégon	1920–1924
Plutarco Elías Calles	1924–1928
Emilio Portes Gil	1928–1930
Pascual Ortíz Rubio	1930–1932
Abelardo Rodríguez	1932–1934
Lázaro Cárdenas	1934–1940

Ruling President

SKILLBUILDER: Reading a Graph

1. What information does the bar graph present?
2. About how much land did President Cárdenas give to small farmers?

FOCUS ON GEOGRAPHY

1. **Region** • Where does more farming occur, in the north or south of Mexico?
2. **Human-Environment Interaction** • What are the most common uses of land in the north of Mexico?
3. **Location** • From looking at this map, why do you think Mexico City is located where it is?

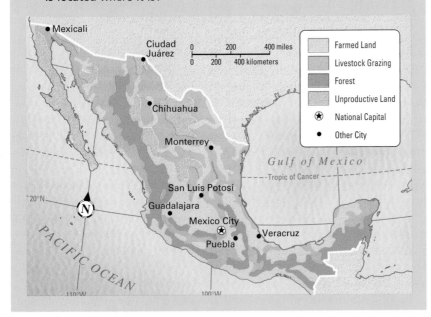

- Mexicali
- Ciudad Juárez
- Chihuahua
- Monterrey
- San Luis Potosí
- Guadalajara
- Mexico City
- Puebla
- Veracruz

Gulf of Mexico
Tropic of Cancer
20°N
PACIFIC OCEAN

	Legend
	Farmed Land
	Livestock Grazing
	Forest
	Unproductive Land
★	National Capital
•	Other City

0 200 400 miles
0 200 400 kilometers

CHAPTER PROJECTS

Interdisciplinary Activity: Art
Making a Poster Research one of Mexico's holidays. Create a poster that explains the focus of the holiday and how it is celebrated. Include photographs or drawings with captions that illustrate various aspects of the holiday.

Cooperative Learning Activity
Creating a News Broadcast With a group of three to five students, create a news show about the experience of Mexicans during the Mexican Revolution. Choose a specific year between 1910 and 1920 and a specific location, such as the National Palace in Mexico City or a battlefront.

- Take on the role of anchor, reporter, or interviewee.
- Write a script for your role.
- Conduct your "broadcast" in front of the class.

 INTERNET ACTIVITY

Use the Internet to do research about climate in Mexico. Focus on one region in Mexico, such as the southern mountains, and how that region's climate affects its people's way of life.

Writing About Geography Write a report of your findings. Include a map or a bar graph that visually presents information on Mexico's climate. List the Web sites you used to prepare your report.

For Internet links to support this activity, go to

RESEARCH LINKS
CLASSZONE.COM

CHAPTER 8

Central America and the Caribbean Islands

SECTION 1 Establishing Independence

SECTION 2 Building Economies and Cultures

SECTION 3 Cuba Today

SECTION 4 Guatemala Today

PACIFIC
OCEAN
ATLANTIC
OCEAN
PACIFIC
OCEAN
INDIAN
OCEAN
CENTRAL AMERICA
AND THE CARIBBEAN
ISLANDS
N

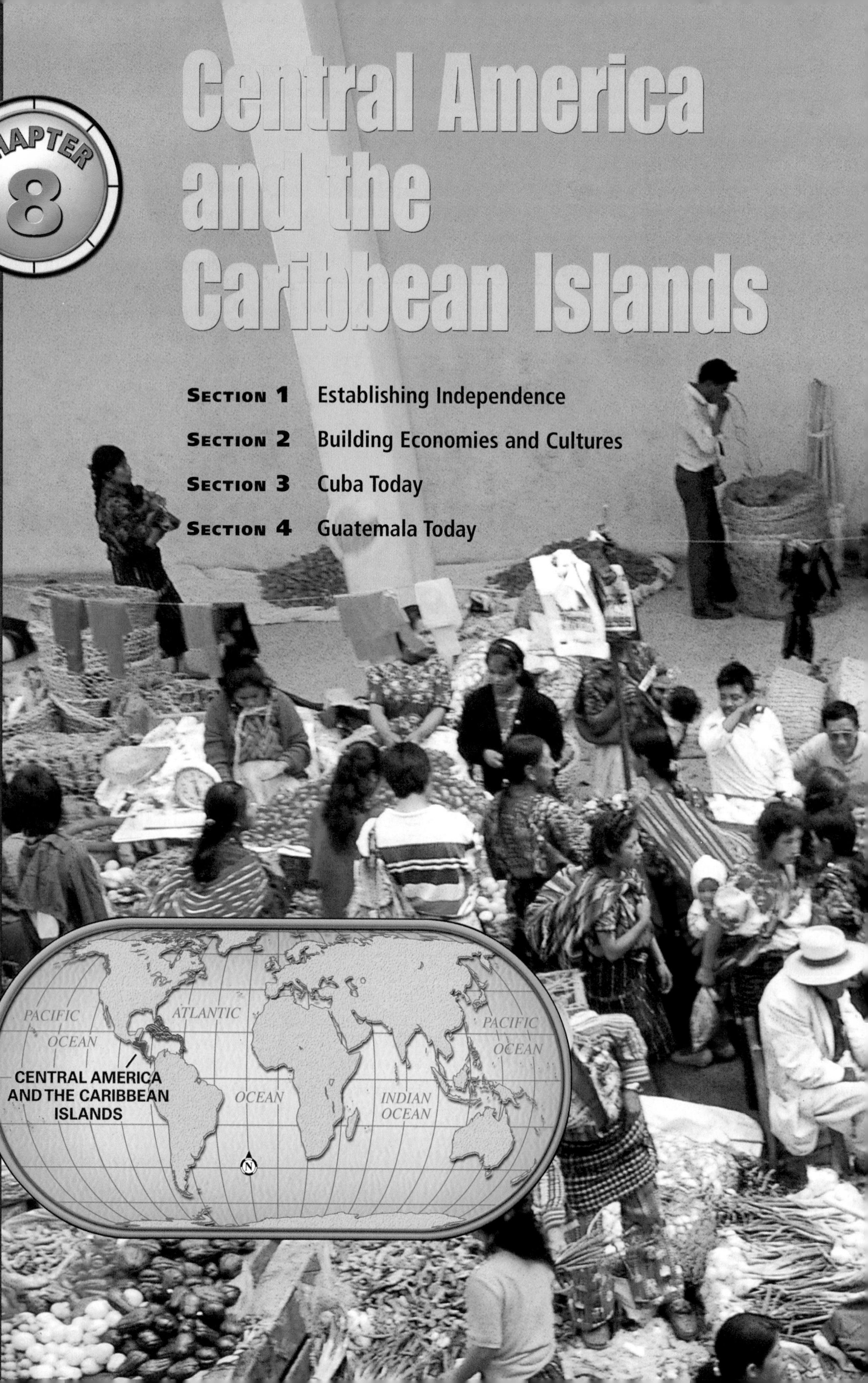

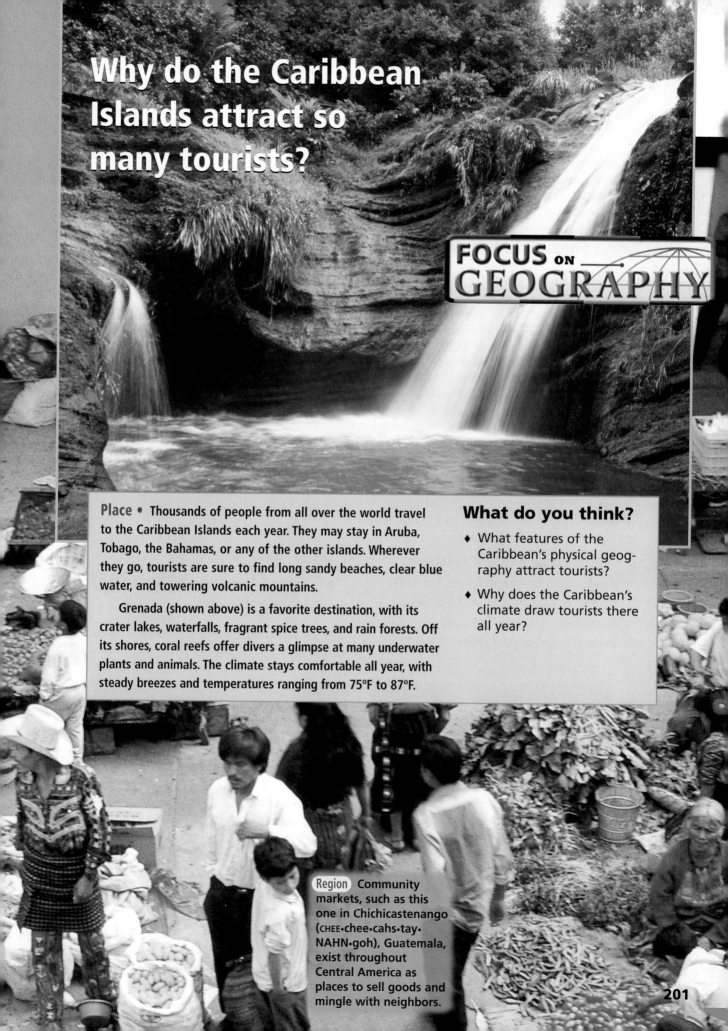

Why do the Caribbean Islands attract so many tourists?

FOCUS ON GEOGRAPHY

Place • Thousands of people from all over the world travel to the Caribbean Islands each year. They may stay in Aruba, Tobago, the Bahamas, or any of the other islands. Wherever they go, tourists are sure to find long sandy beaches, clear blue water, and towering volcanic mountains.

Grenada (shown above) is a favorite destination, with its crater lakes, waterfalls, fragrant spice trees, and rain forests. Off its shores, coral reefs offer divers a glimpse at many underwater plants and animals. The climate stays comfortable all year, with steady breezes and temperatures ranging from 75°F to 87°F.

What do you think?

♦ What features of the Caribbean's physical geography attract tourists?

♦ Why does the Caribbean's climate draw tourists there all year?

Region Community markets, such as this one in Chichicastenango (CHEE•chee•cahs•tay•NAHN•goh), Guatemala, exist throughout Central America as places to sell goods and mingle with neighbors.

201

BEFORE YOU READ

▶▶ *What Do You Know?*

Before you read the chapter, think about what you already know about Central America and the Caribbean Islands. You may have heard Caribbean music like reggae. Perhaps you have seen colorful woven cloth from Central America. Do you know where the Panama Canal is? Have you heard of Fidel Castro?

▶▶ *What Do You Want to Know?*

Decide what else you want to know about Central America and the Caribbean Islands. In your notebook, record what you hope to learn from this chapter.

Place • **This painting shows people working on a Caribbean sugar cane plantation.** ▲

READ AND TAKE NOTES

Reading Strategy: Identifying Problems and Solutions Identifying problems and solutions is a useful strategy for increasing your understanding of what you read. You can make a chart that lists issues. In the chart, identify the problems with those issues and the solutions to the problems to better understand the issues.

- Copy the chart into your notebook.

- As you read the chapter, look for issues related to government and economy.

- Record the problems and solutions involved in each issue on your chart.

Culture • Cubans celebrate a holiday called Carnival. ◀

Issues	Problems	Solutions
Colonization (1492–1800s)		
The Panama Canal (1903–1914)		
Spanish-American War (1898)		
Dictatorships		
Economic Development		
U.S./Cuba Relations		
Civil War in Guatemala		

Establishing Independence

TERMS & NAMES
West Indies
dependency
mulatto
ladino
dictator

MAIN IDEA

Central America and the Caribbean Islands have struggled to become independent nations with democratic governments.

WHY IT MATTERS NOW

The quest for democracy continues in Central America and the Caribbean, as it does elsewhere in the world today.

DATELINE

EXTRA

St. Domingue, Caribbean Islands, 1803

Word has arrived from France that François Dominique Toussaint L'Ouverture died there recently. He was taken to France last year to be imprisoned after leading the slave rebellion here in St. Domingue. The rebellion was so successful that St. Domingue seems just days away from declaring its independence once and for all.

Toussaint was given the nickname L'Ouverture, which means "opening" in French, because he always found an opening in enemy lines. His success in leading the rebellion is staggering when one realizes that his army of former slaves, mostly uneducated, defeated, in turn, the French, the British, and the Spanish.

E. RUNJAT.

Culture • Toussaint has become a hero to many. ▲

Central America and the Caribbean

Central America includes seven nations—Belize, Guatemala, Honduras, El Salvador, Nicaragua, Costa Rica, and Panama. Its neighbors—St. Domingue, now called Haiti, and the other islands of the Caribbean—are known as the **West Indies.** They include 13 nations and 11 dependencies. A **dependency** is a place that is governed by or closely connected with another country. For example, Puerto Rico is a dependency of the United States.

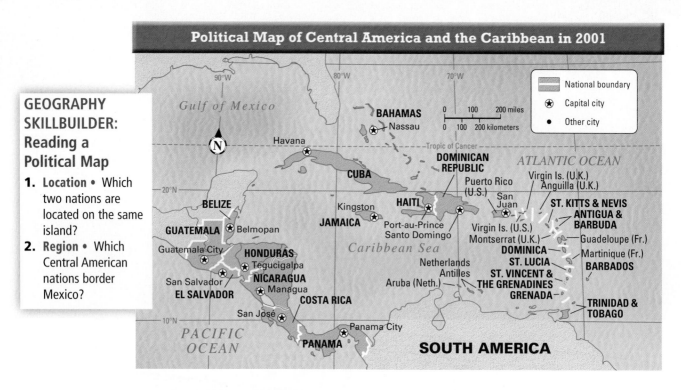

Political Map of Central America and the Caribbean in 2001

GEOGRAPHY SKILLBUILDER: Reading a Political Map

1. **Location** • Which two nations are located on the same island?
2. **Region** • Which Central American nations border Mexico?

Peoples of the Caribbean When Christopher Columbus reached the West Indies in 1492, about 750,000 Native Americans lived there. The Europeans who took over forced Native Americans to work on plantations and in mines. The harsh labor, plus European diseases unknown in the Americas, killed many Native Americans. Others died in battles with the Europeans. Within a few years, nearly all the Native Americans on the islands had died.

Without Native Americans to use for labor, European rulers looked for a new source of workers. By the 1520s, the Spanish began bringing shiploads of enslaved Africans to the West Indies. Other European nations joined in the slave trade. From the 1500s to the mid-1800s, about 10 million enslaved Africans arrived in the West Indies. As a result, many people in the Caribbean today are **mulattos** (mu·LAT·ohz), or people who have African and European ancestry. Few Caribbean people have Native American ancestry.

BACKGROUND

About 75 million people live in Central America and the Caribbean today.

Region • Like this man, many Caribbean people are of African descent. ▼

Central American People In Central America, the situation for the Native Americans was different. When the Spanish arrived in 1501, many Native Americans withdrew to the inland mountains and thus survived what proved to be a deadly encounter with the Spanish elsewhere. Today, one-fifth of Central Americans are Native Americans.

Reading **Social Studies**

A. Finding Causes How did geography help the Native Americans in Central America survive the arrival of Europeans?

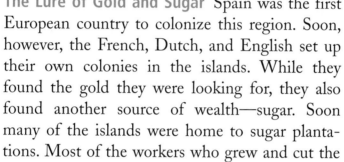

The slave ships also arrived in Central America, bringing Africans to the region. Africans from the Caribbean also migrated to the area. As the years passed, the Spanish, Native Americans, and Africans intermarried. Those people with mixed European and Native American ancestry are called **_ladinos_** (luh·DEE·naws), and they make up about two-thirds of Central America's population today.

Region • Central Americans today reflect the region's rich mix of cultures and people. ▲

From Colonies to Independence

From the 1500s to the 1800s, European nations ruled Central America and the West Indies as colonies. These differed from the dependencies of today. Usually, a dependency is free to break off its connection to the other country, but a colony must either win its independence or be granted it.

The Lure of Gold and Sugar Spain was the first European country to colonize this region. Soon, however, the French, Dutch, and English set up their own colonies in the islands. While they found the gold they were looking for, they also found another source of wealth—sugar. Soon many of the islands were home to sugar plantations. Most of the workers who grew and cut the sugar cane were enslaved.

Becoming Independent By the 1800s, the people of Central America and the Caribbean Islands began to demand their independence. In 1804, the French colony of St. Domingue became the first nation in the region to win independence.

BACKGROUND

After independence, St. Domingue took a new name—Haiti (HAY·tee).

Other nations soon followed St. Domingue's example. In 1821, Guatemala, Honduras, Costa Rica, and Nicaragua declared independence from Spain. At first they united, but since 1839, they have existed as separate nations.

Relations with the United States

The United States of America is the largest neighbor of Central America and the West Indies. U.S. policies have long played a part in shaping the region's history.

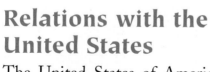

Reggae After the Caribbean island of Jamaica gained independence from Britain in 1962, musicians such as Bob Marley (shown below) developed a new style of music called reggae (REHG·ay). Today, reggae is popular around the world. It is known for its political messages.

With their lyrics, the early reggae singers commented on social and economic problems. Reggae is enjoyed both for pleasure and for its ability to let the poor and the oppressed make their voices heard. Music has played a similar role in many cultures throughout history.

The Panama Canal Until the early 1900s, people who wanted to travel from one side of North or South America to the other had two choices. They could make the long, dangerous trip by land or sail all the way around South America. Because the Isthmus of Panama is about 40 miles wide, by 1900, first France, then the United States were eager to build a canal across it to connect the two oceans.

At that time, Panama was part of the South American nation of Colombia. The United States tried to buy from Colombia a strip of land on the isthmus. Colombia refused, and so the United States urged the people of Panama to break away. Soon, Panama did revolt. After establishing its own country in 1903, Panama agreed to lease the United States land to build a canal. The canal opened in 1914 and soon became one of the most important transportation routes in the world. Now ships only had to sail the 50 miles from one end of the canal to the other.

Human-Environment Interaction • By using the Panama Canal, ships save 2,000 to 8,000 miles, depending on where they start and end their trips. ▲

The Spanish-American War Long after Central America broke free of Spanish rule, Spain continued to control Cuba and Puerto Rico. During the late 1800s, the islanders there rebelled many times but were not able to gain independence.

In 1898, the United States declared war on Spain. It did so partly because it wanted to help the people of Cuba and Puerto Rico gain freedom from Spain. However, the United States also wanted to protect the many sugar cane plantations that U.S. businesses owned on the islands. By the end of the war, which lasted less than a year, Spain had lost its last colonies in the Americas. Puerto Rico became a U.S. dependency, a territory under the control of another nation. Cuba became an independent country, but the U.S. military set up bases there and kept tight control over the country.

Reading
Social Studies

B. Recognizing Effects How did world affairs in the late 1800s affect the Caribbean?

Place • The United States controlled the Panama Canal and the land around it until December 31, 1999, when control passed to Panama. ▶

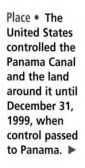

Dictatorships and Democracy

Independence did not necessarily bring freedom to the people of Central America and the West Indies. Only Costa Rica has been a democracy since the beginning of the 20th century.

Dictatorships Nearly all the other countries have spent many years under the rule of dictators. A **dictator** is a person who has complete control over a country's government. At times, dictators ruled Guatemala, Honduras, Panama, El Salvador, Haiti, and the Dominican Republic. Dictators often used violence to grab and keep power.

Culture •
Nicaragua's first female president, Violetta Barrios de Chamorro, governed from 1990 to 1996. ▲

Hopes for Democracy Most countries in Central America and the West Indies now have democratically elected governments. The people of these countries removed most of their dictators, one by one. For example, in 1990, Nicaraguans replaced dictatorial rule by electing Violetta Barrios de Chamorro (vee·oh·LE·tuh BA·ree·ohs day chah·MOH·roh) as president. However, elected leaders sometimes refuse to give up power, thus becoming dictators. Sometimes, elections are not run fairly. Nevertheless, freedom is more widespread than it was 50 years ago.

SECTION 1 ASSESSMENT

Terms & Names

1. Identify:
   (a) West Indies
   (b) dependency
   (c) mulatto
   (d) *ladino*
   (e) dictator

Taking Notes

2. Use a chart like this one to note the effects Europeans had on the Native American populations in Central America and the Caribbean.

In Central America	In the Caribbean

Main Ideas

3. (a) Why are there more Native Americans in Central America today than in the Caribbean?

   (b) Describe the difference between dependencies and colonies.

   (c) List two reasons why the United States declared war on Spain.

Critical Thinking

4. **Identifying Problems**

   Why have some countries in Central America and the Caribbean had trouble establishing democracies?

   Think About

   • the region's history of being controlled by other countries and dictatorship

   • the powers and resources of dictators

ACTIVITY -OPTION- Imagine you lived on the island that became Haiti in 1804. Write a short **biography** of your island's hero, François Dominique Toussaint L'Ouverture.

Building Economies and Cultures

MAIN IDEA	WHY IT MATTERS NOW
The economies and cultures of this region reflect both the colonial past and efforts to modernize.	Though small in size, the region exports its culture and products to the United States and beyond.

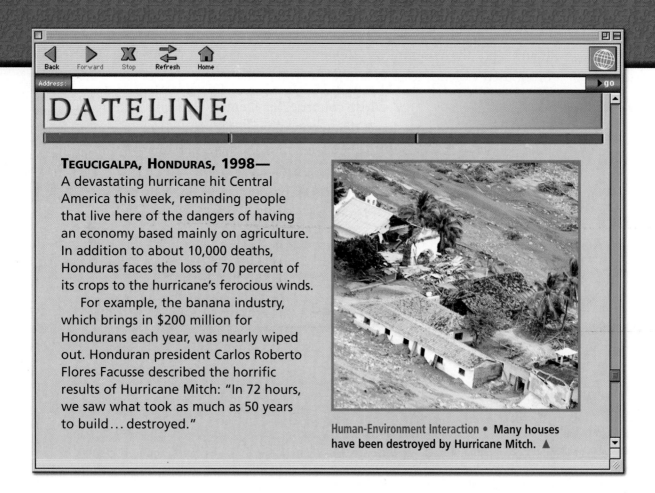

DATELINE

TEGUCIGALPA, HONDURAS, 1998—
A devastating hurricane hit Central America this week, reminding people that live here of the dangers of having an economy based mainly on agriculture. In addition to about 10,000 deaths, Honduras faces the loss of 70 percent of its crops to the hurricane's ferocious winds.

For example, the banana industry, which brings in $200 million for Hondurans each year, was nearly wiped out. Honduran president Carlos Roberto Flores Facusse described the horrific results of Hurricane Mitch: "In 72 hours, we saw what took as much as 50 years to build… destroyed."

Human-Environment Interaction • Many houses have been destroyed by Hurricane Mitch. ▲

The Economies of the Caribbean Islands

In the Caribbean, the economies of most islands have depended on growing one or two crops to sell to other countries. However, the islanders have also worked hard to create new businesses as well as new industries.

Human-
Environment
Interaction •
Many Caribbean
islanders spent
their days
planting and
then harvesting
sugar cane. ▲

The Colonial Period For most of the colonial period, the Caribbean Islands focused mainly on one industry—growing **sugar cane**. From the 1600s to the 1800s, most islanders worked on sugar cane plantations. In the early years, the majority of these workers were enslaved. Even after slavery ended by the late 1800s, most workers owned no land of their own. Instead, they planted, tended, and cut sugar cane on plantations owned by the wealthy.

During the colonial period, most of the islands traded only with their ruling countries. Cuba, for example, sold its sugar to Spain and bought goods from Spain in return. But after the colonial period ended, many of the islands traded mostly with the United States.

Single-Product Economies Sugar was so valuable that plantation owners raised few other crops. Most did not even grow food. Many of the islands had to buy almost all their food from other countries. A country that depends on just one product for almost all its jobs and income has a **single-product economy**.

Economies Must Change A single-product economy can be unstable—if something happens to that single product, the country's economy will be ruined. By the late 1800s, the sugar business in the West Indies was in trouble. People raising sugar cane in other parts of the world offered the West Indies fierce competition. Steam-powered machines allowed these foreigners to process sugar cane at lower prices. The people of the West Indies had to find new ways to make a living.

The islanders found they needed to diversify their economies. To **diversify** an economy means to invest in a variety of industries. People began to raise other crops, such as pineapples and bananas. Industries, such as textiles, medical supplies, and electronic equipment, also developed in the Caribbean.

Reading
Social Studies

A. Analyzing Issues Why did production of sugar elsewhere in the world affect the economies of the Caribbean?

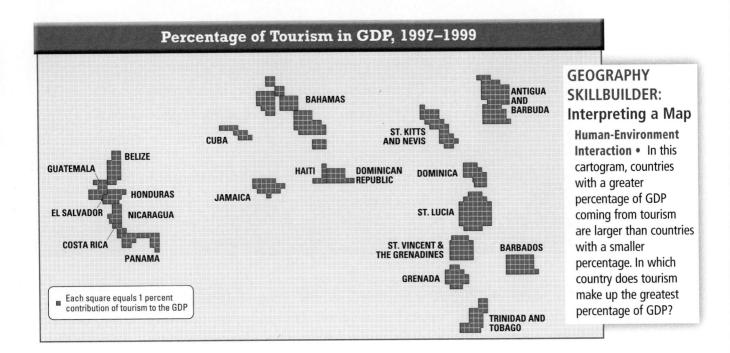

Percentage of Tourism in GDP, 1997–1999

BAHAMAS

ANTIGUA AND BARBUDA

CUBA

ST. KITTS AND NEVIS

BELIZE

GUATEMALA

HAITI

DOMINICAN REPUBLIC

DOMINICA

HONDURAS

JAMAICA

EL SALVADOR

NICARAGUA

ST. LUCIA

COSTA RICA

ST. VINCENT & THE GRENADINES

BARBADOS

PANAMA

GRENADA

■ Each square equals 1 percent contribution of tourism to the GDP

TRINIDAD AND TOBAGO

GEOGRAPHY SKILLBUILDER: Interpreting a Map

Human-Environment Interaction • In this cartogram, countries with a greater percentage of GDP coming from tourism are larger than countries with a smaller percentage. In which country does tourism make up the greatest percentage of GDP?

María Elena Cuadra Movement
In Central America, poverty and unemployment are widespread. In Nicaragua, many women take jobs in factories, like the one shown here, under poor conditions and for low wages.

Since 1994, the María Elena Cuadra Movement of Working and Unemployed Women (MEC) has been working to improve the position of women at work and in the home. MEC protects workers' rights, trains women in new skills, and lends money to women to start their own small businesses.

Tourism Takes Hold One of the most important industries in the Caribbean Islands is tourism. With warm weather and beautiful beaches, the islands attract tourists from around the world. About 8 million tourists flock there each year. On some of the smaller islands, such as Antigua, tourism is now the major industry.

The Economies of Central America

After the Spanish Central American countries became independent in the 1820s, they wanted to increase their trade with other nations. To do so, they needed to develop exports. During the 1800s, several Central American countries began to produce coffee. Soon it became an important export crop for Costa Rica, Guatemala, Honduras, El Salvador, and Nicaragua. In exchange for their exports, Central American countries purchased imports from other parts of the world.

The United States Steps In In the late 1800s, a major new export business got started in Central America. U.S.-based United Fruit Company (UFCO) set up huge banana plantations in the hot, wet lowlands of Central America.

UFCO did a huge amount of business, and bananas became another important Central American product.

Two Crops Are Not Enough The Central American economies grew to depend on bananas and coffee. Whenever the price of these items on the world market fell, Central Americans faced hardship. Like the Caribbean islanders, Central Americans wanted to diversify their economies.

Reading
Social Studies

B. Making Inferences
What are some factors that would cause the price of a product on the world market to fall?

Central American countries have worked to build more factories. Costa Rica, for example, has factories that make machinery, furniture, cloth, and medicine. The countries of the region have also developed tourism as an industry. Visitors arrive by the thousands in Guatemala to see the spectacular ruins of Maya temples. As different businesses grow, Central Americans will not be as dependent on agriculture as they were in the past.

Region •
Coffee grows well in the cool highlands of Central America. ▲

Caribbean Cultures

Each country in the Caribbean has its own particular way of life. Native American, African, and European influences blend differently from place to place.

Languages In the Caribbean, people speak a variety of languages. These reflect the area's history. Look at page 145 of the Unit Atlas to see which languages are spoken in which areas.

Religions Roman Catholicism is the most widespread religion in the West Indies. However, many islanders practice religions that have African influences. In Haiti, elements of Catholic and African religious practices combine in the religion known as voodoo.

Strange ?? but TRUE

A Language Lives On When Europeans arrived on the Caribbean island of St. Vincent in 1635, they encountered a startling mystery. The women of St. Vincent spoke one language, and the men spoke another.

Originally, they all spoke the Arawak language. However, when speakers of the Carib language attacked the Arawak-speaking islands, most of the Arawak-speaking men were killed. Only the female Arawak speakers survived.

The Arawakan women continued to speak their language, while the conquering men spoke the Carib language. Today, the language inherited from the Arawakan women is called Garífuna. Like the woman at the right, 30,000 people living on the Caribbean coast of Central America still speak it.

In Cuba, Yoruba beliefs from Africa combine with Catholic beliefs in the religion called Santeria. In Trinidad, the Shango religion blends Catholic, Baptist, and West African beliefs.

Music Music, too, shows a blending of cultures. From Cuban salsa to Jamaican reggae, much Caribbean music combines African and European styles to make something completely new. The rap music that is popular in the United States also has Caribbean roots. Some of the first rappers to perform in the United States introduced to this country the Jamaican technique of mixing together tracks from different songs.

Central American Cultures

The countries of Central America share a common history. In their cultures, the Native American and Spanish heritages blend.

Languages Look again at the map on page 145. You can see that in most of Central America, people speak Spanish. Central Americans also speak about 80 Native American languages, nearly half of which are Maya languages.

Spotlight on CULTURE

Merengue Dancing is a popular pastime in Latin America. One of the favorite dances (and the national dance of the Dominican Republic) is the merengue (*shown below*). This dance form originated in the neighboring nations of Haiti and the Dominican Republic. It is known for its unique dance step, called a sliding step, in which the dancer always rests his or her weight on the same foot. People commonly explain this step with one of two legends. One legend says that enslaved people developed the step while chained to one another at the leg. Another legend has it that a Dominican war hero, wounded in the leg during a revolt, designed the step. Whatever the true story behind the dance, the merengue did arise as a folk dance in rural areas. Later it became a favorite of ballroom dancers.

THINKING CRITICALLY

1. **Drawing Conclusions**
   What do the two legends about the origins of the merengue's sliding step tell you about the significance of dancing in Latin American culture?

2. **Synthesizing**
   What different roles do you think dancing can play in a culture?

Religions Catholicism is the most widespread religion in Central America. In recent years, however, millions of Central Americans have become Protestants and Mormons. Also, some ancient Maya religious beliefs still thrive. An example is the companion spirit. Maya people today believe that when a person is born, so is an animal. That animal, the companion spirit, lives through the same experiences as the person does. A person usually learns about his or her companion spirit in dreams.

Crafts Many Central American towns are known for their crafts, such as weaving, embroidery, pottery, silversmithing, and basketmaking. Many of the styles and methods used originated with ancient Native Americans. For example, many weavers use a backstrap loom—a 2,000-year-old device consisting of threads that are attached to a fixed post or tree on one end and a belt on the other end.

Culture • By wearing the belt around her waist, the weaver stretches the threads tight to weave on them. ▲

SECTION 2 ASSESSMENT

Terms & Names
1. Identify: (a) sugar cane (b) single-product economy (c) diversify

Taking Notes
2. Use a chart like this one to check off the languages spoken in each region, country, or island mentioned in the text.

	Guatemala	Haiti
Native American		
Spanish		
French		
English		

Main Ideas
3. (a) List some ways in which sugar production affected the lives of Caribbean people.

(b) How have Central American countries diversified their economies?

(c) How do the religions in Central America and the Caribbean reflect the regions' histories?

Critical Thinking
4. Forming and Supporting Opinions How do you think the success of a foreign-owned company affects a country?

Think About
- the importance of UFCO's product to Central American economies
- the jobs created by a successful company
- who receives the company's profits

ACTIVITY -OPTION- A country with a single-product economy risks losing a great deal if that product fails. Make a **chart** of the factors that put the country in this risky position but that it cannot control.

Reading a Political Map

▶▶ Defining the Skill

Political maps show the boundaries of nations and other political areas, such as dependencies. Lines show these boundaries. Often political maps also show capitals and other cities.

▶▶ Applying the Skill

The political map at right shows the nations of Central America. Use the strategies listed below to identify the information shown on the map.

How to Read a Political Map

Strategy ❶ Read the title. It tells you which region's political areas are being represented.

Strategy ❷ Read the key. It tells you what each symbol stands for. This key shows boundaries between nations, national capitals, and other cities.

Strategy ❸ Read the scale. It tells you how many miles or kilometers each inch represents.

Make a Chart

A chart can help you organize information given on maps. The chart below organizes information about the map you just studied.

▶▶ Practicing the Skill

Turn to Chapter 8, Section 1, "Establishing Independence." Study the political map of Central America and the Caribbean on page 204. Make a chart listing the nations of the Caribbean and the capitals that are shown on the map.

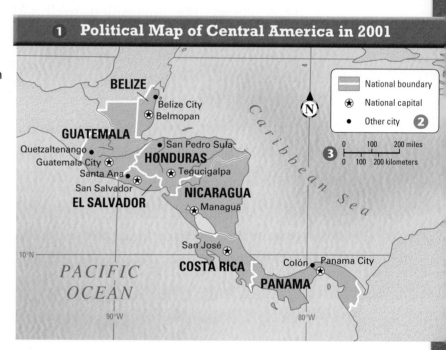

❶ Political Map of Central America in 2001

Key:
- National boundary
- ★ National capital
- • Other city ❷

❸ 0 — 100 — 200 miles / 0 — 100 — 200 kilometers

Central America		
Countries	Capitals	Other Cities
Guatemala	Guatemala City	Quetzaltenango
Belize	Belmopan	Belize City
Honduras	Tegucigalpa	San Pedro Sula
El Salvador	San Salvador	Santa Ana
Nicaragua	Managua	
Costa Rica	San José	
Panama	Panama City	Colón

Cuba Today

TERMS & NAMES
José Martí
Fidel Castro
Communism
malnutrition
Carnival

MAIN IDEA

After Cuba became independent, the country was ruled by a series of dictators. Since 1959, revolutionary leader Fidel Castro has ruled the nation.

WHY IT MATTERS NOW

At the turn of the century, Cuba was the only Communist country in the Western Hemisphere.

DATELINE

SIERRA MAESTRA, CUBA, 1956—Word has leaked out that revolutionary leader Fidel Castro has returned to Cuba. Three years ago, he received a 15-year prison sentence for leading an attack on the government. He was released early, a year ago, at which time he fled to Mexico to organize a group of revolutionaries.

Sources say that he and about 80 of his followers have returned to Cuba, though many of them were killed or captured upon arrival. The rest are hiding out in the Sierra Maestra, mountains in southeastern Cuba. People have been speculating about what kind of revolution may develop now that Castro is back in Cuba.

Place • While hiding deep in the Sierra Maestra, Castro is organizing his followers for revolution. ▲

Independence and Revolution

Long after Mexico and Central America gained independence, Cuba, the largest island in the Caribbean, still suffered Spanish rule. In 1895, Cubans led by **José Martí** continued fighting for the nation's independence. Three years later, the Spanish-American War reached the island. By the end of the war, Cuba had gained its independence from Spain. However, the United States maintained great influence over the nation.

A partnership between the United States and Cuba helped save Cubans from serious diseases, especially malaria and yellow fever. These illnesses killed or weakened many people each year.

In 1900, Dr. Carlos Finlay from Cuba and Dr. Walter Reed from the United States worked together to find the cause of yellow fever. They learned that mosquitoes like the one shown below spread the disease, just as they do malaria. To help put an end to these diseases, the U.S. Army sprayed chemicals that killed off the mosquitoes.

U.S. Ties to Cuba Before the Spanish-American War, the United States wanted to add Cuba to the nation. After the Spanish-American War ended, the United States appointed a military governor for Cuba. From 1899 to 1902, the U.S. Army stayed in Cuba to keep peace and help set up a new government. Most Cubans resented the U.S. presence. However, during these years, Cubans and U.S. soldiers did build many needed roads, bridges, and public schools.

In 1902, the U.S. Army withdrew from Cuba, which then became independent. However, the United States insisted that it still had the right to send soldiers to Cuba any time. The U.S. Navy also kept a large base for its ships at Guantánamo Bay.

Time of Dictatorship After independence, Cuba had a series of leaders. Some were elected, and some took power by force. Most governed as dictators. Cuba's dictators were careful to stay friendly with the United States. They welcomed U.S. businesses and tourists. Havana, Cuba's capital, offered tourists luxury hotels and casinos. Most Cubans, however, remained poor.

Revolution Takes Hold Time and again, Cubans protested against the dictators. In the 1950s, Cubans who were angry at the government found a leader for their cause. He was a young lawyer named **Fidel Castro**. Born in 1927 to a wealthy family, Castro was known for being a dynamic speaker. In college, he developed a deep interest in politics. By late 1956, Castro and a few followers had established headquarters for their revolution in the mountains of southeastern Cuba.

Reading
Social Studies

A. Drawing Conclusions If Cubans resented the U.S. presence in Cuba, why did their dictators stay friendly with the United States?

Culture • The two extremes of life in Cuba are apparent in this contrast of one of Havana's fancy hotels with one Cuban's simple dwelling. ▼

A few at a time, Cubans began to join Castro's small army. The rebel army won several battles against government troops. As the revolution grew stronger, Cuba's dictator, Fulgencio Batista (fool·HEHN·see·oh buh·TEES·tuh), fled the country on January 1, 1959. On January 8, 1959, Castro and his followers marched triumphantly into Havana. More than half a million Cubans greeted them joyfully. In a speech to the crowds, Castro promised that Cuba would have no more dictators.

The revolution had succeeded. Castro became the new commander-in-chief of Cuba's army. By July 1959, he had taken full control of Cuba's government.

A VOICE FROM CUBA

We cannot ever become dictators. Those who do not have the people with them must resort to being dictators. We have the love of the people, and because of that love, we will never turn away from our principles.

Fidel Castro

Cuba in the Cold War Castro took power in Cuba during the Cold War—a period of conflict between the United States and the Soviet Union. Castro needed the friendship of a powerful country. The Soviet Union was eager to have Cuba as an ally. It proved its interest in the smaller country by engaging in large-scale trade with Cuba as well as providing Cuba with weapons. This attention helped Castro choose to side with the Soviet Union in the Cold War.

Cuba Becomes a Communist Country The Soviet Union practiced an economic and political system known as **Communism.** Under this system, the government plans and controls a country's economy—in effect, the government owns the country's farms, factories, and businesses. Soon, Castro began to adopt Communist policies for Cuba's economy. His government took over the big sugar cane plantations, many of which had been owned by U.S. companies. His government then took over U.S. banks, oil refineries, and other businesses on the island.

Human-Environment Interaction • One of Castro's Communist policies was to take government control of farms, such as this one. ▼

In return, the United States cut off all trade with Cuba. Cubans could no longer sell their huge sugar crop to the United States. Instead, the Soviet Union bought Cuba's sugar. The Soviet government also sent weapons, farm machinery, food, and money to Cuba. In 1961, Castro declared that he and Cuba were Communist.

Castro as Dictator While the poor usually supported Castro's policies, many wealthier Cubans did not. They were particularly upset when he redistributed land so that no family or farm owned more than a certain amount. Castro also imprisoned people who spoke out against him. As a result, Cubans who opposed Castro began to flee to the United States and other countries. Over the years, hundreds of thousands of people left Cuba.

Castro has kept a tight hold on power for more than 40 years. Without ever being elected, he has remained head of state. His government has controlled all newspapers and radio and television stations. No one has been allowed to criticize his actions or the government. Despite his 1959 promise, Castro became a dictator.

Place • **In recent years, Cubans like these have continued to protest Castro's policies.** ▲

Reading
Social Studies

B. Clarifying What actions did Castro take that went against his 1959 promise?

Cuba's Economy

Since the Cuban revolution, the Cuban economy has changed in many ways. Since the collapse of the Soviet Union in 1991, Cuba has struggled to maintain its Communist way of life without Soviet aid.

Sugar and the Economy Sugar is Cuba's most important product in the world economy. The yearly sugar cane harvest is a key event for Cuba's economy. Once, workers with machetes cut the tough canes by hand. Then, with Soviet help, Castro's government bought huge machines to cut most of the cane. The cane harvest grew to record size.

While the Soviet Union was powerful, it traded oil, grain, and machinery with Cuba for sugar. Most of these products were worth more than sugar, so the Soviet Union was, in large part, supporting Cuba's economy.

Vocabulary

machete: large, wide-bladed knife

Living in Cuba

As with the economy, ways of life in Cuba have been greatly affected by Communism. Both education and health care reflect these changes.

Education After the revolution, Cuba's government set up many new schools. In the 1960s, teachers and even schoolchildren went into small villages to teach those who could not read or write. Many older people who had never had the chance to go to school learned to read for the first time.

Today, Cuban children must go to public school from ages 6 to 12. They can choose whether to continue their education after that. All schools are free, including college. Besides their academic subjects, students must take classes that teach Communist beliefs.

Health Care Like education, all health care in Cuba is paid for by the government. Cuba's health care system is probably the largest in Latin America. Every small village has a clinic.

However, Cuba had economic problems in the 1990s that affected both education and health care. Lack of fuel for buses and cars prevented some children from getting to school.

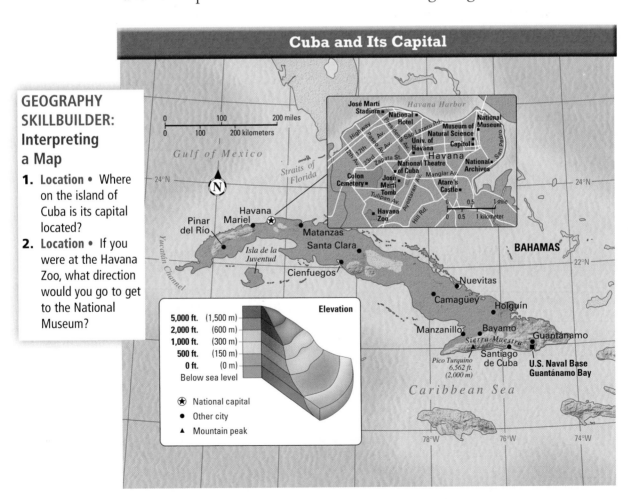

Cuba and Its Capital

GEOGRAPHY SKILLBUILDER: Interpreting a Map

1. **Location** • Where on the island of Cuba is its capital located?
2. **Location** • If you were at the Havana Zoo, what direction would you go to get to the National Museum?

Elevation

5,000 ft.	(1,500 m)
2,000 ft.	(600 m)
1,000 ft.	(300 m)
500 ft.	(150 m)
0 ft.	(0 m)
Below sea level	

★ National capital
● Other city
▲ Mountain peak

Culture • During Carnival, the air fills with the lively music played by musicians such as these drummers. ▲

Food shortages caused malnutrition. **Malnutrition** is poor health due to a lack of eating the right kinds of food. It often causes sickness. From the 1960s to the 1980s, Cuba had almost wiped out malnutrition. Since 1990, malnutrition has again become a problem in Cuba.

Arts, Sports, and Holidays

Both Castro's government and earlier dictators have placed strict limits on what artists, writers, and filmmakers may say in their work. As a result, some Cubans have fled to other countries in search of greater freedom of expression.

However, some art forms thrive in Cuba. Music is part of everyday life there. The unique sound of Cuban music combines African drums and Spanish guitars. Each different style and rhythm has its own name—son, mambo, cha-cha, rumba, salsa.

Sports are also popular in Cuba. The nation's favorite sport is baseball. Cuba's baseball team won a gold medal at the Olympics in 1996.

A favorite Cuban holiday, **Carnival,** takes place each year at the end of July. Cities and villages celebrate the end of the sugar harvest with festivals filled with music and dancing.

SECTION 3 ASSESSMENT

Terms & Names

1. Identify: (a) José Martí (b) Fidel Castro (c) Communism (d) malnutrition (e) Carnival

Taking Notes

2. Use a diagram like this one to show the stages Cuba's government has gone through.

Fight for independence → ☐ → ☐ →

Main Ideas

3. (a) What U.S. actions caused Cubans to resent the United States?

(b) Describe how Fidel Castro instituted Communism in Cuba.

(c) How was the Cuban economy once dependent on the Soviet Union?

Critical Thinking

4. **Drawing Conclusions**

Why might some Cubans think Castro has helped their nation and others think he has hurt it?

Think About

♦ Cuba's possible trade partners
♦ Cuba's health care system
♦ Cuba's education policies

ACTIVITY -OPTION- Reread the sections about the U.S. ties to Cuba. Then make a **poster** displaying information about the relationship.

Guatemala Today

MAIN IDEA

The establishment of a stable government in Guatemala has been a struggle, causing much suffering along the way.

WHY IT MATTERS NOW

Guatemala's increased stability has improved its relationship with its neighbors, such as the United States.

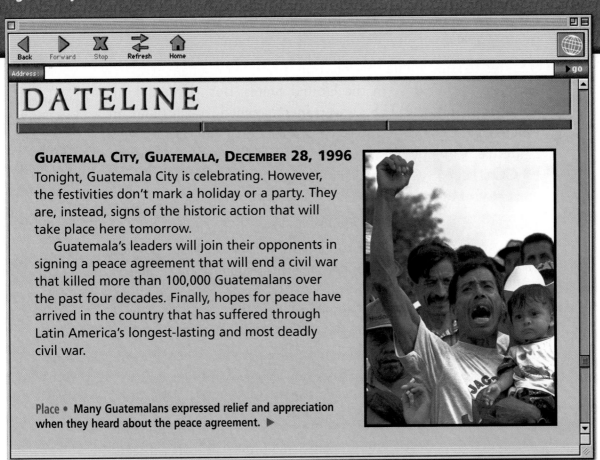

DATELINE

GUATEMALA CITY, GUATEMALA, DECEMBER 28, 1996
Tonight, Guatemala City is celebrating. However, the festivities don't mark a holiday or a party. They are, instead, signs of the historic action that will take place here tomorrow.

Guatemala's leaders will join their opponents in signing a peace agreement that will end a civil war that killed more than 100,000 Guatemalans over the past four decades. Finally, hopes for peace have arrived in the country that has suffered through Latin America's longest-lasting and most deadly civil war.

Place • Many Guatemalans expressed relief and appreciation when they heard about the peace agreement. ▶

History of Government

In 1821, along with three other Central American states, Guatemala gained independence from Spain. It broke from the other states in 1839 to become the nation we know today. Between 1821 and 1839, peasants in the mountains had staged revolts against the government. In 1837, an uneducated farmer, **Rafael Carrera** (rah·fy·EHL kuh·REHR·uh), led a revolt and emerged as a new leader for Guatemala. In 1854, he took over the presidency, which he held until his death in 1865.

From Dictatorial Rule to Reforms After Carrera died, a steady flow of dictators filled Guatemala's presidency. In 1944, a set of military officers revolted and won control of the nation. One of these officers, **Jacobo Arbenz Guzmán** (YAH·koh·boh AHR·bayns gooz·MAHN), saw the need for social reforms in Guatemala. When he became president in 1951, Guzmán decided to develop a market economy and raise Guatemala's standard of living. Guzmán also redistributed 1.5 million acres of land to 100,000 families. As in Mexico, the goal of redistributing land was to give many more people access to land that they could farm.

Place • Born in 1913, Jacobo Arbenz Guzmán was president of Guatemala from 1951 to 1954. ▲

U.S. Ties to Guatemala Serious opposition to Guzmán's redistribution program arose in the United States. Both United Fruit Company and the U.S. government owned much land in Guatemala. Guzmán established a policy of giving farmers any land that was not already being used. Eighty-five percent of UFCO's land in Guatemala was unused. Thus, UFCO was at great risk of losing that land.

The United States Steps In The United States took action in 1954. Accusing Guzmán of supporting Communism—a political system that the United States believed threatened national safety— the U.S. Central Intelligence Agency (CIA) supported an invasion of Guatemala's capital, Guatemala City. A Guatemalan colonel, Carlos Castillo Armas (CAR·lohs kah·STEE·yoh AR·mahs), led the attack. A frightened Guzmán quickly gave in. A new government, backed by the United States, took control of Guatemala.

Place • Rebel forces in Guatemala have included thousands of *ladinos* and Maya people. ▼

Civil War Takes Hold After 1954, Guatemala's government was ruled mainly by military officers. During much of this era, a civil war raged between government forces and rebels who opposed the government. Many people who expressed disagreement with government policy were murdered. More than 100,000 Guatemalans were killed or kidnapped before a peace agreement was reached in 1996.

Reading
Social Studies

A. Synthesizing Given the opposition to the new government after Guzmán's overthrow, do you think it continued social reforms?

Guatemala's Government Today

Guatemala's current constitution was written in 1985. It established the nation's government as a democratic republic with three branches. They are executive, legislative, and judicial.

Government's Three Branches A president heads Guatemala's executive branch. He or she is elected by the people every four years and may not be reelected. The president appoints a cabinet, or a group of advisers, to carry out the government's work.

Guatemala's legislative branch is called Congress. It has 113 members who are elected to four-year terms. Guatemala's Congress is unicameral, or has one chamber. Members of Congress may be reelected.

Guatemala's judicial branch has different levels of courts, somewhat like the United States. Unlike U.S. Supreme Court justices, whom the President appoints to serve for as long as they choose, Guatemala's Supreme Court judges are elected to five-year terms.

State and Local Governments Guatemala is a federal republic, so the national government shares power with state and local governments. Governors head Guatemala's 22 states, called *departamentos* (deh·pahr·tah·MEHN·taws). The president appoints each of the governors. Mayors elected by popular vote oversee the city governments.

Location • Since the 1930s, Guatemala City's National Palace has housed the government's offices. ▲

Guatemala's Economy

At the turn of the century, Guatemala had the largest gross domestic product (GDP) in Central America. It also had the fastest growing GDP in the region.

Agriculture Guatemala's dominant industry is agriculture, which employs more than half of its work force. The nation's economy largely relies on the export of agricultural products. Since 1870, coffee has been Guatemala's leading export. Other agricultural exports include sugar, a spice called cardamom, and bananas.

Banana production began in the early 1900s, when U.S. companies built banana plantations in Guatemala. These fruit companies also developed railroads, ports, and communication systems in order to transport the bananas to foreign markets.

Other Parts of the Economy Guatemala also relies on manufacturing to bring in money. Food, beverages, and clothing are among its manufactured goods. These goods are sold both within Guatemala and as exports to other countries. While other Central American nations purchase many of Guatemala's manufactured goods, the United States purchases more of Guatemala's exports than any other country does.

In past years, Guatemala's economy has boomed with the sale of both textiles and clothing. Also, new nontraditional agricultural products, such as cut flowers and winter fruits, are selling quite well on the international market. Tourism is also a strong industry in Guatemala, which is home to many ancient Maya ruins.

Living in Guatemala

More than half of Guatemala's people are Maya. The rest are *ladinos*. In Guatemala, *ladinos* are either of mixed Maya and Spanish ancestry, or they are of Maya ancestry but no longer practice Maya ways or speak Maya languages. Like the ancient Maya, most of Guatemala's Maya today work in agriculture and live in small rural villages. They speak Maya languages, though many of them also speak Spanish. They wear traditional clothing, much of which they weave by hand.

Education Guatemalan children are required to attend school from the age of 7 through 13. However, about one-third do not. Most of these children live in rural areas that have no schools. Only 15 percent of Guatemalans attend high school.

Human-Environment Interaction • Bananas are produced in mass quantity on Guatemala's many banana plantations. ▲

Reading Social Studies

B. Clarifying Does Guatemala have a single-product economy? Why or why not?

Place • Standing nearly 150 feet high, this Maya temple at Tikal is one of Guatemala's major tourist attractions. ▼

Two Sides of Guatemala Daily life in Guatemala is a matter of extremes. On the one hand, rural Guatemalans have few of the comforts that North Americans take for granted, such as indoor bathrooms, running water, and electricity. Outside the cities, most homes are very small, and many have dirt floors.

On the other hand, urban Guatemalans live in modern homes, attend schools and universities, and go to theaters, museums, and restaurants. Many of the cultural influences in the cities, such as movies, restaurant chains, clothing styles, magazines, cars, and television programs, come from foreign countries. The cultural influences in the rural areas are much more local in origin.

SECTION 4 ASSESSMENT

Terms & Names

1. Identify: (a) Rafael Carrera   (b) Jacobo Arbenz Guzmán   (c) *departamento*

Taking Notes

2. Use a table like this one to keep track of the sequence of events in Guatemala's history.

Year	Event
1837	
1839	
1944	
1951	
1954	
1985	
1996	

Main Ideas

3. (a) Why did the United States feel threatened when Jacobo Arbenz Guzmán established his policy of land redistribution?

   (b) After 1954, how did the Guatemalan government treat people who expressed disagreement with its policies?

   (c) What is Guatemala's leading export?

Critical Thinking

4. **Synthesizing**

   What is the impact of having a powerful nation, such as the United States, be the largest purchaser of Guatemala's exports?

   Think About

   • the role of exports in Guatemala's economy

   • U.S. interventions in Guatemala

**ACTIVITY
-OPTION-**

Write a **paragraph** explaining three facts about Guatemala that you did not know before you read this section.

TERMS & NAMES

Explain the significance of each of the following:

1. West Indies
2. dependency
3. mulatto
4. *ladino*
5. dictator
6. single-product economy
7. diversify
8. Fidel Castro
9. Communism
10. Rafael Carrera

REVIEW QUESTIONS

Establishing Independence *(pages 203–207)*

1. Why did the United States want to build the Panama Canal?
2. What event freed the Caribbean Islands from Spanish rule?

Building Economies and Cultures *(pages 208–213)*

3. What risk did Caribbean islanders face by having single-product economies?
4. What two crops did Central American economies depend on before the countries diversified their economies?

Cuba Today *(pages 215–220)*

5. Why did hundreds of thousands of people flee from Cuba to the United States after Castro took over?
6. How did Cuba's relationship with the Soviet Union affect Cuba?

Guatemala Today *(pages 221–225)*

7. Why did Jacobo Arbenz Guzmán's program of land redistribution upset people in the United States?
8. What are the cultural backgrounds of Guatemala's *ladinos*?

CRITICAL THINKING

Identifying Problems and Solutions

1. Using your completed chart from Reading Social Studies, p. 202, choose one issue, such as dictatorship or colonization, and summarize the problems with it. Then summarize the solutions to the problems.

Drawing Conclusions

2. How do you think Fidel Castro's control of newspapers and television and radio stations has helped keep him in power?

Contrasting

3. Contrast the fates of Native Americans in the Caribbean Islands and in Central America after Europeans took over.

Visual Summary

1 Establishing Independence

- People in Central America and the Caribbean fought first for independence and then for democracy.
  - Central America's people are mostly *ladinos* and Native Americans, while the Caribbean's are largely of African or European descent.

2 Building Economies and Cultures

- The countries of the region had to diversify their economies so they would be more stable.
- The region's languages, religions, and music were influenced by the cultures of the colonizers, the enslaved Africans, and the Native Americans.

3 Cuba Today

- In 1959, Fidel Castro led a revolution and took over Cuba's government. He has ruled ever since.
- Throughout the 1900s, both the United States and the Soviet Union influenced events in Cuba.

4 Guatemala Today

- After decades of struggle, Guatemala's government has become more stable.
- Guatemala's economy relies heavily on agriculture, especially coffee production.
- More than half of Guatemala's people are Maya. The rest are *ladinos*.

SOCIAL STUDIES SKILLBUILDER

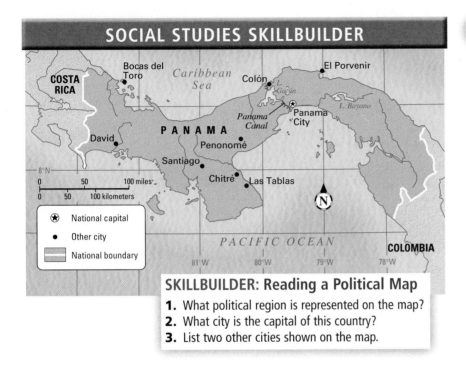

Legend:
- ⊛ National capital
- • Other city
- ▨ National boundary

SKILLBUILDER: Reading a Political Map

1. What political region is represented on the map?
2. What city is the capital of this country?
3. List two other cities shown on the map.

FOCUS ON GEOGRAPHY

1. Place • Look at the map. What physical features do you think would attract tourists to Belize?

2. Human-Environment Interaction • What human-made features might tourists like to see in Belize?

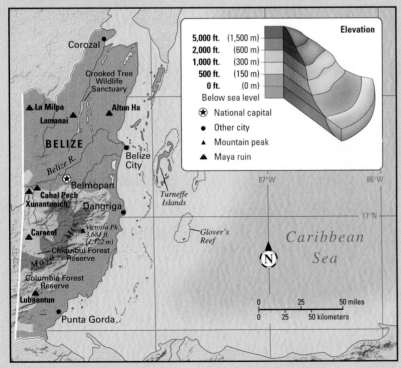

CHAPTER PROJECTS

Interdisciplinary Activity: Language Arts

Writing a Letter Choose one of the Caribbean Islands, such as Grenada or Cuba, to research. Then imagine that you traveled to that island. Write a letter to a friend describing what you saw when you got there. Include photographs or drawings to show your friend what you saw.

Cooperative Learning Activity

Creating a Bulletin Board In a group of three to five students, create a bulletin board about one of the countries in the Caribbean or Central America. Include maps, charts, and pictures to provide different kinds of information about the country.

- Describe the climate of the country.
- List the natural resources that are found there.
- Provide information about the cities.
- Include information about politics and the economy.

ⓘ INTERNET ACTIVITY

Use the Internet to do research about cultural heritage in Central America and the Caribbean. Focus on one country, such as Jamaica or Belize, and how its people have preserved cultural traditions from the past.

Writing About Culture Write a report of your findings. Include any illustrations you found, or make your own drawings. List the Web sites you used to prepare your report.

For Internet links to support this activity, go to

RESEARCH LINKS
CLASSZONE.COM

South America

SOUTH AMERICA

Location The Amazon River winds eastward from the Andes through South America for nearly 4,000 miles.

How has movement from rural to urban areas affected South America?

Movement • Some of the largest and fastest-growing cities in the world are in South America—for example, São Paulo, Brazil, and Buenos Aires, Argentina. Since the mid-1900s, people have been moving from rural to urban areas. Today, three-quarters of all South Americans live in cities.

Although cities often offer more jobs, they also have serious drawbacks. For example, not everyone in South America's cities can find jobs. Others cannot find housing. In some cities, such as Rio de Janeiro, Brazil, some people live in extreme poverty. Because of problems like these, many people, including professionals such as teachers and doctors, have left South America for the United States and other countries that may offer better opportunities.

What do you think?

◆ Why do South Americans leave the countryside and move to cities?

◆ How might South America change when skilled professionals, such as doctors, move to other countries?

CHAPTER 9

READING SOCIAL STUDIES

BEFORE YOU READ

▶▶ *What Do You Know?*

Before you read the chapter, consider what you already know about South America. What do you know about the region's history? What do you know about its role in the world's economy and culture? In particular, what do you know about Brazil and Peru? You may know that Brazil is famous for its successes in soccer. Think about what else you have read or seen on the news or in sports reports. Also consider connections to your own life: Have you ever heard music from South America, such as salsa?

▶▶ *What Do You Want to Know?*

Decide what else you want to know about South America. In your notebook, record what you hope to learn from this chapter.

Region • **This Andean girl plays the region's music, called** *huayno.* ▲

READ AND TAKE NOTES

Reading Strategy: Making Generalizations

Making generalizations is a useful strategy for understanding themes in social studies. A generalization is a conclusion supported by facts. Use the chart of generalizations below to better understand events and situations in South America.

- Copy the chart into your notebook.
- As you read the chapter, look for facts that support each generalization. Examples may be found in more than one section of the chapter.
- Beside each generalization, record the facts that support it.

Place • **People crowd the streets of São Paulo in Brazil.** ▲

Generalizations	Facts
Independence led to different types of governments in South America.	
South American countries are trying to cooperate with one another and with the United States.	
Geography and politics affect the economies of South America.	
Urban growth presents serious problems for some South American countries.	
South America's different cultures contribute to world culture.	

Establishing Independence

MAIN IDEA

After 300 years of rule by Spain and Portugal, South Americans won independence and established their own nations.

WHY IT MATTERS NOW

Because the United States has close economic and political ties with South America, it is important to understand the history of the region.

DATELINE

EXTRA

CAJAMARCA, THE ANDES, 1533

Word has just arrived that the Inca ruler, Atahualpa, was executed by a small group of Spanish adventurers. A few weeks ago, Atahualpa's messengers informed him that the Spanish were coming. Atahualpa commanded 30,000 warriors and saw no reason to worry. However, the Spanish, with cannons and guns, killed around 4,000 of Atahualpa's guards and then captured the Inca king. Atahualpa tried to buy his freedom, offering the Spanish a stack of gold 9 feet high in a room measuring 17 feet by 22 feet. The Spanish accepted the gold—and then executed Atahualpa anyway. Now many fear for the future of the Inca Empire.

Culture • The portrait on the left shows Atahualpa, while the one on the right shows Pizarro. ▲

Europeans Arrive in South America

In 1531, Spanish explorer Francisco Pizarro landed on the coast of what is now the South American country of Peru. He had with him horses, guns, cannons, and about 200 soldiers. His forces began the long climb up into the Andes Mountains, following the Inca road that led to the city of Cajamarca (KAH·hah·MAHR·kah).

Europeans Establish Control When Pizarro first encountered the Inca, he found a kingdom weakened by a bitter civil war. Pizarro quickly captured and executed the Inca ruler, Atahualpa. The Inca Empire soon fell under Spanish control.

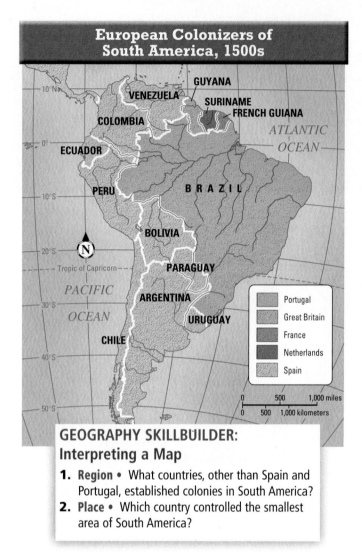

European Colonizers of South America, 1500s

GUYANA
VENEZUELA
SURINAME
FRENCH GUIANA
COLOMBIA
ATLANTIC OCEAN
ECUADOR
B R A Z I L
PERU
BOLIVIA
PARAGUAY
Tropic of Capricorn
PACIFIC OCEAN
ARGENTINA
URUGUAY
CHILE

Portugal
Great Britain
France
Netherlands
Spain

0   500   1,000 miles
0   500   1,000 kilometers

GEOGRAPHY SKILLBUILDER:
Interpreting a Map

1. **Region** • What countries, other than Spain and Portugal, established colonies in South America?
2. **Place** • Which country controlled the smallest area of South America?

Meanwhile, Portugal had claimed what is now Brazil, and so the Portuguese began to settle the region. However, dense rain forests prevented much exploration of the region's interior. The Portuguese therefore built most of their settlements along the Atlantic Coast.

Colonial South America Many Spanish and Portuguese settlers soon made their way to South America. As happened throughout the New World, the arrival of the Europeans led to the deaths of many Native Americans. Millions died from disease or overwork. As the Native American population shrank, the Europeans imported enslaved Africans to work mainly on the large sugar cane plantations in Brazil.

For nearly 300 years, Europeans ruled much of South America. Spain and Portugal between them claimed most of the land. Ships loaded with South American silver, gold, and sugar regularly sailed to these two countries. Both, especially Spain, grew enormously wealthy from their South American colonies.

Independence

In the early 1800s, Spain and Portugal were still taking most of the wealth out of the South American colonies. People of Spanish or Portuguese descent born in South America wanted to share in the political and economic power. They were encouraged by the American Revolution in 1776 and the French Revolution

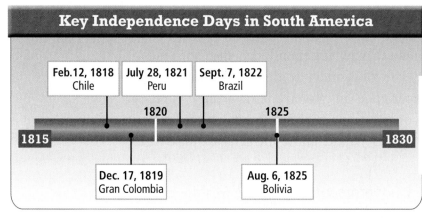

Key Independence Days in South America

Feb.12, 1818 Chile	July 28, 1821 Peru	Sept. 7, 1822 Brazil	

1820   1825

1815   **1830**

Dec. 17, 1819 Gran Colombia   Aug. 6, 1825 Bolivia

SKILLBUILDER: Reading a Time Line

1. For each country on the time line, what event occurred on the date given?
2. On what day did Brazil achieve independence?

in 1789. At the same time, the *mestizos* and mulattos wanted to bring about change because they were often treated no better than slaves. South Americans soon decided to fight for independence.

Gaining Independence Beginning in 1810, two generals led a series of wars for independence. One was **Simón Bolívar** (see·MOHN boh·LEE·var), whose leadership freed the northern parts of South America. The other was **José de San Martín** (san mahr·TEEN). He was responsible for defeating Spanish forces in the south. By 1825, nearly all of Spanish South America was independent.

Meanwhile, Brazil gained its independence without a major war. When the French general Napoleon Bonaparte invaded Portugal in 1807, the Portuguese royal family fled to Brazil. After Napoleon's later defeat, the Portuguese king returned to Portugal in 1821. He left his son Pedro to be regent of Brazil. When the Brazilians demanded their freedom in 1822, Pedro agreed. Brazil then named Pedro its emperor.

Reading
Social Studies

A. Recognizing Important Details How did Brazil gain its independence differently from other South American countries?

Biography

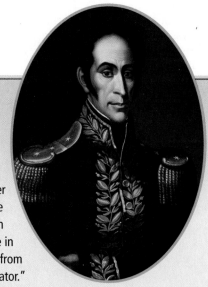

Simón Bolívar Simón Bolívar (shown at right) was born in Caracas, Venezuela, in 1783. As a teenager, Bolívar lived in Spain. He was influenced by the European Enlightenment and the philosophers Voltaire and Rousseau. A dream of freedom and independence for Hispanic America stirred Bolívar's soul, and he returned to South America.

Bolívar became a leader of the revolution in Venezuela in 1810. His clever military tactics led to victory over the Spanish and the creation of the republic of Gran Colombia, which included what are now Colombia, Panama, Venezuela, and Ecuador. Bolívar became president of Gran Colombia and continued fighting farther south. Victorious there, he soon became the president of Peru and Bolivia, which was named for him. Because of his role in gaining South American independence from Spain, Bolívar is often called "the Liberator." He died in Colombia in 1830.

Governments of South America

However, South America's new independence did not lead to a stable, fair society, as revolutionary leaders had hoped. These leaders had little experience in government. Many of them wanted to establish constitutions that set limits on the powers of government. Doing this would allow citizens to participate in government.

Unlimited Governments However, wealthy citizens and former Spanish officials in South America wanted to keep their property and power. They did not want all citizens to have a say in government. To maintain order and to protect their interests, the powerful often gave control of the government to the military. This frequently resulted in unlimited governments, in which one person or one group held total power. In other cases, military leaders used their armies to take over limited governments in South America. By the 1990s, however, the majority of governments in South America were democratic.

Place • General Augusto Pinochet (pee·noh·CHEHT) ruled Chile as a military dictator from 1974 to 1990. ▲

South American Cooperation Simón Bolívar tried to create a united South America—a nation of states like the United States. Although he was not successful, in the late 1800s the U.S. government began encouraging Pan-American unity. *Pan* means "all," so **Pan-American** means "all of the Americas."

In 1948, Latin American nations joined with the United States to form the **Organization of American States** (OAS). The OAS promotes economic cooperation, social justice, and the equality of all people. It encourages democracy within its member nations. For example, OAS officials observe elections to make sure they are run fairly. The organization also helps settle conflicts among its members. In 1979, the OAS established a special court to protect human rights in its member countries.

The countries of South America will probably never join together in the way that Simón Bolívar envisioned. They are, however, working together to achieve justice and a better life for all their people.

Region • An OAS official and a U.S. government official are shown here using a map of South America to discuss Pan-American issues. ▼

The People of South America

Until the 1800s, immigrants to South America came mostly from Spain and Portugal. During the 1880s, South America attracted many more European immigrants.

Immigrants Influence Society The new immigrants helped build South America's economy by establishing a variety of industries. Also, as all immigrants do, they brought their own customs to their new home. For example, the British introduced the game of football (which people in the United States call soccer), and it quickly became a popular sport across South America.

South America's Population Today There are many ethnic groups within South America's population—Native Americans, descendants of Europeans or of enslaved Africans, and people of mixed ancestry. Some of these groups live in particular regions, while others are more widespread. For example, many Africans live in the tropical lowlands where their enslaved ancestors worked. Native Americans make up a large part of the population in the Andean nations of Peru, Bolivia, and Ecuador. The majority of South Americans, however, are either *mestizos* or mulattos.

Region • Welsh settlers started sheep ranches in South America, while Swiss immigrants in Brazil developed the cheese industry. ▼

SECTION 1 ASSESSMENT

Terms & Names

1. **Identify:** (a) Simón Bolívar   (b) José de San Martín   (c) Pan-American
   (d) Organization of American States

Taking Notes

2. Use a chart like this one to list the contributions to South America's history made by the four main groups from which the people of South America are descended.

Group	Contributions
Native Americans	
European Colonists	
Enslaved Africans	
Other Immigrants	

Main Ideas

3. (a) From what South American products did European nations profit?

   (b) How has South America's population changed since the 1500s?

   (c) What challenges have many South American governments faced in recent years?

Critical Thinking

4. **Synthesizing**

   What challenges do you think South Americans faced in their fights for independence?

   Think About

   • differences in wealth between the colonial rulers and the general population

   • who held political power

   • living conditions

Imagine you work for the OAS. Make a **poster** that highlights the benefits the organization offers its members.

Explore the Mysteries of Chichén Itzá

You are a movie director making a documentary film called *Mysteries of the Maya*. You are shooting your film at the ruins of Chichén Itzá, a city of stone deep in the jungle of Mexico's Yucatán Peninsula. Many things about the Maya culture are still a mystery. You want to inform your audience about Chichén Itzá, but you also want to make them feel the mood of the place—awesome and mysterious.

COOPERATIVE LEARNING On these pages you will find challenges that you and your crew will face in making the documentary. Working with your crew, decide which one of these problems you will solve. Divide the work among crew members. Look for helpful information in the Data File. Keep in mind that you will present your solution to the class.

LANGUAGE ARTS CHALLENGE

"As darkness falls, colored lights play on the buildings . . ."

While your film crew visits Chichén Itzá, you are awed by the nighttime "light and sound show." As darkness falls, colored lights play on the buildings, and a narrator tells the Maya's story. How can you include this scene in your film? How can you convey the mood of this site to a TV audience? Choose one of these options. Use the Data File for help.

ACTIVITIES

1. Write a brief (60-second) promotional advertisement to be shown during TV station breaks. Include sketches or descriptions of photographs or art you will use in the commercial. If possible, think of background music, too.
2. As a member of the film crew, write a journal entry describing your experiences at the light and sound show.

CHICHÉN ITZÁ

- **City was founded by Maya** about sixth century A.D.

- The name, which means **"mouth of the wells of Itzá,"** refers to the site's two deep natural wells, or cenotes. The Itzá were a Maya group.

- One **cenote** supplied water. The other, about 200 feet across, was sacred to the rain god. Human sacrifices, mostly young people, were thrown into it, along with gold and jade ornaments.

- The Maya had many gods. **Chac** was the rain god. Kukulcan was pictured as a feathered serpent.

- Major buildings—**Pyramid of Kukulcan** (El Castillo), **Temple of the Warriors, Great Ball Court**— were built about A.D. 900–1200.

- City was abandoned about A.D. 1450.

TEMPLE OF KUKULCAN/ EL CASTILLO ("THE CASTLE")

- Four-sided pyramid represents the **Maya calendar** in several ways.

- Four steep stairways, with 91 steps each, climb each side of the pyramid. Including the top platform, the **steps total 365.** There are 18 flat platforms—the number of months in the Maya calendar.

- At the **spring and fall equinoxes,** sunlight falls on one staircase in a pattern that looks like a serpent creeping down the pyramid.

SCIENCE CHALLENGE

"El Castillo, the pyramid of the serpent god"

From the top of El Castillo, the pyramid of the serpent god Kukulcan, you can see the stone ruins and the jungle surrounding them. This great temple-pyramid is the heart of Chichén Itzá. Maya priests, who were also scientists, studied the skies and made an accurate calendar. This pyramid reflects their knowledge of astronomy. How will your film explain this knowledge? Use one of these options to present information. Look in the Data File for help.

ACTIVITIES

1. Draw a diagram of El Castillo. Write a speech in which the film's narrator uses the diagram to explain the significance of the pyramid's structure and location.
2. Draw a storyboard to show what happens at El Castillo during the spring equinox.

To learn more about Chichén Itzá, visit

RESEARCH LINKS
CLASSZONE.COM

Activity Wrap-Up

As a group, review the way you solved the challenge you chose. Organize your solution and present it to the class.

Building Economies and Cultures

TERMS & NAMES
free-trade zone
economic indicator
urbanization

MAIN IDEA

While South America's countries work to overcome challenges to their economies, their cultures flourish.

WHY IT MATTERS NOW

Cultural elements from South America, such as music, literature, and dance, are popular around the world.

DATELINE

BOGOTÁ, COLOMBIA, SEPTEMBER 9, 2000— All over Bogotá, people are talking about last week's meeting in Brazil's capital, Brasília. It marked the first-ever meeting of the presidents of South America's 12 nations.

Many people here say that holding this meeting in Brazil's capital indicates that Brazil is going to take a leadership role in the region. As one Colombian official in Bogotá said: "We have

Region • Brazil's president, Fernando Henrique Cardoso, sponsored the 12-nation meeting. ▲

serious economic and political problems here. Brazil, the biggest and richest nation in South America, needs to exercise leadership." Indeed, it seems that Brazil has decided to do just that.

Geography and Trade in South America

Many South American nations have found that working together results in greater economic opportunity. Partly this is because they face similar challenges and possibilities. A common factor influencing many of the region's economies is geography. South America's physical geography presents the region with both transportation barriers and transportation corridors.

Barriers South America's transportation barriers have interfered with trade and contacts with other cultures. For example, Portuguese explorers had trouble penetrating the dense Amazon rain forest. Because of this, they built their settlements along the coastline. Today, rain forests and rugged regions such as the Andes still prevent easy travel across the continent.

Corridors South America also has transportation corridors, such as the Amazon River system. Before the Europeans arrived, Native Americans canoed along the Amazon and its tributaries. Today, oceangoing vessels enter the Amazon system on Brazil's north coast. They carry goods such as food, clothing, and tools. They bring back lumber, rubber, animal skins, Brazil nuts, and other raw materials for shipment overseas.

Movement • **Ships like this one can carry goods inland on the Amazon for more than 2,000 miles.** ▲

Spotlight on CULTURE

Gabriela Mistral Chilean poet Gabriela Mistral (1889–1957; shown at right) used poetry to express her deep feelings for the people and land of South America, as in this poem, "Chilean Earth." She particularly loved children, and their rhymes and lullabies influenced her writing.

South Americans and people around the world greatly admire Mistral's work. As the first South American to win the Nobel Prize in Literature, she became a symbol of the hopes and dreams of a whole continent.

THINKING CRITICALLY

1. **Drawing Conclusions**
   What about Chile does Mistral celebrate in this poem?

2. **Forming and Supporting Opinions**
   Why do you think Mistral's poetry inspired South Americans?

Chilean Earth

We dance on Chilean earth
more beautiful than Lia and Raquel:
the earth that kneads men,
their lips and hearts without bitterness.

The land most green with orchards,
the land most blond with grain,
the land most red with grapevines,
how sweetly it brushes our feet!

Its dust molded our cheeks,
Its rivers, our laughter,
and it kisses our feet with a melody
that makes my mother sigh.
For the sake of its beauty,
we want to light up the fields with song.
It is free,
and for freedom we want
to bathe its face in music.

Tomorrow we will open its rocks;
we will create vineyards and orchards;
tomorrow we will exalt its people.
Today we need only to dance!

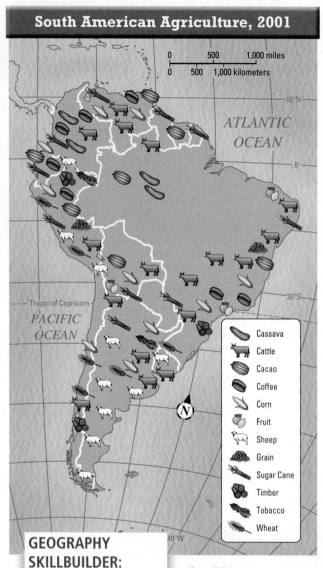

South American Agriculture, 2001

0   500   1,000 miles
0   500   1,000 kilometers

ATLANTIC
OCEAN

10°N

0°

Tropic of Capricorn

PACIFIC
OCEAN

20°S

N

	Cassava
	Cattle
	Cacao
	Coffee
	Corn
	Fruit
	Sheep
	Grain
	Sugar Cane
	Timber
	Tobacco
	Wheat

40°W

GEOGRAPHY SKILLBUILDER: Interpreting a Map

1. **Place** • Name an agricultural product from southern South America.
2. **Region** • Name an agricultural product that is produced in many parts of South America.

Products and Industries of South America

The rich natural resources of South America include abundant minerals and fertile land. However, few South American countries have fully developed their natural resources.

Mineral Resources Under the surface of South America's land lie many precious minerals—including gold, iron ore, lead, petroleum, tin, and copper. Many South American countries mine these minerals for export. For example, Chile mostly mines copper, Bolivia has a great amount of tin, and Colombia supplies the world with emeralds.

Agricultural Products South America is not only rich in mineral resources, but it also boasts some of the largest farms in the world. These farms produce goods for export, such as beef, grain, sugar, wool, bananas, and coffee. However, most of South America's farms are small. On these farms, individual farmers struggle to grow even enough food to feed their families. Many poor farmers have given up and moved to cities, hoping to find jobs there.

Manufacturing The most important South American industrial countries are Venezuela, Chile, Argentina, and Brazil. In fact, Brazil is one of the most important industrial nations in the world. It manufactures enough cars and trucks to supply the entire continent. Brazil also manufactures computers, televisions, and airplanes. In other South American countries, manufactured goods include shoes, furniture, beverages, and textiles.

Economic Cooperation Lack of funding prevents many South American countries from developing manufacturing. To improve their economies, countries may cooperate economically. For example, in 1994, the heads of 34 North and South American countries met in Miami, Florida, at the first Summit of the Americas.

Reading
Social Studies

A. Contrasting How do South America's small farms and large farms differ?

Reading
Social Studies

B. Making Inferences How do you think a high literacy rate can help boost a country's economy?

There, they agreed to create the huge Free-Trade Zone of the Americas, which would include almost every country in North and South America by the year 2005. In a **free-trade zone,** people and goods move across borders without being taxed. Many South Americans are confident that the Free-Trade Zone of the Americas will lead to greater prosperity in the region.

Economic Indicators Economic cooperation among nations can be challenging if some economies are strong and others are weak. Differences can be measured by **economic indicators,** statistics that show how a country's economy is doing. The literacy rate shows the percentage of a country's people who can read and write at an elementary school level. Life expectancy, or the average age to which people in a country live, gives clues about a country's health care and nutrition.

Country	Literacy Rate	Life Expectancy
Argentina	96%	75 years
Bolivia	83%	64 years
Brazil	85%	63 years
Chile	95%	76 years
Colombia	91%	70 years
Ecuador	90%	71 years
Guyana	98%	64 years
Paraguay	92%	74 years
Peru	89%	70 years
Suriname	93%	71 years
Uruguay	97%	75 years
Venezuela	91%	73 years

SKILLBUILDER: Interpreting a Chart

1. Which nation has the highest literacy rate? Which has the lowest?
2. What is the life expectancy in Brazil?

Daily Life in South America

As with all regions, South America is home to both urban and rural areas. Many of the urban areas are enormous. City populations include some very wealthy people and many middle-class people who work in government or business. Millions more, however, live in extreme poverty. Nevertheless, South Americans enjoy a proud tradition of music and literature.

The Urban Setting For the past 50 years or so, South America has experienced major **urbanization,** meaning that many people have moved from the countryside to cities. Multiple factors caused this movement to occur. For example, the growth of manufacturing created more jobs in cities. At the same time, many rural people lived in poverty, without enough land to support their families. The promise of jobs, schools, and health services drew them to cities.

Today, several South American cities rank among the largest in the world. In 2000, São Paulo (sown POW·loh) in Brazil was home to nearly 18 million people, and Buenos Aires (BWAY·nos AIR·ays) in Argentina had nearly 13 million people.

Houses cannot be built quickly enough to keep up with the growing number of people. Large slums surround South America's biggest cities. In these areas, people live in shacks of cardboard, wood scraps, or tin. They often have no electricity or running water.

The Arts Despite the terrible poverty of millions, the arts in South America have thrived. The region's literature is admired throughout the world. The Nobel Prize in Literature has been given to three South Americans—Chilean poets Gabriela Mistral (mih·STRAHL) and Pablo Neruda (neh·ROO·duh), and Colombian novelist Gabriel García Márquez (gar·SEE·uh MAR·kez). Many South American poets and writers express their unique cultural heritage in their work. South American novelists also founded a literary style, magical realism, in which everyday reality mixes with fantasy.

Music, too, is an important part of the culture of South America. The traditional music of the Andean regions, called *huayno,* is played on flutes and drums. Some forms of music, such as salsa, have African roots. As more and more South Americans move to urban areas, musicians there are combining the traditional musical styles with rock and other popular types of music from Europe and North America.

Region •
Peruvians play *huayno* on flutes like the one this girl is using. ▲

SECTION 2 ASSESSMENT

Terms & Names
1. Identify: (a) free-trade zone   (b) economic indicator   (c) urbanization

Taking Notes

2. Use a spider map like this one to show six factors that have influenced South America's economic progress.

South America's Economic Progress

Main Ideas

3. (a) Name one geographic feature that is a transportation barrier and one that is a transportation corridor.

(b) List five of South America's important natural resources.

(c) Name the three South Americans who have won the Nobel Prize in Literature.

Critical Thinking

4. Identifying Problems

What challenges do South American countries face in building strong economies?

Think About

- physical geography
- the needs of a rapidly growing population
- the effects of urbanization

ACTIVITY -OPTION-

Look at the physical map of South America on page 142. Write a short **description** of a way to overcome one of South America's transportation barriers.

Brazil Today

TERMS & NAMES
inflation
São Paulo
Rio de Janeiro
Brasília
Carnival

MAIN IDEA

As the largest country in South America, Brazil has achieved economic success while facing challenges such as unemployment.

WHY IT MATTERS NOW

Brazil's huge land area, population, and economic success enable it to influence its neighbors in South America and North America.

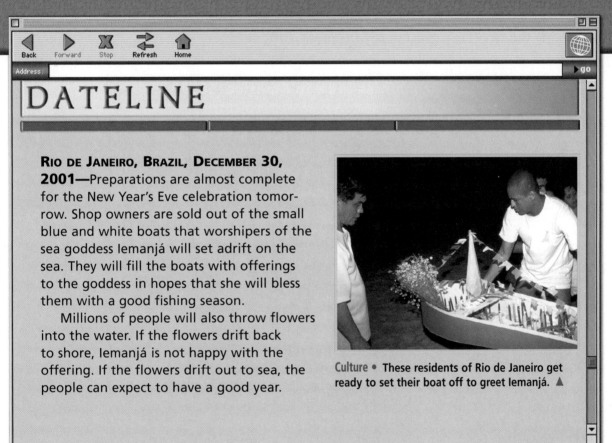

DATELINE

RIO DE JANEIRO, BRAZIL, DECEMBER 30, 2001—Preparations are almost complete for the New Year's Eve celebration tomorrow. Shop owners are sold out of the small blue and white boats that worshipers of the sea goddess Iemanjá will set adrift on the sea. They will fill the boats with offerings to the goddess in hopes that she will bless them with a good fishing season.

Millions of people will also throw flowers into the water. If the flowers drift back to shore, Iemanjá is not happy with the offering. If the flowers drift out to sea, the people can expect to have a good year.

Culture • These residents of Rio de Janeiro get ready to set their boat off to greet Iemanjá. ▲

Brazil: Regional Leader

Almost anything that happens in Brazil is newsworthy—because Brazil is the largest country in South America, covering almost half the continent. Its population of 172 million is close in size to the combined population of all the other South American countries. Brazil's gross domestic product is larger than that of any other South American country.

The Government of Brazil

After gaining independence from Portugal in 1822, Brazil was ruled by a series of emperors. In 1889, Brazil became a constitutional republic. Beginning in 1930, a series of dictators and military leaders ruled Brazil. Democratic government was restored in 1985. Power today is shared by a president, an elected congress, and a court system.

The Economy of Brazil

Brazil has the largest economy in South America. The country's gross domestic product is nearly twice that of Argentina, which is the next largest economy in South America.

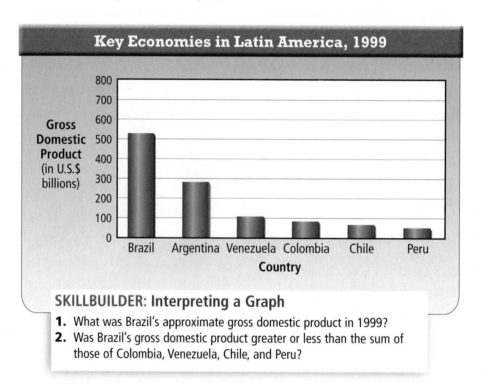

Key Economies in Latin America, 1999

SKILLBUILDER: Interpreting a Graph

1. What was Brazil's approximate gross domestic product in 1999?
2. Was Brazil's gross domestic product greater or less than the sum of those of Colombia, Venezuela, Chile, and Peru?

The Growth of Industry In Brazil, the government controls or influences certain industries to help the economy grow. For example, in the 1950s, the government promoted the building of automobile factories to cut down on the number of cars imported into Brazil. By the late 1980s, Brazil was building more than 1 million vehicles a year, enough to export some to other countries.

Agricultural Production In the world, Brazil is second only to the United States in exporting crops. When it comes to coffee, Brazil produces more than any other country in the world. Brazil is also a leading producer of oranges, bananas, and corn.

Unemployment and Inflation Even though Brazil's economy is the strongest in Latin America, many Brazilians are unemployed. Unemployment results when not enough businesses hire workers, or when workers do not have the education or training they need for the jobs available. Even those who have jobs may face hard times, especially due to inflation. **Inflation** is a general increase in the price of goods or services. It occurs when goods or services are in great demand, allowing producers to charge higher prices for them. The combination of unemployment and inflation has led to much poverty in Brazil.

Place • **Automobile plants supply Brazil with many cars, like these parked in a plant lot, for export each year.** ▲

Reading
Social Studies

A. Synthesizing How would inflation pose challenges even to people who do have jobs?

The People of Brazil

When explorers from Portugal arrived in Brazil in 1500, as many as 5 million Native Americans lived there. During the 1500s, the Portuguese established large sugar cane plantations in northeastern Brazil. At first they enslaved Native Americans to work on the plantations. Soon, however, many Native Americans died of disease. The plantation owners then turned to Africa for labor. Eventually, Brazil brought over more enslaved Africans than any other North or South American country.

Today, Native Americans make up less than 1 percent of Brazil's population. In northeastern Brazil, most people have African ancestors, while many people in Brazil have both European and African ancestors.

BACKGROUND

Of the 10 million to 15 million enslaved Africans brought to North and South America, more than 3.5 million ended up in Brazil.

Strange but TRUE

??

Can Cars Run on Sugar? Brazil's first major export was sugar made from sugar cane (shown at right). However, the plentiful sugar cane isn't just used to make sugar. Today, Brazilians use sugar cane to produce ethanol. Like gasoline, ethanol is a fuel used to run cars.

Nearly half of the cars sold in Brazil run on a gasoline-ethanol mix. Thousands run on ethanol alone. Producing ethanol from sugar cane makes good use of an abundant resource and creates more jobs in the sugar cane industry. Also, its production is less harmful to the environment than is gasoline's.

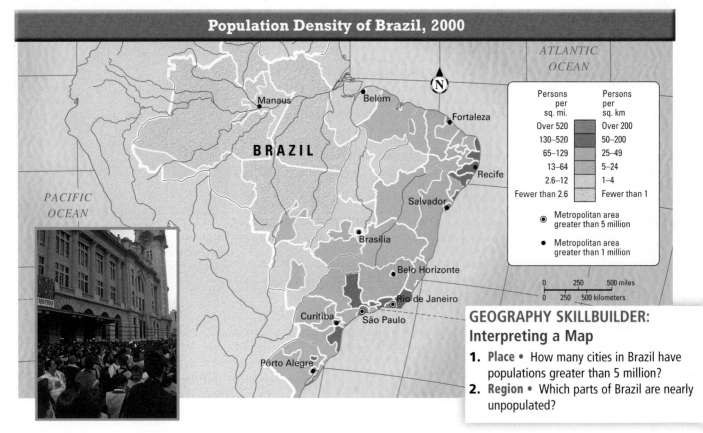

Population Density of Brazil, 2000

ATLANTIC OCEAN

PACIFIC OCEAN

BRAZIL

Manaus
Belém
Fortaleza
Recife
Salvador
Brasília
Belo Horizonte
Rio de Janeiro
Curitiba
São Paulo
Pôrto Alegre

Persons per sq. mi.	Persons per sq. km
Over 520	Over 200
130–520	50–200
65–129	25–49
13–64	5–24
2.6–12	1–4
Fewer than 2.6	Fewer than 1

◉ Metropolitan area greater than 5 million

● Metropolitan area greater than 1 million

0 250 500 miles
0 250 500 kilometers

GEOGRAPHY SKILLBUILDER:
Interpreting a Map

1. **Place** • How many cities in Brazil have populations greater than 5 million?
2. **Region** • Which parts of Brazil are nearly unpopulated?

Place • The overcrowding of Brazil's cities, such as São Paulo, has put many stresses on the nation. ▲

City Populations Today, four out of five Brazilians live in cities. Brazil's two largest cities, **São Paulo** and **Rio de Janeiro,** are growing quickly. In 2000, São Paulo's population was close to 18 million. At the rate it is growing, the population will be more than 20 million in 2015. The national population is also increasing rapidly. In 1999, Brazil's population was almost 172 million. If current trends continue, by 2025 it could reach 210 million.

Because of much crowding along Brazil's Atlantic coast, the government wanted people to move into Brazil's vast interior. In 1956, it decided to create a new capital, **Brasília,** 600 miles inland. Now, like every other city in Brazil, Brasília has problems with overcrowding.

Reading

B. Hypothesizing What problems can rapid population growth cause?

The Culture of Brazil

Brazil's lively culture is a blend of influences from the many cultural groups that have come to Brazil over the centuries. Brazil's music, foods, and religious practices reflect that blend.

A Rich Mix Brazilian languages, religions, and musical traditions all reflect the multiple roots of Brazil's culture. For example, Brazil's official language is Portuguese. Included in Brazilian Portuguese, however, are many words from Tupi-Guarani (TOO•pee-GWAH•ruh•NEE), the language of Native Americans from the interior of northern Brazil.

As for religion, most Brazilians are Catholic, the religion brought to Brazil by the Portuguese. However, the number of non-Catholics is increasing. In 1940, only 5 percent of Brazilians were not Catholic. In 2000, non-Catholics had risen to 20 percent of the population because immigrants and missionaries had brought other religions to Brazil. Even so, more Catholics live in Brazil than in any other country in the world.

In addition, African religions still thrive in Brazil. For example, many people worship the African sea goddess Iemanjá. African influences can also be heard in Brazilian music, such as samba, which is based on African rhythms.

Holidays A Brazilian holiday called **Carnival** highlights the country's cultural diversity. This famous festival occurs during the four days before Lent. Carnival includes huge parades and street parties. In Rio de Janeiro, groups of African Brazilians perform samba dances. The dancers wear elaborate costumes of feathers and brightly colored, sparkling cloth.

Sports Brazilian football, called soccer in the United States, is a sport that most of the country gets excited about. Brazil is often a finalist in the World Cup, the sport's world championship competition. Brazilians enjoy watching professional football; millions of them also enjoy playing the game.

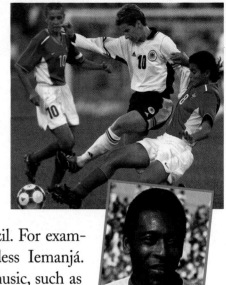

Culture • Top: Players on Brazil's women's soccer team move in for the win. Bottom: Brazilian soccer hero Pelé (PAY·lay) smiles for the crowd. ▲

SECTION 3 ASSESSMENT

Terms & Names

1. Identify: (a) inflation   (b) São Paulo   (c) Rio de Janeiro
             (d) Brasília   (e) Carnival

Taking Notes

2. Use a chart like this one to record key facts about Brazil's geography, history, government, economy, and culture.

Geography	History	Government	Economy	Culture

Main Ideas

3. (a) Why can Brazil be described as an "economic giant"?

   (b) Where do most people in Brazil live today?

   (c) Why did the Brazilian government move the capital inland to Brasília?

Critical Thinking

4. **Drawing Conclusions**

   Why do you think Brazil's economy is the most successful in South America?

   Think About
   - the government's role in the economy
   - natural resources
   - population size

ACTIVITY -OPTION-

Write a **speech** about the different groups that have influenced Brazilian culture. Include descriptions of each group's contributions.

Linking Past and Present

The Legacy of Latin America

Food

People the world over have developed a taste for foods that originated in Latin America. Chile peppers, tomatoes, sweet potatoes, corn, and chocolate are just a few of the Latin American foods regularly found in kitchens and restaurants around the globe.

Natural Rubber

Ancient Latin Americans were the first to make use of natural rubber. Harvested from trees of the genus *Hevea,* native to Brazil, natural rubber is used around the world for everything from erasers to tires for racecars, airplanes, and trucks. The Maya invented chewing gum more than 1,000 years ago. They chewed a rubberlike substance called chicle (CHIHK•uhl), which is made from the sap of the sapodilla tree. Natural chicle was used to make chewing gum in the United States until the 1940s, when it was replaced with artificial ingredients.

Cowboys

Pioneers in the southwestern United States first learned many of the skills of cattle ranching from *vaqueros* (vah•KEH•rohs), Mexican cowboys working on Texas cattle ranches. The *vaqueros* showed the newcomers how to use lariats, saddles, spurs, and branding irons.

Language

Some of the words we use every day come from Spanish or from Native American languages. Examples are *coyote, patio, tomato, cocoa, cafeteria, canyon, corral, chile, lariat, lasso, rodeo,* and *stampede.*

stam·pede (stăm-pēd´) *n.* **1.** A sudden frenzied rush of panic-stricken animals. **2.** A sudden headlong rush or flight of a crowd of people. **3.** A mass impulsive action: *a stampede of support for the candidate. v.* **-ped·ed, -ped·ing, -pedes** —*tr.* **1.** To cause (a herd of animals) to flee in panic. **2.** To cause (a crowd of people) to act on mass impulse. —*intr.* **1.** To flee in a headlong rush. **2.** To act on mass impulse. [Spanish *estampida,* uproar, stampede, from Provençal, from *estampir,* to stamp, of Germanic origin.] —**stam·ped´er** *n.*

Life-Saving Medicines

Native peoples in Latin America, especially in the Amazon rain forest, have been sharing their knowledge of medicinal plants for centuries—to the world's benefit. Two important contributions to modern medicine have been quinine, used to cure malaria, and curare, used to fight serious nerve diseases, such as multiple sclerosis.

Quinine ▲

Find Out More About It!

Study the text and photos on these pages to learn about inventions, creations, and contributions that have come from Latin America. Then choose the item that interests you the most and do research in the library or on the Internet to learn more about it. Use the information you gather to create a poster that celebrates the contribution.

RESEARCH LINKS
CLASSZONE.COM

Peru Today

TERMS & NAMES
oasis
guerrilla warfare
Alberto Fujimori
Quechua

MAIN IDEA

Peru's physical features and its unstable governments have posed challenges to the development of its economy and its people.

WHY IT MATTERS NOW

Peru's economic problems also affect its trading partners, including the United States.

DATELINE

CHINCHA ISLANDS, PERU, 1842— Officials recently announced a major new source of prosperity for Peru. Dried sea-bird droppings, called guano, are now being exported around the world to be used as plant fertilizer.

The idea of using guano as fertilizer came from ancient Inca farmers. Recently, scientific research has confirmed that guano is rich in phosphates and nitrates, which help plants to grow. Fertilizer companies in Britain and other countries are now paying huge sums of money for the right to dig guano from Peru.

Human-Environment Interaction • Guano comes from a number of sea birds, including cormorants like this one. ▲

The Land of Peru

Though Peru is rich in resources, such as guano, variations in its physical geography also present problems. Three types of landforms exist in Peru: mountains, rain forest, and desert. Each type has its own special characteristics, but all three are transportation barriers rather than transportation corridors. Traveling from one part of Peru to another is not easy.

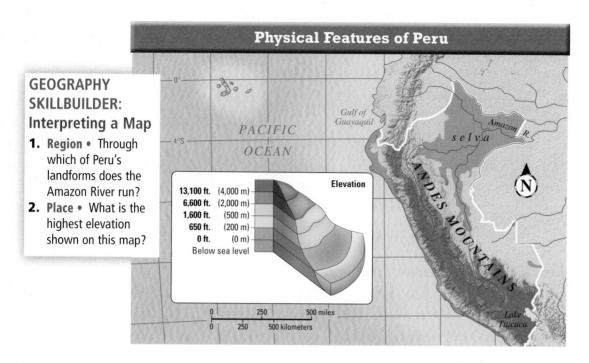

Physical Features of Peru

PACIFIC OCEAN

Gulf of Guayaquil

selva

Amazon R.

ANDES MOUNTAINS

Lake Titicaca

N

0°

4°S

Elevation

13,100 ft. (4,000 m)
6,600 ft. (2,000 m)
1,600 ft. (500 m)
650 ft. (200 m)
0 ft. (0 m)
Below sea level

0   250   500 miles
0   250   500 kilometers

GEOGRAPHY SKILLBUILDER: Interpreting a Map

1. **Region** • Through which of Peru's landforms does the Amazon River run?
2. **Place** • What is the highest elevation shown on this map?

Three Types of Landforms Look at the map above. You can see that the Andes Mountains run the entire length of Peru, dividing the country in two. In places, the mountains are so steep that they are practically impassable. Notice that off the eastern slopes of the Andes stretches rain forest, which is called selva in Spanish. Now look to the west of the Andes, along the Pacific coast. Here the northern stretches of Chile's Atacama Desert reach into Peru. Most of Peru's cities, large farms, and factories are located in the desert, in or near oases. An **oasis** is a fertile region in a desert that formed around a river or spring.

Reading
Social Studies

A. Clarifying Why do you think Peru's cities are located in the desert rather than in other environments?

The Economy of Peru

Peru has many resources, but it also has many problems. The country's harsh geography affects its economy. For example, the cold, rocky highlands and the cool, dry desert cover so much area that there is not enough arable land to feed the growing population.

Place • Because of cold currents in the Pacific Ocean, Peru's desert has an average summer temperature of only 73°F. ▶

Place • At left, a freight train transports copper ingots through Peru. At center, cotton plants grow in Ica, Peru. ▲

Place • Many crates of anchovies are sold in Peru each year. ▲

Agriculture Like many other countries, Peru must import certain foods. These include grains, vegetable oils, and some meats, many of which come from the United States. However, Peruvians do grow sugar cane, cotton, and coffee for export. Also, southern Peru has a large dairy industry that serves markets both in Peru and beyond. Meats from cattle, sheep, alpaca, and goats are also processed and distributed within the country.

Fishing The cold waters along the Pacific Coast are fine fishing grounds. Sardines and anchovies are the most important fish in the Peruvian catch. They are dried and made into fishmeal, which is sold as feed for livestock throughout the world.

Mining Peru is an important supplier of metals such as silver, copper, and bismuth. It also contains oil and gold deposits. However, the richest deposits of minerals in the country exist in dense rain forests and at elevations of over 12,000 feet. Because it is difficult to mine in these locations, Peru's mineral resources have not brought the country the great wealth that they could.

The Government of Peru

Peru declared itself independent of Spain in 1821. The nation was not completely free, however, until December of 1824, when Simón Bolívar finally drove out the Spanish. Following independence, Peru's military leaders began fighting one another. Struggles between military and civilian leaders continued until late in the 20th century.

Guerrilla Warfare Perhaps the greatest struggle in Peru's modern history arose in the early 1980s. At that time, Communist groups rose up to fight against the democracy that they felt was failing Peru. The most powerful of these groups was Sendero Luminoso (sen·DAIR·oh loo·mih·NOH·soh), or Shining Path.

BACKGROUND

Although in Spanish *guerrilla* is pronounced geh-REE-yuh, in English it is pronounced like the word *gorilla*. The word is Spanish for "small-scale war."

Sendero Luminoso fought for changes using **guerrilla warfare,** or nontraditional military tactics characterized by small groups using surprise attacks. The military responded, and many citizens died in the crossfire. Until Sendero Luminoso's leader, Abimael Guzmán Reynoso (ah·bee·mah·EHL gooz·MAHN ray·NAW·saw), was imprisoned in 1992, the civil war continued.

Government in Crisis The 1990s did not bring better times to Peru. From 1990 to 2000, **Alberto Fujimori,** the son of Japanese immigrants, was president. At first, many of Peru's poor rural people supported him. By May 2000, however, he and his officials were accused of corruption. Many resignations followed, and in November, Fujimori abandoned the presidency and fled to Japan. The new president, Alejandro Toledo (al·eh·HAHN·droh toh·LAY·doh), faced the challenge of trying to win back the trust of Peruvians after the government scandals.

Peruvian People and Culture

Today, more Native Americans live in Peru than in any other South American country. Forty-five percent of Peru's people are Native Americans— the descendants of the Inca. Many of these people are **Quechua** (KEHCH·wuh), people who live in the Andes highlands and speak the Inca language Quechua. Along with Spanish, Quechua is one of Peru's official languages. Many people in the highlands speak the language of another Native American group, the Aymara (EYE·mah·RAH). The Inca conquered the Aymara in the 15th century, but the language lived on.

After Native Americans, *mestizos* are Peru's next largest group. Peru's population also includes people with European, African, and Asian ancestors.

Urban and Rural Life Most of Peru's people live in cities or towns. Lima is Peru's capital and its biggest city, with about 7 million people. Lima has grown very quickly, which poses some severe problems. At the dawn of the 21st century, many neighborhoods lacked basic city services, such as electricity, running water, and public transportation.

B. Drawing Conclusions How do you think the violence and corruption in government affected people's daily lives in Peru?

Committee to Protect Journalists In a democracy, freedom of the press helps to prevent wrongdoing by the government. In Peru, for example, many administrators resigned in disgrace after journalists exposed widespread corruption in Alberto Fujimori's administration. Elsewhere, however, many governments have jailed journalists like the one shown below for their reports.

The Committee to Protect Journalists (CPJ) was formed in 1981 to promote freedom of the press. CPJ tracks abuses against the press all over the world, makes the abuses public, and organizes protests.

Many of Peru's rural farmers are very poor. They farm such small plots of land that often they cannot grow enough to feed their families. These rural people, who are mainly Native Americans, often move to the cities in search of a better life. However, many have little education and cannot speak Spanish, making it hard to find work.

Religion Peru's religions reflect multiple cultural traditions. Catholicism is the national religion of Peru, and more than 90 percent of Peruvians are Catholic. However, many Inca religious practices also still exist. At times, the Inca and Catholic customs mix. For example, some villages honor Catholic saints with traditional Inca festivals.

Region • Like this mother and daughter, many Quechua live in the Andes of Ecuador, Peru, and Bolivia. ▲

Literature The literature of Peru reveals modern themes as well as traditional ones. Peru's most famous living novelist, Mario Vargas Llosa (MAHR·yoh VAHR·guhs YOH·suh), is known for his belief that a novel should represent life to the fullest. César Vallejo (SAY·sar vuh·YAY·hoh), a *mestizo,* is Peru's most famous poet and is considered one of the world's best Spanish-language poets. His poetry describes what life is like for Peru's Native Americans and tells about suffering and struggles that all people may face.

SECTION 4 ASSESSMENT

Terms & Names
1. Identify: (a) oasis   (b) guerrilla warfare   (c) Alberto Fujimori   (d) Quechua

Taking Notes
2. Use a chart like this one to list the products generated by each of Peru's industries.

Industry	Products
Agriculture	
Fishing	
Mining	

Main Ideas
3. (a) Describe the three types of landforms in Peru.

   (b) Describe the challenges facing Peru's economy.

   (c) Which group makes up the largest part of Peru's population?

Critical Thinking
4. **Forming and Supporting Opinions**

   Why did Peru's guerrillas use violence to bring about change? Were they right to do so? Explain.

   Think About
   • reasons for discontent in Peru
   • the history of democracy in Peru
   • other possible methods of demanding change

ACTIVITY -OPTION-   Imagine you live in Peru. Write a **short story** describing your daily life, including what you do for work and for recreation.

Reading a Time Line

▶▶ Defining the Skill

A time line is a visual list of dates and events shown in the order in which they occurred. Time lines can be horizontal or vertical. On horizontal time lines, the earliest date is on the left. On vertical time lines, the earliest date is usually at the top.

▶▶ Applying the Skill

The time line below shows the dates of expeditions to explore the Amazon River. Use the strategies listed below to help you read the time line.

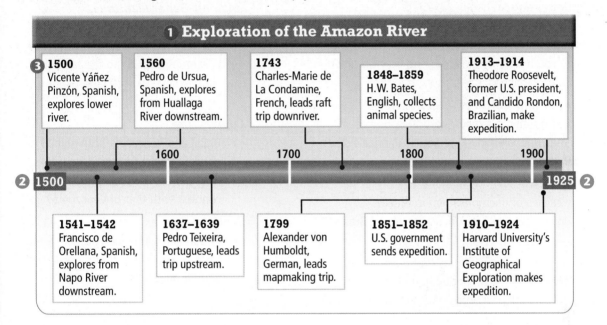

1 Exploration of the Amazon River

3 1500
Vicente Yáñez Pinzón, Spanish, explores lower river.

1560
Pedro de Ursua, Spanish, explores from Huallaga River downstream.

1743
Charles-Marie de La Condamine, French, leads raft trip downriver.

1848–1859
H.W. Bates, English, collects animal species.

1913–1914
Theodore Roosevelt, former U.S. president, and Candido Rondon, Brazilian, make expedition.

2 1500   1600   1700   1800   1900   **1925 2**

1541–1542
Francisco de Orellana, Spanish, explores from Napo River downstream.

1637–1639
Pedro Teixeira, Portuguese, leads trip upstream.

1799
Alexander von Humboldt, German, leads mapmaking trip.

1851–1852
U.S. government sends expedition.

1910–1924
Harvard University's Institute of Geographical Exploration makes expedition.

How to Read a Time Line

Strategy 1 Read the title. It will tell you the main idea of the time line.

Strategy 2 Read the dates at the beginning and the end of the time line. These will show the period of time that the time line covers.

Strategy 3 Read the dates and events in order, beginning with the earliest one. Think about how each event may have influenced later events. Take note of which nations were involved in each expedition.

Strategy 4 Summarize the main idea of the time line. Remember that the title will help you focus on the main idea.

Write a Summary

Writing a summary can help you understand the information shown on a time line. The summary to the right states the time period covered and the main idea of the time line.

> **4** The time line covers the period between 1500 and 1925. During that period of time, people from Europe and the United States explored the Amazon River. The time line shows that on their expeditions, people explored the river, made maps, and collected animal species.

▶▶ Practicing the Skill

Turn to page 233 in Chapter 9, Section 1. Look at the time line entitled "Key Independence Days in South America," and write a paragraph summarizing what you learned from it.

TERMS & NAMES

Explain the significance of each of the following:

1. Simón Bolívar
2. Pan-American
3. free-trade zone
4. urbanization
5. São Paulo
6. Brasília
7. Carnival
8. oasis
9. guerrilla warfare
10. Quechua

REVIEW QUESTIONS

Establishing Independence *(pages 231–235)*

1. What caused the death of so many Native Americans after the arrival of the Europeans in South America?
2. How did many South American nations end up with unlimited governments after independence?

Building Economies and Cultures *(pages 238–242)*

3. List three of South America's major natural resources.
4. Why have so many people moved to South America's cities in the past 50 years?

Brazil Today *(pages 243–247)*

5. What are two causes of unemployment in Brazil?
6. Why did the government of Brazil build the city of Brasília?

Peru Today *(pages 250–254)*

7. Describe the three types of landforms that make up Peru.
8. How does the Native American population in Peru compare in size with the Native American populations elsewhere in South America?

CRITICAL THINKING

Making Generalizations

1. Using your completed chart from Reading Social Studies, p. 230, write a paragraph explaining the facts that support one generalization about South America.

Contrasting

2. Brazil and Venezuela both gained independence from European countries. How did the road to freedom for Brazil contrast with that of Venezuela?

Synthesizing

3. When South American nations form trade blocs, how is that different from uniting politically?

Visual Summary

Establishing Independence

1

- After 300 years of colonial rule, the countries of South America gained independence.
- South America's population today reflects the arrival of immigrants from Europe, Africa, and Asia.

Building Economies and Cultures

2

- Geographic features and growing populations have challenged economic progress in South America.
- The countries of the region work together to benefit all of their economies.

Brazil Today

3

- Brazil is South America's largest and most economically successful country.
- Despite economic success, Brazil still faces unemployment and inflation.

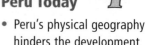

Peru Today

4

- Peru's physical geography hinders the development of its economy.
- Peru has suffered many political problems, such as guerrilla warfare and corrupt government.

SOCIAL STUDIES SKILLBUILDER

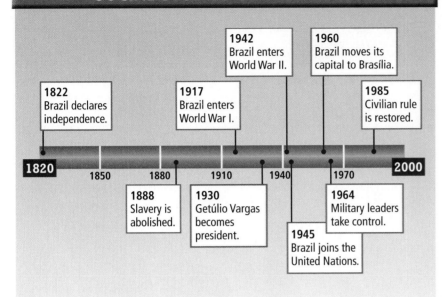

1942
Brazil enters World War II.

1960
Brazil moves its capital to Brasília.

1822
Brazil declares independence.

1917
Brazil enters World War I.

1985
Civilian rule is restored.

1820   1850   1880   1910   1940   1970   2000

1888
Slavery is abolished.

1930
Getúlio Vargas becomes president.

1964
Military leaders take control.

1945
Brazil joins the United Nations.

SKILLBUILDER: Reading a Time Line

1. What period is covered in the time line?
2. What events has Brazil participated in with other countries of the world?
3. Use the time line to write a brief summary of events in Brazil since independence.

FOCUS ON GEOGRAPHY

1. **Region** • How many South American cities had populations over 1 million in 1950?
2. **Movement** • How many more South American cities had populations over 1 million in 2000 than in 1950?
3. **Location** • Are more of South America's cities located on the coast or inland?

1900

1950

2000

 City with population greater than 1 million

CHAPTER PROJECTS

Interdisciplinary Activity: Language Arts

Describing Geography Imagine that you are on an expedition flying over Peru. Record your observations about the long coastline, the mountains, and the jungles you see below you. Write two or three paragraphs describing what you see.

Cooperative Learning Activity

Planning a City In a group of three to five students, plan a new city. Decide on a problem that your country faces, such as overcrowding. Use this city's development to help solve the problem, as was done with Brasília. Describe how the city is organized, what services are provided for the people, and where parks, homes, and businesses are.

- Explain why the new city needed to be built.
- Provide a map of the new city.
- Draw illustrations of important buildings.
- List key services that the city provides.

INTERNET ACTIVITY

Use the Internet to research at least three useful products that come from the Amazon rain forest. Focus on one product, such as medicinal plants, and describe how it is used in different parts of the world.

Writing About Geography Write a report of your findings. Include a map or a chart that shows products from the rain forest and what they are used for. List the Web sites you used to prepare your report.

For Internet links to support this activity, go to

RESEARCH LINKS
CLASSZONE.COM

UNIT 4

Place Completed in A.D. 80, the Colosseum in Rome, Italy, held 50,000 spectators. There they watched battles between gladiators, among other contests. The Colosseum is the largest structure that survives from the Roman Empire.

EUROPE, RUSSIA, AND THE INDEPENDENT REPUBLICS

THE COLOSSEUM

PACIFIC OCEAN

PACIFIC OCEAN

ATLANTIC OCEAN

OCEAN

EUROPE, RUSSIA, AND THE INDEPENDENT REPUBLICS

Climates of Europe, Russia, and the Independent Republics

Legend:

- Desert
- Semiarid
- Mediterranean
- Marine west coast
- Humid subtropical
- Humid continental
- Subarctic
- Tundra
- Highland

Europe, Russia, and the Independent Republics: Physical

120°E

ARCTIC OCEAN

80°N

New Siberian Islands

Laptev Sea

Wrangel Island

East Siberian Sea

Verkhoyansk Range

Cherskiy Range

Lena R.

Kolyma R.

Chukchi Peninsula

RUSSIA

Kolyma Mts.

60°N

Lena R.

Stanovoy Range

Sea of Okhotsk

Kamchatka Peninsula

Bering Sea

Sakhalin Island

PACIFIC OCEAN

Tropic of Cancer

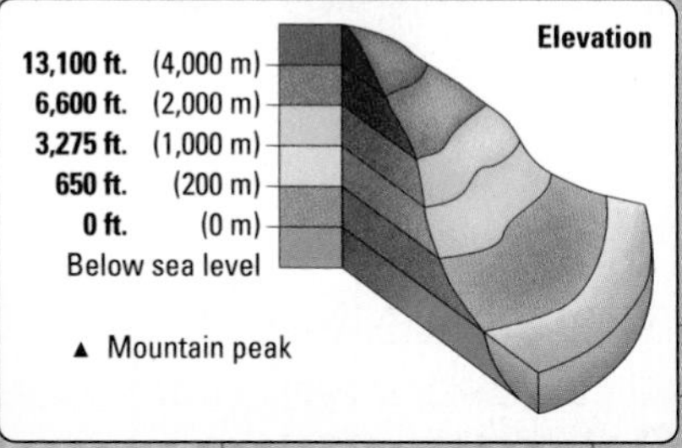

120°E

FAST FACTS

✓ **LONG COASTLINE:**
The coastline of Europe alone is 24,000 miles long. Earth measures 24,902 miles around at the Equator.

✓ **BELOW SEA LEVEL:**
Almost a third of the Netherlands and a large portion of the land by the Caspian Sea are below sea level.

✓ **HIGHEST MOUNTAIN:**
Mt. Elbrus in Russia, 18,510 ft.

✓ **DEEPEST LAKE:**
Lake Baikal, 5,714 ft. deep

✓ **LARGEST INLAND SEA:**
Caspian Sea, 149,200 sq. mi.

✓ **LONGEST RIVER:**
Volga River, 2,193 mi.

Elevation

13,100 ft.	(4,000 m)
6,600 ft.	(2,000 m)
3,275 ft.	(1,000 m)
650 ft.	(200 m)
0 ft.	(0 m)
Below sea level	

▲ Mountain peak

GEOGRAPHY SKILLBUILDER: Interpreting Maps and Visuals

1. **Location** • Which countries have mountains at their borders?
2. **Place** • About how many times larger is the population of Europe, Russia, and the Independent Republics than that of the United States?

Europe, Russia, and the Independent Republics– United States Landmass and Population

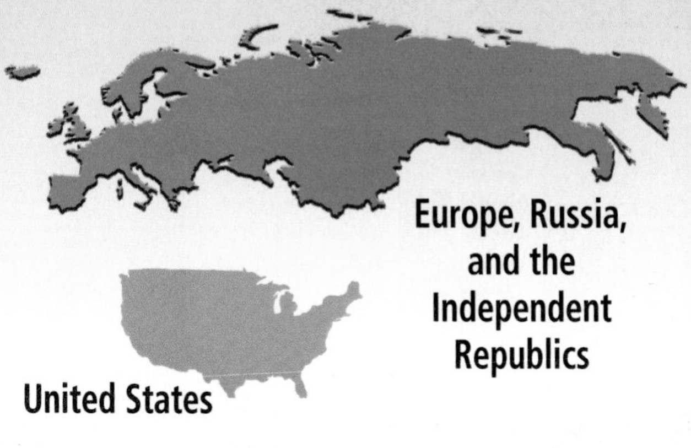

Europe, Russia, and the Independent Republics

United States

LANDMASS

Europe, Russia, and the Independent Republics

10,489,029 square miles

Continental United States

3,165,630 square miles

POPULATION

Europe, Russia, and the Independent Republics
654,628,000

United States
281,421,906

👤 = 50,000,000

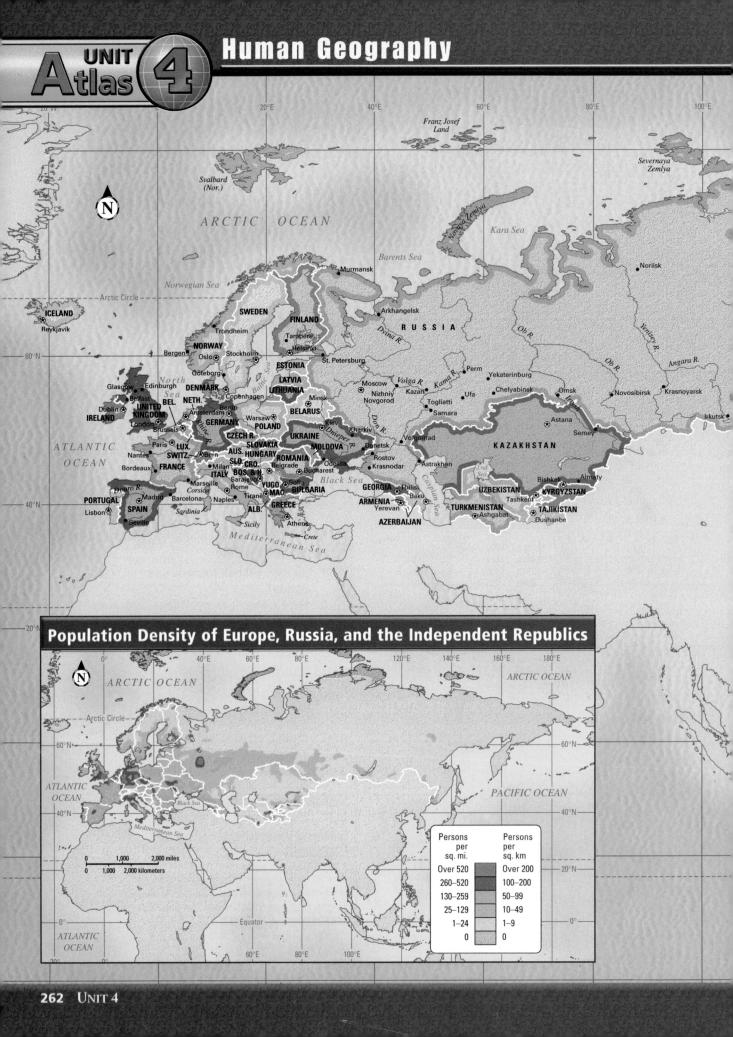

N

ARCTIC OCEAN

Svalbard
(Nor.)

Franz Josef
Land

Severnaya
Zemlya

Novaya Zemlya

Kara Sea

Barents Sea

Murmansk

Norilsk

Arctic Circle

ICELAND

Reykjavik

Norwegian Sea

SWEDEN

FINLAND

Arkhangelsk

RUSSIA

Dvina R.

Ob R.

Yenisey R.

60°N

Trondheim

Tampere

Helsinki

Bergen

NORWAY

Oslo

Stockholm

St. Petersburg

Moscow

Volga R.

Kama R.

Perm

Yekaterinburg

Omsk

Novosibirsk

Krasnoyarsk

Göteborg

ESTONIA

Nizhniy
Novgorod

Kazan

Chelyabinsk

Irkutsk

Glasgow

Edinburgh

DENMARK

LATVIA

LITHUANIA

Minsk

Togliatti

Ufa

Astana

Angara R.

North
Sea

Copenhagen

BEL.

NETH.

BELARUS

Samara

Semey

Belfast

Dublin

UNITED
KINGDOM

Berlin

Amsterdam

Warsaw

Kiev

Kharkiv

Volgograd

KAZAKHSTAN

IRELAND

London

Brussels

GERMANY

POLAND

UKRAINE

Dnieper R.

Don R.

Donetsk

ATLANTIC

OCEAN

Paris

LUX.

Rhine R.

CZECH R.

SLOVAKIA

MOLDOVA

Rostov

Astrakhan

Aral
Sea

Bishkek

Almaty

Nantes

SWITZ.

AUS.

HUNGARY

ROMANIA

Odessa

Krasnodar

Caspian
Sea

UZBEKISTAN

KYRGYZSTAN

Bordeaux

FRANCE

SLO.

CRO.

Belgrade

Bucharest

Black Sea

GEORGIA

Tbilisi

Tashkent

Bern

ITALY

BOS. & H.

YUGO.

Sofia

BULGARIA

ARMENIA

Baku

TURKMENISTAN

TAJIKISTAN

Marseille

Sarajevo

MAC.

Yerevan

Ashgabat

Dushanbe

PORTUGAL

Corsica

Rome

Titane

GREECE

AZERBAIJAN

Douro R.

Madrid

Barcelona

Naples

ALB.

40°N

Lisbon

SPAIN

Sardinia

Athens

Seville

Sicily

Crete

Mediterranean Sea

Population Density of Europe, Russia, and the Independent Republics

N

ARCTIC OCEAN

ARCTIC OCEAN

Arctic Circle

ATLANTIC
OCEAN

60°N

PACIFIC OCEAN

ATLANTIC
OCEAN

Black Sea

40°N

Mediterranean Sea

Persons per sq. mi.	Persons per sq. km
Over 520	Over 200
260–520	100–200
130–259	50–99
25–129	10–49
1–24	1–9
0	0

0   1,000   2,000 miles

0   1,000   2,000 kilometers

Equator

ATLANTIC
OCEAN

Europe, Russia, and the Independent Republics: Political

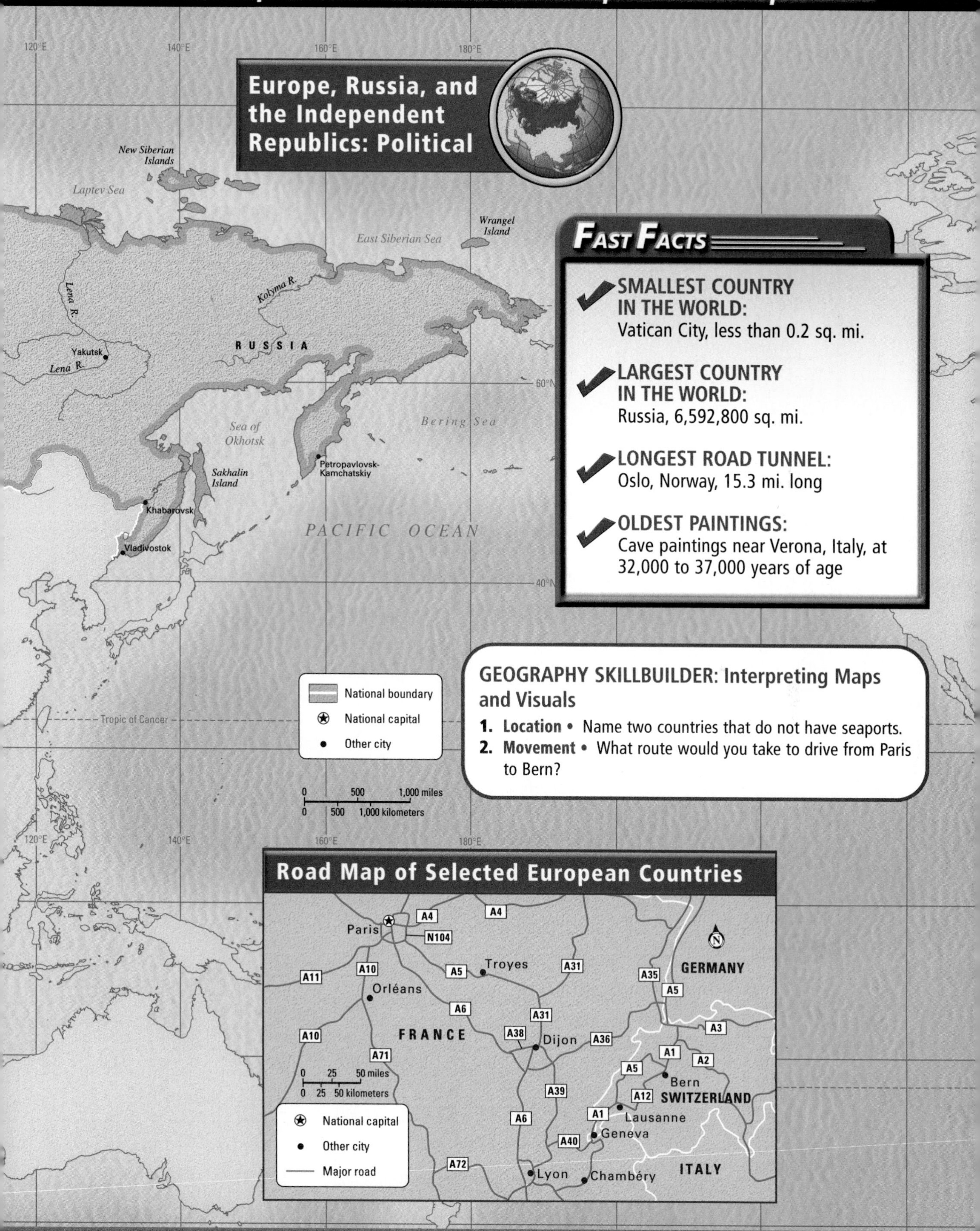

120°E 140°E 160°E 180°E

New Siberian Islands

Laptev Sea

Wrangel Island

East Siberian Sea

Kolyma R.

Lena R.

R U S S I A

Yakutsk

Lena R.

60°N

Bering Sea

Sea of Okhotsk

Sakhalin Island

Petropavlovsk-Kamchatskiy

Khabarovsk

PACIFIC OCEAN

40°N

Vladivostok

Tropic of Cancer

120°E 140°E 160°E 180°E

	National boundary
⊛	National capital
●	Other city

0   500   1,000 miles
0   500   1,000 kilometers

FAST FACTS

✔ **SMALLEST COUNTRY IN THE WORLD:**
Vatican City, less than 0.2 sq. mi.

✔ **LARGEST COUNTRY IN THE WORLD:**
Russia, 6,592,800 sq. mi.

✔ **LONGEST ROAD TUNNEL:**
Oslo, Norway, 15.3 mi. long

✔ **OLDEST PAINTINGS:**
Cave paintings near Verona, Italy, at 32,000 to 37,000 years of age

GEOGRAPHY SKILLBUILDER: Interpreting Maps and Visuals

1. **Location** • Name two countries that do not have seaports.
2. **Movement** • What route would you take to drive from Paris to Bern?

Road Map of Selected European Countries

Paris ⊛ A4   A4
N104
A4
Troyes A31   GERMANY
A11   A10   A5   A35   A5
Orléans
A6   A31
A10   A38   Dijon   A3
FRANCE   A36
A71   A1   A2
A5
A39   Bern   SWITZERLAND
A1   A12
A6   Lausanne
A40   Geneva
A72   ITALY
Lyon   Chambéry

0   25   50 miles
0   25   50 kilometers

⊛	National capital
●	Other city
—	Major road

Country Flag	Country/Capital	Currency	Population (2001 estimate)	Life Expectancy (years)	Birthrate (per 1,000 pop.) (2000)
	Albania Tiranë	Lek	3,510,000	71	19
	Andorra Andorra la Vella	French Franc	68,000	83	11
	Armenia Yerevan	Dram	3,336,000	75	10
	Austria Vienna	Euro*	8,151,000	78	10
	Azerbaijan Baku	Manat	7,771,000	70	15
	Belarus Minsk	Ruble	10,350,000	68	9
	Belgium Brussels	Euro*	10,259,000	78	11
	Bosnia-Herzegovina Sarajevo	Conv. Mark	3,922,000	73	13
	Bulgaria Sofia	Lev	7,707,000	71	8
	Croatia Zagreb	Kuna	4,334,000	73	11
	Czech Republic Prague	Koruna	10,264,000	75	9
	Denmark Copenhagen	Danish Krone	5,353,000	77	12
	Estonia Tallinn	Kroon	1,423,000	70	8
	Finland Helsinki	Euro*	5,176,000	78	11
	France Paris	Euro*	59,551,000	79	13
	Georgia Tbilisi	Lavi	4,989,000	73	9
	Germany Berlin	Euro*	83,029,000	77	9

*On January 1, 2002, the euro became the common currency for 12 of the member nations of the European Union.

DATA FILE

Infant Mortality (per 1,000 live births) (2000)	Doctors (per 100,000 pop.) (1990–1998)	Literacy Rate (percentage) (1991–1998)	Passenger Cars (per 1,000 pop.) (1996–1997)	Total Area (square miles)	Map (not to scale)
41.3	129	83	10 (1990)	11,100	
6.4	253	100	552	174	
41.0	316	98	2	11,506	
4.9	302	100	468	32,378	
83.0	360	99	36	33,436	
15.0	443	100	111	80,154	
5.6	395	99	434	11,787	
25.2	143	86	23	19,741	
14.9	345	98	202	42,822	
8.2	229	98	160	21,830	
4.6	303	99	428	30,448	
4.7	290	100	339	16,637	
13.0	297	99	294	17,413	
4.2	299	100	378	130,560	
4.8	303	99	437	212,934	
53.0	436	99	80	26,911	
4.7	350	100	504	137,830	

Country Flag	Country/Capital	Currency	Population (2001 estimate)	Life Expectancy (years)	Birthrate (per 1,000 pop.) (2000)
	Greece Athens	Euro*	10,624,000	78	10
	Hungary Budapest	Forint	10,106,000	71	9
	Iceland Reykjavik	Krona	278,000	80	15
	Ireland Dublin	Euro*	3,841,000	76	15
	Italy Rome	Euro*	57,680,000	78	9
	Kazakhstan Astana	Tenge	16,731,000	65	14
	Kyrgyzstan Bishkek	Som	4,753,000	67	22
	Latvia Riga	Lat	2,385,000	70	8
	Liechtenstein Vaduz	Swiss Franc	33,000	73	14
	Lithuania Vilnius	Litas	3,611,000	72	10
	Luxembourg Luxembourg	Euro*	443,000	77	13
	Macedonia Skopje	Denar	2,046,000	73	15
	Malta Valletta	Lira	395,000	77	12
	Moldova Chisinau	Leu	4,432,000	67	11
	Monaco Monaco	French Franc	32,000	79	20
	Netherlands Amsterdam	Euro*	15,981,000	78	13
	Norway Oslo	Krone	4,503,000	79	13
	Poland Warsaw	Zloty	38,634,000	74	10

*On January 1, 2002, the euro became the common currency for 12 of the member nations of the European Union.

DATA FILE

Infant Mortality (per 1,000 live births) (2000)	Doctors (per 100,000 pop.) (1990–1998)	Literacy Rate (percentage) (1991–1998)	Passenger Cars (per 1,000 pop.) (1996–1997)	Total Area (square miles)	Map (not to scale)
6.7	392	97	223	50,950	
8.9	357	99	222	35,919	
4.0	326	100	489	39,768	
6.2	219	100	292	27,135	
5.5	554	98	540	116,320	
59.0	353	99	61	1,048,300	
77.0	301	97	32	76,641	
16.0	282	100	174	24,595	
5.1	100	100	592 (1993)	62	
15.0	395	100	242	25,174	
5.0	272	100	515	999	
16.3	204	89	132	9,927	
5.3	261	91	321	124	
43.0	400 (1995)	99	46	13,012	
5.9	664	100	548	0.6	
5.0	251	100	372	16,033	
4.0	413	100	399	125,050	
8.9	236	99	195	124,807	

Country Flag	Country/Capital	Currency	Population (2001 estimate)	Life Expectancy (years)	Birthrate (per 1,000 pop.) (2000)
	Portugal Lisbon	Euro*	10,066,000	76	11
	Romania Bucharest	Leu	22,364,000	70	11
	Russia Moscow	Ruble	145,470,000	67	8
	San Marino San Marino	Italian Lira	27,000	80	11
	Slovakia Bratislava	Koruna	5,415,000	73	11
	Slovenia Ljubljana	Tolar	1,930,000	75	9
	Spain Madrid	Euro*	40,038,000	78	9
	Sweden Stockholm	Krona	8,875,000	80	10
	Switzerland Bern	Franc	7,283,000	80	11
	Tajikistan Dushanbe	Ruble	6,579,000	68	21
	Turkmenistan Ashgabat	Manat	4,603,000	66	21
	Ukraine Kiev	Hryvnya	48,760,000	68	8
	United Kingdom London	Pound	59,648,000	77	12
	Uzbekistan Tashkent	Som	25,155,000	69	23
	Vatican City Vatican City	Vatican Lira/Italian Lira	870 (2000)	N/A	N/A
	Yugoslavia Belgrade	New Dinar	10,677,000	73	11
	United States Washington, D.C.	Dollar	281,422,000	77	15

*On January 1, 2002, the euro became the common currency for 12 of the member nations of the European Union.

DATA FILE

Infant Mortality (per 1,000 live births) (2000)	Doctors (per 100,000 pop.) (1990–1998)	Literacy Rate (percentage) (1991–1998)	Passenger Cars (per 1,000 pop.) (1996–1997)	Total Area (square miles)	Map (not to scale)
6.0	312	91	295	35,514	
20.5	184	98	106	92,042	
20.0	421	100	120	6,592,812	
8.8	252	99	955	23	
8.8	353	100	185	18,923	
5.2	228	99	343	7,819	
5.7	424	97	384	195,363	
3.5	311	100	417	173,730	
4.8	323	100	460	15,942	
117.0	201	99	31	55,251	
73.0	300 (1997)	98	N/A	188,455	
22.0	299	100	97	233,089	
5.7	164	100	434	94,548	
72.0	309	88	37	173,591	
N/A	N/A	100	N/A	0.17	
10.4	203	98	173	39,448	
7.0	251	97	489	3,787,319	

GEOGRAPHY SKILLBUILDER: Interpreting a Chart

1. **Place** • Which country in the region has the highest life expectancy?
2. **Place** • How many fewer cars per thousand people does Greece have than Germany?

CHAPTER
10

Western Europe: Its Land and Early History

EUROPE

ATLANTIC

PACIFIC

OCEAN

PACIFIC

OCEAN

OCEAN

INDIAN
OCEAN

OCEAN

Region Many European cities show their history in their architecture. In Segovia, Spain, an ancient Roman aqueduct lies below the walls of a castle built in the Middle Ages.

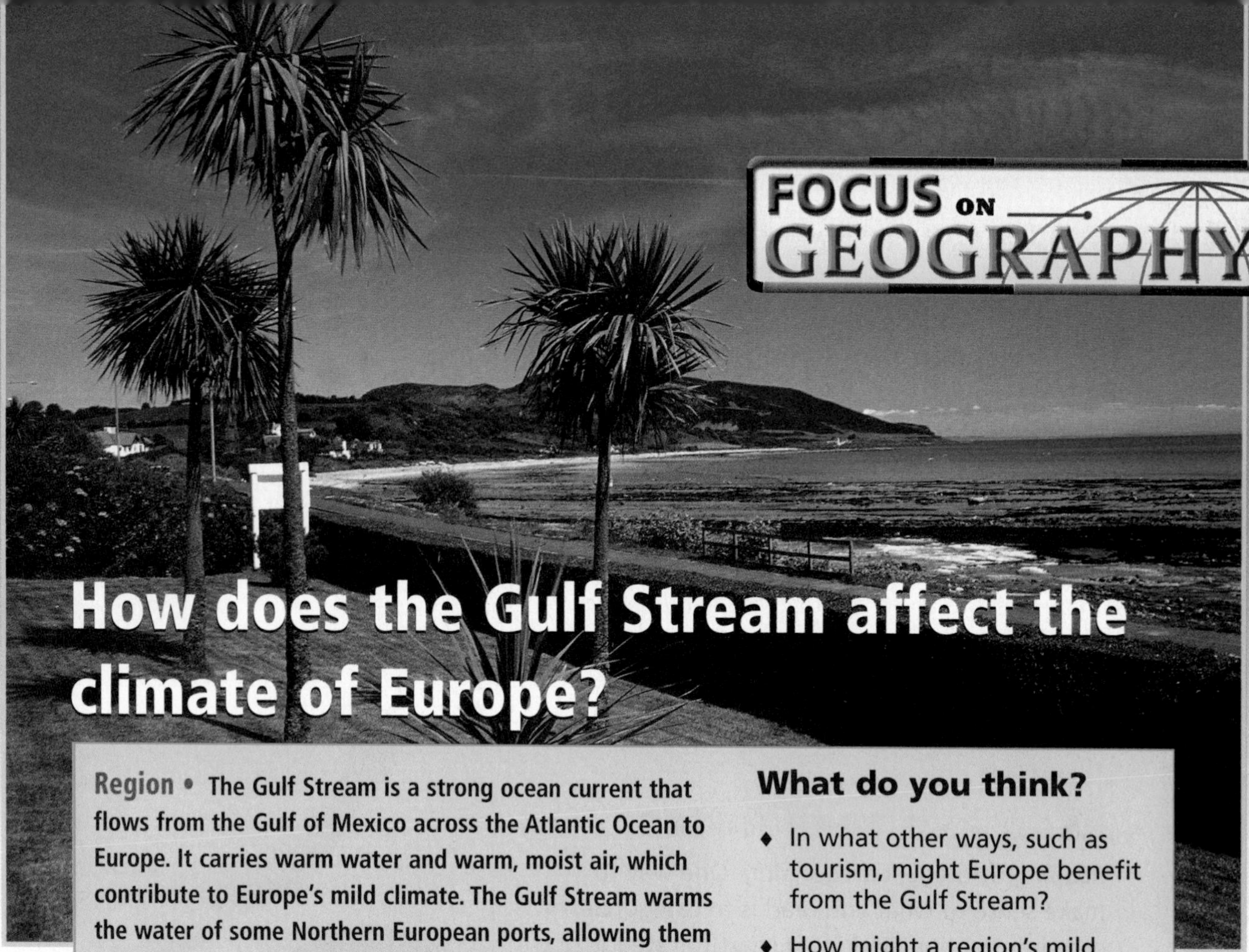

How does the Gulf Stream affect the climate of Europe?

Region • The Gulf Stream is a strong ocean current that flows from the Gulf of Mexico across the Atlantic Ocean to Europe. It carries warm water and warm, moist air, which contribute to Europe's mild climate. The Gulf Stream warms the water of some Northern European ports, allowing them to remain open in the winter when they might otherwise be frozen. Palm trees even grow in Scotland, which is as far north as southern Alaska!

What do you think?

♦ In what other ways, such as tourism, might Europe benefit from the Gulf Stream?

♦ How might a region's mild climate help its economy?

BEFORE YOU READ

▶▶ *What Do You Know?*

Before you read the chapter, think about what you already know about Europe. What are some of its geographical features? What do you know about its early history? Have you ever read myths from ancient Greece or ancient Rome? Have you ever heard of Julius Caesar or Hercules? What do you know about knights and castles from the Middle Ages?

▶▶ *What Do You Want to Know?*

Decide what you want to know about these early periods of European history. Record your questions in your notebook before you read this chapter.

Region • Ancient Greece made important contributions in literature, philosophy, and architecture. ▼

READ AND TAKE NOTES

Reading Strategy: Categorizing One way to make sense of what you read is to categorize, or sort, information. Making a chart to categorize the information in this chapter will help you to understand the contributions made by early European cultures.

• Copy the chart below into your notebook.
• As you read, look for information relating to the categories of social structure, architecture, religion, and arts and sciences.
• Write your notes under the appropriate headings.

Region • The Middle Ages saw the rise of the Catholic Church and the growth of a middle class. ▲

Region • Ancient Rome made its mark in government, law, and engineering. ▲

Time Period	Social Structure	Architecture	Religion	Arts and Sciences
Ancient Greece				
Ancient Rome				
Middle Ages				

A Land of Varied Riches

Mediterranean Sea
peninsula
fjord
Ural Mountains
plain

MAIN IDEA

Europe is a continent with varied geographic features, abundant natural resources, and a climate that can support agriculture.

WHY IT MATTERS NOW

The development of Europe's diverse cultures has been shaped by the continent's diverse geography.

DATELINE

EXTRA

LONDON, ENGLAND, MAY 6, 1994

Rough waters have always made the English Channel, which separates England and France, difficult to cross. Now, however, you can make the trip under the water! Today, a tunnel nicknamed "the Chunnel" opens, allowing high-speed trains to travel between London and Paris in about three hours. The Chunnel—short for Channel Tunnel—was carved through chalky earth under the sea floor and took seven years to build. It is the largest European construction project of the 20th century.

Movement • Eurostar trains make the 31-mile trip under the English Channel in only 20 minutes. ▲

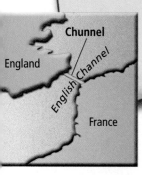

Location • The Channel Tunnel connects England and France. ▲

The Geography of Europe

Today, cars, airplanes, and trains are common forms of high-speed transportation across Europe. Before the 19th century, however, the fastest form of transportation was to travel by water—on top of it, rather than under it.

Western Europe: Its Land and Early History **273**

Waterways Look at the map of Europe on page 277. Water surrounds the continent to the north, south, and west. The southern coast of Europe borders the warm waters of the **Mediterranean Sea.** Europe also has many rivers. The highly traveled Rhine and Danube rivers are two of the most important. The Volga, which flows nearly 2,200 miles through western Russia, is the continent's longest. For hundreds of years, these and other waterways have been home to boats and barges carrying people and goods inland across great distances.

Landforms Several large **peninsulas,** or bodies of land surrounded by water on three sides, form the European continent. In Northern Europe, the Scandinavian Peninsula is home to Norway and Sweden. Along the jagged shoreline of this peninsula are beautiful fjords (fyawrdz). A **fjord** is a long, narrow, deep inlet of the sea located between steep cliffs. In Western Europe, the Iberian Peninsula includes Portugal and Spain. The Iberian Peninsula is separated from the rest of the continent by a mountain range called the Pyrenees (PEER·uh·NEEZ). The entire continent of Europe, itself surrounded by water on three sides, is a giant peninsula.

Reading **Social Studies**

A. Clarifying Why were waterways important for the movement of people and goods?

BACKGROUND

Europe can be divided into four areas: Western Europe, Northern Europe, Eastern Europe, and Russia and its neighboring countries.

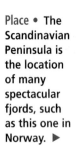

Place • The Scandinavian Peninsula is the location of many spectacular fjords, such as this one in Norway. ▶

Place • The Alps remain snowcapped year-round. ▶

Reading
Social Studies

B. Clarifying
What natural landform separates Europe from Asia?

Mountain ranges, including the towering Alps, also stretch across much of the continent. Along Europe's eastern border, the **Ural Mountains** (YUR·uhl) divide the continent from Asia. The many mountain ranges of Europe separated groups of people from one another as they settled the land thousands of years ago. This is one of the reasons why different cultures developed across the continent.

The Great European Plain Not all of Europe is mountainous. A vast region called the Great European Plain stretches from the coast of France to the Ural Mountains. A **plain** is a large, flat area of land, usually without many trees. The Great European Plain is the location of some of the world's richest farmland. Ancient trading centers attracted many people to this area, which today includes some of the largest cities in Europe—Paris, Berlin, Warsaw, and Moscow.

Climate

Although the Gulf Stream brings warm air and water to Europe, the winters are still severe in the mountains and in the far north. In some of these areas, cold winds blow southward from the Arctic Circle and make the average temperature fall below 0°F in January. The Alps and the Pyrenees, however, protect the European countries along the Mediterranean Sea from these chilling winds. In these warmer parts of southern Europe, the average temperature in January stays above 50°F.

The summers in the south are usually hot and dry, with an average July temperature around 80°F. This makes the Mediterranean coast a popular vacation spot. Elsewhere in Europe, in all but the coldest areas of the mountains and the far north, the average July temperature ranges from 50°F to 70°F.

Natural Resources

Europe has a large variety of natural resources, including minerals. The rich coal deposits of Germany's Ruhr (rur) Valley region have helped to make that area one of the world's major industrial centers. Russia and Ukraine have large deposits of iron ore, which is used to make iron for automobiles and countless other products.

Region • Western Europe benefits from a varied landscape rich in natural resources. ▼

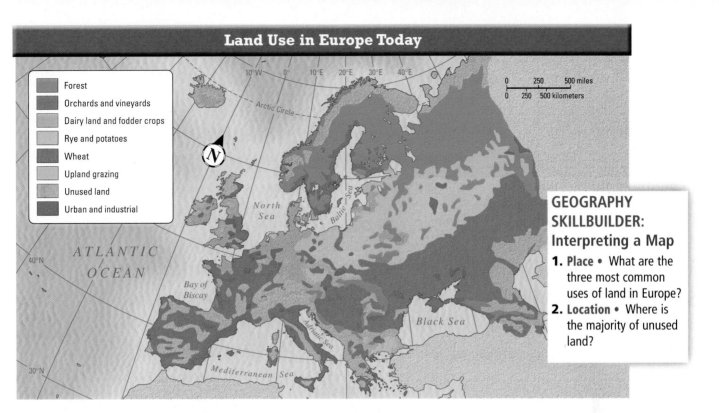

Land Use in Europe Today

Legend:
- Forest
- Orchards and vineyards
- Dairy land and fodder crops
- Rye and potatoes
- Wheat
- Upland grazing
- Unused land
- Urban and industrial

GEOGRAPHY SKILLBUILDER: Interpreting a Map

1. **Place** • What are the three most common uses of land in Europe?
2. **Location** • Where is the majority of unused land?

Vocabulary

precipitation: moisture, including rain, snow, and hail, that falls to the ground

Europe also has rich soil and plentiful rainfall. The average precipitation for the Great European Plain, for example, is between 20 and 40 inches per year. The map above shows the agricultural uses of the land, highlighting the major crops. Notice that few parts of the continent are too cold or too hot and dry to support some form of agriculture. These characteristics have made Europe a world leader in crop production.

SECTION 1 ASSESSMENT

Terms & Names

1. **Identify:**
   - (a) Mediterranean Sea
   - (b) peninsula
   - (c) fjord
   - (d) Ural Mountains
   - (e) plain

Taking Notes

2. Use a spider map like this one to list the different geographic features of Europe, and give a few specific examples of each.

   (spider map with center labeled "Peninsula")

Main Ideas

3. (a) How does the Gulf Stream affect the climate of Europe?

   (b) What separates Europe from Asia?

   (c) How do waterways, such as rivers and seas, strengthen trade in Europe?

Critical Thinking

4. **Recognizing Effects**

   How did Europe's many mountain ranges affect its development?

   Think About
   - climate
   - trade and travel
   - the separation of groups of people

ACTIVITY -OPTION-

Reread the information about the Chunnel. Write a **short story** in which you imagine what it might have been like to work on the Chunnel's construction.

Ancient Greece

TERMS & NAMES
city-state
polis
Aegean Sea
oligarchy
Athens
philosopher
Aristotle
Alexander the Great

MAIN IDEA

The ancient Greeks developed a complex society, with remarkable achievements in the arts, sciences, and government.

WHY IT MATTERS NOW

The achievements of the ancient Greeks continue to influence culture, science, and politics in the world today.

DATELINE

ATHENS, GREECE, FEBRUARY 2, 1997— Five years after construction workers began building the new Athens subway, artifacts from ancient Greek civilization are still being discovered. When completed, the new subway will reduce traffic and air pollution in the capital. Historians and archaeologists, however, have been the first to benefit from this massive public works project.

Workers have discovered statues, coins, jewelry, and gravesites from ancient Greece. Recently, workers digging the foundation for a downtown Athens station found an ancient dog collar decorated with gemstones. Local officials have promised to create

Place • Building the subway in Athens led to spectacular discoveries of ancient artifacts. ▲

permanent displays of some artifacts in stations throughout the new subway system.

The Land and Early History of Greece

The Greek Peninsula is mountainous, which made travel by land difficult for early settlers. Most of the rocky land also contains poor soil and few large trees, but settlers were able to cultivate the soil to grow olives and grapes. The greatest natural resource of the peninsula is the water that surrounds it. The ancient Greeks depended on these seas for fishing and trade, and they became excellent sailors.

Vocabulary

cultivate: to prepare land for growing crops

The Formation of City-States As the ancient Greek population grew, people created city-states. A **city-state** included a central city, called a **polis,** and surrounding villages. Each ancient Greek city-state had its own laws and form of government. The city-states were united by a common language, shared religious beliefs, and a similar way of life.

The Growth of Colonies By the mid-eighth century B.C., the Greeks were leaving the peninsula in search of better land and greater opportunities for trade. During the next 200 years, they built dozens of communities on the islands and coastline of the **Aegean Sea** (ih·JEE·uhn). Some Greeks settled as far away as modern-day Spain and North Africa.

Once established, these distant Greek communities traded with each other and with those communities on the Greek Peninsula. This made a great variety of goods available to the ancient Greeks, including wheat for bread, timber for building boats, and iron ore for making strong tools and weapons.

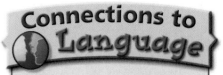

Connections to Language

Metropolis When ancient Greeks moved away from a large polis to a distant community, they referred to their former city-state as their metropolis. In Greek, this means "mother-city." Today, we use the word *metropolis* to mean any large urban area, such as Los Angeles, London, Tokyo, or Athens *(shown below).*

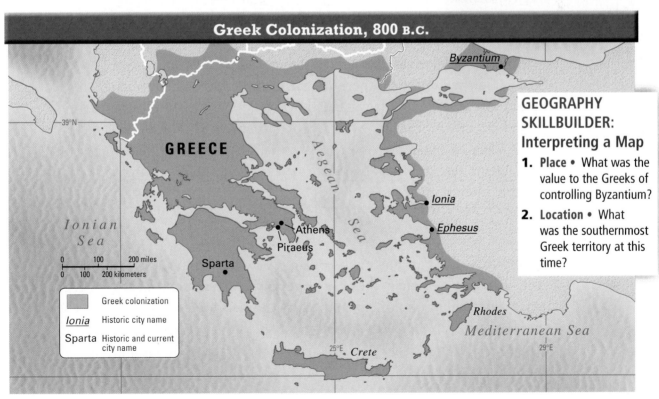

Greek Colonization, 800 B.C.

GREECE

Ionian Sea

Aegean Sea

Byzantium

Ionia

Ephesus

Athens
Piraeus

Sparta

Rhodes

Mediterranean Sea

Crete

0   100   200 miles
0   100   200 kilometers

Greek colonization
Ionia Historic city name
Sparta Historic and current city name

39°N

25°E   29°E

GEOGRAPHY SKILLBUILDER: Interpreting a Map

1. **Place** • What was the value to the Greeks of controlling Byzantium?

2. **Location** • What was the southernmost Greek territory at this time?

Spartan Soldiers Sparta was the only city-state with a permanent army. At age seven, Spartan boys were sent by their families for military training. They had to remain in the army until they were 30 years old.

Individual Forms of Government Some ancient Greek city-states were oligarchies (AHL·ih·GAHR·kees). An **oligarchy** is a system in which a few powerful, wealthy individuals rule. The word *oligarchy* comes from an ancient Greek word meaning "rule by the few." Other city-states were ruled by a tyrant, a single person who took control of the government against the wishes of the community. Still other ancient Greek city-states developed an early form of democracy. The word *democracy* comes from an ancient Greek word meaning "rule by the people." In a democracy citizens, take part in the government.

Athens and Sparta

Athens, centrally located on the Greek Peninsula, was one of the largest and most important ancient Greek city-states. By the end of the sixth century B.C., Athens had developed a democratic form of government. Athenian citizens took part in political debates and voted on laws, but not everyone who lived in Athens enjoyed these rights. Participation in government was limited to free, adult males whose fathers had been citizens of Athens. Women, slaves, and foreign residents could not take part in government.

Athens's chief rival among the other Greek city-states was Sparta. Located in the southernmost part of the Greek Peninsula, Sparta was an oligarchy. It was ruled by two kings, who were supported by other officials. Sparta, like Athens, had a powerful army. Each city-state's army helped protect it from slave rebellions, guard against attack by rival city-states, and defend it from possible foreign invaders.

Learning and the Arts

In 480 B.C., the Persians, who controlled a large empire to the east, tried to conquer the Greek Peninsula. Several Greek city-states, including Athens and Sparta, joined forces to defeat the Persians. In the years following this victory, the ancient Greeks made remarkable achievements in literature, learning, and architecture.

Reading
Social Studies

A. Comparing Compare the three forms of government most common in ancient Greek city-states.

BACKGROUND

After the defeat of Persia, Athens became the most powerful Greek city-state. The most important Athenian leader of the time was Pericles (PEHR·ih·KLEEZ), who lived from c. 495 to 429 B.C.

Literature To honor their gods and goddesses, the ancient Greeks created myths and wrote poems and plays. Some of the greatest Greek plays were written during the fifth century B.C. During that time, the playwrights Aeschylus (EHS·kuh·luhs), Sophocles (SAHF·uh·KLEEZ), and Euripides (yu·RIHP·ih·DEEZ) wrote tragedies, which are serious plays that end unhappily. Many of these stories have been the basis for modern films and operas.

In addition to using the gods as characters, ancient Greek playwrights sometimes poked fun at important citizens, including generals and politicians. Aristophanes (ar·ih·STAHF·uh·NEEZ) was a popular writer of comedies of this type.

Philosophy Ancient Greece was the birthplace of some of the finest thinkers of the ancient world. Socrates (SAHK·ruh·TEEZ) was an important philosopher of the fifth century B.C. A **philosopher** studies and thinks about why the world is the way it is. Socrates studied and taught about friendship, knowledge, and justice. Another great philosopher, Plato (PLAY·toh), was a student of Socrates who studied and taught about human behavior, government, mathematics, and astronomy.

Reading
Social Studies

B. Making Inferences Why do you think philosophers felt the need to teach?

The ancient Greek philosopher Heraclitus (hehr·uh·KLY·tuhs) wrote the following lines.

> **A VOICE FROM ANCIENT GREECE**
>
> One cannot step twice into the same river, for the water into which you first stepped has flowed on.
>
> *Heraclitus*

Many people continue to study and write about the same philosophical questions that these, and other, ancient Greek philosophers explored.

The WORLD'S HERITAGE

Ancient Greek Architecture
Ancient Greek builders created some of the world's most impressive works of architecture. They built several beautiful temples atop the Acropolis (uh·KRAHP·uh·lihs) in Athens, shown at right. The most famous of the temples is the Parthenon (PAHR·thuh·nahn).

In the United States and elsewhere, government buildings, such as courthouses and post offices, have been built similar in style to the Parthenon. This use of ancient architecture echoes the democratic ideals of ancient Greece.

Aristotle At the age of 17, Aristotle (384–322 B.C.) began studying philosophy with Plato. After Plato died, Aristotle received his most important assignment— to teach Alexander, the teenage son of King Philip II of Macedonia.

After teaching Alexander, Aristotle returned to Athens. There he taught and wrote about poetry, government, and astronomy. He started a famous school called the Lyceum (ly•SEE•uhm). Aristotle also collected and studied plants and animals. The work of this brilliant philosopher continues to greatly influence scientists and philosophers today.

The Spread of Greek Culture The city-states of ancient Greece were constantly at war with one another. By the fourth century B.C., this fighting had weakened their ability to defend themselves against foreign invaders. In 338 B.C., King Philip II of Macedonia conquered the land. After Philip died, his son, Alexander—who had been taught by **Aristotle**—took control.

Alexander the Great was an excellent military leader, and his armies conquered vast new territories. As Alexander's empire expanded, Greek culture, language, and ideas were spread throughout the Mediterranean region and as far east as modern-day India. Upon Alexander's death, however, his leading generals fought for control of his territory and divided it among themselves. This marked the end of one of the great empires of the ancient world.

Region • In this mosaic Alexander the Great is shown riding into battle on his beloved horse, Bucephalus (byoo•SEHF•ah•luhs). ▲

SECTION 2 ASSESSMENT

Terms & Names

1. Identify: (a) city-state (b) polis (c) Aegean Sea (d) oligarchy
(e) Athens (f) philosopher (g) Aristotle (h) Alexander the Great

Taking Notes

2. Use a chart like this one to list and describe the ancient Greek achievements in government, literature, and architecture.

Government	Literature	Architecture

Main Ideas

3. (a) Why were the surrounding areas of water an important natural resource of the Greek Peninsula?

(b) Which people were allowed to participate in the government of ancient Athens?

(c) How did Alexander the Great help to spread Greek culture?

Critical Thinking

4. **Summarizing**

Why was the fifth century B.C. a remarkable time in ancient Greek history?

Think About

• warfare

• leaders

• literature and philosophy

ACTIVITY -OPTION- Reread the information about the individual forms of government common in ancient Greece. Present an **oral report** to the class that compares and contrasts two of the forms.

Making a Generalization

▶▶ Defining the Skill

To make generalizations means to make broad judgments based on information. When you make generalizations, you should gather information from several sources.

▶▶ Applying the Skill

The following three passages contain different information on the government of ancient Athens. Use the strategies listed below to make a generalization about Athenian government based on the passages.

How to Make a Generalization

Strategy ❶ Look for all the information that the sources have in common. These three sources all explain about Athenian government.

Strategy ❷ Form a generalization that describes ancient Athenian government in a way that all three sources would support. State your generalization in a sentence.

Make a Chart

Using a chart can help you make generalizations. The chart below shows how the information you just read can be used to generalize about the government of ancient Athens.

❶ Athenian citizens took part in political debates and voted on laws, but not everyone who lived in Athens enjoyed these rights. Participation in government was limited to free, adult males whose fathers had been citizens in Athens.

—*World Cultures and Geography*

In return for playing their parts as soldiers or sailors, ❶ ordinary Athenians insisted on controlling the government.

—*Encyclopaedia Britannica*

Unlike representative democracies or republics, in which one man is elected to speak for many, Athens was a true ❶ democracy: every citizen spoke for himself.

—*Classical Greece*

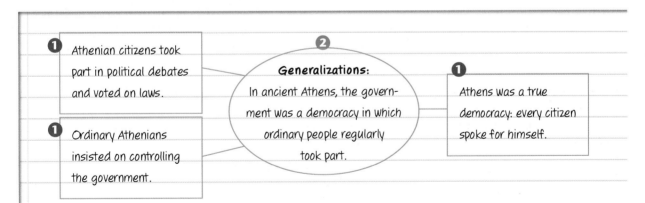

❶ Athenian citizens took part in political debates and voted on laws.

❶ Ordinary Athenians insisted on controlling the government.

❷ **Generalizations:**
In ancient Athens, the government was a democracy in which ordinary people regularly took part.

❶ Athens was a true democracy: every citizen spoke for himself.

▶▶ Practicing the Skill

Turn to Chapter 10, Section 2, "Ancient Greece." Read the sections on literature and philosophy. Also read about ancient Greek writings in an encyclopedia, a library book, or on the Internet. Then make a chart like the one above to form a generalization about the importance of knowledge and learning to the ancient Greeks.

Ancient Rome

TERMS & NAMES
republic
Senate
patrician
plebeian
Julius Caesar
empire
Augustus
Constantine

MAIN IDEA

The ancient Romans made important contributions to government, law, and engineering.

WHY IT MATTERS NOW

The cultural achievements of the Romans continue to influence the art, architecture, and literature of today.

DATELINE

EXTRA

ROME, 295 B.C.

Yet another Roman road was completed today! Rome is famous for its vast network of roadways. Repairing old roads and adding new ones keeps Roman engineers busy. Construction is time-consuming because the lengthy roads, which are paved with large stones, must be carefully planned. However, the benefits are worth the effort.

The roads connect the great city to distant lands under Roman rule. These roadways also enable the army to move quickly. These days, it seems that almost all roads lead to Rome. In fact, when this massive undertaking is finished, Roman roads will stretch for tens of thousands of miles across the land.

Location • All roads lead to Rome—including the Via Appia (VEE•uh APP•ee•uh) shown here. ▲

The Beginnings of Ancient Rome

Ancient Rome began as a group of villages located along the banks of the Tiber River in what is now Italy. There, early settlers herded sheep and grew wheat, olives, and grapes. Around 750 B.C., these villages united to form the city of Rome.

The Formation of the Roman Republic For more than 200 years, kings ruled Rome. Then, in 509 B.C., Rome became a republic. A **republic** is a nation in which power belongs to the citizens, who govern themselves through elected representatives.

The Senate The Roman **Senate** was an assembly of elected representatives. It was the single most powerful ruling body of the Roman Republic. Each year, the Senate selected two leaders, called consuls, to head the government and the military.

Patricians At first, most of the people elected to the Senate were patricians (puh·TRIHSH·uhns). In ancient Rome, a **patrician** was a member of a wealthy, landowning family who claimed to be able to trace its roots back to the founding of Rome. The patricians also controlled the law, since they were the only citizens who were allowed to be judges.

Plebeians An ordinary, working male citizen of ancient Rome—such as a farmer or craftsperson—was called a **plebeian** (plih·BEE·uhn). Plebeians had the right to vote, but they could not hold public office until 287 B.C., when they gained equality with patricians.

The Expansion of the Roman World

Over hundreds of years, Rome grew into a mighty city. By the third century B.C., Rome ruled most of the Italian Peninsula. This gave Rome control of the central Mediterranean.

The city-state of Carthage, which ruled North Africa and southern Spain, controlled the western Mediterranean. To take control over this area as well, Rome fought Carthage and eventually won.

As Rome's population grew, its army also expanded in size and strength. Under the leadership of ambitious generals, Rome's highly trained soldiers set out to conquer new territories one by one.

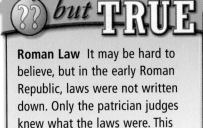

Roman Law It may be hard to believe, but in the early Roman Republic, laws were not written down. Only the patrician judges knew what the laws were. This meant that judges usually ruled in favor of fellow patricians and against plebeians.

The plebeians grew tired of unfair treatment and demanded that the judges create a written code of laws that applied to all Roman citizens. This code, called the Law of the Twelve Tables, was written around 450 B.C. It formed the foundation of Roman law.

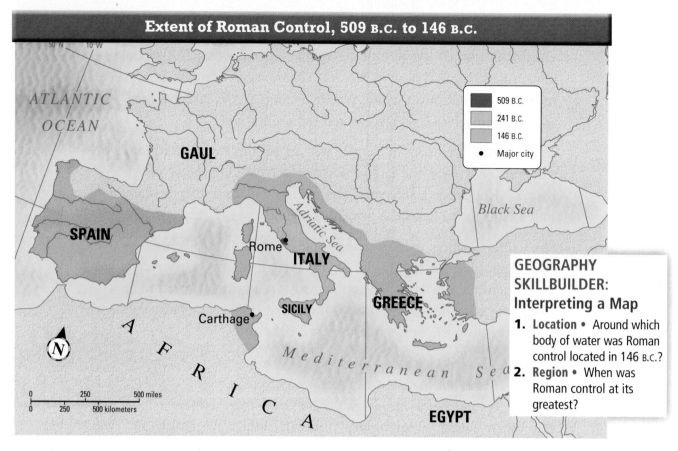

ATLANTIC OCEAN

GAUL

SPAIN

Rome

ITALY

Adriatic Sea

Black Sea

Carthage

SICILY

GREECE

A F R I C A

Mediterranean Sea

EGYPT

509 B.C.
241 B.C.
146 B.C.
• Major city

0   250   500 miles
0   250   500 kilometers

N

GEOGRAPHY SKILLBUILDER: Interpreting a Map

1. **Location** • Around which body of water was Roman control located in 146 B.C.?
2. **Region** • When was Roman control at its greatest?

As Rome's control over its neighbors expanded, its culture and language continued to spread into Spain and Greece. By the end of the second century B.C., the Romans ruled most of the land surrounding the Mediterranean Sea. The ancient Romans even called the Mediterranean *mare nostrum* (MAH•ray NOH•struhm), which means "our sea."

Region • Once in power, Julius Caesar had his likeness stamped on coins such as this one. ▼

From Republic to Empire

As the Roman Republic grew, its citizens became a more and more diverse group of people. Many Romans practiced different religions and followed different customs, but they were united by a common system of government and law. In the middle of the first century B.C., however, Rome's form of government changed.

The End of the Roman Republic <u>**Julius Caesar,**</u> a successful Roman general and famous speaker, was the governor of the territory called Gaul. By conquering nearby territories to expand the land under his control, he increased both his power and his reputation. The Roman Senate feared that Caesar might become too powerful, and they ordered him to resign. Caesar, however, had other ideas.

BACKGROUND

Ancient Gaul included the lands that are modern-day France, Belgium, and parts of northern Italy.

Rather than resign, Caesar fought a long, fierce battle for control of the Roman Republic. In 45 B.C., he finally triumphed and returned to Rome. Caesar eventually became dictator of the Roman world. A dictator is a person who holds total control over a government. Caesar's rule marked the end of the Roman Republic.

The Beginning of the Roman Empire Julius Caesar had great plans to reorganize the way ancient Rome was governed, but his rule was cut short. On March 15, 44 B.C., a group of senators, angered by Caesar's plans and power, stabbed him to death on the floor of the Roman Senate. A civil war then erupted that lasted for several years.

Reading
Social Studies

A. Recognizing Important Details How many years separated the rules of Julius Caesar and Augustus?

In 27 B.C., Caesar's adopted son, Octavian, was named the first emperor of Rome. This marks the official beginning of the Roman Empire. An **empire** is a nation or group of territories ruled by a single, powerful leader, or emperor. As emperor, Octavian took the name **Augustus.**

The Augustan Age Augustus ruled the Roman Empire for more than 40 years. During this time, called the Augustan Age, the empire continued to expand. To help protect the enormous amount of land under his control, Augustus sent military forces along its borders, which now extended northward to the Rhine and Danube rivers.

Region • Sculptures of Augustus were sent all over the Roman Empire to let people know what their leader looked like. ▲

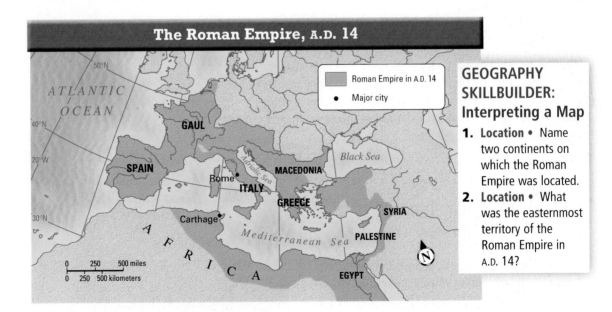

The Roman Empire, A.D. 14

Roman Empire in A.D. 14
• Major city

ATLANTIC OCEAN

50°N
40°N
20°W
30°N

GAUL
SPAIN
Rome
ITALY
Carthage
AFRICA
Mediterranean Sea
Adriatic Sea
MACEDONIA
GREECE
Black Sea
SYRIA
PALESTINE
EGYPT

N

0   250   500 miles
0   250   500 kilometers

GEOGRAPHY SKILLBUILDER: Interpreting a Map

1. **Location** • Name two continents on which the Roman Empire was located.
2. **Location** • What was the easternmost territory of the Roman Empire in A.D. 14?

While the Roman army kept peace, architects and engineers built many new public buildings. Trade increased, with olive oil, wine, pottery, marble, and grain being shipped all across the Mediterranean. Lighthouses were constructed, too, to help ships find their way into port.

The Augustan Age was also a time of great Roman literature. One of the most famous works of the age is the *Aeneid* (ih·NEE·ud). This long poem tells the story of Rome's founding. Augustus himself asked the famous poet Virgil to write it. This period of peace and cultural growth that Augustus created in the Roman Empire was called the "Pax Romana" (pahks roh·MAH·nah). The Pax Romana, or Roman Peace, lasted for 200 years.

Region • A diver holds an artifact from an ancient Roman shipwreck in the Mediterranean Sea. ▲

Spotlight on CULTURE

Architecture Various inventions helped the Roman Empire grow and prosper. In addition to buildings and roads, Roman architects and engineers constructed water systems called aqueducts. Ancient aqueducts were raised tunnels that carried fresh water over long distances.

Built throughout the empire, aqueducts poured millions of gallons of water into Rome and other cities every day. They supplied clean water to private homes, fountains, and public baths. Today, some ancient Roman aqueducts still stand in France, Spain, and even on the outskirts of Rome itself.

THINKING CRITICALLY

1. Analyzing Motives
   Why did Romans want a way to transport water?

2. Hypothesizing
   Do you think the Roman Empire would have grown so large and prosperous without the aqueducts?

The Rise of Christianity

Reading Social Studies

B. Making Inferences How do you think the Roman Empire indirectly helped the spread of Christianity?

In the years following the death of Augustus in A.D. 14, a new religion from the Middle East began to take hold in the rest of the Mediterranean world: Christianity. At first, this religion became popular mainly in the eastern half of the Roman Empire. Many followers there preached about its teachings. Christianity spread along the transportation network constructed by the Romans. By the third century A.D., this religion had spread throughout the empire.

Most earlier Roman leaders had tolerated the different religions practiced throughout the empire. Christians, however, were viewed with suspicion and suffered persecution as early as A.D. 64. Roman leaders and people of other religions even blamed the Christians for natural disasters. Many Christians during this time were punished or killed for their beliefs.

Region • Constantine (died A.D. 337) was the first Christian emperor of Rome. ▼

The First Christian Emperor

Things changed when **Constantine** became emperor of Rome in A.D. 306. In A.D. 312, before a battle, Constantine claimed to have had a vision of a cross in the sky. The emperor promised that if he won the battle, he would become a Christian. Constantine was victorious, and the next year he fulfilled his promise. Christianity became the official religion of the Roman Empire. Today, Christianity has nearly two billion followers worldwide.

SECTION 3 ASSESSMENT

Terms & Names

1. Identify:
   (a) republic
   (e) Julius Caesar
   (b) Senate
   (f) empire
   (c) patrician
   (g) Augustus
   (d) plebeian
   (h) Constantine

Taking Notes

2. Use a chart like this one to outline the achievements of ancient Rome's Augustan Age.

Achievement	Effects

Main Ideas

3. (a) On what waterway is the city of Rome located?

(b) What helped to unite the many different citizens of the Roman Republic?

(c) How did Christianity spread throughout the Roman Empire?

Critical Thinking

4. Drawing Conclusions

Why was ancient Rome able to control most of the land surrounding the Mediterranean Sea?

Think About

• the location of the Italian Peninsula

• Rome's army

• Rome's wars with Carthage

ACTIVITY -OPTION-

Review the information about the beginnings of ancient Rome. Create a **chart** that compares the two important classes of Roman society: patricians and plebeians.

Time of Change: The Middle Ages

TERMS & NAMES
medieval
Charlemagne
feudalism
manorialism
guild
Magna Carta

MAIN IDEA

The Middle Ages was a time of great change in Western Europe.

WHY IT MATTERS NOW

Some developments that occurred during the Middle Ages continue to affect life in Europe today.

DATELINE

ROME, A.D. 476—A Germanic tribe called the Visigoths has attacked our city of Rome and overthrown the emperor, Romulus Augustulus. The Roman army—no longer as large or as well organized as it was during the height of the empire—was unable to fight off the invaders.

After looting the great city, fierce bands of warriors and bandits have continued raiding towns and villages throughout Western Europe. They are stealing jewels and money, killing both people and animals, and even seizing control of entire territories. The Roman Empire seems to have breathed its last breath.

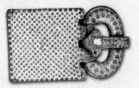

Region • Visigoth artifacts, like these saddle buckles, were found near Rome. ▲

Western Europe in Collapse

As the Roman Empire collapsed in the fifth century, more and more people fled to the countryside to escape invaders from the north and east. Eventually, there was no central government to maintain roads, public buildings, or water systems. Most towns and cities in Western Europe shrank or were totally abandoned. Long-distance travel became unsafe, and trade less common.

Reading
Social Studies

A. Clarifying
Who provided
leadership during
the Middle Ages?

The Beginning of the Medieval Era The period of history between the fall of the Roman Empire and the beginning of the modern world is called the Middle Ages, or **medieval** (MEE·dee·EE·vuhl) era. During this time, many of the advances and inventions of the ancient world were lost. Without a strong central government, many Europeans turned to military leaders and the Roman Catholic Church for leadership and support.

Charlemagne and the Christian Church

Among the most famous military leaders was the Germanic King Charlemagne (SHAHR·luh·mayn). In the late 700s, **Charlemagne,** or Charles the Great, worked to bring political order to the northwestern fringes of what had been the Roman Empire. This great warrior not only fought to increase the size of his kingdom, he also worked to improve life for those who lived there.

A New Roman Emperor Eventually, news of Charlemagne's accomplishments spread to Rome. Although the old empire was gone, Rome was now the center of the Catholic Church. The Pope recognized that joining forces with Charlemagne might bring greater power to the Church.

In 800, the Pope crowned Charlemagne as the new Holy Roman Emperor. During Charlemagne's rule, education improved, the government became stronger, and Catholicism spread. But after Charlemagne's death, Western Europe was once again without a strong political leader.

Region •
Charlemagne
established
order and
supported
education and
culture for a
brief period
in the early
Middle Ages. ▲

The Role of the Church

Throughout Western Europe in medieval times, each community was centered around a church. The church offered religious services, established orphanages, and helped care for the poor, sick, and elderly. They also hosted feasts, festivals, and other celebrations. As communities grew, their members often donated money and labor to build new and larger churches.

Monks and Nuns Some people chose to dedicate their lives to serving God and the Church. These religious people were called monks and nuns. Monks were men who devoted their time to praying, studying, and copying and decorating holy books by hand. Monks lived in communities called monasteries. Many monasteries became important centers of learning in medieval society.

Location •
Convents and monasteries often were located in hard-to-reach areas. ▲

Women who served the Church were called nuns. In the Middle Ages, it was common for a woman to become a nun after her husband died. Nuns prayed, sewed, taught young girls, cared for the poor, and also copied and decorated books. They lived in secluded communities called convents.

Vocabulary

secluded:
to be separate or hidden away

Two Medieval Systems

During the Middle Ages, almost all the land was owned by powerful nobles—lords, kings, and high church officials. The central government was not very strong. The nobles sometimes even controlled the king and constantly fought among themselves. To protect their lands and position, nobles developed a system known as feudalism.

The Feudal System **Feudalism** was a system of political ties in which the nobles, such as kings, gave out land to less powerful nobles, such as knights. In return for the land, the noble, called a vassal, made a vow to provide various services to the lord. The most important was to furnish his lord with knights, foot soldiers, and arms for battle.

The parcel of land granted to a vassal by his lord was called a fief (feef). The center of the lord's fief was the manor, which consisted of a large house or castle, surrounding farmland, villages, and a church. A fief might also include several other manors or castles belonging to the fief-owner's vassals.

Connections to History

The Bayeux Tapestry This famous work of art depicts the invasion of England by William the Conqueror in 1066. The Bayeux (by•YOO) Tapestry is a series of scenes from the point of view of the invaders, who came from Normandy. Normandy is a part of what is now France. The work is an important source of information about not only the conquest of England, but also medieval armor, clothing, and other aspects of culture.

Although called a tapestry, the work is really an embroidered strip of linen about 230 feet long. It includes captions in Latin. The Bayeux Tapestry was probably made by nuns in England about 1092.

Manorialism On the manor, peasants lived and farmed, but they usually did not own the land they lived on. In exchange for their lord's protection, the peasants contributed their labor and a certain amount of the food they raised. Some peasants, known as serfs, actually belonged to the fief on which they lived. They were not slaves, but they were not free to leave the land without the permission of the lord. This system, in which the lord received food and work in exchange for his protection, is known as **manorialism**.

Place • Although castles were large, they were built for defense. Castles were usually located on high ground with a series of walls and towers. ▲

Medieval Ways of Life

Medieval nobles had more power than the peasants. However, the difference in the standard of living between the very rich and the very poor was not as great as the difference today.

Castle Life The manor houses or castles may have been large, but they were built more for defense than for comfort. Thick stone walls and few windows made the rooms cold, damp, and dark. Fires added warmth but made the air smoky. Medieval noble families may have slept on feather mattresses, but lice and other pests were a constant annoyance. Most castles did not have indoor plumbing.

Peasant Life Peasants lived outside the castle walls in small dwellings, often with dirt floors and straw roofs. They owned little furniture and slept on straw mattresses. It was common for peasant families to keep their farm animals inside their homes.

Peasants often worked two or three days a week for their lord, harvesting crops and repairing roads and bridges. The rest of the week they farmed their own small plots. Many days were religious festivals during which no one worked.

The Growth of Medieval Towns

By the middle of the 11th century, life was improving for many people in Western Europe. New farming methods increased the supply of food and shortened the time it took to harvest crops. Fewer farmers were needed, and workers began to leave the countryside in search of other opportunities. People moved back into towns or formed new ones that grew into booming centers of trade. The population increased, and more and more people owned property or started businesses.

Guilds As competition among local businesspeople grew, tradespeople and craftspeople created their own guilds, or business associations. Similar to modern trade unions, a **guild** protected workers' rights, set wages and prices, and settled disputes. Membership in a guild was also a common requirement for citizens who sought one of the few elective public offices.

The Late Middle Ages

Over time, the towns of the late Middle Ages grew in size, power, and wealth. The citizens of these towns began to establish local governments and to elect leaders.

Connections to Economics

The Middle Class In the early Middle Ages, only a small percentage of people in Western Europe were wealthy landowners. Most people worked on manor lands or at some sort of craft. However, those workers who found jobs in towns often were able to save money and build businesses. Eventually, their improved status led to the rise of a middle class.

Unlike nobles, the members of this new middle class did not live off the land they owned. They had to continuously earn money, as most people do today.

Reading Social Studies

B. Analyzing Motives Why did people create guilds?

Governments Challenge the Church The Pope insisted that he had supreme authority over all the Christian lands. Kings and other government leaders, however, did not agree that the Pope was more powerful than they were. This is an issue that continues to be discussed today.

Region • High taxes and failures on the battlefield made King John one of the most hated kings of England. ▼

The Magna Carta The rulers of Western Europe also struggled for power with members of the nobility. In England, nobles rebelled against King John. In 1215, the nobles forced the English king to sign a document called the **Magna Carta** (MAG·nuh KAHR·tuh), or Great Charter. This document limited the king's power and gave the nobles a larger role in the government.

Region • The Magna Carta influenced the creators of the U.S. Constitution. ▲

SECTION 4 ASSESSMENT

Terms & Names

1. Identify:
   (a) medieval
   (b) Charlemagne
   (c) feudalism
   (d) manorialism
   (e) guild
   (f) Magna Carta

Taking Notes

2. Use a flow chart like this one to show how Europe changed over four time periods: A.D. 476, the 800s, the mid-1000s, and the 1200s.

   476
   ↓
   [ ]
   ↓
   800s
   ↓

Main Ideas

3. (a) Why is this era of European history called the Middle Ages?

   (b) Describe the role of the Church in medieval society.

   (c) How did manorialism help both nobles and peasants?

Critical Thinking

4. **Contrasting**

   How did life differ for nobles and peasants under feudalism?

   Think About
   • where they lived
   • what they ate
   • how they did their work

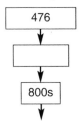

ACTIVITY -OPTION-

Review the information about serfs. Write a series of short **journal entries** describing what a week in the life of a serf might have been like during the Middle Ages.

TERMS & NAMES

Explain the significance of each of the following:

1. peninsula
2. plain
3. city-state
4. Aegean Sea
5. Athens
6. republic
7. empire
8. Constantine
9. feudalism
10. Magna Carta

REVIEW QUESTIONS

A Land of Varied Riches *(pages 273–277)*

1. What is special about Europe's physical environment?
2. Why is the Great European Plain an important region?

Ancient Greece *(pages 278–282)*

3. What helped to unite the separate city-states of ancient Greece?
4. What caused the people of Athens to join forces with their rival city-state, Sparta, in 480 B.C.?

Ancient Rome *(pages 284–289)*

5. Why did the ancient Romans call the Mediterranean Sea "our sea"?
6. Why did the Roman Senate ask Julius Caesar to resign?

Time of Change: The Middle Ages *(pages 290–295)*

7. Why did the people turn to the Roman Catholic Church for leadership and support during the Middle Ages?
8. What contributed to the growth of towns during the Middle Ages?

CRITICAL THINKING

Recognizing Effects

1. Using your completed chart from Reading Social Studies, p. 272, identify changes in art, culture, religion, and social structure from the time of ancient Rome to the Middle Ages.

Hypothesizing

2. Many myths and plays of ancient Greece have been the basis for modern films and dramas. What does this indicate about these ancient stories and characters?

Analyzing Causes

3. How did the long, peaceful reign of Augustus help to promote architecture, literature, and art in the Roman Empire?

Visual Summary

1 A Land of Varied Riches

- The rich natural resources and varied geography of Europe helped to shape its development.

Chunnel

England

English Channel

France

2 Ancient Greece

- The ancient Greeks developed a complex society and system of government.
- The achievements of the ancient Greeks in architecture, literature, and philosophy had a lasting impact on the world.

3 Ancient Rome

- Under strong leadership, ancient Rome experienced a time of great growth.
- Ancient Rome's contributions to government, engineering, and literature influenced Western culture.

4 Time of Change: The Middle Ages

- The social order and government of the Middle Ages transformed Europe into a modern society.

"Across the Roman Empire . . . [T]here were gods to protect the house, gods of healing, in fact gods of all aspects of life."
—*Ancient Rome*

"[The ancient Greeks] believed there were many gods and that those gods controlled the universe."
—*Greek Gods and Heroes*

"Each [Roman] home had a special niche or place for the household gods. Every aspect of nature had its particular spirit too."
—*The New Book of Knowledge*

SKILLBUILDER: Making a Generalization

1. What information do these passages have in common?
2. What generalization can you make from the passages?

FOCUS ON GEOGRAPHY

1. **Location** • What bodies of water does the Gulf Stream flow through on the way to Europe?
2. **Movement** • How might the Gulf Stream help transportation by sea?
3. **Location** • From looking at the map, what countries in Europe do you think are most directly affected by the Gulf Stream?

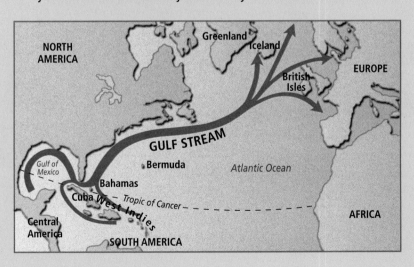

CHAPTER PROJECTS

Interdisciplinary Activity: Language Arts

Writing a Newspaper Report Research the assassination of Julius Caesar by a group of Roman senators in 44 B.C. Write a front-page news article about the event. Include a headline and answers to the *who, what, where,* and *when* questions of good reporting.

Cooperative Learning Activity

Creating a Playbill With a group of two or three students, design and create a playbill, or program for the audience, for a Greek tragedy. Assign responsibilities for the playbill.

- Design a cover illustration.
- List and identify the characters.
- Provide information about the playwright.
- Include a brief summary of the story.

INTERNET ACTIVITY

Use the Internet to research the natural resources of Europe. Focus on one region, such as the Ruhr Valley, the Mediterranean Sea, or the independent republics of Eastern Europe. Identify the major natural resources and explain how they contributed to that region's development.

Presenting Your Findings Organize your research for a class presentation. Include a map that shows the region and its resources. Prepare a short oral report about how that region has developed in modern times. List the Web sites you used to prepare your report.

For Internet links to support this activity, go to

RESEARCH LINKS
CLASSZONE.COM

The Growth of New Ideas

How can trade spread disease?

Movement • In 1347, an epidemic of bubonic plague (boo•BAHN•ihk playg) hit Europe. This plague, also called the Black Death, started in Asia. Caravans and trading ships carried it to port cities on the Mediterranean Sea. The plague spread from Sicily to the Italian Peninsula and then to France, Spain, and England.

The Black Death was carried by fleas that infected both rats and humans. Rats did not die from the plague. Instead, they served as hosts, or carriers, for the disease. By 1349, the horrors of the epidemic reached Switzerland, Austria, and Hungary. Later, it even reached as far north and east as Scandinavia and Russia. Historians estimate that this plague killed one out of every three persons in Europe.

What do you think?

♦ Why might the plague have reached Italy before it spread to England?

♦ How do you think the Black Death might have affected the economy of Europe?

Place The Cape of Saint Vincent is at the southwest tip of Portugal, jutting into the Atlantic Ocean. This was the location of Prince Henry's School of Navigation, where Portuguese sailors learned ways to explore the oceans of the world.

BEFORE YOU READ

▶▶ *What Do You Know?*

Do you know who first sailed around the world? Do you know that Leonardo da Vinci drew plans for a helicopter 400 years before it was actually built? Think of other discoveries, inventions, events, and famous people. What do you think life was like for common people during this time? Think about movies you have seen, books you have read, and what you have learned in other classes about the Renaissance, the Industrial Revolution, and political revolutions in France, Russia, and the United States.

▶▶ *What Do You Want to Know?*

Decide what you know about changes in the West from the Renaissance into the 1800s. In your notebook, record what you hope to learn from this chapter.

READ AND TAKE NOTES

Reading Strategy: Categorizing One way to make sense of what you read is to categorize ideas. Categorizing means sorting information by certain traits, ideas, or characteristics. Use the chart below to categorize details about the topics covered in this chapter.

- Copy the chart into your notebook.
- As you read each section, look for information about ideas, people, and events.
- Record key details in each category.

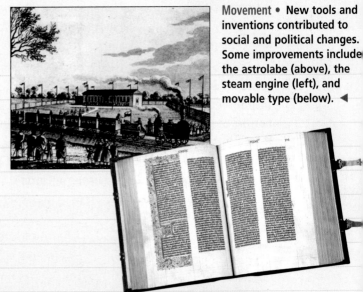

Movement • New tools and inventions contributed to social and political changes. Some improvements include the astrolabe (above), the steam engine (left), and movable type (below). ◀

Influences	New Ideas	People/Achievements	Events/Effects
The Renaissance			
European Exploration and Conquest			
Scientific and Industrial Revolutions			
Political Revolutions			
The Russian Empire			

Renaissance Connections

SECTION 1

TERMS & NAMES

Crusades
Renaissance
Florence
Leonardo da Vinci
William Shakespeare
Reformation
Martin Luther
Protestant

MAIN IDEA

The rebirth of art, literature, and ideas during the Renaissance changed European society.

WHY IT MATTERS NOW

Many accomplishments of the Renaissance are high points of Western culture and continue to inspire artists, writers, and thinkers of today.

DATELINE

EXTRA

PARIS, FRANCE, 1269

Paris is buzzing with activity as thousands of European soldiers assemble here. This is the starting-off point for the eighth Crusade, which has nearly a thousand miles to travel. King Louis IX of France, who is in command, is confident that his armies can restore European power over the Holy Land.

Since the Crusades began in 1096, the Christians have fought against the Muslims and founded four states in the eastern Mediterranean. European power has weakened since then. However, King Louis's army looks ready to recapture the lost territory for Christianity.

Movement • Crusaders will make their way toward the Holy Land. ▲

Europeans Encounter New Cultures

The **Crusades**—a series of military expeditions in the 11th, 12th, and 13th centuries by Western European Christians to reclaim control of the Holy Lands from the Muslims—had a great influence on life in Western Europe. The long distances traveled by the Crusaders opened up trade routes, connecting Western Europeans with people of southwestern Asia and North Africa. This increased contact also helped Europeans rediscover the ideas and achievements of the ancient Greeks and Romans.

BACKGROUND

The Holy Land of the eastern Mediterranean is important to Christians, Jews, and Muslims.

Italian City-States, c. 1350

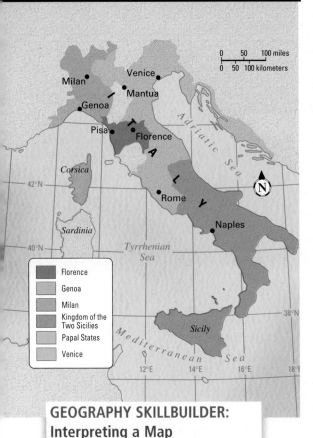

Legend:
- Florence
- Genoa
- Milan
- Kingdom of the Two Sicilies
- Papal States
- Venice

GEOGRAPHY SKILLBUILDER:
Interpreting a Map

1. **Location** • Which city-state does not have access to water?
2. **Location** • Which city-state was in the best position to trade by land and sea with Asia?

Over time, this interest in the ancient world sparked a new era of creativity and learning in Western Europe. This cultural era, which lasted from the 14th to the 16th century, is called the **Renaissance**.

The Rebirth of Europe

The Renaissance began on the Italian Peninsula in the mid-14th century. During this time, many artists, architects, writers, and scholars created works of great importance. These included beautiful paintings, large sculptures, impressive buildings, and thought-provoking literature. As new ideas and achievements spread across the continent of Europe, they changed the way people viewed themselves and the world.

The Italian City-States In the 14th century, the Italian Peninsula was divided into many independent city-states. Some of these city-states, such as **Florence,** were bustling centers of banking, trade, and manufacturing.

BACKGROUND

After Rome fell, many achievements of ancient times were lost. Many books and manuscripts, however, were preserved by Muslim and Christian scholars.

Region • Florence, once a wealthy city-state, remains an important economic and cultural center. The Duomo, shown here, is a symbol of the city's Renaissance past. ▼

Region • The wealthy merchants in Italy built large palaces, called palazzos, such as Florence's Palazzo Medici shown here. ▶

The wealthy businesspeople who lived in these city-states were members of a new class of aristocrats. Unlike the nobles of the feudal system, these aristocrats lived in cities, and their wealth came from money and goods rather than from the lands they owned.

A Changing View of the World Religion was important to people's daily life during the Renaissance, but many wealthy Europeans began to turn increased attention to the material comforts of life.

New wealth allowed aristocratic families to build large homes for themselves in the city centers, decorating them with luxurious objects. They ate expensive food and dressed in fine clothes and jewels, often acquired as a result of the expanded trade routes. Aristocrats also placed increased emphasis on education and the arts.

Learning and the Arts Flourish

BACKGROUND

Some Renaissance architects, such as Filippo Brunelleschi (BROO•nuh•LEHS•kee), studied the ruins of Roman buildings and modeled their new buildings after ancient designs.

Wealthy citizens were proud of their city-states and often became generous patrons. A patron gave artists and scholars money and, sometimes, a place to live and work. They hired architects and designers to improve local churches, to design grand new buildings, and to create public sculptures and fountains. As one Italian city-state made additions and improvements, others competed to outdo it.

Biography

The Medici Family Among the most famous patrons of the Renaissance were the Medici (MEHD•uh•chee). They were a wealthy family of bankers and merchants. In fact, they were the most powerful leaders of Florence from the early 1400s until the 18th century.

Along with Lorenzo, pictured below, the Medici family included famous princes and dukes, two queens, and four popes. Throughout the 15th and 16th centuries, the Medici supported many artists, including Botticelli, Michelangelo, and Raphael. Today, Florence is still filled with important works of art made possible by the Medici.

As part of the competition to improve the appearance and status of their individual city-states, patrons wanted to attract the brightest and best-known scholars and poets of the time. Patrons believed that the contributions of these individuals would, in turn, add to the greatness of their city-states and attract more wealth.

The Visual Arts: New Subjects and Methods Most medieval art was based on religious subjects. Painters and sculptors of the early Renaissance created religious art too, but they also began to depict other subjects. Some made portraits for wealthy patrons. Others created works showing historical scenes or mythological stories.

Leonardo da Vinci One of the most famous artists and scientists of the Renaissance was **Leonardo da Vinci** (lee·uh·NAHR·doh duh VIHN·chee) (1452–1519). Among his best-known paintings are the *Mona Lisa,* a portrait of a young woman with a mysterious smile, and *The Last Supper.* Da Vinci was more than just a talented painter, however.

Throughout his life, da Vinci observed the world around him. He studied the flow of water, the flight of birds, and the workings of the human body. Da Vinci, who became a skilled engineer, scientist, and inventor, filled notebooks with thousands of sketches of his discoveries and inventions. He even drew ideas for flying machines, parachutes, and submarines—hundreds of years before they were built.

The Northern Renaissance

As the new Renaissance ideas about religion and art spread to Northern Europe, they inspired artists and writers working there. The Dutch scholar and philosopher Desiderius Erasmus (ih·RAS·muhs) (1466–1536), for example, criticized the church for its wealth and poked fun at its officials. During the late 16th and early 17th centuries, another writer—the Englishman **William Shakespeare**—wrote a series of popular stage plays. Many of his works, including *Romeo and Juliet* and *Macbeth,* are still read and performed around the world.

Culture •
Leonardo da Vinci completed the painting *La Belle Ferronnière* in 1495. ▲

Reading
Social Studies

A. Contrasting
How did the subject matter of Renaissance art differ from medieval art?

Connections to Math

Perspective During the Renaissance, artists began to use a technique called linear perspective. Linear perspective is a system of using lines to create the illusion of depth and distance. In the drawing below, notice how the perspective lines move toward a single point in the distance, giving the picture depth.

The Reformation

BACKGROUND

In 1516, the English writer Thomas More published a famous book called *Utopia.* It describes the author's idea of a perfect society. Today, the word "utopia" is used to describe any ideal place.

Roman Catholicism was still the most powerful religion in Western Europe. Some of the views of the northern Renaissance writers and scholars, however, were in conflict with the Roman Catholic Church. These new ideas would eventually lead to the **Reformation,** a 16th-century movement to change church practices.

Martin Luther The German monk **Martin Luther** (1483–1546) was one of the most important critics of the church. The wealth and corruption of many church officials disturbed him. Luther also spoke out against the church's policy of selling indulgences—the practice of forgiving sins in exchange for money.

In 1517, Luther wrote 95 theses, or statements of belief, attacking the sale of indulgences and other church practices. Copies were printed and handed out throughout Western Europe. After this, Luther was excommunicated, or cast out and no longer recognized as a member of a church, and went into hiding. While in hiding, he translated the Bible from Latin into German so that all literate, German-speaking people could read it. Under Luther's leadership, many Europeans began to challenge the practices of the Roman Catholic Church.

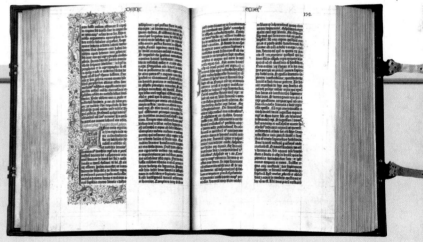

The Printing Press Until the Renaissance, each copy of a book had to be written by hand— usually by monks or nuns. A Renaissance invention, however, changed that forever. Around 1450, a German printer named Johannes Gutenberg (Yoh•HAHN•es GOO•tuhn•BERG) began to use a method of printing with movable type. This meant that multiple copies of books, such as this Bible, could be printed quickly and less expensively.

Although many Renaissance books dealt with religious subjects, printers also published plays, poetry, works of philosophy and science, and tales of travel and adventure. As greater numbers of books were published, more and more Europeans learned to read.

THINKING CRITICALLY

1. **Recognizing Effects**
   What were three effects of the invention of Gutenberg's printing press?

2. **Synthesizing**
   Before the printing press, who produced the books?

A Conflict over Religious Beliefs

Reading Social Studies

B. Clarifying How did Protestants get their name?

Luther's followers were called **Protestants** because they protested events at an assembly that ended the church's tolerance of their beliefs. Many people in Western Europe still supported the church, however. This conflict led to religious wars that ended in 1555. At that time, the Peace of Augsburg declared that German rulers could decide the official religion of their own state.

The Spread of Protestant Ideas By 1600, Protestantism had spread to England and the Scandinavian Peninsula. Protestants pushed to expand education for more Europeans. They did this because being able to read meant being able to study the Bible. They also encouraged translation of the Bible into the native language of each country.

The Counter Reformation The Roman Catholic Church responded to Protestantism by launching its own movement in the mid-16th century. As part of this movement, called the Counter Reformation, the church stopped selling indulgences. It also created a new religious order called the Society of Jesus, or the Jesuits. Jesuit missionaries and scholars worked to spread Catholic ideas across Europe, to Asia, and to the lands of the "new world" across the Atlantic Ocean.

Region ● Martin Luther's writings and actions changed Christianity forever. ▲

SECTION 1 ASSESSMENT

Terms & Names

1. Identify:
- (a) Crusades
- (b) Renaissance
- (c) Florence
- (d) Leonardo da Vinci
- (e) William Shakespeare
- (f) Reformation
- (g) Martin Luther
- (h) Protestant

Taking Notes

2. Use a spider map like this one to chart the characteristics and accomplishments of the Renaissance.

Renaissance Accomplishments

Main Ideas

3. (a) Where and when did the Renaissance begin?

(b) In what ways were the wealthy Europeans of the Renaissance different from the wealthy Europeans of feudal times?

(c) What was the Counter Reformation?

Critical Thinking

4. Hypothesizing

Why do you think Protestantism spread so quickly in Northern Europe?

Think About

- ◆ new methods of printing
- ◆ the ideas of the northern Renaissance
- ◆ the work of Martin Luther

ACTIVITY -OPTION- Write a **letter** to an imagined patron asking for support to create a project—such as a public sculpture, park, fountain, or building—to beautify your community.

Traders, Explorers, and Colonists

TERMS & NAMES
Prince Henry the Navigator
Christopher Columbus
Ferdinand Magellan
circumnavigate
imperialism

MAIN IDEA

European trade and exploration changed the lives of many people on both sides of the Atlantic.

WHY IT MATTERS NOW

Today, citizens of the Americas continue to feel the effects of European exploration and colonization.

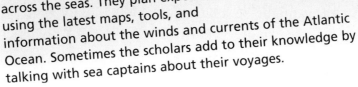

DATELINE

SAGRES, PORTUGAL, 1421— Portugal's Prince Henry may not have journeyed to sea, but he has earned a well-deserved nickname: "The Navigator." He has organized expeditions of sailors to explore the west coast of Africa. Five years ago, Henry also founded a School of Navigation. It is here in Sagres, at Portugal's southwestern tip, which juts into the Atlantic Ocean.

Astronomers, geographers, and mathematicians gather here to study and teach new methods of traveling across the seas. They plan expeditions using the latest maps, tools, and information about the winds and currents of the Atlantic Ocean. Sometimes the scholars add to their knowledge by talking with sea captains about their voyages.

Movement • Prince Henry of Portugal founded the School of Navigation. ▲

Trade Between Europe and Asia

For centuries before the Renaissance, European traders traveled back and forth across the Mediterranean. Merchants commonly journeyed from southern Europe to North Africa and to the eastern Mediterranean. Spices were one of the most important items traded at this time.

The Spice Trade Spices were in great demand by Europeans. Before refrigeration, meat and fish spoiled quickly. To help preserve food and to improve its flavor, people used spices such as pepper, cinnamon, nutmeg, and cloves. These spices came from Asia.

For centuries, Italian merchants from Genoa and Venice controlled the spice trade. They sailed to ports in the eastern Mediterranean, where they would purchase spices and other goods from traders who had traveled across Asia. The Italian merchants would then bring these goods back to Europe.

The Possibility of Great Wealth Transporting goods across these great distances was costly. Everyone along the way had to be paid and wanted to earn a profit. By the time the spices reached Europe, they had to be sold at extremely high prices.

European merchants knew that if they could trade directly with people in Asia, they could make enormous profits. In the 15th century, Europeans began to search for a new route to Asia.

BACKGROUND

In addition to spices, European countries traded for precious metals, which they used to make coins. Metals such as gold and silver were scarce in Europe.

Leaders in Exploration

The small country of Portugal is at the westernmost part of the European continent. Portuguese sailors had navigated the waters of the Atlantic Ocean for centuries. As shown on the map below, they traveled down the west coast of Africa and as far west into the Atlantic as Madeira, the Azores, and the Canary Islands.

Exploring the African Coast In the early 1400s, Portugal's **Prince Henry the Navigator** decided to send explorers farther down the coast of Africa. He believed that if explorers could find a way around Africa, it might be a shortcut to Asia. Portuguese explorers returned home from these expeditions with gold dust, ivory, and more knowledge of navigation. By the time Henry died in 1460, the Portuguese had ventured around the great bulge of western Africa to present-day Sierra Leone.

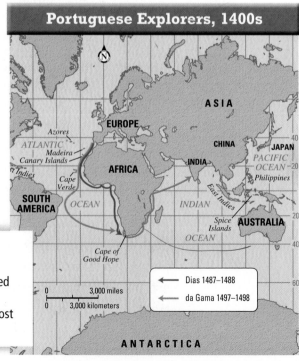

Portuguese Explorers, 1400s

Dias 1487–1488
da Gama 1497–1498

GEOGRAPHY SKILLBUILDER: Interpreting a Map

1. **Movement** • Which explorer reached Asia?
2. **Location** • Which continent was most explored by the Portuguese?

The Race Around Africa Bold Portuguese explorers continued to push farther down the African coast. Finally, in 1488, Bartolomeu Dias (BAHR·too·loo·MAY·oo DEE·uhsh) rounded the southern tip of Africa. The Portuguese named the tip the Cape of Good Hope.

Less than ten years later, Vasco da Gama (vas·KOH deh GAH·muh) led a sea expedition all the way to Asia. Da Gama and his crew traveled for 317 days and 13,500 miles before reaching the coast of India. They were the first Europeans to discover a sea route to Asia. Now, the riches of Asia could be brought directly to Europe. After setting up trading posts along the coast of the Indian Ocean, Portugal ruled these waterways.

Europe Enters a New Age

Portugal was not the only European country to understand that whoever controlled trade with Asia would have great power and wealth. Spain and England quickly entered the race to find a direct sea route of their own.

Christopher Columbus Some explorers believed that the shortest way to Asia was to sail west across the Atlantic Ocean. Queen Isabella of Spain agreed to fund an expedition across the Atlantic.

In August 1492, an Italian named **Christopher Columbus** and 90 crew members left Spain aboard three ships—the *Santa Maria*, the *Pinta*, and the *Niña*. The Atlantic Ocean proved to be wider than maps of the time suggested. On October 12, after weeks at sea, the crew spotted land. Although Columbus thought he had found Asia, they were off the coast of an island in the Caribbean. This was still a great distance from their spice-rich destination.

Ferdinand Magellan In 1519, Spain funded an expedition for the Portuguese explorer **Ferdinand Magellan** (muh·JEHL·uhn). Magellan left Spain with five ships and more than 200 sailors. As they traveled west, the crew battled violent storms and rough seas. Food was in short supply, and starving sailors ate rats and sawdust. Some died of disease.

Reading Social Studies

A. Recognizing Important Details What continent did Columbus reach, and where did he think he was?

Connections to Science

New Ships In the early 15th century, Portuguese shipbuilders designed a sturdy ship called a caravel, pictured below. Built for exploration and trade, the caravel was small and had a narrow body. This helped the ship to cut through waves and to travel in shallow water.

The caravel also used a combination of square and triangular sails. These made sailing easier against strong, shifting winds.

By the time Magellan and his ships reached the Philippines in Asia, the sailors had spent 18 long months at sea. Then, during a battle there, Magellan and several crew members were killed. The expedition returned to Spain after a three-year journey. Only one boat and 18 crew members succeeded. They had to **circumnavigate,** or sail completely around, the world.

Reading
Social Studies

B. Identifying Problems What were the main problems faced by Magellan and his crew?

John Cabot King Henry VII of England did not want Portugal and Spain to claim all the riches of Asia. He funded a voyage by Italian-born Giovanni Caboto, called John Cabot by the English, who believed that a northern route across the Atlantic Ocean might be a shortcut to Asia.

Aboard one small ship, Cabot and 18 crew members sailed west from England in May 1497. When they reached land the following month, Cabot thought they had found Asia. Most likely, they landed in present-day Newfoundland in Canada.

The Outcomes of Exploration

The kings and queens of Europe sent explorers in search of a direct trade route to Asia. These expeditions, however, turned out to have unexpected results.

A Clash of Cultures European countries founded many new colonies along the coastal areas of Africa and North and South America. This practice of one country controlling the government and economy of another country or territory is called **imperialism.** These conquered lands were already home to large, self-ruling populations. They had their own cultural traditions. After the arrival of the Europeans, the lives of these indigenous peoples would never be the same.

Vocabulary

indigenous: born and living in a place, rather than having come from somewhere else

Religious Conversion The European monarchs were Christians. They had strong religious beliefs, and they sent missionaries and other religious officials to help convert conquered peoples to Christianity. The European rulers also hoped that these new converts would help Christianity overcome other powerful religions, especially Islam.

The Spread of Diseases Without knowing it, the European explorers and colonists carried diseases with them, including smallpox, malaria, and measles. These diseases were unknown in the Americas, and killed tens of thousands of people there.

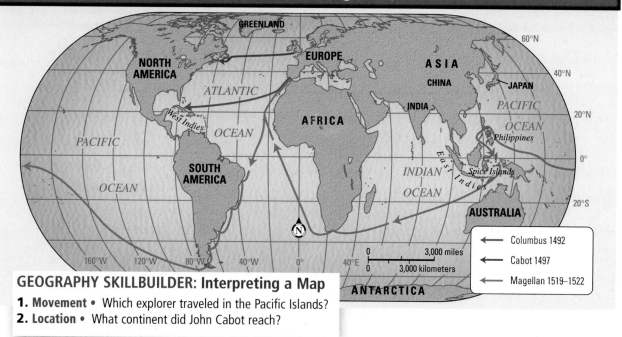

Columbus, Cabot, and Magellan, 1492–1522

GREENLAND
NORTH AMERICA
EUROPE
ASIA
CHINA
JAPAN
ATLANTIC OCEAN
West Indies
AFRICA
INDIA
PACIFIC OCEAN
PACIFIC OCEAN
SOUTH AMERICA
INDIAN OCEAN
East Indies
Philippines
Spice Islands
AUSTRALIA
ANTARCTICA

60°N
40°N
20°N
0°
20°S

160°W 120°W 80°W 40°W 0° 40°E

0   3,000 miles
0   3,000 kilometers

← Columbus 1492
← Cabot 1497
← Magellan 1519–1522

GEOGRAPHY SKILLBUILDER: Interpreting a Map

1. Movement • Which explorer traveled in the Pacific Islands?
2. Location • What continent did John Cabot reach?

Slavery European explorations also led to an expanding slave trade. The Portuguese purchased West Coast African people to work as slaves back in Portugal, where the work force had been reduced by plague. In other colonized areas, such as Mexico and parts of South America, Europeans forced conquered peoples to work the land where they lived. For hundreds of years, Africans and conquered peoples of the Americas would be forced to work under horrible conditions.

SECTION 2 ASSESSMENT

Terms & Names

1. Identify: (a) Prince Henry the Navigator   (b) Christopher Columbus   (c) Ferdinand Magellan
   (d) circumnavigate   (e) imperialism

Taking Notes

2. Use a chart like this one to compare characteristics of the voyages of Christopher Columbus and Vasco da Gama.

Columbus's Voyage	Da Gama's Voyage

Main Ideas

3. (a) Why were spices so important to Europeans?

   (b) Why did Europeans want to find a new route to Asia?

   (c) Name three ways in which European exploration affected the indigenous peoples of North and South America.

Critical Thinking

4. **Making Inferences**

   Why do you think the Portuguese became leaders of European exploration?

   Think About

   • the location of Portugal
   • early Portuguese voyages
   • Prince Henry and his School of Navigation

ACTIVITY -OPTION- Reread the information about Magellan's voyage around the world. Write a **journal entry** describing the events of the voyage from the point of view of a crew member.

Researching Topics on the Internet

▶▶ Defining the Skill

The Internet is a computer network that connects libraries, museums, universities, government agencies, businesses, news organizations, and private individuals all over the world. Each location on the Internet has a home page with its own address, or URL (universal resource locator). With a computer connected to the Internet, you can reach the home pages of many organizations and services. The international collection of home pages, known as the World Wide Web, is an excellent source of up-to-date information about the regions and countries of the world.

▶▶ Applying the Skill

The Web page shown below is the European Reading Room at the Library of Congress Web site. Use the strategies listed below to help you understand how to research topics on the Internet.

How to Research Topics on the Internet

Strategy ❶ Once on the Internet, go directly to the Web page. For example, type http://www.loc.gov/rr/european/extlinks.html in the box at the top of the Web browser and press ENTER. The Web page will appear on your screen.

Strategy ❷ Explore the European Reading Room links. Click any of the links to find more information about a subject. These links take you to other Web sites.

Strategy ❸ Always confirm information you have found on the Internet. The Web sites of universities, government agencies, museums, and trustworthy news organizations are more reliable than others. You can often find information about a site's creator by looking for copyright information or reviewing the home page.

▶▶ Practicing the Skill

Turn to Chapter 11, Section 1, "Renaissance Connections." Reread the section and make a list of topics you would like to research.

For Internet links to support this activity, go to

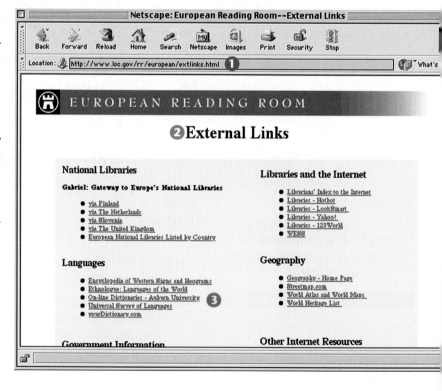

RESEARCH LINKS
CLASSZONE.COM

The Age of Revolution

TERMS & NAMES
Scientific Revolution
Industrial Revolution
labor force
capitalism
French Revolution
Reign of Terror
Napoleon Bonaparte

MAIN IDEA

Scientific, industrial, and political revolutions transformed European society.

WHY IT MATTERS NOW

European revolutions in science, technology, and politics helped to create modern societies throughout the world.

DATELINE

EXTRA

LEIPZIG, GERMANY, APRIL 1839

A new era in German history has begun. The Leipzig-Dresden railway is open for business. Although short rail lines have been in service for a few years, this is the first long-distance railway in this part of Europe.

The steam locomotive that powers the German train was made in England. It is the latest improvement to George Stephenson's "Rocket" train, which set a speed record of 30 mph in 1829. Already, this new form of transportation is changing Europe. The railroads are attracting many passengers and are also ideal for hauling goods. It seems that wherever new train stations are built, growth and prosperity soon follow.

Region • Leipzig's railway will now take passengers all the way to Dresden. ▲

Changes in Science and Industry

The steam-powered locomotive was only one in a long line of technological improvements made in Europe since the 1600s. In fact, scientists and inventors made so many discoveries during these years that Europe experienced both a scientific and an industrial revolution. These periods of great change would help to create modern societies.

Vocabulary

revolution: a period of great change

The Growth of New Ideas **313**

The Scientific Revolution In the 16th and 17th centuries, scientific discoveries changed the way Europeans looked at the world. This led to the **Scientific Revolution.**

In Italy, Galileo Galilei (GAL·uh·LEE·oh GAL·uh·LAY) (1564–1642) studied the stars and planets using a new invention called the telescope. Later in Holland, Antoni van Leeuwenhoek (LAY·vuhn·huk) (1632–1723) used a microscope to explore an unknown world found in a drop of water. The Swedish botanist Carolus Linnaeus (lih·NEE·uhs) (1707–1778) even developed a system to name and classify all living things on Earth.

Culture •
In 1610, Galileo used his telescope to observe that Jupiter had moons. ▲

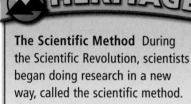

The Industrial Revolution Many inventions of the Scientific Revolution began to change the way people worked all across Europe. Machines performed jobs that once had been done by humans and animals. This brought about such great change that it led to a revolution in the way goods were produced: the **Industrial Revolution.**

Machines were grouped together to make products in large factories. Early factories were built in the countryside near streams and rivers so that they could be powered by water. By the late 1700s, however, new steam engines were used to power the machinery. More and more factories could now be built in cities. People, in turn, moved from the countryside to the cities in search of work.

Reading **Social Studies**

A. Finding Causes How did the Scientific Revolution lead to the Industrial Revolution?

The Workshop of the World

The Industrial Revolution began in England in the late 1700s. The first English factories made textiles, or cloth. The steam-powered machines of the textile industry produced large amounts of goods quickly and cheaply. So many factories were built in England that the country earned the nickname "The Workshop of the World."

Hard Work for Low Pay The Industrial Revolution created a need for workers, or a **labor force,** in cities. The workers who ran the textile machines made up part of this labor force. Most workers could earn more income in cities than on farms, but life could be hard. Factory laborers worked long hours and received low pay. In fact, many families often sent their children to work to help create more income.

In 1838, women and children made up more than 75 percent of all textile factory workers. Children as young as seven were forced to work 12 hours a day, six days a week.

The Spread of Industrialization

The textile industry in 18th-century England was one step in the development of an economic system called **capitalism.** In this system, factories and other businesses that make and sell goods are privately owned. Private business owners make decisions about what goods to produce. They sell these goods at a price that will earn a profit.

Industrialization spread from England to other countries, including Germany, France, Belgium, and the United States. Cities in these countries grew rapidly and became more crowded and dirtier. Diseases, such as cholera (KAHL·uhr·uh) and typhoid (TY·foyd) fever, spread. Smoke from factories blackened city skies, and pollution fouled the rivers.

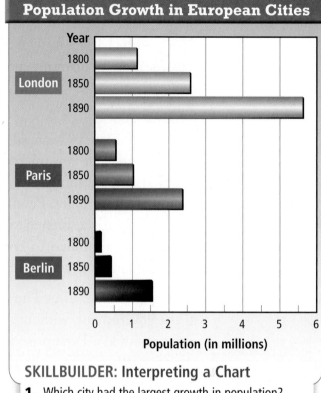

Population Growth in European Cities

Bar graph showing population (in millions) for London, Paris, and Berlin in the years 1800, 1850, and 1890.

Population (in millions)

SKILLBUILDER: Interpreting a Chart

1. Which city had the largest growth in population?
2. What was the population of Paris in 1890?

Place •
Factories, like this one in Sheffield, England, were found throughout Western Europe by the mid-19th century. ▶

The French Revolution

Along with changes in science, technology, and the economy came new ideas about government. In the late 18th century, many ordinary citizens began to fight for more political rights.

Ripe for Political Change By the 1780s, the French government was deeply in debt because of bad investments and the costs of waging wars. Life was miserable for the common working people. Poor harvests combined with increased population had led to food shortages and hunger. People were forced to pay heavy taxes. At the same time, the French king, Louis XVI, and his queen, Marie Antoinette, continued to enjoy an expensive life at court, entertaining themselves and the French nobility.

Storming the Bastille The citizens of France demanded changes in the government, without success. Then, on July 14, 1789, angry mobs stormed a Paris prison called the Bastille (ba·STEEL). The attack on this prison, which reflected the royal family's power, became symbolic of the **French Revolution.**

Revolts spread from Paris to the countryside, and poor and angry workers burned the homes of the nobility. By 1791, France had a new constitution that made all French citizens equal under the law.

Reading
Social Studies

B. Analyzing Motives
Why did the French citizens demand a new government?

Region • The storming of the Bastille remains a symbol of the French Revolution. ▼

The French Republic In 1792, France became a republic. King Louis XVI was found guilty of treason, or betraying one's country. In 1793, he and Marie Antoinette were sentenced to death. They were beheaded on the guillotine (GIHL·uh·teen).

Still, France was not at peace. The new revolutionary leaders refused to tolerate any disagreement. Between 1793 and 1794, these new leaders executed 17,000 people. This period of bloodshed became known as the **Reign of Terror.**

Napoleon French leaders continued to struggle for power until 1799, when General **Napoleon Bonaparte** (nuh·POH·lee·uhn BOH·nuh·PAHRT) took control. The French Revolution and the disorder that followed were finally over.

However, the new sense of equality brought about by the Revolution stirred feelings of nationalism among the French. Nationalism is pride in and loyalty to one's nation. Soon, the citizens of other European nations began to fight for more political power. Slowly, they, too, won more rights.

Region • Napoleon Bonaparte crowned himself emperor of France in 1804. He led France to victory in what became known as the Napoleonic Wars. ▲

SECTION 3 ASSESSMENT

Terms & Names

1. **Identify:**
   - (a) Scientific Revolution
   - (b) Industrial Revolution
   - (c) labor force
   - (d) capitalism
   - (e) French Revolution
   - (f) Reign of Terror
   - (g) Napoleon Bonaparte

Taking Notes

2. Use a chart like this one to list some of the scientific, industrial, and political changes that occurred during the Age of Revolution.

Scientific Changes	Industrial Changes	Political Changes

Main Ideas

3. (a) Describe at least three inventions or discoveries of the Scientific Revolution.

   (b) How did the Industrial Revolution change the way people in Europe worked?

   (c) What changes occurred in France after the French Revolution?

Critical Thinking

4. **Recognizing Effects**

   How did industrialization change the cities to which it spread?

   Think About
   - population
   - diseases
   - the environment

ACTIVITY -OPTION-

Reread the section about the French Revolution. Write a **poem** or **lyrics** for a folk song that describe the events from the point of view of a common citizen or a member of the royal family.

The Russian Empire

TERMS & NAMES
czar
Ivan the Terrible
Peter the Great
Catherine the Great
Russian Revolution

MAIN IDEA

Strong leaders built Russia into a large empire, but the country's citizens had few rights and struggled with poverty.

WHY IT MATTERS NOW

Russia has had a great influence on world politics and is experiencing a period of great change.

DATELINE

MOSCOW, RUSSIA, 1560—Today, the most magnificent church in Moscow opened with a grand celebration. The Cathedral of St. Basil has ten domes—each one unique. The massive structure, built of bricks and white stone, is decorated with brilliant colors.

Ivan IV built this cathedral to celebrate his victory eight years ago over the Tatars (TAH•tuhrz). These Turkish people who live in Central Asia have long threatened Russia's security.

The victory also added the lands of the Tatars, including their capital at Kazan, to our growing empire. Russians everywhere should be proud of Moscow's new church and of the victory it symbolizes.

Place • Ivan IV has honored a Russian victory over the Tatars with the construction of St. Basil's Cathedral. ▲

Ivan IV ▲

Russia Rules Itself

Russia, geographically the world's largest nation, is located in both Europe and Asia. It takes up large parts of both continents, and both continents have helped shape its history.

Mongols from eastern Asia conquered Russia in the 13th century and ruled it for about 200 years. During the 15th century, Russia broke free of Mongol rule. At this time, the most important Russian city was Moscow, located in the west.

Reading
Social Studies

A. Clarifying Why did the Russian people give Ivan IV the nickname Ivan the Terrible?

The First Czars of Russia In 1547, a 16-year-old leader in Moscow was crowned the first **czar** (zahr), or emperor, of modern Russia. His official title was Ivan IV, but the people nicknamed him **Ivan the Terrible.** Ivan was known for his cruelty, especially toward those he viewed as Russia's enemies. During his rule of 37 years, the country was constantly at war.

During the reigns of Ivan the Terrible and the czars who followed him, Russia had an unlimited government. This is a form of government in which a single ruler holds all the power. The people have no say in how the country is run.

Conflicts at Home The first Russian czars were often in conflict with the Russian nobles, who possessed much land and wealth. The czars viewed the nobles as a threat to their control over the people. Ivan the Terrible ordered his soldiers to murder Russian nobles and church leaders who opposed him.

The poor farmers, or peasants, of Russia also suffered under the first czars. New laws forced the peasants to become serfs, who had to remain on the farms where they worked.

Region • Ivan the Terrible is said to have worn this fur-trimmed crown at his coronation in 1547. ▲

The Expansion of Russia

In addition to strengthening their control over the Russian people, the czars wanted to gain new territory. Throughout the 17th and 18th centuries, rulers such as Peter the Great and Catherine the Great conquered neighboring lands.

A Window on the West An intelligent man with big ideas for his country, **Peter the Great** ruled Russia from 1682 to 1725. After defeating Sweden in war and winning land along the Baltic Sea, Peter built a port city called St. Petersburg. This city, which Peter saw as Russia's "window on the west," became the new capital.

One of Peter's goals was to have closer ties with Western Europe. He hoped to use the ideas and inventions of the Scientific Revolution to modernize and strengthen Russia. During his rule, Peter reformed the army and the government and built new schools. He even ordered Russians to dress like Europeans and to shave off their beards. Peter's reforms made Russia stronger, but they did not improve life for Russian peasants.

Movement • Peter the Great brought to Russia many of the improvements of the Scientific and Industrial Revolutions. ▲

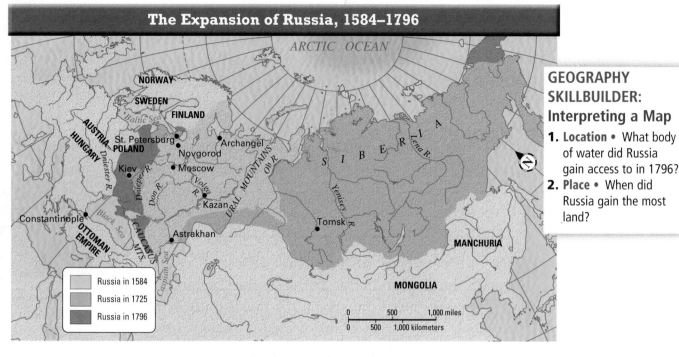

The Expansion of Russia, 1584–1796

GEOGRAPHY SKILLBUILDER: Interpreting a Map

1. **Location** • What body of water did Russia gain access to in 1796?
2. **Place** • When did Russia gain the most land?

Russia in 1584
Russia in 1725
Russia in 1796

A Great Empress <u>**Catherine the Great**</u> took control of Russia in 1762 and ruled until her death in 1796. Catherine added vast new lands to the empire, including the present-day countries of Ukraine (yoo·KRAYN) and Belarus (behl·uh·ROOS). Like Peter the Great, Catherine borrowed many ideas from Western Europe. She started new schools and encouraged art, science, and literature. Catherine also built new towns and expanded trade.

During Catherine's reign, Russia became one of Europe's most powerful nations. The lives of the peasants, however, remained miserable. Catherine thought about freeing them, but she knew the nobles would oppose her. When the peasants rebelled in the 1770s, Catherine crushed their uprising.

Movement • Catherine the Great continued Peter the Great's practice of bringing the ideas of Western Europe to Russia. ▼

A Divided Russia

In the 19th century, Russia remained a divided nation. Most people were poor peasants, and most of the wealth belonged to the nobles. This division would lead to conflict and eventually to a political revolution.

The Nobles Many Russian nobles sent their children to be educated in Germany and France. In fact, many noble families spoke French at home, speaking Russian only to their servants. The Western Europeans introduced many new ideas to the Russian nobles, among them the idea that a nation's government should reflect the wishes of its citizens.

BACKGROUND

Catherine the Great was born in Germany. She came to Russia at 15 to marry the heir to the throne, Peter III. He was a weak ruler, however, and Catherine, supported by the army and the people, overthrew him.

Many Russian nobles were army officers or government officials. Most supported the czar and were proud of Russia's growing power. In 1825, one group of nobles tried to replace the government. Their attempt to gain more power failed.

The Serfs In the 19th century, the Russian serfs still had no land or money of their own. They worked on farms owned by others and received little help from the Russian government.

In 1861, Alexander II decided to end serfdom in Russia. He hoped that freeing the serfs would help his country compete with Western Europe. The serfs had to pay a heavy tax, though, and the land they were given was often not good for farming. Most former serfs felt that they had gained very little.

Bloody Sunday The serfs were not the only unhappy Russians. Many university students, artists, and writers believed that the government's treatment of the serfs was unfair. Some joined groups that tried to overthrow the government. In addition, workers in Russia's cities complained about low pay and poor working conditions.

In 1905, a group of workers marched to the royal palace in St. Petersburg with a list of demands. Government troops shot many of them. News of the events of this "Bloody Sunday" spread across Russia, making people even angrier with the government and czar.

BACKGROUND

In the 1850s, Russia fought the Crimean War against Turkey. Two of Turkey's allies were Britain and France. When Russia lost, Alexander II thought this proved that his country was still far less advanced than Western European nations.

Spotlight on CULTURE

The Hermitage Museum One of the world's greatest and largest art museums is the Hermitage in St. Petersburg. It contains many famous works of art, including French, Spanish, and British paintings. Part of the collection is displayed in the former royal residence, the Winter Palace.

Both Peter the Great and Catherine the Great were collectors of European art. On a trip to Amsterdam in 1716, Peter bought paintings by the famous Dutch artist Rembrandt. Approximately 50 years later, Catherine purchased more than 200 works of art when she visited Germany. These priceless royal collections became part of the Hermitage when it opened as a public museum in 1852.

THINKING CRITICALLY

1. **Analyzing Motives**
   Why did Peter the Great and Catherine the Great collect art from Western Europe?

2. **Making Inferences**
   Why do you think the works of art were displayed to the public in a museum?

The End of the Russian Empire

In 1914, World War I began. Nicholas II—a quiet, shy man who did not want war—ruled Russia, but he failed to keep his country out of the battle. Russia, whose allies included the United Kingdom and France, suffered terrible losses fighting Germany and its allies.

Reading
Social Studies

B. Analyzing Motives Why did Russian workers strike?

During World War I, there were food shortages in the cities and workers went on strike. Russian revolutionaries organized the workers against the czar. Even the Russian army turned against their ruler, and in 1917, Nicholas was forced to give up power. This overturning of the Russian monarchy is known as the **Russian Revolution.**

Nicholas II and the royal family (the Romanovs) were imprisoned by the revolutionaries. On July 17, 1918, they were all shot to death. This execution ended more than 300 years of rule by the Romanov family and nearly 400 years of czarist rule.

Strange but TRUE

Rasputin One of the most influential people at the court of Czar Nicholas II was Rasputin. He came from Siberia in eastern Russia and was a self-styled holy man. Crown prince Alexis suffered from the disease hemophilia, and no doctor in Russia could cure him. Rasputin seemed to mysteriously heal the boy, gaining favor with Nicholas's wife, Czarina Alexandra. However, in 1916, Russian nobles killed Rasputin out of fear of the considerable power and influence the monk had.

SECTION 4 ASSESSMENT

Terms & Names

1. Identify:
(a) czar
(b) Ivan the Terrible
(c) Peter the Great
(d) Catherine the Great
(e) Russian Revolution

Taking Notes

2. Use a chart like this one to describe three characteristics of czars of Russia.

Ivan the Terrible	Peter the Great	Catherine the Great	Nicholas II

Main Ideas

3. (a) What effects did an unlimited government have on Russian peasants?

(b) How did Peter the Great help reform Russia?

(c) Alexander II ended serfdom in 1861, but this did little to help the serfs. Why?

Critical Thinking

4. **Finding Causes**

What events led to the Russian Revolution?

Think About

• the life of the serfs
• Bloody Sunday
• the events of World War I

ACTIVITY -OPTION- Look at the map on page 320 that shows the expansion of Russia. Write a brief **summary** to describe how the Russian nation grew from the 1500s to 1800.

James Watt's Double-Action Steam Engine

Amid the excitement of the Industrial Revolution, James Watt (1736–1819), a Scottish inventor, patented a new steam engine. Steam power had been used for many years, but Watt's invention was an improved, double-action steam engine. This system, in which the steam pushes from both sides of the piston rather than from just one, enhanced efficiency and increased power. Watt's invention helped to advance manufacturing and transportation and influenced later inventions. Watt's double-action steam engine was one of the most important inventions of the Industrial Revolution.

How the Engine Works

Steam from the **boiler** enters the **piston cylinder**. The pressure of the steam pushes the **piston** to one side, moving the **piston rod**. When the piston reaches the end of the stroke, the **slide valve** shifts the steam to the other side of the piston, forcing it back and releasing the steam it compresses as exhaust.

1 As water is converted to steam, its volume increases 1,600 percent.

2 When the steam enters the piston cylinder, it forces the piston rod to one side.

3 As the piston reaches the end of its stroke, the slide valve channels steam to the other side of the piston.

4 The piston rod is pushed back, forcing the "old" steam out as exhaust.

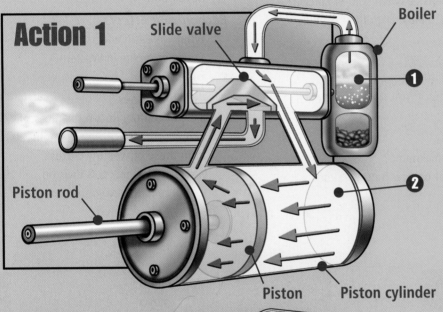

Action 1

Slide valve

Boiler

1

2

Piston rod

Piston   Piston cylinder

Key: | Steam | Exhaust

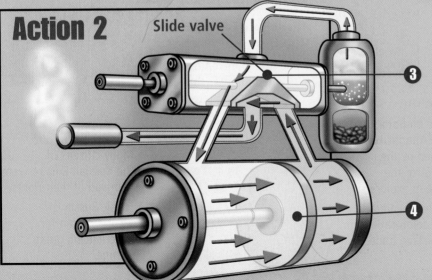

Action 2

Slide valve

3

4

THINKING *Critically*

1. Drawing Conclusions
How did the steam engine help power the Industrial Revolution?

2. Recognizing Effects
How did Watt's steam engine change the lives of working people?

TERMS & NAMES

Explain the significance of each of the following:

1. Renaissance
2. Leonardo da Vinci
3. Reformation
4. Ferdinand Magellan
5. circumnavigate
6. imperialism
7. Industrial Revolution
8. Napoleon Bonaparte
9. Peter the Great
10. Russian Revolution

REVIEW QUESTIONS

Renaissance Connections *(pages 301–306)*

1. How did the subjects chosen by artists change during the Renaissance?
2. Why were the followers of Martin Luther called Protestants?

Traders, Explorers, and Colonists *(pages 307–311)*

3. Why were spices from Asia so expensive when sold in Europe?
4. What did Portuguese explorers bring back from their expeditions to western Africa?

The Age of Revolutions *(pages 313–317)*

5. When and where did the Industrial Revolution begin?
6. What conditions in France during the 1780s led to the French Revolution?

The Russian Empire *(pages 318–322)*

7. How did Ivan the Terrible earn his nickname?
8. What ideas did Catherine the Great borrow from Western Europe?

CRITICAL THINKING

Finding Causes

1. Using your completed chart from Reading Social Studies, p. 300, list the events that led to the growth of cities during the Industrial Revolution.

Recognizing Effects

2. What were the effects of the Crusades on life in Western Europe?

Analyzing Causes

3. In 19th-century Russia, the lives of poor citizens were very different from those of wealthy citizens. How do you think this division led to political revolution?

Visual Summary

1 Renaissance Connections

- European society was transformed by the art, literature, and ideas of the Renaissance.
- The accomplishments of this period are an important part of Western culture.

2 Traders, Explorers, and Colonists

- People on both sides of the Atlantic were changed by the voyages of the European explorers.
- European exploration led to colonization and to the slave trade.

3 The Age of Revolution

- The Age of Revolution resulted in great changes in European society, industry, and politics.
- These changes were felt around the world.

4 The Russian Empire

- Many citizens of the Russian Empire were deprived of their rights.
- Today, Russia is a large nation experiencing great change.

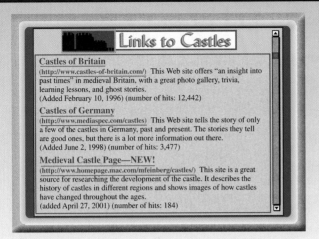

Links to Castles

Castles of Britain
(http://www.castles-of-britain.com/) This Web site offers "an insight into past times" in medieval Britain, with a great photo gallery, trivia, learning lessons, and ghost stories.
(Added February 10, 1996) (number of hits: 12,442)

Castles of Germany
(http://www.mediaspec.com/castles) This Web site tells the story of only a few of the castles in Germany, past and present. The stories they tell are good ones, but there is a lot more information out there.
(Added June 2, 1998) (number of hits: 3,477)

Medieval Castle Page—NEW!
(http://www.homepage.mac.com/mfeinberg/castles/) This site is a great source for researching the development of the castle. It describes the history of castles in different regions and shows images of how castles have changed throughout the ages.
(added April 27, 2001) (number of hits: 184)

SKILLBUILDER: Researching Topics on the Internet

1. What is the subject of this Web site?
2. Which site would you visit to learn about the history of castles?

FOCUS ON GEOGRAPHY

1. **Movement** • How might the path of the plague be related to trade routes?
2. **Place** • Why might the plague have reached Russia later than it reached the other countries in Europe?

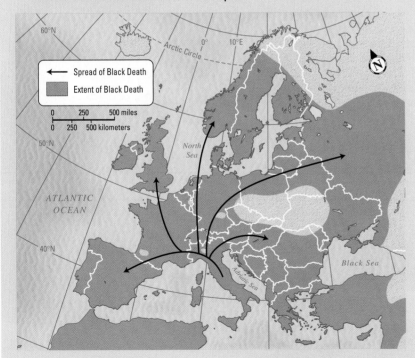

Spread of Black Death
Extent of Black Death

0   250   500 miles
0   250   500 kilometers

ATLANTIC OCEAN

North Sea

Arctic Circle

Black Sea

CHAPTER PROJECTS

Interdisciplinary Activity: Science
Explaining an Invention Research one of the many scientific inventions of Leonardo da Vinci. Write a paragraph that explains how da Vinci came up with his idea and how it works. Find a copy of one of da Vinci's sketches or a photograph of a model, or make your own sketch to illustrate your paragraph.

Cooperative Learning Activity
Tracing a Voyage Work with three or four students to research and make a presentation about the voyage of Ferdinand Magellan, the first explorer to sail around the world.
• How many ships and sailors set out? Who helped finance the trip?
• Create a map of Magellan's route.
• Find details about the hardships the crew faced.
• Include information about what happened to Magellan.

INTERNET ACTIVITY

Use the Internet to research the Scientific Revolution. Focus on the discovery or invention of one great European scientist of the time, such as Galileo Galilei. How did the discovery help change daily life or add to people's knowledge of the world?

Presenting Your Findings Design a poster to explain your findings. Include a diagram or illustration that visually presents information about the scientific discovery. If appropriate, explain how the discovery or invention affects life today.

For Internet links to support this activity, go to

RESEARCH LINKS
CLASSZONE.COM

Europe: War and Change

EUROPE AND
THE FORMER
SOVIET UNION

PACIFIC
OCEAN

ATLANTIC
OCEAN

PACIFIC
OCEAN

INDIAN
OCEAN

OCEAN

Place Berlin's Kaiser Wilhelm Memorial Church remains semi-destroyed as a monument to World War II. Germany has since rebuilt its cities. It is once again an important part of Europe's economy, politics, and culture.

Time
Heure

Nach
Destination
Destination

h

9 h 10 LONDON-WATERLOO

9 h 16 LILLE EUROPE CALAIS

9 h 25 AMIENS AB

9 h 34 ORRY CHAN

LONDON-WATERLOO

FOCUS ON GEOGRAPHY

How has Europe's small landmass affected its history?

Place • The continent of Europe is home to more than 40 countries. Yet, it is approximately the same size as the United States. Since many European nations share borders with several other countries, Europeans often speak three or more languages. Across Europe, approximately 50 languages are spoken.

Europe is densely populated. In fact, the continent has almost three times as many people as the United States. So many people, living so close together, has sometimes led to competition and warfare over land and resources.

What do you think?

♦ How might the differences among Europeans cause conflict?

♦ How might the closeness of so many countries help to unite Europe?

327

BEFORE YOU READ

▶▶ *What Do You Know?*

Do you know that during World War I, armies trained dogs to guard supplies and assist soldiers? What do you know about World War I and World War II? Have you ever seen a movie or read a book about either conflict? What do you hear in the news about current events in Europe? Think about how events in Europe in the past century might have contributed to life there today.

▶▶ *What Do You Want to Know?*

Decide what you know about Europe's history in the 1900s and what it is like there today. In your notebook, record what you hope to learn from this chapter.

Region • The image of the hammer and sickle became the symbol of the Soviet Union. ▲

READ AND TAKE NOTES

Reading Strategy: Analyzing Causes and Effects
Analyzing causes and effects is an essential skill for understanding what you read in social studies, because events are caused by other events or situations. This sequence is called a chain of events. Understanding which causes lead to which events is essential in understanding history and other areas of social studies. Use the chart below to show causes and effects discussed in Chapter 12.

- Copy the chart into your notebook.
- As you read, record causes and effects for each event.

Region • During World War I, armies trained dogs to assist them. ▲

Causes	Event	Effects
	World War I	
	World War II	
	Growth of Soviet Union	

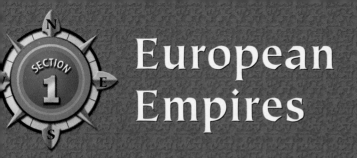

SECTION 1

European Empires

TERMS & NAMES
nationalism
colonialism
Austria-Hungary
dual monarchy

MAIN IDEA

The beginning of the 20th century was a time of change in Europe, as feelings of nationalism began to take hold.

WHY IT MATTERS NOW

Feelings of nationalism continue to lead to conflicts that change the map of Europe.

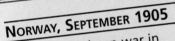

DATELINE

EXTRA

NORWAY, SEPTEMBER 1905

It could have been war in the Scandinavian Peninsula. The armies of Norway and Sweden had begun preparations.

Instead, Sweden ended the crisis peacefully by granting Norway independence. Norway had been under Swedish control since 1814. Although Norway ran its own affairs within the country, Sweden set foreign policy and controlled Norway's international shipping and trade.

Prince Charles of Denmark has been invited to become king of Norway. The Norwegians will vote to approve their new leader. If chosen, he will become King Haakon VII.

The king's role will be largely ceremonial. His chief task will be to help unite the newly independent people of Norway.

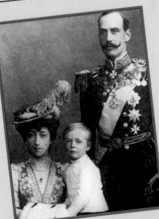

Region • **Prince Charles of Denmark, pictured here with his family, hopes to become King Haakon VII of Norway.**

The Spread of Nationalism

Norway's independence from Sweden was a sign of new ideas that were sweeping across Europe at the time. During the late 19th and early 20th centuries, **nationalism,** or strong pride in one's nation or ethnic group, influenced the feelings of many Europeans. An ethnic group includes people with similar languages and traditions, but who are not necessarily ruled by a common government.

Constitutional Monarchies In part, the spread of nationalism was fueled by the fact that more Europeans than ever before could vote. For centuries, many monarchs had unlimited power. In country after country, however, citizens demanded the right to elect lawmakers who would limit their monarch's authority. This kind of government is called a constitutional monarchy. A constitutional monarchy not only has a king or queen, but also a ruling body of elected officials. The United Kingdom is one example of a constitutional monarchy.

By 1900, many countries in Western Europe had become constitutional monarchies. Citizens of these countries strongly supported the governments that they helped to elect. When one country threatened another, most citizens were willing to go to war to defend their homeland.

The Defense of Colonial Empires At the beginning of the 20th century, many Western European countries—including France, Italy, the United Kingdom, Germany, and even tiny Belgium—had colonies in Asia and Africa. Colonies supplied the raw materials that the ruling countries needed to produce goods in their factories back home. Asian and African colonies, sometimes larger than the ruling country, were also important markets for manufactured goods.

Reading
Social Studies

A. Contrasting
How does a constitutional monarchy differ from a democracy?

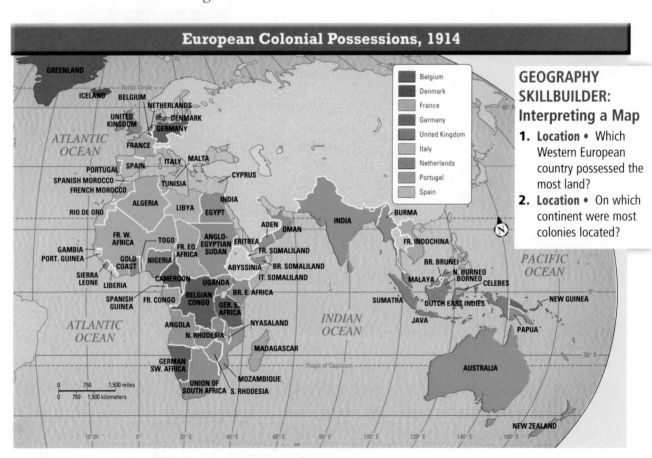

European Colonial Possessions, 1914

Legend:
- Belgium
- Denmark
- France
- Germany
- United Kingdom
- Italy
- Netherlands
- Portugal
- Spain

GEOGRAPHY SKILLBUILDER: Interpreting a Map

1. **Location •** Which Western European country possessed the most land?
2. **Location •** On which continent were most colonies located?

During this period of **colonialism,** Western European nations spent much of their wealth on building strong armies and navies. Their military forces helped to defend borders at home as well as colonies in other parts of the world. Colonies were so important that the ruling countries sometimes fought one another for control of them. They also struggled to extend their territories.

Spotlight on CULTURE

The Ballets Russes Begun in Paris, France, in 1909, the Ballets Russes (ba•LAY ROOS) brought together artists from all across Europe. Under the direction of the famous Russian producer Sergey Diaghilev (dee•AH•guh•LEHF), this dance company became both a critical and a commercial success.

Many talented dancers and choreographers, such as Nijinsky, worked for Diaghilev. In addition, famous composers—including Claude Debussy (duh•BYOO•see) and Igor Stravinsky—wrote music for performances. The Ballets Russes also attracted Pablo Picasso, Marc Chagall, and other great artists to design its sets. It continued until Diaghilev's death in 1929.

THINKING CRITICALLY

1. **Synthesizing**
   How did the Ballets Russes benefit the European art and theater communities?

2. **Clarifying**
   How did the Ballets Russes represent more than a collection of dancers, musicians, and artists?

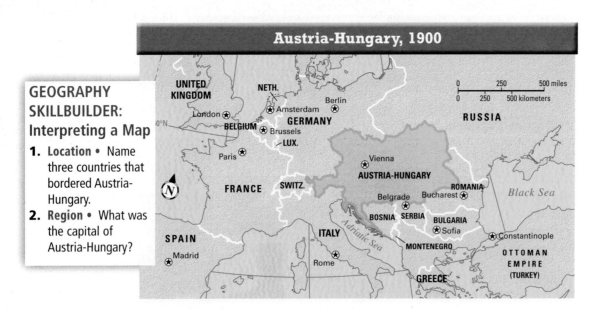

Austria-Hungary, 1900

GEOGRAPHY SKILLBUILDER: Interpreting a Map

1. **Location** • Name three countries that bordered Austria-Hungary.
2. **Region** • What was the capital of Austria-Hungary?

Austria-Hungary By the end of the 19th century, most nations of Western and Northern Europe had become industrialized. The majority of Eastern Europe, including Russia, remained agricultural. These Eastern European countries imported most of their manufactured goods from Western and Northern Europe.

The largest empire in Eastern Europe in 1900 was **Austria-Hungary.** The empire was a **dual monarchy**, in which one ruler governs two nations. As you can see in the map above, Austria-Hungary also included parts of many other present-day countries, including Romania, the Czech Republic, and portions of Poland.

Reading Social Studies

B. Making Inferences Why do you think governing a dual monarchy was difficult?

SECTION 1 ASSESSMENT

Terms & Names

1. **Identify:**   (a) nationalism   (b) colonialism
                    (c) Austria-Hungary   (d) dual monarchy

Taking Notes

2. Look at the map on page 330 that shows European colonial territories. Use a chart like the one below to list the major colonial powers and their colonies.

Nation	Locations of Colonies

Main Ideas

3. (a) Identify one reason for the spread of nationalism in Europe.

   (b) Why did Western European nations spend much of their wealth on armies and navies?

   (c) How did the nations of Eastern Europe differ from those of Western and Northern Europe at the end of the 19th century?

Critical Thinking

4. **Drawing Conclusions**

   Why were their colonies so important to European nations?

   Think About
   • land and people
   • competition among nations
   • the production and sale of goods

ACTIVITY -OPTION-   Reread the information about the Ballets Russes. Write an **outline** of a story or book that might be a good choice for a ballet. Explain your choice.

Europe at War

TERMS & NAMES
World War I
alliance
Adolf Hitler
fascism
Holocaust
World War II
NATO

MAIN IDEA

During the first half of the 20th century, European countries fought each other over land, wealth, and ideals.

WHY IT MATTERS NOW

The changes brought about by the two world wars continue to affect Europe today.

DATELINE

SARAJEVO, BOSNIA-HERZEGOVINA, JUNE 28, 1914—Today, Archduke of Austria-Hungary Franz Ferdinand and his wife, Duchess Sophie, were murdered as they drove through Sarajevo. A nineteen-year-old Serb, Gavrilo Princip, jumped on the Archduke's automobile and fired two shots. The first killed the Duchess. The second killed the Archduke, who was next in line to be emperor of Austria-Hungary.

The Serbians have protested against Austria-Hungary since 1908, when the empire took over Bosnia and Herzegovina (BAHZ•nee•uh HEHRT•suh•GOH•VEE•nuh). Princip has been arrested.

Region • Archduke Franz Ferdinand and his wife, Duchess Sophie, were fatally shot in Sarajevo. ▲

Region • Gavrilo Princip assassinated the future emperor of Austria-Hungary and his wife. ▲

The World at War

Because of the murder of Archduke Franz Ferdinand in 1914, the emperor of Austria-Hungary declared war on Serbia. When Russia sent troops to defend Serbia, Germany declared war on Russia. Russia supported Serbia because both Russians and Serbians share a similar ethnic background—they are both Slavic peoples. This was the beginning of **World War I**.

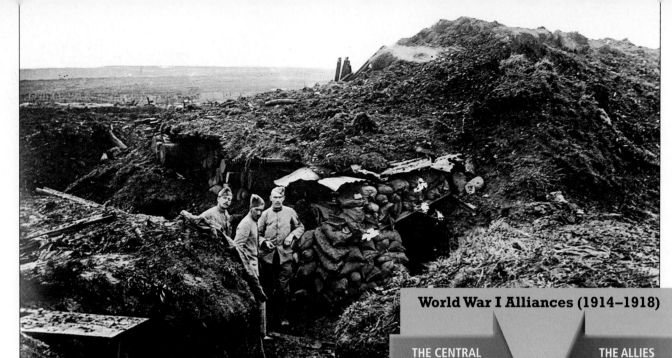

Place • **World War I was primarily fought in trenches, which were dug by the armies for better defense.** ▲

World War I Alliances European rulers wanted other leaders to think twice before declaring war on their countries. To help defend themselves, several countries joined alliances (uh•LY•uhn•sez). An **alliance** is an agreement among people or nations to unite for a common cause. Each member of an alliance agrees to help the other members in case one of them is attacked.

World War I Alliances (1914–1918)	
THE CENTRAL POWERS	**THE ALLIES**
Austria-Hungary	Russia (dropped out in 1917)
Germany	France
Turkey (Ottoman Empire)	United Kingdom
Bulgaria	Italy (joined 1915)
	United States (joined 1917)

When Germany joined the war to support Austria-Hungary, France came in on the side of Russia. Germany then invaded Belgium, which was neutral, to attack France. Because Great Britain had promised to protect Belgium, it, too, declared war on Germany. After German submarines sank four American merchant ships, the United States joined the side of Russia, France, and Great Britain.

The chart above shows the major powers on both sides of World War I. Italy had originally been allied with Germany and Austria-Hungary but joined the Allies after the war began. Russia dropped out of the war completely after the revolution in that country in 1917.

Reading **Social Studies**

A. Recognizing Important Details Why did Great Britain enter World War I?

SKILLBUILDER:

Interpreting a Political Cartoon

1. What does the artist mean by naming the figure "Progress"?
2. Why is the man wearing a gas mask?

World War I was costly in terms of human life. When it was over, nearly 22 million civilians and soldiers on both sides were dead. The Allies had won, and Europe had been devastated.

Europe After World War I

More people were killed during World War I than during all the wars of the 19th century combined. Afterward, people in many countries on both sides of the costly war—and even those not directly involved—were poor, homeless, and without work.

The Allies blamed Germany for much of the killing and damage during the war. In 1919, Germany and the Allies signed the Treaty of Versailles (vuhr·SY).

Strange but TRUE

War Dogs During World War I, dogs were trained to guard ammunition, to detect mines, and to carry messages. Dogs even helped to search for the wounded.

War dogs saved many lives. They were especially helpful in forested areas and at night. These dogs are wearing protective masks to keep them safe from poison gas attacks.

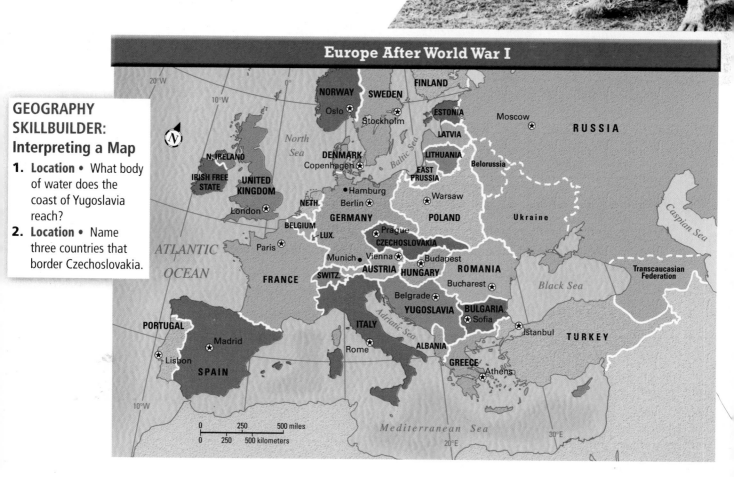

Europe After World War I

**GEOGRAPHY SKILLBUILDER:
Interpreting a Map**
1. **Location** • What body of water does the coast of Yugoslavia reach?
2. **Location** • Name three countries that border Czechoslovakia.

The Treaty of Versailles demanded that Germany be punished by being forced to pay for the damage done to the Allied countries. Germany was also made to give up valuable territory.

A New Map of Europe Additional treaties during the following year also altered the political boundaries of many European countries. As the map on page 335 shows, Austria-Hungary was divided as a result of the war, becoming two separate countries. This allowed several Eastern European ethnic groups that had been part of Austria-Hungary to gain their independence.

World War II

By the 1930s, Germany was still paying for the damage done to the Allied countries during World War I. The German economy was in ruins, and the Germans greatly wished to rebuild their own country. In 1933, citizens elected **Adolf Hitler** and the National Socialist, or Nazi, Party. The Nazi Party believed in fascism. **Fascism** (FASH·IHZ·uhm) is a philosophy that supports a strong, central government controlled by the military and led by a powerful dictator. People believed that this new leader would help Germany recover.

World War II Alliances (1939–1945)

THE AXIS POWERS
Germany
Italy
Japan

THE ALLIES
United Kingdom
France
    (until June 1940)
Soviet Union
    (formerly "Russia")
United States
    (joined in 1941)

Reading
Social Studies

B. Finding Causes
What conditions led Germans to find hope in Adolf Hitler?

BACKGROUND
Like Germany, Italy was also ruled by a fascist dictator after World War I: Benito Mussolini (1883–1945).

Hitler and the Nazi Party Fascists practiced an extreme form of patriotism and nationalism. Fascists also had racist beliefs.

In the 1930s, Hitler unjustly blamed the Jewish citizens of Germany, among other specific groups, for the country's problems. His Nazi followers seized Jewish property and began to send Jews, along with disabled people, political opponents, and others, to concentration camps. During this **Holocaust,** millions of people were deliberately killed, and others starved or died from disease.

In 1934, Hitler took command of the armed forces. Then, in 1939, Hitler's army invaded Poland. **World War II** had begun. By June 1940, Hitler's army had swept through Western Europe, conquering Belgium, the Netherlands, Luxembourg, France, Denmark, and Norway. A year later, Germany invaded the Soviet Union.

WWII Alliances The chart on page 336 shows the major powers on both sides of World War II. As in World War I, the United States at first tried to stay out of the conflict but entered the war after Japan bombed U.S. military bases at Pearl Harbor in Hawaii on December 7, 1941.

Europe After World War II

World War II turned much of Europe into a battleground. By the end of the war, the United States, France, and the United Kingdom occupied Western Europe. The Soviet Union occupied Eastern Europe, including the eastern part of Germany.

Once peace was established, the western allies helped to set up free governments in Western Europe. In 1949, the countries of Western Europe joined Canada and the United States to form a defense alliance called **NATO** (NAY·toh). The members of this alliance, whose name stands for North Atlantic Treaty Organization, agreed to defend one another if they were attacked by the Soviet Union or any other country. Without a common enemy, political differences quickly separated the Soviet Union from Western Europe and the United States.

Place • **The Kaiser Wilhelm Memorial Church in Berlin was nearly destroyed by Allied bombs. The ruins still stand today as a World War II monument. See pages 326–327.** ▲

Biography

Anne Frank In July 1942, during World War II, Anne Frank and her family went into hiding in Amsterdam—a city in the Netherlands. The Frank family were Jewish and were afraid they would be sent to a concentration camp. Anne was only thirteen.

For two years, Anne, her father, mother, sister, and four other people lived in rooms in an attic. Their rooms were sealed off from the rest of the building. While in hiding, Anne kept a diary. Although the family was discovered and Anne died in a concentration camp, her diary was eventually published. Today, this famous book—translated into many languages and the basis for a play and a film—lives on.

Europe: War and Change **337**

Europe After World War II

**GEOGRAPHY SKILLBUILDER:
Interpreting a Map**

1. **Location** • In what country is Berlin located?
2. **Location** • Name three countries that border the Soviet Union.

The Marshall Plan United States Secretary of State George C. Marshall created the Economic Cooperation Act of 1948, also known as the Marshall Plan. This plan provided U.S. aid—agricultural, industrial, and financial—to countries of Western Europe. The Marshall Plan greatly benefited war-torn Europe. It may also have prevented economic depression or political instability.

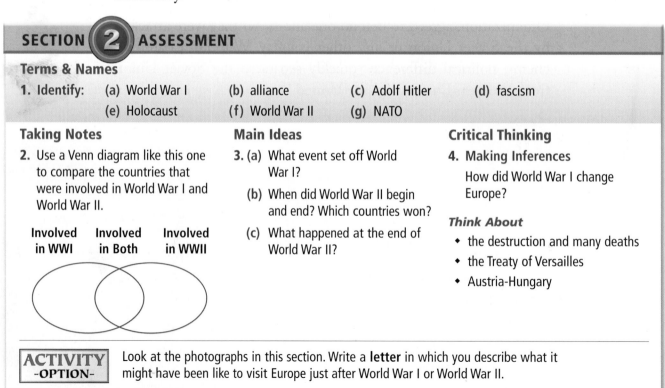

SECTION 2 ASSESSMENT

Terms & Names

1. **Identify:** (a) World War I (b) alliance (c) Adolf Hitler (d) fascism
   (e) Holocaust (f) World War II (g) NATO

Taking Notes

2. Use a Venn diagram like this one to compare the countries that were involved in World War I and World War II.

| Involved in WWI | Involved in Both | Involved in WWII |

Main Ideas

3. (a) What event set off World War I?
   (b) When did World War II begin and end? Which countries won?
   (c) What happened at the end of World War II?

Critical Thinking

4. **Making Inferences**
   How did World War I change Europe?

   Think About
   • the destruction and many deaths
   • the Treaty of Versailles
   • Austria-Hungary

ACTIVITY -OPTION- Look at the photographs in this section. Write a **letter** in which you describe what it might have been like to visit Europe just after World War I or World War II.

Reading a Political Cartoon

▶▶ Defining the Skill

Political cartoons—also known as editorial cartoons—express an opinion about a serious subject. A political cartoonist uses symbols, familiar objects, and people to make his or her point quickly and visually. Sometimes the caption and words in the cartoon help to clarify the meaning. Although a cartoonist may use humor to make a point, political cartoons are not always funny.

▶▶ Applying the Skill

This political cartoon was created in the period between World War I and World War II. However, Europeans were already concerned about developments in Germany.

How to Read a Political Cartoon

Strategy ❶ Read the cartoon's title and any other words. For example, some cartoons have labels, captions, and thought balloons. Then study the cartoon as a whole.

Strategy ❷ If the cartoon has people in it, are they famous? Sometimes the cartoonist wants to comment on a famous person, such as a world leader. Look for symbols or details in the cartoon. For example, in this cartoon a German soldier is climbing out of the Versailles Treaty. Think about the relationships between the words and the images.

Strategy ❸ Summarize the cartoonist's message. What is the cartoonist's point of view about the subject? What does this cartoonist think was the cause of Hitler's rise to power?

Make a Chart

A chart can help you to analyze the information in a political cartoon. Once you understand the cartoon's elements, you can summarize its meaning. Use a chart such as this one to help you organize the information.

Important Words	Hitler Party; Versailles Treaty
Important Symbols/Images	German soldier with "Hitler Party" on his helmet crawling out of the Versailles Treaty that officially ended World War I.
Summary ❸	The terms of the Versailles Treaty led to the rise of Hitler's party in Germany; Hitler's party, symbolized by a soldier, is war-like and threatens Europe.

▶▶ Practicing the Skill

Study the political cartoon in Chapter 12, Section 2, on page 334. Make a chart similar to the one above in which you list the important parts of the cartoon and write a summary of the cartoon's message.

Fionn Mac Cumhail and the Giant's Causeway[1]

FIONN MAC CUMHAIL, more commonly known as Finn MacCool, is a familiar figure in Irish folk tales. He first appears in the ancient Celtic tales known as the Fenian cycle. In the following story, retold by Una Leavy, Fionn is portrayed as a clever giant, hard at work with the Fianna, his band of Irish warriors. They begin to build a bridge from Ireland to Scotland, because, as the boastful Fionn says, "There are giants over there that I'm longing to conquer." Plans suddenly change, however, and Fionn must go home.

1. The Giant's Causeway, which takes its name from this legend, is a striking natural rock formation on the coast of Ireland.

2. The region of Ireland where Fionn and the Fianna are building their bridge to Scotland. It is the location of the actual Giant's Causeway.

Fionn Mac Cumhail and the Fianna worked quickly on the bridge, splitting stones into splendid pillars and columns. Further and further they stretched out into the ocean. From time to time, there came a distant rumble. "Is it thunder?" asked the Fianna, but they went on working. Then one of their spies came ashore. "I've just been to Scotland!" he said. "There's a huge giant there called Fathach Mór. He's doing long jumps—you can hear the thumping. He has a magic little finger with the strength of ten men! He's in training for the long jump to Antrim."[2]

Fionn's face paled. "The strength of ten men!" he thought. "I'll never fight him. He'll squash me into a pancake." But he could not admit that he was nervous, so he said to the Fianna, "I've just had a message from Bláithín, my wife. I must go home at once—you can all take a holiday."

He set off by himself and never did a man travel faster. Bláithín was surprised to see him. "And is the great causeway finished already?" she asked.

"No indeed," replied Fionn.

"What's the matter?" Bláithín asked. So Fionn told her.

"What will I do, Bláithín?" he asked. "There's the strength of ten men in his magic little finger. He'll squish me into a jelly!"

Bláithín laughed. "Just leave him to me. Stoke up the fire and fetch me the sack of flour. Then go outside and find nine flat stones." Fionn did as he was told. Bláithín worked all night making ten oatcakes. In each she put a large flat stone, all except the last. This one she marked with her thumbprint. "Go and cut down some wood," she said. "You must make an enormous cradle."

Fionn worked all morning. The cradle was just finished when there was a mighty rumble and the dishes shook.

"It's him," squealed Fionn.

"Don't worry!" said Bláithín. "Put on this bonnet. Now into the cradle and leave me to do the talking."

"Does Fionn Mac Cumhail live here?" boomed a great voice above her.

"He does," said Bláithín, "though he's away at the moment. He's gone to capture the giant, Fathach Mór."

"I'm Fathach Mór!" bellowed the giant. "I've been searching for Fionn everywhere."

"Did you ever see Fionn?" she asked. "Sure you're only a baby compared with him. He'll be home shortly and you can see for yourself. But now that you're here, would you do me a favor? The well has run dry and Fionn was supposed to lift up the mountain this morning. There's spring water underneath it. Do you think you could get me some?"

"Of course," shouted the giant as he scooped out a hole in the mountain, the size of a crater.

Fionn shook with fear in the cradle and even Bláithín turned pale. But she thanked the giant and invited him in. "Though you and Fionn are enemies, you are still a guest," she said. "Have some fresh bread." And she put the oatcakes before him. Fathach Mór began to eat. Almost at once he gave a piercing yell and spat out two teeth.

"What kind of bread is this?" he screeched. "I've broken my teeth on it."

"How can you say such a thing?" asked Bláithín. "Even the child in the cradle eats them!" And she gave Fionn the cake with the thumbprint. Fathach looked at the cradle. "Whose child is that?" he asked in wonder.

"That's Fionn's son," said Bláithín.

"And how old is he?" he asked then.

"Just ten months," replied Bláithín.

"Can he talk?" asked the giant.

"Not yet, but you should hear him roar!" At once, Fionn began to yell.

"Quick, quick," cried Bláithín. "Let him suck your little finger. If Fionn comes home and hears him, he'll be in such a temper. With an anxious glance at the door, the giant gave Fionn his finger. Fionn bit off the giant's magic little finger. Screeching, the giant bolted from the house. Fionn leaped from the cradle in bib and bonnet and danced his Bláithín round the kitchen.

Reading
THE LITERATURE

Before reading this story, how did you expect Fionn Mac Cumhail to act? Did you expect him to be the hero of the story? Who is? How does the character solve the problem in the story? What skills are used to solve it?

Thinking About
THE LITERATURE

In many European myths and legends, the heroes are powerful and fearless. How does Fionn act in this story? What words does the author use to make clear Fionn's attitude toward the danger he faces? How does he differ from other legendary figures that you have read about?

Writing About
THE LITERATURE

Often, myths are created in order to answer questions about or explain mysteries in the world. This legend explains why the causeway was never finished. How might the story about Fionn be different if the causeway had been finished?

About the Author

Una Leavy, the author of *Irish Fairy Tales & Legends,* is an Irish writer who lives with her husband and children in County Mayo, Ireland.

Further Reading *The Names upon the Harp* by Marie Heaney recounts myths and legends of early Irish literature, including the stories about Fionn Mac Cumhail that make up the Fenian cycle.

The Soviet Union

SECTION 3

TERMS & NAMES
Iron Curtain
puppet government
one-party system
Joseph Stalin
collective farm
Warsaw Pact
Cold War

MAIN IDEA	WHY IT MATTERS NOW
After World War II, the Soviet Union was the most powerful country in Europe, but life for most Soviet citizens was difficult.	Russia, the former Soviet Union, remains powerful and is currently experiencing great change.

DATELINE

EXTRA

WARSAW, POLAND, MAY 14, 1955

Today, the Soviet Union and most Eastern European countries announced that they have signed the Warsaw Treaty of Friendship, Cooperation, and Mutual Assistance. The members of this alliance agree to offer military defense to one another for a period of 20 years.

Yugoslavia is the only country in Eastern Europe that did not sign the agreement.

The new treaty, also called the Warsaw Pact, allows the Soviet Union to keep troops in the countries that are located between the Soviet Union and Western Europe. The Warsaw Pact is a response to the formation of NATO, an alliance that Western European countries joined six years ago.

Region • Warsaw hosted Eastern European officials who signed a military alliance here in the Palace of Culture. ▲

East Against West

After World War II, political differences divided the Soviet-controlled countries of Eastern Europe from those of Western Europe. These differences gave rise to an invisible wall known as the **Iron Curtain**. While there was no actual curtain, people of the East were restricted from traveling outside of their countries. Westerners who wished to visit the East also faced restrictions.

The Strongest Nation in Europe The Union of Soviet Socialist Republics, or USSR, was the official name of the Soviet Union. It included 15 republics, of which Russia was the largest. The Soviet Union entered World War II in 1941, when Germany invaded its borders. German troops destroyed much of the western Soviet Union and killed millions of people. This invasion brought the Soviet Union close to collapse. However, with the defeat of Germany, the Soviet Union rose to become the strongest nation in Europe.

Vocabulary

establish:
set up; create

Region •
The hammer and sickle became the symbol of Soviet Communism. The tools represent the unity of the peasants (sickle) with the workers (hammer). ▲

Communism After World War II, the Soviet Union established Communist governments in Eastern Europe. The Soviets made sure—either by politics or by force—that these new Eastern European governments were loyal to the Soviet Union.

Soviet Control of Eastern Europe The Soviet Union controlled the countries of Eastern Europe through puppet governments. A **puppet government** is one that does what it is told by an outside force. In this case, the Eastern European governments followed orders from Soviet leaders in Moscow.

Reading
Social Studies

A. Making Inferences
How do you think the Soviet Union enforced a one-party system in Eastern Europe?

Most Eastern Europeans did have the chance to vote, but they had only one political party to choose from: the Communist Party. All other parties were outlawed. This meant that there was only one candidate to choose from for each government position. This is an example of a **one-party system.** Soviet citizens could not complain about the government. In fact, they could be jailed for expressing any view that the Soviet leaders did not like.

Movement • The government-controlled factories in the Soviet Union did not produce enough of certain items. When goods that were often in short supply— such as bread and shoes— finally became available, people had to wait in long lines to buy them. ◄

Joseph Stalin

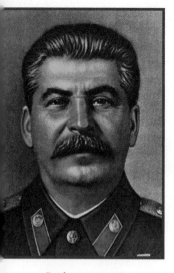

Joseph Stalin (STAH·lihn) (1879–1953) ruled the Soviet Union during World War II. Stalin took power after the death of Vladimir Lenin. Lenin was a Communist leader who had helped overthrow the czar and ruled the Soviet Union from 1917 until his death in 1924. The name Stalin is related to the Russian word for "steel." Stalin was greatly feared, and his rule was indeed as tough as steel. He controlled the government until his death.

Region • Joseph Stalin ruled the Soviet Union from 1928 to 1953. ▲

The Five-Year Plans Under Stalin, the government controlled every aspect of Soviet life. Stalin hoped to strengthen the country with his five-year plans, which were sets of economic goals. For example, Stalin ordered many new factories to be built. The Soviet government decided where and what types of factories to build, how many goods to produce, and how to distribute them. These decisions were based on the Communist theory that this would benefit the most people.

GEOGRAPHY SKILLBUILDER: Interpreting a Map

1. **Region** • Which countries were behind the Iron Curtain but not in the Soviet Union?
2. **Location** • What was the western-most country in the Warsaw Pact?

Region • The Soviet government managed the factories while citizens provided the actual labor. ◄

The Iron Curtain and the Warsaw Pact Nations, 1955

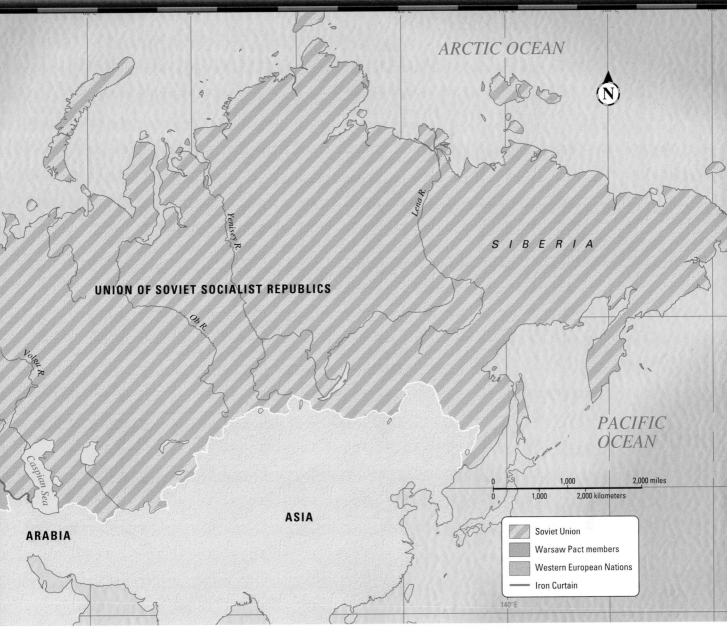

ARCTIC OCEAN

N

SIBERIA

Lena R.

Yenisey R.

UNION OF SOVIET SOCIALIST REPUBLICS

Ob R.

Volga R.

Caspian Sea

PACIFIC OCEAN

ASIA

ARABIA

	Soviet Union
	Warsaw Pact members
	Western European Nations
—	Iron Curtain

0   1,000   2,000 miles
0   1,000   2,000 kilometers

140°E

Soviet Agriculture Stalin also hoped to strengthen the Soviet Union by controlling the country's agriculture. During the 1930s, peasants were forced to move to collective farms. A **collective farm** was government-owned and employed large numbers of workers. All the crops produced by the collective farms were distributed by the government. Sometimes farm workers did not receive enough food to feed themselves and their families.

Region • Similar to urban factory workers, Russian peasants labored on government-controlled collective farms. ▼

The Secret Police Stalin used his secret police to get rid of citizens he did not trust. The secret police arrested those who did not support the Soviet government. Suspects were transported to slave-labor camps in Siberia. Millions of men and women were sent to this remote and bitterly cold region of northeastern Russia. Many never returned home.

The Cold War

From 1941 to 1945, the United Kingdom, the United States, and the Soviet Union shared a goal: to defeat the Axis Powers. They became allies to make that happen. Once the war ended, however, these countries no longer had a common enemy—and had little reason to work together. Most Western European countries were constitutional monarchies or democracies, and most Eastern European countries had Communist, largely Soviet-controlled, governments.

Spotlight on CULTURE

Soviet Film The Russian director Sergey Eisenstein (EYE•zen•stine) (1898–1948), bottom right, made only six movies, but they are among the most important works in film history. The silent film *Battleship Potemkin* (1925), whose poster is to the right, is one of Eisenstein's most famous. It is about a mutiny at sea. The director's use of close-ups and his method of combining short scenes changed the way films were made all over the world.

Just before the start of World War II, Eisenstein made the film *Alexander Nevsky* (1938). It tells the story of a historic battle that the Russians won against German-speaking invaders in the 1200s. This film became very popular during World War II, which it seemed to foreshadow.

THINKING CRITICALLY

1. Clarifying
What influenced Eisenstein to direct war films?

2. Synthesizing
What did Eisenstein want to show about the relationship between Russians and Germans?

Region • The Brandenberg Gate was a part of the Berlin Wall that separated East Berlin from West Berlin. ◄

The members of NATO and the nations in the **Warsaw Pact**—the alliance of Eastern European countries behind the Iron Curtain—refused to trade or cooperate with each other. The countries never actually fought, so this period of political noncooperation is called the **Cold War.** Both sides in the Cold War were hesitant to start a war that would involve the use of newly developed nuclear weapons, which could cause destruction on a global scale.

Reading
Social Studies

B. Comparing
Compare the Soviet Union's fears in the Cold War with those of the United States and Western Europe.

The United States and Western Europe feared that the Soviet Union would influence other countries to become Communist. At the same time, the Soviet Union wanted to protect itself against invasion. This led the countries on either side of the Iron Curtain to view and treat each other as possible threats. The tense international situation caused by the Cold War would continue for almost 40 years.

SECTION 3 ASSESSMENT

Terms & Names

1. Identify: (a) Iron Curtain   (b) puppet government   (c) one-party system   (d) Joseph Stalin
(e) collective farm   (f) Warsaw Pact   (g) Cold War

Taking Notes

2. Use a chart like this one to describe three elements of Joseph Stalin's rule of the Soviet Union.

Five-Year Plans	Agriculture	Secret Police

Main Ideas

3. (a) What happened to the Soviet Union during World War II?

(b) How did the governments of most Western and Eastern European countries differ?

(c) How did Joseph Stalin rule the Soviet Union?

Critical Thinking

4. **Analyzing Motives**

Why do you think the Soviet Union wanted to control the countries of Eastern Europe?

Think About

• the events of World War II

• the location of the Eastern European countries

• the governments of the Soviet Union and Western Europe

ACTIVITY -OPTION- Reread the information about the secret police. Write a dramatic **scene** in which the main character is sent to a labor camp in Siberia.

TERMS & NAMES

Explain the significance of each of the following:

1. nationalism
2. colonialism
3. World War I
4. alliance
5. World War II
6. NATO
7. Adolf Hitler
8. Warsaw Pact
9. Iron Curtain
10. Cold War

REVIEW QUESTIONS

European Empires (*pages 329–332*)

1. What was the largest empire in Eastern Europe in 1900?
2. What is one reason why European nations built up their military?

Europe at War (*pages 333–338*)

3. Why did European countries join alliances?
4. What did the Treaty of Versailles require Germany to do?
5. What country did Germany invade to begin World War II?

The Soviet Union (*pages 342–347*)

6. Why did most Eastern European voters have only one political party to choose from?
7. How did the Iron Curtain affect the lives of Eastern Europeans?
8. Why were both sides in the Cold War hesitant to start a war?

CRITICAL THINKING

Identifying Problems

1. Using your completed chart from Reading Social Studies, p. 328, list some of the causes and effects of World Wars I and II.

Making Inferences

2. Why might a citizen who has helped elect a government be more willing to fight to defend it?

Hypothesizing

3. How do you think Soviet peasants felt about collective farms? Why?

Visual Summary

European Empires *1*

- In early-20th-century Europe, feelings of nationalism arose.
- Western European nations ruled colonial empires.

Europe at War *2*

- Due to a complex set of alliances, most of Europe was drawn into World War I.
- The Treaty of Versailles set the stage for an even more widespread conflict—World War II.

The Soviet Union *3*

- After World War II, the Soviet Union was very powerful.
- However, life was difficult for many Soviet citizens.

SOCIAL STUDIES SKILLBUILDER

A Toast
to <u>Next</u> Thanksgiving:
"Here's hoping we're not the bird!"

Dr. Seuss ©9m

SKILLBUILDER: Reading a Political Cartoon

1. Who is the subject of this cartoon?
2. What do you think the cartoonist, Dr. Seuss, was worried about?

FOCUS ON GEOGRAPHY

1. **Place** • Which areas of Europe are most densely populated?
2. **Place** • Which areas of Europe are least densely populated?
3. **Place** • Why do you think some areas are much more populated than others?

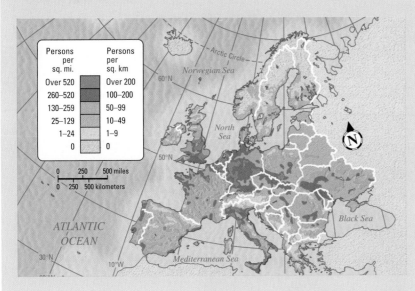

Persons per sq. mi.	Persons per sq. km
Over 520	Over 200
260–520	100–200
130–259	50–99
25–129	10–49
1–24	1–9
0	0

0   250   500 miles
0   250   500 kilometers

CHAPTER PROJECTS

Interdisciplinary Activity: Language Arts

Presenting an Oral Report
Research one of the European colonies in Asia or Africa. What was life like around 1900? Present your findings to the class in an oral report. Be sure to show the location of the colony on a map.

Cooperative Learning Activity

Designing a Monument In a group of three or four students, design a monument to commemorate an event in 20th-century Europe, such as a particular battle from World War I, the Holocaust, or World War II.

• Present background information about the event to the class.
• Display a drawing or a model of the monument.
• Show your suggested location for the memorial on a map.

INTERNET ACTIVITY

Use the Internet to research a European country that was not directly involved in World War I or World War II. Examples include Spain and Switzerland. What can you find out about that country's government and economy? What was life like there during the first half of the 20th century? How was the country affected by the wars?

Presenting Your Findings Write your findings in a report and include illustrations. List the Web sites that you used to prepare your report.

For Internet links to support this activity, go to

RESEARCH LINKS
CLASSZONE.COM

CHAPTER 13

Modern Europe

EUROPE AND RUSSIA

ATLANTIC OCEAN

PACIFIC OCEAN

PACIFIC OCEAN

INDIAN OCEAN

OCEAN

Movement High-speed trains, like this one in France, make travel in Europe very convenient.

118

SNCF

FOCUS ON GEOGRAPHY

How are the new republics of Eastern Europe using natural resources to build their economies?

Human-Environment Interaction • Natural resources are often an important part of a nation's economy. When the Soviet Union broke up in 1991, the newly independent nations of Eastern Europe chose to develop market economies.

In Ukraine, which is rich in coal and iron, mining and manufacturing are major industries. (Ukraine once had vast petroleum and natural gas resources, but heavy production used up much of them.) Estonia, Latvia, and Lithuania have large forests and good farmland. Estonia is also rich in oil shale, which it uses to make electricity.

What do you think?

♦ How do natural resources affect the types of goods a country produces?

♦ Why is it important for countries to use natural resources carefully?

BEFORE YOU READ

▶▶ *What Do You Know?*

Before you read the chapter, think about what you already know about Europe. Do you have family, friends, or neighbors who were born in Europe? Have you read books, such as the Harry Potter series, that take place in Europe? Think about what you have seen or heard about Italy, England, France, or Germany in the news, during sporting events, and in your other classes.

▶▶ *What Do You Want to Know?*

Decide what you know about Europe today. Then, in your notebook, record what you hope to learn from this chapter.

Region • Euros are the most visible symbol of economic unity in Europe. ▲

READ AND TAKE NOTES

Reading Strategy: Comparing Comparing is a useful strategy for understanding how events change societies. As you read this chapter, compare Eastern Europe under Communism with Eastern Europe after Communism. Use the chart below to take notes.

- Copy the chart into your notebook.
- As you read, notice how government, economics, and culture differ under the old and new systems.
- After you read each section, record key ideas on your chart.

Place • Some Christians in Ukraine dye Easter eggs brilliant colors. ▲

Aspect	Under Communism	After Communism
Government		
Economy		
Culture		

Eastern Europe Under Communism

TERMS & NAMES
propaganda
private property rights
Nikita Khrushchev
deposed
détente

MAIN IDEA

The Communist government of the Soviet Union controlled the lives of its citizens.

WHY IT MATTERS NOW

Today, many republics of the former Soviet Union have become independent nations.

DATELINE

EXTRA

THE KREMLIN, MOSCOW, APRIL 12, 1961

A 27-year-old Soviet pilot has become the first person to travel into space. Soviet officials proudly announced today that cosmonaut Yuri Gagarin had orbited Earth in 1 hour and 29 minutes.

His 4.75-ton spacecraft, *Vostok I,* flew at a maximum altitude of 187 miles above the planet. Its top speed was 18,000 miles per hour.

Gagarin graduated from the Soviet Air Force cadet school just four years ago. He is the son of a carpenter and began to study flying while in college. Gagarin's space flight puts the Soviet Union a giant step ahead of the United States in the space race.

Movement • Yuri Gagarin becomes the first human in space. ▶

Soviet Culture

The Soviet space program of the 1950s and 1960s brought international attention to that country. Daily life for citizens of the Soviet Union and of the Eastern European countries under its control, however, was difficult. Most people were poor and had little, if any, say in their government.

Space Dogs Four years before Yuri Gagarin blasted into space, a Russian dog orbited the planet. Her name was Laika (LY·kuh), which means "Barker." Laika, pictured below, was launched into space on *Sputnik 2* in November 1957. The Soviets did not then have the ability to bring a spacecraft down safely, and Laika lived in space for only a few days.

In August 1960, however, the Russians sent two other dogs into space. Named Belka and Strelka, they were the first living creatures to go into space and return safely to Earth.

Creating a National Identity The Soviet government was fearful that some ethnic groups might want to break away from the Soviet Union. To keep this from happening, Soviet leaders tried to create a strong national identity. They wanted people in the republic of Latvia, for example, to think of themselves as Soviets, not as Latvians.

To help achieve its goals, the Soviet government created and distributed **propaganda** (PRAHP·uh·GAN·duh), or material designed to spread certain beliefs. Soviet propaganda included pamphlets, posters, artwork, statues, songs, and films. It praised the Soviet Union, its leaders, and Communism.

Soviet Control of Daily Life To prevent different ethnic groups from identifying with their individual cultures rather than with the Soviet Union, the Soviet government outlawed many cultural celebrations. It destroyed churches and other religious buildings and killed thousands of religious leaders. The members of many ethnic groups were not allowed to speak their native languages or celebrate certain holidays.

The Soviet government also controlled communications media, such as newspapers, books, and radio. This meant that most Soviet citizens could not learn much about other nations around the world.

Literature and the Arts The works of many writers, poets, and other artists who lived during the Soviet era often were banned or censored. Soviet artists were forced to join government-run unions. These unions told artists what kinds of works they could create. Artists who disobeyed were punished. Some were imprisoned or even killed.

Region • This statue, a form of propaganda, displays the Soviet belief in the unity of the worker (hammer) and the farmer (sickle). ▼

ARCTIC OCEAN

Baltic Sea

RUSSIA ESTONIA
LITHUANIA LATVIA
BYELORUSSIA
MOLDAVIA UKRAINE

Black Sea

RUSSIA

GEORGIA
ARMENIA
AZERBAIJAN

Caspian Sea

KAZAKHSTAN

UZBEKISTAN
TURKMENIA KIRGHIZIA
TAJIKISTAN

Bering Sea

0 250 500 miles
0 250 500 kilometers

Caucasian peoples
Indo-European peoples
Uralic and Altaic peoples
Sparsely populated

GEOGRAPHY SKILLBUILDER: Interpreting a Map

1. **Place** • Where in the Soviet Union do most Uralic and Altaic people live?
2. **Region** • What is the most common ethnicity of the Soviet Union?

Sports The leaders of the Soviet Union wanted their country to be seen as equal to, if not better than, other powerful nations. One way to achieve this goal was to become a strong competitor in the Olympics and in other international sports competitions.

The Soviet government supported its top athletes and provided for all their basic needs. It even hired and paid for the coaches and paid for all training. The hockey teams and gymnasts of the Soviet Union were among the best in the world.

The Soviet Economy

In addition to controlling the governments of the Soviet Union and of those Eastern European countries under its influence, Soviet leaders also ran the economy. When the Soviets installed Communist governments in Eastern Europe after World War II, they promised to improve industry and to bring new wealth to be shared among all citizens. This did not happen.

Government Control Communism in the Soviet Union did not support **private property rights**, or the right of individuals to own land or an industry. The Soviets wanted all major industries to be owned by the government rather than by private citizens. So the government took over factories, railroads, and businesses.

Region • Romanian gymnasts, like Nadia Comaneci, won medals at the Olympics. ▼

Modern Europe **355**

The Soviet government decided what would be produced, how it would be produced, and who would get what was produced. These choices were made based on Soviet interests, not on the interests of the republics or of individuals. Communist countries of Eastern Europe were often unable to meet the needs—including bread, meat, and clothing—of their citizens.

Reading **Social Studies**

A. Clarifying Who benefited most from Soviet industry?

Attempts at Change

Starting in the 1950s, Eastern Europeans began to demand more goods of better quality. They also wanted changes in the government. In 1956, Hungary and Poland tried to free their governments and economies from Soviet control. But the Communist army put an end to these attempts at change.

Khrushchev From 1958 until 1964, **Nikita Khrushchev** (KRUSH·chehf) ruled the Soviet Union. During this period, called "The Thaw," writers and other citizens began to have greater freedoms. Khrushchev even visited the United States in 1959, but the thaw in the Cold War did not last. In 1964, with the Soviet economy growing weaker, Khrushchev was **deposed**, or removed from power.

Spotlight on CULTURE

Solzhenitsyn In 1945, army officer Aleksandr Solzhenitsyn (SOHL·zhuh·NEET·sihn), far right, called the Soviet leader Joseph Stalin "the boss." For this, he was sentenced to eight years in slave-labor camps. Later, Solzhenitsyn wrote books about his experiences in those camps. He also wrote a letter against censorship. The government called him a traitor, and in 1969 it forced Solzhenitsyn to leave the writers' union. Five years later, Solzhenitsyn left the country.

Although Solzhenitsyn's works were banned, many Soviet citizens read them in secret. Copies of his and other banned books were passed from person to person across the nation. Through such writings, Soviet citizens learned many things that the government had tried to hide from them.

THINKING CRITICALLY

1. **Analyzing Motives** Why would the Soviet government stop people from reading Solzhenitsyn's books?

2. **Comparing** Compare the censorship of literature in the Soviet Union with censorship in the United States.

Reading
Social Studies

B. Recognizing Important Details How did the Soviet Union maintain control over other Eastern European nations?

The Prague Spring In January 1968 in Czechoslovakia, Alexander Dubček (DOOB·chek) became the First Secretary of the Czechoslovak Communist Party. His attempts to lessen the Soviet Union's control over Czechoslovakia led to a period of improvement called the "Prague Spring." Czech citizens enjoyed greater freedoms, including more contact with Western Europe. In August of that year, however, the Soviet Union sent troops to force a return to strict Communist control. Dubček was later replaced, and Soviet controls were back in place.

Détente The member nations of NATO, which were concerned about starting an all-out war with the Soviet Union, were unable to stop the Soviet control of Eastern Europe. In the 1970s, however, leaders of the Soviet Union and the United States began to have more contact with each other. This led to a period of **détente** (day·TAHNT), or lessening tension, between the members of NATO and the Warsaw Pact nations.

Place • Nikita Khrushchev, the son of a miner and grandson of a peasant, lessened government control of Soviet citizens. ▲

Region • Citizens of Czechoslovakia protested Soviet control in 1968. ◄

Place • The old city of Dubrovnik is in Croatia, a part of the former Yugoslavia, which was a Communist country in Eastern Europe. ▶

Economic Crisis By the 1980s, economic conditions in the Soviet Union and in those countries under its control had still not improved. Even after détente, the Soviet government continued to spend most of its money on the armed forces and nuclear weapons. In addition, people who lived in the non-Russian republics of the Soviet Union now wanted more control over their own affairs. Many citizens began to reject the Soviet economic system, but the Soviet leaders refused to give up any of their power or control.

SECTION 1 ASSESSMENT

Terms & Names

1. Identify:　(a) propaganda　　(b) private property rights　　(c) Nikita Khrushchev
　　　　　　　(d) deposed　　　　(e) détente

Taking Notes

2. Use a chart like this one to list and describe major aspects of Soviet culture.

Aspects of Soviet Culture

Main Ideas

3. (a) Why did Soviet leaders try to create a strong national identity?

(b) What began to happen in Eastern Europe in the 1950s?

(c) Describe the significance of the "Prague Spring."

Critical Thinking

4. **Analyzing Motives**

Why do you think the works of many writers, poets, and artists were banned or censored during the Soviet era?

Think About

◆ what Soviet citizens learned from Solzhenitsyn's works

◆ the government's use of propaganda

◆ what life was like for most Soviet citizens

ACTIVITY -OPTION- Reread the information under "Literature and the Arts" and the Spotlight on Culture feature. Write a **speech** for or against censorship in the arts.

Using an Electronic Card Catalog

▶▶ Defining the Skill

To find books, magazines, or other sources of information in a library, you may use an electronic card catalog. This catalog is a computerized search program on the Internet that lists every book, periodical, or other resource found in the library. You can search for resources in the catalog in four ways: by title, by author, by subject, and by keyword. Once you have typed in your search information, the catalog will give you a list of every resource that matches it. This is called bibliographic information. You can use an electronic card catalog to build a bibliography, or a list of books, on the topic you are researching.

▶▶ Applying the Skill

The screen below shows the results of an electronic search for information about the Danube River. To use the information on the screen, follow the strategies listed below.

How to Use an Electronic Card Catalog

Strategy ❶ To begin your search, choose Subject, Title, Author, or Keyword. The student doing this search chose "Subject" and then typed in "Danube River."

Strategy ❷ Based on your search, the catalog will give you a list of records that match that subject. You must then select one of the records to view the details about the resource. The catalog will then give you a screen like the one to the right. This detailed record lists the author, title, and information about where and when the resource was published, and by whom.

Strategy ❸ Locate the call number for the book. The call number indicates the section in the library where you will find the book. You can also find out if the book is available in the library you are using. If not, it may be available in another library in the network.

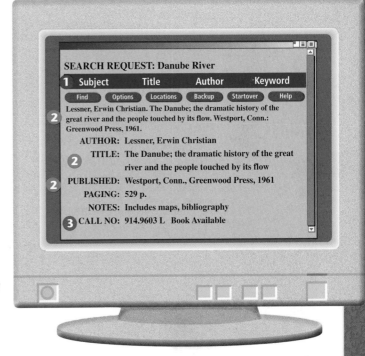

▶▶ Practicing the Skill

Review the text in Chapter 13, Section 1 to find a topic that interests you, such as Yuri Gagarin. Use the Subject search on an electronic card catalog to find information about your topic. Make a bibliography about the subject. Organize your bibliography alphabetically by author. For each book you list, also include the title, city, publisher, and date of publication.

Eastern Europe and Russia

TERMS & NAMES
Mikhail Gorbachev
parliamentary
  republic
coalition government
ethnic cleansing
Duma

MAIN IDEA

After the breakup of the Soviet Union, many former Soviet republics and countries of Eastern Europe became independent.

WHY IT MATTERS NOW

Nations once under Soviet rule are taking steps toward new economies and democratic governments.

DATELINE

THE KREMLIN, MOSCOW, 1988—To reduce military spending, the Soviet Union has begun removing large numbers of troops and arms from Eastern Europe. This latest news is just one of many changes in the Soviet government since Mikhail Gorbachev (GAWR•buh•chawf) came to power three years ago.

Although Gorbachev believes in the ideals of the Soviet system, he thinks that change is necessary to help solve the country's economic and political problems. Since 1985 Gorbachev has reduced Cold War tensions with the United States. At home in the Soviet Union, he has allowed more political and economic freedom.

Region • Mikhail Gorbachev leads the Soviet Union toward a freer society. ▲

The Breakup of the Soviet Union

Mikhail Gorbachev's reforms did not solve the problems of the Soviet Union. The economy continued to get worse. When Gorbachev did not force the countries of Eastern Europe to remain Communist, this further displeased many Communists.

Vocabulary

coup d'état:
the overthrow of
a government,
usually by a small
group in a position
of power; often
shortened to "coup"

In 1991, a group of more traditional Soviet leaders tried to take over the Soviet government. Thousands of people opposed this coup d'état (KOO•day•TAH), and the coup failed. Then, one by one, the Soviet republics declared independence. The Warsaw Pact was dissolved. By the end of 1991, the Soviet Union no longer existed. The huge country had become 15 different nations.

Modern Eastern Europe

Each former Soviet republic set up its own non-Communist government. The countries of Eastern Europe that had been under Soviet control held democratic elections, and many wrote or revised their constitutions.

BACKGROUND

The Central Asian Soviet republics were mostly Muslim. These republics are now the countries of Kazakhstan, Turkmenistan, Uzbekistan, Kyrgyzstan, and Tajikistan.

In some countries, such as the Czech Republic, former Communists were banned from important government posts. In other countries, such as Bulgaria, the former Communists reorganized themselves into a new political party and have won elections. Many different ethnic groups also tried to create new states within a nation or to reestablish old states that had not existed in many years.

Parliamentary Republics Today, most of the countries of Eastern Europe are parliamentary republics. A **parliamentary republic** is a form of government led by the head of the political party with the most members in parliament. The head of government, usually a prime minister, proposes the programs that the government will undertake. Most of these countries also have a president who has ceremonial, rather than political, duties.

Former Soviet Republics and Warsaw Pact Members, 2001

GEOGRAPHY SKILLBUILDER: Interpreting a Map

1. **Location** • Which former Soviet republics and Warsaw Pact members border Russia?
2. **Region** • On which continent are most of these countries located?

In some countries, small political parties have joined forces to work together to form a government. This is called a **coalition government**.

New Economies Under Soviet rule, Eastern Europe struggled economically and its people's freedoms were severely restricted. Although Eastern Europeans gained their freedom, they also faced problems such as inflation and unemployment.

Eastern Europe's countries are changing from command economies to free-market economies. Some countries, such as Slovakia, made this change slowly. Others, such as Poland, reformed their economic system and achieved economic success.

Many former Soviet republics, which did not quickly reform their economic systems, are in bad economic shape. Some of these nations are terribly poor. Struggles for power have led to violence and sometimes civil war. Pollution from the Soviet era threatens people's health. Still, some republics, including Ukraine, Latvia, Lithuania, and Estonia, are making progress as independent nations.

Defense After the breakup of the Soviet Union, Eastern European nations no longer looked to the Soviet government to defend them. Many wanted to become members of NATO. Belonging to NATO would help assure them of protection in case of invasion.

Reading
Social Studies

A. Comparing
Compare a command economy with a free-market economy.

Spotlight on CULTURE

Easter in Ukraine In Ukraine, most Christians belong to the Orthodox Church. These Ukrainians are known for the special way in which they celebrate the Easter holiday. They create beautiful Easter eggs, which are dyed bright colors and covered with intricate designs. These eggs are so beautiful that people around the world collect them.

Ukrainian families also bake a special bread for Easter. They decorate this bread with designs made from pieces of dough. Families bring the bread and other foods to church to be blessed on Easter. These foods then make up the family's holiday feast.

THINKING CRITICALLY

1. Analyzing Issues
Why were Ukrainian Easter eggs not common during the Soviet era?

2. Comparing
Compare how your family prepares for holidays with preparations made by Ukrainians in the Orthodox Church.

In 1999 three new members joined NATO: Poland, Hungary, and the Czech Republic. In 2001 Bulgaria, Romania, Slovakia, Slovenia, and the Baltic states were also working to become NATO members.

War in the Balkan Peninsula

Since the late 1980s, much of Eastern Europe has been a place of turmoil and struggle. Yugoslavia, one of the countries located on Europe's Balkan Peninsula, has experienced terrible wars, extreme hardships, and great change.

Under Tito After World War II, Yugoslavia came under Marshal Tito's (TEE·toh) dictatorship. Tito controlled all the country's many different ethnic groups, which included Serbs, Croats, and Muslims. His rule continued until his death in 1980. Slobodan Milošević (sloh·boh·DON muh·LAW·shuh·vich) became Yugoslavia's president in 1989, after years of political turmoil.

Milosevic Slobodan Milošević, a Serb, wanted the Serbs to rule Yugoslavia. The Serbs in Bosnia began fighting the Croats and Muslims living there. The Bosnian Serbs murdered many Muslims so that Serbs would be in the majority. The Serbs called these killings of members of minority ethnic groups **ethnic cleansing**. Finally, NATO attacked the Bosnian Serbs and ended the war.

Connections to Science

Pollution Soviet leaders thought that industry would improve life for everyone. Developing industry was so important that the Soviet government did not worry about pollution. Few laws were passed to protect the environment.

In the 1970s and 1980s there was not enough money to modernize industry or to reduce pollution. Some areas also could not afford proper sewage systems or recycling plants. Today, Eastern Europe has some of the worst pollution problems on the continent.

The Balkan States, 1991 and 2001

AUSTRIA

HUNGARY

Slovenia

Croatia

Vojvodina

YUGOSLAVIA

Belgrade

ROMANIA

Bosnia and Herzegovina

Serbia

SAN MARINO

Adriatic Sea

ITALY

Montenegro

Kosovo

BULGARIA

Macedonia

ALBANIA

GREECE

National boundaries, 2001
Yugoslavia, 1991
Autonomous province boundaries, 2001
National capital

0   100   200 miles
0   100   200 kilometers

12°E   18°E

In 1995 the Serbs, Croats, and Muslims of Bosnia signed a peace treaty. In 1999 Milošević began using ethnic cleansing against the Albanians in Kosovo, a region of Serbia. NATO launched an air war against Yugoslavia that ended with the defeat of the Serbs. In 2000, public protests led to Milošević's removal. He was subsequently arrested and tried for war crimes by the United Nations.

Modern Russia

Life in Russia has improved since the breakup of the Soviet Union. Russian citizens can elect their own leaders. They enjoy more freedom of speech. New businesses have sprung up, and some Russians have become wealthy.

Unfortunately, Russia still faces serious problems. Many leaders are dishonest. The nation has been slow to reform its economic system. Most of the nation's new wealth has gone to a small number of people, so that many Russians remain poor. The crime rate has grown tremendously. The government has also fought a war against Chechnya (CHECH•nee•yah), a region of Russia that wants to become independent.

Russian Culture The fall of communism helped most Russians to follow their cultural practices more freely. Russians gained the freedom to practice the religion of their choice. They can also buy and read the great works of Russian literature that once were banned. At the beginning of the 21st century, writers and other artists also have far more freedom to express themselves.

New magazines and newspapers are being published. Even new history books are being written. For the first time in decades, these publications are telling more of the truth about the Soviet Union.

Russia's Government Russia has a democratic form of government. The president is elected by the people. The people also elect members of the **Duma** (DOO•muh), which is part of the legislature.

Russian Icons A special feature of Russian Orthodox churches is their beautiful religious paintings called icons (EYE•kahns). Russian icons usually depict biblical figures and scenes. They often decorate every corner of a church.

The greatest Russian icon painter was Andrei Rublev (AHN•dray ruhb•LYAWF). He worked in the late 1300s and early 1400s. Rublev's paintings, one of which is shown below, are brightly colored and highlighted in gold. His work influenced many later painters, and today he is considered one of the world's great religious artists.

Reading Social Studies

B. Identifying Problems What are the main problems that face Russia today?

BACKGROUND

One of the most popular pastimes in Russia is the game of chess. In fact, many of the world's greatest chess players, such as Boris Spassky, have been Russian.

Russia's Natural Resources Today

Legend:
- Forest
- Grassland
- Desert
- Tundra
- Farmland
- Fishing
- Natural gas
- Coal
- Oil
- Iron
- Gold
- Lead

ARCTIC OCEAN

Bering Sea

Sea of Okhotsk

R U S S I A

GEOGRAPHY SKILLBUILDER: Interpreting a Map

1. **Human-Environment Interaction** • Name three of Russia's more common natural resources.
2. **Place** • What is the most common type of land in Russia?

Democracy is still new to the Russian people. Some citizens are working to improve the system to reduce corruption and to ensure that everyone receives fair treatment. Even the thought of changing the government is new to most Russians. Under the Soviets, people had to accept things the way they were.

BACKGROUND

Russian highways are in poor condition. Also, many rivers and major ports are closed by ice in the winter. As a result, most Russian goods are transported by railroad.

Resources and Industry The map above shows Russia's major natural resources. The country is one of the world's largest producers of oil. Russia also contains the world's largest forests. Its trees are made into lumber, paper, and other wood products.

Russian factories produce steel from iron ore. Other factories use that steel to make tractors and other large machines. Since Russian ships can reach both the Pacific and Atlantic oceans, Russia also has a large fishing industry.

Economics Following the lead of Eastern European countries, Russia has been moving toward a free-market economy. Citizens can own land, and foreign companies are encouraged to do business in Russia. These changes have given many Russians more opportunities, but they have also brought difficulties.

Connections to Language

The Russian Language More than 150 million people speak Russian. It is related to other Slavic languages of Eastern Europe, including Polish, Serbian, and Bulgarian.

Russian is written using the Cyrillic (suh•RIHL•ihk) alphabet, which has 33 characters.

Many of the newly independent republics are now returning to the Latin alphabet, used to write English and most other languages of the Western world. The major powers in the world economy base their languages on the Latin alphabet, making communication easier with other countries.

Hello
Привет

Place • Forestry is a major industry in Russia. These harvested logs are being floated downriver to be processed. ▶

Prices are no longer controlled by the government. This means that companies can charge a price that is high enough for them to make a profit. At the beginning of the 21st century, however, people's wages have not risen as fast as prices. Many people cannot afford to buy new products.

Some Russians have done well in the new economy. On the other hand, people with less education and less access to power have not done as well. Also, today most new businesses and jobs are in the cities, which means that people in small towns have fewer job opportunities.

BACKGROUND

The Russian government is unable to enforce tax laws. Many people don't pay their taxes. Without that money, the government cannot provide basic services, such as health care.

SECTION 2 ASSESSMENT

Terms & Names

1. Identify: (a) Mikhail Gorbachev (b) parliamentary republic (c) coalition government
   (d) ethnic cleansing (e) Duma

Taking Notes

2. Use a flow chart like this one to outline the changes in Eastern Europe and Russia from 1988 through 2000.

1988:

   ↓

   ↓

Main Ideas

3. (a) What happened to the governments of the former Soviet republics after independence?

   (b) How have the economies of Eastern European countries changed now that those countries are free?

   (c) In what ways has life in Russia improved since the breakup of the Soviet Union?

Critical Thinking

4. **Making Inferences**

   Why do you think many Eastern European countries would like to join NATO?

   Think About

   • what happened to the Warsaw Pact
   • the economies of Eastern Europe
   • the relationship between Eastern Europe and Russia

ACTIVITY -OPTION-

Reread the information in the Spotlight on Culture feature. Write a short, personal **essay** that describes a special family, school, neighborhood, or holiday celebration in which you participated.

The European Union

TERMS & NAMES
European Union
currency
euro
tariff
standard of living
Court of Human Rights

MAIN IDEA

Europeans want to maintain a high quality of life for all citizens while preserving their unique cultures.

WHY IT MATTERS NOW

A prosperous and culturally diverse Europe provides goods and markets for the rest of the world.

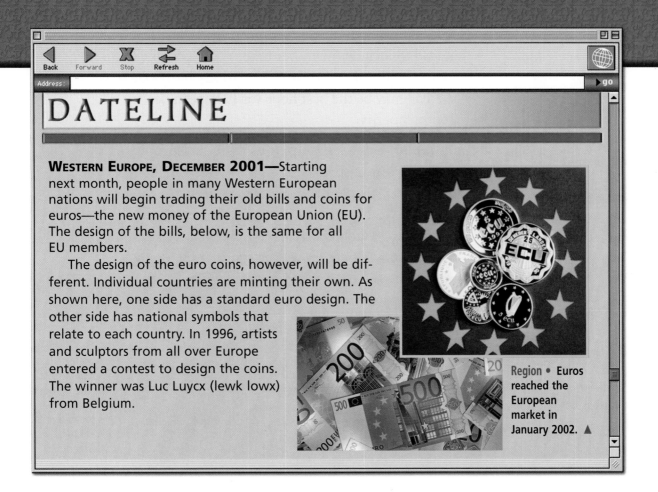

Back Forward Stop Refresh Home

Address: ▸go

DATELINE

WESTERN EUROPE, DECEMBER 2001—Starting next month, people in many Western European nations will begin trading their old bills and coins for euros—the new money of the European Union (EU). The design of the bills, below, is the same for all EU members.

The design of the euro coins, however, will be different. Individual countries are minting their own. As shown here, one side has a standard euro design. The other side has national symbols that relate to each country. In 1996, artists and sculptors from all over Europe entered a contest to design the coins. The winner was Luc Luycx (lewk lowx) from Belgium.

Region • Euros reached the European market in January 2002. ▲

Western Europe Today

Today, in Western Europe, all national leaders share their power with elected lawmakers. Citizens take part in government by voting and through membership in a variety of political parties. The Unit Atlas on pages 260–269 shows modern Europe.

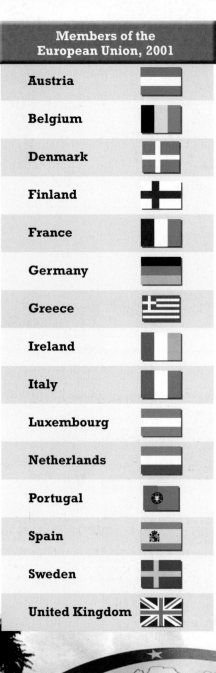
The European Union Many countries of Western Europe belong to a group called the **European Union** (EU). At first, countries joined the EU to encourage trade. This economic group, however, is becoming a loose political union.

Many former Communist countries of Eastern Europe want to join the Union too. They know that membership will help them economically and politically. Eastern European countries, however, cannot automatically join the EU. Many must first make legal, economic, and environmental improvements. The EU has agreed to include them over time. With a possible membership of more than 20 nations by 2003, the EU may be the best hope for European peace and prosperity.

Regional Governments In Western Europe, each nation also has regional governments, similar to those of individual states in the United States. Regional governments are demanding—and receiving—greater power. As a result, many people in Western Europe enjoy increased self-rule and participation in the political process.

BACKGROUND

In 2001, the EU gave initial approval to the Czech Republic, Estonia, Hungary, Poland, and Slovenia to join in the near future.

Region • The headquarters of the European Central Bank is located in Frankfurt, Germany. ◄

EU Economies

BACKGROUND

Some EU nations, including the United Kingdom and Denmark, have not agreed to give up their existing currency.

Traditionally, each European nation has had its own **currency,** or system of money. The EU is meant to make international trade much simpler. With more Europeans using the **euro,** the currency of the EU, currency no longer has to be exchanged every time a payment crosses a border.

Improved Trade To encourage trade, members have also done away with tariffs on the goods they trade with one another. A **tariff** is a duty or fee that must be paid on imported or exported goods, making them more expensive. EU members have lifted border controls as well. This means that goods, services, and people flow freely among these member nations.

Another goal of the EU is to achieve economic equality among its members. To reach this goal, EU members are sharing their wealth. Poorer countries such as Ireland receive money to help them build businesses.

Reading Social Studies

A. Clarifying How would improved trade raise the standard of living?

A Higher Standard of Living Member nations hope that increased trade and shared wealth will help give all citizens of the EU a high standard of living. A person's **standard of living,** or quality of life, is based on the availability of goods and services.

People who have a high standard of living have enough food and housing, good transportation and communications, and access to schools and health care. They also have a high rate of literacy, meaning that most adults are able to read.

Additional Benefits The members of the EU are helping the countries of Eastern Europe to raise their environmental standards. They are willing to pay up to 75 percent of the cost for a new waste treatment system in Romania, for example. The program includes recycling centers for paper, glass, and plastics. It will clean up and close old dumping grounds, which were leaking pollution into the ground water.

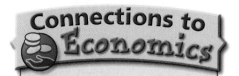

Connections to Economics

Tourism For many European nations, tourism is an important part of the economy. In fact, the continent represents about 60 percent of the world's tourist market. Visitors come to enjoy Europe's climate, historic sites, museums, and food.

Popular destinations include Spain, Italy, Austria, and the United Kingdom. France, below, is the most visited country in the world. In 1999 it hosted more than 73 million tourists.

The EU also runs programs that train people for jobs. As citizens of a member nation, people are not limited to a job in their own country. They may work in any part of the EU. They can even vote in local elections wherever they live. In addition, the Council of Europe's **Court of Human Rights** protects the rights of all its citizens in whichever member country they live.

Cultural Diversity

Although many European nations are part of the EU, they still have their own distinct cultural traditions. These traditions may include different languages, unique foods, certain ways of doing business, and even special games and celebrations. Many of these traditions developed over hundreds of years.

Some nations are a mix of several cultures. In Belgium, for example, Flemings live in the north and speak Dutch. Another major group, the Walloons, lives in the south. They speak French. A third group of German-speaking Belgians lives in the eastern part of the country. Many Belgian cities include people from all three groups.

City Life Many of the world's famous and exciting cities are located in Western Europe. London, Madrid, Paris, Amsterdam, and Rome are just a few of the major centers for the arts, business, and learning. These cities are centuries old, and Europeans work hard to preserve them.

Europeans also take pride in the conveniences that their cities offer. Most major urban areas have excellent public transportation, including subways, buses, and trains. Sidewalk cafés are also popular, where people come to meet friends, eat, and relax.

Reading
Social Studies

B. Identifying Problems What are the main problems facing the European Union?

Region • Many Europeans center their social lives around urban sidewalk cafés, such as this one in Italy. ▼

Region • Quaint small European villages are popular tourist attractions. ▶

BACKGROUND

Many European families cannot make a living on a small farm. The government may offer support to such families, to help preserve the nation's rural culture.

Country Life European cities have much to offer, but the countryside is also popular—especially for vacationers. The Italian region of Tuscany (TUHS·kuh·nee) and the French region of Provence (pruh·VAHNS) are two of the best-known examples of the many beautiful rural areas.

Small European villages may have only a café, a grocery store, a post office, a town square, and a collection of houses. Many families who live in such areas have been farming or raising animals on the same land for generations. Some even live in houses that their families have owned for hundreds of years.

SECTION 3 ASSESSMENT

Terms & Names

1. **Identify:**
   (a) European Union (EU)
   (b) currency
   (c) euro
   (d) tariff
   (e) standard of living
   (f) Court of Human Rights

Taking Notes

2. Use a chart like this one to compare aspects of city life and country life in Europe.

City Life	Country Life

Main Ideas

3. (a) Describe the importance of the new shared currency that is based on the euro.

   (b) Can any European country automatically join the EU? Why or why not?

   (c) List at least two benefits, other than a shared currency, for countries that are members of the EU.

Critical Thinking

4. **Synthesizing**

   Why may the EU be the best hope for European peace and prosperity?

   Think About
   • the number of member countries
   • the goals of the EU
   • modern European conflicts

ACTIVITY -OPTION- Choose one photograph from this section that shows a place in Europe. Write a **postcard** or **e-mail** to a friend or family member as if you were there. What sights and sounds will you describe?

1900 1910 1920 1930 1940 1950 1960 1970   1700 1710 1720 1730 1740 1750 1760 178
1990 2000   1800 1810 1820 1830 1840 1850 1860 187
1890 1900 1910 1920 1930 1940 1950 19
1980 1990 2000

Linking Past and Present

The Legacy of Europe

Movable Type

Before Johann Gutenberg (1400–1468) invented the printing press in Germany, European monks copied books by hand. Movable type made it possible to print multiple copies of books quickly, allowing people access to them. The printing process advanced greatly in the 1930s. By the mid-1940s, printed works included complex illustrations and color. Today, people create text and images and print them directly from their computers.

Early printing press ▲

Nitroglycerin

For almost 20 years, Alfred Nobel (1833–1896), shown at left, worked on developing a way to safely contain and ignite nitroglycerin, a powerful explosive. Eventually, chemists and doctors realized that nitroglycerin widens blood vessels and can be used to treat patients with heart conditions. Given in tablet, patch, or oral-spray form, nitroglycerin has saved countless lives.

Architecture

The White House in Washington, D.C., is one of many buildings in the United States that has been influenced by Roman architecture. Roman buildings often featured vaulted domes, columns, and large interior spaces. This type of architecture has influenced other buildings in the United States, including many banks and courthouses.

Democracy

Around 500 B.C., several Greek city-states established democracies, replacing their single-ruler governments. The word *democracy* derives from two Greek words: *demos,* meaning "people," and *kratos,* meaning "power." Today, the idea of rule by the people is found around the world, from the United States to France to India.

The agora, or marketplace, of ancient Athens was often the scene of political activities. ▲

Find Out More About It!

Study the text and photos on these pages to learn about inventions, creations, and contributions that have come from Europe. Then choose the item that interests you the most and use the library or the Internet to learn more about it. Use the information you gather to create a poster celebrating the contribution.

i RESEARCH LINKS
CLASSZONE.COM

Yacht ▼

Robot ▶

Flamingo ▶

European Languages

Many words of different European languages have made their way into English. For example, the word *dinner* is actually French in origin. As English people traveled and settled around the world, they borrowed words from such European languages as German, Spanish, and Norwegian to use in their everyday communication. Examples of some of these words we use today are *kindergarten* (German), *dinner* (French), *yacht* (Dutch), *corridor* (Italian), *vanilla* (Spanish), *flamingo* (Portuguese), *robot* (Czech), and *ski* (Norwegian).

TERMS & NAMES

Explain the significance of each of the following:

1. propaganda
2. Nikita Khrushchev
3. détente
4. Mikhail Gorbachev
5. ethnic cleansing
6. Duma
7. currency
8. euro
9. tariff
10. standard of living

REVIEW QUESTIONS

Eastern Europe Under Communism *(pages 353–358)*

1. Why did the Soviet government outlaw many cultural celebrations?
2. Explain why most Soviet citizens learned little about other nations around the world.
3. How did the Soviet Union maintain control over Eastern European countries?

Eastern Europe and Russia *(pages 360–366)*

4. How did the Soviet Union change during 1991?
5. List at least three of Russia's major natural resources.

The European Union *(pages 367–371)*

6. What is the importance of the European Union (EU)?
7. Name one benefit of being a member of the EU.
8. Identify at least three of Europe's major centers of the arts, business, and learning.

CRITICAL THINKING

Comparing

1. Using your completed chart from Reading Social Studies, p. 352, compare Eastern Europe under Communism with Eastern Europe after Communism.

Summarizing

2. Outline the changes to the Russian economy since the breakup of the Soviet Union.

Recognizing Important Details

3. What types of changes must Eastern European countries make in order to join the EU?

Visual Summary

Eastern Europe Under Communism

- The Soviet Union's communist government controlled the lives of its citizens.
- Under Nikita Khrushchev, citizens began to have greater freedom.

1

2

Eastern Europe and Russia

- Today, independent nations once under Soviet rule are taking steps toward new economies and greater freedom.

The European Union

- Many European countries are members of an economic and political alliance called the European Union (EU).

3

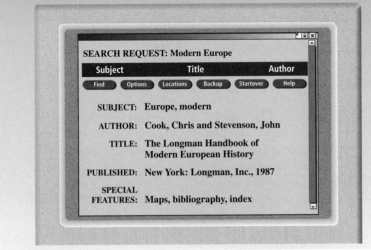

SEARCH REQUEST: Modern Europe

Subject	Title	Author

Find Options Locations Backup Startover Help

SUBJECT: **Europe, modern**

AUTHOR: **Cook, Chris and Stevenson, John**

TITLE: **The Longman Handbook of Modern European History**

PUBLISHED: **New York: Longman, Inc., 1987**

SPECIAL FEATURES: **Maps, bibliography, index**

SKILLBUILDER: Using an Electronic Card Catalog

1. Who wrote this book, and when was it published?

2. Will this book help you find other books related to the subject you researched?

FOCUS ON GEOGRAPHY

1. **Human-Environment Interaction** • Which nation or nations appear to have the largest amounts of farmland?

2. **Place** • Which nation or nations do not have coastal fishing resources?

3. **Place** • Which nation or nations appear to have the smallest amounts of forests?

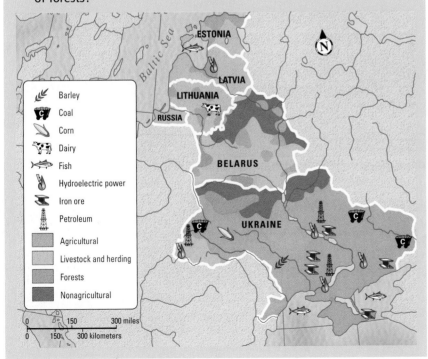

Barley
Coal
Corn
Dairy
Fish
Hydroelectric power
Iron ore
Petroleum
Agricultural
Livestock and herding
Forests
Nonagricultural

ESTONIA
LATVIA
LITHUANIA
RUSSIA
BELARUS
UKRAINE
Baltic Sea

0   150   300 miles
0   150   300 kilometers

CHAPTER PROJECTS

Interdisciplinary Activity: Math

Making an Inflation Chart This activity will help you to understand the effects of inflation on the economy. Look at a flier from a local grocery store. Write the names and prices of five food items in the first column of a chart. Then figure out and record what the prices would be for each item for the next two years.

• To find next year's price: multiply the original price by .03 (the rate of inflation). Add this to the original price.

• To find the following year's price: multiply next year's price by .03 (the rate of inflation). Add that to next year's price.

Cooperative Learning Activity

Creating a New Government Work in a group of three to five students to create a new class government and constitution.

• Assign each student a role in the new government, such as congressperson or president.

• Be sure to outline the responsibilities of each member.

• Write a brief constitution for your government. Include sections outlining basic rights, freedoms, and responsibilities of citizens.

INTERNET ACTIVITY

Use the Internet to do research about the economy in Slovenia. Specifically look for information about the types of industries in Slovenia. What are its major imports and exports?

Writing About Economics Write a short report of your findings. Be sure to list the Web sites that you used to prepare your report.

For Internet links to support this activity, go to

RESEARCH LINKS
CLASSZONE.COM

CHAPTER 14

Europe Today

Place London's Piccadilly Circus is an intersection of major roads, with an Underground, or subway, stop at the center. Piccadilly Circus is a popular tourist attraction and shopping district.

UNDERGROUND

SWEDEN

POLAND

UNITED KINGDOM

GERMANY

ATLANTIC

FRANCE

PACIFIC

PACIFIC

OCEAN

OCEAN

OCEAN

INDIAN
OCEAN

OCEAN

Why is it important for Europeans to protect their seas?

FOCUS ON **GEOGRAPHY**

Human-Environment Interaction • The United Kingdom, Sweden, France, Germany, and Poland have borders along the North Sea or the Baltic Sea. These European seas are major transportation corridors. The North Sea contains one of the world's most important oil deposits. The Baltic Sea has some oil and is heavily used for transporting oil.

Accidents sometimes happen at sea. About three oil spills occur every year in the Baltic Sea. The North Sea has also had major spills. One occurred in November 1998, killing thousands of sea birds. Today, nations are working on ways to prevent spills and to clean up those that occur.

What do you think?

♦ Why is it important for countries to protect the seas?

♦ What effect might oil spills and other pollution have on the seas?

♦ What economic purposes do oceans and seas serve?

PUBLIC SUBWAY

READING SOCIAL STUDIES

BEFORE YOU READ

▶▶ *What Do You Know?*

Did you know that from the end of WW II until 1990, Germany was two separate countries and Poland was controlled by the Soviet Union? Do you have relatives or friends who come from the United Kingdom, Sweden, France, Germany, or Poland? Have you ever seen the Queen of England or the Pope, who is from Poland, on television? Have you heard of the Nobel Prize, which is awarded in Sweden? Think about what you have learned in other classes, what you have read, and what you have heard or seen in the news about these countries.

▶▶ *What Do You Want to Know?*

Consider what you know about the countries covered in Chapter 14. In your notebook, record what you hope to learn from this chapter.

Region • Sweden's Nobel Prize honors great achievements worldwide. ▲

READ AND TAKE NOTES

Reading Strategy: Comparing Comparing is a useful strategy for evaluating two or more similar subjects. Making comparisons also helps you to better understand what you have learned. Use the chart below to compare information about the United Kingdom, Sweden, France, Germany, and Poland.

- Copy the chart into your notebook.
- As you read, look for information for each category.
- Record details under the appropriate headings.

Movement • The German-made Volkswagen Beetle is the best-selling car ever. ▲

Country	Physical Geography	Government	Economy	Culture	Interesting Facts
United Kingdom					
Sweden					
France					
Germany					
Poland					

The United Kingdom

SECTION 1

TERMS & NAMES

London

secede

Good Friday Accord

Charles Dickens

MAIN IDEA	WHY IT MATTERS NOW
The United Kingdom is a small nation in Western Europe with a history of colonization.	British economic, political, and cultural traditions have influenced nations around the world.

DATELINE

EXTRA

BARCELONA, SPAIN, MAY 30, 1999

They did it! Manchester United won the triple crown of soccer. The British fans here are going wild, and their excitement is easy to understand. Manchester United is only the third soccer team to win its league championship, cup titles, and the Champions League final.

Football, or "soccer" as Americans call it, is the world's most popular sport. The British invented a form of the game, called "mob football," in the 1300s. Back then, the playing field was the size of a small town, and there might have been as many as 500 players. A set of rules for the game was developed in 1863. Today, football is the national pastime in the United Kingdom.

Region • Manchester United celebrates after winning soccer's triple crown. ▲

A Kingdom of Four Political Regions

The United Kingdom is a small island nation of Western Europe. Its culture has had an enormous impact on the world. The nation's official name is the United Kingdom of Great Britain and Northern Ireland. **London,** located in southeastern England, is the capital.

Vocabulary

Great Britain: the name for the island that contains Scotland, England, and Wales

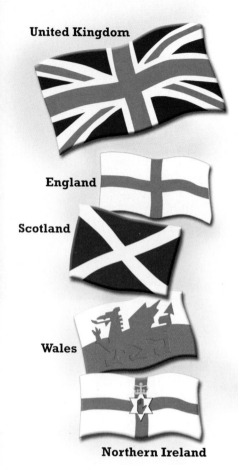

United Kingdom

England

Scotland

Wales

Northern Ireland

Four different political regions make up the United Kingdom: Scotland, England, Wales, and Northern Ireland (see the map below). The British monarchy has ruled over the four regions for hundreds of years.

National Government Today, the government of the United Kingdom is a constitutional monarchy. The British monarch is a symbol of power rather than an actual ruler. The power to govern belongs to Parliament, which is the national lawmaking body.

The British Parliament has two parts. The House of Lords is made up of nobles. Elected representatives make up the House of Commons. The House of Commons is the more powerful of the two houses.

The prime minister leads the government. He or she is usually the leader of the political party that wins the most seats in the House of Commons. The other political parties go into "opposition," which means their role is to question government policies.

Regional Government in Great Britain Recently, the national government of the United Kingdom has returned some self-rule to some regions of Great Britain. In the late 1990s, voters in Wales approved plans for their own assembly, or body of lawmakers. Also at this time, the Scots voted to create their own parliament. Both Wales's assembly and Scotland's parliament met for the first time in 1999.

Vocabulary

monarchy: government by king or queen

Reading
Social Studies

A. Clarifying Who is the head of government in the United Kingdom?

The United Kingdom Today

Legend:
- National boundary
- Regional boundary
- ⊛ National capital
- • Other city

0   50   100 miles
0   50   100 kilometers

GEOGRAPHY SKILLBUILDER: Interpreting a Map

1. **Location** • Which region of the United Kingdom is on a different island?
2. **Location** • Which body of water separates the United Kingdom from France?

BACKGROUND

The roots of division in Northern Ireland go back to at least the 1600s, when English and Scottish colonists settled there. These Protestant settlers took over the lands of Irish Catholics.

Governing Northern Ireland Throughout the 20th century, there were conflicts in Northern Ireland between Irish Catholic nationalists and Irish Protestants who supported the government of the United Kingdom. In fact, during the 1960s, many Irish Catholics wanted Northern Ireland to **secede,** or withdraw from, the United Kingdom. They hoped to unite Northern Ireland with the Republic of Ireland. Irish Protestants—a majority in the region—generally wanted to remain part of the United Kingdom.

In 1969, riots broke out, and the British government sent in troops to stop them. Violence between groups of Protestants and Catholics continued for almost 30 years. In 1998, representatives from both sides signed the **Good Friday Accord**. This agreement set up the Northern Ireland Assembly, which represents both Catholic and Protestant voters. For this government to succeed in Northern Ireland, however, the former enemies will need to work together.

The WORLD'S HERITAGE

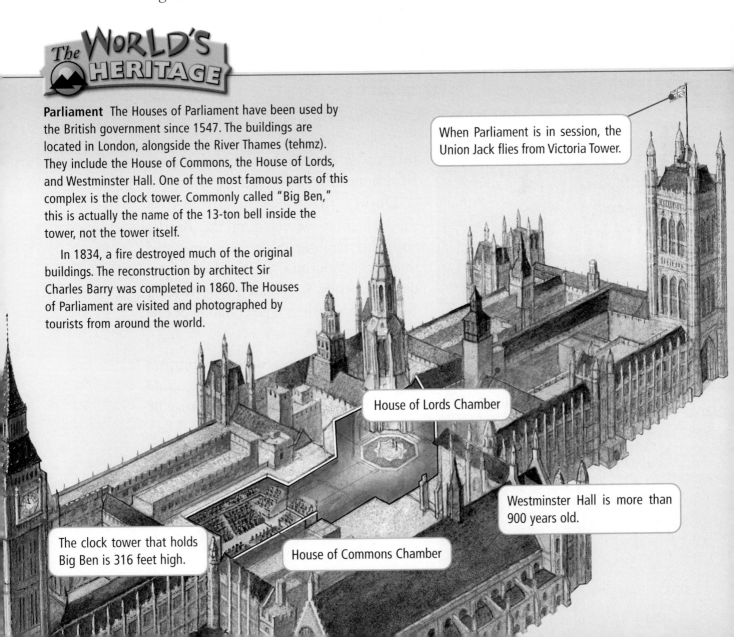

Parliament The Houses of Parliament have been used by the British government since 1547. The buildings are located in London, alongside the River Thames (tehmz). They include the House of Commons, the House of Lords, and Westminster Hall. One of the most famous parts of this complex is the clock tower. Commonly called "Big Ben," this is actually the name of the 13-ton bell inside the tower, not the tower itself.

In 1834, a fire destroyed much of the original buildings. The reconstruction by architect Sir Charles Barry was completed in 1860. The Houses of Parliament are visited and photographed by tourists from around the world.

When Parliament is in session, the Union Jack flies from Victoria Tower.

House of Lords Chamber

Westminster Hall is more than 900 years old.

The clock tower that holds Big Ben is 316 feet high.

House of Commons Chamber

Region • London's New Globe Theater is a replica of the 17th-century playhouse that originally hosted William Shakespeare's works. ◄

Cultural Heritage

The United Kingdom has a rich cultural heritage that includes the great Renaissance playwright William Shakespeare. With a long history as an imperial power, the nation has been exporting its culture around the world for hundreds of years. For example, India, Canada, and other former British colonies modeled their governments on the British parliamentary system. British culture has also set trends in sports, music, and literature.

Music British music influenced the early music of Canada and the United States, both former British colonies. One British tune long familiar to people in the United States is "God Save the Queen." You probably know it as "My Country, 'Tis of Thee." Several countries have put the words of their national anthems to this traditional British melody.

During the 1960s, many British musical groups—including the Beatles and the Rolling Stones—dominated music charts around the world. In later decades, other British singers, including Elton John, Sting, and Dido, became popular favorites.

Literature The best-known cultural export of the United Kingdom, aside from the English language itself, may be literature. In the 19th century, Mary Shelley dreamed up Frankenstein's monster, and Sir Arthur Conan Doyle first wrote about Sherlock Holmes. Another popular author of the time was **Charles Dickens** (1812–1870), who wrote *Oliver Twist* and *A Christmas Carol*.

Region • In the early 1960s, the Beatles became wildly popular, not only in the United Kingdom, but also around the world. ▼

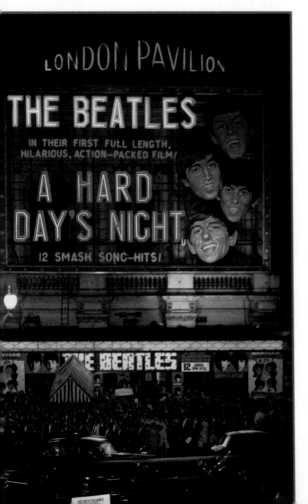

Two gifted British writers of the 20th century are Virginia Woolf and George Orwell. Modern British authors have also given the world many popular stories for young people. They include C. S. Lewis, who wrote *The Chronicles of Narnia,* and J. K. Rowling, who created the Harry Potter books.

Reading
Social Studies

B. Recognizing Important Details Why was the United Kingdom able to spread British culture across the world?

The British Economy

The United Kingdom is an important trading and financial center. Many British citizens also make their living in mining and manufacturing. Factories in the United Kingdom turn out a variety of products ranging from china to sports cars. The nation has plenty of coal, natural gas, and oil to fuel its factories, but it has few other natural resources.

The need for imported goods makes trade another major industry of the United Kingdom. The nation imports many raw materials used in manufacturing. It also imports food, because the farms of this nation produce only enough to feed about two-thirds of its large population.

Region • J. K. Rowling's Harry Potter books have captured the imaginations of children worldwide. ▲

SECTION 1 ASSESSMENT

Terms & Names

1. Identify:
  (a) London
  (b) secede
  (c) Good Friday Accord
  (d) Charles Dickens

Taking Notes

2. Use a chart like this one to describe the major aspects of the United Kingdom's modern government, economy, and culture.

Modern United Kingdom	
Government	
Economy	
Culture	

Main Ideas

3. (a) Identify the four regions that make up the United Kingdom.

(b) What role does the British monarch play in the government of the modern United Kingdom?

(c) What impact has the culture of the United Kingdom had on its colonies and on other parts of the world?

Critical Thinking

4. Analyzing Issues

Why do you think the conflict in Northern Ireland is so difficult to resolve?

Think About

- differences in religious beliefs
- recent changes in British regional governments
- the long period of continued violence

ACTIVITY -OPTION-   Reread the information about British football from the "Dateline" feature that opens the section. Write a **description** of a sport that interests you.

Sweden

TERMS & NAMES
Riksdag
ombudsman
armed neutrality
hydroelectricity
acid rain
skerry

MAIN IDEA

Sweden offers its people a high standard of living, although it also faces environmental problems.

WHY IT MATTERS NOW

Modern Sweden is dealing with environmental issues that affect many countries around the world.

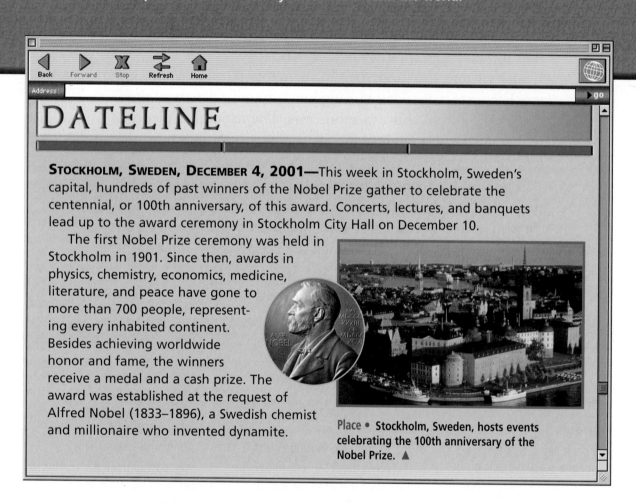

Back   Forward   Stop   Refresh   Home

Address: ▸ go

DATELINE

STOCKHOLM, SWEDEN, DECEMBER 4, 2001—This week in Stockholm, Sweden's capital, hundreds of past winners of the Nobel Prize gather to celebrate the centennial, or 100th anniversary, of this award. Concerts, lectures, and banquets lead up to the award ceremony in Stockholm City Hall on December 10.

The first Nobel Prize ceremony was held in Stockholm in 1901. Since then, awards in physics, chemistry, economics, medicine, literature, and peace have gone to more than 700 people, representing every inhabited continent. Besides achieving worldwide honor and fame, the winners receive a medal and a cash prize. The award was established at the request of Alfred Nobel (1833–1896), a Swedish chemist and millionaire who invented dynamite.

Place • Stockholm, Sweden, hosts events celebrating the 100th anniversary of the Nobel Prize. ▲

Sweden's Government

Sweden is famous for the Nobel Prize, but it is also one of the most prosperous and beautiful countries in Europe. The Kingdom of Sweden shares the Scandinavian Peninsula with Norway in Northern Europe (see the map on page 385). The country is a constitutional monarchy, meaning that the Swedish monarch has only ceremonial powers. He or she cannot make laws. Instead, the people elect representatives to four-year terms in the Swedish parliament, called the **Riksdag** (REEKS·DAHG).

The Riksdag The 349 members of the Riksdag nominate Sweden's prime minister. They also appoint ombudsmen. **Ombudsmen** are officials who protect citizens' rights and make sure that the Swedish courts and civil service follow the law.

Swedish citizens vote to determine how many members of each political party serve in the Riksdag. Before 1976, the Social Democratic Labour Party had been in power for nearly 44 years. Today, the Swedish government includes four other parties.

Region •
Women are active in Swedish government. ▶

Foreign Policy Since World War I, Sweden's foreign policy has been one of **armed neutrality**. This means that in times of war, the country has its own military forces but does not take sides in other nations' conflicts.

Even during peacetime, the Swedish government tries not to form military alliances. Unless Sweden is directly attacked, it will not become involved in war. The country is a strong supporter of the United Nations.

Reading
Social Studies

A. Synthesizing
How does Sweden's neutrality affect its foreign relations?

The Economy and the Environment

Privately owned businesses and international trade are important to Sweden's economy. It exports many goods, including metals, minerals, and wood. Engineering and communications are major industries. The automobile industry also provides many jobs.

Sweden Today

- National boundary
- ⊛ National capital
- • Other city

0   100 miles
0   100 kilometers

Norwegian Sea

Arctic Circle

65°N

SCANDINAVIA

Kiruna

Tornedälven

Umedälven

SWEDEN

Sundsvall

Ljusnan

Gulf of Bothnia

FINLAND

60°N

Falun   Gävle

NORWAY

Karlstad

Uppsala

Örebro   ⊛ Stockholm

ESTONIA

Göteborg

Gotland

Visby

Halmstad

Växjö

LATVIA

Kalmar

Öland

DENMARK

Helsingborg

Malmö

BALTIC SEA

LITHUANIA

GEOGRAPHY SKILLBUILDER:
Interpreting a Map

1. **Location** • Which country shares the Scandinavian Peninsula with Sweden?
2. **Region** • What is the national capital of Sweden?

The Swedish Labor Force After World War II, many Swedes left their towns and villages to find work in the large cities in the south. Today, more than 80 percent of the population lives in these urban areas. Much of Sweden's labor force is highly educated and enjoys a high standard of living.

Place • Many in Sweden's highly educated labor force work in the high-tech and engineering industries. ▲

Power Sources **Hydroelectricity,** or power generated by water, is the main source of electrical power in Sweden. Nuclear power is also widely used. The Swedish government is looking into other, safer sources of energy, which include solar- and wind-powered energy.

Acid Rain Sweden and its neighboring countries share similar environmental problems. One of the most severe problems is **acid rain.** Acid rain occurs when air pollutants come back to Earth in the form of precipitation. These pollutants may soon poison many trees throughout the region. Sweden and neighboring countries are working to clean up the environment by trying to control air pollutants produced by cars and factories.

Region • December 13 is St. Lucia's Day, one of Sweden's most important Christian holidays. ▼

ᵣₑₐding
Social Studies

B. Clarifying What causes acid rain?

Daily Life and Culture

Culturally and ethnically, Sweden is primarily a homogeneous country. Ninety percent of the population are native to Sweden and are members of the Lutheran Church of Sweden. The majority of people speak Swedish.

Since World War II, immigrants from Turkey, Greece, and other countries have brought some cultural diversity to Sweden's population. Today, about one in nine people living in Sweden is an immigrant or the child of an immigrant.

Vocabulary

homogeneous: the same throughout

Recreation Workers in Sweden have many benefits, including long vacations. The Swedes love taking time to enjoy both winter and summer sports. Sweden, with its cold weather and many hills and mountains, is a great place for cross-country and downhill skiing. Skating, hockey, and ice fishing are also popular.

Place • Sweden's cold winters have made downhill and cross-country skiing popular. ▶

Many small islands, called **skerries,** dot the Swedish coast. In the summer, many people visit these islands to hike, camp, and fish. Tennis, soccer, and outdoor performances such as concerts are popular as well.

Contributions to World Culture Sweden is well-known for its contributions to drama, literature, and film. The late 19th-century and early 20th-century plays of August Strindberg are produced all over the world. Astrid Lindgren's children's books, including *Pippi Longstocking* (1945), still delight readers everywhere. Ingmar Bergman is famous for the many great films he directed.

SECTION 2 ASSESSMENT

Terms & Names

1. Identify:
- (a) Riksdag
- (b) ombudsman
- (c) armed neutrality
- (d) hydroelectricity
- (e) acid rain
- (f) skerry

Taking Notes

2. Use a spider map like this one to outline the major aspects of Sweden's government, economy, and culture.

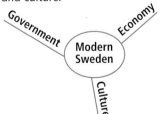

Government
Economy
Modern Sweden
Culture

Main Ideas

3. (a) On which European peninsula is Sweden located? What other country shares this peninsula?

(b) What happened to the Swedish labor force after World War II?

(c) How has immigration since World War II changed the population of Sweden?

Critical Thinking

4. Evaluating Decisions

What do you think might be the advantages and disadvantages of armed neutrality for Sweden?

Think About

- Sweden's location
- the damage and expense of war
- the benefits of alliances

ACTIVITY -OPTION- Reread the "Dateline" feature at the beginning of this section. Write a short **description** of which category you would like to earn a Nobel Prize in and why.

Spend a Day in Renaissance Florence

You are a traveler visiting Florence, Italy, in the year 1505. It is exciting to be here now. All over Europe, people have heard about the Renaissance, or cultural rebirth, that is taking place in this beautiful city. Artists, architects, writers, and scientists are turning out brilliant work. In the day you spend here, you want to learn about this new cultural movement. You want to be able to tell people at home about Renaissance Florence.

COOPERATIVE LEARNING On these pages are challenges you will encounter as you tour Renaissance Florence. Working with a small group, choose one of these challenges to solve. Divide the work among group members. Look for helpful information in the Data File. Keep in mind that you will present your solution to the class.

LANGUAGE ARTS CHALLENGE

"Florence is home to brilliant artists and writers."

Why did the Renaissance start here? Florence is home to brilliant artists and writers. Successful merchants and craftworkers, along with several powerful families, have made the city rich. Many wealthy people are patrons, or sponsors, of artists' work. You are curious about the people of Florence. Who are the leading figures? What is life like here? Choose one of these options to discover the answers. Use the Data File for help.

ACTIVITIES

1. Choose one major figure who lived in Florence during the Renaissance and research his or her life. Then write a short first-person monologue in which, speaking as that person, you describe your life and work.
2. Imagine you are an ordinary young Florentine living in 1505—for example, a goldsmith's apprentice. Write journal entries for a week in your life.

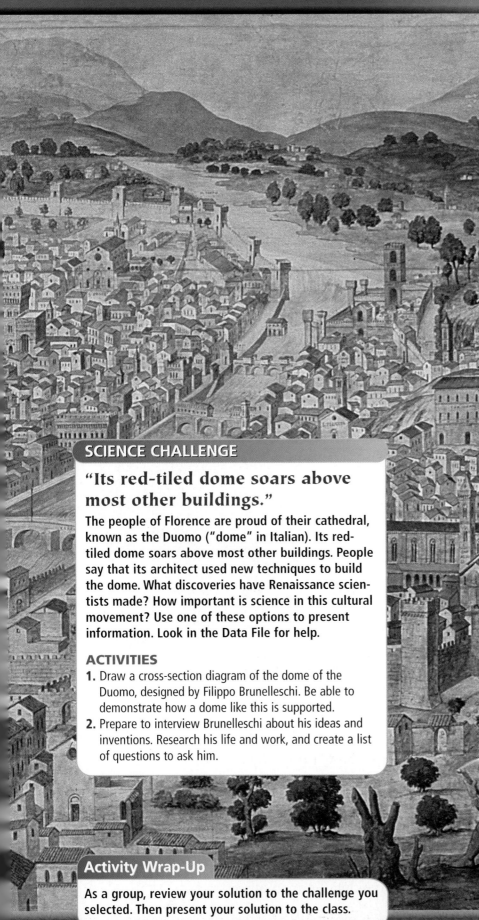

SCIENCE CHALLENGE

"Its red-tiled dome soars above most other buildings."

The people of Florence are proud of their cathedral, known as the Duomo ("dome" in Italian). Its red-tiled dome soars above most other buildings. People say that its architect used new techniques to build the dome. What discoveries have Renaissance scientists made? How important is science in this cultural movement? Use one of these options to present information. Look in the Data File for help.

ACTIVITIES

1. Draw a cross-section diagram of the dome of the Duomo, designed by Filippo Brunelleschi. Be able to demonstrate how a dome like this is supported.
2. Prepare to interview Brunelleschi about his ideas and inventions. Research his life and work, and create a list of questions to ask him.

Activity Wrap-Up

As a group, review your solution to the challenge you selected. Then present your solution to the class.

LANDMARKS OF RENAISSANCE FLORENCE

- Florence is built on both sides of the **Arno River**. Its population during the Renaissance was about 100,000. Most of the famous buildings are on the right bank. Besides its artists, Renaissance Florence was known for its craftworkers, such as goldsmiths and leatherworkers.

- The **Duomo** stands on the Piazza del Duomo, an open square. In 1418, Filippo Brunelleschi won a contest to build a dome over the unfinished church. He invented new methods and machines to build it. As in earlier domes, vaults or pointed arches support the dome. Brunelleschi added a circular support wall, called a drum, to build it higher.

- The **Ponte Vecchio** ("Old Bridge"), built in 1345, is one of several bridges across the Arno River. Shops, especially those of goldsmiths, line both sides of the bridge.

- The **Pitti Palace**, built in 1458, is on the left bank of the river.

MAJOR FIGURES OF THE RENAISSANCE

- **Filippo Brunelleschi** (1377–1446), architect of the Duomo and the Pitti Palace.

- **Dante** (1265–1321), poet, author of *Divine Comedy*. Dante pioneered the usage of everyday language, instead of Latin, in literature.

- **Isabella d'Este** (1474–1539), noblewoman and patron of many artists.

- **Leonardo da Vinci** (1452–1519), painter, sculptor, engineer, scientist.

- **Michelangelo** (1475–1564), sculptor, painter, architect; sculptor of *David* (1504).

- **Raphael** (1483–1520), painter and architect.

To learn more about Renaissance Florence, go to

RESEARCH LINKS
CLASSZONE.COM

France

TERMS & NAMES
Charles de Gaulle
French Resistance
Jean Monnet
socialism
European Community
impressionism

MAIN IDEA

France was ruined politically and economically by World War II but has since made a full recovery.

WHY IT MATTERS NOW

France is an important member of the European Union and continues to influence the world's economy and cultures.

DATELINE

EXTRA

PARIS, FRANCE, AUGUST 26, 1944

Paris is free! The church bells are still ringing from yesterday's celebrations. After four long years of German control, Paris finally has been liberated. General Charles de Gaulle returned from the United Kingdom yesterday and celebrated the liberation by leading a parade from the Arc de Triomphe to Notre Dame Cathedral.

The liberation of Paris is the result of a two-and-a-half-month advance of Allied forces from the beaches of Normandy in northern France. The French Resistance in Paris began disrupting the German occupiers on August 19, and yesterday, the French army entered Paris.

Region • The liberation of Paris is a significant symbolic victory for the Allies. ▲

Region • Charles de Gaulle is a hero to the French. ▲

The Fifth Republic

During World War II, **Charles de Gaulle** (1890–1970) was a general in the French army. After Germany conquered France in 1940, de Gaulle fled to the United Kingdom. There, he became the leader of the French in exile and stayed in contact with the French Resistance. The **French Resistance** established communications for the Allied war effort, spied on German activity, and sometimes assassinated high-ranking German officers.

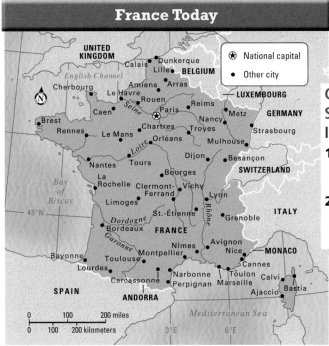

France Today

- ⊛ National capital
- ● Other city

UNITED KINGDOM

English Channel

Calais • Dunkerque
Lille • BELGIUM
Amiens • Arras
Cherbourg • Le Havre • Rouen • Reims
Caen • Seine • Paris
Brest • Chartres • Troyes • Nancy • Metz • LUXEMBOURG
Rennes • Le Mans • Orléans • GERMANY
Nantes • Tours • Dijon • Strasbourg
Loire • Bourges • Besançon • Mulhouse
La Rochelle • Clermont-Ferrand • Vichy • SWITZERLAND
Limoges • St.-Étienne • Lyon
Dordogne • Grenoble • ITALY
Bordeaux • FRANCE • Rhône
Garonne • Nîmes • Avignon • MONACO
Bayonne • Toulouse • Montpellier • Nice
Lourdes • Narbonne • Toulon • Cannes
Carcassonne • Perpignan • Marseille • Calvi
SPAIN • Bastia
ANDORRA • Ajaccio
Mediterranean Sea

Bay of Biscay

45°N

0   100   200 miles
0 100 200 kilometers
3°E   6°E

GEOGRAPHY SKILLBUILDER:
Interpreting a Map

1. **Location** • Name three countries that border France.
2. **Location** • Which bodies of water does France have access to?

On December 21, 1958, Charles de Gaulle was elected president of France. He reorganized the French constitution and instituted the Fifth Republic of France.

The Government of the Fifth Republic France is a parliamentary republic. Governmental power is split between the president and parliament. The president is elected by the public to a seven-year term; beginning in 2002, the president will serve a five-year term. The president's primary responsibilities are to act as guardian of the constitution and to ensure proper functioning of other authorities.

Parliament has two parts: the Senate and the National Assembly. The president chooses a prime minister, who heads parliament and is largely responsible for the internal workings of the government. The French government is very active in the country's economy.

A Centralized Economy

World War II left France poor and in need of rebuilding. The National Planning Board, established by **Jean Monnet** (moh•NAY) in 1946, launched a series of five-year plans to modernize France and set economic goals for the country.

Reading
Social Studies

A. Comparing
Compare the term and role of the president of France with the president of the United States.

Connections to History

Lascaux Cave Paintings On September 12, 1940, while hiking in the hills of Lascaux (lah•SKOH) near the town of Montignac in southern France, four teenage boys discovered ancient cave paintings. They found the caves after their dog fell in a hole in the ground.

Henri Breuil (broy), one of the first archaeologists on the scene, counted more than 600 images of horses (shown here), deer, and bison. The cave paintings are about 17,000 years old, making them some of the oldest works of art yet discovered.

The result of these plans was a mixed economy, with both public and private sectors. The French government nationalized, or took over, major banks; insurance companies; the electric, coal, and steel industries; schools; universities; hospitals; railroads; airlines; and even an automobile company.

This nationalization of industry is a form of socialism. **Socialism** is an economic system in which some businesses and industries are controlled by the government. The government also provides many health and welfare benefits, such as health care, housing, and unemployment insurance. However, today the French government is slowly placing more of the economy under the control of private companies.

Energy The French economy grew rapidly after 1946, and the country's industry was powered mainly by coal, oil, and gas. When worldwide oil prices rose in the 1970s, the French economy suffered. In the 1980s, France turned to nuclear power so that its economy would be less dependent on oil. Today France draws 75 percent of its power from nuclear energy, a higher percentage than any other nation in the world.

Most famous for its wines, France also exports grains, automobiles, electrical machinery, and chemicals. Although only about 7 percent of the labor force works on farms, France exports more agricultural products than any other nation in the European Community.

The **European Community** is an association developed after World War II to promote economic unity among the countries of Western Europe. Its success gave rise to greater unity, both politically and economically, in the European Union.

Reading
Social Studies

B. Analyzing Motives Why does France produce a large amount of nuclear energy?

BACKGROUND

Tourism is a major industry in France. The country hosts more than 70 million visitors annually, making it the most visited country in the world.

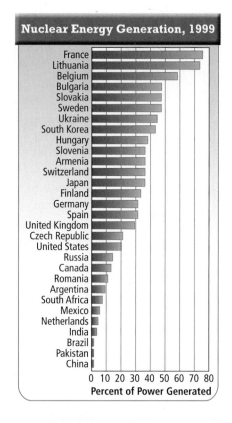

Nuclear Energy Generation, 1999

	Percent of Power Generated
France	
Lithuania	
Belgium	
Bulgaria	
Slovakia	
Sweden	
Ukraine	
South Korea	
Hungary	
Slovenia	
Armenia	
Switzerland	
Japan	
Finland	
Germany	
Spain	
United Kingdom	
Czech Republic	
United States	
Russia	
Canada	
Romania	
Argentina	
South Africa	
Mexico	
Netherlands	
India	
Brazil	
Pakistan	
China	

0 10 20 30 40 50 60 70 80
Percent of Power Generated

Region • Nuclear power plants are a common sight in the French countryside. ▼

The Culture of Paris

Paris, the capital city of France, is famous for its contributions to world culture, most especially in the arts. Nicknamed "City of Light," Paris has long been an intellectual and artistic center.

Edouard Manet (muh·NAY) (1832–1883) helped influence one of the most important art movements of modern times, impressionism. **Impressionism** is an art style that uses light to create an impression of a scene rather than a strictly realistic picture. Manet inspired such artists as Claude Monet (moh·NAY), Pierre Renoir (ruhn·WAHR), and Paul Cézanne (say·ZAHN). This group of artists worked together in Paris and shared their thoughts and opinions of art.

Region • Monet and his family often modeled for Manet, as in this 1874 painting, *Monet Working on His Boat in Argenteuil.* ▲

Paris's Musée d'Orsay and the Louvre (loove) house two of the greatest collections of fine art in the world. The School of Fine Arts leads a tradition of education and art instruction that has produced artists such as Pierre Bonnard (baw·NAHR) (1867–1947) and Balthus (1908–2001).

Literature France has a rich tradition of literature as well. Marcel Proust, who wrote *Remembrance of Things Past,* was an influential writer in the early 20th century. Other significant writers include Albert Camus (kah·MOO), who wrote *The Stranger,* and Simone de Beauvoir (boh·VWAHR), author of *The Mandarins.*

SECTION 3 ASSESSMENT

Terms & Names

1. Identify:
   (a) Charles de Gaulle
   (d) socialism
   (b) French Resistance
   (e) European Community
   (c) Jean Monnet
   (f) impressionism

Taking Notes

2. Use a chart like this one to list the major aspects of French government, economy, and culture.

	Major Aspects
Government	
Economy	
Culture	

Main Ideas

3. (a) What role does the French government play in the country's economy?

   (b) What is France's primary source of power?

   (c) Name three contributions of French culture to the world.

Critical Thinking

4. Clarifying

   How was the liberation of Paris a symbolic victory?

   Think About

   • the actions of the French Resistance
   • the cultural life of Paris

ACTIVITY -OPTION-

Reread the text on Manet. Draw an impressionist **portrait** of a classmate, friend, or family member.

Germany

TERMS & NAMES
Berlin Wall
reunification
Ludwig van
  Beethoven
Rainer Maria Rilke

MAIN IDEA

Germany has overcome many obstacles to become both a unified and a modern nation.

WHY IT MATTERS NOW

Germany has helped to shape recent European history and contemporary Western culture.

DATELINE

BERLIN, GERMANY, OCTOBER 3, 1990— It is just past midnight. Church bells are ringing, fireworks are exploding, bands are playing, and the streets are filled with celebrating Germans. At midnight, the treaty to reunite East and West Germany became official. Germany is whole once more!

Just a year ago, the Berlin Wall—a 103-mile-long barrier of concrete and barbed wire—still separated East and West Berlin. Constructed in 1961, the Wall kept East Germans from escaping from their Communist government to democratic West Germany. Then, in 1989, as the Communist government weakened, the Wall came down.

Location • Germans celebrate unification in front of the Reichstag, the seat of the federal government. ▲

A Divided Germany

Today, the reunified nation of Germany is one of the largest countries in Europe. When World War II ended in 1945, however, Germany was divided. United States, French, and British soldiers occupied the new West German nation, and Soviet soldiers occupied the new East Germany.

Location • The largest remaining sections of the Berlin Wall, which stand up to 15 feet high, are covered with paintings and signatures. ▲

West Germany The United States helped West Germany set up a democratic government. In part, the United States supported the new nation because it was located between the Communist countries of Eastern Europe and the rest of Western Europe.

With the help of U.S. loans, West Germany experienced a so-called economic miracle. In 20 years, it rebuilt its factories and became one of the world's richest nations. Its economy later became the driving force behind the European Union.

East Germany In contrast to West Germany, East Germany remained poor. Most East Germans saw West Germany, and Western Europe in general, as a place where people had better lives. East Germany's Communist government, however, discouraged contact between east and west.

By 1989, the Soviet Union's control of Eastern Europe was weakening. Hungary, a Soviet ally, relaxed control over its borders with Western Europe. East Germans began crossing the Hungarian border into Austria and eventually made their way into West Germany. After the **Berlin Wall** came down in 1989, more East Germans fled to West Germany.

Germany Today

GEOGRAPHY SKILLBUILDER: Interpreting a Map

1. **Location** • Which country is nearest to Germany's national capital?
2. **Place** • Which was larger, East or West Germany?

- - - - Former border of East and West Germany
──── National boundary
⊛ National capital
● Other city

Reunified Germany

Since the 1990 **reunification,** or the reuniting of East and West Germany, the German government has spent billions of dollars rebuilding the eastern part of the country. The effort has included roads, factories, housing, and hospitals. The city of Berlin, once again the nation's capital, was also rebuilt. The newly reunified nation also restored the Reichstag (RYK·shtahg), where the Federal Assembly meets.

However, reunification has also caused tensions between "Ossies" (OSS·eez) and "Wessies" (VEHSS·eez). Many Ossies complain about the lack of jobs and the cost of housing. Many Wessies complain about paying taxes to rebuild the nation and to help support the former East Germans.

Region • The new Volkswagen Beetle is typical of German car design, known for its simplicity and style. The first Volkswagen was designed by Ferdinand Porsche (POOR·sheh) in 1934. ▲

Reading Social Studies

Clarifying Why did East Germany need to be rebuilt and not West Germany?

Vocabulary

Ossies: former East Germans

Wessies: former West Germans

German Culture

Germany's rich cultural traditions may help to unite its people, who are especially proud of their music and literature. Germans are also famous for designing high-quality products, such as cars, electronic appliances, and other complex machinery.

Music Three of Germany's best-known composers are Johann Sebastian Bach (bahck) (1685–1750), George Frederick Handel (HAHN·duhl) (1685–1759), and **Ludwig van Beethoven** (LOOD·vig vahn BAY·TOH·vuhn) (1770–1827). Their music is still performed and recorded all over the world. German composer Richard Wagner (VAHG·nuhr) (1813–1883) wrote many operas, including a series based on German myths and legends known as the Ring Cycle.

Biography

Beethoven Perhaps the best-loved German composer is Ludwig van Beethoven. Beethoven began to lose his hearing when he was in his 20s. By the time he was 50, he was almost deaf.

Beethoven refused to let his deafness stop him from creating music, however. "I will grapple with Fate, it shall not overcome me," he wrote. In 1824, he finished his Ninth Symphony, which ends with a section containing the well-known "Ode to Joy." An orchestra played this same symphony at an open-air concert during the destruction of the Berlin Wall.

Place •
Half-timber architecture, shown here, is common throughout Germany. ▲

Literature One of the greatest writers in the German language was **Rainer Maria Rilke** (RIHL·kuh) (1875–1926). His poems, which are still admired and studied today, were a way for Rilke to communicate his feelings and experiences.

BACKGROUND

More than 100 million people around the world speak German.

Other important 20th-century German authors include Günter Grass (grahs) (b. 1927) and Thomas Mann (man) (1875–1955). Grass has written about the horrors of World War II, the setting for his novel *The Tin Drum*. Both writers were awarded the Nobel Prize in Literature—Mann in 1929 and Grass in 1999.

SECTION 4 ASSESSMENT

Terms & Names

1. **Identify:**
   (a) Berlin Wall
   (b) reunification
   (c) Ludwig van Beethoven
   (d) Rainer Maria Rilke

Taking Notes

2. Use a chart like this one to compare aspects of Germany before and after reunification.

Before Reunification	After Reunification

Main Ideas

3. (a) Describe the economic miracle that occurred in West Germany.

   (b) Why has there been tension between the Ossies and the Wessies?

   (c) On what projects has Germany spent billions of dollars since 1990?

Critical Thinking

4. **Synthesizing**

   What makes Germany an important European country?

   Think About

   ◆ its location

   ◆ its size

   ◆ its role in modern history

ACTIVITY -OPTION- Reread the "Dateline" feature at the beginning of the section. Write a **short story** describing what it might have been like to celebrate the reunification of Germany in 1990.

Making an Outline

▶▶ Defining the Skill

Before writing a research report, you must decide on your topic and then gather information about it. When you have all of the information you need, then you begin to organize it. One way of organizing your information before writing the report is to make an outline. An outline lists the main ideas in the order in which they will appear in the report. It also organizes the main ideas and supporting details according to their importance. The form of every outline is the same. Main ideas are listed on the left and labeled with capital Roman numerals. Supporting ideas are indented and labeled with capital letters. Supporting details are indented farther and labeled with numerals.

▶▶ Applying the Skill

The outline to the right is for a biography of Marie Curie, one of the great physicists of all time. Use the strategies listed below to help you learn how to make an outline.

How to Make an Outline

Strategy ❶ Read the main ideas of this report. They are labeled with capital Roman numerals. Each main idea will need at least one paragraph.

Strategy ❷ Read the supporting ideas for each main idea. These are labeled with capital letters. Notice that some of the main ideas require more supporting ideas than others.

Strategy ❸ Read the supporting details that are included in this outline. These are labeled with numerals. The writer of this outline did not include the supporting details for some of the supporting ideas. It is not necessary to include every piece of information that you have. An outline is intended merely as a guide for you to follow as you write the report.

Strategy ❹ A report can be organized in different ways. This biography is organized chronologically, that is, according to time. It starts with Curie's birth and ends with her legacy after death. The outline follows the order of events in her life. A report can be organized in other ways, such as comparing and contrasting or according to advantages and disadvantages. The outline should clearly reflect the way the report is organized.

❶ I. Who Was She?
    A. Polish-born physicist
❷ B. Birth and early life
    C. Schooling
       1. In secret in Poland (women were not allowed to enter
❸   higher education)
       2. In France at the Sorbonne
❹   a. license of physical sciences, 1893
         b. license of mathematical sciences, 1894
II. The Physicist
    A. Life and work with husband, Pierre Curie
       1. Discoveries
         a. polonium, summer 1898
         b. radium, fall 1898
       2. Nobel Prize in Physics, 1903
         a. shared with Henri Becquerel
         b. Marie was the first woman to ever be awarded
          a Nobel Prize
    B. Her own accomplishments
       1. Became the first female professor at the Sorbonne
         a. took over Pierre's position after his death, 1906
       2. Her research on radioactivity was published, 1910
       3. Nobel Prize in Chemistry, 1911

▶▶ Practicing the Skill

Look through Chapter 14 and find a topic that interests you. Gather information about that topic, and then write an outline for a report about that topic. Be sure to use the correct outline form.

Poland

SECTION
5

TERMS & NAMES
Solidarity
Lech Walesa
Czeslaw Milosz
censorship
dissident

MAIN IDEA

Poland has gone through the difficulties of establishing a new democratic government and a new economic system.

WHY IT MATTERS NOW

Poland is an excellent example of the success that has been achieved by the newly independent Eastern European nations.

DATELINE

EXTRA

GDAŃSK, POLAND, 1980

In response to recent increases in food prices, many strikes have broken out across Poland. Today's strikes are much larger than the strikes that occurred in 1976. The shipyards in Gdańsk have 17,000 striking workers. One of the strikers' demands is the right to form labor unions. The recent strikes are yet another sign of the country's weakening economy, which has continued to decline over the past decade. Poland's attempts to improve its economic health by borrowing money from other nations have not helped, as the government is unable to repay those loans.

Place • Polish workers protest poor conditions under the Communist government. ▲

Political and Economic Struggles

The strikes and riots of the 1970s and 1980s were not the first actions Polish citizens took against their government. In 1956, Polish workers had rioted to protest their low wages.

In fact, there have been political and economic struggles in Poland since World War II ended in 1945. At that time, Communists took over the government and set strict wage and price controls.

Poland Today

GEOGRAPHY SKILLBUILDER:
Interpreting a Map

1. **Location** • Name a port city in Poland.
2. **Location** • How many different countries border Poland?

Solidarity In 1980, labor unions throughout Poland joined an organization called **Solidarity**. This trade union was led by **Lech Walesa** (LEK wah·LEHN·suh), an electrical worker from the shipyards of Gdańsk (guh·DAHNSK).

In the beginning, Solidarity's goals were to increase pay and improve working conditions. Before long, however, the organization set its sights on bigger goals. In late 1981, members of Solidarity were calling for free elections and an end to Communist rule. Even though Solidarity had about 10 million members, the government fought back. It suspended the organization, cracked down on protesters, and arrested thousands of members, including Walesa.

BACKGROUND

Poland's capital and largest city is Warsaw. The nation's citizens are called Poles.

Region • In 1980, Solidarity leader Lech Walesa gained the support of labor unions. Ten years later, he became Poland's president. ◄

Region • Poland's senate helps ensure that all the country's citizens have representation. ◀

A Free Poland

In the late 1980s, economic conditions continued to worsen in Poland. The government asked Solidarity leaders to help them solve the country's economic difficulties. Finally, the Communists agreed to Solidarity's demand for free elections.

When the elections were held in 1989, many Solidarity candidates were elected, and the Communists lost power. In 1990, Lech Walesa became the president of a free Poland.

A New Constitution Today, Poland is a parliamentary republic. The country approved a new constitution in 1997. This constitution guarantees civil rights such as free speech. It also helps to balance the powers held by the president, the prime minister, and parliament.

Parliament Poland's parliament is made up of two houses. The upper house, or senate, has 100 members. The lower house, which has 460 members, chooses the prime minister. Usually, as in the United Kingdom, the prime minister is a member of the largest party or alliance of parties within parliament.

A number of seats in parliament are reserved for representatives of the small German and Ukrainian ethnic groups in Poland. In this way, all Polish citizens are ensured a voice in their government.

A Changing Economy

Besides a new government, the Poles have also had to deal with a changing economy. In 1990, Poland's new democratic government quickly switched from a command economy to a free market economy. Prices were no longer controlled by the government, and trade suddenly faced international competition.

Reading
Social Studies

A. Recognizing Important Details What led to free elections in Poland?

BACKGROUND

The Polish president, who is elected every five years, is the head of state.

Inflation Although Polish shops were able to sell goods that had not been available before, prices rose quickly—by almost 80 percent. With this inflation, or a continual rise in prices, people's wages could not keep up with the cost of goods.

Many Polish companies, which could not compete with high-quality foreign goods, went out of business. This, in turn, resulted in high unemployment. As more and more people lost their jobs, Poland's overall standard of living fell.

Region • With Poland's economy on the rise, unemployment has decreased. ▲

An Improving Economy In time, new Polish businesses found success, giving more people work. Inflation started to drop. By 1999, inflation was down to around 7 percent. By 2000, Poland no longer needed the economic aid it had been receiving from the United States.

One way to measure the strength of a country's economy is to look at consumer spending. Between 1995 and 2000, Poles bought new cars at a high rate of half a million each year. Today, Poland has 2 million small and medium-sized businesses. The success of these small businesses is another sign of Poland's healthy economy.

Poland's Culture

The history of Poland has been one of ups and downs. In the 1500s and 1600s, Poland was a large and powerful kingdom. By 1795, Russia, Prussia, and Austria had taken control of its land, and Poland ceased to exist as an independent country. Poland did not become a republic until 1918, after World War I. Throughout the centuries, however, Poland has had a rich culture.

Literature Polish literature is full of accounts of struggles for national independence and stories about glorious kingdoms won and lost by heroic patriots.

One of Poland's best-known writers of recent times is **Czeslaw Milosz** (CHEH•slawv MEE•LAWSH) (b. 1911). Milosz published his first book of poems in the 1930s. After World War II, he worked as a diplomat in the United States and then France.

BACKGROUND

A famous Polish general and patriot, Thaddeus Kosciusko (KAHS•ee•UHS•koh), fought on the side of the colonists during the American Revolution.

Milosz, who became a professor at the University of California at Berkeley, won the Nobel Prize in Literature in 1980.

Reading
Social Studies

B. Analyzing Motives Why did the Communist government control the media?

Censorship Under Communist rule, the Polish media were controlled by the government. The government decided what the media could and could not say. It outlawed any information that did not support and praise the accomplishments of Communism. As a result of this **censorship,** many writers could not publish their works. Some of them became dissidents. A **dissident** is a person who openly disagrees with a government's policies.

Supporting the Arts In order to help Polish writers, the government now allows publications printed in Poland to be sold tax-free. To help Polish actors, screenwriters, and directors, movie theaters are repaid their costs for showing Polish movies. Public-sponsored television stations are supported not only by free-market advertising but also by fees the public pays to own television sets.

Place • In 1978, Poland's pride was greatly boosted when Polish-born John Paul II was elected pope. He was the first non-Italian to be elected pope in 456 years. ▲

SECTION 5 ASSESSMENT

Terms & Names

1. **Identify:** (a) Solidarity (b) Lech Walesa (c) Czeslaw Milosz
   (d) censorship (e) dissident

Taking Notes

2. Use a chart like this one to compare and contrast one aspect of Poland with the same aspect of the United Kingdom, Sweden, France, or Germany.

Poland	Other Country

Main Ideas

3. (a) How did the Polish government respond to Solidarity's goals?

   (b) What was the outcome of Poland's free election in the late 1980s?

   (c) Describe the recent changes in the economy of Poland.

Critical Thinking

4. **Summarizing**

   How would you describe what life was like in Poland before the changes of 1990?

   Think About

   • strikes and riots
   • the Communist government
   • censorship

ACTIVITY -OPTION- Reread the information about Solidarity. Write a short **speech** that might have been given to gain support for the organization in the 1980s.

TERMS & NAMES

Explain the significance of each of the following:

1. London
2. Good Friday Accord
3. armed neutrality
4. hydroelectricity
5. Charles de Gaulle
6. socialism
7. Berlin Wall
8. reunification
9. censorship
10. dissident

REVIEW QUESTIONS

The United Kingdom (pages 379–383)

1. What are the two houses that form the British Parliament? Which is more powerful?
2. Why is it necessary for the United Kingdom to import foods and other goods?

Sweden (pages 384–387)

3. What role do ombudsmen play in the Swedish government?
4. Why is Sweden an excellent place for skiing?

France (pages 390–393)

5. What is France's main source of energy?
6. Identify at least three Impressionist painters.

Germany (pages 394–397)

7. What role did the United States government play in West Germany after World War II?
8. Identify at least three famous German composers.

Poland (pages 399–403)

9. Why is Lech Walesa important to modern Poland?
10. Describe the new constitution that Poland approved in 1997.

CRITICAL THINKING

Comparing

1. Using your completed chart from Reading Social Studies, p. 378, compare the governments and economies of the United Kingdom, Sweden, France, Germany, and Poland.

Hypothesizing

2. One of Sweden's severe environmental problems is acid rain. Why might it be difficult for a country to solve this problem?

Making Inferences

3. Why do you think it was important to the United States that West Germany have a democratic government?

Visual Summary

The United Kingdom *1*

- British economic, political, and cultural traditions have influenced nations around the world.

Sweden *2*

- Sweden offers its people a high standard of living.
- Sweden is dealing with environmental issues such as nuclear power and acid rain.

France

- France has made a speedy recovery from World War II.

3

Germany *4*

- Germany has overcome many obstacles to become a unified and modern nation.

Poland *5*

- Poland is an example of the success made possible by the recent independence of Eastern European nations.

Jacques Cousteau (koo•STOH) (1910–1997) was the most famous undersea explorer of the 20th century. While serving in the French navy in 1943, Cousteau invented the Aqua-Lung, also known as scuba gear. *Scuba* stands for "self-contained underwater-breathing apparatus." Scuba gear allowed divers to more freely explore the depths of the oceans, which cover more than three-fifths of Earth's surface. Cousteau became a household name after he popularized underwater exploration through books, films, and a television series.

SKILLBUILDER: Making an Outline

Outline the text above.

1. **Place** • How many airports does the map show in Germany? What cities are they located in or near?
2. **Movement** • Describe at least two possible routes that connect London and Stockholm.
3. **Place** • Which cities in Poland are located along major rail lines?

Interdisciplinary Activity: Art

Preparing a Written Report Research the life and work of a well-known painter, sculptor, or other artist from the United Kingdom, Sweden, France, Germany, or Poland. Use your findings to write a short report. Be sure to include a description or a copy of at least one important work of art.

Cooperative Learning Activity

Researching a Festival In a group of three students, organize a classroom presentation about a festival or holiday that is celebrated in the United Kingdom, Sweden, France, Germany, or Poland. What is the importance of the festival? When is it celebrated? What kinds of activities or foods are associated with it?

- Research information about different festivals or holidays and select one that interests your group.
- Decide what form your presentation will take.
- Discuss how the festival compares with others that are familiar to you.

INTERNET ACTIVITY

Use the Internet to research a major tourist site in the United Kingdom, Sweden, France, Germany, or Poland. Focus on one location, such as Edinburgh, Stockholm, Paris, Munich, or Warsaw. What special attractions or activities does that location offer to visitors?

Presenting Your Findings Write up your findings and include illustrations of the location. Be sure to list the Web sites you used to help you prepare your report.

For Internet links to support this activity, go to

RESEARCH LINKS
CLASSZONE.COM

UNIT 5

Place The Blue Mosque was built in the 17th century in Constantinople (now Istanbul, Turkey). On the land around the mosque, there is a religious school, a public bath, souvenir shops, and a kitchen to feed the poor.

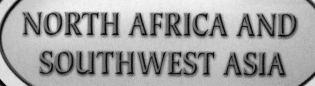

NORTH AFRICA AND SOUTHWEST ASIA

Chapter 15	North Africa and Southwest Asia: Place and Times
Chapter 16	North Africa and Southwest Asia Today

THE BLUE MOSQUE
ATLANTIC
OCEAN
PACIFIC
OCEAN
PACIFIC
OCEAN
N
NORTH AFRICA AND SOUTHWEST ASIA

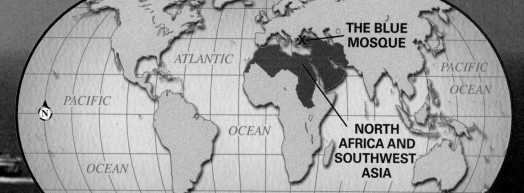

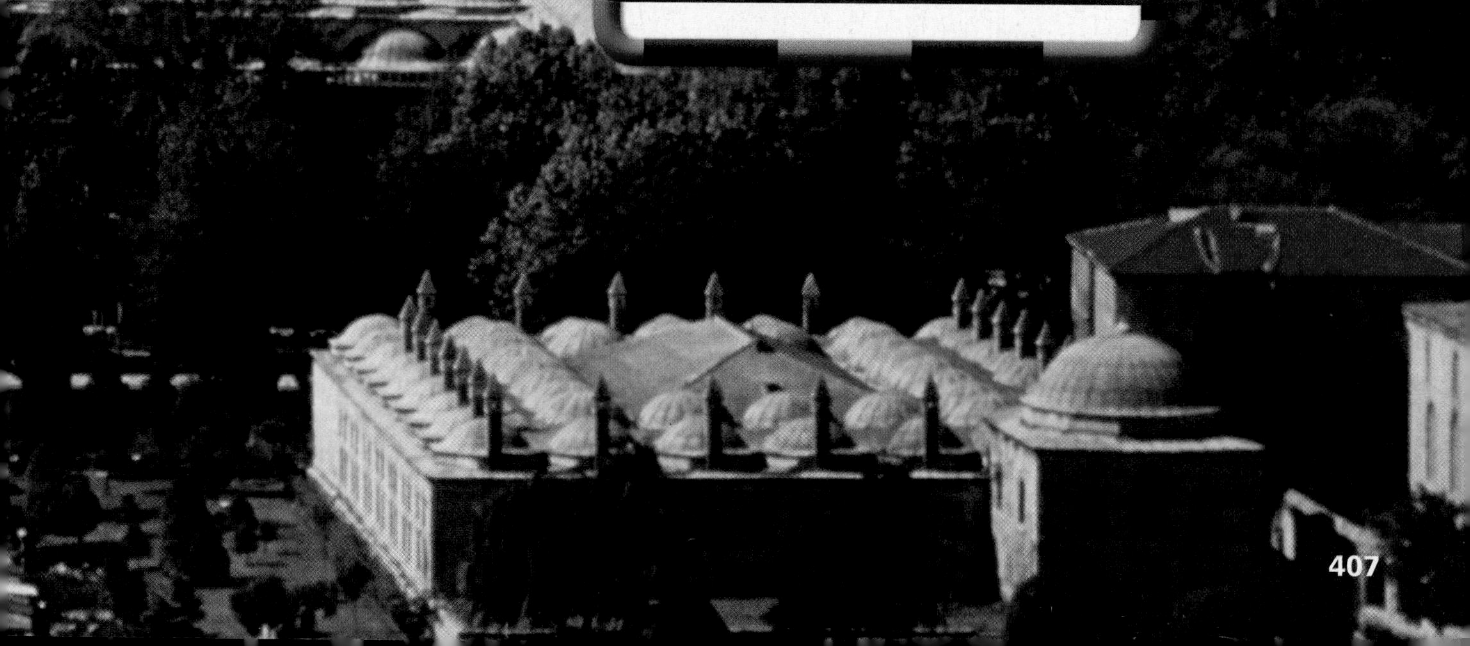

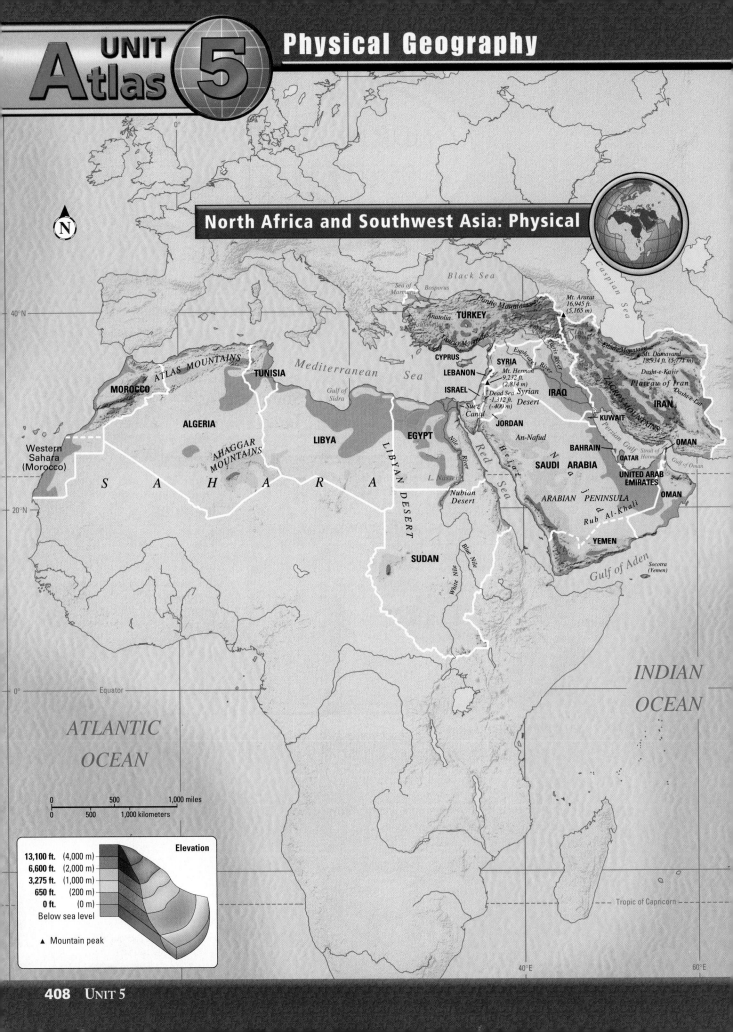

North Africa and Southwest Asia: Physical

N

ATLANTIC OCEAN

INDIAN OCEAN

Black Sea

Sea of Marmara

Bosporus

Caspian Sea

Ponte Mountains

Mt. Ararat
16,945 ft.
(5,165 m)

Anatolia

TURKEY

Dardanelles

Taurus Mountains

Elburz Mountains

Mt. Damavand
18,934 ft. (5,771 m)

CYPRUS

SYRIA

Euphrates River

Tigris River

Dasht-e-Kavir

LEBANON

Mt. Hermon
9,232 ft.
(2,814 m)

Plateau of Iran

Dasht-e-Lut

ISRAEL

Dead Sea
-1,312 ft.
(-400 m)

Syrian Desert

IRAQ

IRAN

Mediterranean Sea

Gulf of Sidra

ATLAS MOUNTAINS

TUNISIA

MOROCCO

ALGERIA

LIBYA

EGYPT

Suez Canal

JORDAN

KUWAIT

Zagros Mountains

Persian Gulf

Strait of Hormuz

Gulf of Oman

OMAN

An-Nafud

BAHRAIN

QATAR

UNITED ARAB EMIRATES

OMAN

Western Sahara (Morocco)

AHAGGAR MOUNTAINS

LIBYAN DESERT

Nile River

Red Sea

Hejaz

SAUDI ARABIA

Nejd

ARABIAN PENINSULA

Rub Al-Khali

S   A   H   A   R   A

L. Nasser

Nubian Desert

SUDAN

White Nile

Blue Nile

YEMEN

Gulf of Aden

Socotra (Yemen)

Equator

Tropic of Capricorn

Scale

```
0        500      1,000 miles
0    500   1,000 kilometers
```

Elevation

13,100 ft.	(4,000 m)
6,600 ft.	(2,000 m)
3,275 ft.	(1,000 m)
650 ft.	(200 m)
0 ft.	(0 m)
Below sea level	

▲ Mountain peak

North Africa and Southwest Asia: Precipitation

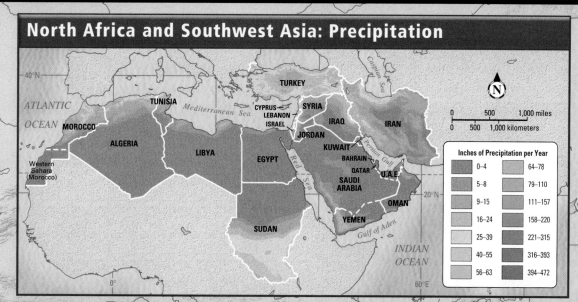

Inches of Precipitation per Year	
0–4	64–78
5–8	79–110
9–15	111–157
16–24	158–220
25–39	221–315
40–55	316–393
56–63	394–472

Comparisons of Landmass and Population of the United States, North Africa, and Southwest Asia

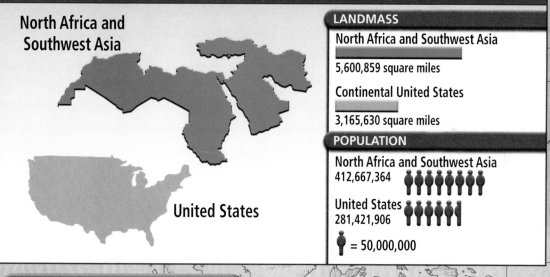

North Africa and Southwest Asia

United States

LANDMASS

North Africa and Southwest Asia
5,600,859 square miles

Continental United States
3,165,630 square miles

POPULATION

North Africa and Southwest Asia
412,667,364

United States
281,421,906

= 50,000,000

FAST FACTS

✔ **WORLD'S LONGEST RIVER:**
Nile, 4,132 mi.

✔ **WORLD'S LARGEST DESERT:**
Sahara, 3,350,000 sq. mi.

✔ **WORLD'S HIGHEST RECORDED TEMPERATURE:** 136°F at El Azizia, Libya, on September 13, 1922

✔ **WORLD'S LARGEST SUPPLY OF OIL:**
259 billion barrels of proven oil reserves in Saudi Arabia

✔ **DRIEST AREA IN THE WORLD:**
Nearly two-thirds of this region is desert.

GEOGRAPHY SKILLBUILDER: Interpreting Maps and Visuals

1. **Region** • Name three countries that get less than 10 inches of rain per year.
2. **Region** • Name the countries that border the Red Sea.

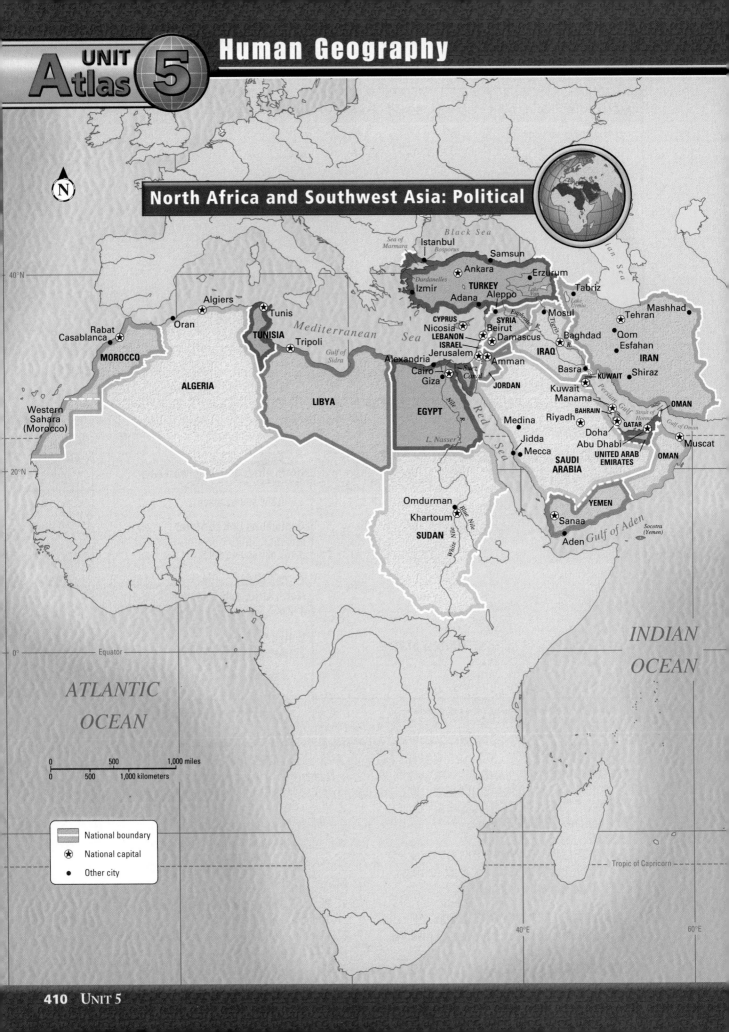

North Africa and Southwest Asia: Political

Black Sea
Sea of Marmara
Istanbul
Bosporus
Samsun
40°N
Dardanelles
Ankara
Erzurum
Izmir
TURKEY
Aleppo
Tabriz
Adana
Lake Van
Mashhad
CYPRUS
Nicosia
SYRIA
Mosul
Tehran
Beirut
LEBANON
Damascus
Baghdad
Qom
ISRAEL
Esfahan
Alexandria
Jerusalem
Amman
IRAQ
IRAN
Cairo
Suez Canal
Basra
Shiraz
Giza
KUWAIT
JORDAN
Kuwait
Manama
OMAN
Medina
Riyadh
BAHRAIN
Strait of Hormuz
Gulf of Oman
Jidda
Doha
QATAR
Mecca
Abu Dhabi
Muscat
SAUDI
UNITED ARAB
OMAN
ARABIA
EMIRATES

Algiers
Tunis
Oran
TUNISIA
Mediterranean
Rabat
Tripoli
Casablanca
Gulf of Sidra
MOROCCO
Sea
ALGERIA
LIBYA
Western
Sahara
(Morocco)
EGYPT
Nile R.
20°N
L. Nasser
Red Sea

YEMEN
Omdurman
Sanaa
Khartoum
Blue Nile
Aden *Gulf of Aden*
Socotra
SUDAN
White Nile
(Yemen)

Iran Sea

INDIAN
OCEAN

0°
Equator

ATLANTIC
OCEAN

	500	1,000 miles
0	500	1,000 kilometers

Tropic of Capricorn

40°E
60°E

Legend:
- National boundary
- ⊛ National capital
- ● Other city

Religions of North Africa and Southwest Asia

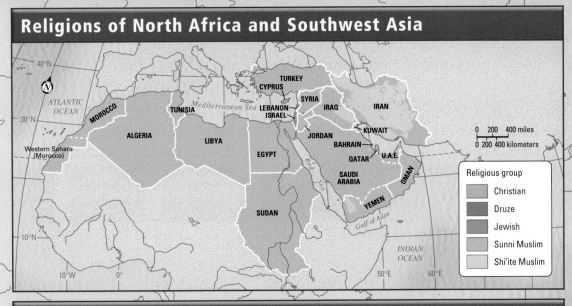

Religious group	
	Christian
	Druze
	Jewish
	Sunni Muslim
	Shi'ite Muslim

Ethnic Groups of North Africa and Southwest Asia

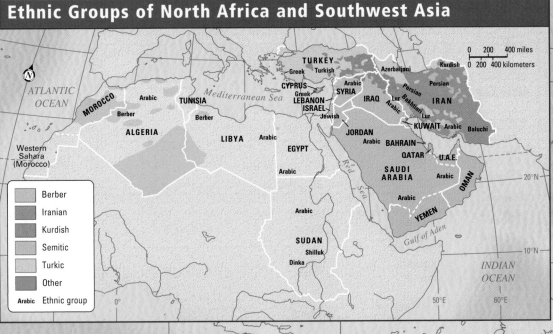

	Ethnic group
	Berber
	Iranian
	Kurdish
	Semitic
	Turkic
	Other
Arabic	Ethnic group

FAST FACTS

✔ **LARGEST COUNTRY (in land area):**
Sudan, with 966,757 sq. mi.

✔ **LARGEST ETHNIC GROUP WITHOUT A COUNTRY:**
The Kurds, with 20 million living in Iran, Iraq, Syria, and Turkey

✔ **ORIGIN OF MAJOR RELIGIONS:**
Islam, Judaism, and Christianity all originated in this area.

✔ **LOWEST POPULATION DENSITY:**
Libya, with 7.5 people per sq. mi.

GEOGRAPHY SKILLBUILDER: Interpreting Maps and Visuals

1. **Movement** • What is the largest ethnic group in this region?
2. **Region** • What is the most common religion in this region?

Country Flag	Country/Capital	Currency	Population (2001 estimate)	Life Expectancy (years)	Birthrate (per 1,000 pop.) (2000 estimate)
	Algeria Algiers	Dinar	31,736,000	70	23
	Bahrain Manama	Dinar	645,000	73	21
	Cyprus Nicosia	Pound	763,000	77	13
	Egypt Cairo	Pound	69,537,000	63	25
	Iran Tehran	Rial	66,129,000	70	18
	Iraq Baghdad	Dinar	23,332,000	67	35
	Israel Jerusalem	New Shekel	5,938,000	79	19
	Jordan Amman	Dinar	5,453,000	77	26
	Kuwait Kuwait	Dinar	2,042,000	76	22
	Lebanon Beirut	Pound	3,628,000	71	20
	Libya Tripoli	Dinar	5,241,000	75	28
	Morocco Rabat	Dirham	30,645,000	69	23
	Oman Muscat	Rial Omani	2,622,000	72	38
	Qatar Doha	Riyal	769,000	72	16
	Saudi Arabia Riyadh	Riyal	22,757,000	68	38
	Sudan Khartoum	Pound	36,080,000	57	39

DATA FILE

Infant Mortality (per 1,000 live births) (2000)	Doctors (per 100,000 pop.) (1992–1998)	Literacy Rate (percentage) (1995–2000)	Passenger Cars (per 1,000 pop.) (1996–1997)	Total Area (square miles)	Map (not to scale)
42.2	85	62	17	919,595	
14.0	100	85	242	268	
7.4	255	97	316	3,572	
65.7	202	51	20	385,230	
28.1	85	79	26	636,300	
62.4	55	58	32	167,975	
7.6	385	96	224	7,992	
32.1	166	87	40	34,342	
9.8	189	79	318	6,880	
29.4	210	92	325	3,950	
26.4	128	76	126	678,400	
37.0	46	44	39	274,461	
23.9	133	59	108	82,009	
16.4	126	79	151	4,416	
36.3	166	63	89	865,000	
69.2	9	46	1	966,757	

Country Flag	Country/Capital	Currency	Population (2001 estimate)	Life Expectancy (years)	Birthrate (per 1,000 pop.) (2000)
	Syria Damascus	Pound	16,729,000	68	31
	Tunisia Tunis	Dinar	9,705,000	74	17
	Turkey Ankara	Lira	66,494,000	71	19
	United Arab Emirates Abu Dhabi	Dirham	2,407,000	74	18
	Yemen Sanaa	Rial	18,078,000	60	43
	United States Washington, D.C.	Dollar	281,422,000	77	15

The Blue Mosque in Istanbul ◄

Queen Hatshepsut ▲

The Dead Sea ▲

DATA FILE

Infant Mortality (per 1,000 live births) (2000)	Doctors (per 100,000 pop.) (1992–1998)	Literacy Rate (percentage) (1996–1998)	Passenger Cars (per 1,000 pop.) (1991–1998)	Total Area (square miles)	Map (not to scale)
35.2	144	79	9	71,498	
30.1	70	67	28	63,378	
33.3	121	82	53	300,948	
13.4	181	79	144	32,278	
67.4	23	43	15	203,796	
7.0	251	97	489	3,787,319	

GEOGRAPHY SKILLBUILDER: Interpreting a Chart

1. **Region** • How much higher is Lebanon's literacy rate than Iran's?
2. **Region** • In general, how can a country's literacy rate be a predictor of its infant mortality rate in this region?

A shadoof in Egypt ▼

Palestinians in Israel ▲

An oil well in Saudi Arabia ▲

CHAPTER 15

North Africa and Southwest Asia: Place and Times

Region The Sahara stretches across much of North Africa.

How have sheep contributed to the spread of deserts in North Africa?

Human-Environment Interaction • Overgrazing, or allowing live-stock such as sheep and goats to eat too much vegetation, has con-tributed to the spread of deserts in North Africa. Desertification from overgrazing is particularly bad in northwestern countries such as Morocco.

As population increases, more strain is put on fragile areas. When people plant too many crops, graze too many animals, or cut down trees in the dry lands—especially during periods of drought—the land becomes unusable. People have difficulty growing food, and famine may follow. Countries in North Africa are working to change political, economic, and social problems that contribute to desertification.

What do you think?

♦ What might cause people to plant or graze their animals on dry lands?

♦ What can countries do to prevent desertification?

BEFORE YOU READ

▶▶ *What Do You Know?*

Before you read the chapter, consider what you already know about North Africa and Southwest Asia. Look at a physical map of the region, and think about features, such as the Sahara. How might living in a desert affect the lives of people who live there? What do you know about the pyramids of ancient Egypt? Are you familiar with any of these sacred books—the Hebrew Scriptures, the Christian Bible, or the Qur'an of Islam? Many of the events in these books took place in this region. Try to imagine the changes that have occurred here in 5,000 years of human history.

Place • **Ziggurats were stepped towers on which temples were built in ancient Mesopotamia.** ▲

▶▶ *What Do You Want to Know?*

Decide what you know about the physical features of the region and about ancient Mesopotamia, Egypt, and the Muslim Empires. In your notebook, record what you hope to learn from this chapter.

READ AND TAKE NOTES

Reading Strategy: Making Generalizations Making generalizations is a useful strategy for understanding universal themes in social studies. A generalization is a statement expressed in general terms but supported by detailed evidence. As you read this chapter, think about how the civilizations that arose in North Africa and Southwest Asia influenced world history. Use the chart below to record details that support each generalization.

Culture • **The Qur'an is the sacred book of Islam.** ▲

- Copy the chart into your notebook.
- As you read, notice how civilization has developed in this region.
- Beside each generalization, record some key details that support it.

Generalizations	Supporting Details
1. Bodies of water provide resources for people in North Africa and Southwest Asia.	
2. Complex civilizations developed religions and laws in ancient Mesopotamia.	
3. An ancient Egyptian culture based on shared beliefs and goals left a monumental legacy.	
4. Three of the world's major religions began in Southwest Asia.	
5. Islamic beliefs and achievements spread throughout the world.	

SECTION 1

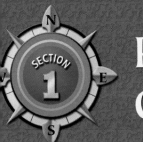

Physical Geography

TERMS & NAMES
fertile
hunter-gatherer
irrigation

MAIN IDEA

Water and the lack of it has shaped this region of flooding rivers, little rainfall, and surrounding seas.

WHY IT MATTERS NOW

Today the region enjoys the benefits of rich oil resources, but its people continue to struggle with problems of both dry land and flooding rivers.

DATELINE

EXTRA

MESOPOTAMIA, 3000 B.C.

Yesterday, the yearly spring flooding of the Euphrates River began. The river is high this year because of heavy rains. Farmers from nearby villages are afraid their homes will be lost. But they need the rich soil the swollen river brings. As soon as the river settles back in its bed, they can begin to plant.

It's like this every year. The gods tell the river to bring good soil, and the river obeys. To Mesopotamians, it means that life will go on.

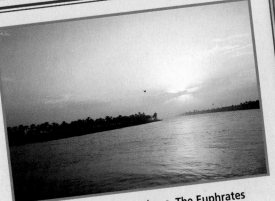

Human-Environment Interaction • **The Euphrates River brings rich soil to the land.** ▲

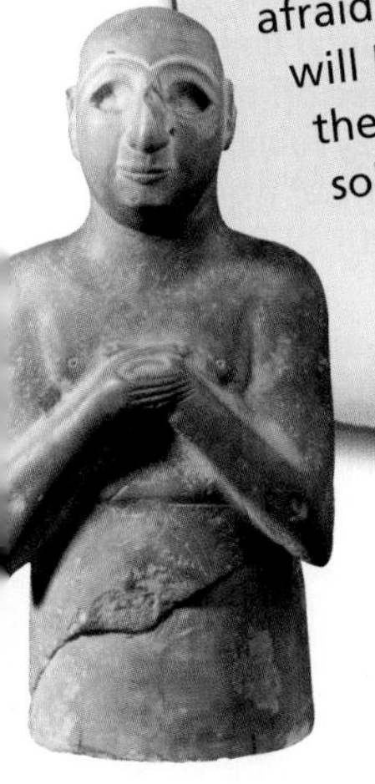

Culture • **Utu was one of the gods the Mesopotamians prayed to.** ▲

Rivers and Deserts

Water and the lack of it has shaped North Africa and Southwest Asia, a region where little rain falls. Seas of sand cover the deserts, which are dry all year. In these deserts, water is found only in oasis areas. Other areas have depended on the annual flooding of the rivers to make the soil **fertile,** or productive. Fertile soil provides the nutrients that plants need to grow.

Three Rivers

Some of the ancient peoples who lived in North Africa and Southwest Asia benefited from three major rivers in the region—the Nile, the Tigris (TY·grihs), and the Euphrates (yoo·FRAY·teez). The 4,000-mile-long Nile, the longest river in the world, flows from its source in east central Africa to the Mediterranean in northeast Egypt. The Tigris and Euphrates flow to the southeast from Turkey into the northern end of the Persian Gulf. (See the Unit Atlas map on page 408).

From Hunter-Gatherers to Farmers Thousands of years ago, **hunter-gatherers** roamed the east coast of the Mediterranean and the valleys formed from the rivers. These people found food by hunting, fishing, and gathering wild grains, fruits, and nuts. For 99 percent of the time human beings have been on Earth, they have been hunter-gatherers. Eventually, hunter-gatherers settled permanently in places where they could raise animals and grow crops. Some places where hunter-gatherers may have first become farmers are the valleys of the Nile, Tigris, and Euphrates rivers about 8,000 years ago.

How Rivers Enrich the Soil Most of the soil in the desert regions of North Africa and Southwest Asia is not good for farming. It contains a lot of salt or sand. Only the rivers make farming possible. In summer, when melted snow flowing from the Ethiopian mountains raises the level of the Nile, the river floods. Heavy spring and summer rains also cause the Nile to flood. When these flooding waters flow over the riverbanks, they leave behind fertile soil that has been carried from one area to another.

Snows also melt in the Turkish highlands, where the Tigris and Euphrates rivers begin. As a result, these rivers also flood yearly, bringing fertile soil into the river valleys.

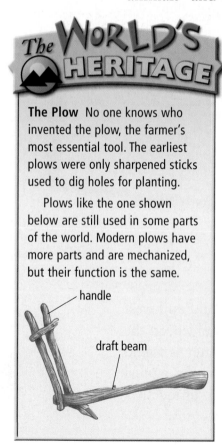

The Plow No one knows who invented the plow, the farmer's most essential tool. The earliest plows were only sharpened sticks used to dig holes for planting.

Plows like the one shown below are still used in some parts of the world. Modern plows have more parts and are mechanized, but their function is the same.

handle

draft beam

Human-Environment Interaction • **Hunter-gatherers lived off the food they found in the natural world.** ▲

Reading
Social Studies

Finding Causes Why might farming have begun in the valleys of the Nile, Tigris, and Euphrates rivers?

Human-Environment Interaction • This modern irrigation system is in the Draa Valley in Morocco. ▼

Human-Environment Interaction • For thousands of years farmers in the region have used simple irrigation tools, such as this shadoof, to water the land. ▲

Irrigation Few places in the region are close enough to the three major rivers to depend on them for deposits of fertile soil. Farmers in other areas have had to develop **irrigation** methods, or ways of bringing water to dry land.

Surrounding Waters

The Mediterranean Sea, the Red Sea, and the Persian Gulf have shaped the climate, resources, and societies of the region. The Mediterranean is the largest body of water in the region. The mild climate of the lands around the Mediterranean attracted settlers. Early civilizations formed on its eastern shores.

Trade Routes Since ancient times, the Red Sea has been an important trade route. Goods and ideas that have traveled through the Red Sea have shaped the cultures that lie on either side of it. The Persian Gulf has also been an important trade route. Today, it draws the interest of the world because of its key position in the middle of oil-rich Southwest Asia.

Energy from an Ancient Sea Millions of years ago, a huge sea covered North Africa and Southwest Asia. When sea creatures died, their remains sank to the bottom.

Strange but TRUE

The Dead Sea It's not actually a sea—it's a lake—and it's not completely dead—some bacteria can survive in its salty depths. The Dead Sea has an area of about 394 square miles. At 1,312 feet below sea level, it is the lowest point on Earth, and it is about ten times saltier than any ocean. Salt and minerals make the water so dense, you can easily float on it.

Black Sea

★ Ankara

TURKEY

Mediterranean Sea

0   100   200 miles
0   100   200 kilometers

Desert and dry scrub	Deciduous forest
Temperate grassland	Mixed forest
Mediterranean vegetation	

Average Yearly Temperature

Fahrenheit	Celsius
73–81	23–27
68–73	20–23
63–68	17–20
55–63	13–17

Black Sea

Ankara ★

0   200   400 miles
0   200   400 kilometers

30°E

Average Yearly Precipitation

inches	centimeters
40–80	102–203
20–40	51–102
10–20	25–51
0–10	0–25

Black Sea

Ankara ★

0   200   400 miles
0   200   400 kilometers

30°E

GEOGRAPHY SKILLBUILDER: Interpreting a Map

1. **Place** • How does the amount of yearly precipitation affect the type of vegetation that grows?
2. **Location** • What is the average yearly temperature in Ankara?

Over long periods of time, mud and sand and other materials were deposited on top of them. Heat and pressure from these materials changed the dead matter into petroleum, or oil.

Turkey Not all of North Africa and Southwest Asia is hot and dry. Turkey is cooler than the rest of the region and gets more rain. As a result, instead of deserts, Turkey has grasslands and even forest areas.

SECTION **1** ASSESSMENT

Terms & Names

1. **Identify:**   (a) fertile   (b) hunter-gatherer   (c) irrigation

Taking Notes

2. Use a spider map like this one to map the importance of water in North Africa and Southwest Asia.

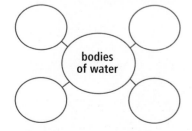

bodies of water

Main Ideas

3. (a) How did the area around the Persian Gulf come to be a rich source of petroleum?

(b) How did hunter-gatherers in North Africa and Southwest Asia become farmers?

(c) How did rivers in Southwest Asia enrich the soil?

Critical Thinking

4. **Analyzing Causes**

Why might the earliest farming communities have developed along the Nile, Tigris, and Euphrates rivers?

Think About

♦ needs of farmers

♦ annual flooding

ACTIVITY -OPTION-   Make a **chart** of the major rivers and bodies of water discussed in this section and list the effects each has had on the region.

Ancient Mesopotamia and the Fertile Crescent

TERMS & NAMES
Hammurabi
Fertile Crescent
Sumerian
ziggurat
class system
cuneiform
scribe

MAIN IDEA

Ancient Mesopotamia's complex civilization, based on city-states, developed a code of laws and a written language.

WHY IT MATTERS NOW

Mesopotamia's achievements led the way to the law codes and written languages in use today.

DATELINE

BABYLON, HAMMURABI'S EMPIRE, 1750 B.C.— Emperor Hammurabi has unveiled a huge black stone containing 282 laws given to him by the god Shamash. For one of the first times ever, a code of laws has been presented to the people of the empire.

According to the Code of Hammurabi, punishment for breaking the law will depend upon the status of the offender and the victim. Most serious crimes, such as murder, will be punished by death. If a house falls down on its owner, the builder of the house will be killed. If the owner's son is killed, then the builder's son will be killed as well. The idea is that a crime should be repaid with a similar punishment. Many of the laws can be boiled down to this statement: "An eye for an eye, a tooth for a tooth."

Culture • Emperor Hammurabi receives a code of laws from the god Shamash, patron of justice. ▲

The Mesopotamian City-State

Hammurabi (HAM·uh·RAH·bee), a famous emperor of ancient Mesopotamia, ruled from 1792 to 1750 B.C. (See the map on page 424.) Mesopotamia, which means "land between the rivers" in Greek, covers about the same area as modern Iraq, northeast Syria, and part of southeast Turkey. The region is sometimes called the **Fertile Crescent** because of its shape and fertile soil.

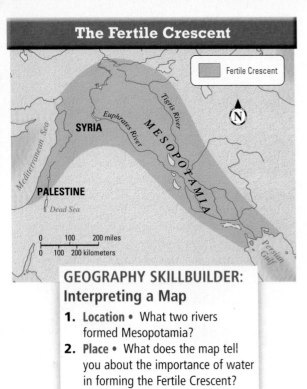

Fertile Crescent

SYRIA

MESOPOTAMIA

Euphrates River

Tigris River

Mediterranean Sea

PALESTINE

Dead Sea

Persian Gulf

0   100   200 miles
0   100   200 kilometers

GEOGRAPHY SKILLBUILDER:
Interpreting a Map

1. **Location** • What two rivers formed Mesopotamia?
2. **Place** • What does the map tell you about the importance of water in forming the Fertile Crescent?

City-States Around 3000 B.C., the **Sumerians,** the first inhabitants of the area, organized the first city-states. A city-state is made up of a city and the areas it controls. Three major challenges influenced the development of city-states. One was the threat of hostile invaders. To protect themselves, the Sumerians surrounded their cities with strong, high walls. The second challenge was lack of water. There was very little rainfall in the region. City-states built and maintained irrigation canals for local use.

The third challenge involved trade. The Sumerians lacked stones, metals, and timber for building and had to import these materials. The Sumerians wanted to export grain, dates, and cloth, but trade was risky. Traders often had to cope with bandits, pirates, and wild animals. Well-protected city-states would have helped traders feel more confident about doing business.

Government by Priests and Kings Mesopotamian city-states were centers of religious worship. The Sumerians believed in many gods. The most important gods, Enlil and Utu, controlled the rain and sun. Other gods, such as Inanna, Goddess of Love and War, cured diseases and helped kings fight wars. Each city-state built a temple to a specific god. The people believed this god was the city's special guardian. The temple was built on a pyramid-shaped tower called a **ziggurat.** From the winding terraces wrapped around the ziggurat, people could watch celebrations honoring their god.

Temple priests were the first governors of Mesopotamian city-states. When the city-states began to argue about land and water rights, leaders were elected to defend their interests. Later these rulers became kings. Each king chose who would rule after his death. From then on, the city-states were governed by two groups. The priests controlled religious and economic life, and the king controlled political and military life.

Reading
Social Studies

A. Recognizing Effects What were three effects of the founding of city-states?

Place • This is the gateway to a ziggurat built around 1250 B.C. ▼

From Kings to Emperors Occasionally, kings conquered other city-states. Sometimes these kings allowed the conquered cities to keep worshiping their own special gods. They let the ruling families and temple priests keep local control. Other kings built empires from the lands they had conquered. An empire is a group of countries under one ruler's control. These emperors demanded that the conquered people honor them as gods. Local rulers could no longer turn to their own gods for advice. Now they had to take orders directly from the emperor.

Reading
Social Studies

B. Analyzing Causes How did some kings become emperors?

The Class System

Mesopotamia had a **class system**. This meant society was divided into different social groups. Each social group, or class, possessed certain rights and was protected by law. The most favored classes enjoyed more rights than anyone else.

The Three Classes Kings, priests, and wealthy property owners were at the top of the class system. The middle class included skilled workers, merchants, and farmers. Skilled workers specialized in one craft, such as making pottery or spinning thread. Merchants often sold goods brought from other Mesopotamian cities or from other countries. Farmers worked fields that belonged to the temple or the palace.

Many workers in Mesopotamia were enslaved. These people were at the bottom of the class system. Some had been captured in war. Others sold themselves and their families into slavery to pay off a debt. Once they paid the debt, their masters had to set them free. Even former slaves had some rights in Mesopotamian society.

Culture •
These necklaces, earrings, and headress were worn by a Sumerian queen. ▲

Place •
People in Mesopotamia raised animals, caught fish, raised crops, and traded goods. ▶

A Culture Based on Writing

The Sumerians developed one of the first systems of writing, called **cuneiform** (KYOO•nee•uh•FAWRM). With this wedge-shaped writing, they kept lists and records. They sent business letters. They recorded their history, their religious beliefs, and their knowledge of medicine, mathematics, and astronomy. Few Sumerians actually learned to read and write. Schools trained **scribes** to be society's record keepers and meet the different needs of the temple, the royal government, and the business world.

Educating Scribes Only the wealthy could afford to send their children to school. Most of these children were boys, but a few girls also studied at the schools—called tablet houses. Most scribes were children of government officials, priests, and wealthy merchants. Some were orphans who had been adopted by rich people and sent to school. The school day lasted from sunrise to sunset. There were about 600 different characters which students had to memorize. Students who misbehaved were punished by "the man in charge of the whip." Here is how one student scribe described his monthly school schedule:

The Development of Cuneiform The Sumerians created one of the world's first written languages more than 5,000 years ago. Cuneiform—which means "wedge-shaped"—developed from pictographs. Early pictographs looked like the object they represented, such as a fish or a bird. Sumerians used a pen made from a sharpened reed to draw pictographs in vertical rows on soft clay tablets. Over time, the pictograph forms became more simplified and people began to write in horizontal rows. Eventually the forms became wedge-shaped. Scribes began using a pen that created the wedge-shaped signs when it was pushed into the clay.

THINKING CRITICALLY

1. **Analyzing Information** Why do you think Sumerians wrote on clay tablets?

2. **Contrasting** What were the differences between early pictographs and cuneiform writing?

fish

picture writing → cuneiform

A VOICE FROM SUMERIA

The reckoning of my monthly stay in the tablet house is (as follows):

My days of freedom are three per month.
Its festivals are three days per month.
Within it, twenty-four days per month
(is the time of) my living in the tablet house.
They are long days.

a student scribe

Scribes Played Many Roles Scribes did more than make lists, keep records, and write letters for their employers. Some wrote literary and scientific works of their own. Certain lullabies and love songs were written by women scribes. Traveling scribes from Mesopotamia shared their writings with people from neighboring countries.

Since few people in Mesopotamia could read, scribes read out loud to audiences. One favorite tale was about a flood that covered the earth. It is one of a collection of tales in a book called *The Epic of Gilgamesh*, which relates the adventures of a semi-divine hero.

Culture • The hero Gilgamesh was both a king and a god. ▲

SECTION (2) ASSESSMENT

Terms & Names

1. **Identify:**
   (a) Hammurabi
   (b) Fertile Crescent
   (c) Sumerian
   (d) ziggurat
   (e) class system
   (f) cuneiform
   (g) scribe

Taking Notes

2. Use a chart like this one to show how building city-states solved challenges faced by the Mesopotamians.

Challenge	Solution

Main Ideas

3. (a) Why do geographers refer to Mesopotamia as the Fertile Crescent?

   (b) How did some Mesopotamian kings become emperors?

   (c) How did scribes contribute to Mesopotamian civilization?

Critical Thinking

4. **Forming and Supporting Opinions**

   Are the laws set forth in Hammurabi's Code too harsh?

   Think About
   - the meaning of justice
   - the reasons for punishment
   - the role mercy plays in justice

ACTIVITY -OPTION-   Design a **mural** of ancient Mesopotamia showing the roles and activities of typical citizens.

Comparing Climate and Vegetation Maps

▶▶ Defining the Skill

A climate map shows the climate of a country or region. Climate has two important factors—average temperature and precipitation. A vegetation map shows what grows in the region. It shows, for example, whether the region has forests or deserts. The climate of a region influences its vegetation. The key shows what each map color means.

▶▶ Applying the Skill

The maps shown here are of the country of Morocco in northwestern Africa. The top map shows Morocco's climate and the bottom map shows its vegetation.

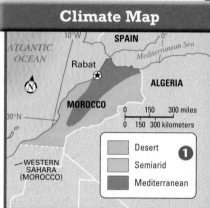

How to Compare Climate and Vegetation Maps

Strategy ❶ Look at the climate map. Read the key to see what types of climates are represented on the map. Then study the map to see where each of those climate types can be found in the country of Morocco.

Strategy ❷ Look at the vegetation map. Read the key, and then look at the map. What kind of vegetation is found in Morocco, and where?

Strategy ❸ Compare the maps. Look at the different climates and at the vegetation in those areas. What kind of vegetation grows where there is little rain? What kind grows where it rains some of the year?

Make a Chart

A chart can help you organize the information that you gain from comparing the two maps. The chart below lists the types of vegetation found in Morocco and the kind of climate that vegetation is located in.

❸

Climate	Vegetation
Desert	Desert and dry shrub
Semiarid	Temperate grassland
Mediterranean	Mediterranean shrub

▶▶ Practicing the Skill

Turn to page 422 in Chapter 15, Section 1. Look at the climate map and the vegetation map found there. Create a chart to organize and analyze the information found in those two maps.

Ancient Egypt

SECTION 3

TERMS & NAMES
papyrus
pyramid
pharaoh
hieroglyphics
Re
Horus

MAIN IDEA

The civilization of the ancient Egyptians developed in response to both its desert environment and the flooding waters of the Nile River.

WHY IT MATTERS NOW

The ancient Egyptian civilization is a model of a well-organized society with limited natural resources.

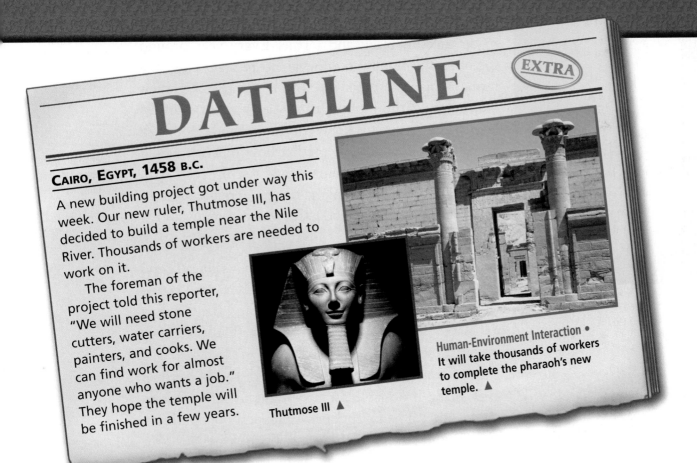

DATELINE

EXTRA

CAIRO, EGYPT, 1458 B.C.

A new building project got under way this week. Our new ruler, Thutmose III, has decided to build a temple near the Nile River. Thousands of workers are needed to work on it.

The foreman of the project told this reporter, "We will need stone cutters, water carriers, painters, and cooks. We can find work for almost anyone who wants a job." They hope the temple will be finished in a few years.

Thutmose III ▲

Human-Environment Interaction •
It will take thousands of workers to complete the pharaoh's new temple. ▲

Ancient Egypt and the Nile

Many of the temples and other monumental structures of ancient Egypt still stand. Without the Nile River, however, they probably would never have been built. As the Greek historian Herodotus (hih·RAHD·uh·tuhs) said approximately 2,500 years ago, Egyptian civilization was "the gift of the Nile."

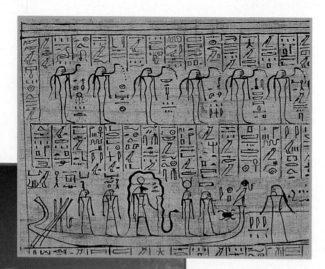

The River in the Sand Desert covers most of Egypt. The sands spread for hundreds of miles to the west and the south, discouraging outsiders from invading. The Nile River, which runs through the desert, is sometimes called "the river in the sand."

The Nile's yearly floods deposited tons of silt in the river valley. The deposits made the soil black and fertile. Every year, around October, the floodwaters began to retreat. Then the farmers planted their seeds. They harvested their crops during the months the Nile was at its lowest levels. The Egyptians knew the Nile would flood each year. But they could not predict how much it would flood or how high the water would rise. In years with very low floods, there might not be enough food. In years with very high floods, the waters would destroy fields and homes.

Vocabulary

silt:
particles of earth and rock that build up in rivers or streams

Reading
Social Studies

A. Identifying Problems What problems did the Nile River cause Egyptian farmers?

Taming the Nile The ancient Egyptians found ways to manage the unpredictable river. They built canals to carry water from the Nile to the parts of the land the flooding water did not reach. They strengthened the riverbanks to keep the river from overflowing.

Egyptian towns and cities were spread along the Nile River valley. The Nile made it possible for Egyptians living in distant places to come together. The Egyptians were expert boat builders. They built harbors and ports for large cargo boats. The Nile provided such good transportation that there were few roads in ancient Egypt. Because goods moved easily along the Nile, trade was very profitable.

The Nile's Gifts The ancient Egyptians used Nile mud to make pottery and bricks. They made a paperlike material called **papyrus** (puh·PY·ruhs) from the papyrus plant. This tall plant grew in marshes and swamps around the Nile. In fact, the English word *paper* comes from "papyrus." It was easier to write on papyrus than on the bulky clay tablets the Mesopotamians used.

Place • **Papyrus reeds grow along the Nile River.** ▲

Place • In 1922, the tomb of Egyptian king Tutankhamen (TOOT•ahng•KAH•muhn) was found almost exactly as it had been left thousands of years before. Although his tomb may be the most famous, Tutankhamen was not buried in a pyramid. He was buried in an area now known as the Valley of the Tombs of the Kings. ◄

The Great Builders

The Egyptians noticed that bodies buried in the sand on the edge of the desert resisted decay. It may have affected their beliefs in an afterlife. The concept of an afterlife played a central role in ancient Egyptian life and culture. It led the Egyptians to build huge **pyramids,** as well as many other temples and monuments.

Vocabulary

afterlife:
a life believed to follow death

The Pyramids Pyramids are easily recognized by their shape. Four triangular sides on a rectangular base meet at a single point. The Egyptians built the pyramids for their kings, or **pharaohs** (FAIR•ohz). Each pyramid is a palace where an Egyptian king planned to spend the afterlife.

BACKGROUND

Nubia (NOO•bee•uh), a country to the south of Egypt, was a source of the gold the Egyptians used in their pyramids.

Materials and Labor To build the pyramids, the Egyptians used large blocks of stone. A single pyramid might contain 92 million cubic feet of stone, enough to fill a large sports stadium. The tips of pyramids were often capped with gold.

Building a pyramid was complicated. The pharaoh appointed a leader to organize the project. The leader and his staff used **hieroglyphics**—a writing system that uses pictographs to stand for words or sounds—to make lists of the workers and supplies they needed for the project.

Citizenship IN ACTION

Recording the Past The great statues and monuments of ancient Egypt have lasted thousands of years, but they will not last forever. They are threatened by pollution and other changes in the environment. Now a nonprofit group called INSIGHT (Institute for the Study and Implementation of Graphic Heritage Techniques) is using the latest technology, such as digital photography and laser scanning, to record Egypt's cultural heritage.

Working with archaeologists, INSIGHT volunteers record ancient tombs, temples, and statues before they fall apart or are destroyed. The results will be used for research and educational purposes.

Hatshepsut (hat•SHEHP•soot) was the first woman to rule Egypt. Like male pharaohs, she wore a tightly braided false beard.

Hatshepsut came to the throne around 1500 B.C., when her husband, the pharaoh Thutmose II, died. The throne passed to Thutmose III, Hatshepsut's son. Because he was a child, Hatshepsut acted as ruler. Even when he grew up, she refused to give him the throne. Instead, she had herself proclaimed pharaoh and ruled for 20 years.

She encouraged foreign trade and building projects, including a number of magnificent temples.

The Egyptians had no cutting tools or machines to get the stone they needed. Removing the stone and shaping it into blocks was very difficult work. The work was also dangerous. Every Egyptian family had to help with the project. They either worked as laborers or provided food for the workers.

The Pharaoh and the Gods

Egyptians believed that the ruling pharaoh was the living son of the sun god, **Re** (RAY). The pharaoh was also linked with **Horus,** the sun god. The pharaoh was not only ancient Egypt's chief judge and commander in chief, he was also the chief religious figure. His religious example guided the common people in their daily lives and in their preparations for the afterlife.

Religion in Daily Life Temples were everywhere in ancient Egypt. Some were dedicated to major gods, like Re. Others were dedicated to local gods. Pharaohs had temples built in their honor so that people could worship them.

Ordinary citizens did not gather for prayer in the temples. Only priests carried out the temple rituals. Smaller buildings stood outside the temple grounds where common people could pray or leave offerings to the gods. Many private homes also contained small shrines where family members worshiped their gods and honored the spirits of dead family members.

Reading
Social Studies

B. Making Inferences How important was their religion to Egyptians?

Culture • Egyptian artists' drawings followed rules. Eyes and shoulders were drawn as if from the front, the rest of the body sideways. Important people were drawn larger than others. ▶

Preparing for the Afterlife Average Egyptians were not buried in pyramids. They made careful preparations for the afterlife, however. Family members were responsible for burying their dead relatives and tending their spirits. Egyptians believed they could help the dead person live comfortably in the afterlife. They prevented bodies from decaying by treating them with preservatives, or mummifying them. The Egyptians filled tombs with items for the dead to use in the afterlife and they decorated the tombs with art. They also made regular offerings to honor the dead.

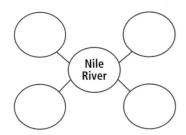

Culture • Osiris and Isis were the Egyptian god and goddess of the dead. ◄

Culture • A mask covers this mummy's face. ▲

SECTION 3 ASSESSMENT

Terms & Names

1. **Identify:**
   (a) papyrus
   (b) pyramid
   (c) pharaoh
   (d) hieroglyphics
   (e) Re
   (f) Horus

Taking Notes

2. Use a spider map like this one to record all the ways the Nile River benefited the ancient Egyptians.

   (◯ ◯ ◯ **Nile River** ◯ ◯)

Main Ideas

3. (a) Why did the Egyptians build pyramids?

   (b) How did the use of hieroglyphics help Egyptian builders?

   (c) Why was the pharaoh so important to the Egyptians?

Critical Thinking

4. **Summarizing**

   How did belief in an afterlife affect the culture of the ancient Egyptians?

   Think About
   ◆ burial practices
   ◆ buildings

ACTIVITY -OPTION- Suppose that you are an ancient Egyptian. Write a **journal entry** about the daily work of an inhabitant of ancient Egypt.

Technology: 3500 B.C.

The Potter's Wheel

Archaeologists can trace the origin of the wheel back to flat stones used to make pottery about 8,500 years ago. An ancient potter's wheel consisted of a stone, wood, or baked-clay disk resting on a short stone or clay stand. A potter's helper would spin the disk while the potter shaped clay. The spinning motion allowed potters to make symmetrical containers. Some ancient potters had artists decorate their finished pots. By 3500 B.C., the Sumerians of Mesopotamia had developed the first true potter's wheel, which rotated at a much greater speed.
This enabled potters to produce larger quantities of containers, helping to turn pottery into an industry.

> The wheel has provided not only a surplus of goods to be traded far and wide but also a means of transporting them.

> The potter's wheel makes possible the mass production of a wide variety of inexpensive goods.

> Archaeologists study broken pieces of pottery, called potsherds, to learn about lifestyles and practices of past civilizations.

> The centrifugal force of the spinning wheel causes the clay to move outward, allowing the potter to form stronger, lighter vessels and to fashion such useful features as spouts.

THINKING Critically

1. Drawing Conclusions
As production of pottery increased, the amount of decoration decreased. Why?

2. Making Inferences
Which mechanical devices used today were adapted from the wheel?

Birthplace of Three Religions

TERMS & NAMES

Abraham

Judaism

Jesus

Christianity

Muhammad

Islam

Muslim

Qur'an

MAIN IDEA

Southwest Asia was the birthplace of Judaism, Christianity, and Islam.

WHY IT MATTERS NOW

Today, these three religions continue to attract believers and influence world events.

DATELINE

JERUSALEM, JUNE 10, 1967—The third war between Arab States and Israel ended today—after just six days of fighting. Israeli forces have gained control of Jerusalem's Old City, which has been in the hands of the Arabs since the first Arab-Israeli war in 1948.

The Old City includes sites sacred to three religions. Muslims revere the Dome of the Rock, built over the rock from which Muhammad made a night journey to heaven. The Wailing Wall, all that remains of the ancient Temple of Solomon, is sacred to the Jews. The Christian Church of the Holy Sepulcher marks the spot where Jesus Christ is believed to have been buried after his crucifixion.

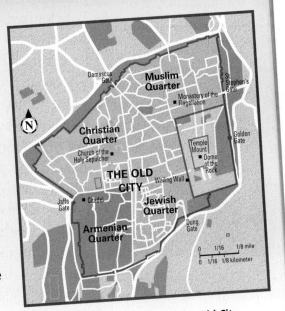

Location • This map of Jerusalem's Old City section shows the location of many sacred sites. ▲

Three Religions

Jerusalem is a city in which Jews, Christians, and Muslims have lived for centuries. These religions all share common traits. They all got their start in Southwest Asia.

The members of each group believe that there is only one god, a belief called monotheism. The Sumerians and Egyptians believed in many gods, a belief called polytheism. In addition, each religion was first led by a single person and has a set of sacred writings.

Movement • **Abraham led his household into the land of Canaan.** ▲

Place • **The Wailing Wall is all that remains of Solomon's Temple.** ▲

Abraham and the Origin of Judaism

The Hebrew people were the first monotheists. They believed in a god they called Yahweh. According to the Hebrew scripture, Yahweh spoke to a man named **Abraham.** Abraham was from the city of Ur, in southeastern Mesopotamia. Yahweh told Abraham to leave his native land. Abraham obeyed and settled in Canaan, which is now in the land of Israel. Abraham's descendants are known as Jews, and their religious belief is called **Judaism.**

Vocabulary

scripture:
sacred writing

How Judaism Adapted over Time The story of Judaism is the story of exile. In 586 B.C., the Babylonians from southern Mesopotamia destroyed the First Temple built by the Jews in Jerusalem. The Jews were exiled to Babylon. They continued to worship by praying and reading their holy texts.

About 50 years later, the Persians took control of Mesopotamia. The Persian ruler Cyrus allowed the Jews to return to Jerusalem and rebuild their Temple. Much later, the Jews came under Roman control. The Jews revolted against Rome in A.D. 66. Jerusalem and the Second Temple were destroyed in the struggle.

Vocabulary

exile:
forced removal from one's native country

Although the Temple was never rebuilt, Judaism did not die out. Jewish teachers and religious leaders encouraged their people to replace worship in the Temple with prayer, study, and good deeds. For the next 1,800 years, most Jews lived outside Jerusalem. They hoped that Jerusalem might once again become the home of Judaism.

Jesus and the Birth of Christianity

Sometime during the years 8 to 4 B.C., a Jewish boy named **Jesus** was born in Bethlehem, a small town in ancient Palestine. (See the map on page 439.) The story of his life is told in the four Gospels, part of the Christian scripture collected in the Bible. The first of the Gospels was written about 30 years after Jesus died.

Early Life According to the Gospels, Jesus grew up in Galilee, a region in northern Palestine. His father trained him to be a carpenter.

Culture • This famous painting, *The Last Supper* by Leonardo da Vinci, shows Jesus with his disciples shortly before his death. ◄

Vocabulary

baptize:
to purify and admit into a new way of life

disciple:
a follower of the teachings of another

When he was about 30, his cousin John the Baptist baptized him. For the next three years, he traveled around the countryside, preaching a religion of love and forgiveness and performing miracles. People flocked to hear his words. Disciples gathered around him.

The Jewish people believed that someday a Messiah, or savior, would come to lead them out of exile. Some people believed Jesus was the Messiah. He came to be called Christ, the Greek word for *messiah*. Those who believed in him and his teachings were called Christians.

Final Days Some government and religious leaders considered Jesus' teachings and his large following a threat to their own power. When Jesus came to Jerusalem to celebrate the Jewish feast of Passover, the authorities decided to get rid of him. Judas Iscariot, one of the 12 disciples who were closest to Jesus, betrayed him to the authorities. Jesus was arrested. After a brief trial, he was crucified and died. He was put into a tomb. After three days, according to his disciples, he was resurrected and later went up into heaven.

Vocabulary

crucify:
to put to death by fastening the hands and feet to a cross

resurrect:
to bring back to life

Place • Many Christians believe Jesus was buried at the site of the Church of the Holy Sepulcher in Jerusalem. ▼

Beginnings of Christianity Jesus' disciples spread his teachings and their belief that he was the Messiah promised in Jewish scripture. From its roots in Judaism, a new religion developed called **Christianity**. It is based on the life and teachings of Jesus. Eventually, the new religion spread to other parts of the world. Today, only a small number of Christians live in Southwest Asia, the region where Christianity began. (See the Unit Atlas map on page 411.)

Muhammad, the Prophet of Islam

Less than 600 years after Christ's death, a third monotheistic religion arose in Southwest Asia. A man named **Muhammad** (mu·HAM·ihd) was born in Mecca (MEHK·uh) about A.D. 570.

He is the founder of **Islam,** a religion whose followers believe there is one god and that Muhammad is his prophet. A believer in Islam is called a **Muslim.**

Vocabulary

prophet:
a person who speaks through divine inspiration

One day about A.D. 610, according to Muslim beliefs, when Muhammad was alone, he heard a voice commanding him: "Recite in the name of your Lord who created! He created man from that which clings. Recite; and thy Lord is Most Bountiful, He who has taught by the pen, taught man what he knew not."

Place • The Sultan of Morocco donated this copy of the Qur'an to the city of Jerusalem. ▼

Muhammad's Teachings Muhammad believed that the command came from the angel Gabriel, who was revealing to him the will of God. For the next 22 years, Gabriel continued to send revelations to Muhammad. Later, the revelations were collected into the **Qur'an** (kuh·RAN), the sacred text of Islam. Muhammad told other people about the divine messages he received. He criticized the wealthy people of Mecca for turning their backs on the poor and needy. He encouraged them to reject their wicked ways and to worship the one true God.

Reading
Social Studies

Comparing What did the founders of Judaism, Christianity, and Islam have in common?

The leaders of Mecca thought Muhammad's teachings threatened their traditions and businesses. Some plotted to kill him. In 622, Muhammad and a group of followers escaped to the nearby city of Medina (mih·DEE·nuh), where they were welcomed. Muslims date the beginning of their calendar from this important year in their history.

SECTION 4 ASSESSMENT

Terms & Names

1. **Identify:** (a) Abraham (b) Judaism (c) Jesus (d) Christianity
   (e) Muhammad (f) Islam (g) Muslim (h) Qur'an

Taking Notes

2. Use a time line like this one to write important dates in the early history of Judaism, Christianity, and Islam.

   586 B.C. |—+—+—+—+—| A.D. 622

Main Ideas

3. (a) What do Judaism, Christianity, and Islam have in common?

   (b) What role did Jesus' disciples play in establishing Christianity?

   (c) What does the Qur'an contain?

Critical Thinking

4. **Making Inferences**

   Why do you think Judaism was able to flourish in exile for so many centuries?

   Think About

   ◆ religious beliefs
   ◆ the role of religious leaders and teachers

ACTIVITY -OPTION- Suppose that you have just seen and heard one of the religious leaders mentioned in this section. Write a **letter** to a friend describing your experience.

Holy Places of Three Religions

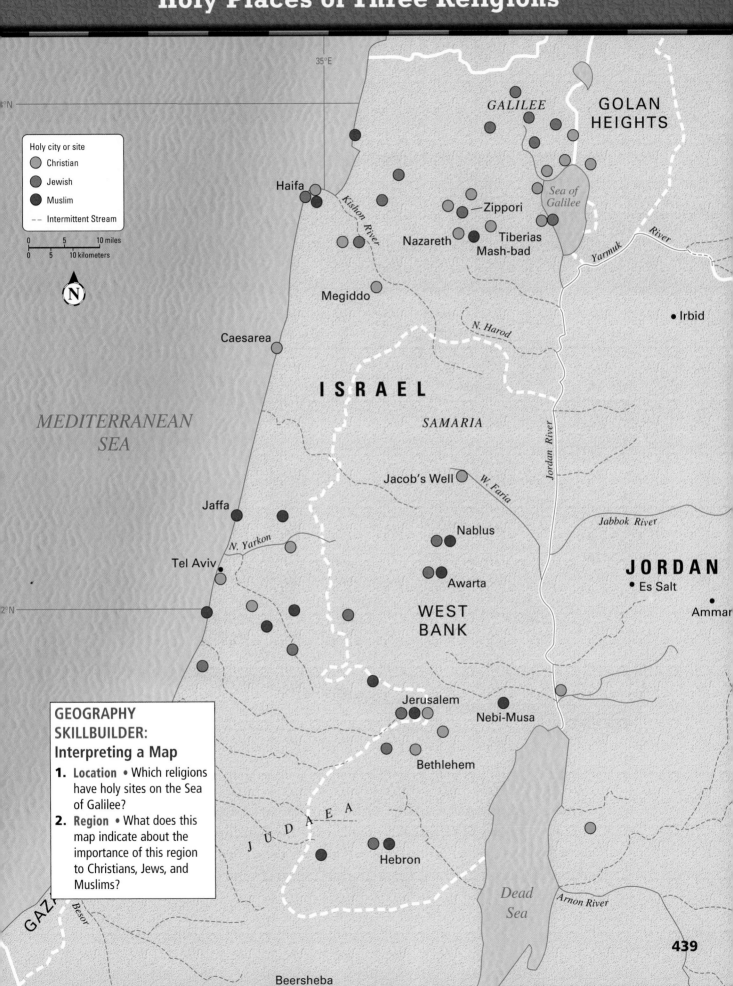

GALILEE

GOLAN HEIGHTS

Holy city or site
- ○ Christian
- ● Jewish
- ● Muslim
- –– Intermittent Stream

0   5   10 miles
0   5   10 kilometers

N

Haifa

Kishon River

Zippori

Sea of Galilee

Nazareth

Tiberias

Mash-bad

River

Yarmuk

Megiddo

N. Harod

• Irbid

Caesarea

ISRAEL

SAMARIA

Jordan River

MEDITERRANEAN SEA

Jacob's Well

W. Faria

Jabbok River

Jaffa

N. Yarkon

Nablus

JORDAN

Tel Aviv

Awarta

• Es Salt

2°N

WEST BANK

Ammar

Jerusalem

Nebi-Musa

GEOGRAPHY SKILLBUILDER: Interpreting a Map

1. **Location** • Which religions have holy sites on the Sea of Galilee?
2. **Region** • What does this map indicate about the importance of this region to Christians, Jews, and Muslims?

Bethlehem

J U D A E A

Hebron

Dead Sea

Arnon River

GAZA

Besor

439

Beersheba

Muslim Empires

TERMS & NAMES
Five Pillars of Islam
caliph
theocracy
Ottoman Empire
Constantinople
Suleiman I
Janissary
Sultan Mehmed VI

MAIN IDEA

Islamic beliefs and culture spread throughout Southwest Asia and much of the world.

WHY IT MATTERS NOW

Islam, the world's second largest religion, influences society and governments in most Southwest Asian countries today.

DATELINE

EXTRA

MECCA, ARABIA, 9TH DAY OF DHUL HIJJAH, A.D. 622

The Prophet Muhammad today preached a sermon to 140,000 followers who have come to Mecca from all over Arabia on a pilgrimage. In his sermon, Muhammad reviewed all his teachings over the years. Many say it was the most important sermon he has ever preached. Some fear it may be his last.

He began by saying, "O People, lend me an attentive ear, for I know not whether after this year I shall ever be among you again." It is well-known that for the past few years the Prophet has been anxious to spread word of his religion wherever he can.

Place • Mecca is the holiest city in Islam. ▲

The Five Pillars of Islam

The most important teachings of Muhammad are summed up in the **Five Pillars of Islam.** All members of the Muslim community believe in the central importance of these five religious duties. The Five Pillars of Islam unite Muslims around the world.

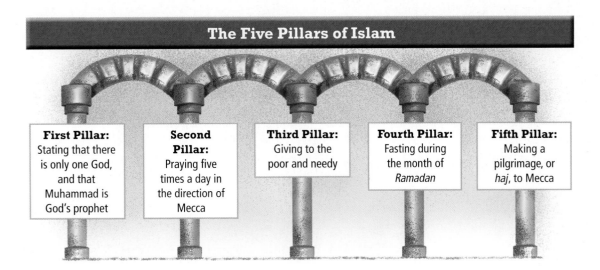

The Five Pillars of Islam

First Pillar: Stating that there is only one God, and that Muhammad is God's prophet

Second Pillar: Praying five times a day in the direction of Mecca

Third Pillar: Giving to the poor and needy

Fourth Pillar: Fasting during the month of *Ramadan*

Fifth Pillar: Making a pilgrimage, or *haj*, to Mecca

Muslim Empires

Muhammad died without choosing someone to continue his work. His close associates soon selected a **caliph** (KAY·lihf) to succeed him. The title of caliph was used by rulers of the Muslim community from 632 until 1924. The caliph's duty was to spread God's rule. In carrying out this task, the caliphs founded a new empire, the caliphate. The caliphate was a **theocracy** (thee·AHK·ruh·see), a government ruled by a religious leader.

Conquest, Trade, and Learning The caliphs created a vast trading system throughout their empires. Islamic ideas spread as books were exchanged along trade routes. Metalwork, pottery, and fabrics exposed other people to new and unique Muslim artwork.

In the early Middle Ages, Muslims collected and translated important books and papers in order to preserve knowledge. During the 1100s and 1200s, these texts were translated from Arabic into Hebrew and Latin. These translations helped European scholars study the knowledge of the ancient world. They could see how Islamic thinkers had further developed this knowledge.

Islam in Europe The caliphs conquered Christian Spain and introduced Islamic culture there. They had hoped to spread their influence elsewhere in Europe. In 732, however, that hope was dashed. Muslim armies trying to capture Tours, in what is now west-central France, were defeated by Charles Martel (sharl mahr·TEHL), Charlemagne's grandfather. By 1400, however, the Muslims had succeeded in conquering parts of Europe.

Reading
Social Studies

A. Analyzing Causes How did the caliphs' trading system lead to the spread of culture?

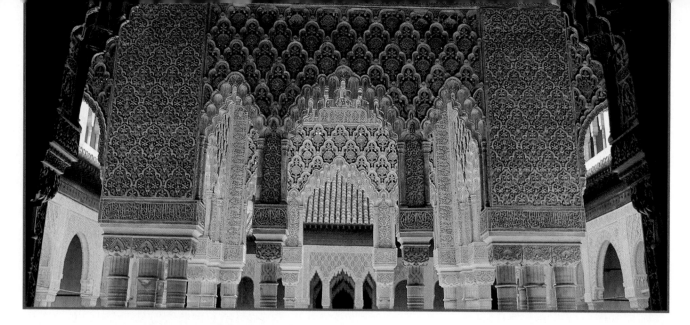

The Ottoman Empire

The Muslim **Ottoman Empire** controlled what is now Turkey and parts of North Africa, Southwest Asia, and Southeast Europe. The Ottomans made **Constantinople,** called Istanbul in present-day Turkey, their capital city. The rulers of the Ottoman Empire were called sultans. The vast Ottoman Empire included people of different backgrounds. The sultans were tolerant of other religions. Christians and Jews could pay a tax that allowed them to worship as they pleased. Some achieved prominent positions in banking and business.

Culture • The influence of Islamic art left its mark in southern Spain, where Muslims built such works of art as the Alhambra, a magnificent palace. ▲

Region • Suleiman I was a 16th-century sultan of the Ottoman Empire. ▼

Suleiman, "The Magnificent" From 1520 to 1566, **Suleiman I** (SOO•lay•MAHN) ruled the Ottoman Empire. Christians called Suleiman "The Magnificent." Muslims called him "The Lawgiver." Suleiman published a code of laws that established a system of justice throughout his empire. Suleiman's chief architect, Sinan (suh•NAHN), transformed Christian Constantinople into an Islamic capital. Sinan designed famous mosques in Istanbul and elsewhere in the Ottoman Empire. As long as Suleiman ruled the Ottoman Empire, it was the richest and most powerful empire in Europe and Southwest Asia.

Reading
Social Studies

B. Forming and Supporting Opinions Do you think Suleiman I deserved to be called "The Magnificent"?

Slaves and Soldiers

Not everyone shared in the empire's wealth and glory. Many people were slaves, often prisoners from conquered nations. They served at court or in the homes of wealthy people. Many of the male slaves became soldiers.

The Janissaries A special group of soldiers loyal to the sultan, called **Janissaries,** developed in the late 1300s out of a small force of slaves. By the 1600s, they had become so powerful that even the sultans feared them. They refused to learn modern ways of fighting, however, and grew weak. In 1826, a group of Janissaries attacked the sultan. Forces loyal to the sultan fired on the attacking Janissaries, killing 6,000. The sultan then disbanded the force.

Culture • Three Janissaries (on the right) stand in front of their sultan. ▲

The Decline of the Ottoman Empire

Over the centuries, the Ottoman Empire grew weak. It fought wars constantly to hold on to its empire. By the 1800s, the empire came close to bankruptcy several times. It also had trouble competing in trade with industrialized Europe. **Sultan Mehmed V** fought on the losing side of World War I. After the war ended, the empire lost control of Arab lands. By 1924, the Ottoman Empire no longer existed. The modern country of Turkey had taken its place.

SECTION 5 ASSESSMENT

Terms & Names

1. Identify:
   (a) Five Pillars of Islam
   (b) caliph
   (c) theocracy
   (d) Ottoman Empire
   (e) Constantinople
   (f) Suleiman I
   (g) Janissary
   (h) Sultan Mehmed V

Taking Notes

2. Use a time line like this one to record major events in the spread of Islamic empires.

632 — — — — 1924

Main Ideas

3. (a) How did the caliphs contribute to the growth of Islamic empires?

   (b) What regions of the world did the Ottoman Empire include?

   (c) What was Constantinople?

Critical Thinking

4. **Hypothesizing** How might the modern world be different if Muslim armies had won the battle of Tours?

Think About
   • cultural change
   • religious differences

ACTIVITY -OPTION- Create an illustrated **report** on the religious buildings of Judaism, Christianity, or Islam.

ASSESSMENT

TERMS & NAMES

Explain the significance of each of the following:

1. fertile
2. irrigation
3. Hammurabi
4. Fertile Crescent
5. pyramid
6. hieroglyphics
7. Re
8. Muhammad
9. caliph
10. theocracy

REVIEW QUESTIONS

Physical Geography *(pages 419–422)*

1. What makes it possible to farm the desert near the Nile?
2. Name the three important bodies of water that helped to shape the region of North Africa and Southwest Asia.

Ancient Mesopotamia and the Fertile Crescent *(pages 423–427)*

3. What three problems faced the city-states of Mesopotamia?
4. List the three classes of people in Mesopotamia.

Ancient Egypt *(pages 429–433)*

5. Why did the ancient Egyptians build canals on the Nile?
6. Why did the ancient Egyptians fill their tombs with everyday items?

Birthplace of Three Religions *(pages 435–438)*

7. What do Judaism, Christianity, and Islam have in common?
8. Why is Jerusalem an important city for both Jews and Christians?

Muslim Empires *(pages 440–443)*

9. Why did the Muslims call Suleiman I "The Lawgiver"?
10. What caused the Ottoman Empire to grow weak?

CRITICAL THINKING

Comparing

1. Use the details in your completed chart from Reading Social Studies, p. 418, to compare the religion of ancient Egypt with the religion of Mesopotamia.

Evaluating Decisions

2. The nonprofit group INSIGHT is using technology to record Egypt's culture. (See page 431.) Based on the amount of work involved, do you think the work of INSIGHT is a good idea? Why or why not?

Making Inferences

3. The Greek historian Herodotus called Egypt "the gift of the Nile." What do you think he meant?

Visual Summary

1 Physical Geography

- The climate, resources, and soil conditions of North Africa and Southwest Asia are determined by the water and rainfall of the region.
- Dry land and flooding rivers still affect the region today.

2 Ancient Mesopotamia and the Fertile Crescent

- A complex civilization arose as Mesopotamia struggled with challenges.
- Early achievements in Mesopotamia led the way for later societies.

3 Ancient Egypt

- Environment influenced the development of civilization in ancient Egypt.
- The ancient Egyptians created a well organized and complex civilization.

4 Birthplace of Three Religions

- Three major world religions began in Southwest Asia.
- Judaism, Christianity, and Islam have a great deal in common.

5 Muslim Empires

- Islamic beliefs have spread through Southwest Asia and other parts of the world.
- These beliefs influence both society and government.

SOCIAL STUDIES SKILLBUILDER

Natural Vegetation in Algeria, Libya, and Egypt ▼

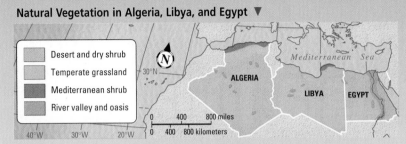

Desert and dry shrub
Temperate grassland
Mediterranean shrub
River valley and oasis

ALGERIA
LIBYA
EGYPT

0   400   800 miles
0   400   800 kilometers

Precipitation (Rainfall) in Algeria, Libya, and Egypt ▼

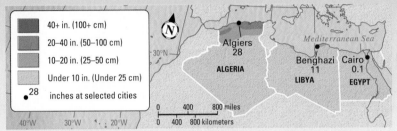

40+ in. (100+ cm)
20–40 in. (50–100 cm)
10–20 in. (25–50 cm)
Under 10 in. (Under 25 cm)
•28   inches at selected cities

Algiers 28
ALGERIA
Benghazi 11
LIBYA
Cairo 0.1
EGYPT
Mediterranean Sea

0   400   800 miles
0   400   800 kilometers

SKILLBUILDER: Comparing Precipitation/Climate and Vegetation Maps

1. What type of vegetation would you expect to find in these countries?
2. What does the precipitation map tell you about the availability of drinking water in these countries?
3. What relationship do you see between the two maps?

FOCUS ON GEOGRAPHY

1. **Region** • This map shows degrees of desertification in North Africa. What do you think the green areas represent?
2. **Human-Environment Interaction** • Which countries have lost the greatest amount of land to the desert?

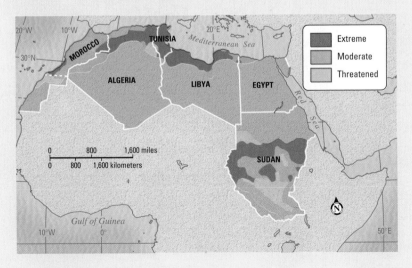

MOROCCO
TUNISIA
Mediterranean Sea
ALGERIA
LIBYA
EGYPT
Red Sea
SUDAN
Gulf of Guinea

Extreme
Moderate
Threatened

0   800   1,600 miles
0   800   1,600 kilometers

CHAPTER PROJECTS

Interdisciplinary Activity: Language Arts

Writing a Letter Imagine you are learning to be a scribe in Mesopotamia. Write a letter home to your parents describing your training and the responsibilities you will be taking on.

Cooperative Learning Activity

Writing a Documentary In a group of three to five students, plan a documentary about one of the female rulers of ancient Egypt. Choose a ruler, such as Hatshepsut, Nefertiti, or Cleopatra, and do research to find out when she ruled, how she came to power, and what she accomplished in her rule.
• Write the script for your documentary.
• Locate or create illustrations.
• Present your documentary to the class.

INTERNET ACTIVITY

Use the Internet to do research about hieroglyphics, the picture writing of the ancient Egyptians. Find out how many types of picture symbols there were, how they were organized, and the sounds, words, actions, or ideas they represented.

Making a Poster Create a poster that shows hieroglyphic symbols and what they represent and include an explanation. Try to create some simple sentences or signs to "translate." Report your finding to the class. List the Web sites you used to prepare your report.

For Internet links to support this activity, go to

RESEARCH LINKS
CLASSZONE.COM

CHAPTER 16

North Africa and Southwest Asia Today

NORTH AFRICA
AND SOUTHWEST
ASIA

ATLANTIC
OCEAN

PACIFIC
OCEAN

PACIFIC
OCEAN

INDIAN
OCEAN

How have rich oil deposits affected Southwest Asia and the world?

FOCUS ON **GEOGRAPHY**

Human-Environment Interaction • Enormous amounts of petroleum, or oil, lie beneath the land surrounding the southern and eastern shores of the Mediterranean Sea, a region often called the Middle East. Experts believe the Middle East supplies about 40 percent of the world's oil. Other countries have come to depend on the oil produced here. The importance of providing energy resources for the planet has given the region great political and economic power. The governments of Middle Eastern nations try to control the price and amount of oil that is produced in their region.

What do you think?

♦ How are politics and economics related in the Middle East?

♦ How might the importance of this region change as nations develop alternative sources of energy?

Place A wealth of goods is sold in this vast indoor bazaar in Istanbul, Turkey.

447

BEFORE YOU READ

▶▶ *What Do You Know?*

Before you read the chapter, consider what you know about North Africa and Southwest Asia today. You may know something about countries like Israel, Saudi Arabia, Iran, Egypt, Turkey, and Iraq from televised news reports about conflicts in this area. Think about the region's role as a major producer of oil. You, or people you know, may have been born in the region or may have lived or visited there. Review what you have learned about recent history and current events in this part of the world.

▶▶ *What Do You Want to Know?*

Decide what you want to know about contemporary North Africa and Southwest Asia. In your notebook, record what you hope to learn from this chapter.

Region • These girls live in Cairo, Egypt, the largest city in the region. ▼

READ AND TAKE NOTES

Reading Strategy: Identifying Problems and Solutions Recognizing problems and how they are solved will help you understand complicated issues you read about in social studies. Use the chart below to identify problems, solutions, and new problems discussed in Chapter 16.

- Copy the chart into your notebook.

- As you read, look for information related to each problem listed on the chart. Some issues are discussed more than once.

- Take notes on solutions that have been tried and problems that resulted.

Region • This sign is in three languages—Hebrew, Arabic, and English. ▲

Problems	Solutions	Resulting Problems
History of foreign influence		
Changes in world markets		
Severe water shortage		
Poverty in villages in Egypt		
Lack of a homeland for Jews		
Forced modernization in Turkey		

A Troubled Century

TERMS & NAMES
mandate
Palestine
Arab-Israeli Wars
Kurd
Persian Gulf War

MAIN IDEA

Today's conflicts in North Africa and Southwest Asia have roots in the history of the region.

WHY IT MATTERS NOW

Regional conflicts affect the security and well-being of people around the world.

DATELINE

EXTRA

SÈVRES, FRANCE, AUGUST 10, 1920

Turkey's Ottoman Empire, the "sick man of Europe" is dead at last. Today, Turkey agreed to surrender most of its territory to Great Britain and France. Revolts by Arab nationalists in recent years had weakened the once-great empire. Being on the losing side in the recent World War marked its end. Mesopotamia and Palestine will now be under British control. Syria, which includes Lebanon, goes to the French.

Region • European nations divided up the Ottoman Empire at the Sèvres conference. ▲

European Nations Take Over

When World War I ended, the history of modern Southwest Asia and North Africa began. During the war, the Turkish Ottoman Empire had sided with Germany against Great Britain, France, and Russia. After the Ottoman Empire's defeat, most of its former territory was divided between Great Britain and France. The stage was set for major conflicts that still trouble the region today. (See the map on page 454.)

Independence Days in Southwest Asia and North Africa

Country	Controlling Power	Taken Over	Achieved Independence
Algeria	France	1847	July 5, 1962
Bahrain	Great Britain	1880	August 15, 1971
Egypt	Great Britain	1882	February 28, 1922
Iraq	Great Britain	1920	October 3, 1932
Jordan	Great Britain	1921	May 25, 1946
Kuwait	Great Britain	1899	June 19, 1961
Lebanon	France	1920	November 22, 1943
Libya	Italy	1932	December 24, 1951
Morocco	France (1/3 under Spain)	1912	March 2, 1956 (April 1956 from Spain)
Oman	Portugal	late 1500s	1650
Qatar	Great Britain	1916	September 3, 1971
Sudan	Egypt/Great Britain	1898	January 1, 1956
Syria	France	1920	April 17, 1946
Tunisia	France	1881	March 20, 1956
United Arab Emirates	Great Britain	1952	December 2, 1971
Yemen	Great Britain	1882	1967 (South Yemen) May 22, 1990 (union of North and South Yemen)

SKILLBUILDER: Interpreting a Chart

1. Which European nation controlled the most countries in the region?

2. In which century did most countries on the chart achieve independence?

A History of Foreign Control Europeans had been taking control of the region since before the 19th century. After World War I, this control often took the form of mandates. A **mandate** is a country placed under the control of another power by international agreement. The European powers promised to give their mandates independence by a certain date. Countries that were not mandates often had to fight for independence.

Conflict Over Palestine

After World War I, Great Britain controlled **Palestine,** an Arab region that was also the land the Jews had lived in 2,000 years earlier. Starting in the late 1800s, Jews fleeing persecution in Eastern Europe had begun migrating there again. After World War II and the Holocaust, many Jews were left homeless and the number who wanted to migrate to Palestine increased.

Palestine, however, was already home to Arabs who had no desire to see their homeland become a Jewish state. Arabs in other countries backed them up. In 1947, Great Britain asked the United Nations to solve the problem. The United Nations divided Palestine—one part for Jews and another for Arabs. The Jews accepted the plan, but the Arabs did not. In May 1948, Jewish leaders declared Israel an independent state. Iraq, Syria, Egypt, Jordan, and Lebanon immediately declared war on Israel. The Israelis won the first of the **Arab-Israeli Wars.** (See the map on page 451.)

Reading Social Studies

A. Summarizing What was the main source of conflict between the Jews and Arabs in Palestine?

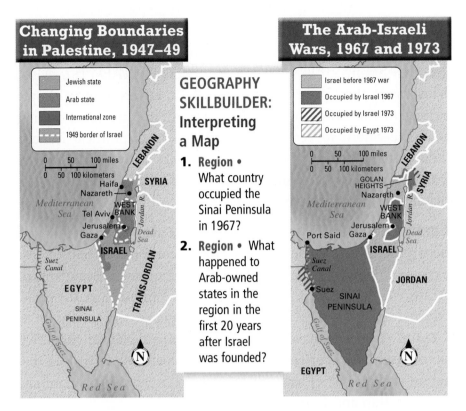

Changing Boundaries in Palestine, 1947–49

- Jewish state
- Arab state
- International zone
- 1949 border of Israel

0   50   100 miles
0   50   100 kilometers

LEBANON
SYRIA
Haifa
Nazareth
Mediterranean Sea
Tel Aviv — WEST BANK
Jerusalem
Gaza
Dead Sea
ISRAEL
Jordan R.
Suez Canal
TRANSJORDAN
EGYPT
SINAI PENINSULA
Gulf of Suez
Red Sea
N

GEOGRAPHY SKILLBUILDER: Interpreting a Map

1. **Region** • What country occupied the Sinai Peninsula in 1967?
2. **Region** • What happened to Arab-owned states in the region in the first 20 years after Israel was founded?

The Arab-Israeli Wars, 1967 and 1973

- Israel before 1967 war
- Occupied by Israel 1967
- Occupied by Israel 1973
- Occupied by Egypt 1973

0   50   100 miles
0   50   100 kilometers

LEBANON
SYRIA
GOLAN HEIGHTS
Nazareth
Mediterranean Sea
WEST BANK
Jerusalem
Port Said   Gaza
Dead Sea
ISRAEL
Jordan R.
Suez Canal
JORDAN
Suez
SINAI PENINSULA
Gulf of Suez
EGYPT
Red Sea
N

Palestine Refugees About 700,000 Palestinian Arabs had to leave their homes. They became refugees living in other Arab countries. In 1964, some Palestinian people formed the Palestine Liberation Organization (PLO). The PLO's goal is the establishment of an independent Palestinian state.

Continuing Conflict In 1967 and 1973, Israel won the third and fourth of the Arab-Israeli Wars. Conflict continued even in peacetime. Over the years, territory passed back and forth between Israel and Arab countries. (See the map above.)

Attempts at Peace In 1979, Egypt became the first Arab country in the region to make peace with Israel. Leaders of Egypt and Israel discussed the Palestinians' wish for their own state. Ten years later, Palestinian Arabs rebelled in the territories controlled by Israel. Most countries around the world sided with the Palestinians. Finally, in 1993, Israel and the PLO signed an agreement. The PLO recognized Israel's right to exist. Israel returned land to the Palestinians. The next year, Israel and Jordan signed a peace treaty. In 2000, however, another Palestinian uprising broke out.

Sources of Conflict

The conflict between Israel and the Arab countries is partly due to religious differences between Jews and Muslims. Religious conflicts between Christians and Muslims have erupted in Egypt, Lebanon, and Sudan. Conflicts also occur within religions.

Sunnis and Shi'ites Islam, for example, has two main sects, or groups—Sunnis (SUN·eez) and Shi'ites (SHEE·YTS). Most Muslims in the region are Sunni. In Iran, however, most people belong to the Shiah branch of Islam. Shi'ites are more willing than the Sunni to accept religious leaders as political leaders. This difference has contributed to conflict between the neighboring countries of Iran and Iraq. The most powerful Iraqis belong to the Sunni branch of Islam.

Reading Social Studies

B. Contrasting What is an important difference between Sunnis and Shi'ites?

Region • Hebrew (top) is the official language of Israel. Arabic (bottom) is the language of many other countries in the region. ▼

Conflict Between Ethnic Groups Trouble also occurs within and between countries when ethnic groups come into conflict. For example, like most people in the region, Iraqis are descendants of Arabs who spread out from the Arabian Peninsula in the 600s. Most Iranians, however, are Persian, people originally from Central Asia who have lived on the Iranian plateau for 3,000 years. Arabs and Persians have different histories and speak different languages. These differences contribute to conflicts between Iran and Iraq.

Nationalism Some ethnic groups want to have a country of their own instead of being part of a multi-ethnic nation. The **Kurds,** for example, are a mountain people who live in Armenia, Georgia, Iran, Iraq, Lebanon, Syria, and Turkey. Their independence movements have been defeated in Turkey, Iran, and Iraq. Many Kurds have died in these struggles.

Vocabulary

ethnic group: people who share a common and distinctive culture, heritage, and language

Fundamentalism Muslim fundamentalists believe Islam should be strictly observed. In 1979, Shi'ite leader Ayatollah Khomeini (EYE·yuh·TOH·luh koh·MAY·nee) took over the government of Iran. Khomeini and his followers objected to the way the former shah, or ruler, had been westernizing the country. Khomeini's government passed laws forbidding the sale of alcohol and limiting the freedom of women. Such fundamentalist movements have also arisen in other countries in the region, often leading to battles between people who hold opposing points of view.

Vocabulary

ayatollah: respected religious leader

Place • These Kurdish children live in Antalya, Turkey. ▼

Recent Wars

The neighboring countries of Iran and Iraq had long disputed who owned the oil-rich territory between them. In 1980, Iraq, led by its absolute ruler Saddam Hussein, invaded Iran.

The Iran-Iraq War The war lasted eight years. As many as one million people died, including soldiers as young as 11 and 12. Neither side could gain a clear victory. In 1988, both countries finally signed a cease-fire agreement developed by the United Nations.

Human-Environment Interaction • Iraq devastated Kuwait when Iraq released oil into the Persian Gulf and torched Kuwait's oil fields. ▼

The Persian Gulf War In 1990, Iraq invaded the small oil-rich country of Kuwait. The United Nations imposed a trade embargo to prevent Iraq from importing goods or exporting oil. The embargo took away most of Iraq's income, but Hussein continued to fight. On January 16, 1991, the **Persian Gulf War** began when a multi-national armed force began missile attacks on Iraq, followed by a ground attack on February 24. One hundred hours later, Iraq surrendered. Iraq was out of Kuwait, but Saddam Hussein stayed in power. Both Kuwait and Iraq suffered widespread destruction in the war.

> **Vocabulary**
>
> **embargo:** a government order forbidding trade with other countries

SECTION 1 ASSESSMENT

Terms & Names

1. Identify: (a) mandate (b) Palestine (c) Arab-Israeli Wars (d) Kurd
(e) Persian Gulf War

Taking Notes

2. Use a time line like this one to write the dates of major wars in Southwest Asia and North Africa.

1948 ├──┼──┼──┼──┤ 1991

Main Ideas

3. (a) How have European nations contributed to turmoil in Southwest Asia and North Africa?

(b) In what ways has religion been a source of conflict in this region?

(c) What are some of the different ethnic groups in this region and how have they come into conflict?

Critical Thinking

4. Forming and Supporting Opinions

Do you think the United Nations should be more involved in settling conflicts in Southwest Asia and North Africa?

Think About

* the system of mandates
* conflict in the region
* the UN in the Persian Gulf War

ACTIVITY -OPTION-   Trace a **map** of the countries of Southwest Asia and North Africa. Write each country's name and the year it achieved independence on the map.

Reading a Historical Map

▶▶ Defining the Skill

Historical maps show an area of the world as it was in the past. Different historical maps contain different kinds of information. Some show trade routes or routes of exploration. Some show how an empire or nation has increased or decreased in size. Some show how political boundaries have changed over time. The map key tells what the symbols, lines, and colors on a historical map represent.

▶▶ Applying the Skill

The historical map below shows how the Ottoman Empire gradually collapsed. During the 15th and 16th centuries, the Ottoman Empire was one of the most powerful empires in the world. It lasted for more than 600 years, but by 1922 the empire was gone.

How to Read a Historical Map

Strategy ❶ Read the title to learn the time period that is shown on the map.

Strategy ❷ Read the key. Shown first on this key is a dotted line, which represents the boundary of the Ottoman Empire in 1807. Look at the map and find that boundary. As you follow the boundary, notice which bodies of water it touches and which continents it covers.

Strategy ❸ Look at each color on the key and the time period represented by that color. Then look for each color on the map. Some of the color regions are scattered. Be sure to locate all of them.

Strategy ❹ Read the map. Notice when different regions were lost to the Ottoman Empire. Some of these regions became independent; others fell under the rule of other nations.

Write a Summary

Writing a summary will help you gain a clearer understanding of the map. The paragraph to the right summarizes the information from this historical map.

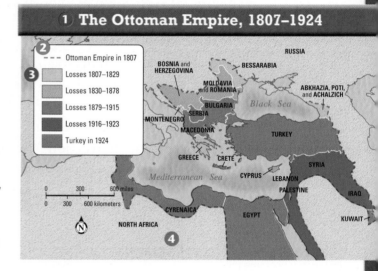

❶ **The Ottoman Empire, 1807–1924**

❷ - - - - Ottoman Empire in 1807
❸ Losses 1807–1829
Losses 1830–1878
Losses 1879–1915
Losses 1916–1923
Turkey in 1924

SUMMARY In 1807 the Ottoman Empire stretched from Bosnia and North Africa in the west to Kuwait in the east, and from Russia in the north to Egypt in the south. Beginning in 1807, the area claimed by the Ottomans was gradually taken over by Greece, Austria-Hungary, Italy, and Great Britain.

▶▶ Practicing the Skill

Turn to page 451 in Chapter 16, Section 1. Look at the historical map entitled *Changing Boundaries in Palestine, 1947–49*, and then write a paragraph summarizing what you learned from it.

Resources and Religion

TERMS & NAMES
OPEC
primary product
secondary product
petrochemical
haj
Ramadan

MAIN IDEA

Oil resources are a powerful influence on the region's economies, and religion, especially Islam, is a powerful influence on its culture.

WHY IT MATTERS NOW

Peace in Southwest Asia and North Africa depends on prosperity and the ability of different religions to coexist.

DATELINE

KHUZISTAN PROVINCE, PERSIA (IRAN), 1908—A British company has just discovered oil here in Khuzistan. Both the British and the Persians expect it to bring their countries great wealth. The Shah of Iran (Persia) has given British businessman William Knox D'Arcy the rights to drill for oil here. D'Arcy plans to create the Anglo-Persian Oil Company and to begin exporting oil by 1912. The world's increasing dependence on oil for energy has led experts to predict that the value of oil will increase dramatically. The Middle East, they say, has the potential to become the greatest oil-producing area in the world.

Human-Environment Interaction • Workers lay an oil pipeline in the Khuzistan plain. ▶

Human-Environment Interaction • British businessman William Knox D'Arcy was the principal founder of the oil industry in Iran. ▲

The Importance of Oil

Oil was soon discovered in other countries of Southwest Asia and North Africa. Great Britain, France, the United States, and other western countries made agreements with the oil-rich nations to build and run companies to develop the oil fields. Today, nearly half the world's oil is found here, mainly in Saudi Arabia, Iran, Kuwait, and Iraq. Saudi Arabia, the world's largest oil-producing country, is also one of the largest oil exporters to the United States.

Gaining Control After World War II, many nations in the region chose to nationalize, or have their governments take over the running of, their oil industries. In 1960, four of these countries—Iran, Iraq, Saudi Arabia, and Kuwait—joined with Venezuela, an oil-rich country in South America, to form the Organization of Petroleum Exporting Countries, or **OPEC**. OPEC would decide the price and amount of oil produced in each country each year. In a world dependent on oil as its major energy source, OPEC had a great deal of power. In 1973, OPEC placed an embargo on the export of oil to countries that supported Israel. As a result, the price of gasoline shot way up as its supply went down, leading to shortages.

Reading Social Studies

Analyzing Causes How did OPEC's oil embargo lead to a rise in the price of gasoline?

Developing New Products Since the early 1900s, oil has been the most important **primary product,** or raw material, in Southwest Asia and North Africa. The countries of the region export mostly primary products. (See the map below.) Many countries have also developed **secondary products,** or goods manufactured from primary products. In Iraq, for example, date palms are an important primary product. From them, industries in Iraq manufacture date syrup, paper from palm leaves, and other secondary products.

Products of Southwest Asia and North Africa, 2000

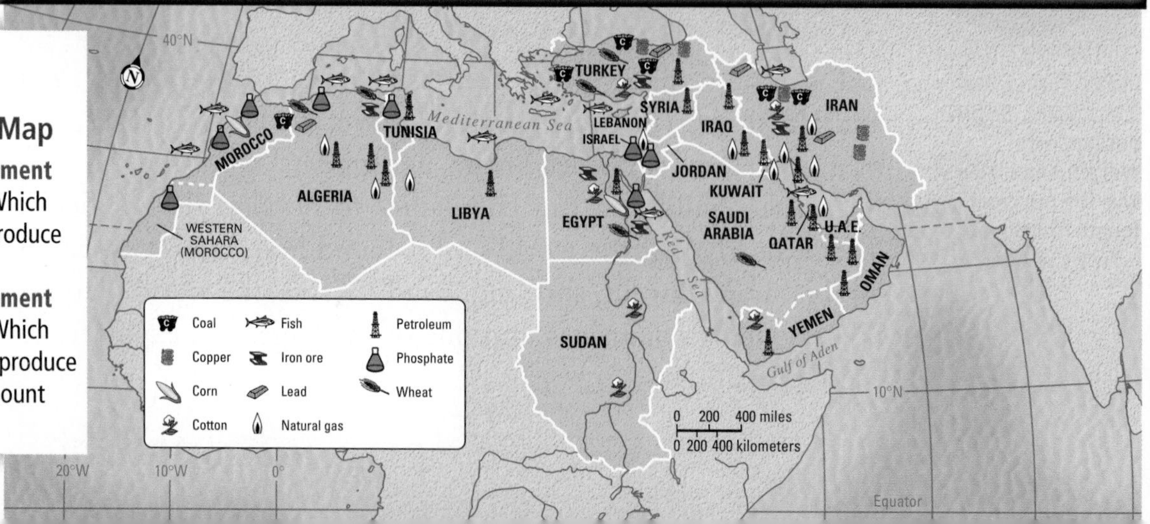

**GEOGRAPHY SKILLBUILDER:
Interpreting a Map**

1. **Human-Environment Interaction** • Which five countries produce cotton?
2. **Human-Environment Interaction** • Which three countries produce the greatest amount of oil?

Legend:
- Coal
- Copper
- Corn
- Cotton
- Fish
- Iron ore
- Lead
- Petroleum
- Phosphate
- Wheat
- Natural gas

Map labels: MOROCCO, WESTERN SAHARA (MOROCCO), ALGERIA, TUNISIA, LIBYA, EGYPT, SUDAN, Mediterranean Sea, TURKEY, SYRIA, LEBANON, ISRAEL, IRAQ, IRAN, JORDAN, KUWAIT, SAUDI ARABIA, QATAR, U.A.E., OMAN, YEMEN, Red Sea, Gulf of Aden, Equator

Scale: 0 200 400 miles / 0 200 400 kilometers

Oil Industries The oil-rich countries also use the oil to make secondary products. For over 30 years, Saudi Arabia and other Persian Gulf countries have been refining crude oil in modern refineries. They also make **petrochemicals** from crude oil and natural gas. Petrochemicals are used in the manufacture of cosmetics, plastics, synthetic materials, detergents, fertilizers, and many other products.

Religion in the Region

BACKGROUND

The Israeli city of Haifa is the world center of the Bahai religion, which split off from Islam. Bahais believe in the equality of men and women and a universal God.

Islam is the dominant religion in the region, but not the only one. Jews and Christians have lived there for thousands of years. Most Jews in the region moved to Israel once it was created, but small communities of Jews remain in Turkey, Egypt, and Iran. Many Christians left after the breakup of the Ottoman Empire. Today the Copts of Egypt and the Maronites of Lebanon are the region's two largest Christian communities.

The Influence of Islam on Culture

Every country in the region shows the influence of Islam. The Five Pillars of Islam (see page 441) are woven into the fabric of daily life. People stop to pray five times a day, no matter what they are doing—at home, in the streets, at school, at work. Radio and television stations air programs devoted to readings from the Qur'an many times a day. All Muslims try to go on a *haj*, or pilgrimage to Mecca, once in a lifetime.

Place • During a *haj*, the holy city of Mecca is packed with pilgrims. ▲

Ramadan During the ninth month of the Islamic year, called **Ramadan** (RAM·uh·DAHN), Muslims fast from sunrise to sunset. Only the very young or sick or those on a journey are allowed to eat or drink during this time. During Ramadan, believers eat a light breakfast before dawn. Then they do not eat or drink again until dusk. The joyous *'Id al-Fitr* (ihd uhl·FIHT·uhr), the Feast of the Breaking of the Fast, ends Ramadan and lasts for several days.

The Muslim Calendar For Muslims, the calendar begins the year Muhammad fled to Medina, A.D. 622 according to the Western calendar. Each Islamic year has 12 months of about 29 days each, which makes the Islamic year about 11 days shorter than the Western year. Each day starts at sunset.

Westernization vs. Traditional Culture

Many people in Southwest Asia and North Africa think western nations exert too much influence over their culture. Others are more open to westernization, adopting aspects of the way of life common in Europe and the United States. Fast-food restaurants, T-shirts, television, and rap music are examples of westernization. So are many technological advances in business, science, medicine, and agriculture. Some people in the region believe westernization will give them a higher standard of living and an easier, more exciting, more enjoyable way of life. For others, the loss of their traditional culture is too great a price to pay.

The Roles of Women

Women in the region have different roles in society. In countries like Israel, Jordan, and Egypt, many women are well educated and hold important positions in business, politics, and the military. In some countries, however, religious beliefs limit the roles women can play. For example, Saudi Arabian women have fewer rights than do Saudi men. Women are not allowed to attend gatherings with men, and they are forbidden to drive cars. A Saudi woman may have only one husband, but a Saudi man is allowed by Islamic law to have up to four wives. Very few Saudi women work outside the home. Those that do usually teach in all-girl schools or treat patients at maternity clinics.

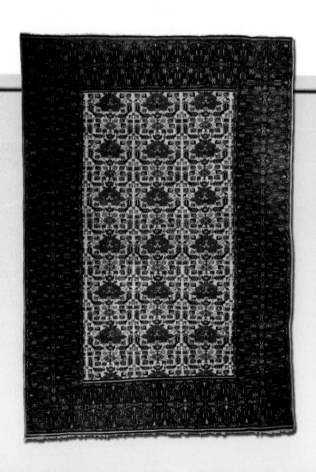

Persian Carpets Persians—now called Iranians—have been making carpets for more than 2,500 years. The first Persian carpets were woven for nomads who needed protection from the cold. Brightly colored intricate designs made the carpets valuable for their beauty. Craftspeople spent months and even years carefully weaving dyed sheep's wool into artistic patterns. Today Persian carpets decorate palaces, important buildings, and museums.

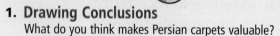

THINKING CRITICALLY

1. **Drawing Conclusions**
   What do you think makes Persian carpets valuable?

2. **Summarizing**
   What role have Persian carpets played in Iranian culture?

Culture • **This woman is wearing a** *chador.* ▲

Clothing and Culture

Clothing reveals much about the region's cultures. In Israel, for instance, some women and men dress in fashionable Western clothing. Orthodox Jewish women, however, wear more modest dress as their religious beliefs dictate. Orthodox men often wear black suits and hats and grow long ringlets of hair in front of their ears. In some Islamic countries, women wear *chadors,* floor-length cloaks that cover everything but the women's eyes. In Iran and Saudi Arabia, such clothing is not a choice; it's the law. Men, too, dress and grow facial hair as Islamic law demands.

A Disappearing Nomadic Culture

Once nomads lived in the desert places of the region. Most nomads herded sheep from place to place in search of grazing lands. Other nomads escorted camel caravans of traders across the desert. Today, only one percent of the population is nomadic. Now trucks, not camels, cross the desert on paved roads. Droughts have decreased grazing lands. Governments encourage nomads to settle down. They have also made it more difficult for nomads from other countries to cross their borders.

Vocabulary

nomads: people with no fixed home who move about in search of food, water, and grazing land

---

SECTION **2** ASSESSMENT

Terms & Names

1. Identify: (a) OPEC (b) primary product (c) secondary product (d) petrochemical
(e) *haj* (f) Ramadan

Taking Notes

2. Use a chart like this one to list major products in Southwest Asia and North Africa.

Primary Products	Secondary Products

Main Ideas

3. (a) How are oil resources important to Southwest Asia and North Africa?

(b) How does Islam affect the culture of the region?

(c) What is the status of women in most Islamic countries?

Critical Thinking

4. Critical Thinking

What makes it difficult for nomadic peoples in Southwest Asia and North Africa to continue their traditional way of life?

Think About

◆ modern technology
◆ climatic conditions
◆ government actions

Make a **poster** showing crude oil and the products made from it. Label them as primary or secondary products.

Explain the Pyramids of Ancient Egypt

You are a tour guide and Egyptologist—an expert on ancient Egypt. Your specialty is the age of pyramid building, about 4,700 to 4,200 years ago (c. 2686–2160 B.C.). Pyramids, large and small, were built as tombs for the pharaohs of the Old Kingdom and members of their families. The most famous are the three pyramids at Giza, near Cairo, where you work. In the course of your work, tourists come to you with questions about the pyramids. You want to find interesting ways to share your knowledge with them.

COOPERATIVE LEARNING On these pages are challenges you will meet while dealing with visitors to the pyramids. Working with a small group, choose one challenge to solve. Divide the work among group members. Look for helpful information in the Data File. Keep in mind that you will present your solution to the class.

MATH CHALLENGE

". . . the Great Pyramid of Khufu was the world's tallest structure."

The three pyramids at Giza were built for Khufu, his son Khafre, and his grandson Menkure. For more than 4,300 years, the Great Pyramid of Khufu was the world's tallest structure. Khafre's pyramid is almost as big. How can you explain these huge structures to your visitors? Choose one of these options. Look in the Data File for information.

ACTIVITIES

1. Make an accurate drawing of the Great Pyramid of Khufu on graph paper, using the measurements given. Use blocks or clay to build a scale model.
2. How does the present height of the Great Pyramid compare with its original height? How does its height compare with the heights of the pyramids of Khafre and Menkure? Express your answers as percentages.

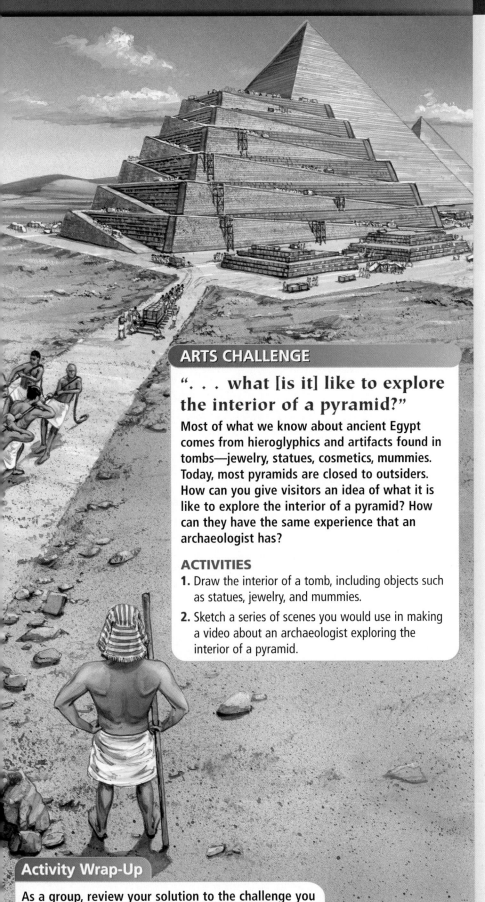

ARTS CHALLENGE

"... what [is it] like to explore the interior of a pyramid?"

Most of what we know about ancient Egypt comes from hieroglyphics and artifacts found in tombs—jewelry, statues, cosmetics, mummies. Today, most pyramids are closed to outsiders. How can you give visitors an idea of what it is like to explore the interior of a pyramid? How can they have the same experience that an archaeologist has?

ACTIVITIES

1. Draw the interior of a tomb, including objects such as statues, jewelry, and mummies.

2. Sketch a series of scenes you would use in making a video about an archaeologist exploring the interior of a pyramid.

Activity Wrap-Up

As a group, review your solution to the challenge you selected. Then present your solution to the class.

DATA FILE

THE PYRAMIDS OF EGYPT

- The pyramids at Giza were one of the **Seven Wonders of the Ancient World.** The oldest of all the wonders, they are the only ones that still stand today.

- Builders used mainly **limestone** and **granite blocks.** Originally, the pyramids were faced with smooth, white limestone. Vandals have stripped off most of this surface stone.

- Building the **Great Pyramid** took about 20 years. Ancient historians said that it took 100,000 workers. Archaeologists today, however, think that there were **20,000 to 30,000 workers.** The workers were probably not slaves, but farmers and villagers who worked in exchange for food and the chance to serve their god-king.

GREAT PYRAMID OF KHUFU

- Oldest and largest of pyramids at Giza, built about **4,500 years ago.**

- Square base: length of each side about **756 feet.**

- Original height: **481 feet;** now about 451 feet.

- Covers about **13 acres**—about seven city blocks.

- Contains about **2.3 million blocks** of stone, each weighing about 2.5 tons.

PYRAMID OF KHAFRE

- Square base: length of each side about **708 feet.**

- Original height: **471 feet.**

- Covers about **11.5 acres.**

PYRAMID OF MENKURE

- Square base: length of each side about **356.5 feet.**

- Original height: **218 feet.**

- Covers about **2.9 acres.**

To learn more about the pyramids, go to

RESEARCH LINKS
CLASSZONE.COM

SECTION 3

Egypt Today

TERMS & NAMES
King Farouk
Gamal Abdel Nasser
Aswan High Dam
tradeoff
Anwar Sadat
Muslim Brotherhood
fellahin

MAIN IDEA	WHY IT MATTERS NOW
Egypt's modernization has brought progress and problems.	Egypt often sets the pace in the region for social and political change.

DATELINE

EXTRA

CAIRO, EGYPT, NOVEMBER 17, 1869

Today is a red-letter day for Egypt. The Suez Canal is open at last. Trade will surely increase now that ships can travel easily between the Mediterranean and Red seas. Not all Egyptians are happy about the canal, however.

More than ten years and 120,000 Egyptian lives have gone into building it. Egyptians wonder whether Egypt will benefit from the Suez Canal or whether Britain and France will continue to control the region. Only time will tell.

Place • Ships sail for the first time through the newly opened Suez Canal. ▲

Location • The Suez Canal connects the Mediterranean Sea and the Red Sea. ▲

The Suez Canal

The Suez Canal was the grand project of Egyptian ruler Ismail Pasha (ihs·MAH·eel PAH·shuh). He wanted it built to make Egypt the equal of Western nations. But the cost of the canal and other expensive projects drove Egypt into bankruptcy. Ismail had to sell Egypt's shares in the Suez Canal Company to the British government. From then until 1956, Great Britain had some control over Egypt.

From Ancient to Modern Times

Great Britain was not the first foreign power to rule Egypt after the time of the pharaohs. For 2,500 years, Egypt was under foreign influence. It was conquered in turn by Persians, Macedonians, and Romans. Arab Muslims from the Arabian peninsula invaded in A.D. 639–642. A military group called the Mamelukes (MAM·uh·LOOKS) seized control in about 1250 and ruled until Ottoman troops invaded in 1517. From the late 1700s to the early 1900s, France and then Great Britain controlled much of Egypt. Britain gave up absolute control in 1922, and Egypt became a monarchy, a country ruled at first by King Fuad (FOO·ahd), and after 1936 by his son, **King Farouk** (fuh·ROOK). Foreign policy, defense, and communications, however, remained under British control.

Place • Gamal Abdel Nasser was President of Egypt for 16 years. ▼

Nasser Takes Over An Egyptian army officer, **Gamal Abdel Nasser,** resented the weakness of his government and the strong British influence on his country. In 1952, he and other officers overthrew King Farouk. The next year Egypt became a republic. Nasser was Egypt's leader from 1954 to 1970.

Controlling the Nile Nasser's most significant accomplishment was the construction of the **Aswan High Dam,** begun in 1956, to control the flooding of the Nile River. The dam gives Egyptian farmers a more dependable source of water for their crops and allows them to grow crops year round. It also gives Egypt electrical power and has made fishing an important industry.

Human-Environment Interaction • The Aswan High Dam, opened in 1971, cost about $1 billion to build. ▼

The Nile River and the Aswan High Dam, 2001

25°E   30°E

Mediterranean Sea

Alexandria
Port Said
Cairo
Suez Canal

EGYPT

Nile R.

Red Sea

Aswan High Dam   Aswan

Lake Nasser

NUBIAN DESERT

N

0   150   300 miles
0   150   300 kilometers

GEOGRAPHY SKILLBUILDER: Interpreting a Map

1. **Location** • What is the location of the Aswan High Dam?
2. **Human-Environment Interaction** • What does the map show you about the dam's importance to Egypt?

Place • Egyptian women campaigned for the vote in Cairo in the 1920s. ▲

Biography

Anwar Sadat, 1918–1981
Anwar Sadat (below, left) took part in the 1952 seizure of the government of King Farouk. When President Nasser died in 1970, Vice President Sadat was elected President.

Sadat led Egypt to war with Israel in 1973. A few years later, however, he became the first Arab leader to seek peace between the two countries. He shared the 1978 Nobel Peace Prize with Israeli Prime Minister Menachem Begin (right, below). In 1979, Israel and Egypt signed a peace treaty. Muslim extremists objected to Sadat's peace treaty with Israel and his close ties with the United States. On October 6, 1981, extremists assassinated him.

Because of the dam, however, the river no longer deposits the rich soil from the south as it did during yearly flooding. Instead, over 100 million tons of earth settle behind the dam each year. Farmers now have to use artificial fertilizers which pollute the water. The Aswan High Dam is an example of a tradeoff. A **tradeoff** is an exchange of one benefit for another.

Rights for Women Women were active in the movement for Egyptian independence in the years from 1919 to 1922, yet were denied the vote. Although they gradually acquired the right to higher education, women were still subject to the Muslim Personal Status Law, which gave men far more rights in marriage. Women continued to demand their rights. In 1956, in Nasser's new government, they gained the right to vote and to run for office. A revised Muslim Personal Status Law in 1979 somewhat improved women's rights within the family. In 2000, Egypt passed a law making it easier for women to get a divorce.

A Search for Peace Egypt actively opposed Israel for many years. However, in 1979, led by President **Anwar Sadat**, Egypt became the first Arab state to sign a peace treaty with Israel. Egypt also led the region in opposing Iraq's 1990 invasion of Kuwait. Egypt has tried to settle arguments between Iraq and the United Nations. In the fall of 2000, President Hosni Mubarak met with other regional leaders to talk about how to end Israeli-Palestinian violence.

The Muslim Brotherhood Not everyone in Egypt values freedom and compromise. The **Muslim Brotherhood** is an extremist Muslim group which insists that Egypt be governed solely by Islamic law. The Brotherhood claims the Egyptian government is being untrue to the principles of Islam by working with Israel and the United States.

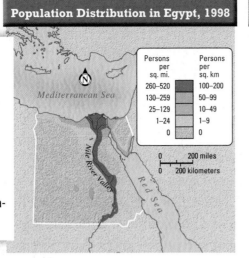

Population Distribution in Egypt, 1998

Persons per sq. mi.	Persons per sq. km
260–520	100–200
130–259	50–99
25–129	10–49
1–24	1–9
0	0

Mediterranean Sea

Nile River Valley

Red Sea

0 — 200 miles
0 — 200 kilometers

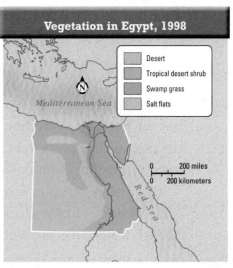

Vegetation in Egypt, 1998

- Desert
- Tropical desert shrub
- Swamp grass
- Salt flats

Mediterranean Sea

Red Sea

0 — 200 miles
0 — 200 kilometers

GEOGRAPHY SKILLBUILDER: Interpreting a Map

1. **Place** • What do you notice about the Nile River on each map?
2. **Human-Environment Interaction** • What relationship do you notice between population and vegetation?

The Land and the People

Most of Egypt consists of desert lands where no one can live. Just about all of Egypt's 70 million people live in a narrow strip of land along either side of the Nile or in a few desert oases. Some live in big cities. Others farm the fields made fertile by the Nile.

Egyptian Cotton Cotton is a major primary product and agricultural export. Cotton-growing developed in Egypt during the 1860s when the Civil War in the United States disrupted cotton exports from southern states. Egypt produces some of the finest cotton in the world. It has also developed a textile industry that manufactures cotton yarns and cotton fabrics as secondary products.

Village Life More than half the population of Egypt lives in villages. Most villagers are **fellahin** (FEHL·uh·HEEN), or peasant farmers. The fellahin are some of the poorest Egyptians. Most rent land or work in their own fields. Many do not know how to read or write. Many fellahin children do not go to school.

Fellahin wear traditional Arab clothing. Men wear pants and loose-fitting, hooded gowns. Women wear long, flowing gowns. Like poor people in the cities, they eat a simple diet of bread and beans, which leads to malnutrition. Infectious diseases, such as tuberculosis, also afflict the fellahin. Only a lucky few are ever treated by doctors.

Reading
Social Studies

A. Identifying Problems What are the main problems the fellahin face?

Human-Environment Interaction • These fellahin raise sheep. ▼

Africa's Largest City

Life in Egyptian cities is different from life in rural areas. Cairo (KY·roh) is the capital of Egypt. The city's older inhabitants remember when the city had gardens, trees, and birds. Now those gardens have been paved over. The city is crowded and polluted, and the population continues to grow. Thousands of people leave Egypt's villages every year and come to Cairo looking for work. Instead, they find unemployment and overcrowding.

Reading
Social Studies

B. Analyzing Causes What is the main reason for Cairo's increase in population?

The total population of ancient Egypt was never more than four million people. Only about 5 percent of the population lived in cities. In 2000, the population of Cairo alone was more than 12 million. Cairo now has more people than any other African city.

Life in Cairo Cairo has both historic and modern sections. Many poor people live in the older sections. Some poor Cairenes live in cemeteries or on roofs. Others live in poorly built apartment buildings. Many have no steady work. Some are unskilled workers in factories. Others work in the city's small shops that sell jewelry and tourist souvenirs. Cairo's newer areas are along the west bank of the Nile. Most well-educated Cairenes live near the government buildings, foreign embassies, hotels, museums, and universities located there. They are doctors, lawyers, teachers, factory managers, and government officials.

The WORLD'S HERITAGE

The Pyramids and the Great Sphinx
The current residents of Cairo, Egypt, live in the shadows of some of the ancient world's most magnificent architecture—the pyramids and the Great Sphinx.

Egyptians built the pyramids as tombs for their kings more than 4,000 years ago. Near the pyramids, they also carved an enormous sphinx—a mythological creature with a lion's body and human head—out of natural rock. The head of the Great Sphinx is fashioned to look like King Khafre (c. 2575–c. 2465 B.C.).

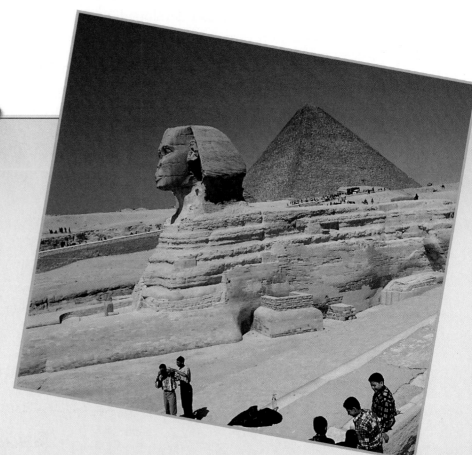

Place • Cairo is a huge city crowded with buildings, cars, and millions of people. ▶

Place • These girls live in Cairo within sight of the Sphinx and pyramids of ancient Egypt. ▼

The Region's Cultural Leader

Egypt has been the Arab world's cultural leader for over a century. It has led the region in education. In 1829, it opened the first modern school for girls in the Arab world. In the 1950s, it became the first Arab country to require that all children attend elementary school. It has also had a strong feminist movement for many years. Arabs throughout the region get much of their information and entertainment from Egyptian television, radio, movies, newspapers, and magazines.

SECTION 3 ASSESSMENT

Terms & Names

1. Identify:
   (a) King Farouk
   (b) Gamal Abdel Nasser
   (c) Aswan High Dam
   (d) tradeoff
   (e) Anwar Sadat
   (f) Muslim Brotherhood
   (g) fellahin

Taking Notes

2. Use a time line like this one to write the dates when control of Egypt changed hands.

639–642 |—|—|—|—|—|| 1952

Main Ideas

3. (a) What were Nasser's major achievements?

   (b) How have Egyptian women's rights improved over the last century?

   (c) What has Egypt done to improve the search for peace in the region?

Critical Thinking

4. **Evaluating Decisions**

   Do you think the building of the Aswan Dam was a worthwhile tradeoff?

   Think About

   ◆ its value to farmers
   ◆ the consequences of pollution

ACTIVITY -OPTION- Write a **letter** telling about daily life as a young person in Cairo or in a farming village along the Nile.

Thread by Thread

OVER THE PAST 60 YEARS, wars in Southwest Asia have left a bitter legacy of anger, frustration, and despair. Despite continuing conflicts, however, many people in the region share a hope for peace. The author of this poem, Bracha Serri, believes that one day peace will be achieved.

Thread by thread
knot by knot
like colonies of ants
we weave a bridge

Thread by thread
piece by piece
knitting embroidering
sewing decorating
thread by thread
we weave
the map of conciliation.[1]

1. Friendship.

Rachel's is white
Yemima's purple
Amal's is green
Salima's rose-colored
thread by thread
we stitch together
torn hearts
bind the map of conciliation.

I pray for the life of Ami and Nitsi
you pray for Ilan, Shoshi and Itsik
and she prays
for Jehan, Asheraf and Fahed
with the same tear.
Word and another word
prayer and another prayer
and our heart is one
we embroider in hope
with the sisterhood of workers
a map of love
to tear down the borders . . .

Reading
THE LITERATURE

What technique does the poet use to let the reader know that the "weavers" are people from different countries or ethnic backgrounds? Why is that important?

Thinking About
THE LITERATURE

Why do you think this poem is called "Thread by Thread"? What do the threads represent? Who are the weavers and what are they making?

Writing About
THE LITERATURE

Describe how you think the finished cloth would look. What size and shape would it be? What colors would it have in it? Where would it be placed or displayed?

About the Author

Bracha Serri, born in Yemen, grew up speaking Arabic. Later, her family moved to Israel. Serri has written, "I want my childhood spoken language, Arabic, to come together with my university education in linguistics. . . . I feel I have written my poems for women who do not have a voice, who can't speak up for themselves."

Further Reading *The Space Between Our Footsteps,* edited by Naomi Shihab Nye, contains poems by more than 100 poets and artists from 19 Southwest Asian countries.

Israel Today

TERMS & NAMES
Zionism
kibbutz
Law of Return
Orthodox Jews
Rosh Hashanah
Yom Kippur
secular

MAIN IDEA

Israel's current problems are rooted in a long and complicated history.

WHY IT MATTERS NOW

Peace in the region depends on peace between Israelis and Palestinians.

DATELINE

TEL AVIV, PALESTINE, JULY 14, 1921— Newcomers from America arrived here today after a long and difficult trip. All have been active in the movement to establish a Jewish homeland in Palestine. Goldie Mabovitch and her husband, Morris Myerson, born in Russia, hope to join a kibbutz. Riots in the port city of Jaffa delayed their arrival. Palestinian Arabs are protesting the immigration of Jews from America, Russia, and other countries who plan to settle in the land the Arabs consider their own.

Movement • Jewish immigrants from Europe arrive in Palestine. ▲

Movement • Goldie Mabovitch, who later adopted the Hebrew name Meir (to burn brightly) became prime minister of Israel in 1969. ▲

From Zionism to a Modern State

After A.D. 70, when the Romans destroyed the Temple in Jerusalem, Jews no longer had a country of their own. They lived scattered around the world, but still considered Palestine their homeland. **Zionism** was a Jewish movement that encouraged Jews to return to that homeland, which many called Zion. In the late 1800s, Jews began immigrating there and establishing colonies.

Reading
Social Studies

A. Analyzing Motives What were the Jewish immigrants' main reasons for forming kibbutzim?

Life on a Kibbutz Many new arrivals came from Eastern Europe, where Jews were often denied the right to be landowners. Seizing the chance to own land, even in the desert, the newcomers formed communities called kibbutzim. A **kibbutz** (kih·BUTS; *kibbutzim* is the plural) is a farming village whose members own everything in common. Members share labor, income, and expenses. The people of the kibbutzim saw themselves as brave, hard-working pioneers.

A VOICE FROM ISRAEL

The kibbutz would break new ground, literally; it would make the parched earth bloom and beat back the attacks of marauders who sought to destroy our pioneering lives.

David Ben Gurion

Kibbutzim Today About 270 kibbutzim still exist in Israel today. Some manufacture and sell products or welcome tourists. Others are still farming communities. Israel produces nearly all of its food. To improve the dry soil, Israelis practice drip irrigation. Tubes in the ground deliver the exact amount of water each plant needs.

The People of Israel

Israel was established in 1948 as a Jewish state. Judaism is the state religion. Hebrew is the official language. Of its six million inhabitants, over 80 percent are Jews. The Declaration of the Establishment promised that Israel would treat all its inhabitants equally. Some Israelis feel their country has not always lived up to that promise.

Place •
A modern kibbutz sprawls over a desert landscape. ▲

Palestinian Arabs About 20 percent of the people in Israel are Palestinian Arabs. These Arab Israelis carry Israeli passports and vote. Arab politicians serve in Israel's government. However, Arab Israelis do not live as well as Jewish Israelis. Most do not have equal rights and opportunities in jobs, job training, higher education, and housing. In 1996, Arabs were elected to 11 of the 120 seats in the Knesset, the Israeli parliament, the most they had ever won. In October 2000, the Israeli government announced that it planned to spend a billion dollars on schools, housing, and new jobs for Arab Israelis.

Some Palestinians are refugees from Israel who fled to the Gaza Strip and the West Bank after the 1948 Arab-Israeli War. (See the map on page 451.) Israel occupies these territories. Constant tension between Arabs and Israelis often leads to violence.

Women in Israel Even before Israel was a state, its women were encouraged to work outside the home. To free mothers from child-care duties, children on kibbutzim lived and slept in separate children's houses and visited their parents during evenings and weekends. An American-educated woman, Golda Meir (MY·uhr), was the prime minister of Israel from 1969 to 1974.

Culture • Israeli women must serve in the military for two years; men must serve for three. ▲

The Law of Return

Since 1948, Israel has taken in nearly 3 million Jewish immigrants. The 1950 **Law of Return** states that Jews anywhere in the world can immigrate to Israel and become citizens.

Recent Immigrants In 1987, the USSR finally allowed Jews within its borders to emigrate. Within three years, 300,000 arrived in Israel. Many were skilled engineers and technicians. Because of their numbers, however, they had a hard time finding jobs and good housing.

In the 1980s, Israel began a policy of airlifting groups of Jews from countries such as Yemen, Albania, and Ethiopia and bringing them into Israel. Ethiopia's 38,000 Jews were airlifted between 1984 and 1999. These people had been so isolated they had thought they were the only Jews left in the world.

Reading
Social Studies

B. Making Inferences Why might Jews in other countries want to emigrate to Israel?

Connections to Citizenship

B'Tselem Many Israelis are concerned about abuses of power by their own government. That was why the Israeli Center for Human Rights in the Occupied Territories, or B'Tselem, was founded in 1989. B'Tselem documents and reports human rights violations against the mostly Palestinian residents of Gaza and the West Bank. Such violations include housing discrimination, torture, killing, and the taking of land by Israeli security forces. B'Tselem believes that educating the public about these abuses is the best way to bring about change in Israeli policy in the Occupied Territories.

Many had never used electricity or running water. Although poorly educated, they had useful skills such as blacksmithing, weaving, and pottery making that helped them fit into Israeli society.

Religion in Israel Today

Only about one in four of Israel's Jews strictly follows Jewish law. They are called **Orthodox Jews.** These Jews believe that Jewish law should help form government policy. Orthodox rabbis have official control over marriage, divorce, and burial. They also limit what Israeli Jews can do on the Sabbath and holidays. **Rosh Hashanah** (RAWSH huh·SHAW·nuh) is the Jewish New Year. **Yom Kippur** (YAWM KIHP·uhr) is the Day of Atonement, a day for fasting and reflecting on one's sins. It is the holiest day in the Jewish year. No government employee can work on these Jewish High Holy Days. No newspapers appear on either holiday. Most of Israel's Jews are **secular,** meaning that religious practices play a less important role in their lives. They are more interested in living a modern way of life. Many resent Orthodox control of daily life.

Movement • Jewish children from Ethiopia make a new home in Israel. ▲

SECTION 4 ASSESSMENT

Terms & Names

1. Identify:
(a) Zionism
(b) kibbutz
(c) Law of Return
(d) Orthodox Jews
(e) Rosh Hashanah
(f) Yom Kippur
(g) secular

Taking Notes

2. Use a cause-and-effect chart like this one to write the reasons for Jewish immigration to Palestine.

Causes [ ] [ ] [ ]
           ↓   ↓   ↓
Effect | Jewish immigration to Palestine |

Main Ideas

3. (a) Why did early Jewish settlers in Israel establish kibbutzim?

(b) Why have Russian Jews faced problems fitting in to Israeli society?

(c) What are the major differences between Orthodox and secular Jews?

Critical Thinking

4. Forming and Supporting Opinions

How well do you think Israel has lived up to its promise to treat all its inhabitants equally?

Think About

• the treatment of Palestinian Arabs

• the treatment of women

• the treatment of immigrants

ACTIVITY -OPTION- Write an **interview** you might have with a new immigrant to Israel. Include information on where the immigrant comes from, the date and method of arrival, reasons for coming, and reactions to a new land.

Linking Past and Present

The Legacy of North Africa and Southwest Asia

Religion

Three major religions—Judaism, Christianity, and Islam—began in Southwest Asia. Judaism is based on the laws Moses received from God, which are written in the Torah. Christianity is based on the teachings of Jesus, which appear in the New Testament. Islam is based on the teachings of the prophet Muhammad and the sacred text called the Qur'an. The teachings and beliefs of Judaism, Christianity, and Islam spread east and south through Asia, north and west to Europe, south through Africa, and west to the Americas. All three religions share a belief in one God and encourage people to live a life of tolerance and peace.

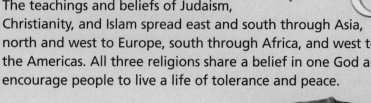

Cosmetics

Archaeologists believe that cosmetics were used as early as 4000 B.C. Ancient Egyptians used plants and powdered minerals to make cosmetics. During and after the Renaissance, the use of cosmetics flourished in Europe, as both men and women made up their faces. Italy and France became cosmetic-manufacturing centers. By the 1900s, people of all social classes were using cosmetics. Since the 1930s, the cosmetic industry has developed into a big business.

Writing

About 5,500 years ago, Mesopotamians began to use what is considered the first developed system of writing. They made marks that represented words on wet clay tablets, some of which survive today. Two thousand years later, the Egyptians developed a sophisticated writing system, known as hieroglyphics, in which pictures were used to represent sounds and words. Today, people continue to communicate, not only by writing with pen and paper but also by using electronic mail.

Banking

Almost 5,500 years ago, before the invention of coins or paper money, a form of banking existed in ancient Mesopotamia. In Italy in the 1200s, banking took place on benches in the street. In fact, the word *bank* comes from the Italian word *banco,* which means "bench." By the 1600s, customers of banks in England were using written drafts, or checks, to make payments. Modern banking is electronic. Though some people use written checks, many take advantage of automated teller machines and telephone-banking systems to meet their banking needs.

Find Out More About It!

Study the text and photos on these pages to learn about inventions, creations, and contributions that have come from North Africa and Southwest Asia. Then choose the item that interests you the most and, in a short essay, describe how your life would be different if it did not exist.

RESEARCH LINKS
CLASSZONE.COM

Lever

A lever is a rod or bar that pivots on a fulcrum, acting like a seesaw to help people perform work. Early people used levers to move and lift heavy rocks. In 1500 B.C., Egyptians used the shadoof—a lever with weights on one end and a bucket on the other—to lift water from rivers and canals into their fields. They also developed a balance scale based on the lever. Balance scales and wheelbarrows are examples of levers we use today.

Forks

Though the ancient Greeks first used kitchen forks for carving and serving meat, it was not until the 800s that nobles in Southwest Asia used forks for dining. For the next 900 years, wealthy people continued to use forks for eating. Because the common people believed forks were unnecessary and even odd, they continued to use their hands, knives, and spoons for eating. Forks were not commonly used in the West until the 1800s.

Turkey Today

MAIN IDEA

Turkey's culture blends modern European and traditional Islamic ways.

WHY IT MATTERS NOW

Turkey is an important military ally and trade partner of the United States and Europe.

DATELINE

ANKARA, TURKEY, NOVEMBER 25, 1925—No more fez. Turkish leader Mustafa Kemal has declared that Turkish men are no longer allowed to wear the fez, their traditional head covering.

According to the new Hat Law, hats are now the acceptable head covering for men. Muslim women are being strongly encouraged to give up the veil. These changes are in keeping with Kemal's drive to westernize Turkey. Many Turks are happy to see Turkey become more like Europe. Others are unhappy with this move away from the traditional Islamic way of life.

Culture • Turkish men are getting used to wearing hats. ▲

Culture • The fez will become a thing of the past. ▲

Between Two Worlds

If you look at Turkey on the map on page 479, you will see that it is joined to Southwest Asia on the east and to Europe on the west. The question after World War I was: Would Turkey be like its Islamic neighbors and hold on to its traditions, or would it become more like the West? Its powerful new ruler, **Mustafa Kemal** (kuh·MAHL), believed in westernization, by force if necessary.

A Powerful Ruler

Mustafa Kemal was the founder of modern Turkey. He had been a Turkish officer and war hero for the Ottoman forces during World War I. The Ottomans had continued to rule Turkey even after the empire became weak. Turkey fought on the losing side during the war, which weakened it even more. In 1920, Great Britain occupied Turkey.

Mustafa Kemal Becomes Atatürk Kemal opposed Britain's action. He organized Turkey's first **Grand National Assembly,** or legislature. The assembly elected Kemal president. At his suggestion, the assembly officially adopted the name Turkey, the land of the Turkish people. In 1923, Kemal declared Turkey a republic and got rid of the old Islamic government the following year.

While Kemal was in the Ottoman army, he spent time in European cities. He admired the way of life he saw there. He believed adopting modern, "Western" ways and ideas would benefit Turkey. Over the next nine years, Kemal introduced his changes. The Western alphabet replaced the Arabic alphabet. The Western calendar replaced the Islamic calendar.

Before 1934, many Turks used only first names. In 1934, a new law required the use of last names. The National Assembly gave Kemal the name **Atatürk,** which means "Father of Turks."

Reading
Social Studies

Forming and Supporting Opinions Which of Mustafa Kemal's changes do you think had the greatest effect on Turkish life?

Changes Brought by Modernization

For nearly 1,000 years, Islamic law had shaped Turkish life. Atatürk, however, believed in secular government. He closed all institutions that had been founded on Islamic law. He replaced religious schools with secular schools. Since people were used to having Islam play a major role in all aspects of their lives, many protested Atatürk's reforms.

Women in Turkey Turkish women benefited from Atatürk's reforms. He made it easier for women to divorce their husbands. Marriages could no longer be arranged by a woman's parents unless she agreed. Men were no longer able to have more than one wife at the same time.

Women could now also vote and run for office. In the mid-1930s, women were elected to the national parliament. The world's first woman supreme court justice was a Turk. For several years during the 1990s, a woman named **Tansu Ciller** was Turkey's prime minister.

Rights and Freedoms Today

Turkey adopted its most recent constitution in 1982. The Turkish Constitution promises freedom of religion, freedom of speech, freedom of the press, and other rights. The government, however, does not always live up to these promises. It sometimes limits freedoms. Turkish journalists can be arrested for writing articles against the government. The government also bans some publications.

The Kurds The Kurds are a group of people who live in the mountainous regions of southeastern Turkey, Iraq, Iran, and Syria. They have been fighting for their own state since 1984. The Turkish government has made suspected Kurd fighters leave their homes. It limits the right to teach Kurdish in schools. It also limits the use of Kurdish in television and radio programs.

International Alliances

Turkey and the United States are both members of the North Atlantic Treaty Organization (NATO). This alliance was formed in 1949 to keep the Soviet Union and its allies from attacking non-Communist countries in Western Europe. Turkey joined the alliance in 1952. When the Soviet Union fell apart in 1991, some NATO members felt the alliance was no longer necessary. Turkey disagreed because NATO membership helps protect its borders. Membership also gives Turkey a say in major decisions other members make.

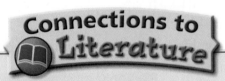

Connections to Literature

Looking for Troy Two of the world's best-known epic poems tell about a long-ago war in the eastern Mediterranean. In the *Iliad,* Greeks besiege the city of Troy. Greek soldiers hide inside a giant wooden horse to trick the Trojans into opening the gates of the city. The photo at right shows a model of the Trojan Horse. In the *Odyssey,* the hero, Odysseus, has many adventures on his way home from the same war. Both poems may have been composed by the Greek poet Homer sometime around 800 B.C.

While many people thought the Trojan War was just a legend, Heinrich Schliemann, a German archaeologist, dreamed of finding the real Troy. In the 1870s, he began to dig at a site in northwestern Turkey. He found ruins of palaces and golden artifacts. In fact, Schliemann had found Troy—but not the city of the poems. Over centuries, people had built new cities on the ruins of older ones. Archaeologists think that the seventh city down on the site is the Troy of the *Iliad.* It was destroyed about 1250 B.C.

Joining the European Union Most of Turkey's trade is with Western Europe. In 1987, Turkey applied to join the European Union (EU). The EU was reluctant to accept Turkey, partly because of the size of its population. There are not enough jobs in Turkey for all the people who want them. Two million Turks have gone to Germany to work. Millions more work in other European countries. Workers from EU countries are allowed to move freely within the region. European countries worried that membership in the EU would let more Turkish workers into their countries than they could handle.

Region •
The city of Istanbul is partly in Europe and partly in Asia. ▲

SECTION 5 ASSESSMENT

Terms & Names

1. **Identify:**
   (a) Mustafa Kemal
   (b) Grand National Assembly
   (c) Atatürk
   (d) Tansu Ciller

Taking Notes

2. Use a chart like this one to list changes made by Mustafa Kemal.

Old Ways	New Ways
1.	
2.	
3.	
4.	
5.	

Main Ideas

3. (a) How does Turkey limit the rights of the Kurds?

   (b) How did Atatürk's reforms benefit women?

   (c) Why does Turkey value its membership in NATO?

Critical Thinking

4. **Analyzing Issues**

   How does the issue of unemployment affect Turkey's chances of joining the European Union?

   Think About
   • Turkey's population
   • jobs in Europe

ACTIVITY -OPTION- Write a **dialogue** between two Turks, one who welcomes Mustafa Kemal's changes and one who opposes them.

TERMS & NAMES

Explain the significance of each of the following:

1. Arab-Israeli Wars
2. OPEC
3. primary product
4. Aswan High Dam
5. Anwar Sadat
6. Zionism
7. kibbutz
8. Yom Kippur
9. Mustafa Kemal
10. Tansu Ciller

REVIEW QUESTIONS

A Troubled Century *(pages 449–453)*

1. What was the United Nations solution to the conflicting claims of Arabs and Zionists to Palestine?

Resources and Religion *(pages 455–459)*

2. Why is oil the most important resource in the region?
3. How does Islam influence the culture of the region?

Egypt Today *(pages 462–467)*

4. Why did France and Britain build the Suez Canal?
5. What are the main benefits and drawbacks of the Aswan Dam?
6. How is life in Egypt's rural areas different from life in Cairo?

Israel Today *(pages 470–473)*

7. Why do Jews and Arabs come into conflict in Israel?
8. Why has immigration caused problems in Israel today?

Turkey Today *(pages 476–479)*

9. What changes did Mustafa Kemal make in Turkey?
10. Why has Turkey had difficulty joining the European Union?

CRITICAL THINKING

Identifying Problems

1. Using your completed chart from Reading Social Studies, p. 448, list times when the solution to a problem in the region caused a new problem.

Analyzing Motives

2. Why have Muslim fundamentalists and others objected to westernization?

Comparing

3. Compare the progress of women's rights in modern-day Turkey to those of women in modern-day Saudi Arabia.

Visual Summary

1 A Troubled Century

- The conflicts of the past have contributed to problems today in North Africa and Southwest Asia.

2 Resources and Religion

- Oil and Islam are major factors in the region's economy and culture.

Egypt Today 3

- Modernization has brought both benefits and problems to Egypt.

4

Israel Today

- Conflict continues because both Jews and Arabs claim the land of Israel.

5 Turkey Today

- Modern Turkey is the result of Mustafa Kemal's forcible westernization of a traditional Islamic culture.

SKILLBUILDER: Reading a Historical Map

1. What color represents the Iraqi invasion of Kuwait?
2. How are the boundaries of present-day borders shown?
3. Write a brief summary of the information in the map.

FOCUS ON GEOGRAPHY

1. **Location** • Where are most of the crude oil reserves in the region located?
2. **Region** • Name two countries with very little of this resource.
3. **Region** • How might this difference in oil reserves cause problems in the region?

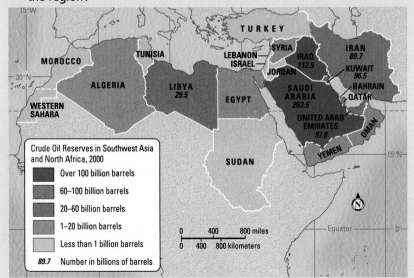

CHAPTER PROJECTS

Interdisciplinary Activity: Language Arts

Writing a Speech Imagine that you are a member of the United Nations involved in a debate about peace in Palestine. Write a short speech urging peace between the Israelis and the Palestinians. Review the history of the conflict and mention the rights of both sides. Suggest steps that the parties can take to achieve peace.

Cooperative Learning Activity

Make a Presentation In pairs, present information to the class about religious celebrations that involve fasting. Choose one celebration, such as Ramadan, Lent, or Yom Kippur, and research the celebration.

• Write a paragraph that explains the celebration.
• Arrange illustrations on a piece of poster board or an overhead projector.
• Present your information to the class.

INTERNET ACTIVITY

Use the Internet to research one major city—Cairo, Istanbul, or Tel Aviv. Find out what a tourist would need to know before a visit. What language is spoken? What will the climate be? What historic sites would a tourist want to see?

Writing a Tourist Brochure Create a tourist brochure of your findings. Include a map or illustrations of the sites a tourist would expect to see. Include important information a tourist would need. List the Web sites you used to prepare your report.

For Internet links to support this activity, go to

RESEARCH LINKS
CLASSZONE.COM

UNIT 6

Place Elephants are one of many kinds of animals that inhabit the 5,700-square-mile Serengeti National Park in Tanzania, Africa. The Serengeti Plain is the last place in Africa where vast land-animal migrations take place.

AFRICA SOUTH OF THE SAHARA

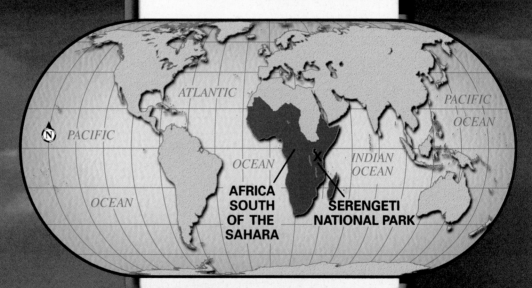

ATLANTIC

PACIFIC

PACIFIC

OCEAN

OCEAN

INDIAN
OCEAN

OCEAN

OCEAN

**AFRICA
SOUTH
OF THE
SAHARA**

**SERENGETI
NATIONAL PARK**

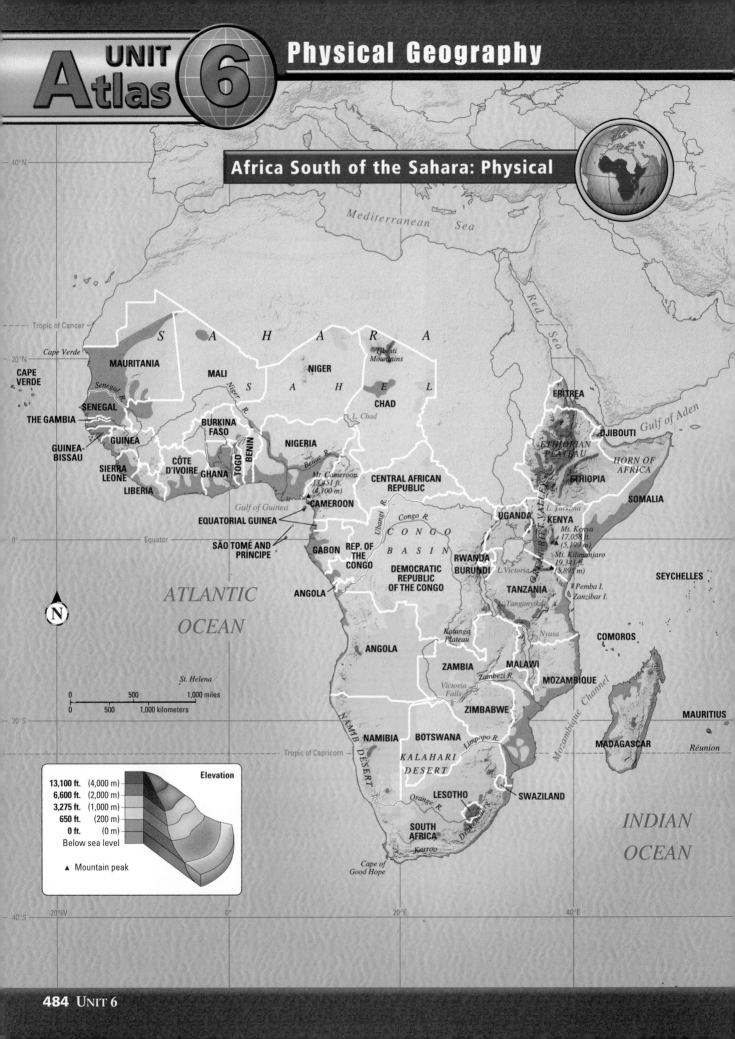

Africa South of the Sahara: Physical

Mediterranean Sea

40°N

Tropic of Cancer

Cape Verde

20°N

CAPE VERDE

MAURITANIA

MALI

NIGER

Tibesti Mountains

CHAD

L. Chad

ERITREA

Red Sea

DJIBOUTI

Gulf of Aden

Senegal R.

SENEGAL

THE GAMBIA

GUINEA-BISSAU

GUINEA

SIERRA LEONE

BURKINA FASO

Niger R.

S A H E L

NIGERIA

Benue R.

ETHIOPIAN PLATEAU

ETHIOPIA

HORN OF AFRICA

CÔTE D'IVOIRE

GHANA

TOGO

BENIN

LIBERIA

Mt. Cameroon 13,451 ft. (4,100 m)

CAMEROON

CENTRAL AFRICAN REPUBLIC

SOMALIA

Gulf of Guinea

EQUATORIAL GUINEA

SÃO TOMÉ AND PRÍNCIPE

Ubangi R.

Congo R.

C O N G O

B A S I N

UGANDA

L. Turkana

KENYA

Mt. Kenya 17,058 ft. (5,199 m)

Equator

0°

GABON

REP. OF THE CONGO

DEMOCRATIC REPUBLIC OF THE CONGO

RWANDA

BURUNDI

L. Victoria

Mt. Kilimanjaro 19,341 ft. (5,895 m)

SEYCHELLES

ANGOLA

TANZANIA

Pemba I.

Zanzibar I.

L. Tanganyika

ATLANTIC OCEAN

Katanga Plateau

Nyasa

COMOROS

ANGOLA

ZAMBIA

MALAWI

MOZAMBIQUE

St. Helena

Zambezi R.

Victoria Falls

ZIMBABWE

Mozambique Channel

MAURITIUS

0   500   1,000 miles
0   500   1,000 kilometers

20°S

Tropic of Capricorn

NAMIBIA

BOTSWANA

Limpopo R.

MADAGASCAR

Réunion

KALAHARI DESERT

INDIAN OCEAN

Elevation

13,100 ft.	(4,000 m)
6,600 ft.	(2,000 m)
3,275 ft.	(1,000 m)
650 ft.	(200 m)
0 ft.	(0 m)

Below sea level

▲ Mountain peak

LESOTHO

Orange R.

SWAZILAND

Drakensberg

SOUTH AFRICA

Karroo

Cape of Good Hope

40°S

20°W

0°

20°E

40°E

Resources of Africa South of the Sahara

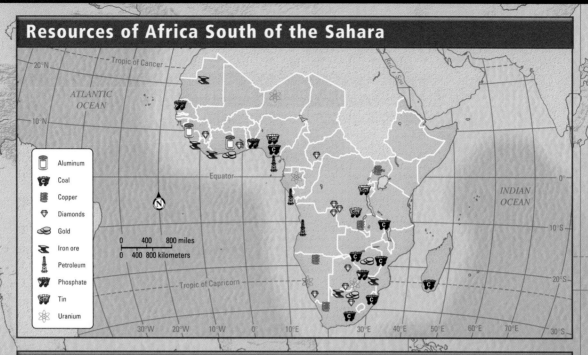

Legend:
- Aluminum
- Coal
- Copper
- Diamonds
- Gold
- Iron ore
- Petroleum
- Phosphate
- Tin
- Uranium

0 400 800 miles
0 400 800 kilometers

Africa South of the Sahara–U.S. Landmass and Population

Africa South of the Sahara

United States

LANDMASS

Africa South of the Sahara
8,389,419 square miles

Continental United States
3,165,630 square miles

POPULATION

Africa South of the Sahara
625,535,088

United States
281,421,906

 = 50,000,000

FAST FACTS

COUNTRY WITH LEAST RAINFALL:
Namibia, with 10.63 in. per yr.

MOST DIAMONDS:
Africa produces about 50 percent of the world's diamonds.

GOLD RESERVES:
South Africa produces 495 tons of gold per year—about 30 percent of the world's total—and accounts for more than half of the world's known reserves.

GEOGRAPHY SKILLBUILDER: Interpreting Maps and Visuals

1. **Place** • Which country has the greatest number of mineral resources?
2. **Region** • Find Lesotho on the map on page 484. What are some issues that might arise due to its location?

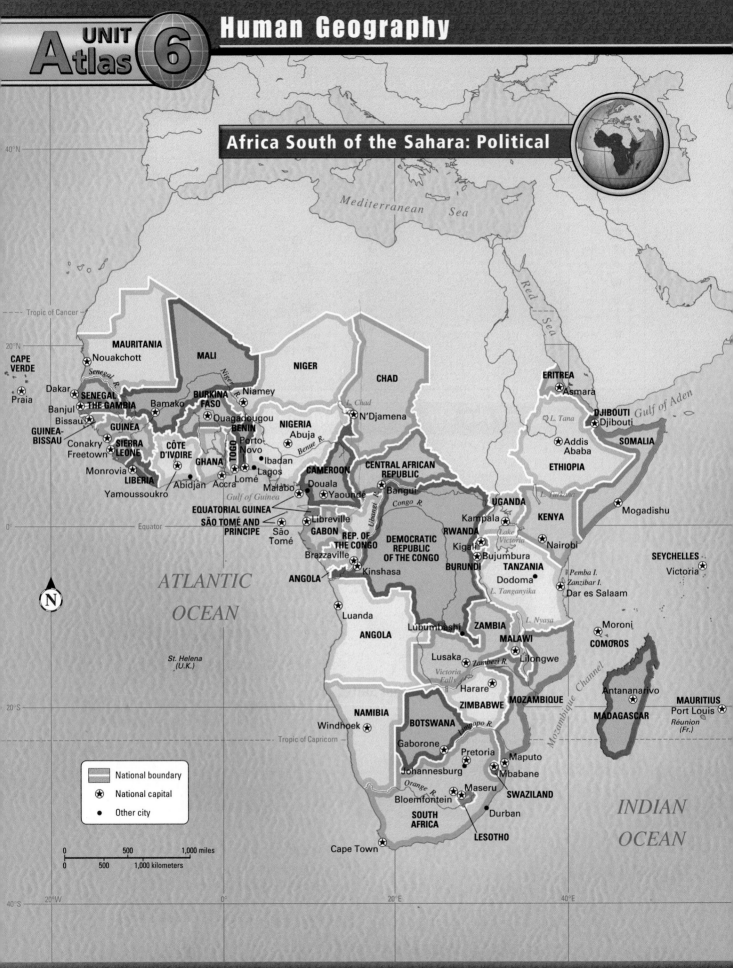

Africa South of the Sahara: Political

Mediterranean Sea

MAURITANIA
• Nouakchott

CAPE VERDE
• Praia

Dakar •
SENEGAL
THE GAMBIA
Banjul •
Bissau •
GUINEA-BISSAU
Conakry •
Freetown •
SIERRA LEONE
Monrovia •
LIBERIA
Yamoussoukro •

MALI

Senegal R.

Bamako •
BURKINA FASO
Ouagadougou •
CÔTE D'IVOIRE
GHANA
Abidjan • Accra •

NIGER
Niamey •
BENIN
TOGO
Lomé •
Porto-Novo •
Ibadan •
Lagos •

NIGERIA
Abuja •
Benue R.

CHAD
N'Djamena •
L. Chad

CAMEROON
Douala •
Yaoundé •
Malabo •
EQUATORIAL GUINEA
SÃO TOMÉ AND PRINCIPE
São Tomé •
GABON
Libreville •

CENTRAL AFRICAN REPUBLIC
Bangui •
Ubangi R.
Congo R.

ERITREA
Asmara •
L. Tana

DJIBOUTI
Djibouti •
Addis Ababa •
ETHIOPIA

SOMALIA

Gulf of Aden

Red Sea

UGANDA
Kampala •
RWANDA
Kigali •
BURUNDI
Bujumbura •
Lake Victoria
L. Turkana

KENYA
Nairobi •
Mogadishu •

REP. OF THE CONGO
Brazzaville •
Kinshasa •
DEMOCRATIC REPUBLIC OF THE CONGO

TANZANIA
Dodoma •
Dar es Salaam •
Zanzibar I.
Pemba I.
L. Tanganyika

SEYCHELLES
Victoria •

ANGOLA
Luanda •

Lubumbashi •

ZAMBIA
Lusaka •
Zambezi R.
Victoria Falls
L. Nyasa

MALAWI
Lilongwe •

COMOROS
Moroni •

ATLANTIC OCEAN

St. Helena (U.K.)

ANGOLA

ZIMBABWE
Harare •

MOZAMBIQUE

Mozambique Channel

NAMIBIA
Windhoek •

BOTSWANA
Gaborone •

Limpopo R.

MADAGASCAR
Antananarivo •

MAURITIUS
Port Louis •
Réunion (Fr.)

Pretoria •
Johannesburg •
Orange R.
Bloemfontein •
Maseru •
LESOTHO
SOUTH AFRICA
Maputo •
Mbabane •
SWAZILAND
Durban •

INDIAN OCEAN

Cape Town •

Gulf of Guinea

Equator

Tropic of Cancer

Tropic of Capricorn

20°N

0°

20°S

40°S

20°W   0°   20°E   40°E

N

Legend:
- National boundary
- ⊛ National capital
- • Other city

0   500   1,000 miles
0   500   1,000 kilometers

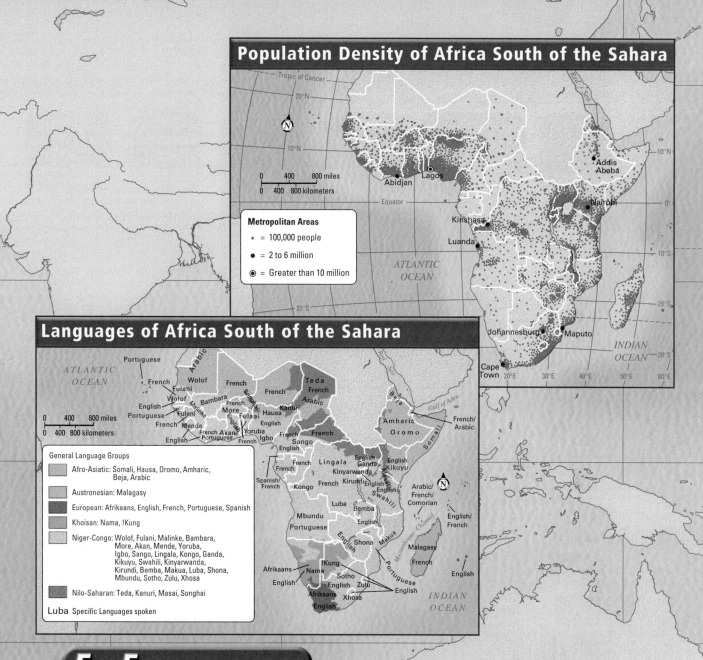

Population Density of Africa South of the Sahara

Tropic of Cancer

20°N

10°N

10°N

400   800 miles

400   800 kilometers

Abidjan Lagos

Addis Ababa

Equator

Nairobi

Kinshasa

0°

Luanda

Metropolitan Areas

• = 100,000 people

● = 2 to 6 million

◎ = Greater than 10 million

10°S

ATLANTIC
OCEAN

20°S

Johannesburg Maputo

INDIAN
OCEAN

30°S

Cape Town 20°E   30°E   40°E   50°E   60°E

Languages of Africa South of the Sahara

Portuguese

Arabic

ATLANTIC
OCEAN

French Wolof French

Teda
French

Fulani

Wolof

Arabic

Bambara French

English Malinke More Kanuri

Portuguese Fulani Hausa Beja

French Mende Fulani English

0   400   800 miles

0 400 800 kilometers

French Akan Yoruba Amharic

English Portuguese Igbo French Oromo

French/Arabic

Gulf of Aden

Sango

English French

Somali

General Language Groups

Afro-Asiatic: Somali, Hausa, Oromo, Amharic, Beja, Arabic

French Lingala English English

Ganda English

Spanish/French Kongo French Kinyarwanda Kikuyu

Arabic/French/Comorian

Kirundi English

Austronesian: Malagasy

Luba Swahili

European: Afrikaans, English, French, Portuguese, Spanish

Bemba English/French

Khoisan: Nama, !Kung

Mbundu English

Niger-Congo: Wolof, Fulani, Malinke, Bambara, More, Akan, Mende, Yoruba, Igbo, Sango, Lingala, Kongo, Ganda, Kikuyu, Swahili, Kinyarwanda, Kirundi, Bemba, Makua, Luba, Shona, Mbundu, Sotho, Zulu, Xhosa

Portuguese Makua

Malagasy

Shona French

English/French

Nilo-Saharan: Teda, Kanuri, Masai, Songhai

Afrikaans Nama Kung English

Luba Specific Languages spoken

English Sotho

English Zulu English

Afrikaans Xhosa

INDIAN
OCEAN

English

FAST FACTS

✔ **LARGEST FAMILY OF LANGUAGES:**
Niger-Congo language family, with 890 known member languages

✔ **FEWEST PHONES:**
Africa has less than 2 percent of the world's telephone lines. Most Africans have to travel two hours to find a phone. Eighty percent of Africa's population has never placed a phone call. More people use the Internet in London than in all of Africa.

✔ **MOST SPARSELY POPULATED:**
After Mongolia, Namibia is the most sparsely populated country in the world, with 5.7 people per square mile.

GEOGRAPHY SKILLBUILDER: Interpreting Maps and Visuals

1. **Movement** • In which two countries is Afrikaans spoken?
2. **Place** • Name two countries that have low population densities.

Country Flag	Country/Capital	Currency	Population (2001 estimate)	Life Expectancy (years)	Birthrate (per 1,000 pop.) (2000)
	Angola Luanda	Readjusted Kwanza	10,366,000	47	48
	Benin Porto-Novo	CFA Franc	6,591,000	50	45
	Botswana Gaborone	Pula	1,586,000	44	32
	Burkina Faso Ouagadougou	CFA Franc	12,272,000	47	47
	Burundi Bujumbura	Franc	6,224,000	47	42
	Cameroon Yaoundé	CFA Franc	15,803,000	55	37
	Cape Verde Praia	Escudo	405,000	68	37
	Central African Republic Bangui	CFA Franc	3,577,000	45	38
	Chad N'Djamena	CFA Franc	8,707,000	48	50
	Comoros Moroni	Franc	596,000	59	38
	Congo, Democratic Republic of the Kinshasa	Congolese Franc	53,625,000	49	48
	Congo, Republic of the Brazzaville	CFA Franc	2,894,000	48	40
	Côte d'Ivoire Yamoussoukro	CFA Franc	16,393,000	47	38
	Djibouti Djibouti	Djibouti Franc	461,000	48	39
	Equatorial Guinea Malabo	CFA Franc	486,000	50	41
	Eritrea Asmara	Birr	4,298,000	55	43
	Ethiopia Addis Ababa	Birr	65,892,000	46	45

DATA FILE

Infant Mortality (per 1,000 live births) (2000)	Doctors (per 100,000 pop.) (1997–1998)	Literacy Rate (percentage) (1996–1998)	Passenger Cars (per 1,000 pop.) (1991–1998)	Total Area (square miles)	Map (not to scale)
125.0	8	42	21	481,351	
93.9	6	38	6	43,483	
57.2	24	76	53	231,804	
105.3	3	22	3	105,869	
74.8	6	46	2	10,759	
77.0	7	74	7	183,591	
76.9	17	73	29	1,557	
96.7	4	44	3	240,534	
109.8	3	39	1	459,752	
77.3	7	59	18	719	
108.6	7	59	7	905,365	
108.6	25	78	10	132,047	
112.2	9	45	11	124,503	
115.0	14	62	31	8,958	
108.0	25	81	9	10,830	
81.8	3	52	2	10,830	
116.0	4	36	0.8	471,776	

Country Flag	Country/Capital	Currency	Population (2001 estimate)	Life Expectancy (years)	Birthrate (per 1,000 pop.) (2000)
	**Gabon** Libreville	CFA Franc	1,221,000	52	38
	**Gambia, The** Banjul	Dalasi	1,411,000	45	43
	**Ghana** Accra	Cedi	19,894,000	58	34
	**Guinea** Conakry	Franc	7,614,000	45	42
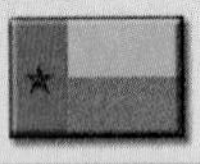	**Guinea-Bissau** Bissau	CFA Franc	1,316,000	45	42
	**Kenya** Nairobi	Shilling	30,766,000	49	35
	**Lesotho** Maseru	Maloti	2,177,000	53	33
	**Liberia** Monrovia	Dollar	3,226,000	50	50
	Madagascar Antananarivo	Malagasy Franc	15,983,000	52	44
	**Malawi** Lilongwe	Kwacha	10,548,000	39	41
	**Mali** Bamako	CFA Franc	11,009,000	53	47
	**Mauritania** Nouakchott	Ouguiya	2,747,000	54	41
	**Mauritius** Port Louis	Rupee	1,190,000	70	17
	**Mozambique** Maputo	Metical	19,371,000	40	41
	**Namibia** Windhoek	Rand	1,798,000	46	36
	**Niger** Niamey	CFA Franc	10,355,000	41	54
	**Nigeria** Abuja	Naira	126,636,000	52	42

DATA FILE

Infant Mortality (per 1,000 live births) (2000)	Doctors (per 100,000 pop.) (1997–1998)	Literacy Rate (percentage) (1996–1998)	Passenger Cars (per 1,000 pop.) (1991–1998)	Total Area (square miles)	Map (not to scale)
87.0	19	63	21	103,346	
130.0	4	35	7	4,127	
56.2	6	69	5	92,100	
98.0	13	36	2	94,925	
130.0	17	37	3	13,948	
73.7	13	81	10	224,960	
84.5	5	82	3	11,720	
139.1	2	38	9	43,000	
96.3	11	65	4	226,658	
126.8	2	58	3	47,747	
122.5	5	38	3	478,764	
92.0	14	41	7	397,955	
19.4	85	84	61	790	
133.9	4	42	4	302,328	
68.3	30	81	38	318,000	
123.1	4	15	4	489,189	
77.2	19	61	5	356,669	

Country Flag	Country/Capital	Currency	Population (2001 estimate)	Life Expectancy (years)	Birthrate (per 1,000 pop.) (2000)
 R	**Rwanda** Kigali	Franc	7,313,000	39	43
 ★★	**São Tomé and Príncipe** São Tomé	Dobra	165,000	64	43
 ★	**Senegal** Dakar	CFA Franc	10,285,000	52	41
	**Seychelles** Victoria	Rupee	80,000	71	18
	Sierra Leone Freetown	Leone	5,427,000	45	47
 ★	**Somalia** Mogadishu	Shilling	7,489,000	46	47
	**South Africa,** Pretoria/Cape Town/Bloemfontein	Rand	43,586,000	55	25
	**Swaziland** Mbabane	Lilangeni	1,104,000	38	41
	**Tanzania** Dar es Salaam	Shilling	36,232,000	53	42
 ★	**Togo** Lomé	CFA Franc	5,153,000	49	42
	**Uganda** Kampala	Shilling	23,986,000	42	48
	**Zambia** Lusaka	Kwacha	9,770,000	37	42
	**Zimbabwe** Harare	Dollar	11,365,000	40	30
	**United States** Washington, D.C.	Dollar	281,422,000	77	15

DATA FILE

Infant Mortality (per 1,000 live births) (2000)	Doctors (per 100,000 pop.) (1997–1998)	Literacy Rate (percentage) (1996–1998)	Passenger Cars (per 1,000 pop.) (1991–1998)	Total Area (square miles)	Map (not to scale)
120.9	4	64	2	10,169	
50.8	47	73	30	372	
67.7	8	36	12	76,124	
8.5	132	84	85	178	
157.1	7	31	4	27,699	
125.8	4	24	2	246,200	
45.4	56	85	102	471,445	
107.7	15	78	29	6,705	
98.8	5	74	2	364,898	
79.7	8	55	17	21,853	
81.3	4	65	1	91,134	
109.0	7	76	16	290,585	
80.0	14	87	3	150,820	
7.0	251	97	489	3,787,319	

GEOGRAPHY SKILLBUILDER: Interpreting a Chart

1. **Place** • How many more doctors per 100,000 people does Cape Verde have than Burkina Faso?
2. **Place** • How much higher is Lesotho's literacy rate than Guinea's?

CHAPTER 17

Africa South of the Sahara: Geography and History

ATLANTIC

PACIFIC

PACIFIC

OCEAN

OCEAN

OCEAN

INDIAN
OCEAN

OCEAN

**AFRICA SOUTH
OF THE SAHARA**

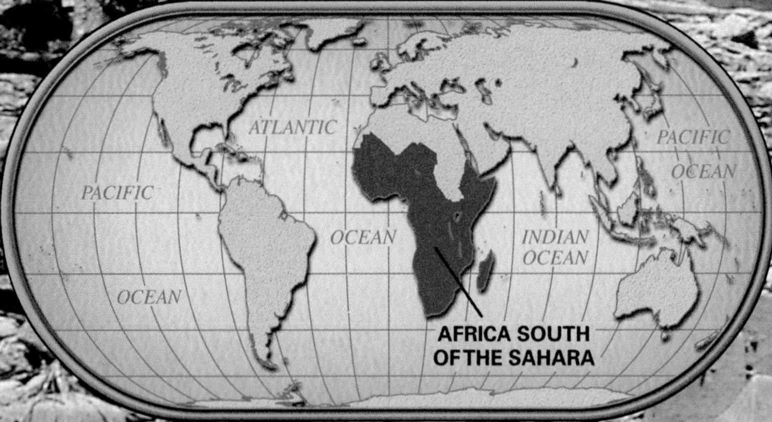

Who owns a country?

Place • This 1892 drawing of a British imperialist illustrates the United Kingdom's claim on Africa. In the late 1800s, many European nations wanted to control a piece of the continent. By the early 1900s, all but two African nations were colonized by European powers. What did Africans think about this? Who owned Africa: the Africans or the European colonizers?

What do you think?

♦ Why do you think the artist drew the British man with his feet planted on Egypt and South Africa?

♦ What are the benefits and disadvantages of being a colony?

Place Most Africans live in villages, not in cities. The cliffside dwellings of the Tellem tribe are built above a Banani village in Mali.

495

READING SOCIAL STUDIES

BEFORE YOU READ

▶▶ *What Do You Know?*

Africa south of the Sahara is a land rich in natural resources. Despite this, many countries in this part of Africa do not have strong economies. What do you know of Africa's early history? How did Europeans affect the development of this region? Reflect on what you have learned in other classes, what you have read, and what you have seen in movies or on television about the countries in Africa south of the Sahara.

▶▶ *What Do You Want to Know?*

Decide what you know about Africa south of the Sahara. In your notebook, record what you hope to learn from this chapter.

Place • **Baule gold masks sometimes represent the face of an enemy killed in battle.** ▲

READ AND TAKE NOTES

Reading Strategy: Analyzing Causes and Effects
As you read about history, it is important to understand not only historical events, but also why the events happened (causes) and what resulted from the events (effects). Use the chart below to record the causes and effects of processes that shaped the history of Africa south of the Sahara.

- Copy the chart into your notebook.
- As you read, look for information about the geographic and human processes listed on the chart.
- Record the causes and effects of each process.

Culture • **Traditional dances in Zambia are used for tribal ceremonies and entertainment.** ▲

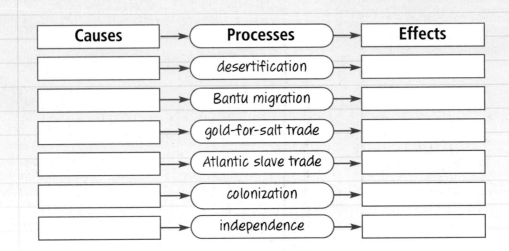

Causes	→	Processes	→	Effects
	→	desertification	→	
	→	Bantu migration	→	
	→	gold-for-salt trade	→	
	→	Atlantic slave trade	→	
	→	colonization	→	
	→	independence	→	

The Geography of Africa South of the Sahara

TERMS & NAMES
plateau
Great Rift Valley
Sahel
desertification
drought
savanna
nonrenewable resource
renewable resource

MAIN IDEA

Africa south of the Sahara is a region with dramatically different landforms and climates. This provides for a variety of natural resources.

WHY IT MATTERS NOW

Tourists come from all over the world to explore this region's natural landscapes.

DATELINE

EXTRA

BAMAKO, MALI, MARCH 8, 2000

Families in Mali are watching in despair as their farmland turns to sand. This problem—called desertification—is affecting many families in Africa. Experts have come to Mali for a United Nations–sponsored meeting to decide what can be done. In the past, efforts have focused on grand plans, such as planting thousands of trees to stop the advancing desert. When there was no money to water the trees, they died. Soon, the desert marched on.

Today's plans are more modest. One idea is to convince villagers to collect firewood from far away, leaving trees near

Human-Environment Interaction • This brushwood fence is an attempt to stabilize sand dunes and fight against the advance of the desert. ▲

the sand in place. Another idea is to change how people farm so that soil doesn't blow away. In these small ways, experts hope they can stop desertification.

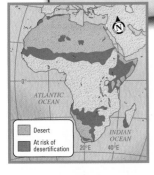

Region • More than half of Africa is desert or dry land. ▲

The African Continent

The natural changes in Africa's lands, such as desertification, affect its people. Africa is roughly three times the size of the United States. About 225 million years ago, Africa was the center of Earth's only continent, called Pangaea (pan•JEE•uh). Pangaea began to break up into separate continents that drifted apart over many millions of years. The piece that became Africa stayed where it was. Africa's shape has changed very little over time.

Landforms of Africa South of the Sahara

Africa has two major land types: lowlands and highlands. Locate the two regions on the Unit Atlas map on page 484. The lowlands are in the north and west, and the highlands are in the south and east. Several peaks rise out of the highlands of Kenya and Tanzania. The highest is Mount Kilimanjaro. The name *Kilimanjaro* comes from the Swahili (swah·HEE·lee) phrase *kilima njaro*, which means "shining mountain." From the sweltering rain forest below, Kilimanjaro looks as though it is shining in the sun. That's because its peak is snowcapped all year even though Kilimanjaro sits almost on the Equator.

Plateaus   Look again at the Unit Atlas map on page 484. Most of Africa south of the Sahara—both highlands and lowlands—lies on a high plateau. A **plateau** is a raised area of relatively level land. The African plateau rises from coastal plains along much of the north and west coastlines. Steep cliffs line much of the southern and eastern coasts, rising sharply from the Atlantic and Indian oceans. The east side of the plateau is higher than the west, at about 5,000 feet above sea level. The western plateau averages about 1,500 feet above sea level.

BACKGROUND

Mount Kilimanjaro is a volcanic massif, or large, independent mountain mass. It is made up of three distinct parts: Kibo, Mawensi, and Shira. Kibo is still actively volcanic and, as the highest peak, has a permanent ice cap.

Region • The Congo Basin is drained by the 2,900-mile-long Congo River (also called the Zaire River). ▼

Place • Mount Kenya, at 17,058 feet, is the second highest mountain in Africa. It is an extinct volcano. ▼

Region • The Great Rift Valley is nearly 4,000 miles long. It is 9,850 feet below sea level at its deepest point. ▷

Rifts The tectonic plates on which Africa sits have been slowly pulling apart for 50 million years. The separation of the plates has been forming a series of broad, steep-walled valleys called rifts. The rifts make up the **Great Rift Valley,** which stretches from the Red Sea to Mozambique. Locate the valley on the Unit Atlas map on page 484. The Great Rift Valley will become larger and larger as East Africa pulls away from the rest of the continent. Eventually, East Africa may become an island. The island of Madagascar was formed in this way. Look again at the map on page 484 to find where Madagascar fit before it broke away.

Waterways of Africa South of the Sahara

Reading
Social Studies

A. Summarizing
What are some benefits provided by Africa's lakes and rivers?

Parts of the Great Rift Valley have filled with water to form huge lakes, such as Lake Tanganyika. Africa's largest lake, Lake Victoria, is pictured at the bottom of this page. It lies in a shallow basin between two rift valleys on the borders of Uganda, Kenya, and Tanzania. Lakes and rivers provide fresh water and fish. However, waterfalls and rapids make boat travel difficult.

Rivers Many of Africa's rivers have exceptional features. The Nile River, flowing northward out of the mountains of central Africa, is the world's longest river. The Okavango River crosses Angola, Namibia, and Botswana before emptying into marshes north of the Kalahari Desert. The Zambezi River features many powerful waterfalls, including Victoria Falls. The mist from these falls can be seen 25 miles away.

Place • Lake Victoria is the second largest freshwater lake in the world. It is the major source of the Nile River. ▼

Africa's Deserts			
Desert	Area (sq. mi)	High Temp.	Annual Rainfall
Sahara	3,320,000	136°F	1" to 5"
Kalahari	360,000	115°F	<5" south; more northeast
Namib	52,000	over 100°F	0.5" to 2"

SKILLBUILDER: Reading a Chart
1. **Place** • Which desert is the largest?
2. **Place** • Which desert is the hottest?

Many Climates

Four major climatic regions of Africa south of the Sahara are desert (arid), semiarid, tropical, and equatorial. The different temperatures and amounts of rainfall affect which plants and animals live in each region.

Desert and Semiarid Regions Desert climates are found in the Sahara to the north and the Namib (NAH·mihb) and Kalahari to the south. These areas have little rain, high temperatures, and few plants and animals. Around the desert areas are semiarid regions that also have high temperatures but have more rainfall than the deserts.

The **Sahel** (suh·HAYL) is a semiarid region south of the Sahara. This area is experiencing **desertification**—a process by which a desert spreads. **Drought,** or the lack of rain, is one cause of desertification. The lack of rain causes fewer plants to grow. Without plants, soil blows away, leaving a dry, barren landscape. Other causes are overgrazing and overuse of the land for farming. People in Africa and around the world are trying to stop this process because a lack of enough arable land contributes to the widespread hunger in many African countries.

Tropical and Equatorial Regions The tropical climate extends from the semiarid areas toward the Equator. There is a rainy season of up to six months, and the rest of the year is dry.

Savannas, found in both semiarid and tropical areas, are flat grasslands with scattered trees and shrubs. More than 4.5 million square miles of Africa are savannas. Many African animals, including lions, elephants, giraffes, and zebras, live on these grasslands.

The equatorial region has two rainy seasons and two brief dry seasons each year. Located at the Equator, this climate has high temperatures year-round and annual rainfall of 50 to 60 inches.

Reading
Social Studies

B. Analyzing Issues How does the great area of desert and semiarid land impact the lives of many Africans?

Citizenship IN ACTION

Helping the Hungry Since 1977, a global volunteer organization called the Hunger Project has been working to end hunger in developing nations. In Africa, where poverty and hunger are widespread, the Hunger Project is sponsoring the African Woman Food Farmer Initiative.

So far, the program has loaned money to more than 14,000 women farmers like this one, in eight countries. The initiative has also provided health, nutrition, and literacy training for 9,000 more women in agriculture.

Rain forests with trees as tall as 195 feet grow here. Many animals, including the chimpanzee, gorilla, hippopotamus, and African gray parrot, live in the rain forest.

Resources of Africa South of the Sahara

Africa is rich in mineral resources, such as gold and diamonds, that form over hundreds of millions of years. Other plentiful minerals are copper, tin, chrome, nickel, and iron ore. **Nonrenewable resources,** such as copper and diamonds, cannot be replaced or can be replaced only over millions of years.

Renewable resources can be used and replaced over a relatively short time period. The renewable resources of this region include trees used to make wood products, cocoa beans, cashew nuts, peanuts, vanilla beans, coffee, bananas, rubber, sugar, and tea. Africa's natural wildlife and historic sites are important resources that draw tourists from all over the world.

Strange but TRUE ??

The Fish That Did Not Die In 1938, off the coast of South Africa, some fishermen caught something surprising. The blue fish in their net was 5 feet long, weighed about 127 pounds, and had several rows of small, pointed teeth. The fishermen had never seen anything like it. Nor, according to scientists, should they have.

The fish, a coelacanth (SEE•luh•KANTH), was thought to have been extinct for 70 million years. Now here was proof that it wasn't. However, they aren't plentiful. It wasn't until 1952 that a second live coelacanth was found. Only a few hundred exist today.

SECTION **1** ASSESSMENT

Terms & Names

1. **Identify:**
   (a) plateau
   (b) Great Rift Valley
   (c) Sahel
   (d) desertification
   (e) drought
   (f) savanna
   (g) nonrenewable resource
   (h) renewable resource

Taking Notes

2. Use a chart like this one to list some of this region's renewable and non-renewable resources.

Renewable Resources	Nonrenewable Resources

Main Ideas

3. (a) Describe the landforms and waterways of Africa.

   (b) Describe four climatic regions of Africa south of the Sahara.

   (c) Explain the differences between renewable and nonrenewable resources. Give examples of each.

Critical Thinking

4. **Using Maps**

   Look at the map of Africa on page 486. Has the Great Rift Valley affected modern political boundaries in Africa? Explain your answer.

   Think About

   ◆ the location of the Great Rift Valley

   ◆ current national borders in Africa

ACTIVITY -OPTION- Draw a **commemorative stamp** honoring a climatic region or landform in Africa south of the Sahara.

African Cultures and Empires

MAIN IDEA	**WHY IT MATTERS NOW**
Africa south of the Sahara has a rich and significant history.	Many scientists think Africa south of the Sahara is the cradle of the human race. The oldest fossil remains of humans have come from this region.

DATELINE

SOUTHERN AFRICA, A.D. 500—There is a group of newcomers in the area. They come from the north and speak languages unlike ours. Instead of hunting in the forests as we do, they raise animals for food. They plant grain in fields near their settlement.

The newcomers, who call themselves "Bantu," have sharp spears and blades made of a cold, dark metal. They use a short, sharp metal tool for digging—much better than our stone and wood tools. Many of our people have begun to trade goods for the newcomers' fine tools and pottery.

Movement • This woman is one of many Bantu who have settled in southern Africa. ▲

The First Humans

The roots of the Bantus can be traced back thousands of years. Fossil evidence shows that the first known humans lived in Africa several million years ago. **Paleontologists,** or scientists who study fossils, have discovered human remains in Kenya, South Africa, and other African nations. Fossilized human footprints 3.6 million years old have been found in Tanzania. It is now known that humans in Africa were the first to develop language, tools, and culture. Then, over tens of thousands of years, they migrated to other continents.

Early African Farmers

The first humans lived in small groups. For food, they collected berries, plants, and nuts and hunted wild animals. As plants and animals became scarce in one place, the people moved on. During this time, a group known as Bantu lived in what is now Cameroon. Around 5,000 years ago, the Bantu became farmers instead of hunter-gatherers. They learned to grow grain and herd cattle, sheep, and other animals. Later, they learned how to work with iron to make tools and weapons.

On the Move The Bantu began to move to other parts of Africa around 1000 B.C. Perhaps the desert was spreading, or they needed more land for a growing population. For about 2,000 years, the Bantu gradually spread across the continent. Their great movement is called the **Bantu migration.** In their new homes, they learned to grow and use different plants. In some places, the native hunter-gatherers lived in separate villages or moved away, as did the Sans, or Bushmen. In other places, the Bantu and the local people, such as the Pygmies, intermarried. Over time, the Bantu culture became widespread throughout Africa. Today, many Africans speak Swahili, Zulu, and other Bantu languages.

Culture • These headdresses represent Tyi Wara—an antelope spirit who, according to Bantu mythology, taught the first people how to grow crops. ▲

Reading
Social Studies

A. Recognizing Effects How did the Bantu migration influence the character of Africa south of the Sahara?

2,000 Years of Bantu Migration

GEOGRAPHY SKILLBUILDER:
Interpreting a Map

1. **Place** • Use the Unit Atlas map on page 486 and this map to name two countries in which the Bantu people lived c. 500 B.C.
2. **Region** • About how many miles from east to west did the area of the Bantu migration measure after A.D. 1000?

Original Bantu Area

Equator

Congo River

Lake Victoria

ATLANTIC OCEAN

N

INDIAN OCEAN

Lake Malawi

Zambezi River

Tropic of Capricorn

Bantu migration, c. 500 B.C.

Bantu migration, date unknown (between 500 B.C. and A.D. 500)

Bantu migration, after A.D. 500

Bantu migration, after A.D. 1000

| 0 | 500 | 1,000 miles |
| 0 | 500 | 1,000 kilometers |

20°W   0°   40°E   60°E

Trade Networks

Eventually, the Bantu built permanent villages. Trade routes began to develop between these communities across Africa.

The Salt Trade Salt was as precious to ancient Africans as gold and diamonds. People needed salt each day to stay alive. They also used it to preserve food. However, most of Africa south of the Sahara had no salt deposits. The closest source was in the Sahara, where giant salt slabs, some as heavy as 200 pounds, were mined. A vast trade network developed between the salt mines and the area south of the Sahara. To get salt, people in southern Africa traded gold, slaves, ivory, and cola nuts.

Camels and Caravans African trade expanded even further when the Arabian camel was introduced to Africa in the A.D. 600s. Camels are well adapted for long treks across the desert. Using camels, salt traders could carry goods from the savannas and forests across the desert to Northern Africa. There they traded for goods from Europe and Asia, such as glass from Italy or cotton and spices from India. The desert trade was profitable but risky. Robbers lived in the desert. For protection, traders traveled together in caravans.

Why Camels Are Well Adapted to Desert Travel

A double row of **long, curly eyelashes** keeps sand out of eyes, and **bushy eyebrows** shield eyes from the sun.

Fur-lined ears filter out sand.

The fat-filled hump provides many days' worth of energy.

A large mouth, 34 **sharp teeth,** and a **tough mouth lining** enable the camel to eat thorn bushes.

Long, thin legs have powerful muscles; a camel can walk 25 miles in a day and carry 330 pounds of cargo.

Broad, flat feet don't sink into the sand.

An Empire Built by Trade

In the fourth century A.D., a kingdom called Ghana arose in the Niger River Valley. Ancient Ghana's location allowed it to control trade between northern and southern Africa. Traders had to pay a tax in gold nuggets to pass through the kingdom on their way to Europe and Southwest Asia. In addition, ancient Ghana had many gold mines. Ghana had so much gold from these two sources that the kingdom was called the Land of Gold.

Reading
Social Studies

B. Synthesizing
Why was Ghana called the Land of Gold?

People eagerly traded gold for other precious items, such as salt. The merchants of Ghana also traded gold and slaves for cooking utensils, cloth, jewelry, copper, and weapons.

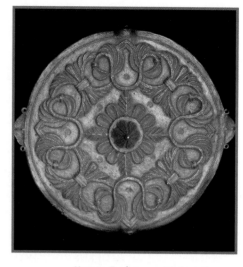

Human-Environment Interaction •
This 18th- or 19th-century gold jewelry from Ghana was probably worn by members of an Ashanti king's court. ▲

The Mali Empire

Muslim armies began a war with Ghana in 1054. The fighting continued for many years and interfered with the trade upon which Ghana depended. This weakened the empire. By the 1200s, the people under Ghana's rule began to break away.

Mali Absorbs Ghana Around 1235, a Muslim leader named Sundiata united warring tribes. He then brought neighboring states under his rule to create the Mali Empire. In the year 1240, he took control of what was left of the Ghana Empire. The Mali Empire included most of the area that Ghana had ruled, along with lands to the east.

Culture • **This daughter of a Fanti chief continues a long tradition of Ghanian royalty by wearing gold jewelry and ornaments.** ▶

Africa South of the Sahara: Geography and History **505**

It controlled trade routes across the Sahara and from the south, as well as along the Niger River. Many rulers and people of Mali became Muslims but still continued to practice their traditional religions, too.

Mali's Golden Age **Mansa Musa** ruled Mali from about 1312 to 1332. Under his rule, Mali expanded and flourished. In 1324, he made a religious pilgrimage to Mecca in Arabia. During his journey, he persuaded Muslim scholars and artisans to return to Mali with him. Timbuktu, Mali's major city, became a cultural center. Architects built beautiful mosques in and around the city. Scholars brought their knowledge of Islamic law, astronomy, medicine, and mathematics. Universities in several West African cities became centers of Islamic education.

Culture • Mansa (emperor) Musa spread interest in Mali as he traveled to Arabia. Tales of his wealth reached as far away as Europe. ▲

The Songhai Empire

Mali's power declined after Mansa Musa's death in 1337. Eventually, Mali was conquered by nearby Songhai. Like Mali and Ghana had in the past, Songhai controlled trade across the Sahara. It ruled neighboring states, and by the early 1500s was larger than Mali had been. Timbuktu again became a center of Muslim culture. In the early 1590s, a Moroccan army defeated the Songhai Empire.

SECTION 2 ASSESSMENT

Terms & Names

1. Identify: (a) paleontologist   (b) Bantu migration   (c) Mansa Musa

Taking Notes

2. Use a time line like this one to list important events in this region's history.

1000 B.C.
↓
| |
↓
| A.D. 1600 |

Main Ideas

3. (a) How did the introduction of the camel influence trade in ancient Africa?

(b) What were the two most valuable minerals in ancient Ghana? Why?

(c) How did a location in the Niger River valley help empires flourish?

Critical Thinking

4. **Recognizing Effects**

What were the effects of Mansa Musa's pilgrimage on Mali?

Think About

- who came to Mali after the pilgrimage
- what changes occurred in the culture of Mali

ACTIVITY -OPTION-   Make a **diorama** showing a camel caravan traveling through the Sahara, carrying salt to people in southern Africa.

The Impact of Colonialism on African Life

MAIN IDEA

The slave trade and colonialism destroyed traditional cultures and social systems in Africa south of the Sahara.

WHY IT MATTERS NOW

Africa is still recovering from the effects of the slave trade and colonialism.

DATELINE

EXTRA

THE ROYAL PALACE, KONGO, JULY 6, 1526

King Affonso of Kongo has sent a letter to the king of Portugal, protesting the criminal behavior of Portuguese merchants and sailors in Kongo. Traders are kidnapping the young men of his kingdom to sell into slavery. They use European goods to bribe Kongolese to capture their own people. Even noblemen and the king's own relatives have been taken.

Affonso says that European ways are corrupting the Kongolese. Some of the king's courtiers believe the slave trade can bring Kongo a great deal of wealth. But the king's position remains firm.

Movement • Elmina is a slave-trading fortress through which the Portuguese move enslaved Africans. ▲

Movement • Enslaved Africans were forced to wear shackles like these. ▲

Africa Before the Europeans

Before Europeans came, Africans had varied ways of life under different kinds of governments. Kings ruled great empires like Mali and Songhai. Some states had aspects of democratic rule. Some groups had no central government. Some Africans lived in great cities like Timbuktu, while others lived in small forest villages. Some were nomadic hunters, and some were skilled artists who sculpted masks and statues of wood, gold, or bronze.

The Slave Trade

Slavery existed in Africa long before Europeans arrived. Rulers in Mali and Songhai had thousands of slaves who worked as servants, soldiers, and farm workers. Villages raided one another to take captives and sell them. Often, a slave could work to earn his or her freedom. In the 1400s, however, Europeans introduced a form of slavery that devastated African life and society.

From Africa to the Americas In the early 15th century, European traders began to sell slaves. They raided towns to capture unwilling Africans. Some Africans captured in wars were sold to European traders by other Africans. One estimate is that 10 to 12 million Africans were forced into slavery and sent to European colonies in North and South America from 1520 to 1860. Many more were captured but died of disease or starvation before arriving. About 1750, movements to stop the slave trade had begun. By 1808, the United States, the United Kingdom, and Denmark had made it illegal to bring in slaves from Africa. However, it would take longer for countries to make owning a slave illegal.

Impact on Africa In addition to the Africans captured and sold, many were killed during raids. About two-thirds of those taken were men between the ages of 18 and 30. Slave traders chose young, strong, healthy people, leaving few behind to lead families and villages. African cities and towns did not have enough workers. Family structures were destroyed.

BACKGROUND

Conditions on slave ships were so bad that about 16 percent of slaves died during transport.

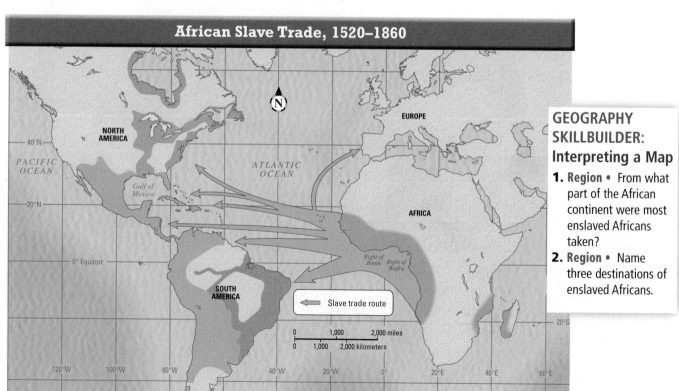

African Slave Trade, 1520–1860

NORTH AMERICA

EUROPE

PACIFIC OCEAN

ATLANTIC OCEAN

Gulf of Mexico

AFRICA

Bight of Benin   Bight of Biafra

40°N
20°N
0° Equator

SOUTH AMERICA

Slave trade route

20°S

0   1,000   2,000 miles
0   1,000   2,000 kilometers

120°W   100°W   80°W   40°W   20°W   0°   20°E   40°E   60°E

GEOGRAPHY SKILLBUILDER: Interpreting a Map

1. **Region** • From what part of the African continent were most enslaved Africans taken?
2. **Region** • Name three destinations of enslaved Africans.

European Colonialism

When Europeans ended the slave trade, they did not lose interest in Africa. The Industrial Revolution had changed economies in Europe and the United States. Africa could supply both raw materials, such as minerals, and new markets for goods.

Explorers and Missionaries Europeans knew little about the interior of Africa, but many were curious. Scientists and explorers were interested in African wildlife and natural resources. European missionaries also traveled to Africa. A **missionary** is a person who goes to another country to do religious and social work. Missionaries wanted to convert Africans to Christianity and bring education and health care to Africa. Many also taught European ways of thinking, which often conflicted with, and destroyed, African traditions.

Competition for Africa In the 19th century, European nations began to compete for control of Africa. Each wanted the biggest or richest colonies and control of trade. To avoid wars over territory, European and U.S. leaders met in Berlin in 1884. There, and in later meetings, they discussed how to divide Africa. No Africans were consulted. Over the next 20 years, Belgium, France, the United Kingdom, Germany, Italy, Spain, Portugal, and the Ottoman Empire all established colonies in Africa. By 1912, only Ethiopia and Liberia remained independent.

The WORLD'S HERITAGE

A Wealth of Animals When European explorers came to Africa, they saw impressive sights—lions and cheetahs stalking zebras, elephants trumpeting messages to their young, giraffes delicately nibbling the tops of trees. Today, Tanzania's Serengeti National Park is where modern explorers watch animals in the wild—animals that most non-Africans have seen only in zoos.

The Serengeti is home to an astonishing variety of life. It is also the last place in Africa where huge migrations of animals take place. The sight of a million gnus, zebras, and gazelles moving majestically through the park is one of the wonders of the world.

European Colonies in Africa, 1912

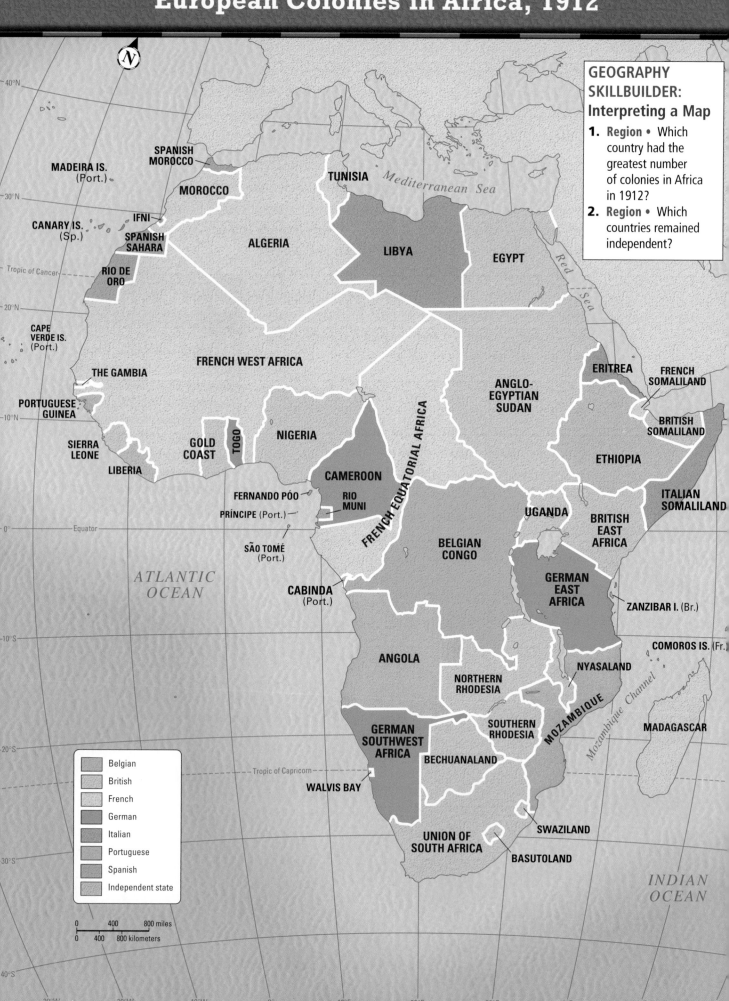

GEOGRAPHY SKILLBUILDER:
Interpreting a Map

1. **Region** • Which country had the greatest number of colonies in Africa in 1912?
2. **Region** • Which countries remained independent?

MADEIRA IS. (Port.)

SPANISH MOROCCO

TUNISIA

Mediterranean Sea

MOROCCO

IFNI

CANARY IS. (Sp.)

SPANISH SAHARA

ALGERIA

LIBYA

EGYPT

Red Sea

RIO DE ORO

Tropic of Cancer

CAPE VERDE IS. (Port.)

FRENCH WEST AFRICA

THE GAMBIA

ANGLO-EGYPTIAN SUDAN

ERITREA

FRENCH SOMALILAND

PORTUGUESE GUINEA

SIERRA LEONE

GOLD COAST

TOGO

NIGERIA

BRITISH SOMALILAND

ETHIOPIA

LIBERIA

CAMEROON

FERNANDO PÓO

RIO MUNI

ITALIAN SOMALILAND

PRÍNCIPE (Port.)

FRENCH EQUATORIAL AFRICA

UGANDA

BRITISH EAST AFRICA

Equator

SÃO TOMÉ (Port.)

BELGIAN CONGO

GERMAN EAST AFRICA

ATLANTIC OCEAN

CABINDA (Port.)

ZANZIBAR I. (Br.)

COMOROS IS. (Fr.)

ANGOLA

NYASALAND

NORTHERN RHODESIA

MOZAMBIQUE

Mozambique Channel

MADAGASCAR

GERMAN SOUTHWEST AFRICA

SOUTHERN RHODESIA

BECHUANALAND

Tropic of Capricorn

WALVIS BAY

SWAZILAND

UNION OF SOUTH AFRICA

BASUTOLAND

INDIAN OCEAN

Legend:
- Belgian
- British
- French
- German
- Italian
- Portuguese
- Spanish
- Independent state

0   400   800 miles
0   400   800 kilometers

Impact of Colonial Rule

When Europeans divided Africa, most colonizers cared mainly about gold, diamonds, and other resources. The Europeans knew little about Africa's political and social systems. Many Europeans looked down on Africa's rich cultures and tried to make Africans more like Europeans.

Europeans also worsened conflicts among ethnic groups. For example, the Belgian rulers of Rwanda-Burundi insisted that everyone carry identity cards saying whether they were **Hutu,** the ethnic majority, or **Tutsi,** the minority that had ruled the Hutu. Many people did not know which of these they were. The Belgians decided that anyone who owned more than ten cows was Tutsi. The Tutsi got the best education and jobs. Soon the Hutu were resentful, and a violent conflict began. In 1994, the conflict between the Hutu and the Tutsi escalated into a brutal civil war. The Tutsi were victorious and formed a new government in Rwanda.

Movement • During and after the civil war, thousands of Tutsi were massacred, and thousands of Hutu refugees, such as these, were driven from their homeland. ▼

SECTION 3 ASSESSMENT

Terms & Names

1. Identify: (a) missionary   (b) Hutu   (c) Tutsi

Taking Notes

2. Use a chart like this one to list the ways in which Europeans changed Africa, and the effects of the changes on African life.

Change	Effect

Main Ideas

3. (a) How did Europeans change the institution of slavery in Africa?

   (b) Why did European interest in Africa turn from the slave trade to colonization?

   (c) How is the modern conflict between the Hutu and Tutsi a result of the actions of European rulers?

Critical Thinking

4. **Comparing**

   How was the way of life of many Africans different after the arrival of Europeans?

   Think About

   • goals of missionaries and European countries

   • history and traditions of ethnic peoples

ACTIVITY -OPTION- Write an **opinion paper** explaining the negative effects of colonization.

Interpreting a Chart

▶▶ Defining the Skill

A chart organizes information in a visual form. The information is simplified or summarized and then arranged so that it is easy to read and understand.

▶▶ Applying the Skill

The chart below lists the population, number of radios, and number of televisions in several West African nations and the United States. Use the strategies listed below to help you interpret the chart.

How to Interpret a Chart

Strategy ❶ Read the title to learn the main idea of the chart.

Strategy ❷ Read the labels across the top and down the first column of the chart. The labels in the column list the countries represented in the chart. The labels across the top tell what information is provided for each country.

Strategy ❸ Study the information in the chart. Read down the columns to compare one country with another. Read across the rows to see the communications available in each country.

Strategy ❹ Summarize the information in the chart. The title helps you clarify the main idea of the chart.

❶ **Communication in Western Africa and the United States, 2000**

❷ Country	Population	Radios	Televisions
Benin	❸ 6.6 million	620,000	60,000
Ghana	❸ 19.9 million	4,400,000	1,730,000
Liberia	❸ 3.2 million	❸ 790,000	❸ 70,000
Mali	11 million	570,000	45,000
Niger	10.4 million	680,000	125,000
Nigeria	126.6 million	23,500,000	6,900,000
United States	284.5 million	575,000,000	219,000,000

❹ This chart compares the population, the number of radios, and the number of televisions in several West African nations and the United States. In the countries of Benin and Mali, there are very few radios and televisions compared with the number of people. For example, in Mali there is one television for every 244 people. In the United States, there is more than one radio per person. In Nigeria, there is one television for every 18 people.

Write a Summary

To gain a clear understanding of the information in this chart, write a summary. It is possible to produce other data from the information in this chart. To find out how many people there are for one television or radio in each nation, divide the population by the number of televisions or radios. The paragraph above summarizes the chart.

▶▶ Practicing the Skill

Turn to page 500 in Chapter 17. Study the chart titled "Africa's Deserts," and write a paragraph that summarizes the information in that chart.

The Road to Independence

TERMS & NAMES
racism
diversity
apartheid

MAIN IDEA

During the 20th century, African nations gained independence from their colonial rulers.

WHY IT MATTERS NOW

Many independent nations in Africa are now struggling to form democratic governments.

DATELINE

NAIROBI, KENYA, DECEMBER 12, 1963— Thousands of Kenyans watched today as the British flag was lowered for the last time over the former colony. The new national flag of independent Kenya was raised in its place.

The new flag's stripes of black, red, and green stand for the country's people, their struggle for independence, and the country's rich resources. The center symbol is a Masai shield and spears.

To mark the change from British rule, Prince Philip of England attended the ceremony. All over Kenya, people cheered their new country, shouting "Uhuru!" the Swahili word for freedom.

Place • Prince Philip and Kenya's President Jomo Kenyatta attend the ceremony marking Kenya's independence. ▲

Culture • This flag is a symbol of Kenya's independence. ▲

Moving Toward Independence

Colonial rule in Africa disrupted social systems and governments, and robbed Africa of resources. Many Africans objected, but they did not have enough power to act. During the 1920s and 1930s, colonial rulers sent a few Africans to attend universities in Europe and the United States. These educated young people started to dream of independence. Nationalism grew strong.

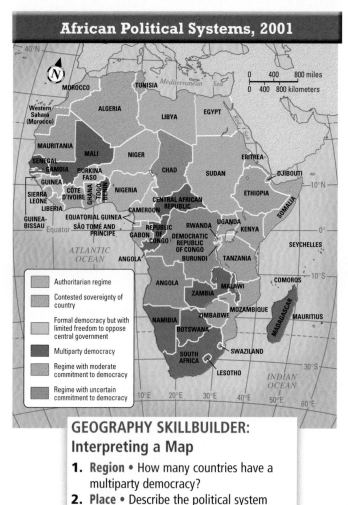

African Political Systems, 2001

Authoritarian regime

Contested sovereignty of country

Formal democracy but with limited freedom to oppose central government

Multiparty democracy

Regime with moderate commitment to democracy

Regime with uncertain commitment to democracy

GEOGRAPHY SKILLBUILDER:
Interpreting a Map

1. **Region** • How many countries have a multiparty democracy?
2. **Place** • Describe the political system in Cameroon.

Journey to Freedom

European nations wanted to keep their colonies for their valuable resources although they were expensive to maintain. Many Europeans believed that Africans were unable to govern themselves. This attitude is an example of **racism,** the unfounded belief that one race is inferior to another race.

Pan-African Congresses Educated Africans believed they could govern themselves. African men had fought for the European Allies during World War I, and thousands had died. Ex-soldiers wanted self-rule. Pan-Africanism, an idea that people of African descent around the world should work together for their freedom, attracted more supporters. In 1919, the first Pan-African Congress was organized. Africans again fought in World War II. After this war, many felt that they now deserved independence.

A VOICE FROM AFRICA

...We are determined to be free. We want education. We want the right to earn a decent living; the right to express our thoughts and emotions, to adopt and create forms of beauty. We demand for Black Africa autonomy and independence....

The Pan-African Congress, 1945

Reading
Social Studies

A. Analyzing Causes How did the two world wars and the Pan-African congresses affect the struggle for African independence?

At the fifth Pan-African Congress in 1945, there were 90 delegates; 26 were from all over Africa. Several were men who would become the political leaders of their countries, including Kwame Nkrumah of Ghana and Jomo Kenyatta of Kenya.

New African Countries

Between 1951 and 1980, most of the colonies in Africa south of the Sahara gained independence. For some countries, the path to nationhood was smooth. For others, it was not. Nigeria and South Africa had different experiences in achieving independence.

Nigeria: Diversity Brings Division

Before Nigeria gained independence from the United Kingdom in 1960, it had experienced a well-organized government, rich resources, and a strong economy under British rule. It was hoped that Nigeria's **diversity**—its many different cultures and viewpoints—would be a source of strength. Many Nigerians are Muslim, while others are Christian or follow traditional African religions. Nigerians speak more than 400 languages. However, instead of being a source of strength, this diversity caused problems.

Reading
Social Studies

B. Finding Causes What led to the 1966 rioting in Nigeria?

Riots and War The slave trade and colonial rule had worsened hostility between the ethnic groups in Nigeria. Many Nigerian politicians focused on their ethnic group and not the whole country. Some leaders stole money and gave or took bribes.

Spotlight on CULTURE

Yam Festivals People celebrate what is precious to them. In Ghana, Nigeria, and Côte d'Ivoire, the yam is traditionally the most important crop. Among the Igbo people of Nigeria, a man's first prayer to God is for children. His second is for many yams.

Every year, people in these countries celebrate the harvest of the new yams with special dances and ceremonies. Côte d'Ivoire's King Kofti is shown at right accepting offerings at the Yam Festival. Yam paste is prepared in a large bowl.

Among the Akan people of Aburi in Ghana, a priest begins the festival by slicing and dropping three pieces from a yam. If the pieces fall skin-side down, the village will have good luck. If the slices fall cut-side down, trouble is ahead.

THINKING CRITICALLY

1. **Comparing** How is the American holiday Thanksgiving similar to the Yam Festival?

2. **Making Inferences** Why do you think a priest is involved with the Yam Festival in Ghana?

In 1966, deadly riots broke out, and many people were killed. The next year, people in the eastern part of Nigeria announced the formation of a separate country, Biafra. After three years of civil war between Biafran Nigerians and the Nigerian army, Biafra was defeated and rejoined Nigeria. Since then, military leaders have primarily ruled Nigeria.

Independence of South Africa

The United Kingdom gave South Africa independence in 1910. This action did not bring freedom to most South Africans. Only white South Africans could vote, and many laws were passed to restrict nonwhites.

In 1948, an official policy of racial segregation known as **apartheid** (uh·PAHRT·HYT) was adopted. Apartheid strictly separated people by color. Many people resisted apartheid. Protesters held marches, went on strike, and sometimes became violent. Although many protesters were jailed or killed, they did make progress. In 1991, apartheid ended. In 1994, for the first time, all South African adults could vote.

Place • Signs such as these were common in South Africa during apartheid. Everything from businesses to bathrooms was segregated. ▲

BACKGROUND

The word *apartheid* is from the Afrikaans language. It means "apartness."

SECTION 4 ASSESSMENT

Terms & Names

1. **Identify:**   (a) racism   (b) diversity   (c) apartheid

Taking Notes

2. Use a Venn diagram like this one to list the similarities and differences between the processes of independence for Nigeria and for South Africa.

Nigeria   South Africa

Main Ideas

3. (a) What factors strengthened the movement among Africans for independence?

(b) How did Nigeria's diversity create problems after the country gained independence?

(c) How did opportunities for South African citizens to participate in and influence the political process change in the 1990s?

Critical Thinking

4. **Hypothesizing**

Do you think possessing African colonies helped or hurt the economies of European countries?

Think About

• the cost of running a colony
• Africa's resources

ACTIVITY -OPTION-   Design a **logo** or write a **motto** for a modern-day Pan-African Congress. Remember to represent African peoples around the world.

Technology: 1100

House of Stone

Scattered throughout the interior of southeastern Africa are hundreds of stone ruins archaeologists believe date to A.D. 1100–1500. The most spectacular, Great Zimbabwe, covers almost 1,800 acres. The word *zimbabwe* means "house of stone."

For centuries Europeans wondered about the origins of this city. In the early 1900s, archaeologists proved that its builders were ancestors of the present-day Shona people. Artifacts from India, China, and Asia have been found at the site. They show that the area was a trade center for gold, ivory, cloth, beads, and ceramics. Trade in Great Zimbabwe was controlled by a few wealthy people.

Trade routes of Great Zimbabwe

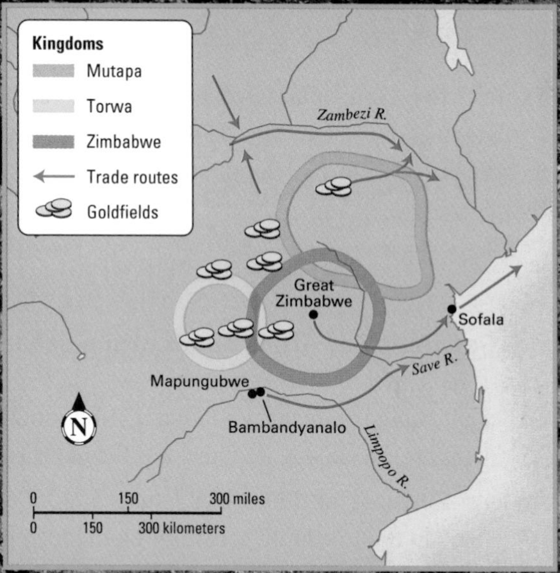

Kingdoms
- Mutapa
- Torwa
- Zimbabwe
- ← Trade routes
- Goldfields

Zambezi R.

Great Zimbabwe

Sofala

Mapungubwe

Save R.

Bambandyanalo

Limpopo R.

N

0   150   300 miles
0   150   300 kilometers

Builders used 900,000 granite slabs to create stone walls. The slabs were laid together without any type of mortar.

Natural weathering causes slabs of granite to break off hills in this area. Builders of Great Zimbabwe cut these slabs into smaller pieces and used them to create the stone walls.

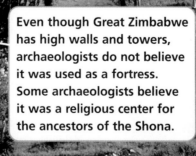

Even though Great Zimbabwe has high walls and towers, archaeologists do not believe it was used as a fortress. Some archaeologists believe it was a religious center for the ancestors of the Shona.

THINKING Critically

1. Drawing Conclusions
The stone walls and towers of Great Zimbabwe were not built to protect the city. Why did its builders construct the walls and towers?

2. Making Inferences
How do trading networks of today differ from those of Great Zimbabwe?

ASSESSMENT

CHAPTER 17

TERMS & NAMES

Explain the significance of each of the following:

1. plateau
2. Great Rift Valley
3. Sahel
4. desertification
5. drought
6. savanna
7. Bantu migration
8. Mansa Musa
9. racism
10. diversity

REVIEW QUESTIONS

The Geography of Africa South of the Sahara
(pages 497–501)

1. What climatic regions are found in Africa south of the Sahara?
2. What are rift valleys, and how are they formed?

African Cultures and Empires *(pages 502–506)*

3. How did Bantu culture spread through much of Africa?
4. How did kingdoms of Ghana, Mali, and Songhai become powerful?

The Impact of Colonialism on African Life *(pages 507–511)*

5. How did the European slave trade affect life in this region?
6. What factors did European countries consider while dividing up Africa?

The Road to Independence *(pages 513–516)*

7. What events increased the determination of Africans to gain independence from European rule?
8. What were some of the problems that accompanied independence in some African countries?

CRITICAL THINKING

Finding Causes

1. Using your completed chart from Reading Social Studies, p. 496, explain the causes and effects of desertification.

Analyzing Motives

2. Why were European nations so interested in establishing colonies in Africa?

Recognizing Effects

3. How did slave trade and colonialism in the past make it difficult for African leaders to build new, independent nations?

Visual Summary

1 The Geography of Africa South of the Sahara

- Africa south of the Sahara is a region of highlands and lowlands, with a variety of landforms and rich resources.

2 African Cultures and Empires

- Africa is the cradle of humankind.
- For over a thousand years (A.D. 400–1600), Africans built great empires based on trade.

3 The Impact of Colonialism on African Life

- Slave trade weakened African social systems by removing many healthy, young people from Africa.
- In the late 1800s, European nations divided Africa and established colonies, destroying existing governmental and social systems.

4 The Road to Independence

- In the late 20th century, most European colonies in Africa became independent nations.

SOCIAL STUDIES SKILLBUILDER

Major Lakes of Africa South of the Sahara

Name of Lake	Location	Area (sq. miles)	Length (miles)	Greatest Depth (feet)
Victoria	Tanzania, Uganda, Kenya	26,828	200	270
Tanganyika	Tanzania, Democratic Republic of the Congo, Zambia, Burundi	12,700	420	4,708
Nyasa	Malawi, Mozambique, Tanzania	11,600	360	2,316
Turkana (Rudolf)	Ethiopia	2,473	154	240

SKILLBUILDER: Interpreting a Chart

1. **Region** • What information does this chart present?
2. **Place** • Which lake is the largest in area? Which is the deepest?
3. **Place** • Which country has part of three major lakes within its borders? What are the lakes' names?

FOCUS ON GEOGRAPHY

Compare this map of Africa in 1886 with the map of Africa in 1912 on page 510.

1. Which two European countries had the most colonies in Africa?
2. What happened to African borders between 1886 and 1912?

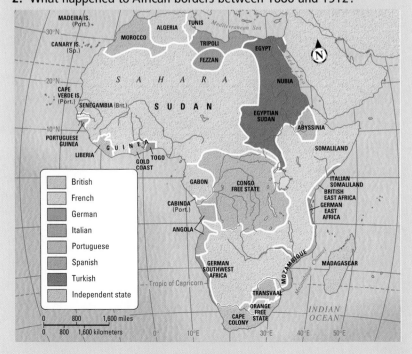

Legend:
- British
- French
- German
- Italian
- Portuguese
- Spanish
- Turkish
- Independent state

CHAPTER PROJECTS

Interdisciplinary Activity: Science

Investigating a Process Africa's geological history makes it a major source of diamonds. Research and report on how diamonds are formed deep in the earth, how they are mined in Africa, and how different kinds of African diamonds are used. Use encyclopedias, science references, and other sources for your report. Include photographs or drawings if possible.

Cooperative Learning Activity

Creating an Art Display In a group of three to five classmates, gather photocopies, museum postcards, or magazine clippings showing art forms from at least four countries in Africa south of the Sahara. Each student in the group can choose a country. Organize your collection on the bulletin board around a map of Africa. Use string to connect each object to its country and label with the following information:

- The country where the art was created
- When the art was made
- How it was used

INTERNET ACTIVITY

Use the Internet to research wildlife parks and refuges in Africa south of the Sahara. Where are they located? What are their goals? What problems do they face?
Writing About Geography Prepare a written or oral report on one park. Discuss its climate and landforms, its animals, and the opportunities for visitors. Include information on how the country manages and protects its endangered wildlife.

For Internet links to support this activity, go to

CHAPTER 18

Western and Central Africa

SECTION 1 History and Political Change

SECTION 2 Economies and Cultures

SECTION 3 Nigeria Today

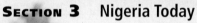

PACIFIC OCEAN

ATLANTIC OCEAN

PACIFIC OCEAN

INDIAN OCEAN

WESTERN AND CENTRAL AFRICA

How can an entire town move across a country?

FOCUS ON **GEOGRAPHY**

Movement • Many African villages are far away from pharmacies, stores, airports, and other modern services.

In the Democratic Republic of the Congo, dense forests separate many villages from cities and towns.

Instead of building roads, the Congolese use their rivers as highways. Great barges run up and down the Congo River, carrying thousands of people on each trip. These barges are moving towns, with clinics, churches, markets, restaurants, and more.

What do you think?

♦ In what other ways do you think Africans use their waterways?

♦ What benefits do you think the barge offers over airplane travel in the Democratic Republic of the Congo?

Place Most African towns and villages host daily or weekly outdoor markets. Many of the vendors live in the countryside and travel into town to sell their goods.

BEFORE YOU READ

▶▶ *What Do You Know?*

Western and Central African countries export many products to the United States, including gold and the cacao beans used to make chocolate. What else do you know about this region? Did you know that Liberia was founded by Americans? How did European colonialism affect the region? Reflect on what you have learned in other classes, what you read in Chapter 17, and what you have seen in the news about recent events in this area.

▶▶ *What Do You Want to Know?*

Decide what else you want to know about Western and Central Africa. In your notebook, record what you hope to learn from this chapter.

Culture • Cameroon's soccer team celebrated after winning the gold medal at the Olympic Games in 2000. ▼

READ AND TAKE NOTES

Reading Strategy: Making Inferences Making inferences is an important skill in reading social studies. Making inferences involves thinking beyond the text and interpreting the information you read. To make inferences, read carefully and use common sense and previous knowledge to make connections between ideas. Use the chart below to record inferences you can build on as you read.

- Copy the chart into your notebook.

- Read each statement. Use what you know to make inferences. Record your interpretations, connections, and ideas.

- As you read, record key evidence that confirms, changes, or builds on your inferences.

Culture • At one time only royalty in Ghana could wear this colorful Kente cloth. Today, it is popular among all Ghanaians. ▲

Statements	My Inferences	Key Evidence
European colonial powers divided Africa. Territories created by colonial powers became separate countries.		
In most African countries, governments are either too strong or too weak.		
Most countries of Western and Central Africa have a mix of different types of economies.		
Africa is culturally diverse. Before colonial rule, Africa had many different types of societies. There are some things that most of the peoples of Western and Central Africa have in common.		
Nigeria has more than 250 ethnic groups. Conflicts among these groups have sometimes led to civil war. This diversity has also led to a rich artistic and literary heritage.		

History and Political Change

TERMS & NAMES
coup d'état
OAU
mediate
ECOWAS

MAIN IDEA

Since gaining independence, some of the countries of Western and Central Africa have had trouble establishing stable governments.

WHY IT MATTERS NOW

Unstable governments are the basis for many conflicts in Western and Central Africa.

DATELINE

EXTRA

BERLIN, GERMANY, FEBRUARY 26, 1885

The competition for the riches of Africa has caused growing conflict. But today, the countries of Europe finally agreed on the rules for dividing up the African continent. The rules will enable the countries to claim land in Africa without going to war with one another.

When the powers of Europe take land in Africa, they must make sure that no other country has already claimed that land. Also, the agreement will allow open trade among the colonies. All countries will be able to freely move goods on the Congo River. At last, the takeover of Africa will be orderly.

Region • This political cartoon makes clear that European nations have been fighting for control of African lands and resources. ▲

Human-Environment Interaction • Explorers, such as Sir Henry Morton Stanley, have helped Europeans learn about Africa. Sir Henry is the first European to explore the entire Congo River. ▲

Dividing Western and Central Africa

European nations divided the African continent in the late 1800s. They were not thinking about creating new nations. Their goal was to control Africa's rich resources. To avoid war with one another, the European powers made trades. They traded one advantage—such as coastal land—for another.

New Maps of West Africa

When Europeans divided Africa, they ignored traditional borders between Africa's ethnic groups. They used other factors to draw new maps, such as the location of rivers or lakes.

Let's Make a Deal Look at The Gambia on the political map of Africa on page 486. The country is only 30 miles across at its widest point. How was a country with such strange borders formed? In 1816, the British bought an island at the mouth of the Gambia River. They used the island as a base to extend their control over the banks of the river. However, France claimed all the land around the river. When the Europeans drew borders in the late 1880s, the British kept The Gambia, with access to the river. In return, the French got more land for Senegal.

Dividing the Congo Basin European interest in a river affected borders in Central Africa too. The Congo River is the second-longest river in Africa. Belgium, France, and Portugal all wanted to claim the river and the lands around it. That rivalry was the main reason for the conference in Berlin that you read about on page 523. At the conference, the three nations agreed to divide the huge Congo Basin. King Leopold of Belgium took the land that is now the Democratic Republic of the Congo as his personal property. France possessed what is now the Republic of the Congo. Portugal controlled what is present-day Angola.

Human-Environment Interaction • The Gambia's width was in large part determined by the firing range of the British gunboats that patrolled the Gambia River. ▲

Reading **Social Studies**

A. Analyzing Motives Why was controlling a river so important to the Europeans?

Governments in Western and Central Africa

When African nations became independent, many of their colonial borders stayed the same. These borders split ethnic groups and regions that historically had been united, making it difficult for many modern African nations to establish stable governments.

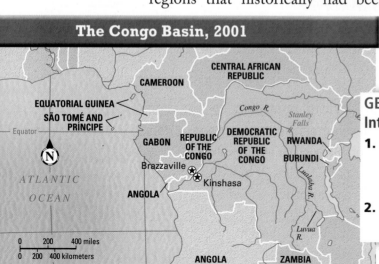

The Congo Basin, 2001

GEOGRAPHY SKILLBUILDER: Interpreting a Map

1. **Region •** What physical feature forms the border between the Republic of the Congo and the Democratic Republic of the Congo?
2. **Place •** What is the capital of the Republic of the Congo?

Since 1963, about 200 African governments have been ousted by coups d'état (KOO day·TAH). A **coup d'état** is an overthrow of a government by force. Two of the many countries that have struggled to create stable democratic governments are the Democratic Republic of the Congo and Ghana.

Government in the Democratic Republic of the Congo

In 1960, the former Belgian Congo gained independence, but a series of coups d'état toppled each established government. Five years later, an army general, Joseph Désiré Mobutu, took power. Mobutu tried to wipe out all traces of colonialism. He changed the name of the country to Zaire (ZY·eer) and his own name to Mobutu Sese Seko (SAY·say SAY·koh). He made people wear African-style clothing and take names that were African instead of Belgian.

Place • This banknote was printed in 1993, four years before Zaire became the Democratic Republic of the Congo. ▼

Mobutu ruled as a dictator, calling the people of Zaire his "children." He allowed no criticism of his rule. At the same time, he built up a personal fortune by stealing government money intended for roads, schools, and hospitals.

BACKGROUND

Joseph Kabila was not elected president. He was chosen by his father's handpicked parliament.

Civil War A brutal civil war began in Zaire in 1994. It resulted in Laurent-Désiré Kabila overthrowing Mobutu's government. Kabila changed the country's name to the Democratic Republic of the Congo. However, the country was not a true democracy, and civil war started again. Kabila was assassinated in 2001. His son, Joseph Kabila, replaced him as president.

Government in Ghana

In 1957, the British colony of Gold Coast became the first independent country in Africa south of the Sahara. The new nation took its name, Ghana, from a great ancient empire. The country's first leader was Kwame Nkrumah (uhn·KROO·muh). Nkrumah wanted to make Ghana modern. He built a new seaport, roads, and railroads to make shipping natural resources to factories and sending manufactured goods to stores easier and cheaper. Foreign trade improved. Ghana also became the first country in Africa south of the Sahara to have compulsory primary education.

Place • Kwame Nkrumah is shown here, at left, shortly after Ghana gained independence. ▼

Reading
Social Studies

B. Drawing Conclusions Why do you think some African leaders have decided to change their nations' names?

Western and Central Africa **525**

Place • This billboard in Accra, Ghana, showed Jerry John Rawlings (center) with the two candidates for the presidency in 2000. ▲

Military Rulers Although Nkrumah helped the new nation, he ruled as a dictator. He sent his opponents to prison. Some were tortured and killed. In 1966, the police and the army organized a coup d'état against Nkrumah. The coup d'état leaders freed political prisoners. They tried to help small businesses. Still, conditions in Ghana grew worse. People lost their jobs and did not have money for food. They went on strike to protest. When military leaders tried to take control, fighting began, and more coups d'état followed. In 1979, Jerry John Rawlings, a soldier, took power.

The Coming of Democracy In 1992, Rawlings allowed an election to take place. Ghana then became more democratic. A new constitution and parliament put limits on his power. In 2000, Rawlings became the first modern African military ruler to give up power peacefully. Elections brought in a new president. Today, Ghana is one of the most stable nations in Africa. In 1998, UN Secretary General Kofi Annan commented on Ghana's success.

Reading
Social Studies

C. Forming and Supporting Opinions What do you think of Rawlings's decision to give up power peacefully? Why might he have decided to do so?

A VOICE FROM GHANA

I grew up in Ghana at the time when we were fighting for independence, and so I saw lots of changes in my youth. I saw that it was possible to challenge the status quo and do something about it. And change did occur.

Kofi Annan, 1998

Vocabulary

status quo: existing state of affairs

Citizenship IN ACTION

Aid for Children In cities all over Africa, growing numbers of children can be found living on the streets. In Accra, Ghana, which has thousands of street children (shown at right), two local organizations are working to help them: Street Girls Aid (S.Aid) and Catholic Action for Street Children (CAS).

CAS provides places where children can wash, eat, rest, take classes, or simply play. For teenage mothers with children, S.Aid offers daycare so the mothers can work. Both groups provide health care and counseling to help children cope with the harshness of life on the streets.

Region • In 2001, the OAU was being transformed into the African Union, whose new Secretary General, Amara Essy, is shown here on the right. ▶

Nations Helping Nations

Like Ghana, many African nations have had to struggle for peace and democracy. Some nations are working together to help one another. In 1963, the **OAU,** or the Organization of African Unity, was formed. The organization tries to promote unity among all Africans. For example, the OAU would like to establish a single currency for Africa. The OAU also mediates disputes between countries. To **mediate** means to help find a peaceful solution.

ECOWAS The nations of Western Africa also cooperate economically. **ECOWAS,** or the Economic Community of West African States, was formed in 1975. It works to improve trade within Western Africa and with countries outside the region. ECOWAS also has mediated disputes between countries in Western Africa and tried to end government corruption.

SECTION 1 ASSESSMENT

Terms & Names

1. Identify: (a) coup d'état   (b) OAU   (c) mediate   (d) ECOWAS

Taking Notes

2. Use a chart like this one to compare the governments of the Democratic Republic of the Congo and Ghana.

Democratic Republic of the Congo	Ghana

Main Ideas

3. (a) What was the impact of European colonization on the governments of modern Africa?

(b) What example was given in this section of a government with unlimited power? What example was given in this section of a government with limited power?

(c) How did Kwame Nkrumah influence Ghana?

Critical Thinking

4. **Making Inferences**

Why do you think it was important for the power of Jerry John Rawlings, the former president of Ghana, to be limited?

Think About

• other dictatorships around the world

• the progression of human rights

ACTIVITY -OPTION- Pretend you have been commissioned by the OAU to design a common currency for all of Africa. Draw a **model** or write a **description** of your design.

Linking Past and Present

The Legacy of Africa South of the Sahara

Music

Music has always played an important role in the daily life of Africa south of the Sahara. Characteristic of the music are its complex rhythms. Hand clapping, drums, and iron bells produce different rhythmic patterns. Over the years, the music of Africa south of the Sahara has influenced music around the world. Jazz, a popular type of music that began in the early 1900s in the United States, is based on a combination of European harmonies and African rhythms.

Swahili Language

Swahili, also called Kiswahili, is a widespread language on the eastern coast of Africa. It evolved from the mixing of East African and Arab cultures. Swahili also includes words adapted from the English of British colonists, such as *penseli* (pencil), *basi* (bus), and *baiskeli* (bicycle). Today, it continues to be the language spoken in the business community and is one of the languages of Tanzania, Kenya, and Uganda.

Gold

For nearly 1,000 years, Africans south of the Sahara have used their prized possessions—gold and ivory—as signs of wealth and power. They have also traded these valuable materials for other commodities, such as glass, precious stones, and ceramics. Many European settlers came to South Africa to take part in the gold industry. Today, South Africa is the continent's largest gold producer.

Find Out More About It!

Study the text and photos on these pages to learn about inventions, creations, and contributions that have come from Africa south of the Sahara. Then choose the item that interests you the most and use the library or the Internet to learn more about it. Use the information you gather to write a short essay about how what you researched relates to you.

RESEARCH LINKS
CLASSZONE.COM

Coffee

More than 1,000 years ago, coffee trees grew in Ethiopia. Coffee beans were first used as a food. In the 1400s, coffee as a beverage was popular in Arabia, Egypt, and Turkey. In the following centuries, it was introduced to Europe and to North America. Today, coffee comes in many varieties and blends and is served as a hot or a cold beverage. It is also used to flavor ice cream and other treats.

Sculpture

The earliest evidence of African sculpture outside of Egypt dates from around 500 B.C. in Nok, located in what is now Nigeria. Archaeologists have found baked-clay heads and figures made by the Nok people. In the 1400s, sculptures of kings and thrones were created to show respect for royalty. They also represented the wealth of a region. Today, many African sculptures continue to be based on traditional themes. Artists create sculptures for religious and social purposes as well as for the retail and tourist trade.

Economies and Cultures

TERMS & NAMES
subsistence farming
cash crop
rite of passage

MAIN IDEA

The economies in Western and Central Africa are mostly a mix of traditional and market economies.

WHY IT MATTERS NOW

Economic development is one of the keys to sustaining democracy in Africa.

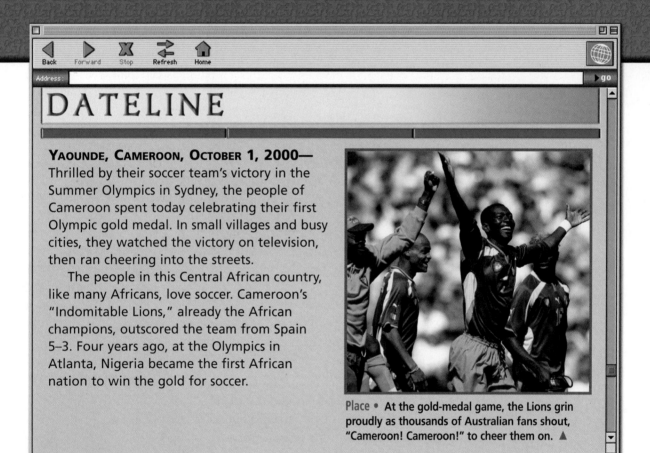

Back | Forward | Stop | Refresh | Home

Address: ▶ go

DATELINE

YAOUNDE, CAMEROON, OCTOBER 1, 2000— Thrilled by their soccer team's victory in the Summer Olympics in Sydney, the people of Cameroon spent today celebrating their first Olympic gold medal. In small villages and busy cities, they watched the victory on television, then ran cheering into the streets.

The people in this Central African country, like many Africans, love soccer. Cameroon's "Indomitable Lions," already the African champions, outscored the team from Spain 5–3. Four years ago, at the Olympics in Atlanta, Nigeria became the first African nation to win the gold for soccer.

Place • At the gold-medal game, the Lions grin proudly as thousands of Australian fans shout, "Cameroon! Cameroon!" to cheer them on. ▲

Economies of Western and Central Africa

Culture • These gold medals are from the 2000 Olympic Games. ▲

Many Africans share not only a passion for soccer but also a common economic history. Most African countries once had traditional economies, which followed age-old trading customs. Colonial governments introduced market economies, in which goods were bought and sold. Government-controlled economies, or command economies, became common after independence. Today, most African countries again have market economies.

Agriculture in Western and Central Africa

Reading Social Studies

A. Clarifying Is subsistence farming done for profit or need?

Most people in Western and Central Africa are farmers. Many practice **subsistence farming.** That is, they grow food, such as millet and sorghum, mainly to feed their own households. During the colonial era, European and African business owners started large plantations. They grew tropical crops—sugar cane, coffee, and cacao—for export. A crop grown only for sale is called a **cash crop**.

Edible Exports Have you eaten or used anything from Africa today? Chances are you have. Côte d'Ivoire (KOHT dee•VWAHR), formerly Ivory Coast, is the world's largest producer and exporter of cacao beans, which are used to make chocolate. Coastal West African countries also export coffee, bananas, pineapples, palm oil, peanuts, and kola nuts. Central African countries produce coffee, rubber, and cotton. These exports bring many African countries income for development, such as building roads and schools.

African Artisans

Although the majority of people are farmers, some have other jobs. Some people craft items out of metal, leather, or wood. These workers make things such as iron hoes, leather shoes, and beautiful pieces of art. Other people are entertainers and musicians. Musicians act as the historians in some traditional African societies. Their skills and stories are passed down from generation to generation.

Culture • Kente cloth, exported from West Africa, has become popular in many non-African countries. ▼

African Minerals

Almost every type of mineral in the world can be found somewhere in Africa. Valuable minerals exported from Central and Western Africa include diamonds, gold, petroleum, manganese, and uranium. Many Africans earn their living by working in mines.

Connections to Science

Disappearing Tusks Ivory from African elephant tusks has been used to make items such as piano keys, jewelry, and billiard balls. Many elephants have been killed for their tusks, which you can see below. To protect elephants, ivory products were banned internationally in the 1980s. However, the demand for ivory is still so great that people continue to hunt elephants illegally for their tusks.

Because elephants born without tusks are not hunted, they live and reproduce. Often their offspring are tuskless. Biologists have noted that about 30 percent of African elephants are now tuskless—an impressive increase from 1 percent in the 1930s.

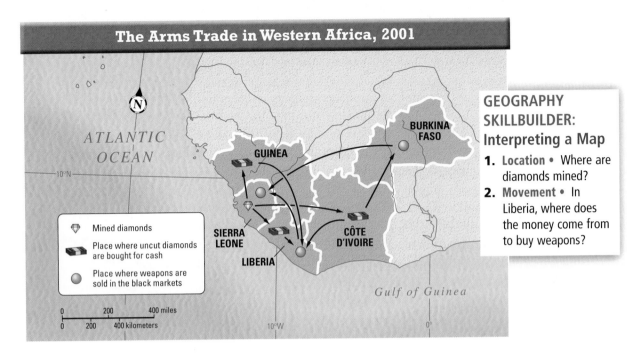

The Arms Trade in Western Africa, 2001

ATLANTIC OCEAN

SIERRA LEONE

LIBERIA

GUINEA

BURKINA FASO

CÔTE D'IVOIRE

Gulf of Guinea

Mined diamonds

Place where uncut diamonds are bought for cash

Place where weapons are sold in the black markets

0   200   400 miles
0   200   400 kilometers

GEOGRAPHY SKILLBUILDER: Interpreting a Map

1. **Location** • Where are diamonds mined?
2. **Movement** • In Liberia, where does the money come from to buy weapons?

Diamonds for Weapons Africa's mineral wealth is sometimes used to help fund wars. During Angola's civil war, the government used income from oil exports to buy weapons, while rebel forces traded diamonds for guns. Diamonds have also been exported illegally to support brutal wars in Sierra Leone and the Democratic Republic of the Congo. In Sierra Leone, diamonds were smuggled out of the country in small envelopes and sold to buy weapons for rebel forces. World diamond markets are working to prevent the sale of "conflict diamonds."

Ways of Life in Western and Central Africa

In Western and Central Africa, hundreds of different ethnic groups speak more than 1,000 languages. People practice many different religions, including Islam and Christianity. Most Africans live in small villages, but more Africans are moving to large, crowded cities, such as Lagos, Nigeria, or Accra, Ghana. City living has put strains on traditional African family life and culture.

Family Structure Society in Western and Central Africa is based on extended families that include children, parents, grandparents, and other close relatives such as aunts and cousins. Some ethnic groups trace ancestry through the mother's family; others, through the father's family. People share both work and free time with their family.

Reading
Social Studies

B. Making Inferences What aspects of city life do you think would put new strains on Africans from small villages?

Place • Many African extended families live in compounds such as this one. In addition to living areas, there are storage buildings and an open space for community life. ◄

Social Status

In many African societies, older people have higher status and more influence than younger ones. For example, when men of the Igbo people in Nigeria gather for discussions, they sit in order of age. The eldest men are served food and drink first. In some African communities, each age group has different responsibilities. Men of the most senior rank settle legal disputes and police the village. Female elders punish behavior that harms women, such as unfair treatment by husbands.

Seats of Art In Central and Western Africa, artists—not carpenters—make the most valued piece of household furniture: the stool. The Ashanti of Ghana believe that a person's spirit flows into a stool each time the person sits on it. Because of this, each individual in a household has his or her own stool. Nobody else is allowed to sit on the stool.

Each stool is decorated with special carvings that indicate the person's social status. The stools of the Luba people living in the Democratic Republic of the Congo reflect the importance the Luba place on their ancestors. Like the one at the right, most Luba stools feature a carving of an important ancestor of the owner.

THINKING CRITICALLY

1. **Recognizing Important Details**
   What do you think is the symbolism of the carved person holding up the seat of the stool?

2. **Drawing Conclusions**
   Why do you think the artist made this figure a woman?

Culture • These young boys of the Ituri forest in the Congo dance in outfits made of straw and woven cords during a rite of passage. ▶

Because age is so important, a special ceremony, which is called a **rite of passage,** marks the transition from one stage of life to another. A major rite of passage occurs when young men and women are recognized as adults. However, this tradition is dying out in parts of Africa. Some younger people are gaining higher status because they have skills that are needed. For example, as people move to cities, educated youths who can speak a European language are highly valued.

SECTION 2 ASSESSMENT

Terms & Names

1. Identify: (a) subsistence farming (b) cash crop (c) rite of passage

Taking Notes

2. Use a chart like this one to list characteristics of this region's economy and way of life. How might the economy affect how people live?

Economy	Way of Life

Main Ideas

3. (a) What types of economies are present in Western and Central Africa?

(b) How is the use of Africa's mineral resources both beneficial and harmful to Africans?

(c) How is African family structure similar to and different from American family structure?

Critical Thinking

4. Drawing Conclusions

Do you think Africans will continue to have rites of passage in the future? Why or why not?

Think About

- how city life is affecting African societies
- other societies around the world

Many Americans participate in rites of passage, such as baptisms, weddings, and funerals. Pretend you are studying American culture. Make a **poster** illustrating an American rite of passage.

Drawing Conclusions

▶▶ Defining the Skill

You are drawing conclusions when you read carefully, analyze what you read, and form an opinion based on facts about the subject. Often you must use your own common sense, your experiences, and your previous knowledge of a subject to draw a conclusion.

▶▶ Applying the Skill

The passage to the right is about the years following independence in the Democratic Republic of the Congo. Use the following strategies to help you draw conclusions based on the passage.

How to Draw Conclusions

Strategy ❶ Read the passage carefully. Pay attention to the statements that can be proved to be true.

Strategy ❷ Locate the facts in the passage and list them in a diagram. Use your common sense, your experiences, and your previous knowledge to understand how the facts relate to one another.

Strategy ❸ Apply your common sense, experiences, and previous knowledge to the new facts from the passage, and then write a conclusion based on your gathered evidence.

Make a Diagram

A diagram is a way of organizing facts. The diagram to the right shows how to organize the facts and inferences from the passage above and a conclusion that could be drawn from them.

▶▶ Practicing the Skill

Turn to pages 531–532 and reread the passage entitled "African Minerals." Make a diagram like the one to the right to draw conclusions from the passage.

In 1960, the country then known as the Belgian Congo gained independence. Five years later, Mobutu Sese Seko seized power and renamed the country Zaire. Mobutu ruled Zaire until 1997. ❶ Even though this country has some of the richest resources in Africa—copper, gold, and diamonds—Mobutu led the country into greater poverty. ❶ He put much of the country's money into his personal bank accounts. ❶ Mobutu ruled like a dictator, requiring men who worked in the government to dress like him and allowing only his political party to have any power.

❶ In 1997, Laurent Kabila led a rebel army into Zaire from the east and took over the government of Zaire. ❶ He immediately renamed the country the Democratic Republic of the Congo. Many people in Congo hoped that Kabila would work to improve life there, but instead, he led the country into war with neighboring nations. ❶ When Kabila seized power, Mobutu fled to Morocco, where he died in 1997. ❶ At the time of his death, there was no mention on radio or television in Congo that he died.

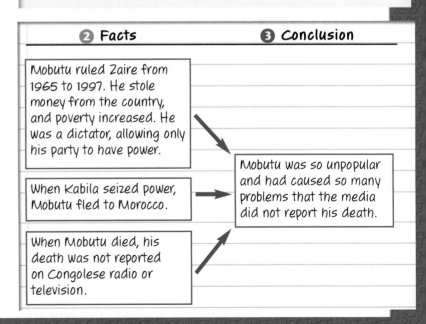

❷ Facts	❸ Conclusion
Mobutu ruled Zaire from 1965 to 1997. He stole money from the country, and poverty increased. He was a dictator, allowing only his party to have power.	Mobutu was so unpopular and had caused so many problems that the media did not report his death.
When Kabila seized power, Mobutu fled to Morocco.	
When Mobutu died, his death was not reported on Congolese radio or television.	

Nigeria Today

MAIN IDEA

Nigeria has a rich diversity of peoples and resources.

WHY IT MATTERS NOW

Nigeria's diversity has caused civil war, from which the country is currently recovering.

DATELINE

ZAZZUA, HAUSALAND, ANCIENT NIGERIA, 1566—The Queen is dead! Long live the Queen! This week the peaceful and prosperous reign of Queen Bakwa came to an end. Her daughter, Amina, was crowned queen. Unlike her peace-loving mother, Queen Amina is a warrior in the Zazzua cavalry.

At her crowning, she announced her intention to force other West African rulers to honor her and allow Hausa traders to travel safely through their lands. She also intends to build earthen defense walls around all of Zazzua's towns. She will begin her first military campaign in three months' time.

Place • These earthen defense walls are known as *ganuwar Amina*, or "Amina's walls." ▲

A Look at Nigeria

Queen Amina's 16th-century military conquests helped make the present-day nation of Nigeria very diverse. Its land includes several types of environments, such as tropical rain forests, mangrove swamps, and savannas. Its people and cultures come from more than 250 ethnic groups. Nigeria has a long history and a rich artistic heritage. However, like other African countries, Nigeria faced violence on the way to becoming a modern democracy.

History of Nigeria's People

Culture • **This sculpture was made by a Nok artist at least 1,500 years ago.** ▲

The Nok people were one of the earliest known cultures in the land that is now Nigeria. By about 500 B.C., they occupied the central plateau. They were skilled in ironworking and weaving.

Today, about 60 percent of Nigerians belong to one of three major ethnic groups: the **Yoruba** (YAWR·uh·buh), the **Igbo,** and the **Hausa** (HOW•suh). The first Yoruba established their kingdom on the west bank of the Niger River. The Igbo were part of the Nri kingdom in the southeast, and the Hausa built cities in the northern savannas.

The Yoruba Most of the Yoruba today live in southwestern Nigeria. Before colonial rule, Yoruba society was organized around powerful city-states. Yoruba men grew yams, peanuts, millet, beans, and other crops on land around the cities. Artists and poets had great prestige in traditional Yoruba society. Yoruba women specialized in marketing and trade. Their businesses made some women wealthy and independent.

The Igbo For thousands of years, the Igbo have lived in the southeast region of Nigeria. Igbo villages are fairly democratic, with leaders being chosen rather than inheriting their position. They are known for their metalworking, weaving, and woodcarving. In British colonial times, many Igbo held jobs in business and government.

Culture • **An Igbo woman paints a python on a house wall.** ▲

The Hausa The Hausa are the largest ethnic group in Nigeria. Almost all Hausa are Muslims. Most live in farming villages in northern Nigeria. Crafts such as leatherworking, weaving, and blacksmithing have been passed down through generations.

Reading Social Studies

A. Comparing How do the current locations of Nigeria's three ethnic groups compare with their original locations?

GEOGRAPHY SKILLBUILDER: Interpreting a Map

1. **Culture** • Which of Nigeria's ethnic groups covers the largest area?
2. **Location** • Which ethnic groups live alongside Lake Chad?

Ethnic Groups of Nigeria, 2001

NIGER · Sokoto · L. Chad · Fulani · BURKINA FASO · CHAD · Kano · Hausa · Kanuri · Maiduguri · Kaduna · BENIN · Jos · GHANA · TOGO · Bida · Abuja · Mumuye · Yola · Ilorin · Nupe · NIGERIA · Yoruba · Oshogbo · Tiv · Wukari · Ibadan · Ilesha · Makurdi · Mambila · Abeokuta · Edo · Enugu · Lagos · Benin City · Igbo · CAMEROON · CENTRAL AFRICAN REPUBLIC · Owerri · Ijo · Ibibio · Gulf of Guinea · Port Harcourt

0 100 200 miles
0 100 200 kilometers

• City
TOGO Country
Igbo Ethnic group

Becoming a Democracy

Region • Cassava plants grow in Nigeria's tropical climate. Nigerians eat the cassava's starchy root, shown below. It must be prepared carefully, since it is poisonous if eaten raw. ▼

In the 1800s, the United Kingdom colonized the northern and southern areas of what is now Nigeria. English became the common language. The two regions were united in 1914. In the 1920s, Nigerians began to work toward separating from British rule. Nigeria finally gained independence in 1960.

When oil was found in eastern Nigeria, the Igbo people there declared their independence. They set up the Republic of Biafra (bee•AF•ruh). Civil war raged from 1966 to 1970, causing a million deaths from fighting or starvation. After the war, military rulers took over. People had little freedom. Sometimes elections were held, but leaders often ignored the results. Finally, in May 1999, Nigeria had a free election. Former military ruler Olusegun Obasanjo was elected president.

Reading
Social Studies

B. Recognizing Important Details What event prompted the Igbo people to declare independence from Nigeria?

Nigeria's Economy

Nigeria has more than 123 million people—the largest population in Africa. More than half of Nigerians are farmers. Huge areas of the country have rubber, cacao, peanut, and palm oil plantations. The country has rich deposits of oil and natural gas. Oil is Nigeria's main export, supplying more than 90 percent of government income. Minerals, such as coal, iron ore, tin, lead, limestone, and zinc, are also important to the economy. Factories produce cars, cement, chemicals, clothing, and processed foods.

Biography

Wole Soyinka Wole Soyinka (WOH•leh shaw•YIHNG•kuh), a Yoruba man, was born in Abeokuta, Nigeria, in 1934. In 1986, Soyinka became the first black African to receive the Nobel Prize in literature. Soyinka (shown on the left) is best known for his plays, which combine African stories and European drama. He has also written novels, essays, and poetry. At the same time, he has been a voice for democracy, justice, and freedom of speech.

Soyinka's outspoken ideas got him into trouble with Nigeria's military rulers, and he was thrown into prison. After he was released, he left Nigeria. Soyinka lived in France and the United States for many years. He returned to Nigeria in 1998 to work for democratic reforms.

Nigerian Art and Literature

Nigeria's many cultures and ethnic groups have produced a rich mix of artistic styles. Yoruban artists have been making metal sculptures for about a thousand years. Yoruba also carve masks and figures out of wood. Decorated calabashes, or gourds, are another example of Nigerian art. Dried, hollow gourds are used as food containers or musical instruments. Baskets are made from local plants. Basket weavers turn practical containers into works of art.

Nigerians are also famous for their literature. Nigerian writers such as Amos Tutuola, Ben Okri, and **Wole Soyinka** have used folktale themes. Their novels and plays combine these themes with modern-day concerns such as human rights.

Human-Environment Interaction • **This decorated bowl was made from a calabash.** ▲

SECTION 3 ASSESSMENT

Terms & Names

1. **Identify:** (a) Yoruba   (b) Igbo   (c) Hausa   (d) Wole Soyinka

Taking Notes

2. Use a chart like this one to list the three major ethnic groups of Nigeria and give facts about each.

Group	Facts

Main Ideas

3. (a) How could a drought affect Nigeria's economy?

 (b) How did the discovery of oil affect Nigeria after it gained independence?

 (c) How are Nigeria's modern writers influenced by the past?

Critical Thinking

4. **Synthesizing**

 What relationship exists between Nigerian society and history and its art and literature?

 Think About

 • what modern Nigerian artists and writers are concerned about

 • how the past affects modern artists

Make a **mask** inspired by Nigeria's history, economy, or peoples.

ASSESSMENT

TERMS & NAMES

Explain the significance of each of the following:

1. coup d'état
2. mediate
3. ECOWAS
4. subsistence farming
5. cash crop
6. rite of passage
7. Yoruba
8. Igbo
9. Hausa
10. Wole Soyinka

REVIEW QUESTIONS

History and Political Change (pages 523–527)

1. What factors influenced the way in which European nations divided Western and Central Africa?
2. Describe the rule of Mobutu Sese Seko in the Democratic Republic of the Congo.
3. What were some positive and negative aspects of Nkrumah's leadership of Ghana?

Economies and Cultures (pages 530–534)

4. How do most people in Western and Central Africa earn a living?
5. What is the basis of society in most African countries? How is this changing?

Nigeria Today (pages 536–539)

6. Where does Nigeria's population rank in Africa?
7. What are the three major ethnic groups in Nigeria? In what region does each live?
8. What are some important resources and products of Nigeria's economy?

CRITICAL THINKING

Recognizing Effects

1. Using your completed diagram from Reading Social Studies, p. 522, summarize one of your inferences and the evidence you based it on.

Drawing Conclusions

2. How would the establishment of plantations growing cash crops affect a society used to subsistence farming? Try to think of both positive and negative effects.

Analyzing Issues

3. How does their ethnic diversity both help and hurt modern African nations?

Visual Summary

1 History and Political Change

- Colonial rule upset traditional forms of government and natural boundaries, causing problems for modern countries in Western and Central Africa.
- Ethnic violence, corrupt officials, and military rule have made it hard for many countries to establish stable, democratic governments.

2 Economies and Cultures

- Most people in Western and Central Africa are subsistence farmers, but cash crops and minerals are also important in the economy.
- The extended family is the basis of society in Africa south of the Sahara.

Nigeria Today 3

- Nigeria has a large population, valuable resources, and a rich cultural history, but it has faced problems since gaining independence.
- The Hausa, Yoruba, and Igbo are the largest of Nigeria's more than 250 ethnic groups.

Endangered Animals in Western and Central Africa

Animal	Range	Reasons for Decline
Cheetah	Africa to India	Habitat destruction, fur trade
Gorilla	Central and Western Africa	Habitat destruction, capture of young, fur trade
Black Rhinoceros	Africa south of the Sahara	Habitat destruction, overhunting for horn
White Rhinoceros	Central Africa	Habitat destruction, overhunting for horn

SKILLBUILDER: Drawing Conclusions

1. What information does this chart present?
2. From this information, what can you conclude about how humans affect wild animals in Africa?

FOCUS ON GEOGRAPHY

1. **Movement** • In which direction would you travel on most of the roads and railroads in Liberia?
2. **Human-Environment Interaction** • Why do you think the roads follow the paths they do?
3. **Movement** • Which forms of transportation are available for someone wishing to travel from Sulima, Sierra Leone, to Gbarnga, Liberia?

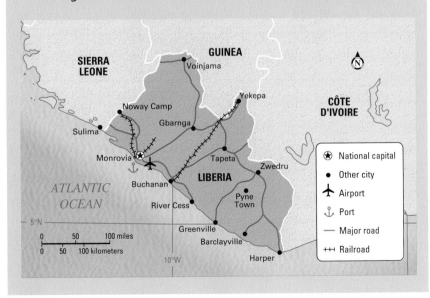

CHAPTER PROJECTS

Interdisciplinary Activity: Music

Exploring World Music Many musicians from Western and Central Africa, such as Youssou N'dour, have become internationally known. American jazz also grew out of African musical traditions. Learn more about an aspect of African music in a local music store or other music resource. Find and listen to music by one artist or in a certain style. Share your discoveries with the class.

Cooperative Learning Activity

Creating a Newspaper In a group of three to five classmates, write and produce a four-page newspaper, *Nigeria Today*, about current events in Nigeria. Write short articles about:

- Politics and economics
- Weather
- Human-interest stories
- Arts
- Sports

Find information and photographs on Web sites and in the library.

INTERNET ACTIVITY

Choose a country in Western or Central Africa other than Nigeria and use the Internet to research it and prepare a country study. Include information about topics such as population, language, religion, type of government, ethnic groups, and important crops and products.

Writing About Geography Make a one-page chart or poster summarizing your findings. If possible, include a photograph from a Web site you used to prepare your display.

For Internet links to support this activity, go to

RESEARCH LINKS
CLASSZONE.COM

Eastern and Southern Africa

Culture Tradition meets modern technology as two Masai girls in Masai Mara National Reserve in Kenya peer through the viewfinder of a long-range camera.

ATLANTIC

PACIFIC

PACIFIC
OCEAN

OCEAN

INDIAN
OCEAN

OCEAN

**EASTERN AND
SOUTHERN AFRICA**

How might a country's wealth lead to its poverty?

Human-Environment Interaction • In Burundi in Eastern Africa, your wealth and status in society are determined by the number of Ankole cattle you own. The more of these crescent-horned animals you own, the more important you are. Because of this, many Burundi families eat a mainly vegetarian diet rather than kill one of their cattle for food.

Hundreds of thousands of Ankole cattle are overgrazing Burundi's limited grasslands. This leads to soil erosion and desertification. Many other herding societies in Eastern and Southern Africa are experiencing the same problem.

What do you think?

- In the United States, what are some equivalents to owning Ankole cattle?

- As soil erosion continues, what might happen to Burundi's Ankole cattle?

READING SOCIAL STUDIES

BEFORE YOU READ

▶▶ *What Do You Know?*

Does your family own anything made of gold? If so, chances are that the gold came from Eastern or Southern Africa. What do you know about this region? What do you know about its people? What kinds of animals are found there? Recall what you read in Chapters 17 and 18, what you have learned in other classes, and what you have read or seen in the news about Kenya, South Africa, and the other countries of this region.

▶▶ *What Do You Want to Know?*

Decide what you know about Eastern and Southern Africa. In your notebook, record what you want to learn from this chapter.

Place • Mogadishu, the capital of Somalia, is one of many African cities devastated by civil war. ▲

READ AND TAKE NOTES

Reading Strategy: Predicting Predicting means using what you know to make an educated guess about what is going to happen. This is an important skill in social studies. Scholars look at the past and present to try to predict the future.

- Copy the chart into your notebook.
- As you read, record information about past and present situations in each category. If you find predictions about the future, record those also.
- After you read, review your information and use it to write your own predictions.

Place • Nairobi, Kenya, is a rapidly growing city with a population in 2000 of over 2 million. ▲

	Past	Present	Future
Government			
People			
Economy			
Culture			
South Africa			
Kenya			

History and Governments

MAIN IDEA

There is a great diversity of cultural groups in Eastern and Southern Africa.

WHY IT MATTERS NOW

This diversity has contributed to several conflicts as different countries work to establish stable democratic governments.

EXTRA

HADAR, ETHIOPIA, NOVEMBER 1974

Three to three and a half million years ago, a humanlike being died beside a lake in Africa. This month, her remains were found by Donald Johanson and Maurice Taieb. After studying the skeleton, scientists determined that the female had been approximately three and a half feet tall, and she might have walked on two legs. Humans and their ancestors are the only known mammals that walk on two legs rather than four.

Discoveries such as this skeleton are very rare. One of the discoverers said, "They're even harder to find than diamonds, but they're the key to understanding human origins."

Place • Scientists named the newly discovered skeleton "Lucy." Lucy's brain was about one-third the size of a modern human brain. ▶

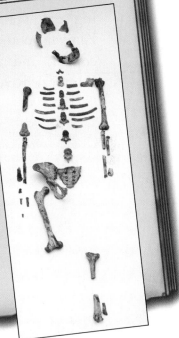

Early Humans in Eastern and Southern Africa

The oldest fossils of human ancestors have been found in African sites ranging from Ethiopia to South Africa. Tools of stone made about 2.5 million years ago have also been found in Eastern Africa. Slowly, early humans spread across Africa before migrating to other continents. The humans that remained in Africa became farmers and herders.

Early Eastern and Southern African Kingdoms

As the human population in Africa grew, societies became more complex. People began to trade with other regions. The income from trade helped build kingdoms.

The Aksum Empire Approximately 2,000 years ago, a great trading empire called Aksum (AHK·SOOM) developed in what is now Ethiopia. Find Aksum on the map below. Ships carried goods from Southern Africa, Arabia, Europe, and India to Aksum. About A.D. 350, King Ezana of Aksum became a Christian. Christianity spread throughout Ethiopia. When Islam came to Arabia, Aksum lost much of its trade because the Muslim Arabians preferred to trade with other Muslim nations.

Human-Environment Interaction • Making stone tools is difficult. This symmetrical hand axe found in Tanzania had to be carefully chipped into shape. ▲

Trade in Zimbabwe and Mozambique Around A.D. 700, trading empires arose in Southern Africa, in what are now Zimbabwe and Mozambique. These empires were rich in gold, copper, and iron. The mined metals were sent down the Zambezi River and then shipped across the Indian Ocean.

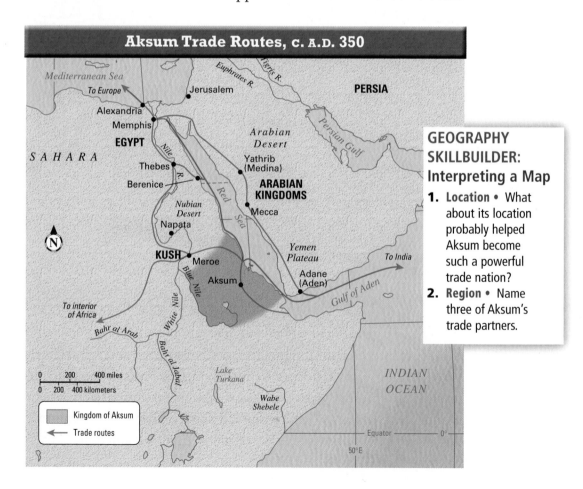

Aksum Trade Routes, c. A.D. 350

GEOGRAPHY SKILLBUILDER: Interpreting a Map

1. **Location •** What about its location probably helped Aksum become such a powerful trade nation?
2. **Region •** Name three of Aksum's trade partners.

The Africans traded their precious metals for textiles and spices from India, and silk and porcelain from China. Porcelain is a hard, white, glasslike material first made by the Chinese.

The Shona was one of the great trading empires of the lower Zambezi River from about 1100 to 1500. Its people created walled stone structures. These stone enclosures were called *zimbabwes* (zihm·BAHB·weez). The **Great Zimbabwe** is a spectacular stone ruin of a city made up of three parts. The Great Enclosure is the largest single ancient structure in Africa south of the Sahara. The Hill Complex, begun in 900, is the oldest section. The Valley Ruins include remnants of earthen and mud brick buildings. This city was abandoned in the 1400s. (See page 517 for more about the Great Zimbabwe.)

BACKGROUND

In the late 1800s, figurines of a bird were found in the ruins of the Great Zimbabwe. This Zimbabwe Bird is depicted on the flag of the present-day country of Zimbabwe, which you can see on page 492.

Other Eastern and Southern African Societies

Eastern and Southern Africa had other societies besides the great trade kingdoms. Two of these societies were the Masai (mah·SY) and the Zulu (ZOO·loo).

The Masai and the Zulu The **Masai** once lived in nearly all of Kenya and about half of what is now Tanzania in Eastern Africa. They raised grazing animals, especially cattle. The Masai were nomads who moved from place to place so their animals would have fresh land to graze. Land generally belonged to the whole group, not to one person or family. In the 1800s, the Masai began fighting among themselves over water and grazing rights. Many Masai warriors died in these wars. Long periods without rain followed, during which many Masai cattle died. The Masai society was weakened by these events.

Strange but TRUE

Floating Seeds Many sailors on trading vessels heading to and from the eastern coast of Africa saw huge seed pods floating on the ocean's surface. The seed pods were called *cocos de mer*, or coconuts of the sea.

It wasn't discovered until the late 1700s that the pods came from giant fan palm trees on the Seychelles Islands just north of Madagascar. The seeds of these trees are the largest in the world—some reaching 50 pounds in weight. It can take up to 10 years for a *coco de mer* to ripen.

Place • **A typical Masai village is set up in a circle. This layout helps the Masai defend their villages from attack.** ▼

The <u>Zulu</u> migrated to Southern Africa about 1,800 years ago. They have traditionally lived in settled villages, grown grains, and raised cattle. In 1815, a man named Shaka Zulu became chief of the Zulu. He led his people in a series of wars to expand Zulu territory. As the Zulu conquered other peoples, they made them Zulu as well. Shaka Zulu held unlimited power. Anyone who disagreed with him could be killed. Shaka's half-brother assassinated him in 1828.

European Colonization Soon after the death of Shaka Zulu, the Zulu began losing land to European settlers. The British and Germans then invaded Masai territory in the 1880s and 1890s. The Masai, weakened by war and drought, were no longer powerful. The Europeans quickly took the lands they wanted. The Masai were forced to live on reserves—small territories set aside for them. By the late 1800s, the United Kingdom, Germany, and France had claimed most of Eastern and Southern Africa.

Region • The Zulu, like this warrior chief, were members of a highly organized military society. ▲

African Independence

World Wars I and II weakened Europe. After the wars, European nations began to lose control of their African colonies. This paved the way for the independence of African nations. Most of the countries of Eastern Africa, such as Kenya, Tanzania, Rwanda, and Burundi, became independent between 1960 and 1964. Most of the countries of Southern Africa achieved independence later. Almost all of the new African governments were democracies, but many of them were subsequently overthrown and became dictatorships. Today, many African nations are again turning toward democracy.

Reading
Social Studies

A. Clarifying What events in Europe enabled African nations to gain their independence?

Place • These women and children in Mogadishu have struggled through years of brutal civil war in Somalia. ▼

Government in Somalia

From 1969 to 1991, Somalia was governed by a dictator, Siad Barre (SEE·ahd bah·RAY), who had unlimited power. In the 1980s, more than 100 leading citizens published an open letter criticizing the government. An open letter is a letter that is published in a newspaper. In the United States it is legal to publish letters criticizing leaders. In Somalia it was not. Forty-five of those who signed the open letter were arrested.

The arrests led to more protests. By 1990, fighting forced Barre to agree to reform his government. In 1991, he was driven from office. Since then, twelve clans have been fighting for control of the government.

Government in Rwanda

Through much of the 1900s, Rwandan women could not own land, hold jobs, or participate in government. In 1991, a new constitution was passed. It gave women the right to own prop-

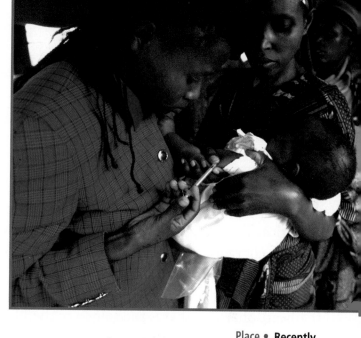

Place • Recently, Rwandan women have gained the right to own property and to work in fields such as medicine. ▲

erty and hold jobs, but the new laws were not enforced. Then, in 1994, a civil war began in Rwanda. So many men were killed that women began taking over as heads of households. Finally, as a result of the deadly wars, women were able to claim their constitutional rights. Since the conflict, more laws benefiting women have been passed. Today, not only can a Rwandan woman own property, but she can inherit property as well.

Reading
Social Studies

B. Analyzing Issues How did civil war in Rwanda lead to enforcement of women's rights?

SECTION 1 ASSESSMENT

Terms & Names

1. **Identify:**   (a) Great Zimbabwe   (b) Masai   (c) Zulu

Taking Notes

2. Use a flow chart like this one to show the different societies that have flourished in Southern Africa.

```
┌─────────────────────────┐
│     The Aksum Empire     │
└─────────────────────────┘
            ↓
┌─────────────────────────┐
│                         │
└─────────────────────────┘
            ↓
┌─────────────────────────┐
│                         │
└─────────────────────────┘
```

Main Ideas

3. (a) Explain how location helped build trade empires in ancient Ethiopia, Zimbabwe, and Mozambique.

   (b) What factors contributed to the weakening of the Masai society?

   (c) Describe how the lives of women in Rwanda have changed in recent years.

Critical Thinking

4. **Clarifying**
   What led to the downfall of Siad Barre in Somalia?

   Think About
   • how Barre ruled Somalia
   • the actions of the citizens

ACTIVITY
-OPTION-

Imagine you are a Rwandan woman in 1992. Write an **open letter** criticizing the government for not enforcing your constitutional rights.

Discover the Source of the Nile

You are proud to be part of a daring expedition to the heart of Africa. The trip, which begins in 1856, is sponsored by the Royal Geographical Society. Its leaders are two of Britain's best-known explorers—John Hanning Speke and Richard Burton. They are chasing a legend—that there is a great lake in the heart of Africa that is the source of the Nile—and you are the newest member of their team.

COOPERATIVE LEARNING On these pages are challenges your expedition will face as you search for the source of the Nile. Working with a small group of other explorers, decide which one of these challenges you will solve. Divide the work among group members. Look for helpful information in the Data File. Keep in mind that you will present your solution to the class.

SCIENCE CHALLENGE

"The African rain forest is full of hazards, from warring tribes to malaria to deadly snakes."

Exploring Africa is dangerous, especially in the mid-1800s. The African rain forest is full of hazards, from warring tribes to malaria to deadly snakes. While your expedition is deep in the jungle, you and your companions must be your own doctors. How can you keep yourself and others in the expedition healthy? Choose one of these options. Use the Data File for help.

ACTIVITIES

1. Research dangers and diseases you may encounter in the rain forest. Make a list of the safety equipment and medicines you will pack for the expedition.

2. Write a short manual on tropical diseases common in East Africa.

GEOGRAPHY CHALLENGE

". . . others are likely to challenge you."

Recently, Speke left the main expedition, and he now believes that he has found the Nile's source at Lake Ukerewe. He has renamed this huge lake Victoria, after the British queen. With him went a small group of people, and you are one of them. You are sure of your discoveries, but others are likely to challenge you. You need to demonstrate exactly how you found the source of the Nile. Choose one of these options. Use the Data File for help.

ACTIVITIES

1. Draw or trace a large map of East Africa that you can display on an easel. Make notes for a lecture-demonstration in which you will trace your route to show where the Nile begins.

2. Make a tabletop clay model of the lakes region of East Africa, including Lakes Victoria and Albert.

Activity Wrap-Up

As a group, review your solution to the challenge you selected. Then present your solution to the class.

DATA FILE

DISCOVERY TIME LINE

- February 1858: **Speke** and **Burton** are the first Europeans to reach Lake Tanganyika.

- July 1858: Speke breaks off from Burton, travels north, and finds and names **Lake Victoria.**

- 1860–1862: Speke and **James Grant** map Lake Victoria. Speke finds and names **Ripon Falls,** where the Nile flows out of the lake. The explorers start to follow the Nile but are stopped by local warfare.

- 1863: Speke passes on stories of another great lake to **Samuel W. Baker** and **Florence von Sass,** who find and name **Lake Albert.** It feeds into the White Nile.

AFRICA'S GREAT LAKES

- **Lake Victoria,** Uganda-Tanzania: area, 26,828 sq. mi.; length, 250 mi.; maximum depth, 270 ft.

- **Lake Tanganyika,** Tanzania-Congo: area, 12,700 sq. mi.; length, 420 mi.; maximum depth, 4,823 ft.

- **Lake Albert** (Mobuto), Congo-Uganda: area, 2,075 sq. mi.; length, 100 mi.; maximum depth, 168 ft.

- **Lake Turkana** (Rudolf), Kenya: area, 2,473 sq. mi.; length, 154 mi.; maximum depth, 240 ft.

EXPLORERS SEEKING THE SOURCE OF THE NILE

- **John Hanning Speke** (1827–1864): British soldier, discoverer of Lake Victoria.

- **Sir Richard Burton** (1821–1890): discoverer of Lake Tanganyika, looked for source of White Nile, also explored India and Arabia.

To learn more about Nile exploration, go to

RESEARCH LINKS
CLASSZONE.COM

Economies and Cultures

MAIN IDEA	WHY IT MATTERS NOW
The economies of Eastern and Southern Africa are based primarily on agriculture.	Billions of dollars of U.S. aid goes to this region to boost its economy.

DATELINE

ETHIOPIA, 1985—Ethiopia has been experiencing a widespread famine for a year. In 1984, a drought hit Northern Ethiopia and other parts of Eastern Africa. Nearly all crops failed. Many nations sent food, but it was not enough. Almost one million Ethiopians have died of starvation.

The government has moved 600,000 people to Southern Ethiopia, where conditions are better. Another 100,000 went to Somalia, 10,000 to Djibouti, and 300,000 to Sudan. Currently, there is no end in sight to this tragedy.

Region • The drought has killed not only crops, but also many of Ethiopia's animals. ▲

Agriculture in Eastern and Southern Africa

Agriculture is the primary industry of countries in Eastern and Southern Africa, even though drought is a serious problem. An exception is the area around Lake Victoria, which tends to get enough rain to support many different kinds of crops. People in this area grow bananas, strawberries, sweet potatoes, and yams. Cash crops such as coffee and cotton are grown in parts of Kenya, Rwanda, Burundi, and Uganda.

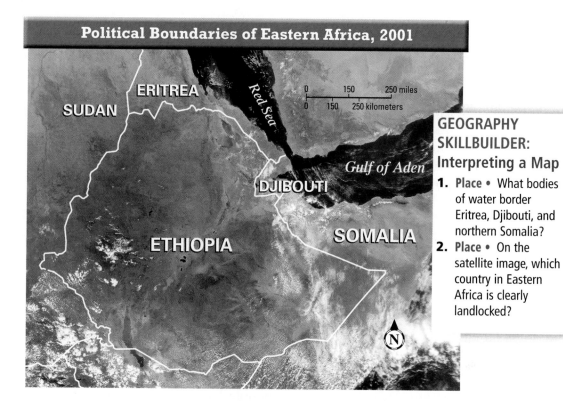

Political Boundaries of Eastern Africa, 2001

SUDAN
ERITREA
Red Sea
Gulf of Aden
DJIBOUTI
ETHIOPIA
SOMALIA

0 150 250 miles
0 150 250 kilometers

N

GEOGRAPHY SKILLBUILDER: Interpreting a Map

1. **Place •** What bodies of water border Eritrea, Djibouti, and northern Somalia?
2. **Place •** On the satellite image, which country in Eastern Africa is clearly landlocked?

Pastoralism In some areas of Africa, there is not enough rain to grow any crops. Somalia and most of Kenya receive less than 20 inches of rain each year. People survive by raising grazing animals, such as cattle, sheep, or goats. This way of life is called **pastoralism.** Many pastoralists are nomads. Today, because of Africa's increasing population, there are fewer places for nomads to graze their animals. As a result, the land is suffering from **overgrazing,** or the process in which animals graze grass faster than it can grow back. Overgrazing is a cause of desertification in Africa.

Place • Tanzanian fishermen spread nets along the shore of Lake Victoria. This cichlid is one of the native fish threatened by the Nile perch in the lake. ▼

Fishing Africa's large lakes support commercial fishing. Lake Victoria was once home to almost 500 native species of fish. Most of these fish were too small to support a large fishing industry. The large Nile perch was then introduced into Lake Victoria. Since then, nearly all the native fish have disappeared. Today, commercial fishing of the Nile perch has brought many jobs to the area and provided an important export.

Place • Sorghum is a cereal grain plant native to Africa. It is a mainstay in the diets of 500 million people in more than 30 countries. ▲

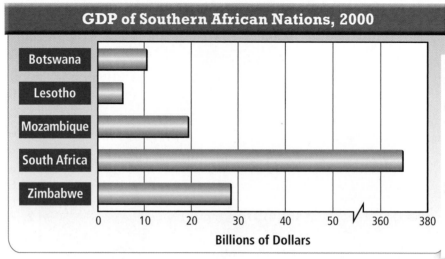

GDP of Southern African Nations, 2000

Botswana
Lesotho
Mozambique
South Africa
Zimbabwe

0   10   20   30   40   50   360   380
Billions of Dollars

SKILLBUILDER:
Interpreting
a Chart

1. Which of these countries had the largest GDP in 2000? the smallest?

2. Which country had a GDP about two times the size of Lesotho?

Africa's Economic Strength

Eastern Africa is the poorest region on the continent. Countries in Southern Africa have more diverse economies than do those in Eastern Africa. This means people have more ways to earn a living. For example, several countries in Southern Africa are rich in mineral resources, so there are jobs in mining. South Africa and Zimbabwe also have many manufacturing jobs. South Africa has by far the strongest economy in the region. In 2000 it had a Gross Domestic Product, or GDP, of approximately $369 billion.

Reading
Social Studies

A. Analyzing Causes What contributes to South Africa's strong economy?

The Beat Goes On People have made and played drums since at least 6000 B.C. In many African cultures, drums are more than musical instruments. The Yoruba used drums that imitate the pitch and pattern of human speech to transmit messages over many miles. These "talking" drums would, for example, send the message to an unpopular king that his people wanted him to resign. In Uganda, kettledrums were used to symbolize the king's power and offer him protection. Sacrifices of cattle were regularly made to the drums to give them a life force.

THINKING CRITICALLY

1. Making Inferences
What status do you think drum players hold in African society? Why?

2. Analyzing Motives
Why do you think the Yoruba people would use drums instead of a human messenger to send messages to their king?

Reading Social Studies

B. Making Inferences Why do you think good transportation and communication will improve Southern Africa's economies?

Transportation and Communication The countries of Southern Africa work together to improve the economy of the region. This includes improving transportation and communication among countries. For example, the railway lines of Botswana, Namibia, Lesotho, South Africa, and Swaziland are linked. These lines carry goods from all areas of Southern Africa to major ports along the Atlantic and Indian coasts.

Cultures of Eastern and Southern Africa

Marriage and kinship are changing in Eastern and Southern Africa as people move to cities. **Kinship** means family relationships. Economic activity brings people together; as they trade goods, they trade ideas. Their behavior and attitudes change as well.

BACKGROUND

The Tumbuka healers of Malawi use special songs and dances to diagnose and cure their patients' diseases.

Music in Eastern and Southern Africa In Eastern and Southern Africa, musical traditions of many different cultural groups come together. One characteristic of Southern African music is repetition. The Shona people of Zimbabwe make *mbira* (ehm·BEER·uh) music. *Mbira* music forms patterns of repetition using different voices or instruments. In Zulu choral music, individual voices singing different parts enter a song at various points in a continuous cycle. This creates a rich and varied pattern of sound. Another traditional way of making music is called *hocketing.* Groups of musicians play flutes or trumpets. Each musician plays one note. Then they rotate, or take turns, playing one note after another to create a continuous, freeform song.

Culture • Joseph Shabalala, founder of the South African vocal group Ladysmith Black Mambazo, performs with women dancers in traditional Zulu dress. ▼

Ancient Churches Ethiopia adopted Christianity in the 500s. In the 1200s, King Lalibela of Ethiopia commissioned 11 churches to be built in the town of Roha. The town was later renamed after the emperor. All of the churches were carved from solid volcanic rock. A network of tunnels was built to connect the churches. Today, a community of approximately 1,000 monks presides over these ancient churches and the pilgrims who visit them.

Changing the Tune African musical traditions moved across North America, South America, and Europe because of the slave trade and European colonization. African musicians have added elements of European, West Asian, and American music to their own styles to create new types of music. *Jiti*, for example, is a type of Shona *mbira* music that follows the traditional *mbira* rhythms using an electric guitar.

Religion in Eastern and Southern Africa

Today, about 85 percent of Southern and Eastern Africans practice Islam or Christianity. Only 15 percent practice a traditional African religion. Many traditional African religions focus on the worship of sky gods, ancestors, or spirits of rivers and of Earth. However, like Islam and Christianity, African religions recognize one supreme creator. Many Africans practice a traditional African religion that is combined with another religion.

SECTION ② ASSESSMENT

Terms & Names

1. Identify: (a) pastoralism   (b) overgrazing   (c) kinship

Taking Notes

2. Using a spider map like the one shown, fill in details that describe each type of economic activity. Add more lines as necessary.

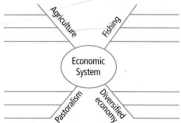

Main Ideas

3. (a) What geographic factors are responsible for the location of pastoralism in Eastern Africa?

(b) How did cultural borrowing affect African music? How did it affect other types of music around the world?

(c) What religious belief is common to all the major religions practiced by Africans?

Critical Thinking

4. **Recognizing Important Details**

Describe unique characteristics of the music of some African peoples. What influence do they have in common?

Think About

• the variety of African music

• how Africans incorporate European, West Asian, and American music

---

ACTIVITY
-OPTION-

Imagine you have moved from a community of nomads in Kenya to South Africa. Write a **letter** describing what your life was like as a nomad and what kind of job you might find in your new home.

Reading a Satellite Image

▶▶ Defining the Skill

A satellite image is a photograph taken from a satellite. Photographs taken from satellites can be of continents or neighborhoods. A satellite image of a large area shows water, land, and clouds. The color of the land indicates whether it is desert, forest, farmland, or mountains.

▶▶ Applying the Skill

This satellite image shows the continent of Africa. Use the strategies listed below to help you interpret the image.

How to Read a Satellite Image

Strategy ❶ Distinguish the land from the water. Water on a satellite image is blue or green. Notice the cloud formations, which appear as white on the image.

Strategy ❷ Look at the land. Areas that are desert are light tan. Mountainous areas are gray. Dark green areas show places where there is vegetation, or forests and farmland.

Strategy ❸ Compare the satellite image with the political map of Africa in the Unit Atlas on page 486. Use the chart below to match the regions on the satellite image as closely as possible with countries. Because of clouds, you cannot see the land in all parts of Africa.

Make a Chart

A chart will help you organize the information found on the satellite image and on the political map of Africa.

Color on Satellite Map	Land Type	Countries
Light tan	Desert	Northern Africa
Orange	Semiarid	Sudan, Chad, Eastern Ethiopia, Namibia, Botswana
Dark green	Forest, farmland	Central Africa, Mozambique, Zimbabwe
Gray	Mountains	Ethiopia, Kenya

▶▶ Practicing the Skill

Turn to the satellite image shown on page 553. Compare that satellite image with the political map on page 486. Make a chart like the one shown above to organize the information found on the map and photo.

MY FATHER's FARM

NIGERIA, with over 123 million people, has the largest population of any country in Africa. More than half of all Nigerians live in rural villages. In this selection, the Nigerian writer Isaac Olaleye vividly describes his father's farm in a small village called Erin in western Nigeria. In the language of the Yoruba people, *erin* means "laughter."

In the heart of a great tropical forest
In space and solitude
Lies my father's farm.
In the acres of solitude
Grow rows of yams,[1]
White like sugar,
Their vines, mounting stakes,
Are clothed in pea green.

*

In the acres of solitude grow:
Rows of yams
The color of vanilla ice cream,
Rows of yams
Smooth as eggshells,
Rows of yams,
Gray like blueberries,
Rows of yams,
Yellow like lemons, and
Rows of yams,
Smooth and creamy as butter.

1. Throughout southern Nigeria, roots—especially yams, taro, and cassava— are the main crops grown on small farms.

Their vines, all mounting stakes,
And their leaves glowing green—
Yellowish green to emerald.
All the colorful rows delight me.
On my father's farm,
Where it is quiet enough to hear
Bees and flies as they buzz and hum
Through another busy day.

*

In the acres of solitude
Maize waves in the gentle wind.
Popondo beans hug one another.
Tomatoes sit on pumpkins.
The black-eyed peas climb the maize.
Sweet peas smother the okra
And while peppers flash
The color of danger,
White cotton balls
Laugh at them all.

Reading THE LITERATURE

What techniques does the poet use to describe the variety and texture of the yams growing in the fields of his father's farm? How does the poet use language, particularly verbs, to give the vegetables human traits?

Thinking About THE LITERATURE

At what time of year is this poem set? How can you tell? How might the images differ if the poem described the farm during another season of the year? during a drought?

Writing About THE LITERATURE

In the second stanza of "My Father's Farm," the poet uses repetition and similes. Do these devices enhance the poem? In what ways?

About the Author

Isaac Olaleye (b. 1941) was born and grew up in Nigeria. In addition to the poetry collection in which this poem appears, he has written several books for young people about Nigeria. As an adult he lived for several years in England before settling in the United States.

Further Reading "My Father's Farm" is one of 15 poems by Isaac Olaleye in the book *The Distant Talking Drum.* These poems capture daily life in a Nigerian village by treating such topics as a market day, a tropical rainstorm, and village weavers.

South Africa Today

TERMS & NAMES
veldt
Afrikaner
Boer
African National Congress
Nelson Mandela
sanction
Willem de Klerk

MAIN IDEA	WHY IT MATTERS NOW
South Africa is working to rebuild itself in the aftermath of apartheid.	Since the end of apartheid, South Africa has become a democracy.

DATELINE

EXTRA

WITWATERSRAND MAIN REEF, SOUTH AFRICA, 1896

Gold! Ten years ago, George Harrison, an Australian prospector, discovered gold in the Witwatersrand Main Reef. Most people, including Harrison, thought the find wasn't worth much. Harrison sold his claim for approximately $14. But many people were wrong.

The gold buried in the Witwatersrand is one of the biggest deposits in the world. Many expect these mines will soon produce 20 percent of the world's gold supply. Prospectors from all over the world are coming to the sleepy town of Johannesburg. Already, its population has passed 100,000.

Location • Johannesburg's growth is especially surprising considering that it is hundreds of miles from the nearest railroad, port, or major river. ▲

Place •
The discovery of gold nuggets has drawn many people to South Africa. ▲

Geography of South Africa

Mineral-rich South Africa is located at the southern tip of Africa. The Witwatersrand, also called the Rand, remains the world's largest and richest gold field. It also contains diamonds, uranium, and platinum. Since South Africa is south of the Equator, winter is in July and summer is in January. Most of South Africa is on a plateau. Much of it is flat grassland called the **veldt** (vehlt), where farmers raise cattle, corn, fruit, potatoes, and wheat.

Place • The Dutch landed at Table Bay and later established Cape Town nearby. ◄

History of South Africa

South Africa was home to Khoisan and Bantu peoples for more than 1,500 years. The Khoisan were herders and hunters, and the Bantu were farmers.

European Settlers In 1652, the Dutch founded the Cape Town colony. Their descendents, called **Afrikaners,** make up more than half of modern South Africa's white population. Over time, Dutch settlers left Cape Town to become pastoral farmers. Known as **Boers,** they developed their own culture and fought with Africans over land.

German, French, and British settlers followed the Dutch during the 1700s and 1800s. The Cape Town colony came under British control in the early 1800s. Africans resisted British efforts to force them out of the region. Thousands of Boers established two independent states in the 1850s and followed a policy of apartheid.

Wealth and War The discovery of diamonds and gold in the second half of the 19th century renewed European interest in the area. It also attracted prospectors and settlers from Australia, the United States, and Eastern Europe. Between 1899 and 1902, the British and the Boers fought each other in the South African War. Africans supported the British in hopes of gaining some equal rights. The British won and the Boer states came under British rule. Black protest organizations were formed when their situation did not improve.

BACKGROUND

Cape Town later became the legislative capital of South Africa. The country also has an administrative capital in Pretoria and a judicial capital in Bloemfontein.

Reading
Social Studies

A. Analyzing Motives What drew Europeans to South Africa?

Nelson Mandela (1918–) Nelson Mandela, below, led the fight against apartheid. He continued to inspire his followers during his 26 years in prison for protest activities. In 1990, South African President Willem de Klerk helped obtain Mandela's release. In 1991, Mandela became president of the African National Congress. Amid escalating violence, Mandela and de Klerk worked to end apartheid. In 1993, they shared the Nobel Peace Prize for their efforts.

In 1994, Mandela became president of South Africa. His Truth and Reconciliation Commission investigated crimes committed under apartheid. He worked to improve the living standards of the black population and helped enact a new constitution.

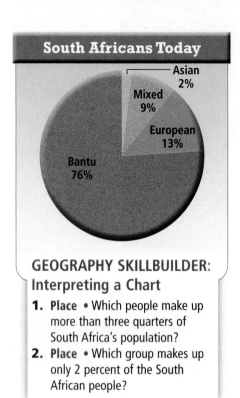

South Africans Today

Asian 2%
Mixed 9%
European 13%
Bantu 76%

GEOGRAPHY SKILLBUILDER:
Interpreting a Chart

1. **Place** • Which people make up more than three quarters of South Africa's population?
2. **Place** • Which group makes up only 2 percent of the South African people?

A Nation of Apartheid

In 1910, the British colony became the Union of South Africa. Afrikaners retained a political voice in the new nation. Racial segregation or separation continued under several new laws. Nonwhites were discriminated against concerning where they could live and travel, what jobs they could hold, and whether they could attend school. Many were forced to leave their homes. Apartheid became the official policy of South Africa in 1948 under the rule of the Afrikaner Nationalist Party.

The African National Congress The ANC,
or **African National Congress,** was a group of black Africans that opposed apartheid. When the government responded to their passive resistance during the 1950s with arrests and violence, the ANC became more aggressive in their protests. **Nelson Mandela** emerged as a leader of the ANC and the anti-apartheid movement. The fight continued for decades. Hundreds of demonstrators were killed, and thousands more were arrested.

Apartheid Ends Strikes had a negative impact on the economy and forced the government to change some of the apartheid laws in the 1970s and again in the 1980s. In 1985, the United States and Great Britain agreed to impose economic sanctions against South Africa. A **sanction** is a measure taken by nations against a country violating international law. **Willem de Klerk,** a white South African who opposed apartheid, became president in 1989. He helped to repeal many apartheid laws and to release from jail those who had worked to eliminate the policy.

Reading
Social Studies

B. Recognizing Important Details What were the main ways in which apartheid affected the lives of black South Africans?

Provinces of South Africa, 2001

⊛ National capital
★ Provincial capital
▭ Provincial boundary

0   150   300 miles
0   150   300 kilometers

NORTHERN PROVINCE
Pietersburg ★
Mafikeng ★   Pretoria ★ Nelspruit ★
NORTH-   ⊛★ MPUMALANGA
WEST   Johannesburg
        GAUTENG
Kimberley ★ FREE STATE   Ulundi ★
                          KWAZULU/
              ⊛ Bloemfontein   NATAL
30°S
NORTHERN
CAPE
                EASTERN
                CAPE
ATLANTIC   Bisho ★   INDIAN
OCEAN   WESTERN   OCEAN
          CAPE
     Cape ⊛
     Town
15°E   25°E   30°E

GEOGRAPHY SKILLBUILDER:
Interpreting a Map

1. **Place** • Name South Africa's three national capitals.
2. **Region** • How many provinces are there in South Africa?

In 1993, a new constitution gave all adults the right to vote. Nelson Mandela was elected president, served one five-year term, and retired in 1999. Thabo Mbeki (uhm·BAY·kee) then became president.

A New Era for South Africa

Today, the constitution of South Africa guarantees the same rights to everyone in South Africa. However, most black South Africans remain very poor. The government is working to provide better housing and to bring electricity and water to communities without them. South Africa continues to have the strongest economy in Southern Africa.

Cultures of South Africa Like its people, the cultures of South Africa are very diverse. For example, South Africa has 11 official languages. Although there are many official languages, English is understood by almost every South African because it is the language used in schools and universities. South African art and music are other examples of the country's diverse culture. Jazz and jive have combined with Zulu and Sotho rhythms to make a new, vibrant musical style.

Culture • South Africa's diverse cultures create a wide range of music and art. Zulu beadwork is one example. ▲

SECTION ③ ASSESSMENT

Terms & Names

1. **Identify:**
   (a) veldt
   (b) Afrikaner
   (c) Boer
   (d) African National Congress
   (e) Nelson Mandela
   (f) sanction
   (g) Willem de Klerk

Taking Notes

2. Use a chart like this one to list some of the reasons for conflicts between African and European groups during colonization.

European Group	Reason for Conflict

Main Ideas

3. (a) How have the veldt and the Witwatersrand contributed to South Africa's economy?

   (b) How did Nelson Mandela and the ANC influence South Africa's history?

   (c) How is apartheid related to South Africa's current political, social, and economic conditions?

Critical Thinking

4. **Recognizing Effects**

   What actions did South Africa and other nations take to change the policy of apartheid?

   Think About
   - the ANC's efforts
   - policies of the United States and Great Britain

ACTIVITY -OPTION-

Create a **poster** urging South Africans to vote. List several reasons why voting is important.

Kenya Today

MAIN IDEA

Kenya is a beautiful land that has rich natural resources.

WHY IT MATTERS NOW

In the future, Kenya may become the engine for economic growth in Eastern Africa.

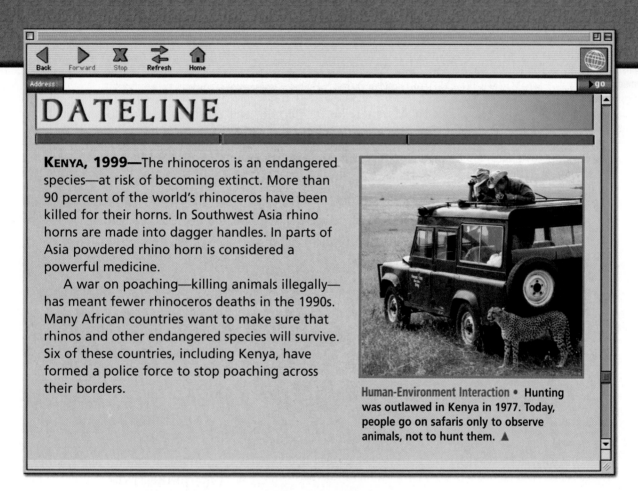

DATELINE

KENYA, 1999—The rhinoceros is an endangered species—at risk of becoming extinct. More than 90 percent of the world's rhinoceros have been killed for their horns. In Southwest Asia rhino horns are made into dagger handles. In parts of Asia powdered rhino horn is considered a powerful medicine.

A war on poaching—killing animals illegally—has meant fewer rhinoceros deaths in the 1990s. Many African countries want to make sure that rhinos and other endangered species will survive. Six of these countries, including Kenya, have formed a police force to stop poaching across their borders.

Human-Environment Interaction • Hunting was outlawed in Kenya in 1977. Today, people go on safaris only to observe animals, not to hunt them. ▲

Geography of Kenya

Kenya, on Africa's east coast, lies directly on the Equator. Its national park system is home to many threatened species, including rhinoceros, elephants, and cheetahs. Most of Kenya's human population lives in the highlands in the southwest, where there is rich soil and plenty of rain. Nairobi, the capital and largest city, and Mount Kenya are found here. Kenya's coast has tropical beaches and rain forests. The remaining three-quarters of Kenya are covered by a plain that is too dry for farming. Kenyans who live here are herders.

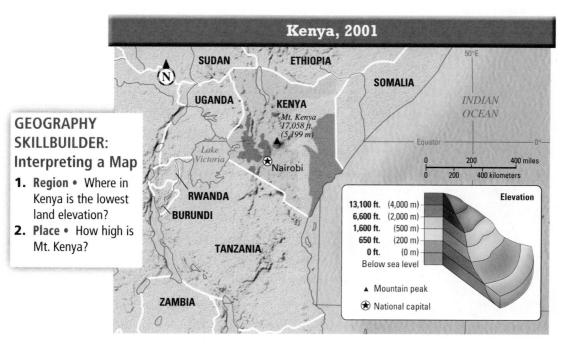

Kenya, 2001

GEOGRAPHY SKILLBUILDER:
Interpreting a Map

1. **Region** • Where in Kenya is the lowest land elevation?
2. **Place** • How high is Mt. Kenya?

SUDAN ETHIOPIA
SOMALIA
UGANDA KENYA
Mt. Kenya 17,058 ft. (5,199 m)
INDIAN OCEAN
Lake Victoria
⊛ Nairobi
RWANDA
BURUNDI
Equator 0°
TANZANIA

0	200 400 miles
0	200 400 kilometers

ZAMBIA

Elevation
13,100 ft. (4,000 m)
6,600 ft. (2,000 m)
1,600 ft. (500 m)
650 ft. (200 m)
0 ft. (0 m)
Below sea level

▲ Mountain peak
⊛ National capital

Culture • The Masai people migrated to Kenya a few thousand years ago. Masai warriors carried leather shields such as this one to help defend themselves and their animals from attack. ▼

Early History of Kenya

The ancestors of modern Kenyans began arriving in Kenya approximately 3,000 years ago. They were farmers, herders, and hunters from other parts of Africa. Some were part of the Bantu migration. Others came from the northeast. Greek, Roman, and Arabian traders and sailors often visited Kenya's coast along the Indian Ocean. Arabs set up trading posts there about 1,200 years ago. Portuguese sailors arrived in the early 1500s and took control of these trading posts. In the late 1800s, Kenya became a British colony. It gained independence in 1963.

Government of Kenya

Kenya's first prime minister, Jomo Kenyatta, ruled from 1963 until 1978, when he died in office. Vice President Daniel arap Moi then became prime minister. Moi's party was the only political party. By the early 1990s, however, many Kenyans became dissatisfied with this political system. One problem was that Moi gave special favors to people of his own ethnic group, the Kalenjin. After Kenyans held violent demonstrations in 1991, Moi agreed to allow a **multiparty system.** This meant that other parties could offer ideas for new laws and policies that might be different from Moi's ideas. Despite the change, Moi remained in power. Some people believe that Moi won the 1992 and 1997 elections through fraud.

Culture • Prime Minister Moi takes this baton, a symbol of his authority, to every public function he attends. ▼

Culture • Most Kenyans wear Western clothing, but a few rural groups still dress in their traditional native clothing. ▲

The People of Kenya

Thirty to forty different ethnic groups live in Kenya today. The Kikuyu are the largest group, making up approximately 20 percent of the population. Other large ethnic groups include the Kalenjin, Kamba, Luhya, and Luo. Most groups have their own language. Many people also know Swahili (swah·HEE·lee) and use it to communicate with other groups. **Swahili** is a Bantu language that includes many Arabic words. Swahili and English are the official languages of Kenya.

Education Education is very important to Kenyans. About 80 percent of Kenya's children go to elementary school. Government-run elementary schools are free, but students must pay tuition to attend high school. Most parts of Kenya have government-run schools. However, Kenyans value education so much that some have built their own schools in places where the government has not started them yet. These schools are called *harambee* schools. *Harambee* means "pulling together" in Swahili.

How Kenyans Earn a Living About 80 percent of Kenyans work in agriculture. The most profitable cash crops are coffee and tea. Farmers also grow bananas, corn, pineapples, and sugar cane. Tourism brings the most money into Kenya's economy. More than 500,000 tourists visit Kenya each year. Tourists come to visit the national parks to see the antelope, buffalo, elephants, giraffes, lions, and other native animals. Kenya protects these animals as an important natural resource.

A. Drawing Conclusions Why do you think Swahili has Arabic influences?

BACKGROUND

The Masai Mara National Reserve in Kenya and the Serengeti National Park in Tanzania include a combined 6,345 square miles.

Human-Environment Interaction • One of Kenya's most famous tourist attractions are the flamingos of Lake Nakuru. Unfortunately, their population is declining because the lake is polluted. ◄

Place • Each month thousands of people move to Nairobi. The majority of newcomers are men. ▲

Nairobi

Nairobi is Kenya's capital. The city's name comes from a Masai word meaning "place of cool waters." With 2 million people, Nairobi is the biggest city in Eastern Africa. It has restaurants, bookstores, museums, and skyscrapers. Many foreign companies have offices in Nairobi. Every year, many Kenyans leave their rural homes to move to Nairobi. Not all of them find life in the city as easy as they had hoped. They are often unable to find work. Also, Nairobi suffers from water shortages and power outages. Despite these problems, many residents enjoy the big-city lifestyle that can be found in Nairobi.

Reading
Social Studies

B. Identifying Problems What are the main problems Kenyans face after they move to Nairobi?

SECTION 4 ASSESSMENT

Terms & Names

1. Identify: (a) multiparty system   (b) Swahili   (c) *harambee*

Taking Notes

2. Use a time line like this one to document key events in Kenya's history.

| 1000 B.C., first Kenyans |
| ↓ |
| A.D. 800s, first Arab trading posts |
| ↓ |
| |

Main Ideas

3. (a) Why do most Kenyans live in the highlands?

   (b) Describe Kenya's government under Prime Minister Moi. How did it change in the 1990s?

   (c) How does the educational system of Kenya compare with that of the United States?

Critical Thinking

4. **Synthesizing**

   What problems might be caused by the system of languages in Kenya?

   Think About

   • the many ethnic groups
   • the use of Swahili and English

ACTIVITY -OPTION-   Imagine that you are on vacation in Kenya. Design a **postcard** to send home. Draw and write about some of the things you have seen on your visit.

TERMS & NAMES

Explain the significance of each of the following:

1. Zulu   **2.** pastoralism   **3.** overgrazing   **4.** kinship   **5.** veldt

6. Afrikaner   **7.** Nelson Mandela   **8.** sanction   **9.** multiparty system   **10.** *harambee*

REVIEW QUESTIONS

History and Governments *(pages 545–549)*

1. Why did the Masai and Zulu lose control of their own lands?

2. Explain how civil war in the recent histories of Somalia and Rwanda caused changes in each country.

Economies and Cultures *(pages 552–556)*

3. Why do so many people of Eastern Africa live as nomadic pastoralists?

4. How has the music of Eastern Africa changed?

South Africa Today *(pages 560–563)*

5. How have South Africa's rich natural resources affected events in its history?

6. How did apartheid limit the lives of nonwhites in South Africa?

Kenya Today *(pages 564–567)*

7. Why did Kenyans become dissatisfied with the government of Daniel arap Moi?

8. Describe the city of Nairobi.

CRITICAL THINKING

Forming and Supporting Opinions

1. Use your completed chart from Reading Social Studies, p. 544, to list three predictions for Africa's future. Explain your predictions.

Comparing

2. Compare the leadership shown by Somalia's Siad Barre, Kenya's Daniel arap Moi, and South Africa's Willem de Klerk.

Making Inferences

3. The Nobel Peace Prize is awarded to people who have done the most to create peace in the world. What did Nelson Mandela do to earn this award?

Visual Summary

1 History and Governments

- The history of Eastern and Southern Africa spans millions of years and includes trading empires, European settlement, and independence.

- Nations of Eastern Africa have suffered under colonial governments and rulers with unlimited powers. They now are trying to achieve democracy and freedom.

2 Economies and Cultures

- Most Eastern and Southern African nations are poor due to lack of rainfall, but Southern Africa has a more diverse economy.

- Eastern and Southern Africa have rich cultural heritages.

3 South Africa Today

- South Africa was first settled 2,000 years ago and was later colonized by the Dutch, French, Germans, and British.

- South Africa has the largest economy in Africa south of the Sahara.

4 Kenya Today

- Kenya has a varied geography, including beaches, plains, rain forests, and highlands that are home to many wild animals.

- Education is very important to Kenyans.

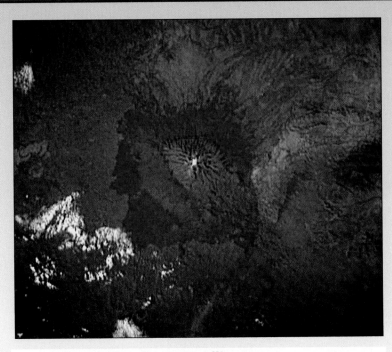

SKILLBUILDER: Reading a Satellite Image

1. **Place** • Locate Mount Kenya. Is it snow-covered? How can you tell?
2. **Region** • Describe the surrounding landforms.

FOCUS ON GEOGRAPHY

1. **Region** • What is the most common use of land in Southern Africa?
2. **Region** • What is most land used for in Eastern Africa?
3. **Region** • Use the Unit Atlas map on page 486 to identify two countries on this map in which nomadic herding is the main land use.

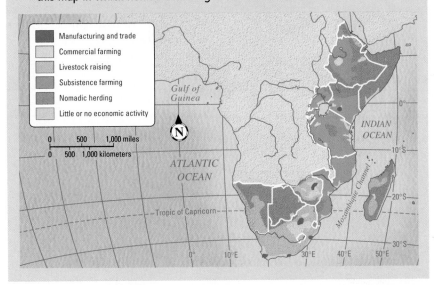

Legend:
- Manufacturing and trade
- Commercial farming
- Livestock raising
- Subsistence farming
- Nomadic herding
- Little or no economic activity

0   500   1,000 miles
0   500   1,000 kilometers

Gulf of Guinea

ATLANTIC OCEAN

INDIAN OCEAN

Mozambique Channel

Tropic of Capricorn

0°   10°E   30°E   40°E   50°E

0°

10°S

20°S

30°S

CHAPTER PROJECTS

Interdisciplinary Activity: Art
African Art Research the art produced by the Shona, Zulu, or another Eastern or Southern African group. Then choose a piece you especially like. Show it to your classmates, and tell what you like about it.

Cooperative Learning Activity
Create an African Collage Work in a group of two or three classmates. Make a collage about the daily lives and culture of one ethnic group living in Eastern or Southern Africa.
- Meet with your team and choose a group to research.
- Learn how and where the people live.
- Make pictures and write poems or sentences about your African group. As a team, make a collage of your work.

INTERNET ACTIVITY

Use the Internet to learn more about the climate and vegetation of one region of Eastern or Southern Africa. Learn how climate and vegetation affect people's lives.

Writing About Geography Write a report of your findings. Create drawings, diagrams, or charts to show information. Include a list of Internet sites you used to gather information.

For Internet links to support this activity, go to

RESEARCH LINKS
CLASSZONE.COM

UNIT 7

Place The Grand Palace is the former residence of the king of Siam, the country now known as Thailand. The palace complex was constructed in 1782 in Bangkok, the national capital.

SOUTHERN ASIA

SOUTHERN
ASIA

ATLANTIC

PACIFIC
OCEAN

PACIFIC

N

OCEAN

THE
GRAND
PALACE

OCEAN

INDIAN
OCEAN

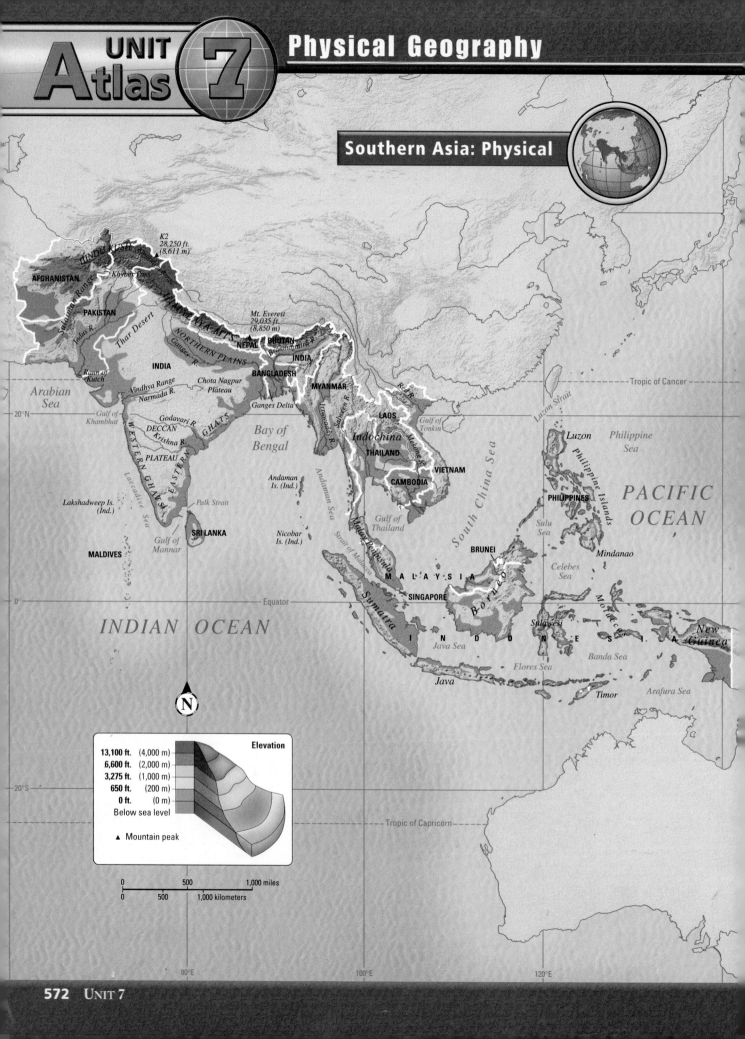

Southern Asia: Physical

AFGHANISTAN

HINDU KUSH

K2
28,250 ft.
(8,611 m)

Khyber Pass

PAKISTAN

Sulaiman Range

Indus R.

Thar Desert

HIMALAYA MTS.

Mt. Everest
29,035 ft.
(8,850 m)

NORTHERN PLAINS

Ganges R.

NEPAL

BHUTAN

Brahmaputra R.

INDIA

BANGLADESH

Rann of
Kutch

Vindhya Range

Narmada R.

Chota Nagpur
Plateau

INDIA

Ganges Delta

MYANMAR

Irrawaddy R.

Salween R.

Red R.

LAOS

Gulf of
Tonkin

Arabian
Sea

20°N

Gulf of
Khambhat

Godavari R.

DECCAN

Krishna R.

WESTERN GHATS

PLATEAU

EASTERN GHATS

Bay of
Bengal

Andaman
Is. (Ind.)

Andaman Sea

Indochina

THAILAND

Mekong R.

VIETNAM

CAMBODIA

Tropic of Cancer

Luzon Strait

Luzon

Philippine
Sea

Philippine Islands

PACIFIC
OCEAN

Lakshadweep Is.
(Ind.)

Laccadive
Sea

Palk Strait

SRI LANKA

Gulf of
Mannar

Nicobar
Is. (Ind.)

Strait of Malacca

Gulf of
Thailand

Malay Peninsula

PHILIPPINES

Sulu
Sea

Mindanao

Celebes
Sea

MALDIVES

BRUNEI

MALAYSIA

Sumatra

SINGAPORE

Borneo

Moluccas

New
Guinea

0°

Equator

INDIAN OCEAN

INDONESIA

Java Sea

Sulawesi

Banda Sea

Flores Sea

Java

Timor

Arafura Sea

20°S

N

Elevation

13,100 ft. (4,000 m)
6,600 ft. (2,000 m)
3,275 ft. (1,000 m)
650 ft. (200 m)
0 ft. (0 m)
Below sea level

▲ Mountain peak

0   500   1,000 miles
0   500   1,000 kilometers

Tropic of Capricorn

80°E

100°E

120°E

Precipitation in Southern Asia

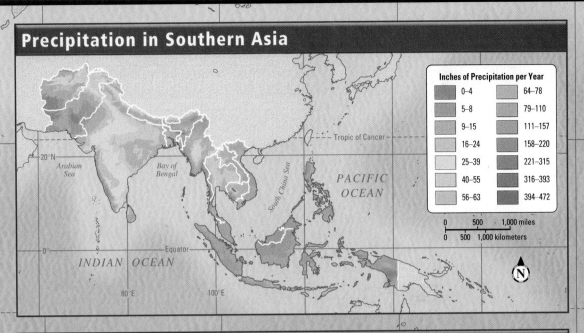

Inches of Precipitation per Year

0–4	64–78
5–8	79–110
9–15	111–157
16–24	158–220
25–39	221–315
40–55	316–393
56–63	394–472

Tropic of Cancer

20°N

Arabian Sea

Bay of Bengal

South China Sea

PACIFIC OCEAN

0°

Equator

INDIAN OCEAN

80°E   100°E

0   500   1,000 miles
0   500   1,000 kilometers

N

Southern Asia–United States Landmass and Population

Southern Asia

United States

LANDMASS

Southern Asia

3,685,718 square miles

Continental United States

3,165,630 square miles

POPULATION

Southern Asia
1,878,880,000

United States
281,421,906

= 50,000,000

FAST FACTS

✔ **MOST RAIN IN ONE MONTH:**
Meghalaya, India, July 1861, 366 in.

✔ **WORLD'S LARGEST RIVER DELTA:**
Ganges delta, Bangladesh

✔ **WORLD'S LARGEST ARCHIPELAGO:**
Indonesia, 3,231 mi., 17,000 islands

✔ **HUGE TSUNAMI:**
Java and Sumatra, 1883, 120-ft.-high wave

GEOGRAPHY SKILLBUILDER: Interpreting Maps and Visuals

1. **Location** • What mountain range lies in the north of India?
2. **Place** • Which two rivers form the Ganges delta?

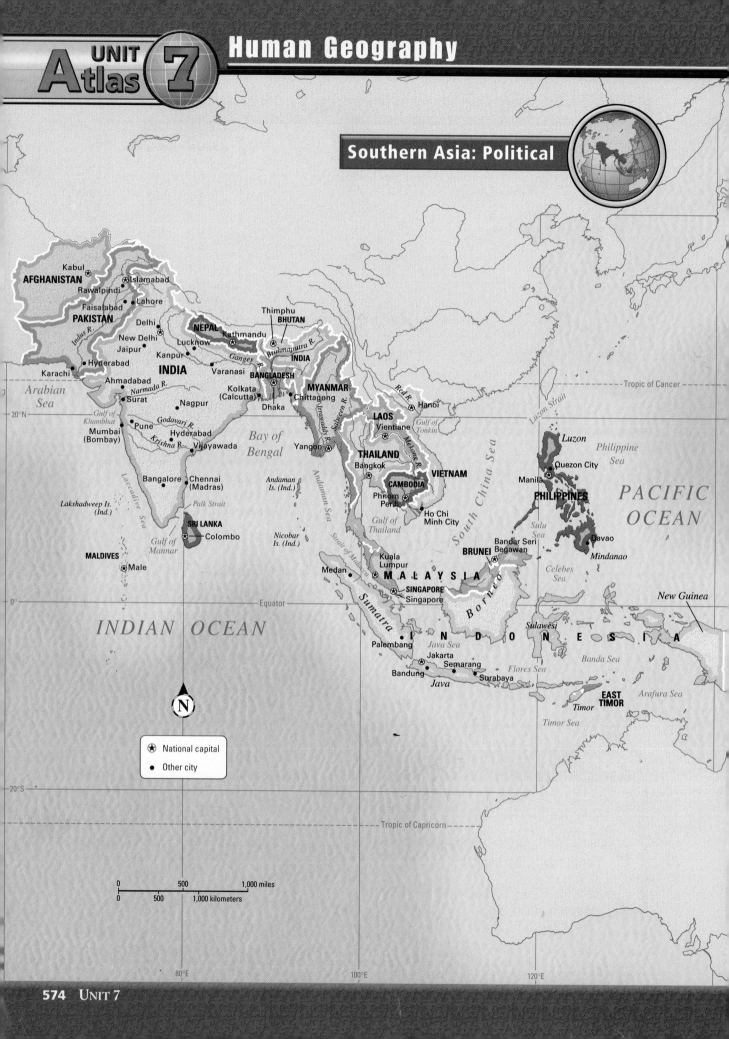

Southern Asia: Political

National capital ⊛
Other city •

Religions of Southern Asia

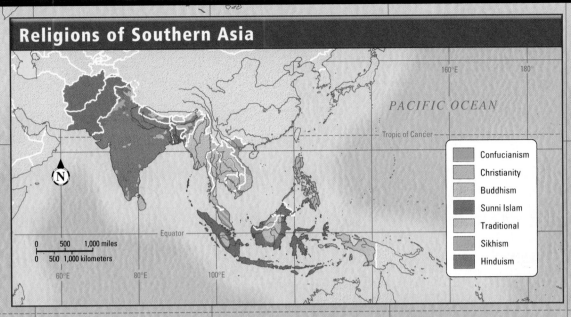

	Confucianism
	Christianity
	Buddhism
	Sunni Islam
	Traditional
	Sikhism
	Hinduism

PACIFIC OCEAN

Tropic of Cancer

Equator

0   500   1,000 miles
0   500   1,000 kilometers

Population Density of Southern Asia

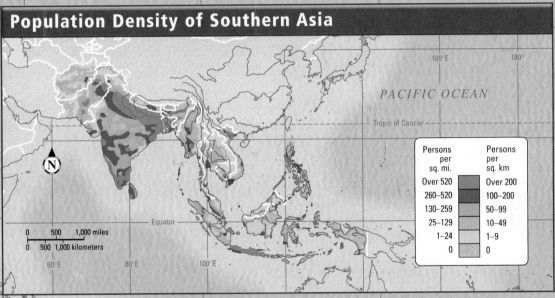

PACIFIC OCEAN

Tropic of Cancer

Equator

0   500   1,000 miles
0   500   1,000 kilometers

Persons per sq. mi.	Persons per sq. km
Over 520	Over 200
260–520	100–200
130–259	50–99
25–129	10–49
1–24	1–9
0	0

FAST FACTS

✔ **WORLD'S SECOND LARGEST COUNTRY POPULATION:**
India, 1,002,142,000 (2000)

✔ **WORLD'S TALLEST BUILDING:**
Petronas Towers, Kuala Lumpur, Malaysia, 1,483 ft.

✔ **WORLD'S LARGEST PRODUCER OF TEA:**
Assam, India, 1,700,000 lbs. per yr.

✔ **SINKING CITY:**
Bangkok, Thailand, sinking at about 3 in. per yr.

GEOGRAPHY SKILLBUILDER: Interpreting Maps and Visuals

1. **Region** • What country has the largest Hindu population?
2. **Place** • Which country shares borders with India and Afghanistan?

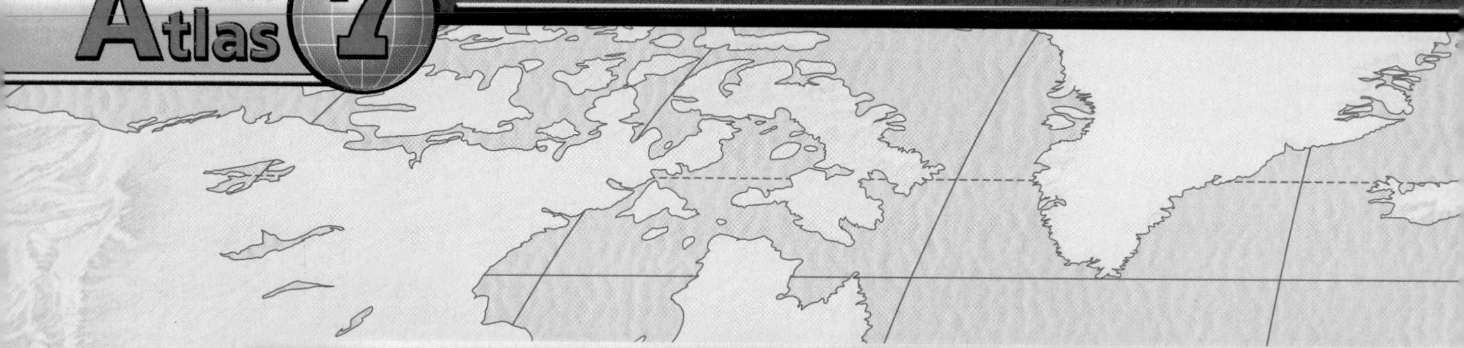

Country Flag	Country/Capital	Currency	Population (2001) (estimate)	Life Expectancy (years) (2000)	Birthrate (per 1,000 pop.) (2000)
	**Afghanistan** Kabul	Afghani	26,813,000	46	43
	**Bangladesh** Dhaka	Taka	131,270,000	59	27
	**Bhutan** Thimphu	Ngultrum	2,049,000	66	40
	**Brunei** Bandar Seri Begawan	Dollar	344,000	71	25
	**Cambodia** Phnom Penh	Riel	12,492,000	56	38
	**East Timor*** Dili	Dollar	737,000	50	25
	**India** New Delhi	Rupee	1,029,991,000	61	27
	**Indonesia** Jakarta	Rupiah	228,438,000	64	24
	**Laos** Vientiane	Kip	5,636,000	51	41
	**Malaysia** Kuala Lumpur	Ringgit	22,229,000	73	25
	**Maldives** Male	Rufiyaa	311,000	71	35
	**Myanmar** Yangon	Kyat	41,995,000	54	30
	**Nepal** Kathmandu	Rupee	25,284,000	57	36
	**Pakistan** Islamabad	Rupee	144,617,000	58	39
	**Philippines** Manila	Peso	82,842,000	67	29
	**Singapore** Singapore	Dollar	4,300,000	78	13

*East Timor became an independent country on May 20, 2002.

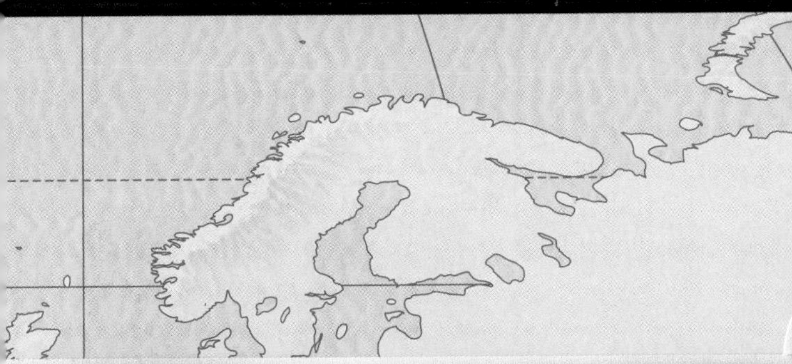

DATA FILE

Infant Mortality (per 1,000 live births) (2000)	Doctors (per 100,000 pop.) (1992–1999)	Literacy Rate (percentage) (1996–1999)	Passenger Cars (per 1,000 pop.) (1996–1999)	Total Area (square miles)	Map (not to scale)
149.8	11	32	2	250,775	
82.2	20	40	1	55,126	
70.7	16	42 (1995)	1	16,000	
24.0	85	88	441	2,226	
80.8	30	65 (1993)	1.2	69,898	
120.9	N.A.	48	23	5,641	
72.0	48	56	4	1,195,063	
45.7	16	84	12	779,675	
104.0	24	57	1.7	91,428	
7.9	66	84	143	128,727	
27.0	40	96	3	115	
82.5	30	83	0.7	261,789	
78.5	4	39	N/A	54,362	
91.0	57	44	8	310,403	
35.3	123	95	9	115,651	
3.2	163	91	95	225	

Country Flag	Country/Capital	Currency	Population (2000 estimate)	Life Expectancy (years) (2000)	Birthrate (per 1,000 pop.) (2000)
	Sri Lanka Colombo	Rupee	19,409,000	72	18
	Thailand Bangkok	Baht	61,798,000	73	16
	Vietnam Hanoi	Dong	79,939,000	66	20
	United States Washington, D.C.	Dollar	281,422,000	77	15

Mohandas Gandhi ▼

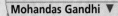

The Shwezigon Pagoda, a Buddhist temple in Myanmar ▲

The Ganges River Valley ▲

DATA FILE

Infant Mortality (per 1,000 live births) (2000)	Doctors (per 100,000 pop.) (1992–1998)	Literacy Rate (percentage) (1996–1999)	Passenger Cars (per 1,000 pop.) (1996–1999)	Total Area (square miles)	Map (not to scale)
17.3	37	91	12	25,332	
22.4	24	94	25	198,455	
36.7	48	94	1	130,468	
7.0	251	97	489	3,787,319	

GEOGRAPHY SKILLBUILDER: Interpreting a Chart

1. **Place** • How much lower is Singapore's birthrate than India's?
2. **Region** • How much higher is the literacy rate in the Philippines than in Laos?

Dancer in Rasa Lila drama in India ▼

Boys in Indonesia studying the Qur'an ▲

Central Highlands in Sri Lanka ▲

CHAPTER 20

Southern Asia: Place and Times

Place The temple complex at Angkor Wat, Cambodia, is dedicated to the Hindu god Vishnu. Built in the 1100s, it covers almost one square mile.

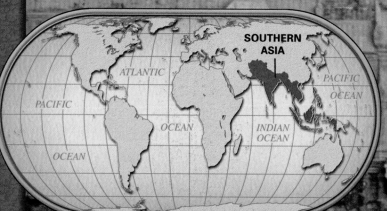

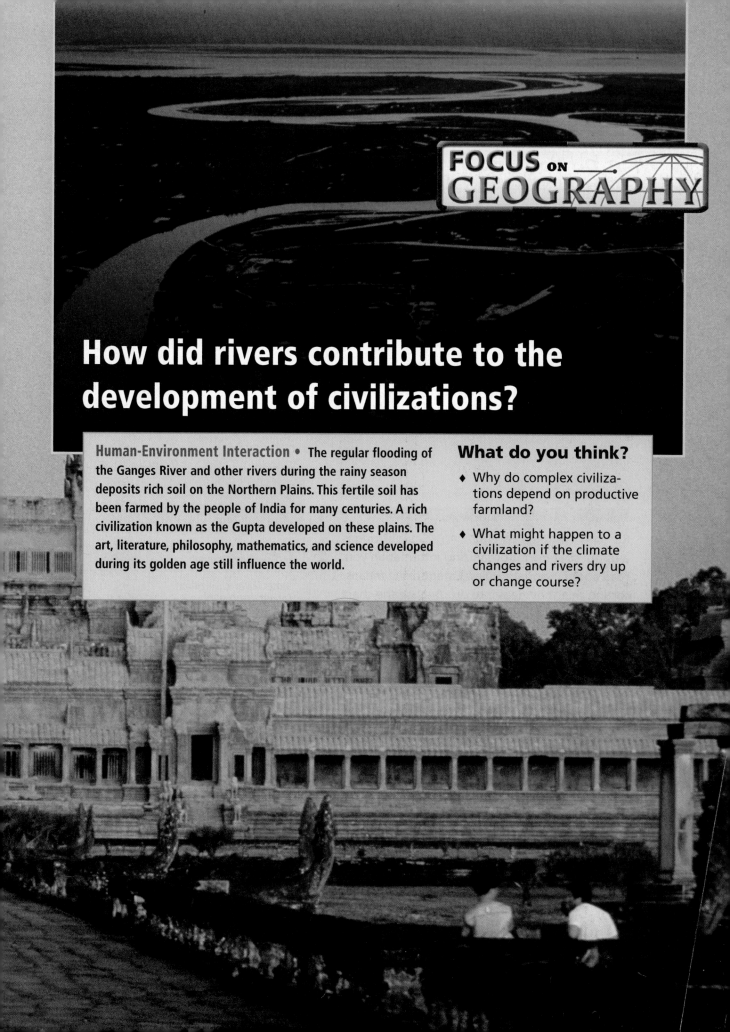

How did rivers contribute to the development of civilizations?

Human-Environment Interaction • The regular flooding of the Ganges River and other rivers during the rainy season deposits rich soil on the Northern Plains. This fertile soil has been farmed by the people of India for many centuries. A rich civilization known as the Gupta developed on these plains. The art, literature, philosophy, mathematics, and science developed during its golden age still influence the world.

What do you think?

♦ Why do complex civilizations depend on productive farmland?

♦ What might happen to a civilization if the climate changes and rivers dry up or change course?

READING SOCIAL STUDIES

BEFORE YOU READ

▶▶ *What Do You Know?*

Before you read the chapter, consider what you already know about Southern Asia. What stories have you read or heard about climbing the Himalayas, the highest mountains in the world? What do you know about explorers who have traveled the area's rain forests? What do you know about India? Have you read or heard about Hinduism or Buddhism, the major religions of Southern Asia? Reflect on what you have learned in other classes, what you have read, and what you may have seen in documentaries or news reports about the history of this region.

▶▶ *What Do You Want to Know?*

Decide what you know about Southern Asia. In your notebook, record what you hope to learn from this chapter.

Culture • Shiva is one of the Hindu gods worshiped in Southern Asia. ◀

Place • Mohenjo-Daro was once a thriving city in Southern Asia. ▼

READ AND TAKE NOTES

Reading Strategy: Categorizing Categorizing is a useful strategy for organizing information you read about in social studies. Categorizing means sorting things or ideas into groups. Use the chart at the right to categorize information about the geographic and human factors that shaped the ancient history of Southern Asia.

- Copy the chart into your notebook.
- As you read, look for information about geographic features and human civilization.
- When you reach the end of a section, record key details next to the appropriate headings.
- Note that the geography of Southeast Asia is discussed in Section 1 and Section 3.

Factors	Impact of Geography/ Contributions of Civilizations
South Asia	
Geography of Indian Subcontinent	
Indus River Civilization (about 2500–1700 B.C.)	
Aryans (1700 B.C.)	
Hinduism	
Buddhism (500 B.C.)	
Mauryan Dynasty (about 324–185 B.C.)	
Gupta Dynasty (A.D. 320–500)	
Southeast Asia	
Geography	
Location	
Early Advances	
Southeast Asian empires (6th century A.D.)	

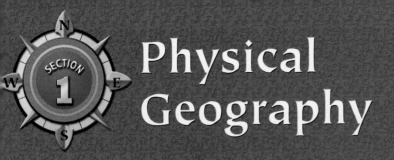

Physical Geography

TERMS & NAMES
subcontinent
Himalayas
Northern Plains
delta
sediment
Deccan Plateau
archipelago
monsoon

MAIN IDEA

Southern Asia's geography affects how the region's people live.

WHY IT MATTERS NOW

Studying the geography of Southern Asia will help you understand its history, economy, and customs.

DATELINE

EXTRA

NEPAL, SOUTHERN ASIA, MAY 29, 1953

Today, New Zealander Sir Edmund Hillary and Sherpa tribesman Tenzing Norgay became the first people to reach the top of Mount Everest in the Himalayas. Using oxygen canisters and boots and clothing with special insulation, the two men overcame the tremendous cold, high winds, and thin air to reach their goal. "We didn't know if it was humanly possible to reach the top of Mount Everest," said Hillary of their adventure. "And even using oxygen as we were, if we did get to the top, we weren't at all sure whether we wouldn't drop dead or something of that nature." Hillary and Tenzing survived and will go down in history as the first people to stand atop the highest mountain in the world.

Human-Environment Interaction •
Tenzing Norgay (on the right) and Sir Edmund Hillary relax after their historic climb. ▲

The Variety of Southern Asia

The Unit Atlas maps on pages 572–573 show the great variety and contrasts in the geography of Southern Asia. There are the vast snow-capped mountain ranges, such as the Himalayas, and wet low-lying rain forests. Some people live in the mountains, while others live deep in the tropical rain forest or in the desert. Some places are dry, and others get plenty of water—some, in fact, get too much.

Southern Asia is divided into two regions, South Asia and Southeast Asia. South Asia includes Afghanistan, Bangladesh, Bhutan, India, the Maldives, Nepal, Pakistan, and Sri Lanka (sree LAHNG•kuh). The South Asian subcontinent includes the countries of India, Pakistan, Bangladesh, Nepal, and Bhutan. A **subcontinent** is a large landmass that is part of a continent, but is geographically separate from it. India is the largest country on the subcontinent and in Southern Asia. It is the second most populous country in the world, next to China.

Geographic Regions of South Asia

The subcontinent has three main geographic regions—the Northern Mountain Rim, the Northern Plains, and the Deccan (DEHK•uhn) Plateau. Just off the coast are two island countries, Sri Lanka and the Maldives. Each of these regions has distinctive landforms and climate that affect how people live.

The Northern Mountain Rim The Northern Mountain Rim is made up of several mountain ranges. The Hindu Kush Mountains are located to the west and the **Himalayas** to the east. The Karakoram Range lies between the two, extending along the northern border of Pakistan. These mountains form a wall that separates the subcontinent from the rest of Asia.

BACKGROUND

Geologists believe that the South Asian subcontinent was once part of the African continent. It broke away 200 million years ago. Forty million years ago, this subcontinent crashed into Asia and created the Himalayas.

Reading
Social Studies

A. Making Inferences How might these mountains have made trade and travel by water important in ancient times?

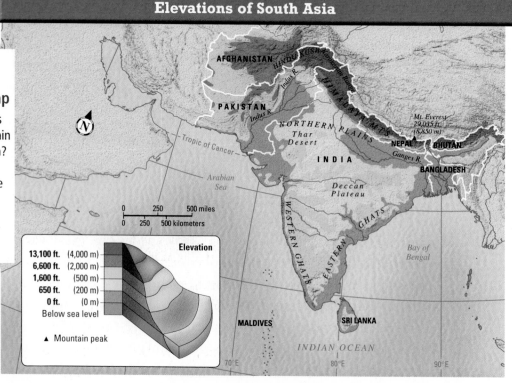

Elevations of South Asia

GEOGRAPHY SKILLBUILDER: Interpreting a Map

1. **Location** • What is the highest mountain range in South Asia?
2. **Region** • How would you compare land elevations in Bangladesh with land elevations in Pakistan?

Elevation

13,100 ft. (4,000 m)
6,600 ft. (2,000 m)
1,600 ft. (500 m)
650 ft. (200 m)
0 ft. (0 m)
Below sea level

▲ Mountain peak

However, there are some mountain passes that since ancient times have allowed travelers and invaders from Asia to get through the mountain barrier. The Khyber Pass, for example, connects the two modern-day countries of Pakistan and Afghanistan.

The Himalayas stretch for 1,500 miles across northern India and Nepal. They are 200 miles wide at some points, and many peaks are more than four and a half miles high. The tallest mountain in the world, Mount Everest, is almost five and a half miles high. This is taller than 23 Empire State Buildings stacked on top of one another. The terrain is rough in this region with few safe roads. It is also difficult to farm. As a result, fewer people live in this part of South Asia.

The Northern Plains The **Northern Plains** lie between the Himalayas and southern India. This region includes the Ganges (GAN·JEEZ) and Indus River valleys. The Ganges flows through Bangladesh and empties into the Bay of Bengal. The Indus River flows through Pakistan and empties into the Arabian Sea. The Indus and the Ganges rivers form large deltas where they empty into the sea. A **delta** is a triangular deposit of soil at the mouth of a river. The map on page 584 shows that the Ganges River delta is mostly within Bangladesh.

Human-Environment Interaction • People in heavily populated Bangladesh crowd aboard a Ganges River ferryboat. ▶

The Ganges River carries rich sediment from the Himalayas to the plains. **Sediment** includes minerals and debris that settle at the bottom of a river. During the rainy season, the Northern Plains flood, and the sediment from the Ganges River is deposited there. This makes the plains a fertile farming area.

Because of the fertile soil, parts of the Northern Plains are densely populated. In Bangladesh, for example, more than 130 million people live in an area smaller than the state of Wisconsin. In ancient times, the Indus River valley was also fertile and densely populated. Today, however, the valley is mostly desert, and few people live in this hot, dry region.

The Deccan Plateau As you can see from the map on page 584, the **Deccan Plateau** makes up most of southern India. The plateau has mineral deposits, as well as forests where elephants roam. Mountains border the plateau to the east and west—the Eastern and Western Ghats (gawts). The Western Ghats are the higher peaks, reaching 8,000 feet at the southern tip of India. A coastal plain runs between the mountains and the oceans on both coasts. Along these coastal plains the soil is fertile and water is plentiful. In the interior part of the plateau, between the mountain ranges, the soil is not as rich. People do farm there but water supplies are unreliable and it is hot year round. Fewer people live on the Deccan Plateau than in the Northern Plains.

Place • An elephant gets its tusks washed at an elephant training camp in Mudumalai National Park. ▲

Sri Lanka and the Maldives The islands of Sri Lanka and the Maldives lie south and southwest of India. Sri Lanka is a picturesque, mountainous island, 23 miles off the southern tip of India. Parts of it receive a great deal of rain.

The Maldives is a country made up of more than 1,200 low, flat coral islands called atolls. People live on only about 300 of these islands. The Maldives stretch south for 400 miles. The highest elevation in the entire chain is just over six feet above sea level.

Place • **The central highlands of Sri Lanka have mountains that reach over 7,000 feet and offer some spectacular scenery.** ◄

Place • **Mount Merapi, called the Fire Mountain, is the most active volcano in Indonesia.** ◄

Regions and Nations of Southeast Asia

Southeast Asia contains both a mainland region and many islands. The countries that make up Southeast Asia include Brunei, Cambodia, Indonesia, Laos, Malaysia, Myanmar (Burma), the Philippines, Singapore, Thailand, and Vietnam.

Mainland Southeast Asia The mainland lies on two peninsulas—the Indochinese Peninsula and the Malay Peninsula. The countries of mainland Southeast Asia are Cambodia, Laos, Myanmar, Thailand, Vietnam, and part of Malaysia. The Mekong River drains more than 313,000 square miles of this region. It starts in the highlands of the Plateau of Tibet and ends in the South China Sea. It flows through Laos, central Cambodia, and into Vietnam. This area is a major rice-producing region and is densely populated.

Islands of Southeast Asia The islands of Southeast Asia include Borneo, part of which belongs to the country of Malaysia, the island of Singapore, and the archipelagoes of Indonesia and the Philippines. An **archipelago** (AHR•kuh•PEHL•uh•GOH) is a group of islands.

Indonesia is the largest nation in Southeast Asia. It extends over an area about three times the size of Texas, and it has the fourth largest population in the world. Indonesia is made up of 17,000 islands that were formed by volcanoes.

Reading
Social Studies

C. Making Inferences How do you think the Mekong River contributes to growing crops in this region?

Southern Asia: Place and Times **587**

More than 6,000 of these islands are inhabited. The islands have a tropical climate with a lot of rain, but the soil is not very fertile. Still, more than half the people of Indonesia are farmers.

The 7,100 islands of the Philippines cover an area about the size of the state of Arizona. Only 800 of these islands are inhabited. Nearly half of the Philippine people are farmers.

Climate and Monsoons

Most of South Asia has three seasons—cool, hot, and rainy. The higher elevations are usually cooler. Much of India's weather is milder in the cool season. Sometimes frost forms on the Northern Plains. However, most of southern India is hot all year round.

Southeast Asia's climate has less variety. It is hot and rainy. Heavy seasonal winds and rains are common both to South Asia and Southeast Asia.

The Monsoon Cycle The period from June through September marks the coming of the monsoon winds and the rainy season. A **monsoon** is a seasonal wind that blows over the northern part of the Indian Ocean. From April through October, the monsoon blows from the southwest, building up moisture over the ocean and bringing heavy rains to South Asia and Southeast Asia. From November through March, the monsoon blows from the northeast.

South Asia and Southeast Asia have different monsoon cycles. In South Asia, heavy monsoon rains fall from June through October. November through February is mostly cool and dry. Because March through late May is hot and humid, the monsoon rains in June bring great relief. In India, school starts in June, after the rains begin. Children take their main vacation during the spring, when it is too hot to study. The monsoon rains reach as far north as the Himalayas. However, there is very little rain in most of western Pakistan.

The World's Most Destructive Volcano Krakatau (KRAK•uh•TOW), a volcanic island between Java and Sumatra in Indonesia, is pretty quiet these days (see below). In 1883, however, it erupted with explosions so loud they were heard in Australia and Japan, thousands of miles away. Krakatau's volcanic eruption caused tidal waves that killed 36,000 people. The eruption blew nearly 5 cubic miles of rock into the air and spewed out volcanic ash at least 17 miles high, throwing the region into darkness for days. This ash, blown around Earth for two years, caused amazing sunsets worldwide.

In Southeast Asia, there are two seasons. The summer monsoon lasts from April to September. During this time, there are heavy rains. The winter season from October through March is cool and dry.

Depending on Rain Agriculture depends on the timing of the monsoons. If the monsoons come too early, the farmers do not have time to plant their seeds. If the rains do not arrive or if they arrive too late, the crops fail. Sometimes the monsoons bring too much rain, resulting in severe flooding that ruins crops, damages property, and is dangerous to people.

Reading
Social Studies

D. Compare and Contrast How does this cycle of hot, cool, and rainy seasons compare with the cycle of seasons where you live?

Culture • **These women in India are celebrating Teej, a festival for welcoming the coming of the monsoons.** ▶

SECTION 1 ASSESSMENT

Terms & Names

1. Identify:
(a) subcontinent
(b) Himalayas
(c) Northern Plains
(d) delta
(e) sediment
(f) Deccan Plateau
(g) archipelago
(h) monsoon

Taking Notes

2. Use a chart like this one to record important information about South Asia and Southeast Asia.

	South Asia	Southeast Asia
Countries		
Major Regions		
Major Rivers		
Monsoon Cycle		

Main Ideas

3. (a) Describe three distinctive regions of South Asia.

(b) Where is the Mekong River? Which countries does it flow through?

(c) Name two nations in Southeast Asia that are archipelagoes.

Critical Thinking

4. Compare and Contrast

Compare the Northern Plains with the Deccan Plateau. How are they similar? How are they different?

Think About

• location

• fertility of the soil and population density

Photocopy a **map** of Southeast Asia. Using highlighter markers, spotlight the places you have learned about in Section 1. Share your map with the class.

India and Its Neighbors, 2001

National boundary

⭐ National capital

• Other city

0   250   500 miles

0   250   500 kilometers

N

AFGHANISTAN

Kabul ⭐

Indus R.

⭐ Islamabad
Rawalpindi

Faisalabad   Lahore

Indus R.

PAKISTAN

Hyderabad

Karachi

Tropic of Cancer

Delhi •
New Delhi ⭐

Jaipur •

Kanpur •

NEPAL   Kathmandu ⭐

Lucknow •

Thimphu ⭐
BHUTAN

Brahmaputra R.

INDIA

Ganges R.

Varanasi •

BANGLADESH

Dhaka ⭐

20°N   Arabian   Ahmadabad •

Sea   Narmada R.

Surat •

INDIA

Nagpur •

Mumbai   (Bombay) •

Pune •

Krishna R.

Hyderabad •

Godavari R.

Vijayawada •

Kolkata
(Calcutta) •

Chittagong •

Bay of
Bengal

Andaman Is.
(Ind.)

Lakshadweep
(Ind.)

Laccadive

Bangalore •

Chennai
(Madras) •

10°N

10°N

Andaman Sea

Sea

Gulf of
Mannar

Colombo ⭐ SRI LANKA

Nicobar Is.
(Ind.)

MALDIVES   ⭐ Male

GEOGRAPHY SKILLBUILDER: Interpreting a Map

1. **Location** • What country is both east and west of Bangladesh?

2. **Location** • What is the absolute location of the capital of Sri Lanka?

INDIAN OCEAN

0°

0°

Equator

80°E   90°E

Ancient India

TERMS & NAMES
Mohenjo-Daro
Aryan
Sanskrit
Hinduism
Vedas
caste
Ashoka

MAIN IDEA

The people of ancient India established social and cultural practices that became widespread throughout the region.

WHY IT MATTERS NOW

The scientific and cultural contributions of ancient India affect our lives today.

DATELINE

MAURYAN EMPIRE 232 B.C.—The great Emperor Ashoka died yesterday. He was dearly loved by his people, and millions will mourn his death. Horrified by the suffering and bloodshed he saw at the battle of Kalinga in 262 B.C., Ashoka embraced the teachings of Buddhism.

From that point on, he put his beliefs into action and ruled his people without violence. Who can possibly step forward to take the place of our great leader?

Place • Three lion figures top this pillar at Sarnath, one of many pillars Ashoka had erected during his reign. ▲

The Indus River Valley Civilization

Ashoka's empire was built on a civilization whose roots were more than 2,000 years old. Around 2500 B.C., a brilliant civilization developed in the Indus River valley. Sometimes called the Harappan civilization after one of its major cities, it flourished until about 1700 B.C. in an area that is mostly in present-day Pakistan. This civilization, which existed at the same time as ancient Egyptian civilization, stretched west to what is now Kabul, Afghanistan, and east to what is now Delhi, India. Its center was the rich farmland along the Indus River and its tributaries. The map on page 593 shows the extent of this civilization.

The civilization of the Indus River valley came to an end around 1700 B.C. No one knows for sure why the civilization ended. Some think the cause was a climate change—like a severe decrease in rainfall—while others think the urban centers were conquered and destroyed.

Hundreds of towns existed in the Indus River valley. There were two major cities: Harappa and **Mohenjo-Daro** (moh·HEHN·joh·DAHR·oh). Mohenjo-Daro was a large city with well-built homes and public buildings. Canals brought water from wells to farms outside the city walls.

Reading
Social Studies

A. Making Inferences Why do you think this civilization developed in the Indus River valley rather than on the plains?

The Aryan Influence on South Asia

Around 1700 B.C., the **Aryans** (AIR·ee·uhnz) came to South Asia. These people migrated from southern Russia through passes in the Hindu Kush. The time of the Aryan arrival suggests that the Aryans played a role in the fall of the Harappan civilization, although there is no proof. Over time, the Aryan people and the people of the Indus River valley produced a new blend of culture in northern India.

A New People, a New Civilization The Aryans were different from the people of the Indus River valley. They spoke another language called **Sanskrit.**

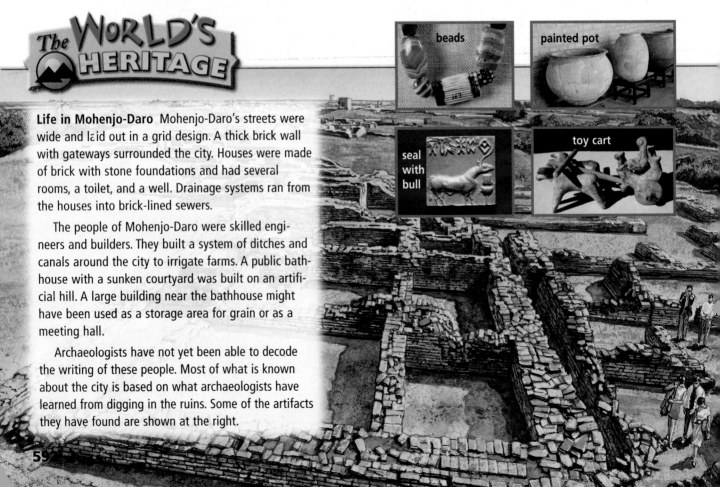

The WORLD'S HERITAGE

Life in Mohenjo-Daro Mohenjo-Daro's streets were wide and laid out in a grid design. A thick brick wall with gateways surrounded the city. Houses were made of brick with stone foundations and had several rooms, a toilet, and a well. Drainage systems ran from the houses into brick-lined sewers.

The people of Mohenjo-Daro were skilled engineers and builders. They built a system of ditches and canals around the city to irrigate farms. A public bathhouse with a sunken courtyard was built on an artificial hill. A large building near the bathhouse might have been used as a storage area for grain or as a meeting hall.

Archaeologists have not yet been able to decode the writing of these people. Most of what is known about the city is based on what archaeologists have learned from digging in the ruins. Some of the artifacts they have found are shown at the right.

beads

painted pot

seal with bull

toy cart

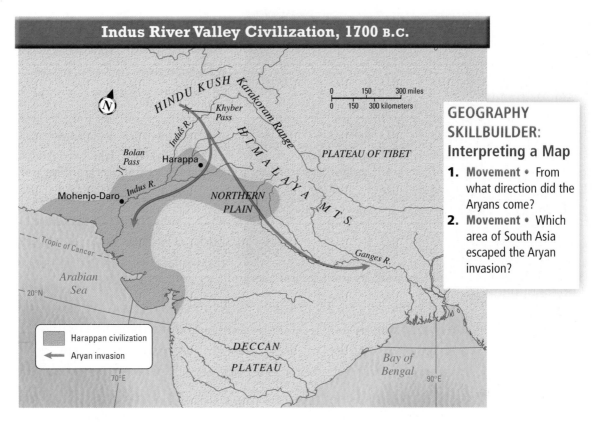

Indus River Valley Civilization, 1700 B.C.

Harappa
Mohenjo-Daro
Bolan Pass
Khyber Pass
HINDU KUSH
Karakoram Range
Indus R.
PLATEAU OF TIBET
HIMALAYA MTS.
NORTHERN PLAIN
Ganges R.
Tropic of Cancer
Arabian Sea
20°N
DECCAN PLATEAU
Bay of Bengal
70°E
90°E

0   150   300 miles
0   150   300 kilometers

Harappan civilization
Aryan invasion

GEOGRAPHY SKILLBUILDER: Interpreting a Map

1. **Movement** • From what direction did the Aryans come?
2. **Movement** • Which area of South Asia escaped the Aryan invasion?

The Aryans had not settled in cities but were nomads and herders. Because the Aryans got their food and clothing from the animals they raised, they measured wealth by the number of cattle a person owned.

New Technology The Aryans brought new technology, animals, and ideas with them to South Asia. Sometime after 1000 B.C., the Aryans discovered iron ore in the Ganges River valley. Iron plows improved agriculture, and with the Aryan adoption of some local ways—like growing rice—they began to settle in towns. The Aryans also developed new iron weapons. These weapons were stronger than those of the Harappan people. Improved weapons and the introduction of the horse enabled the Aryans to rule northern India.

Reading
Social Studies

B. Drawing Conclusions How did the Aryans' use of iron help them settle and control India?

Hinduism—A Way of Life

People of ancient India developed the religion of **Hinduism**, based on certain Aryan practices. Aryan priests chanted hymns in praise of their gods. For a long time, these hymns were passed down through oral tradition. Later, these hymns and other Aryan religious beliefs were written down and became part of the **Vedas** (VAY•duhz), or Books of Knowledge. The Vedas contain writings on prayers, hymns, religious rituals, and philosophy.

Culture • The god Vishnu is said to take ten forms, including a fish, a tortoise, and a boar. Here, he is half man and half lion. ▲

Karma and Reincarnation

The ideas of karma and reincarnation are central to Hinduism. Karma is the idea that a person's actions determine what will happen after his or her death. Reincarnation is the idea that after death a person's soul is reborn into a different body. Hindus believe that the cycle of birth, death, and rebirth occurs many times.

BACKGROUND

Hindus worship many gods and goddesses. Most Hindu families have a shrine to a god or goddess set up in their homes.

Each person's status in life is determined by his or her behavior in previous lives. A person who leads a virtuous life may be reborn as a wealthy or wise person. A person who lives an immoral life may be reborn as a poor or sick person.

The Caste System One of the main characteristics of Hinduism is the caste system. A **caste** is an inherited social class. Each person is born to a particular caste for his or her lifetime. Caste determines a person's job, marriage partner, and friends. The Hindu caste system was strongly influenced by the Aryan tribal social system, which was organized around the belief that people are not equal.

Reading Social Studies

C. Analyzing Issues How do the caste system and the idea of reincarnation work together?

The Hindu caste system is based on four major classes—priests, warriors and princes, merchants and farmers, and laborers. Another group, once known as untouchables, has traditionally been considered inferior to the four major castes. Untouchables did the work that no one else wanted to do and were generally shunned by society. Today, the Hindu caste system is made up of thousands of castes and subcastes, but the four major castes are still the most important. The government and other groups are working to reduce the influence the caste system has on society.

Culture • The god Shiva may be represented in various forms. Here he is shown as the Lord of the Dance. ▶

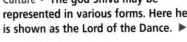

The Maurya and Gupta Dynasties

Two dynasties made important contributions to India. These dynasties were the Maurya and the Gupta. The contributions made by the people of these cultures still affect our lives today.

The Mauryan Empire The first Indian empire was called the Maurya (324–185 B.C.). It was founded by the descendants of the Aryans who moved eastward from the region of the Indus River valley civilization. One of its emperors, **Ashoka,** created a unified government. He built a palace of stone and religious monuments. The Mauryans were known for their fine sculpture and sandstone carvings.

The Golden Age and the Gupta Dynasty The Gupta Dynasty (A.D. 320–500) ruled during India's golden age in science, art, and literature. Most Gupta rulers were Hindus. However, both Hinduism and Buddhism were practiced throughout the empire at that time. Hindu and Buddhist beliefs inspired many artists. They created sculptures and paintings of Hindu gods and goddesses. Many temples were built that contained images of characters from Hindu mythology. Gupta architects hollowed out the solid stone of mountainside cliffs to create Buddhist temples. In the city of Ajanta, 30 Buddhist temples are carved into the side of a mountain.

Place • The Buddhist temples at Ajanta are carved into granite cliffs. The walls inside are covered with beautiful paintings. ▲

Ashoka Ashoka has been called one of the greatest emperors in world history. He ruled India's Mauryan Empire from 269 B.C. until his death in 232 B.C.

As a ruthless conqueror, Ashoka extended the Mauryan Empire over almost the entire subcontinent of South Asia. However, during one bloody battle, Ashoka became horrified at what he saw. He wrote, "150,000 persons were . . . carried away captive, 100,000 were [killed] and many times that number died." Ashoka vowed that this would be his last war, and he converted to the Buddhist religion.

He began to preach nonviolence and compassion for all living things and appointed "Officers of Righteousness" to relieve suffering among the people. Throughout the kingdom, the "principles for a just government" were carved in stone (shown at left) and displayed for all to see.

Literature Sanskrit literature blossomed during the Gupta Dynasty. Kalidasa, who lived during the fifth century A.D., was the greatest poet and playwright of his age. His plays were used to teach moral principles and were filled with creativity and mystery.

Mathematics Gupta mathematicians made many important discoveries. They developed the concept of zero and the numerals that we use today. Centuries after the Gupta Empire fell, Europeans learned these numerals and the concept of zero from the Islamic civilizations of Southwest Asia. Europeans called this number system *Arabic*, the name still used today.

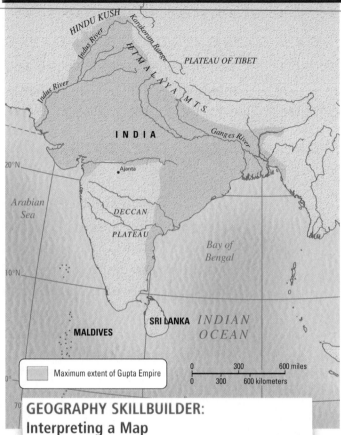

The Gupta Empire

Maximum extent of Gupta Empire

GEOGRAPHY SKILLBUILDER:
Interpreting a Map
1. **Location** • How far north did the Gupta Empire reach?
2. **Movement** • In which part of the Deccan Plateau would you expect to find influences from the Gupta Empire?

SECTION 2 ASSESSMENT

Terms & Names
1. **Identify:** (a) Mohenjo-Daro   (b) Aryan   (c) Sanskrit   (d) Hinduism
             (e) Vedas   (f) caste   (g) Ashoka

Taking Notes
2. Use a spider map like the one below to record information about changes the Aryans brought to ancient India.

Religion: Language: Aryans   Tools: Weapons: Animals:

Main Ideas
3. (a) Describe the city of Mohenjo-Daro.

   (b) Describe three aspects of Hinduism.

   (c) Why is the Gupta Dynasty considered a golden age in science, art, and literature?

Critical Thinking
4. **Analyze**

   Why do you think the originally nomadic Aryans settled in India?

   Think About
   • where the Aryans came from and the geography of the subcontinent
   • the civilization the Aryans encountered
   • the discoveries the Aryans made in India

ACTIVITY
-OPTION-
Suppose you could go back in time to visit Mohenjo-Daro, the Mauryan Empire, or the Gupta Dynasty. Write a **paragraph** explaining which period you would visit and why.

Reading an Elevation Map

▶▶ Defining the Skill

When you learn to read an elevation map, you will be able to tell how high above sea level the land in a region is. Land that is at sea level is at the same height, or level, as the sea. Land rises from that point. (In some inland areas, however, the land is actually below sea level.) The highest point above sea level on Earth is the peak of Mount Everest. It stands 29,028 feet above sea level. Elevation maps use color to show the height of the land. The key gives a color code for level of elevation. Usually, darker green areas are at or close to sea level. Light yellow or tan areas are the highest above sea level.

▶▶ Applying the Skill

The elevation map at the right shows the country of Pakistan. Pakistan, a country in southern Asia, has its southern border on the Arabian Sea. Its northern border is in the Hindu Kush mountain range and the Karakoram Range. Both ranges have mountain peaks higher than the highest peaks in the Rocky Mountains of the United States. Use the strategies below to help you read the elevation map.

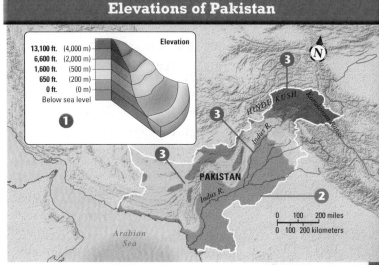

Elevations of Pakistan

How to Read an Elevation Map

Strategy ① Read the key. Notice how land closest to sea level is a dark green. Land that is highest above sea level is dark brown.

Strategy ② Look at the map. Find each of the elevation regions indicated on the key.

Strategy ③ Find the two highest mountain peaks. Follow the flow of the Indus River. Find the mountain pass. A pass is an opening in the mountain range where people have made roads or laid railroad lines because it is the easiest place to get from one side of the range to the other.

Write a Summary

A summary will help you understand the information found in the elevation map. The paragraph to the right summarizes the information found in the map of Pakistan.

▶▶ Practicing the Skill

Turn to page 584 in Chapter 20, Section 1. Read the map, "Elevations of South Asia," and then write a paragraph summarizing the information found in that map.

> The southern border of Pakistan is on the Arabian Sea. Land along that border is at sea level and then rises dramatically to the northern regions of Pakistan, where some of the highest peaks on Earth can be found. The Indus River flows from an area of more than 6,600 feet through a region of less than 500 feet, until it reaches the sea. In the west of Pakistan are several mountain ranges that reach up to 5,000 feet. Pakistan is a country of great variety in elevation.

Ancient Crossroads

TERMS & NAMES
Buddhism
Siddhartha Gautama
Four Noble Truths
Eightfold Path
Khmer
Angkor Wat

MAIN IDEA

The culture of ancient Southeast Asia was heavily influenced by traders and travelers from China, India, and other countries.

WHY IT MATTERS NOW

The culture of modern Southeast Asia still reflects the influence of ancient Indian and Chinese cultures.

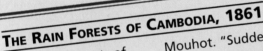

EXTRA

THE RAIN FORESTS OF CAMBODIA, 1861

In the rain forests of Southeast Asia, a young French explorer has made a startling discovery. He stumbled onto what appears to be one of the largest and most impressive archaeological discoveries in history. "We hacked our way through the dense [rain forest]," said Henri Mouhot. "Suddenly the huge stone towers of an ancient city, some of them 200 feet high, appeared before us." Experts believe this city may have been built by the Khmer people, who ruled a vast empire in the region about 600 years ago.

Place • Henri Mouhot has discovered the extraordinary lost city of Angkor. ▲

Crossroads of Culture

The ancient city that Mouhot found was Angkor. It contains an impressive temple complex dating back to the time when the region was one of the crossroads of the ancient world. A crossroads is a place where people, goods, and ideas from many areas come together. In ancient times, travelers from India, China, and other countries came to Southeast Asian shores and made a lasting impression on the region.

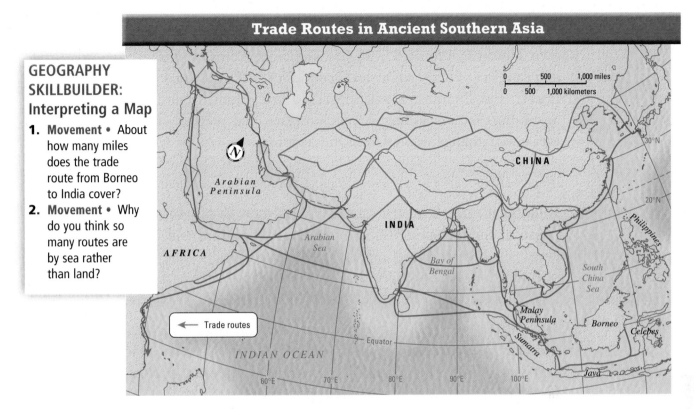

Trade Routes in Ancient Southern Asia

GEOGRAPHY SKILLBUILDER:

Interpreting a Map

1. **Movement** • About how many miles does the trade route from Borneo to India cover?
2. **Movement** • Why do you think so many routes are by sea rather than land?

BACKGROUND

Coastal traders used monsoon winds to sail their ships. They waited for favorable winds before sailing from India to Southeast Asia. When the winds shifted, the traders would sail back.

Reading
Social Studies

A. Analyzing What effect did India have on Southeast Asia?

Early History Many important skills were developed in ancient Southeast Asia, including making tools from bronze, growing yams and rice, and sailing. In the past, historians thought that people from China or India brought these skills to the region. But now it seems clear that this knowledge was developed in Southeast Asia. Bronze Age items found in Thailand have been dated as far back as 3000 B.C. That is before bronze work was done in China. Eight to nine thousand years ago, rice was grown in Thailand. Yams and other roots were grown in Indonesia between 15,000 and 10,000 B.C. This is one of the earliest examples of agriculture ever found.

Trade and Travel Look at the map above. You can see that the central position of Southeast Asia made it a likely crossroads of trade for the area. Southeast Asia is in the center of the sea trading routes of the South Pacific and the Indian Ocean. Traders from India began to visit Southeast Asia around A.D. 100. Southeast Asian goods reached both India and China. From there, they traveled on to Southwest Asia and East Africa.

Southeast Asian trade goods included rice, tea, timber, and spices such as cloves, nutmeg, ginger, and pepper. Gold and other metals were also traded. Many ideas were shared as well. Religious ideas and knowledge spread. Skills such as farming and metalworking, as well as art forms and techniques, crossed to and from Southeast Asia.

Influence of India Southeast Asia had a thriving culture of its own. However, it learned from and adopted customs from traders and travelers of other countries. Around A.D. 100, traders, Hindu priests, and Buddhist monks began to bring Indian culture to Southeast Asia, including art, architecture, and religion. These ideas were gradually adopted in the region.

Buddhism in Southeast Asia

<u>Buddhism</u> came from the same religious roots as Hinduism. It began in India around 500 B.C., although Hinduism and Islam eventually became more important religions in India. The ideas of Buddhism, however, spread to East and Southeast Asia, where it is still strong today. It is one of the major religions of the world.

The Signs of the Buddha The founder of Buddhism was <u>Siddhartha Gautama</u> (sih·DAHRTH·uh GAW·tuh·muh). He grew up as a wealthy prince and a member of the warrior class. Gautama lived in luxury in a palace with his wife and son.

One day, while out driving, he saw an old man. On other days, he saw a sick man, a corpse, and a holy man. Gautama interpreted these as signs to show him that life involves aging, sickness, and death. He believed that the holy man was a sign telling him to leave his family and seek the causes of human suffering.

For the next six years, Gautama was a wandering monk. He practiced self-denial and ate very little. However, he did not discover the cause of human suffering. One day, he decided to stop living a life of self-denial. He sat under a tree and began to meditate. Through meditation, Gautama gained enlightenment, or religious awakening. He now felt that he knew the reasons for human suffering and how to escape from it. News of his experience spread. People began to call him the Buddha, or the Enlightened One.

Buddhist Teachings The Buddha had once studied Hinduism. He was influenced by the Hindu beliefs in karma and reincarnation. These taught that life is a continuing cycle of death and rebirth. However, he did

Culture •
According to legend, the Buddha was sitting under a bodhi tree when he received enlightenment and the inspiration for his religious teachings. ▼

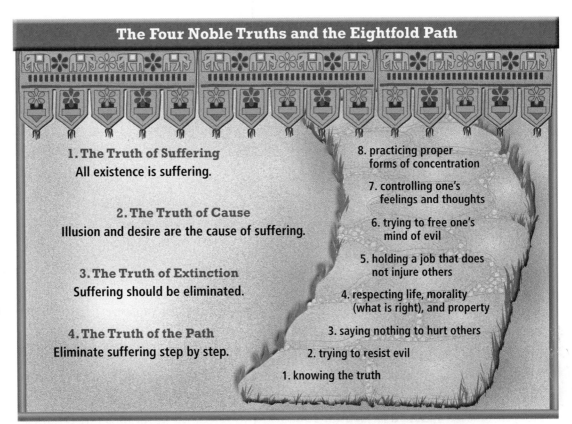

The Four Noble Truths and the Eightfold Path

1. **The Truth of Suffering**
   All existence is suffering.

2. **The Truth of Cause**
   Illusion and desire are the cause of suffering.

3. **The Truth of Extinction**
   Suffering should be eliminated.

4. **The Truth of the Path**
   Eliminate suffering step by step.

8. practicing proper forms of concentration

7. controlling one's feelings and thoughts

6. trying to free one's mind of evil

5. holding a job that does not injure others

4. respecting life, morality (what is right), and property

3. saying nothing to hurt others

2. trying to resist evil

1. knowing the truth

Culture • People in many parts of the world today still try to follow the teachings of the Buddha. ▶

not like the part of Hindu philosophy that was based on the Vedas, the ancient Aryan texts. In particular, he rejected the caste system and the role of priests.

The basic teachings of Buddhism are the **Four Noble Truths.** The first truth is that life is full of pain. The second truth is that suffering comes from the desire for possessions. The third truth explains that if people stop desiring these possessions, they will no longer suffer. The Buddha taught that the goal of life is to be free from desires and pain. Then one can progress to nirvana (neer·VAH·nuh), a state of happiness and peace.

Reading
Social Studies

B. Making Inferences What challenges might a person face in trying to follow the Eightfold Path?

The fourth truth says that people can escape suffering by following the Middle Way. The Middle Way is a set of guidelines called the **Eightfold Path.** These eight guidelines are as follows: right understanding, right purpose, right speech, right conduct, right means of livelihood, right effort, right awareness, and right meditation.

The Spread of Buddhism After the Buddha's death, his followers spread the new faith throughout southern India, Sri Lanka, and Southeast Asia. Buddhism also spread to Tibet, central Asia, China, Korea, and Japan. Buddhists organized schools and spiritual communities where monks and nuns could live and work.

Indian Influence in Southeast Asia

As the influence of India spread, new images and religious art became part of Southeast Asian culture. Historians can trace these images from one country to another. Empires were founded on the beliefs of Hinduism, Buddhism, and, later, Islam. The success of empires often depended on the ongoing popularity of these beliefs.

Empire of the Khmer In the sixth century A.D., the **Khmer** (kmair) people established a great kingdom in present-day Cambodia. This kingdom was Hindu and very much influenced by Indian culture. The Khmer built great Hindu temples, including the huge complex, **Angkor Wat.** The Khmer kingdom spread through much of Southeast Asia. Then, as Buddhism grew in influence, the number of Hindu followers declined, and the Khmer lost power. The Khmer retreated south to the area near the city of Phnom Penh.

Reading
Social Studies

C. Making Inferences How do you think Buddhism spread to other areas?

Indian influence in the form of Buddhism was also felt in the island nations of Southeast Asia. In Indonesia, a huge Buddhist temple called Borobudur was built in the sixth century. The builders used about 2 million cubic feet of stone to build the temple. It is shaped like a pyramid, with three terraces, or levels, which contain relief carvings. At the center, the temple is 103 feet high.

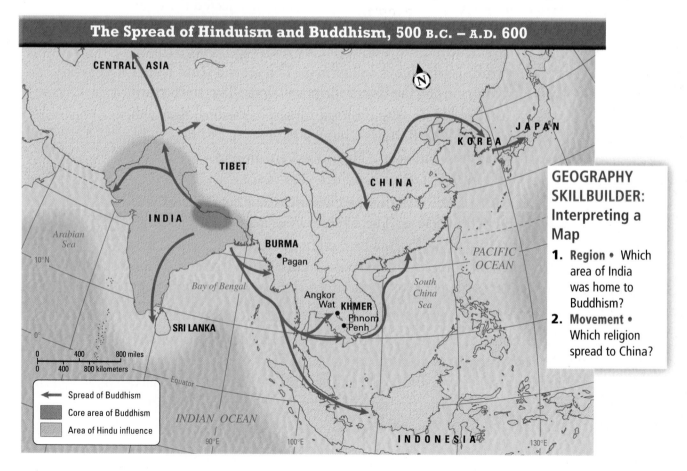

The Spread of Hinduism and Buddhism, 500 B.C. – A.D. 600

Spread of Buddhism
Core area of Buddhism
Area of Hindu influence

GEOGRAPHY SKILLBUILDER: Interpreting a Map

1. **Region** • Which area of India was home to Buddhism?
2. **Movement** • Which religion spread to China?

Place •
Borobudur is located in Indonesia on the large island of Java. The temple has three levels. Each represents a stage of spiritual perfection. ▲

Place • The Ananda temple is located at Pagan, the old capital city of Myanmar, which was an important Buddhist center. ▲

Indian culture also spread to Myanmar. There, Buddhism was firmly in place by the fifth and sixth centuries. In the 11th century, the powerful king Anawrahta established a strong Buddhist kingdom in the capital city of Pagan. There were soon thousands of Buddhist temples and buildings in the kingdom. The most famous is the Ananda temple.

SECTION 3 ASSESSMENT

Terms & Names
1. **Identify:** (a) Buddhism (b) Siddhartha Gautama (c) Four Noble Truths (d) Eightfold Path (e) Khmer (f) Angkor Wat

Taking Notes
2. Use a graphic organizer like the one below to show the ideas and goods that came into and out of Southeast Asia.

Southeast Asia

Main Ideas
3. (a) Why is Southeast Asia a crossroads for trade and cultural exchange?

(b) How did Buddhism affect Southeast Asia?

(c) Why did the Khmer kingdom decline?

Critical Thinking
4. **Making Inferences**

Why do you think Southeast Asians adopted Indian culture?

Think About

• the level of development of Indian civilization

• the activity of Buddhist and Hindu monks

 ACTIVITY -OPTION- Imagine you are a traveler from ancient India, passing through the Khmer Empire. Write a **letter** home describing some of the sights you see and your feelings about them.

ASSESSMENT

TERMS & NAMES

Explain the significance of each of the following:

1. subcontinent
2. sediment
3. archipelago
4. monsoon
5. Aryan
6. Hinduism
7. caste
8. Buddhism
9. Siddhartha Gautama
10. Khmer

REVIEW QUESTIONS

Physical Geography *(pages 583–589)*

1. What are the three major geographical regions of South Asia?
2. How do the monsoons affect South Asia and Southeast Asia?

Ancient India *(pages 591–596)*

3. What did the Aryan people bring to the Indus Valley, and what did they learn from the civilization that was already in place?
4. What are the main beliefs and characteristics of Hinduism?
5. When did India's golden age occur, and what were its major contributions?

Ancient Crossroads *(pages 598–603)*

6. How did early travelers to Southeast Asia influence that region's culture?
7. How is Buddhism similar to and different from Hinduism?
8. How did Hindu and Buddhist beliefs affect the empires of Southeast Asia?

CRITICAL THINKING

Identifying Effects

1. Using your completed chart from Reading Social Studies, p. 582, write two or three sentences describing how Buddhism affected Southern Asia.

Making Inferences

2. If you were an archaeologist, what would you conclude about the people who inhabited Mohenjo-Daro, based on the evidence that currently exists?

Comparing and Contrasting

3. In what ways are Buddhism and Hinduism similar and different?

Visual Summary

1 Physical Geography

- The physical geography of South Asia and Southeast Asia includes mountains, plateaus, river deltas, and islands.

- Landforms and climate continue to influence where people settle and what they do for a living.

Ancient India 2

- Merging with the existing culture, the Aryan people influenced the development of social structure and religion in ancient India.

- Hinduism provided instruction for daily life as well as inspiration for artists and emperors.

3 Ancient Crossroads

- As a crossroads for trade and culture, ancient Southeast Asia shared goods and ideas with places as far away as India, China, and Africa.

- Hinduism and Buddhism became the foundation of several powerful empires in Southeast Asia.

SOCIAL STUDIES SKILLBUILDER

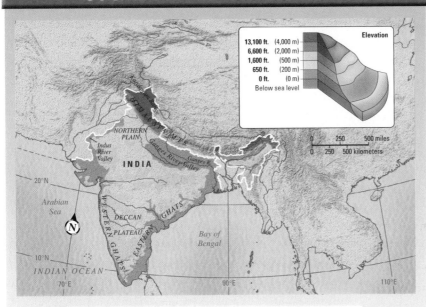

SKILLBUILDER: Reading an Elevation Map

1. What kind of information does this map present?
2. What does the map illustrate about the geographic features of India?

FOCUS ON GEOGRAPHY

1. **Region** • From what mountain range does the river flow that nourished the first ancient Indian civilization?
2. **Movement** • What mountain range did ancient Aryan invaders of India cross?
3. **Location** • The Ganges River delta lies next to what body of water?

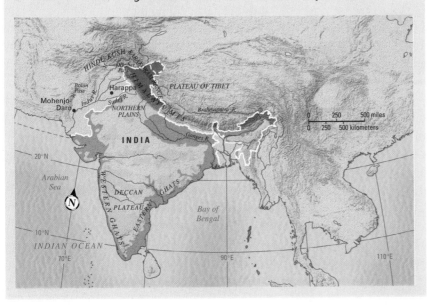

CHAPTER PROJECTS

Interdisciplinary Projects: Art

Making a Collage Research some of the visual arts of Southern Asia. Using encyclopedias, books, or the Internet, try to find as many examples as you can. Look for examples of costumes, jewelry, painting, sculpture, and architecture—in other words, the things that people of the region found beautiful or important. Use sketches or photocopies of these images to create a collage. Include a caption for each image.

Cooperative Learning Activity

Writing a Play In a group of three or four students, write a biographical sketch about one of the people in this chapter—perhaps Ashoka or Siddhartha Gautama. You might also invent a character, such as an Indian trader, a Buddhist monk, or a Gupta or Khmer emperor. Create a situation in which that person is trying to convince other people of his or her views and beliefs. One student might support those views and beliefs, and another student might disagree with them.

- Write a script for the play.
- Assign the roles of the central character, supporters, and critics.
- Perform the play for your class.

INTERNET ACTIVITY

Use the Internet to research floods in the Ganges River valley. Try to find information about floods that have been influenced by deforestation and soil erosion in Tibet.

Writing About Geography Write a report about what you have learned and present it to the class. List the Web sites you used to prepare your report.

For Internet links to support this activity, go to

CLASSZONE.COM

India and Its Neighbors

INDIA AND ITS NEIGHBORS

ATLANTIC

PACIFIC OCEAN

PACIFIC OCEAN

OCEAN

INDIAN OCEAN

Place Bathers descend steps called ghats to reach the Ganges River. To Hindus, it is the holiest river in India.

How has a sudden increase in population affected South Asia?

Place • By the beginning of the 21st century, South Asia had a population of well over 1 billion people. Its annual rate of growth is so high that it will soon have more people than China. Rapid population growth has put pressure on the region's resources and environment. There are not enough jobs for everyone. Many people live in poverty. India, which is the most heavily populated country in the region, struggles to feed its people. Farms are being overplanted in India. Its forests are disappearing as trees are cut down to create more farmland.

What do you think?

♦ Why is it important for countries to control population growth?

♦ How do you think continuing population growth will affect life in South Asia?

BEFORE YOU READ

▶▶ *What Do You Know?*

Before you read the chapter, consider what you know about India and its neighbors. Who was Gandhi? Have you ever seen a Bengal tiger? How high is Mount Everest? What spices go into curry? Where do *The Jungle Books* take place? Reflect on what you read in Chapter 20 and what you have seen or heard in the news about India, Pakistan, and other countries in South Asia.

▶▶ *What Do You Want to Know?*

Decide what you know about India and its neighbors. In your notebook, record what you hope to learn from this chapter.

Place • **Farmers in Afghanistan still use traditional methods.** ▲

READ AND TAKE NOTES

Reading Strategy: Sequencing To sequence means to put events in the order in which they happened. Sequencing can help you understand how events lead to other events. Use the chart to the right to record key events in the histories of India and Pakistan and to note differences and similarities.

- Copy the chart into your notebook.
- As you read, look for dates and key events.
- In the top two boxes, record events and important details next to the dates.
- In the row of three boxes, record important details about India and Pakistan since 1947.

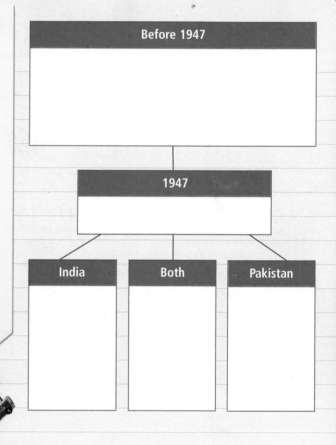

Before 1947

1947

India	Both	Pakistan

Place • **The sitar is a popular instrument in India.** ◀

MAIN IDEA

The movements of people and ideas through the nations of South Asia have produced a varied and exciting history.

WHY IT MATTERS NOW

Similarities and differences among these nations have led to both development and conflict.

DATELINE

EXTRA

RAMNURGER, NEAR BENARES ON THE GANGES RIVER, APRIL 19, 1796

A British ship anchored in the river yesterday after sailing many months from England. Today, boatmen and British sailors outfitted in our native cotton dress have been working madly to load the ship. They hope to sail before the monsoon winds and storms begin. Hundreds of boxes of tea, spices, and cotton fabric will travel back to England.

Movement • Despite great risk, ships from Great Britain, France, and Portugal sail to India and other parts of South Asia to carry back valuable spices, tea, and other goods. ▲

Islam Comes to India

The coast of India has been a site of trade for centuries. Arabs were trading along the coast of India a thousand years before the British arrived. Early in the eighth century A.D., Muslims from Arabia conquered northwest India. They converted many of the people of this region to their religion, Islam. Even today, the people of this region (what is now Afghanistan and Pakistan) are Muslim.

Turks and Mongols Beginning in the 11th century A.D., Turkish Muslims from what is now Afghanistan attacked northwest India, replacing the Arabs. By 1206, the Turkish kingdom stretched south to the Deccan Plateau. The region was ruled from the city of Delhi by a sultan. During this time, Mongols from Central Asia began spreading west and south. Because of the mountains in the northeastern part of South Asia, the Mongols never invaded the region. Many people who were threatened by the Mongols fled across the mountains into South Asia. These artists, teachers, government officials, and religious leaders brought with them their culture and learning.

Location •
The Hindu Kush
Mountains in
northern
Pakistan helped
to keep out
invaders. ▲

Vocabulary

sultan:
emperor

The Mughal Empire

Culture • **Akbar,**
shown here
crossing the
Ganges, had
his life story
told in words
and pictures in
the *Akbarnama,*
or *The Memoirs
of Akbar.* ▼

In the year 1526, Babur (BAH·buhr), a Mughal (moo·GUHL) ruler and a Muslim, invaded southward with his army. Eventually, his kingdom included northern India and land west into Afghanistan. Babur involved local leaders in his government and built trade routes, strengthening his rule. Babur's reign was the beginning of the great **Mughal Empire.**

Vocabulary

Mughal:
Muslim Turks
from what is
now Turkistan

Akbar, Mughal Emperor The third Mughal emperor, Akbar, was a strong and intelligent leader who was careful to include both Hindus and Muslims in his government. His policies made India a place where both Hindus and Muslims could live in peace. He taxed people according to the size and value of their land, which meant that poor farmers were not taxed as heavily as they had been before. Akbar was a strong supporter of the arts. He provided studios for painters and gave awards to the best among them. He also created a position for the official Hindu poet of the nation.

End of the Empire During the period of the Mughal Empire, many new trade routes over land and water were established, making travel between regions easier. The trade routes also connected the empire with other parts of the world. In this way new ideas and inventions made their way into South Asia. Then, in the year 1707, with the death of the last Mughal emperor, the empire eventually collapsed.

Reading
Social Studies

**A. Drawing
Conclusions** How
would trade routes
help to strengthen
an empire?

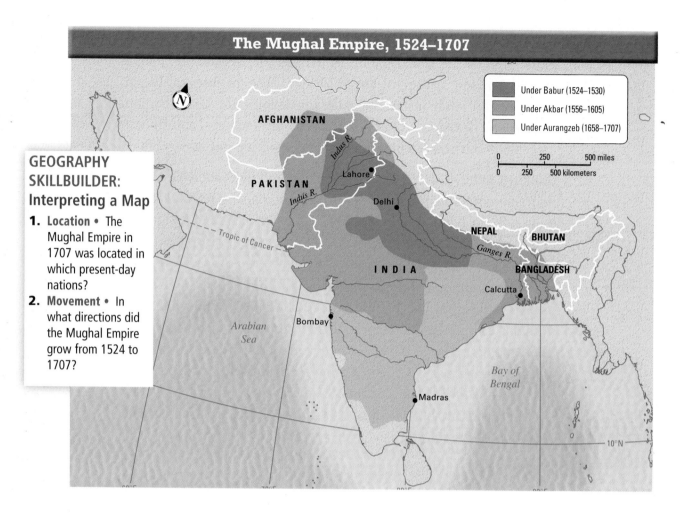

The Mughal Empire, 1524–1707

AFGHANISTAN

PAKISTAN

Indus R.

Indus R.

Lahore

Delhi

NEPAL

BHUTAN

Ganges R.

INDIA

BANGLADESH

Calcutta

Tropic of Cancer

Arabian
Sea

Bombay

Bay of
Bengal

Madras

10°N

Legend:
- Under Babur (1524–1530)
- Under Akbar (1556–1605)
- Under Aurangzeb (1658–1707)

0   250   500 miles
0   250   500 kilometers

GEOGRAPHY SKILLBUILDER: Interpreting a Map

1. **Location •** The Mughal Empire in 1707 was located in which present-day nations?
2. **Movement •** In what directions did the Mughal Empire grow from 1524 to 1707?

Arrival of the British

In 1600, Queen Elizabeth I of England gave trade rights to the East India Company, an organization of English merchants, to trade in India and East and Southeast Asia. The Mughals agreed to let the British set up factories and trading centers. The East India Company shipped spices, tea, cotton, silk, indigo (used for dyeing), sugar, and saltpeter (used for gunpowder) to England. Gradually, the British increased their power. By 1818, after the Rajputs and other groups agreed to be ruled by the British, Great Britain's strength in the region was undeniable.

Movement • The British brought railroads to India, such as this steam train in Darjeeling, shown in 1930. ▼

India and Its Neighbors **611**

India's Neighbors and Great Britain In 1796, Great Britain took possession of the island nation of Sri Lanka, then called Ceylon, and the island nation of the Maldives. The nations of Nepal, Bhutan, and Afghanistan never became colonies of Great Britain, though the British tried to colonize Afghanistan. Nepal and Bhutan depended on their mountainous frontiers to keep out foreigners.

Making India British The British army and navy, merchants, and Christian missionaries came to India, bringing new technology for railroads, the telegraph, steamships, and new methods of irrigation. They also introduced the British legal system, with new laws regarding landownership, and made English the official language.

Indians responded to the British in different ways. Some chose to live just as they had before the British arrived. Others chose to interact economically with the British by working for and with them while maintaining their traditions. Still others studied the British traditions and adopted what seemed useful while keeping their own traditions. Among the higher castes, parents sent their children to British schools so that they could learn English and become successful.

Reading
Social Studies

B. Comparing
Which changes brought by the British were cultural and which were technological?

Independence

In 1885, the **Indian National Congress** was formed to provide a forum where Indians could discuss their problems. Muslims formed the **Muslim League** in 1906. After World War I, Indians began to think of independence. They had a great leader in **Mohandas Gandhi.**

Biography

Mohandas Gandhi (GAHN•dee) Gandhi was born in India in 1869. He learned about discrimination when, as a young boy, he saw that no matter how wealthy and well educated Indians were, they were treated as second-class citizens by the British. Gandhi studied law in England and then spent the rest of his life working for justice for the Indian people.

He encouraged his followers to use nonviolence to resist the British and bring about social change. Gandhi believed that the forces of goodness and truth had powerful effects on people. As part of this belief, he went on hunger strikes and organized labor strikes and marches to force the British to grant India its independence.

The Indian people call Gandhi the *Mahatma*, which means "Great Soul." They honor him as the father of their nation. His ideas have influenced many people who have worked for justice around the world.

Gandhi used nonviolence to impress upon the British the need for independence. He also wanted all Indians to be treated equally. He wanted women to have the same freedoms as men. He encouraged Hindus and Muslims to find peaceful ways to solve their problems. For example, to protest the British monopoly of salt, Gandhi led a 240-mile walk to the coast to gather sea salt.

Vocabulary

monopoly: The sale of a good by only one company

Eventually, Great Britain realized that it would have to leave India, but the Indian National Congress and the Muslim League disagreed about how the new government would be formed. Muslims were afraid of losing power because Hindus were the majority in India. The solution was to divide India into two separate countries, India for the Hindus and Pakistan for the Muslims. The two countries were formed and granted independence in 1947. Sri Lanka became independent in 1948, and the Maldives in 1965.

BACKGROUND

On the Unit Atlas Map on page 574, find India, Pakistan, and Bangladesh. Before independence, this entire region was India.

Movement •
Gandhi led his countrymen to the coast at Dandi to protest the British sale of salt. ▲

SECTION 1 ASSESSMENT

Terms & Names

1. Identify:
  (a) Mughal Empire   (b) Indian National Congress
  (c) Muslim League   (d) Mohandas Gandhi

Taking Notes

2. Use a Venn diagram like the one below to compare and contrast the rule of the Mughals and the British in India.

Mughals   British

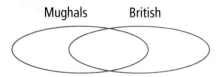

Main Ideas

3. (a) How did Islam reach India?

  (b) Name three achievements of the Mughal emperors.

  (c) Why did the British colonize India?

Critical Thinking

4. Making Inferences

Do you think it was easier for rich Indians or poor Indians to live under British rule? Explain.

Think About

• how Indians responded to British rule

• the opportunities for Indians of different castes

ACTIVITY -OPTION-   Imagine being a reporter for an Indian newspaper and attending a speech given by Gandhi. Write a **short article** reporting on the speech and giving your reaction to it.

Qanats

Because much of their country has little or no rainfall, Iranians have relied on a system of collecting and transporting water that was developed more than 2,500 years ago. The ancient Iranians, known as Persians, dug 30-to-100-foot shafts at the feet of mountains to tap into the water table. They built underground tunnels called *qanats* (KAH•NAHTS) that followed the slope of the land. These *qanats* collect water that seeps into the ground from melting snow and from rivers and streams. Although they are expensive to build and difficult to maintain, the *qanats* carry water to villages as much as 50 miles away for drinking and irrigating fields. They supply more than 75 percent of Iran's water.

1 At the base of a mountain range, melting snow and rainwater collect underground on top of a layer of solid rock. The water table slopes downward farther and farther from the surface.

2 Workers dig a well as deep as 100 feet to reach the water table. This is called the mother well.

3 Shafts are dug at regular intervals so that villages can draw water and workers can maintain the tunnel.

4 Workers build a shaft and haul out soil. Then they use stone, soil, and existing mineral and salt deposits to line the tunnel.

THINKING Critically

1. Drawing Conclusions
What is a drawback of the *qanat* system?

2. Recognizing Effects
How would a drought affect the *qanat* system?

Governments

TERMS & NAMES
Taliban
martial law
Dalit
Indira Gandhi
panchayat

MAIN IDEA

The countries of South Asia have different types of governments, but all face the challenges of economic growth and poverty.

WHY IT MATTERS NOW

As the nations of the world grow more and more connected, any individual nation's success becomes important to all.

DATELINE

NEW DELHI, INDIA, AUGUST 15, 1947— Jawaharal Nehru, India's first prime minister, has today solemnly declared India a free and independent nation. At 8:30 A.M. the new government was sworn in. Prime Minister Nehru then unfurled India's flag, the Tricolor, which flew for the first time from the Council House against a free sky.

In February, the British government had announced its willingness to grant India its independence. On June 3, Lord Mountbatten, viceroy of India, took to the airwaves to explain the method by which power would be transferred from one government to another. Yesterday, the nation waited breathlessly for midnight to arrive. After 300 years of colonial rule, India has won her freedom at last.

Place • Indians celebrate independence in the streets of Calcutta and other cities and towns throughout India. ▲

South Asia's Governments

Since independence, the nations of South Asia have chosen different forms of government. Some are republics. In a republic, the people elect leaders to represent them. Some countries, such as India, chose a parliamentary form of government. Others chose to be constitutional monarchies. In a constitutional monarchy, the king or queen serves a mostly ceremonial role, while the prime minister and cabinet actually run the government.

Afghanistan In 1964, a new constitution established a constitutional monarchy for Afghanistan. The monarchy collapsed in 1973 as the result of a coup. In 1979, the Soviet Union invaded Afghanistan and established a Communist government. A UN agreement forced Soviet troops to withdraw from Afghanistan in 1989, leaving behind an Afghani Communist government. This government was overturned and an Islamic republic was declared, but it did not have support from enough people and was too weak to maintain power.

A group of fundamentalist Muslims, the **Taliban,** took control of the government. Under the Taliban, people must follow strict rules. Women cannot go to school or hold jobs, nor can they go out in public without a male relative. Punishment for breaking rules includes being whipped or even executed.

The Taliban has been at war with opposing Muslim groups for many years. Although the Taliban has received help from a few other nations, such as Pakistan, most of the world has spoken out against the Taliban government. In 2001, the Taliban was accused of harboring terrorists responsible for the attacks on the United States made on September 11 of that year.

Culture • Bhutan is ruled by a king. This is King Jigme Dorji Wangchuk (JIHG•may DAWR•jee WAHNG•chook) in 1998. ▼

Bangladesh Bangladesh gained independence from Pakistan in 1971 and adopted its constitution in 1972. The constitution gives Bangladesh a parliamentary form of government, with a prime minister and a president. However, in 1975, and several times since, the military has taken over the government.

Bhutan For three centuries, Bhutan was ruled jointly by two types of leaders—one spiritual and the other political. In 1907, the spiritual ruler withdrew from public life, and since then Bhutan has had a king only. In 1953, an assembly, which meets twice a year to pass laws, was formed. Then, in 1968, a Council of Ministers was created to advise the king. The king appoints ministers, but the assembly must approve them.

The Maldives In 1965, the Maldives gained independence from Great Britain and became a republic three years later. The Citizens' Council has 48 members, 40 elected by the people and 8 appointed by the president. The president also appoints the judges, who follow Islamic law in making their judgments.

Nepal For centuries, Nepal was ruled exclusively by kings. The prime minister replaced the king as the country's ruling official. In 1962, Nepal became a constitutional monarchy and all political parties were banned. In the 1990s, the king allowed the formation of political parties. Soon, some had gained enough power to force a change in the government. The Nepalese wrote a new constitution and established a new parliamentary system.

Pakistan Pakistan gained independence from Great Britain in 1947. The constitution of 1947 gave Pakistan a parliamentary government. However, in 1958, **martial law** was declared. The military took control of the government and maintained power until 1988. Today, Pakistan is a republic, with a prime minister and a president, both of whom must be Muslim.

Reading
Social Studies

A. Recognizing Important Details What two attitudes do Pakistanis have about the role of Islam in their government?

People in Pakistan have differing views about the role of Islam in the government. Some think Islam is what holds the people together as one nation. Others feel that Islam does not meet the needs of all the groups in the country and that it has actually pulled people apart.

Sri Lanka In 1948, Sri Lanka gained independence from Great Britain. Today, it is a democracy with a president as its leader. As in the United States, two political parties struggle for power in the government.

Culture • President Chandrika Kumaratunga (chan·DREE·kah kum·ruh·TUNG·ah), of Sri Lanka, opens the country's new Parliament in November 2000. ▲

The World's Largest Democracy

India is the world's largest democracy. Approximately 370 million Indians voted in the 1999 elections. The country's official head of state is the president. However, India's prime minister actually runs the government.

Place • The prime minister of Pakistan works in the Offices of Government in Islamabad, the capital. ▶

India's constitution went into effect in 1950, protecting Indians from being treated unfairly. According to the constitution, all Indians are assured the same basic rights. These include the rights of free speech and religion, which are protected in the courts.

The Changing Caste System India's new constitution stated that even the lowest and poorest classes could vote. The poor are also represented in the government. Special programs reserve jobs for people of the lower castes and secure places for them in schools. The **Dalits** (formerly called "untouchables") have gained political power. They were outside the caste system and considered even lower than the lowest caste. Today, they vote for leaders, though more changes are needed to ensure the Dalits have equal rights in the government and the economy.

Women in India After independence from Britain, Indian women gained many new rights. Finally, all women were granted the right to vote. It is now against the law in India to discriminate on the basis of gender.

Indian women began working at jobs that had been held only by men. Women became teachers and doctors. They were elected to public office. **Indira Gandhi** became India's first woman prime minister in 1966.

Culture • **An Indian woman has her finger marked before voting in a 1999 election in Gujarat.** ▲

Nonviolence The Jain (JYN) religion was founded in India in the sixth century B.C. Its followers believe that people should never harm a living being, including the smallest insect. The Jain belief in nonviolence led to its use as a powerful political weapon.

Instead of leading an armed revolt, Gandhi used nonviolence as a tactic to drive the British out of India. The idea of nonviolence inspired American civil rights leader Martin Luther King, Jr. (shown at left below with his wife and Prime Minister Nehru). King used nonviolent methods, including marches and demonstrations, to fight against the discrimination of African Americans in the United States.

Village Life and Grass-roots Democracy

Since ancient times, small rural Indian villages have governed themselves. Today they are governed by the *panchayat* system. A *__panchayat__* is a village council. India's constitution allows these councils to govern themselves. The *panchayat* collects taxes for maintaining schools and hospitals. It builds roads and digs wells for drinking water. The councils also take care of primary school education in India.

Three Levels The *panchayat* works on three levels. The first level represents a village or a group of small villages. The second level is made up of *panchayat* chiefs from 100 villages. The third level represents an entire district. Some districts have as many as ten million people.

Today, there are over 3 million *panchayat* representatives in India. By law, one-third of them must be women. The constitution also makes room for the Dalits and other minorities to participate in the *panchayat* system.

Reading Social Studies

B. Contrasting How are the three levels of *panchayats* different from one another?

SECTION 2 ASSESSMENT

Terms & Names

1. **Identify:** (a) Taliban (b) martial law (c) Dalit (d) Indira Gandhi (e) *panchayat*

Taking Notes

2. Use a chart like the one below to list the countries of South Asia and the features of their governments.

Country	Features of Government

Main Ideas

3. (a) Name three kinds of government found in South Asia.

(b) What kind of government does India have?

(c) Describe the responsibilities of the *panchayat*.

Critical Thinking

4. **Synthesizing**

How did India's 1950 constitution change the lives of women and members of the lower castes?

Think About

• the treatment of the lower castes and women before 1950

• what it means to live in a democracy

ACTIVITY -OPTION- Choose one of the following nations: Bhutan, Nepal, or Sri Lanka. Use the Internet to find a recent news story about it. **Summarize** the story for your class.

Interdisciplinary Challenge

Tour the Ganges River

You are a guide leading a group tour of the Ganges River in India and Bangladesh. Since ancient times, this great river has been central to Indian life and culture. The Ganges rises in an ice cave in the Himalayas and flows southeast across a wide plain into the Bay of Bengal. As it nears the coast, the river splits into many channels—the "Mouths of the Ganges"— which have built up a huge delta. You want your tour group to understand the river's importance over the centuries.

COOPERATIVE LEARNING On these pages are challenges you will encounter as you plan your tour of the Ganges. Working in a small group, choose one of these challenges. Divide the work among group members. Look in the Data File for helpful information. Keep in mind that you will present your solution to the class.

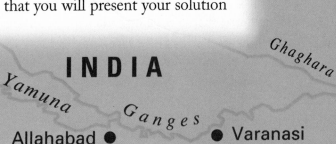

CHINA

Brahmaputra

Himalayas

NEPAL

Delhi

INDIA

Yamuna

Ganges

Ghaghara

Ganges

Allahabad ● ● Varanasi

HISTORY CHALLENGE

"So much has happened in the Ganges region . . ."

To start your tour, give your group an overview of the Ganges and its place in history. So much has happened in the Ganges region; for centuries, cities and villages along the Ganges have been centers of trade, industry, and religion. How can you give your group a sense of place? What should the group learn from this trip? Choose one of these options. Use the Data File for help.

ACTIVITIES

1. Choose one city or region along the Ganges. Make a time line of major events that took place there, starting with its early history.
2. Design a travel brochure for a city in the Ganges Basin. Include a list of historical monuments and other attractions.

Brahmaputra

MATH CHALLENGE

". . . plan a travel schedule . . . and keep to it."

Along the course of the Ganges are many historic cities and other attractions. One important part of a tour guide's job is to plan a travel schedule, or itinerary, and keep to it. Your trip is scheduled to take about four weeks. How will you plan your river journey? How will you divide your time? Choose one of these options to present information, using the map and the Data File for help.

ACTIVITIES

1. Prepare a four-week itinerary for the Ganges tour. List the places your group will visit and the time you will spend at each of them.

2. By riverboat, your trip from Kanpur to Allahabad—a distance of about 115 miles—takes about ten hours. After a stop for sightseeing, you leave Allahabad at 11:00 P.M. Your next stop is Varanasi, about 90 miles downriver. If you travel at the same speed as before, will you get to Varanasi in time for breakfast?

Brahmaputra

INDIA

BANGLADESH

Hugli

Mouths of the Ganges

Kolkata ●

Bay of Bengal

Activity Wrap-Up

As a group, review your solution to the challenge you selected. Then present your solution to the class.

DATA FILE

THE GANGES

- **Length:** 1,557 mi.
- Headwaters in Himalayas: **Alaknanda** and **Bhagirathi** are main streams; other tributaries enter along river's course.
- Ganges Basin is one of the most densely populated areas in the world.

Major Tributaries

- **Yamuna:** flows from Himalayas past Delhi and Agra.
- **Brahmaputra** (also called Jamuna): joins Ganges in Bangladesh to form delta.

Important Sites in the Ganges Basin

- **Patna:** center of Asoka's empire (third century B.C.).
- **Agra:** on Yamuna River, site of **Taj Mahal;** once capital of Mogul Empire.
- **Allahabad:** at junction of Yamuna and Ganges rivers; a holy place to Hindus.
- **Varanasi** (Benares): Hindu holy city; pilgrims come to bathe in the river.
- **Delhi/New Delhi:** on Yamuna River, India's capital city; once a Mogul capital.
- **Kolkata (Calcutta):** on Hugli River, major channel of the Ganges; was capital of British India, now capital of West Bengal.
- **Dhaka:** capital of Bangladesh.

INDIA

Population: 1.01 billion; population density: 799/sq. mi.; 28 percent urban.

Area: about 1.3 million sq. mi.

BANGLADESH

Population: 129.2 million; population density: 2,324/sq. mi.; 24 percent urban.

Area: 55,600 sq. mi.

To learn more about the Ganges River, go to

RESEARCH LINKS
CLASSZONE.COM

Economies

TERMS & NAMES

jute

information technology

Green Revolution

MAIN IDEA

The countries of South Asia have economies that have changed and grown in the last century.

WHY IT MATTERS NOW

As the economies of South Asia's countries grow, these nations have more influence on the economies of their neighbors.

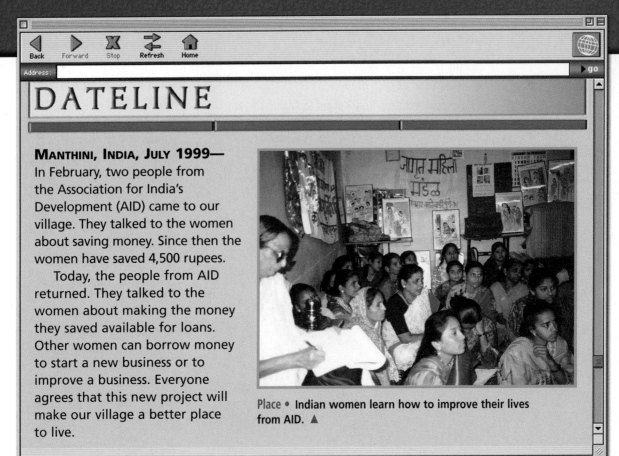

DATELINE

MANTHINI, INDIA, JULY 1999— In February, two people from the Association for India's Development (AID) came to our village. They talked to the women about saving money. Since then the women have saved 4,500 rupees.

Today, the people from AID returned. They talked to the women about making the money they saved available for loans. Other women can borrow money to start a new business or to improve a business. Everyone agrees that this new project will make our village a better place to live.

Place • Indian women learn how to improve their lives from AID. ▲

Developing Economies

Organizations like AID are helping the developing nations of South Asia to move from traditional economies to market economies. Most people in South Asia live in rural areas. They have low incomes and literacy levels and depend on traditional farming methods to survive. They are farmers, shepherds, and herders.

BACKGROUND

You read about traditional and market economies in Chapter 4. Look back to pages 105–106 if you need to review.

Afghanistan In the 1960s and 1970s, Afghanistan worked to strengthen its economy. It built roads, dams, power plants, and factories. It provided education to more people and began irrigation projects. Then Afghanistan was invaded by the Soviet Union. The invasion was followed by civil war. Afghanistan has not returned to the improvement program of four decades ago. Today, Afghanistan is one of the poorest countries in the world. Most people work on farms, raising livestock. Only 12 percent of the land in Afghanistan is arable, and only half of that is cultivated in any year. Wheat is the chief crop, though cotton, fruits, and nuts are also grown.

Bangladesh Agriculture is a major part of the economy in Bangladesh. About three-fifths of the workers are farmers. The most important cash crops are rice, jute, and tea. Bangladesh supplies one-fifth of the world's **jute**, a fibrous plant used to make twine, bags, sacks, and burlap. Irrigation projects have reached many farms, but the monsoon rains bring floods and disaster to many farmers.

Bangladesh has almost no mineral resources, so its few industries are based on agricultural products, such as bamboo, which is made into paper at mills.

Bhutan and Nepal The economies of Bhutan and Nepal are similar. Until the 1950s and 1960s, both countries were largely isolated from the outside world. There were no highways or automobiles. Bhutan did not have a currency. People bartered for goods rather than using money. Since that time, with financial help from other countries and organizations, both countries have been working to modernize their economies. For example, they have built major roads allowing the transport of goods and people, especially tourists.

The Maldives The Maldives is one of the world's poorest nations. The majority of its workers fish or build or repair boats. Tourism has become an important industry as well. Nearly all the food people eat is imported, including rice, which is one of the main foods in people's diets.

Reading
Social Studies

Making Inferences How might the monsoon season affect a subsistence farmer?

India and Its Neighbors **623**

PakistanPakistan is the richest country in South Asia. Half of its work force is employed in agriculture, forestry, and fishing. Pakistan is the third-largest exporter of rice in the world. Its important industries are fabric and clothing, sugar, paper, tobacco, and leather.

Human-Environment Interaction • **Many people in the Maldives earn a living by fishing.** ▲

Sri Lanka Sri Lanka depends on agriculture and tourism. Its most important agricultural product is rice, followed by tea, rubber, and coconuts. Sri Lanka has not yet been able to benefit much economically from its many mineral resources.

India Although some regions of India have many valuable resources, millions of India's people are among the world's poorest. Most people work in agriculture. More than half of the farms are smaller than three acres. Farmers practice what is known as subsistence farming, which means they grow only enough food to live on. Rice and wheat are India's most important crops. Because many people do not eat meat, chickpeas and lentils are important sources of protein in the diet.

There is a growing information technology industry in India. **Information technology** includes computers, software, and the Internet. Since 1991, India's software exports have been doubling every year.

Human-Environment Interaction • **Village women plant rice, one of the chief crops in India. They carry the new rice shoots to the fields in flat baskets, which they then place on their backs as protection from the sun.** ▶

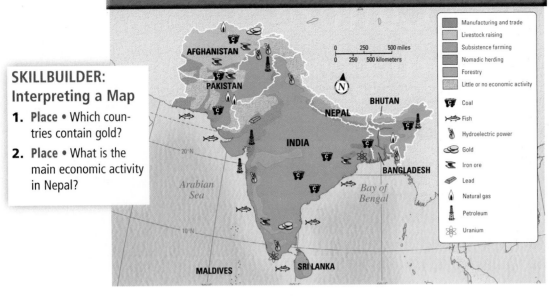

South Asia Economic Activities and Resources, 2000

Legend:
- Manufacturing and trade
- Livestock raising
- Subsistence farming
- Nomadic herding
- Forestry
- Little or no economic activity
- Coal
- Fish
- Hydroelectric power
- Gold
- Iron ore
- Lead
- Natural gas
- Petroleum
- Uranium

SKILLBUILDER:
Interpreting a Map
1. **Place** • Which countries contain gold?
2. **Place** • What is the main economic activity in Nepal?

The Green Revolution

In the 1960s, the **Green Revolution** introduced farmers to varieties of grain that were more productive, the widespread use of pesticides, and different methods for farming. In India, farmers grew more rice and wheat than they needed. Much of this surplus was set aside in case of a poor growing season. Some was exported. The Green Revolution had some negative results too. The use of chemicals damaged the land and polluted rivers.

The cost of such new methods is too high for some small farmers. As a result, many farmers in South Asia still use old farming techniques despite their governments' efforts to introduce reform.

SECTION 3 ASSESSMENT

Terms & Names

1. **Identify:** (a) jute   (b) information technology   (c) Green Revolution

Taking Notes

2. Use a chart like the one below to list the important economic activities of South Asian countries.

Country	Economic Activity

Main Ideas

3. (a) How do most people in the countries of South Asia make a living?

(b) What new technology is becoming an important part of India's economy?

(c) Why was the Green Revolution important in South Asia? What were its negative effects?

Critical Thinking

4. **Identifying Problems**

What are the main problems faced by South Asian countries as they move from traditional economies to market economies?

Think About

- their natural resources
- levels of economic development, including rates of poverty and literacy

ACTIVITY -OPTION- Choose a nation in South Asia. Imagine you are a government official applying to an international aid agency for help. Write a **letter** describing your economy and what it needs to develop further.

The Culture of India

TERMS & NAMES

Taj Mahal

Mahabharata

dialect

Indo-Aryan

Dravidian

dowry

MAIN IDEA	WHY IT MATTERS NOW
India's rich cultural heritage has its roots in a long history and the influences of other cultures.	The languages, arts, and traditions of India, a country with over a billion people, have an international influence.

DATELINE

AGRA, NORTHERN INDIA, 1648
With tears in his eyes, Shah Jahan watched today as workers put the finishing touches on the Taj Mahal. The building is made of rare white marble and is decorated with semiprecious stones, such as lapis lazuli, crystal, and jade. The Taj Mahal is to be the tomb of Shah Jahan's wife, who died giving birth to their 14th child. "Some day, when I depart," Shah Jahan said, "we will lie here together forever."

Culture • The Taj Mahal has taken 20,000 workers 22 years to build. ▲

The Taj Mahal

The Mughal emperor Shah Jahan built the **Taj Mahal** for his beloved wife, Mumtaz Mahal. This white marble building with its onion-shaped domes and thin towers is one of the finest examples of Islamic architecture in the world. Today, it is India's most famous building and a symbol of India's rich artistic heritage.

India and the Arts

Literature Two great works of world literature come from India. One, the **Mahabharata** (MAH·huh·BAH·ruh·tuh), is an epic poem, which means that it tells a lengthy story, in a grand style, of one or more heroes. The *Ramayana* is another famous epic poem. Both the *Mahabharata* and the *Ramayana* have influenced painters, dancers, and other writers in India. Both are important because they tell about the growth of Hinduism.

Music and Film India has several styles of music, and each style is unique to a region of India. Music is played and sung in concerts, at parties, or in religious settings. Indians also love to see movies. India makes more films every year than any other country, including the United States. In rural areas, movie vans travel to villages to show films outdoors.

Culture • Long-necked stringed instruments, like the sitars (sih·TAHRS) shown here, are used to play North Indian classical music. ▲

The Languages of India

The constitution of India now recognizes 18 official languages. However, Indians speak hundreds of other languages and dialects. A **dialect** is a regional variety of a language. Most languages in India come from one of two families: Indo-Aryan or Dravidian.

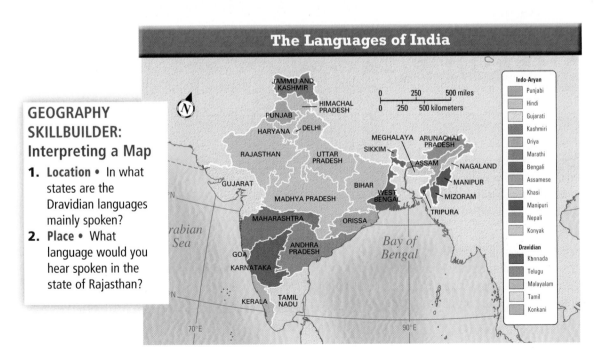

GEOGRAPHY SKILLBUILDER: Interpreting a Map

1. **Location** • In what states are the Dravidian languages mainly spoken?
2. **Place** • What language would you hear spoken in the state of Rajasthan?

The Languages of India

Indo-Aryan
- Punjabi
- Hindi
- Gujarati
- Kashmiri
- Oriya
- Marathi
- Bengali
- Assamese
- Khasi
- Manipuri
- Nepali
- Konyak

Dravidian
- Kannada
- Telugu
- Malayalam
- Tamil
- Konkani

JAMMU AND KASHMIR
HIMACHAL PRADESH
PUNJAB
HARYANA
DELHI
RAJASTHAN
UTTAR PRADESH
MEGHALAYA
SIKKIM
ARUNACHAL PRADESH
ASSAM
NAGALAND
MANIPUR
GUJARAT
BIHAR
MIZORAM
WEST BENGAL
TRIPURA
MADHYA PRADESH
MAHARASHTRA
ORISSA
Arabian Sea
GOA
ANDHRA PRADESH
Bay of Bengal
KARNATAKA
KERALA
TAMIL NADU

0   250   500 miles
0   250   500 kilometers

70°E   90°E

The Indo-Aryan Language Family **Indo-Aryan** languages are related to the Indo-European language family, which comes from the ancient Aryan language Sanskrit and includes almost all European languages. Today, about three-fourths of the people in northern and central India speak Indo-Aryan languages.

The Dravidian Language Family About one-fourth of all Indians speak Dravidian languages. **Dravidian** was the language spoken centuries ago in India. As invaders moved into the north, the speakers of Dravidian moved south.

English English, which came to India with British colonialism, is spoken by less than 5 percent of the population. However, because it is the language of business, government, and science, English is important in India.

Religion in Daily Life

Most people in India are Hindus. There are no rules dictating how Hinduism is practiced, nor is there one Hindu church. Many Hindus are vegetarians. Some Hindus perform daily rituals on behalf of their gods. The caste system, which is still in place in India, is less rigid than it once was.

Many Muslims who had been living in India moved to Pakistan and East Pakistan, now Bangladesh. Today, 14 percent of Indians are Muslim.

Reading
Social Studies

A. Drawing Conclusions What problems might exist when neighbors speak different languages?

BACKGROUND

Look back to Chapters 15 and 20 to review what you read about Islam and Hinduism.

The *Mahabharata* One of the greatest works of world literature comes from India. The epic poem the *Mahabharata* is the longest poem in the world. It was composed over a period of about 800 years, from about 400 B.C. to A.D. 400. The *Mahabharata* tells the story of two warring families, the five Pandava brothers (shown at right) and the Kauravas.

One famous section of the poem is called the *Bhagavad-Gita*. In this section, Arjuna, the leader of the Pandavas, receives good advice from his chariot driver, who is actually the god Krishna in disguise.

THINKING CRITICALLY

1. **Clarifying** How do you know that more than one person must have created the *Mahabharata*?

2. **Making Inferences** What do you think might happen to the events in a story created like the *Mahabharata*?

The Family in India

Family is important to Indians. Often, several related families live together. Parents choose a bride or groom for their children from a family of the same caste. Parents may consider a potential mate's education, financial status, or even horoscope to help them make a decision.

Parents prefer sons to daughters, partly because men have more power in this society. Women who have male children have greater influence in their families. These attitudes are beginning to change. Also, when a woman marries, her parents must provide a **dowry,** money or property given by a bride to her new husband and his family. This can be expensive, especially for rural families. As India modernizes, this practice, too, is beginning to change.

Reading
Social Studies

B. Analyzing Motives Why might parents want to arrange their child's marriage?

Culture • A bride and groom circle a fire four times as part of a Hindu wedding ceremony. ▲

Family Meals A typical meal varies from region to region in India. In the south and east, a meal usually includes rice. In the north and northwest, people eat a flat bread called a *chapati* (chuh·PAH·tee). Along with rice or *chapatis,* a meal may include beans or lentils, some vegetables, and maybe yogurt. Chili peppers and other spices like cardamom, cinnamon, and cumin give the food extra flavor. Meat is rarely eaten, either because it is forbidden by religion or because it is so expensive.

SECTION 4 ASSESSMENT

Terms & Names

1. Identify:
   (a) Taj Mahal
   (e) Dravidian
   (b) *Mahabharata*
   (f) dowry
   (c) dialect
   (d) Indo-Aryan

Taking Notes

2. Use a spider map like the one below to list the unique traits of India's culture.

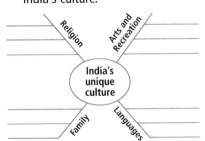

Religion

Arts and Recreation

India's unique culture

Family

Languages

Main Ideas

3. (a) Why are there so many official languages in India?

   (b) What religion plays the biggest role in Indian culture?

   (c) How is family an important part of Indian life?

Critical Thinking

4. **Finding Causes**

   Why do you think English is the language of business and government in India?

   Think About
   • India's colonial history
   • the country's cultural diversity

ACTIVITY -OPTION-   Develop a **plot** for an Indian movie. Describe it in a paragraph, and share your idea with a classmate.

Understanding Point of View

▶▶ Defining the Skill

The phrase *point of view* refers to the particular opinions or beliefs that a person holds. Education, religious beliefs, and life experiences all contribute to a person's point of view. Understanding point of view makes it possible to understand and explain a historical figure's opinions and actions.

▶▶ Applying the Skill

The passage to the right explains the differences and similarities between Mohandas Gandhi and Jawaharlal Nehru, who was the prime minister of India from 1947 until 1964. Use the strategies listed below to help you analyze their points of view.

How to Understand Point of View

Strategy ❶ Look for statements that reveal a person's point of view on a particular subject. Gandhi believed that government could not guarantee a person's rights. Nehru, on the other hand, had faith in the power of government.

Strategy ❷ Look for clues about why people hold the opinions they do. In these paragraphs you learn about Gandhi's and Nehru's childhoods, their educations, and their experiences as young men. How do these things influence their opinions?

Strategy ❸ Summarize the information given for each person that explains their opposing opinions.

Write a Summary

Writing a summary will help you understand differing points of view. The paragraph below and to the right summarizes the passage about Gandhi and Nehru.

▶▶ Practicing the Skill

Turn to page 625 in Section 3. Read "The Green Revolution." Then write a summary like the one on the right to understand the farmers' opposing points of view.

INDIAN INDEPENDENCE

Two of the men who led India in its struggle for independence from Great Britain, Mohandas Gandhi and Jawaharlal Nehru, had different ideas about how a fair and just society should be achieved.

❷ Gandhi grew up in a rural area of India, where he saw how difficult life was for many Indians. Through hard work and study he became a lawyer. Gandhi then lived in South Africa, a country that discriminated against people because of race. For 20 years he worked for the rights of Indian workers there. ❶ He saw how important it was for everyone in a country to have equal rights. At the same time, he did not trust that a government could provide people with those rights. He felt that each person individually had to seek ways to live in a fair and honorable manner.

❷ Nehru's father was a respected and wealthy lawyer, and Nehru had many privileges while growing up. Like Gandhi, Nehru went to England to study law. But when he finished his studies, he traveled around Europe, seeing other societies and learning about other governments. ❶ He came to believe that a government could be successful in granting its people equal rights and that it could do so by dividing up the land among all the people.

❸
Gandhi believed that government could not grant equal rights. He felt that each person, individually, could work for the good of the whole. Nehru, on the other hand, felt that government could grant equality by making sure that everyone had land.

Pakistan

TERMS & NAMES
Mangla Dam
Tarbela Dam
Punjabi
Sindhi
Urdu

MAIN IDEA

Conflict between Muslims and Hindus in colonial times led to the creation of Pakistan.

WHY IT MATTERS NOW

Political and religious conflict continues to make this region unstable.

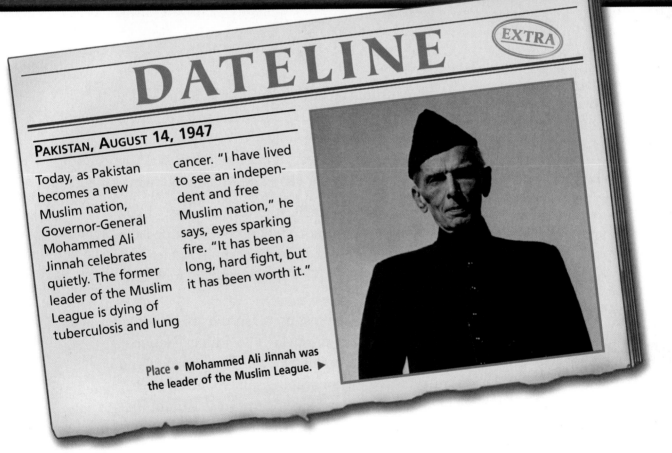

DATELINE

EXTRA

PAKISTAN, AUGUST 14, 1947

Today, as Pakistan becomes a new Muslim nation, Governor-General Mohammed Ali Jinnah celebrates quietly. The former leader of the Muslim League is dying of tuberculosis and lung cancer. "I have lived to see an independent and free Muslim nation," he says, eyes sparking fire. "It has been a long, hard fight, but it has been worth it."

Place • Mohammed Ali Jinnah was the leader of the Muslim League. ▶

History of Pakistan

Great Britain granted independence to Pakistan and India on the same day. Both South Asian countries have a long and sometimes common history. The Indus River flows through eastern Pakistan, from the mountains in the north to the Arabian Sea. This river valley was the site of one of the world's oldest civilizations. Over time, invaders and immigrants crossed the Himalayas and the Hindu Kush Mountains to reach this fertile area.

Culture •
The city of
Mohenjo-Daro
thrived over
4,000 years
ago in the
Indus River
valley. ◄

In A.D. 712, Arab Muslims brought Islam to the Indus Valley region. Then, around the year 1000, Muslims from Central Asia built their own kingdom in the Indus River valley. Lahore (luh·HAWR), today one of the biggest cities in Pakistan, was the capital of their kingdom and a major center of Muslim culture.

The British Influence In the 1600s, the British East India Company set up trading posts in India, which then included the region that is now Pakistan. When the Mughal Empire, which had been ruling India, grew weak in the 1700s, the company took control of India.

With British rule, the Muslims lost power in the government, and over time, the Hindus gained power. The Indian National Congress was controlled by Hindus, so Muslims formed the Muslim League in 1906 as a way of keeping some political power. As India moved closer to independence from Great Britain, the Muslim League, led by Mohammed Ali Jinnah, called for an independent Muslim state.

Pakistan Becomes a Nation Differences between Hindus and Muslims led to violence. Neither the British nor the Indian National Congress could find a way to settle the differences between the two groups. So on August 14, 1947, at the same time that India gained independence, Pakistan was declared a separate Muslim nation. Millions of Muslims living in India moved to Pakistan, and Hindus in Pakistan moved to India.

Reading
Social Studies

Using Maps Use the map below to find the locations of the four provinces of Pakistan.

Pakistan Divides When Pakistan became a nation, it included two regions—East Pakistan and West Pakistan—separated from each other by 1,000 miles. This distance made Pakistan a difficult country to rule. Although most people of East and West Pakistan were Muslim, they had many differences. Many East Pakistanis were angry that West Pakistan was in charge of the government. War broke out between East and West Pakistan. When the war ended, over a million people had lost their lives. In 1971, East Pakistan became the country of Bangladesh.

The Land of Pakistan

Pakistan (once West Pakistan) is divided into four provinces: Baluchistan, North-West Frontier, Punjab, and Sindh. Most Pakistanis live in the northeast province of Punjab.

Western and northern Pakistan are dry and mountainous, with few river valleys suitable for farming. The provinces of Sindh and Punjab are less mountainous, and although there is not much rain, the Indus River flows through them. About two-thirds of the people in Pakistan are farmers and herders who irrigate their land with water from the Indus River.

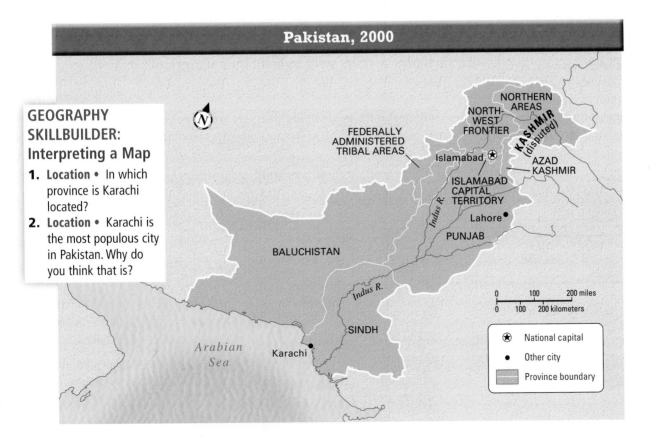

Pakistan, 2000

GEOGRAPHY SKILLBUILDER:
Interpreting a Map

1. **Location** • In which province is Karachi located?
2. **Location** • Karachi is the most populous city in Pakistan. Why do you think that is?

NORTHERN AREAS

NORTH-WEST FRONTIER

KASHMIR (disputed)

FEDERALLY ADMINISTERED TRIBAL AREAS

Islamabad ⊛

AZAD KASHMIR

ISLAMABAD CAPITAL TERRITORY

Indus R.

Lahore •

PUNJAB

BALUCHISTAN

Indus R.

SINDH

Arabian Sea

Karachi •

| 0 | 100 | 200 miles |
| 0 | 100 | 200 kilometers |

⊛ National capital
• Other city
▮ Province boundary

River Power In 1967, Pakistan finished building the **Mangla Dam** on the Jhelum River in northeast Pakistan. The dam was built to control floodwaters and to provide hydroelectricity. In 1976, Pakistan opened one of the world's largest dams, the **Tarbela Dam.** Located on the Indus River, it is used for flood control and irrigation. In 1994, the Tarbela Dam began to produce hydroelectricity as well.

Connections to Technology

Drawbacks to Dams Dams can be useful for many things, such as irrigation and the production of electricity. Pakistan's Mangla Dam has stopped floods from destroying harvests (see below). Dams can also have negative effects. When a dam is built, hundreds of thousands of people may be forced to move because water that is held back by the dam covers nearby land and homes.

Fertile land can become unproductive because it becomes water-logged or because the salinity, or salt content, increases. Water has salt in it, and the salt stays behind in the soil. Over time, the salt content increases, and few plants will then grow in the soil. Wildlife suffers when rising waters disturb their natural habitats. In many countries, including Pakistan and India, there has been widespread opposition to dam building.

Language and Religion

Language divides the people of Pakistan, but the religion of Islam unites them. Each of Pakistan's four provinces has a unique culture with its own customs and languages.

Languages in Pakistan There are more than 20 languages spoken in Pakistan, of which **Punjabi** and **Sindhi** are the most common. Punjabi is spoken mostly in rural areas, and it is usually not written. **Urdu,** which is Pakistan's official language, is taught in schools. Students also learn their regional language. No single language is spoken by everyone in Pakistan, and in every province many different languages are spoken.

Movies made in Pakistan are usually in Punjabi or Urdu. The most popular newspapers are in Urdu, Sindhi, or English. This variety of languages has caused conflict among Pakistanis.

Culture • To read all the signs in Lahore, you would need to know several languages. ◄

Religion in Pakistan The country's official name is the Islamic Republic of Pakistan. More than 97 percent of Pakistanis are Muslim. Public schools base their teaching on Islam. Except in the homes of the wealthy and educated, women follow the rules of purdah.

Vocabulary

purdah:
the practice of keeping women secluded

Modern Conflict in Pakistan

In 1947, when India and Pakistan became independent, each nation claimed the region of Kashmir. Find Kashmir on the map on page 633. This region is important to both nations because of its water resources. India and Pakistan have failed to reach an agreement about the future of Kashmir. Within South Asia, Hindus and Muslims have fought over whether Kashmir should join India or Pakistan or become independent.

Culture • **Benazir Bhutto became the leader of Pakistan in 1988. She was the first Muslim woman ever elected to lead an Islamic state.** ▲

Relations between Pakistan and India grew increasingly tense in 1998 when both nations tested nuclear weapons and then refused to sign a nuclear test-ban treaty. Since then, both nations have tested nuclear weapons and relations have not improved, though efforts continue to be made by Pakistan and India, with help from other nations.

SECTION **5** ASSESSMENT

Terms & Names

1. Identify: (a) Mangla Dam (b) Tarbela Dam (c) Punjabi
(d) Sindhi (e) Urdu

Taking Notes

2. Use a chart like the one below to outline the history of Pakistan from its earliest beginnings to its creation as a modern nation in 1947.

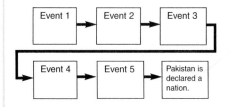

Main Ideas

3. (a) Why was Pakistan created in 1947?

(b) Why are rivers an important natural resource in Pakistan?

(c) What religion do most Pakistanis follow?

Critical Thinking

4. **Drawing Conclusions**

Why do you think it is important for India and Pakistan to solve the problem of Kashmir peacefully?

Think About

• the results of conflicts between India and Pakistan

• the reason relations between the two countries grew worse in 1998

ACTIVITY -OPTION- Draw a **political cartoon** that shows how the use of so many languages affects Pakistan.

TERMS & NAMES

Explain the significance of each of the following:

1. Mughal Empire
2. Mohandas Gandhi
3. Indira Gandhi
4. *panchayat*
5. jute
6. Green Revolution
7. dialect
8. dowry
9. Mangla Dam
10. Sindhi

REVIEW QUESTIONS

History *(pages 609–613)*

1. How did the East India Company influence India's history?
2. What was Mohandas Gandhi's contribution to India's independence?

Governments *(pages 615–619)*

3. What kinds of governments do the nations of South Asia have?
4. What rights did India's 1950 constitution give some people?

Economies *(pages 622–625)*

5. How are the economies of South Asian nations changing?
6. What is being done to improve the economies of South Asia?

The Culture of India *(pages 626–629)*

7. What languages are spoken in India and why?
8. What role does family play in the lives of most Indians?

Pakistan *(pages 631–635)*

9. What was the Muslim League, and what did it accomplish?
10. How has Pakistan taken advantage of its natural resources?

CRITICAL THINKING

Sequencing Events

1. Using your completed chart from "Reading Social Studies," p. 608, explain why India's independence was inevitable.

Evaluating Decisions

2. Based on what you know about India-Pakistan relations since 1947, was the partition of Pakistan a good idea?

Forming and Supporting Opinions

3. What is your opinion of Gandhi's philosophy of nonviolence?

Visual Summary

History *1*

- The early invasion of India by Muslims sowed the seeds of conflict that continues today.
- Britain's influence in the region lasted from the 17th century until Indian independence in 1947.

Governments *2*

- Most South Asian countries are republics that became independent from British rule in the 20th century.

Economies *3*

- The region's countries have traditional economies in which most people are farmers or market economies in which most people make money and buy what they need.

The Culture of India *4*

- The diversity of cultures in India has its roots in a long history.
- Family plays an important role in the lives of most Indians.

Pakistan *5*

- Pakistan is united by the common religion of Islam.
- Pakistan's history has been marked by conflict with other peoples in South Asia.

SOCIAL STUDIES SKILLBUILDER

"[A]dvance is certain when people are liberated and educated. . . . Conquest of illiteracy comes first."

John Kenneth Galbraith

Country	Literacy Rate	Gross Domestic Product (GDP) per capita
Sri Lanka	90 percent	$3,800
India	52 percent	$1,600
Afghanistan	32 percent	$800

SKILLBUILDER: Understanding Point of View

1. How does the table support the ideas expressed in the quotation?
2. If a different table showed you that Afghanistan's GDP per capita was $1,600, what might you conclude?

FOCUS ON GEOGRAPHY

1. Location • According to this population density map, which parts of India have the most people?

2. Human-Environment Interaction • What is likely to happen if India's population continues its rapid growth?

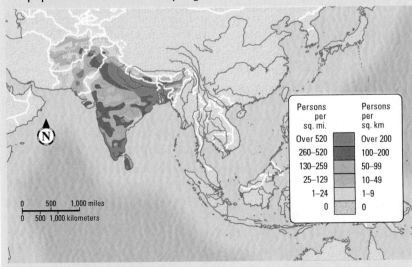

Persons per sq. mi.	Persons per sq. km
Over 520	Over 200
260–520	100–200
130–259	50–99
25–129	10–49
1–24	1–9
0	0

0   500   1,000 miles
0   500 1,000 kilometers

CHAPTER PROJECTS

Interdisciplinary Projects: Architecture

Making a Diorama Choose one of the buildings or cities described in the chapter. Find out more about it. Make a diorama showing the inside of the building or the layout of the city you have chosen.

Cooperative Learning Activity

Designing a Travel Brochure With a group of three to five students, design a travel brochure for someone who is visiting South Asia for the first time. Include details about the region's history, geography, governments, economies, and cultures.

- Take on the roles of editor, art director, and writers.
- Work on a rough draft of the text, a layout of the brochure, and ideas for photographs.
- Share your completed brochure with the class.

INTERNET ACTIVITY

Use the Internet to research the current leaders of India, Pakistan, and Afghanistan. These may be individuals or groups. Focus on their beliefs and their ideals—what they hope for their countries. Find a statement from each leader that you think best expresses beliefs and ideals.

Writing About Geography Write a report about what you have learned and present it to the class. Include a table showing the leaders of each country. List the Web sites you used to prepare your report.

For Internet links to support this activity, go to

RESEARCH LINKS
CLASSZONE.COM

The Sandstorm

IN *SHABANU: DAUGHTER OF THE WIND,* Suzanne Fisher Staples tells about 11-year-old Shabanu, the youngest child in a family of nomadic camel herders. Shabanu lives in the Cholistan Desert with her parents; her older sister, Phulan; her grandfather; and an aunt with two young children. She also has a camel named Mithoo and a pet dog named Sher Dil. In this hot and dry area of Pakistan, blinding sandstorms can strike without warning. When they do, they threaten the lives of the people who make the desert their home and of the camels they depend on for their livelihood.

O ne night Phulan shakes me awake in the middle of a deep sleep.

"Shabanu!" she shouts from such a great distance I can barely hear her.

She yanks the quilt away, and suddenly my skin is pierced by thousands of needles. The wind is howling around us. I can't see anything when I open my eyes, but I can tell by the sound and feel that it's a monstrous sandstorm, the kind few living things survive without protection. Phulan pulls me by the hand, but I yank away.

"Mithoo!" I stumble about the courtyard, tripping over huddled chickens, clay pots, and bundles of reeds that have broken away from the entrance. "Mithoo!"

Hands outstretched, I feel my way around the courtyard wall, where Mithoo normally sleeps. When I get to where the reeds were stacked on their stalks, lashed side by side and tied to cover the doorway, there is a gaping hole. Quickly I make my way around the courtyard again. Mithoo is gone.

1. A loose robe, worn by Islamic women, that covers the body and most of the face; also spelled *chador.*

2. A freshwater pond that serves as a water supply for desert nomads.

"You can't find him without a light and something to put over your eyes!" Phulan shouts, pulling on my arm. Together we drag the bed through the doorway. Mama struggles to close the window shutters and Phulan and I manage to push the door shut and wedge the bed against it. Dadi lights a candle and swears softly as the light fills the room. Grandfather and Sher Dil are missing too.

"Where can he have gone?" Mama gasps, her eyes bright with fear. Grandfather had been sound asleep, and the storm must have wakened him.

Dadi uses the candle to light the kerosene storm lantern and pulls the bed away from the door. Mama throws a shawl around his shoulders. He pulls it over his head and I follow him out to the courtyard, where *khar* shrubs, their shallow roots torn from the dry sand, tumble and hurl themselves against the walls.

With my *chadr*[1] over my face, I can open my eyes enough to see the haze of the lantern in Dadi's hand, the light reflecting from the dust in a tight circle around him.

Auntie has already closed up her house, and Dadi pounds on the door for several minutes before she opens it again and we slip inside.

"Have you seen Grandfather?" asks Dadi.

"And Mithoo and Sher Dil?" I shout.

She stands in the center of her house, mouth open and speechless, her hands raised helplessly. My cousins stand behind her skirt, their eyes wide. From between her feet Sher Dil's black nose glistens in the lamplight. But no Grandfather and no Mithoo.

"Come to our house," Dadi orders her, handing me the lantern. "I'll close up here. Shabanu, come back for me," he says, bending to light Auntie's storm lantern.

When I return, Dadi holds the light so we can see each other.

"Mithoo will be fine," he says, and I know it is a warning not to ask to look for him. "When the wind has died and it's light, we'll find him standing near a tree by the *toba*."[2]

Reading
THE LITERATURE

In this selection, the author draws on almost all of the five senses to help the reader understand what it might be like to live through a sandstorm. Find an example of how each sense is used to make the account more vivid.

Thinking About
THE LITERATURE

What role does nature play in the lives of Shabanu and her family? How does the author make clear the challenges of living in the Cholistan Desert?

Writing About
THE LITERATURE

In this story, Shabanu and her family work together to survive the sudden sandstorm. How do the members of the family help one another overcome the dangers of the storm?

About the Author

Suzanne Fisher Staples (b. 1945) has traveled widely as a reporter for a global news service. In 1979, she went to work in Southern Asia, covering such events as the civil war in Afghanistan. A 1985 trip to Pakistan, where she conducted a study of poor rural women, led her to write *Shabanu*. Staples currently lives in Florida.

Further Reading *The Land I Lost* by Huynh Quang Nhuong takes the reader to a tiny village in the central highlands of Vietnam, years before the Vietnam War. The book has won many awards, including selection as an ALA Notable Book.

Southeast Asia Today

SECTION 1   History and Governments

SECTION 2   Economies and Cultures

SECTION 3   Vietnam Today

Human-Environment Interaction
People harvest tea leaves in a field near Bao Loc, Vietnam. Tea growing began in Southeast Asia when the Dutch brought seeds to Java from Japan.

How has migration influenced Southeast Asia's culture?

Movement • The first people to live in mainland Southeast Asia probably came from southern China and South Asia. Later, the ethnic groups known as the Mon, Khmer, and Thai slowly moved south into the Indochinese Peninsula, where they set up rich kingdoms. Over the centuries, the region's wealth attracted Chinese settlers and merchants from India and Arabia. All these groups brought their unique cultures and religions with them. These and other influences blended to form the culture of Southeast Asia.

What do you think?

♦ How does the migration of people into a region affect its culture?

♦ What challenges face modern nations made up of many different ethnic groups and religions?

BEFORE YOU READ

▶▶ *What Do You Know?*

Before you read the chapter, think about what you know about Southeast Asia. What countries make up this region? What do you know about the region's governments and economies? Have you ever seen a movie about the Vietnam War? What do you know about Vietnam today? Recall what you know from other classes, what you have read, and what you have seen on television.

▶▶ *What Do You Want to Know?*

In your notebook, record what you hope to learn from this chapter.

Culture • Puppets made from water buffalo hides are used in the ancient art of shadow theater. ▼

READ AND TAKE NOTES

Reading Strategy: Drawing Conclusions To draw conclusions, look at the facts and then use your common sense and experience to decide what the facts mean. Use the chart below to gather facts and draw conclusions about Southeast Asia.

- Copy the chart into your notebook.

- As you read, record facts and examples that answer each question. Look for specific information, as shown.

- After you read, review the facts and examples, decide what they mean, and record your conclusions.

Place • Singapore is a busy and wealthy city in Southeast Asia. ▲

	Facts/Examples	Conclusions
How are Southeast Asian nations linked to other countries?		
What forms of government are in the region?		
What factors affect economies in Southeast Asia today?		
What factors shape cultures in the region?		
What are the effects of the Vietnam War?		

History and Governments

TERMS & NAMES
mandala
military dictatorship
East Timor

MAIN IDEA

Southeast Asia has experienced a variety of cultural and governmental influences throughout its history.

WHY IT MATTERS NOW

The current governments of the nations of Southeast Asia are relatively new and unstable.

DATELINE

EXTRA

BURMA, 1274

Today, the famed traveler from Italy arrived. Marco Polo has come to Southeast Asia with his family. He is carrying important papers from a religious leader known as the Pope, but mostly he wants to see the land, the people, and the cultures. When he returns home, he plans to write a book about his adventures. Marco Polo marveled at our beautiful temples. He noted that they are "covered with gold, a full finger's breadth in thickness." Perhaps there is nothing quite so beautiful in Italy.

Culture • Marco Polo will return to Italy to share the wonders of the East. ▲

New Cultures in Southeast Asia

Seven hundred years before Marco Polo's visit, Southeast Asia had come under the influence of two stronger, more advanced cultures: China and India. China made Vietnam part of its empire. Vietnam was not able to gain its independence until A.D. 939. India never ruled any part of Southeast Asia, but its culture spread throughout the region and had a lasting influence.

Influences of China and India New religions—Hinduism, Buddhism, and Confucianism—came to Southeast Asia from China and India. So did writing systems, literature, and ideas about government and social class. Indian ideas about government were especially important.

Southeast Asian Governments Instead of states or nations, Southeast Asia was made up of mandalas. A **mandala** (MUHN·duh·luh) had at its center a ruler who worked to gain support from others. The ruler used trade and business to influence others and maintain power. Mandalas varied. Some were larger than others, some depended on agriculture, and some had more advanced technology. The mandala system stayed in place in many parts of Southeast Asia until the 19th century. One ancient mandala, called Oc Eo, was located in southern Vietnam. Ships from this port carried goods to and from places as far away as Rome. Over time, the mandalas developed into states, and the people began to think of themselves as belonging to these states. Because of trade and communication, new ideas were exchanged among the peoples of the region and between the region and other parts of the world. Each state took what it wanted from these new ideas and developed into a unique nation.

Reading
Social Studies

A. Summarizing How did nations develop out of mandalas?

The WORLD'S HERITAGE

Cambodia's Temple Treasures
Angkor (ANG·kawr) was an early civilization in northwestern Cambodia between the 9th and 15th centuries. Its capital, also called Angkor, contains temples that are among the world's greatest works of art and architecture.

One of these temples, Angkor Wat, is particularly splendid. It was built to honor the Hindu god Vishnu. This huge pyramid-shaped temple covers almost one square mile. Its stonework is covered with richly carved scenes from Hindu mythology. For centuries after the city and its magnificent temples were abandoned, jungle growth hid them until their rediscovery around 1860. Later, war kept admirers away. Today, efforts are under way to restore Angkor Wat as a world monument to Cambodian culture.

Culture • Today, most Indonesians, like these boys studying the Qur'an, are Muslims. ▲

New Religions Trade with other parts of the world also brought Christianity and Islam to Southeast Asia. In the ninth or tenth century, Muslim traders brought Islam to the region, especially to the islands of Sumatra and Java, part of what is now Indonesia. Islam spread gradually throughout the other islands of Indonesia and Malaysia.

In the early 1500s, Christian missionaries came to Southeast Asia from Portugal, France, and Spain. The Spanish missionaries met with success in the Philippines, where there was no organized religion to combat, although each group of Filipinos had its own set of beliefs. Today, about 90 percent of Filipinos are Christians. However, in the rest of Southeast Asia, the missionaries were not as successful. Buddhist monks worked to keep the missionaries from making converts.

European Colonialism

Europeans came to Southeast Asia as traders as well as missionaries. The Portuguese were the first to arrive, in 1509. The Spanish, the Dutch, the British, and the French all followed. These European traders came for wealth—spices, gems, and gold—not power. For the most part, the Europeans controlled port cities and nothing more for the first three centuries.

Strange but TRUE

Dragons of Komodo On Komodo (kuh•MOH•doh) Island and a few other islands in Indonesia lives one of Earth's most fearsome creatures. Its body is covered with scales, and its tail is long and powerful. It has sharp teeth, long claws, and a yellow tongue that flicks in and out. If this description makes you think of a storybook dragon, you are not alone.

Hundreds of years ago, Chinese fishermen thought the same thing when they called this creature a dragon. Komodo dragons are really lizards. In fact, they're the largest living lizards in the world. Some Komodo dragons grow more than 10 feet long and weigh as much as 200 pounds. They're so strong that they can overpower and eat deer, wild pigs, and water buffalo. They have even been known to attack people.

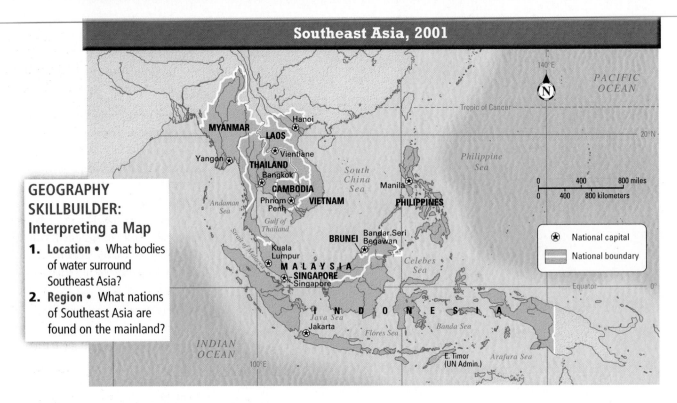

PACIFIC
OCEAN

Tropic of Cancer

MYANMAR

Hanoi

LAOS

20°N

Yangon · Vientiane

Philippine
Sea

THAILAND

Bangkok

South
China
Sea

CAMBODIA

Manila

Andaman
Sea

Phnom
Penh · VIETNAM

PHILIPPINES

Gulf of
Thailand

BRUNEI

Bandar Seri
Begawan

Kuala
Lumpur

Celebes
Sea

Strait of Malacca

MALAYSIA

SINGAPORE

Singapore

Equator

0°

INDONESIA

Java Sea

Jakarta

Banda Sea

INDIAN
OCEAN

Flores Sea

Arafura Sea

E. Timor
(UN Admin.)

100°E

0   400   800 miles
0   400   800 kilometers

⊛ National capital
▭ National boundary

**GEOGRAPHY
SKILLBUILDER:
Interpreting a Map**

1. **Location** • What bodies
   of water surround
   Southeast Asia?
2. **Region** • What nations
   of Southeast Asia are
   found on the mainland?

Then, in the 19th and early 20th centuries, these European nations began to colonize the nations of Southeast Asia. The Philippines was under Spanish rule until 1898, when it came under the rule of the United States. Cambodia, Laos, and Vietnam were all ruled by France. The British ruled Burma, most of Malaysia, and Singapore, and the Dutch ruled Indonesia. Only Thailand never became a colony.

During World War II, the Japanese pushed out most Europeans from the region. When the war ended in 1945, Cambodia, Vietnam, Laos, Malaysia, and Indonesia fought for independence. The Philippines won independence peacefully.

Contributions of the Europeans The Spanish learned of the chile pepper in North America and brought it to Southeast Asia. Immediately, the chile pepper became a familiar part of the diet in Southeast Asia. Coffee came to the region with the Dutch. Today, coffee is an important crop in Indonesia, Laos, and Vietnam.

Culture • **King
Bhumibol
Adulyadej**
(POO·mee·POHN
ah·DOON·luh·DAYT)
is the longest-
reigning monarch
in Thailand's
history. His duties
are mainly
ceremonial. ▼

After Independence

After gaining independence, many nations in Southeast Asia found themselves in turmoil. Political parties fought one another to gain power. In Vietnam, Myanmar, and Indonesia, the military eventually took control of the government. Over the next 20 years, the nations of Southeast Asia worked out their own unique government systems.

Governments Brunei, Malaysia, Cambodia, and Thailand are all constitutional monarchies. Indonesia, the Philippines, and Singapore are republics. Myanmar was also a republic, but in 1988, the military overthrew the government. Since then, it has been a **military dictatorship,** ruled by one man whose power comes from the military. Laos and Vietnam are both Communist states.

East Timor The island nation of **East Timor** declared its independence from Portugal in 1975. A month later, the neighboring country of Indonesia invaded and took over. The United Nations said the people of East Timor could decide their government for themselves. In 1999, they voted for independence.

However, Indonesia did not accept the people's ruling. The United Nations has accused the Indonesian army of killing and deporting people because of the vote. UN peacekeeping forces were stationed in East Timor. In August 2001, East Timor held its first democratic elections.

Aung San Suu Kyi (OWNG·SAHN·SOO·CHEE) Suu Kyi was born in Burma, now called Myanmar, in 1945. In 1988, she became the leader of a new national movement against the brutal military dictatorship that controlled Myanmar. She and millions of followers used peaceful methods to protest human rights abuses and to demand a democratic government. The military killed thousands of protesters. Suu Kyi was put under house arrest. In 1991, she won the Nobel Peace Prize.

NATIONAL LEAGUE FOR DEMOCRACY

SECTION 1 ASSESSMENT

Terms & Names

1. Identify: (a) mandala   (b) military dictatorship   (c) East Timor

Taking Notes

2. Use a cluster map like this one to take notes on ways the Chinese, Indian, European, and other cultures influenced Southeast Asian culture.

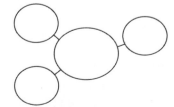

Main Ideas

3. (a) Who brought Islam and Christianity to Southeast Asia?

(b) Why did European nations come to Southeast Asia?

(c) How is the government of Thailand different from the government of the Philippines?

Critical Thinking

4. Analyzing Causes

Why do you think many of the newly independent Southeast Asian nations came under the control of military dictators?

Think About

• the political and social confusion many countries find themselves in when their colonial rulers leave

• the role of the military

ACTIVITY -OPTION-   Make a **chart** showing the countries of Southeast Asia and each country's system of government.

Linking Past and Present

The Legacy of Southern Asia

Architecture

Even before the rise of Buddhism in the 5th century B.C., people in India made burial mounds for their dead. When the Buddha died, similar mound-shaped structures called stupas became symbols of his death and of Buddhism. Stupas became more elaborate over time. This architectural form spread throughout the Buddhist world and can be found in the pagodas—religious buildings—of Korea, Japan, and China, as well as in shrines in Sri Lanka and temples in Java.

Theater and Dance

In ancient times, theater and classical dance productions were held in the temples and royal courts of India. Spectators watched dancers act out stories of Hindu gods and myths, especially from famous epics. The two most famous epics are the *Ramayana* (ruh•MAH•yuh•nuh) and the *Mahabharata* (MAH•huh•BAH•ruh•tuh). Folk dancing, another dance form, was popular in rural areas. Modern dance in Southern Asia includes elements of both classical and folk dancing.

Cities

One of the first cities in the world, Mohenjo-Daro, was built along the Indus River in what is now Pakistan. After archaeologists discovered the 4,000-year-old city in 1922, they spent years excavating its ruins. What they unearthed was a city laid out in a grid pattern, with streets, houses, assembly halls, storerooms, public baths, and a sewer system. Many modern cities are laid out in grids, and some cities in India have public baths similar to the ones found in Mohenjo-Daro.

Find Out More About It!

Study the text and photos on these pages to learn about inventions, creations, and contributions that have come from Southern Asia. Then choose the item that interests you the most and use the library or the Internet to research the subject and learn more about it. Use the information you gather to create a diorama to share with the class.

RESEARCH LINKS
CLASSZONE.COM

Black Tea

Though tea bushes were found growing wild in Assam, India, in the 1820s, it was not until the mid-1880s that India began to export tea. Workers used a process that turned green leaves to a brownish black color to produce a blend known as black tea. Though tea had been grown in China for more than 3,000 years, by 1888 England was importing more tea from Southern Asia than from China. Today, some of the best black teas come from India.

Sanskrit Language

Sanskrit, the oldest written language of India, was first brought to India around 1500 B.C. The language has distinctive sounds, as well as complex grammar rules. Some of India's modern languages—Hindi, Bengali, and Punjabi—are based on Sanskrit. Though by 100 B.C. Sanskrit was no longer being spoken, it is still used in many Hindu ceremonies and in scholarly works and teachings.

Economies and Cultures

SECTION 2

TERMS & NAMES

developing nation
Bahasa Indonesian
pagoda
thatch
batik

MAIN IDEA

The economically and culturally unique nations of Southeast Asia trade with most of the world.

WHY IT MATTERS NOW

Southeast Asia's successes contribute to the strength of other economies.

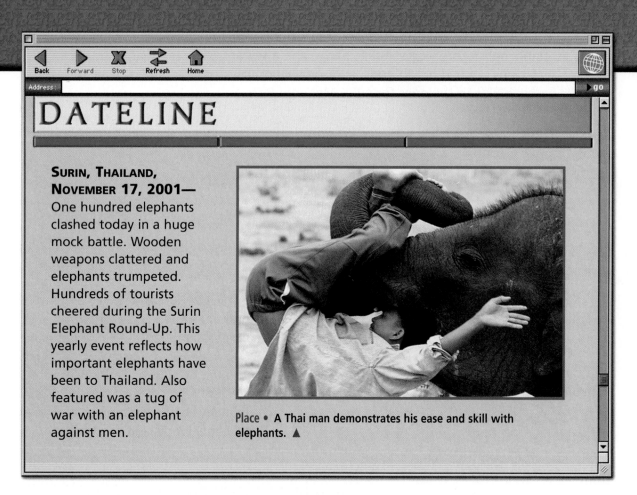

DATELINE

SURIN, THAILAND, NOVEMBER 17, 2001— One hundred elephants clashed today in a huge mock battle. Wooden weapons clattered and elephants trumpeted. Hundreds of tourists cheered during the Surin Elephant Round-Up. This yearly event reflects how important elephants have been to Thailand. Also featured was a tug of war with an elephant against men.

Place • A Thai man demonstrates his ease and skill with elephants. ▲

An Agricultural Economy

Events such as elephant roundups take place in rural areas, where three-fourths of the people in Southeast Asia live, many of them on small farms where they grow rice to feed their families, not to sell for profit. Many nations of Southeast Asia are **developing nations.** They are working to improve their economies and to help people live safe, healthy, successful lives.

Small Farms and Factories The Green Revolution and irrigation have helped some farmers grow more food. But many others have small plots of land and cannot afford to buy fertilizers, chemicals, and modern equipment. They must rely on good weather and hard work for successful harvests.

Place • The people of Singapore enjoy a high standard of living. ▲

In the past 50 years, industry has become more important in Southeast Asia. Small factories that process crops, make clothing and fabric, and produce small electronic parts are the most common. Many people have moved into the larger cities looking for work.

Singapore The small country of Singapore is an exception in Southeast Asia. Virtually everyone lives in the city, also called Singapore. Though small in size, Singapore is one of the richest nations in the world and has one of the busiest ports. The production of electronic goods is its most important industry, and more than half of these goods are exported.

The Cultures of Southeast Asia

The people of Southeast Asia live in widely differing geographical regions. In rural communities, people's lives have not changed much in the past century. In the big cities, however, history and tradition stand side by side with modern architecture, automobiles, and fast-food restaurants.

Languages In Indonesia, the Philippines, and Myanmar, where communities are separated by water, dense forests, or mountains, people speak many languages. However, most people from Indonesia also speak **Bahasa Indonesian** (bah·HAH·suh), the national language. In places where there is a large Chinese population, dialects are spoken. Indians who live in parts of Southeast Asia speak Hindi or Tamil.

Reading Social Studies

Drawing Conclusions
How can geography affect the languages of a nation?

Languages of Southeast Asia, 2002

Country	Official Language	Other Languages Spoken
Brunei	Malay	English, Chinese
Cambodia	Khmer	French, English
Indonesia	Bahasa Indonesian	English, Dutch, Javanese, local dialects
Laos	Lao	French, English, local languages
Malaysia	Bahasa Malay	English, Chinese dialects, Tamil, Hindi, Telugu, Malayalam, Punjabi, Thai, local languages
Myanmar	Burmese	Local languages
Philippines	Filipino, English	Local languages
Singapore	Mandarin Chinese, Malay, Tamil, English	
Thailand	Thai	English, local languages and dialects
Vietnam	Vietnamese	Chinese, English, French, Khmer, local languages

SKILLBUILDER: Reading a Chart
1. Which country has the most official languages? Why do you think that is?
2. Why do you think French is spoken in several countries?

Religions A form of Buddhism is the most common religion in mainland Southeast Asia. Islam, brought by Muslims who came to Southeast Asia several centuries ago, is practiced in Malaysia, the Philippines, Thailand, and Indonesia. Spanish and Portuguese missionaries spread the Catholic faith, which is most important today in southern Vietnam and the Philippines. Protestantism and Hinduism are also practiced in the region.

Architecture Statues of the Buddha can be seen in temples all over Southeast Asia. Often the temples consist of one or more **pagodas,** or towers, built in many levels, with sculptures or carvings of Buddha on each level. Houses, built of wood or bamboo, have roofs made of **thatch,** or woven palm fronds. In areas where there is flooding from monsoons, houses are built on stilts.

Wayang Kulit For over 1,000 years, shadow puppet theater has been a popular form of entertainment in Java, Bali, Thailand, and Cambodia. The most famous shadow theater is the Javanese *wayang kulit*. It tells ancient Hindu stories, such as the *Mahabharata*. To perform *wayang kulit*, the puppeteer sits behind a screen, moving the puppets (which are made from water buffalo hides) with rods connected to their bodies and arms. A light shines behind the puppets, casting shadows on the screen, and the audience sees only the shadows.

THINKING CRITICALLY

1. Drawing Conclusions
What does the popularity of this art form tell you about Indonesian culture?

2. Making Inferences
How can you tell from the design of these puppets that Javanese craftspeople are highly skilled?

Culture •
Weaving is an important part of Laotian culture. ▲

Culture • This Thai dance tells the story of the *Ramayana*. ▲

Dance Dancing is a popular art form in much of Southeast Asia. A dance might tell a story from history or the *Ramayana*, one of India's great epic poems. Dancers must train for years. They wear elaborate and beautiful costumes. The motions of their hands often tell the story.

Weaving Weavers in Southeast Asia use available resources. In the Philippines, fabrics are sometimes made of pineapple fiber. In Indonesia, weavers make cotton **batik** (buh·TEEK), using wax and dye to make intricate patterns on fabric. In Laos, they weave cotton and silk from fibers that are grown in Laos.

SECTION 2 ASSESSMENT

Terms & Names

1. Identify:
   (a) developing nation
   (b) Bahasa Indonesian
   (c) pagoda
   (d) thatch
   (e) batik

Taking Notes

2. Use a chart like this one to list important characteristics of the economies and cultures of Southeast Asia.

Economic Characteristics	Cultural Characteristics

Main Ideas

3. (a) Where do most of the people in Southeast Asia live?
   (b) How have the economies of Southeast Asia changed in the past 50 years?
   (c) What are the three main religions in Southeast Asia?

Critical Thinking

4. **Synthesizing**

   Why are so many languages spoken in Southeast Asia?

   Think About
   • the region's varied history and cultural influences
   • how geography contributes to the development of different ethnic groups and their languages

ACTIVITY -OPTION- Trace a **map** of Southeast Asia from the Unit Atlas on page 572. Draw arrows and write labels to show the paths of cultural influences.

Distinguishing Fact from Opinion

▶▶ Defining the Skill

A fact is a piece of information that can be proved to be true. Statements, statistics, and dates all may be facts. An opinion, on the other hand, is a belief, feeling, or judgment that is expressed by someone. An opinion cannot be proved to be true. Being able to distinguish fact from opinion is one part of critical thinking. It helps you know whether to trust an argument or to change your own opinion when someone is trying to influence you.

▶▶ Applying the Skill

The passage to the right tells about an unusual law in the country of Singapore. Use the strategies below to help you distinguish fact from opinion.

How to Distinguish Fact from Opinion

Strategy ❶ Look for facts, or information that can be proved to be true.

Strategy ❷ Look for statements that express a person's opinion, judgment, or feeling.

Strategy ❸ Think about how the facts in the passage could be checked for accuracy. Where might you look to see if they are true? Identify the facts and opinions expressed in the passage. List the facts and opinions in a chart. Also list where you could look to prove a fact.

A SINGAPORE LAW

❶ In 1992, Singapore began a program to stop littering. People caught tossing litter have to put on bright yellow vests and spend 12 hours sweeping up garbage. They may also be fined up to $2,940. And if they are caught several times, they have to attend a meeting where they learn about the costs of pollution. The punishment seems to be working. One woman who was sweeping garbage said, ❷ "Anyway, it is very embarrassing."

Make a Chart

The chart below lists some of the statements from the passage and shows whether they are facts or opinions.

Statement	❸ Can It Be Proved?	Fact or Opinion?
In 1992, Singapore began a program to stop littering.	Yes. Check a newspaper story or the laws in Singapore.	Fact
People caught littering have to sweep garbage for up to 12 hours.	Yes. Check a newspaper story or a magazine article.	Fact
"Anyway, it is very embarrassing."	No. This statement expresses a person's feelings.	Opinion

▶▶ Practicing the Skill

Turn to page 643 in Chapter 22, Section 1, and read the Dateline. Make a chart like the one above in which you list key statements and then determine whether they are facts or opinions.

Vietnam Today

TERMS & NAMES
Ho Chi Minh
Politburo
doi moi
supply and demand
Tet

MAIN IDEA

Vietnam has struggled for centuries to be a unified nation.

WHY IT MATTERS NOW

The United States and other countries have established new trade relations with a unified Vietnam.

DATELINE

SAIGON, SOUTH VIETNAM, APRIL 30, 1975—At last the war between North and South Vietnam is over. Saigon, the capital of South Vietnam, has fallen. Few thought this day would ever come. At this moment, North Vietnamese citizens and soldiers march victoriously toward Saigon.

Hundreds of South Vietnamese fought to climb aboard the last helicopters lifting Americans off the roof of the United States embassy. The thousands left behind worry about what will happen to them now.

Place • Helicopters evacuate Americans and some Vietnamese from defeated South Vietnam. ▲

A History of Struggle

The Vietnam War was only the latest in a series of wars and invasions that the people of Vietnam had endured. China ruled Vietnam for more than a millennium, until A.D. 939. During this time, the Chinese built roads and waterways. They introduced the use of metal plows, farm animals, and improved methods of irrigation. Though China strongly influenced life in Vietnam, the Vietnamese protected their own culture and traditions.

China invaded Vietnam again in 1407, but in 1428, after ten years of fighting, the Vietnamese were able to force out the Chinese. For a time, Vietnam enjoyed peace and prosperity. But during the 1500s and again in the 1600s, Vietnam was disrupted by civil wars. It has not enjoyed a long period of peace and growth like the one in the 1400s since.

French Rule In 1858, Napoleon III, the ruler of France, invaded Vietnam. He wanted to increase the size of his empire and benefit from more trade in Southeast Asia. Gradually, over the next 25 years, France took control of all of Vietnam, Cambodia, and Laos.

The French transported natural resources such as rice, coal, gems, and rubber out of Vietnam. They exported French goods to Vietnam, making the Vietnamese buy them at higher prices than they would have paid for goods made in neighboring countries. The French failed to bring health care and education to the people of Vietnam. Because of irrigation, there was more land to farm, but most farmers could not afford the land. During the first half of the 20th century, 3 percent of landowners in southern Vietnam owned 45 percent of the land. Peasants, who made up 70 percent of the landowners, owned only about 15 percent of the land.

War

Over time, the Vietnamese organized against the French. Some people, especially in northern Vietnam, also looked to China for help. **Ho Chi Minh** (HOH CHEE MIHN), who studied Communism in the Soviet Union and China, became a leader in Vietnam's independence movement.

North and South Vietnam France tried to maintain its rule over Vietnam, but Ho Chi Minh and his government began fighting the French. He received support from the Communist government in China. The United States government, worried that Communism would spread to Vietnam and other parts of the world, sent money and weapons to the French.

In 1954, an agreement was signed that again divided Vietnam into two parts: Communist North Vietnam and U.S.-supported South Vietnam. In South Vietnam, no government was able to rule successfully, and soon the Vietminh began looking for ways to overthrow South Vietnam's government and unite all of Vietnam as a Communist nation.

Place • Ho Chi Minh was president of North Vietnam from 1954 to 1969. ▲

BACKGROUND

The organization that led Vietnam's independence movement was called the Vietminh.

Reading
Social Studies

A. Analyzing Motives
Why did the Vietnamese want to be independent from France?

Movement • Over 500,000 U.S. troops were in Vietnam in the late 1960s. ▼

Place • Many people in the United States protested the war in Vietnam. ▲

The United States Intervenes Not wanting South Vietnam to fall to Communism, the United States provided it with military support. In 1965, the United States went a step further and began bombing North Vietnam. By 1973, however, opposition to the war by citizens in the United States led to the withdrawal of troops.

North Vietnam overwhelmed South Vietnam, and the war ended in 1975. Three million Vietnamese died during the war, and four million were wounded. Bombs and chemical weapons destroyed much of Vietnam, leaving more than half the people homeless. The country reunited in 1976 as the Socialist Republic of Vietnam. Several hundred thousand South Vietnamese fled to the United States and other nations.

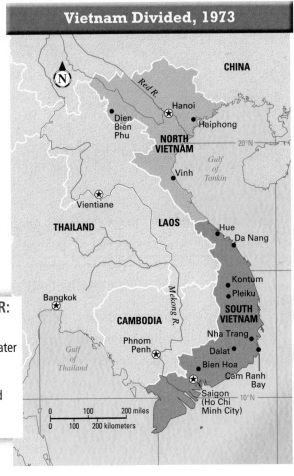

Vietnam Divided, 1973

GEOGRAPHY SKILLBUILDER:
Interpreting a Map

1. **Movement** • What body of water does the Red River flow into?
2. **Location** • Why might the capital city of Hanoi be located where it is?

Vietnam Today

Vietnam is now a communist nation. People elect representatives to the National Assembly, which then chooses the prime minister. A group called the **Politburo** (PAHL·iht·BYUR·oh) heads the only political party, the Communist Party. The Communist Party and especially the Politburo have a major role in the government.

The Government and the Economy In a Communist nation, the government owns and runs industries and services. The government makes almost all decisions about the economy. After the Vietnam War, many people lived in poverty, while many educated people left the country. It was a difficult time for the new government. In an effort to improve the economy, the government restricted trade with other nations. Instead, this made the economic situation worse.

In 1986, the government began a policy called *doi moi* (doy moy), or "change for the new." Under *doi moi,* individuals gain more control of some industries. The state still owns the land, but farmers decide how to work it. Businesses can control prices, which rise and fall according to **supply and demand**. The price of a good goes up or down depending on how many people want it and how much of that good is available.

Place • **People live in houseboats on the Saigon River in Ho Chi Minh City.** ▲

Farming and Industry Most of the farmland in Vietnam is in the deltas of the Red and Mekong rivers. Almost four-fifths of the farmland is planted with rice, the main staple of the Vietnamese diet. There are also plantations for growing rubber, bananas, coffee, and tea. The most profitable industry in Vietnam is food processing. Seafood is frozen or canned and then exported to nations such as Japan, Germany, and the United States. Also important is silk, which is produced in Vietnam, woven into textiles, and exported around the world.

Opening Doors Perhaps the biggest boost to the Vietnamese economy occurred when Vietnam opened up trade with the rest of the world. Foreigners started businesses and invested in Vietnam, bringing money and modern technology with them.

In 1994, the United States began trading again with Vietnam. This is when the two nations reopened diplomatic relations. The governments now communicate and work together.

Reading
Social Studies

B. Recognizing Effects Why might it have taken so long for diplomatic relations between Vietnam and the United States to be reopened?

Living in Vietnam

In the large cities of Vietnam, many people live in apartment buildings. One apartment may house children, their parents, and their grandparents. In the country, families live in stone houses in the north and in houses built of bamboo and wood in the warmer south. Many people do not have electricity or running water, and get their water from wells or creeks.

Along the Mekong River, many people live in houseboats or in houses built on stilts to be safe from floods. In the mountains, people may live in longhouses (long, narrow buildings that hold up to 30 or 40 people). A fireplace in the middle of the house is used for cooking and warmth. A hole in the roof lets out the smoke.

Holidays The most important holiday is **Tet,** the Vietnamese New Year. This three-day festival includes parades, feasts, dances, and family gatherings. Tet marks the beginning of spring. People bring tree buds indoors to blossom. Fireworks light up the skies. Families feast on dried fruit, pickled vegetables, candy, and fish, duck, or meat in rice cakes. To start the New Year, people wear new clothes, pay debts, and settle old arguments. Children may receive gifts of money wrapped in red rice paper.

SECTION 3 ASSESSMENT

Terms & Names

1. **Identify:** (a) Ho Chi Minh (b) Politburo (c) *doi moi*
   (d) supply and demand (e) Tet

Taking Notes

2. Use a sequence chart like this one to list the main events that led to the reunification of Vietnam in 1976.

1858: Napoleon III invades Vietnam
↓
↓
↓
↓
↓
1976: Vietnam reunited

Main Ideas

3. (a) Why did Ho Chi Minh want independence from France?

   (b) Why did the United States wage war against North Vietnam?

   (c) How is Vietnam governed today?

Critical Thinking

4. **Contrasting**

   Contrast the effects of Chinese and French rule on Vietnam.

   Think About

   - the contributions of China to the culture of Vietnam
   - the reasons foreign powers wanted to rule Vietnam
   - the response of the Vietnamese to French rule

ACTIVITY -OPTION- How do former enemies learn to get along? Think of a way to encourage good relations between the United States and Vietnam. Share your **idea** with your classmates.

TERMS & NAMES

Explain the significance of each of the following:

1. mandala
2. military dictatorship
3. East Timor
4. Bahasa Indonesian
5. batik
6. Ho Chi Minh
7. Politburo
8. *doi moi*
9. supply and demand
10. Tet

REVIEW QUESTIONS

History and Governments *(pages 643–647)*

1. In what ways was the culture of Southeast Asia shaped by other cultures?
2. How did World War II and the end of colonialism affect Southeast Asia?

Economies and Cultures *(pages 650–653)*

3. How do most of the people in Southeast Asia make a living?
4. In what ways are people in Southeast Asia culturally different from one another?

Vietnam Today *(pages 655–659)*

5. Why were Ho Chi Minh and the Vietminh trying to overthrow the government of South Vietnam?
6. What two government policies contributed to Vietnam's growing economy?

CRITICAL THINKING

Drawing Conclusions

1. Using your completed chart from Reading Social Studies, p. 642, decide whether or not it is in the best interests of Southeast Asian countries to develop industries that will enable them to increase their international trade. List the facts and examples that support your conclusion.

Clarifying

2. Why do you think Southeast Asian nations were in political turmoil after the colonial powers withdrew?

Forming and Supporting Opinions

3. What personal qualities did Ho Chi Minh need to possess in order to lead Vietnam's independence movement?

Visual Summary

1 History and Governments

- India and China greatly influenced the culture of Southeast Asia.
- When European colonialism ended, Southeast Asian nations established their own governments including constitutional monarchies, republics, military dictatorships, and Communist states.

2 Economies and Cultures

- Most of the people in Southeast Asia make their living by farming, but industry is growing.
- Language, religion, and art in Southeast Asia are a blend of local and foreign influences.

Vietnam Today 3

- Vietnam struggled against France, China, the United States, and itself before being reunited as a single, independent country in 1976.
- Today Vietnam is a Communist nation that encourages world trade, including trade with the United States.

SOCIAL STUDIES SKILLBUILDER

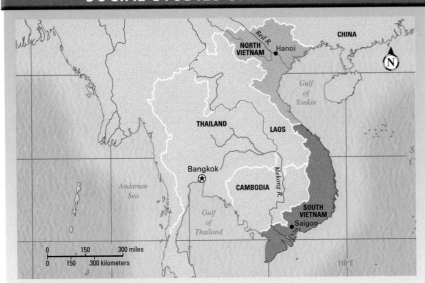

SKILLBUILDER: Distinguishing Fact from Opinion

In the 1960s, a military adviser to the president of the United States might have made the following statement:

> Vietnam borders two other Southeast Asian countries. If the North Vietnamese Communists win, all of Southeast Asia will fall to Communism. To prevent that, we should support the South Vietnamese.

1. Look at the map and read the statement. Which part is factual? Which part is an opinion?
2. Based on the facts, do you agree with the opinion? Why or why not?

FOCUS ON GEOGRAPHY

1. **Movement** • From where did early invaders to Vietnam come?
2. **Place** • Which kingdom included much of present-day Myanmar?
3. **Location** • Why do you think China and India, but not Europe, had a great influence on Southeast Asia?

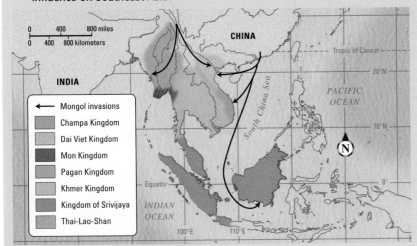

CHAPTER PROJECTS

Interdisciplinary Activity: Literature

Storytelling Find and memorize a folk tale from one of the Southeast Asian countries. Retell the story discussed in the chapter to your classmates. Be sure to remember all the important details and make it exciting for your listeners.

Cooperative Learning Activity

Creating a Newscast In a group of three to five students, create a television or radio newscast about a significant event in the chapter. For example, you might focus on the withdrawal of Europeans from Southeast Asia, the invasion of East Timor by Indonesia, or the Vietnam War.

- Take on the roles of director, writers, and anchors.
- Work on a rough draft of the report and practice delivering the news broadcast.
- Perform your final version of the news broadcast for the class.

INTERNET ACTIVITY

Use the Internet to research education in Southeast Asia. Choose one country and find out as much information as you can about how children are educated and what it's like to be a student in that country.

Writing About Geography Write a report about your findings. Include photographs and drawings to illustrate your information. List the Web sites you used to prepare your report.

For Internet links to support this activity, go to

RESEARCH LINKS
CLASSZONE.COM

UNIT 8

Place The Great Wall of China stretches for thousands of miles. Built to defend China from foreign invaders, the Great Wall was constructed in stages from the 7th century B.C. to the 15th century A.D.

EAST ASIA, AUSTRALIA, AND THE PACIFIC ISLANDS

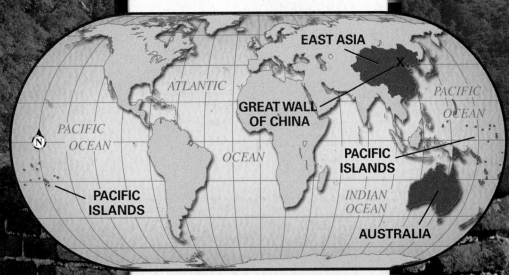

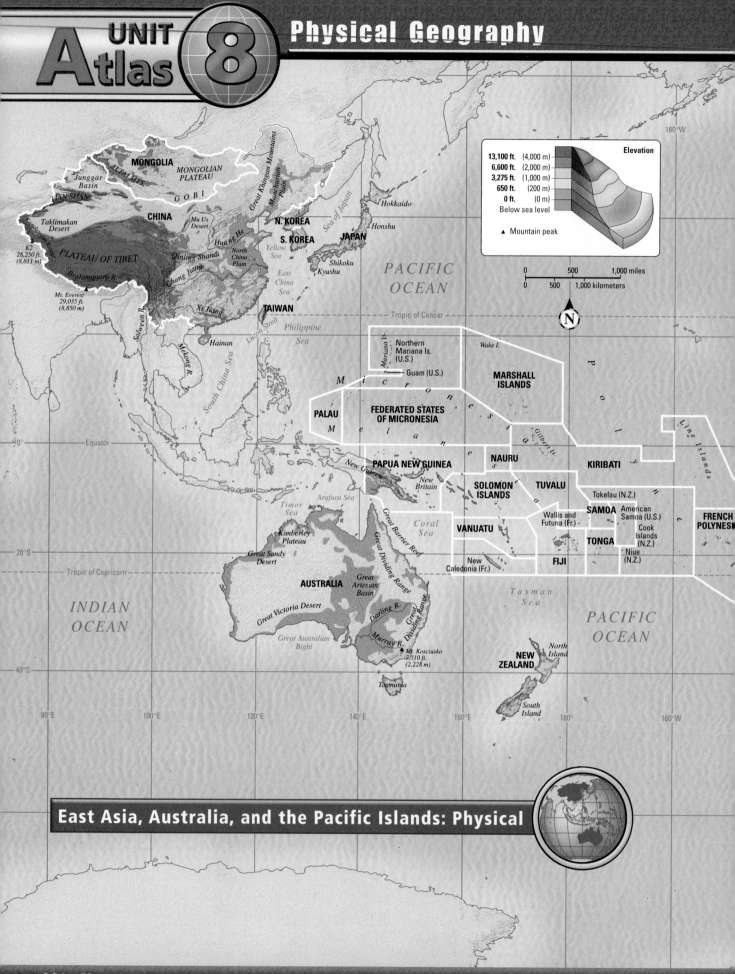

MONGOLIA

MONGOLIAN PLATEAU

Junggar Basin

ALTAI MTS.

Great Khingan Mountains

Manchurian Plain

G O B I

TIAN SHAN

Hokkaido

Taklimakan Desert

CHINA

Mu Us Desert

N. KOREA

Sea of Japan

Honshu

K2 28,250 ft. (8,611 m)

Huang He

S. KOREA

JAPAN

Yellow Sea

Shikoku

PLATEAU OF TIBET

Qinling Shandi

North China Plain

Kyushu

PACIFIC OCEAN

Brahmaputra R.

Chang Jiang

East China Sea

Mt. Everest 29,035 ft. (8,850 m)

Xi Jiang

TAIWAN

Tropic of Cancer

Salween R.

Hainan

Philippine Sea

Luzon Strait

Wake I.

Mekong R.

Mariana Is.

Northern Mariana Is. (U.S.)

MARSHALL ISLANDS

South China Sea

Guam (U.S.)

M i c r o n e s i a

PALAU

FEDERATED STATES OF MICRONESIA

Equator

M e l a n e s i a

P o l y n e s i a

Gilbert Is.

Line Islands

PAPUA NEW GUINEA

NAURU

KIRIBATI

New Guinea

New Britain

SOLOMON ISLANDS

TUVALU

Tokelau (N.Z.)

Arafura Sea

Timor Sea

Wallis and Futuna (Fr.)

SAMOA

American Samoa (U.S.)

FRENCH POLYNESIA

VANUATU

Cook Islands (N.Z.)

Kimberley Plateau

Great Barrier Reef

Coral Sea

TONGA

Great Sandy Desert

New Caledonia (Fr.)

FIJI

Niue (N.Z.)

Tropic of Capricorn

Great Dividing Range

AUSTRALIA

Great Artesian Basin

Tasman Sea

INDIAN OCEAN

Great Victoria Desert

Darling R.

Great Dividing Range

PACIFIC OCEAN

Great Australian Bight

Murray R.

Mt. Kosciusko 7,310 ft. (2,228 m)

North Island

NEW ZEALAND

Tasmania

South Island

Elevation

13,100 ft.	(4,000 m)
6,600 ft.	(2,000 m)
3,275 ft.	(1,000 m)
650 ft.	(200 m)
0 ft.	(0 m)
Below sea level	

▲ Mountain peak

0   500   1,000 miles
0   500   1,000 kilometers

N

East Asia, Australia, and the Pacific Islands: Physical

Vegetation of East Asia, Australia, and the Pacific Islands

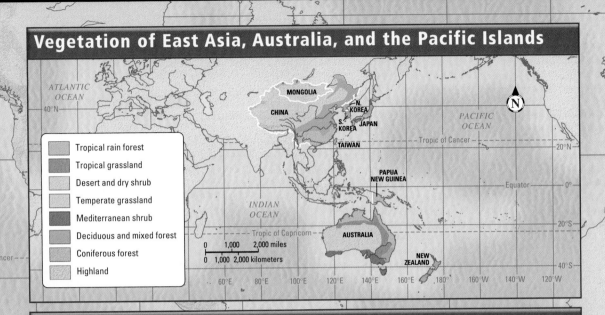

Legend:
- Tropical rain forest
- Tropical grassland
- Desert and dry shrub
- Temperate grassland
- Mediterranean shrub
- Deciduous and mixed forest
- Coniferous forest
- Highland

0   1,000   2,000 miles
0   1,000 2,000 kilometers

East Asia, Australia, and the Pacific Islands–United States Landmass and Population

United States

East Asia, Australia, and the Pacific Islands

LANDMASS

East Asia, Australia, and the Pacific Islands
7,837,975 square miles

Continental United States
3,165,630 square miles

POPULATION

East Asia, Australia, and the Pacific Islands
1,515,889,363

United States
281,421,906

= 50,000,000

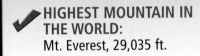

PITCAIRN

FAST FACTS

✔ **HIGHEST MOUNTAIN IN THE WORLD:**
Mt. Everest, 29,035 ft.

✔ **LONGEST RIVER:**
Chang Jiang, 3,915 mi.

✔ **WORLD'S GREATEST VOLCANIC ERUPTION:**
Taupo Volcano, New Zealand, around A.D. 130; 33 billion tons of debris from the eruption covered 20,000 sq. mi.

✔ **ONLY IN AUSTRALIA:**
Kangaroos, koalas, and platypuses are found in the wild only in Australia.

GEOGRAPHY SKILLBUILDER: Interpreting Maps and Visuals
1. **Location** • Name three rivers in East Asia.
2. **Place** • Which country in the region has tropical grassland?

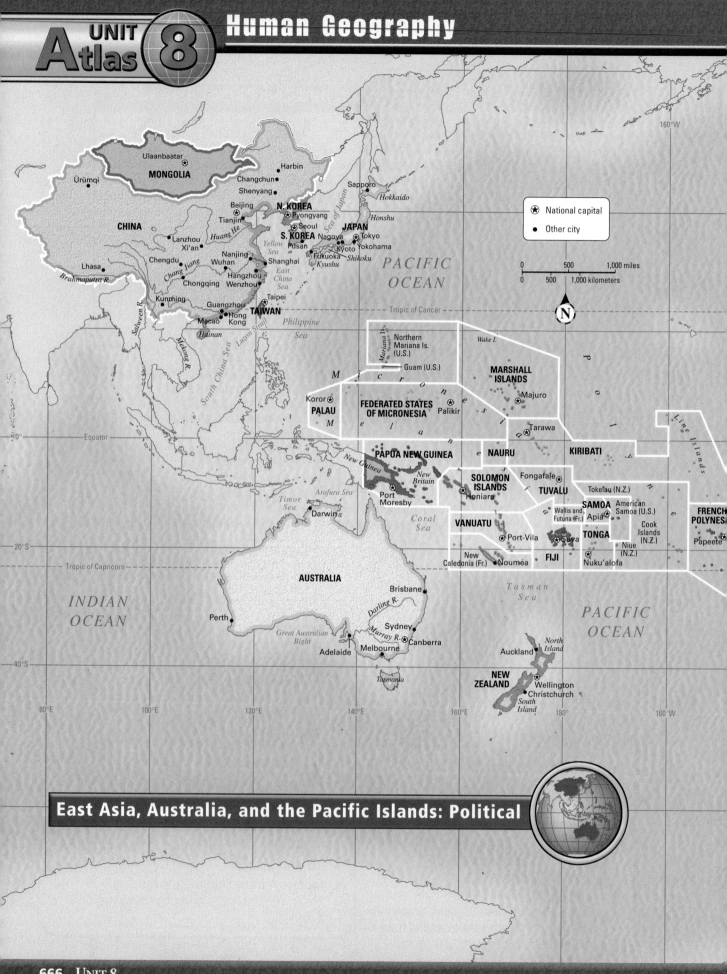

National capital
Other city

MONGOLIA
Ulaanbaatar
Ürümqi
Harbin
Changchun
Shenyang
Sapporo
Hokkaido
CHINA
Beijing
N. KOREA
Pyongyang
Tianjin
Seoul
S. KOREA
Honshu
Sea of Japan
Lanzhou
Xi'an
Huang He
Yellow
Sea
Pusan
Nagoya
JAPAN
Tokyo
Yokohama
Kyoto
Fukuoka
Shikoku
Kyushu
PACIFIC
OCEAN
Lhasa
Chengdu
Chang Jiang
Nanjing
Wuhan
Shanghai
Brahmaputra R.
Hangzhou
Chongqing
Wenzhou
East
China
Sea
Kunming
Guangzhou
Taipei
Salween R.
Macao
Hong
Kong
TAIWAN
Hainan
Mekong R.
Luzon Strait
Philippine
Sea
South China Sea
Tropic of Cancer

Northern
Mariana Is.
(U.S.)
Mariana Is
Wake I.
MARSHALL
ISLANDS
Guam (U.S.)
Majuro
Koror
PALAU
FEDERATED STATES
OF MICRONESIA
Palikir
M i c r o n e s i a
Tarawa
P o l y n e s i a
Equator
M
e l a n e s i a
NAURU
KIRIBATI
Line Islands
New Guinea
PAPUA NEW GUINEA
New
Britain
SOLOMON
ISLANDS
Fongafale
TUVALU
Tokelau (N.Z.)
Port
Moresby
Honiara
SAMOA
American
Samoa (U.S.)
FRENCH
POLYNES
Arafura Sea
Wallis and
Futuna (Fr.)
Apia
Cook
Islands
(N.Z.)
VANUATU
Timor
Sea
Darwin
Coral
Sea
Port-Vila
Suva
TONGA
Niue
(N.Z.)
Papeete
New
Caledonia (Fr.)
Nouméa
FIJI
Nuku'alofa
Tropic of Capricorn
INDIAN
OCEAN
AUSTRALIA
Brisbane
Tasman
Sea
PACIFIC
OCEAN
Perth
Darling R.
Sydney
Great Australian
Bight
Murray R.
Canberra
North
Island
Auckland
Adelaide
Melbourne
Tasmania
NEW
ZEALAND
Wellington
Christchurch
South
Island

PACIFIC
OCEAN

0 500 1,000 miles
0 500 1,000 kilometers

N

80°E 100°E 120°E 140°E 160°E 180° 160°W
160°W

East Asia, Australia, and the Pacific Islands: Political

The International Date Line

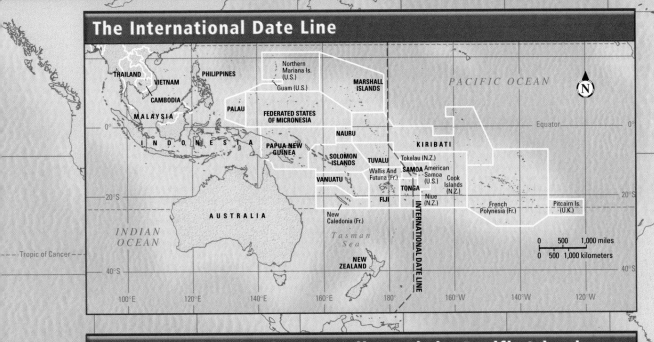

Religions of East Asia, Australia, and the Pacific Islands

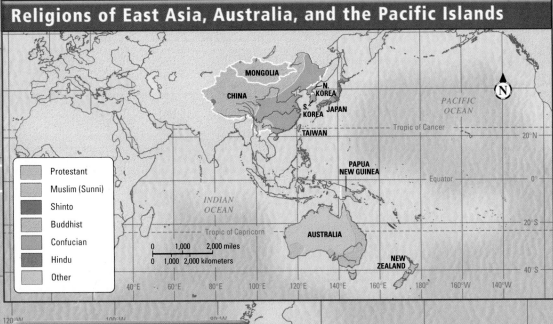

Legend:
- Protestant
- Muslim (Sunni)
- Shinto
- Buddhist
- Confucian
- Hindu
- Other

FAST FACTS

✔ **LARGEST POPULATION IN THE WORLD:**
China, 1,273,111,000 (2001 estimate)

✔ **SPARSEST POPULATION IN THE WORLD:**
Mongolia, 4.4 people per sq. mi.

✔ **LARGEST CITY IN THE WORLD:**
Tokyo, 26,444,000 (2000)

GEOGRAPHY SKILLBUILDER: Interpreting Maps and Visuals

1. **Place** • Which country in this region has no coast?
2. **Location** • Name an island in this region that is on the other side of the International Date Line from Vanuatu.

Country Flag	Country/Capital	Currency	Population (2001 estimate)	Life Expectancy (years)	Birthrate (per 1,000 pop.) (2000 estimate)
	**Australia** Canberra	Australian Dollar	19,358,000	79	13
	**China** Beijing	Renminbi	1,273,111,000	71	15
	**Fiji** Suva	Dollar	844,000	67	22
	**Japan** Tokyo	Yen	126,772,000	80	9
	**Kiribati** Tawara	Australian Dollar	94,000	62	33
	**Marshall Islands** Majuro	U.S. Dollar	71,000	65	26
	**Micronesia, Fed. States of** Palikir	U.S. Dollar	135,000	66	33
	**Mongolia** Ulaanbaatar	Tugrik	2,655,000	63	20
	**Nauru** Yaren Administrative Center	Australian Dollar	12,000	61	19
	**New Zealand** Wellington	New Zealand Dollar	3,864,000	77	15
	**North Korea** Pyongyang	Won	21,968,000	70	21
	**Palau** Koror	U.S. Dollar	19,000	67	18
	**Papua New Guinea** Port Moresby	Kina	5,049,000	56	34
	**Samoa** Apia	Tala	179,000	68	31
	**Solomon Islands** Honiara	Dollar	480,000	71	37
	**South Korea** Seoul	Won	47,904,000	74	14
	**Taiwan** Taipei	New Taiwan Dollar	22,370,000	75	13

DATA FILE

Infant Mortality (per 1,000 live births) (2000)	Doctors (per 100,000 pop.) (1994–1999)	Literacy Rate (percentage) (1996–1998)	Passenger Cars (per 1,000 pop.) (1996–1997)	Total Area (square miles)	Map (not to scale)
5.3	240.0	100	453	2,967,909	
31.4	161.7	82	4	3,704,427	
12.9	48.0	92	37	7,055	
3.5	193.2	99	367	143,619	
62.0	30.0	90	N/A	277	
30.5	42.0	93	N/A	70	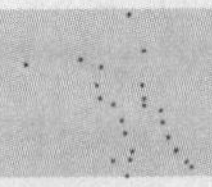
46.0	57.0	90	N/A	1,055	
34.1	243.3	83	8	604,247	
25.0	157.0	99	N/A	8.2	
5.5	217.0	100	391	103,736	
26.0	297.0	99	N/A	46,609	
19.2	110.0	98	N/A	191	
77.0	7.0	72	5	178,260	
25.0	34.0	98	7	1,209	
25.3	14.0	54	N/A	11,500	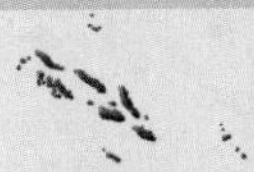
11.0	136.1	98	2	38,022	
6.6	100.0	94	198	13,887	

Country Flag	Country/Capital	Currency	Population (2000 estimate)	Life Expectancy (years)	Birthrate (per 1,000 pop.) (2000 estimate)
	Tonga Nuku'alofa	Pa'anga	104,000	71	27
	Tuvalu Fongafale	Australian Dollar	11,000	64	22
	Vanuatu Port-Vila	Vatu	193,000	65	35
	United States Washington, D.C.	Dollar	281,422,000	77	15

Easter Island stone heads ▼
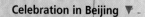

Celebration in Beijing ▼

An Aborigine artist ▼

DATA FILE

Infant Mortality (per 1,000 live births) (2000)	Doctors (per 100,000 pop.) (1994–1999)	Literacy Rate (percentage) (1996–1998)	Passenger Cars (per 1,000 pop.) (1996–1997)	Total Area (square miles)	Map (not to scale)
19.0	44	93	31	270	
24.8	30	95	N/A	9	
39.0	12	36	21	5,700	
7.0	251	97	489	3,787,319	

GEOGRAPHY SKILLBUILDER: Interpreting a Chart

1. **Place** • How much lower is Vanuatu's literacy rate than New Zealand's?
2. **Place** • How much larger is Australia's population than Kiribati's?

Terraced rice fields in China ▼

A Chinese family ▼

A Shinto archway in Japan ▲

CHAPTER 23

East Asia, Australia, and the Pacific Islands: Land and History

EAST ASIA

ATLANTIC

PACIFIC OCEAN

PACIFIC OCEAN

OCEAN

INDIAN OCEAN

PACIFIC ISLANDS   AUSTRALIA

Place Mount Uluru, also called Ayers Rock, stands out against the flat desert of Australia's Red Center, the vast interior part of Australia. Uluru is the largest single rock in the world.

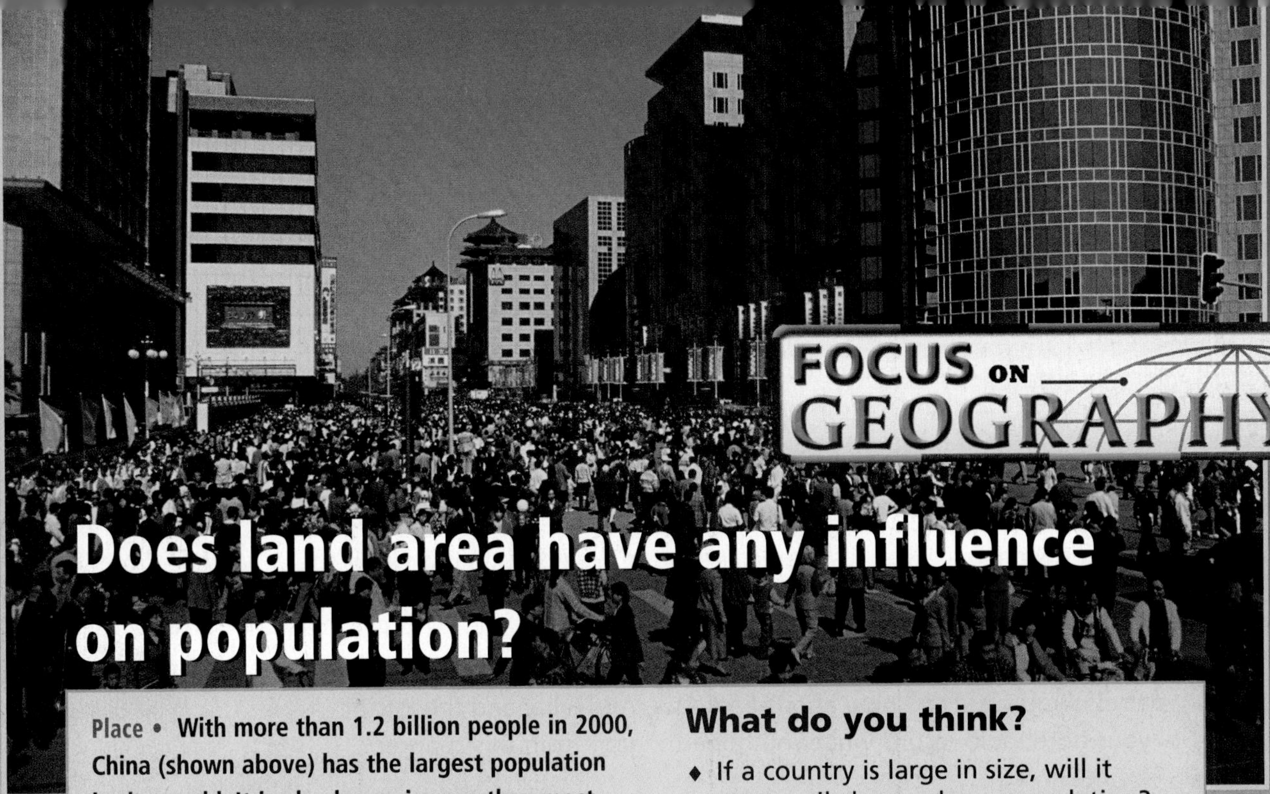

Does land area have any influence on population?

Place • With more than 1.2 billion people in 2000, China (shown above) has the largest population in the world. It is also larger in area than most countries, with 3.6 million square miles of land.

Australia, on the other hand, is home to 19 million—a population that is 63 times smaller than China's. However, Australia's land area, at 2.9 million square miles, is only slightly smaller than China's. In effect, the two countries are similar in land area, but their population sizes are dramatically different.

What do you think?

♦ If a country is large in size, will it necessarily have a large population? What other factors contribute to population size? Think about natural resources, social conditions, and climate.

♦ How do the physical features of a country affect where people can or will live? Does harsh physical geography in some parts of a country affect the overall population, or just the population density?

BEFORE YOU READ

▶▶ *What Do You Know?*

Before you read the chapter, consider what you already know about East Asia, Australia, and the Pacific Islands. What are the geographic features of these areas? Have you seen a television program about the Ring of Fire or about Australia's Outback? You may have learned about ancient China and ancient Japan in other classes. Do you know who Confucius was or who the Japanese samurai warriors were? Do you know anyone who has visited the Great Wall of China, which is the world's longest wall?

Place • China's emperors lived in the Forbidden City, which still stands in the capital, Beijing. ▲

▶▶ *What Do You Want to Know?*

Decide what else you want to know about East Asia, Australia, and the Pacific Islands. In your notebook, record what you hope to learn from this chapter.

READ AND TAKE NOTES

Reading Strategy: Comparing and Contrasting
Comparing and contrasting places helps you understand more about each one. Comparing means looking for similarities, while contrasting means looking for differences. Making a comparing and contrasting chart for the countries in this chapter will help you better understand them.

- Copy the chart into your notebook.

- As you read the chapter, look for information about the geography and civilizations of ancient China and ancient Japan.

- Record key details under the appropriate headings in the chart.

Culture • Japanese warriors called samurai wore intricate suits of armor. ◀

	Ancient China	Ancient Japan
Geography		
Government		
Religion/Philosophy		
Discoveries/Inventions		
Trade/International Relations		

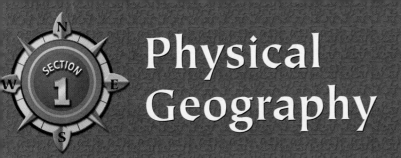

Physical Geography

TERMS & NAMES
Mount Everest
Mount Fuji
Ring of Fire
typhoon
outback
Great Barrier Reef

MAIN IDEA

The physical features of East Asia, Australia, and the Pacific Islands are the result of different geological processes.

WHY IT MATTERS NOW

Understanding these countries' physical features helps us to understand their political and economic roles in the world.

DATELINE

EXTRA

YOKOHAMA, JAPAN, SEPTEMBER 1, 1923

Today, as thousands of people in Tokyo and in Yokohama were preparing to have lunch, a powerful earthquake struck. Walls bulged and buildings lurched as though made of cardboard.

Hundreds of thousands of houses completely collapsed, trapping unknown numbers of victims. The ground heaved and tossed, and in one area the earth was lifted 24 feet high. The massive uplifting of the ground caused thousands of landslides.

Some of the worst damage was caused by the fires that followed the quake. When the tremors began, people were cooking on stoves. Within minutes, kitchen fires sprang up throughout the cities. Many people who survived the quake died in the fires. As night falls, the entire city of Tokyo is in flames.

Human-Environment Interaction • It will take many people a long time to clean up the wreckage from the earthquake. ▲

The Lands of the Region

Japan is one among many countries in the region of East Asia, Australia, and the Pacific Islands, which you can see on page 666 of the Unit Atlas. East Asia includes China, Japan, North Korea, South Korea, Mongolia, and Taiwan. Australia is an island, a nation, and a continent all its own, with New Zealand as a nearby neighbor. The thousands of Pacific Islands are grouped into three subregions—Melanesia, Micronesia, and Polynesia.

China

Look at the map below. Notice that the geography within China's boundaries varies greatly. Over much of China's area, mountains rise to great heights. Rivers and plains cover the eastern part of China. To the southwest, the land rises to high plateaus, and to the northwest, it stretches out in long, dry deserts.

China's Mountains Look again at the map. You can see that China's highest mountains are in the west. The Himalayas run along China's southwestern border, dividing China from Nepal. The highest peak in the Himalayas—and in the world—is **Mount Everest,** at 29,035 feet. Notice also the Plateau of Tibet. It spreads across one-fourth of China's land and is the highest plateau on Earth, earning it the nickname "roof of the world."

China's Great Rivers China's three great rivers are the Huang He (hwahng huh), the Chang Jiang (chahng jyahng), and the Xi Jiang (shee jyahng). They all start in the highlands and flow east. The southernmost is the Xi Jiang, as you can see on the map.

BACKGROUND

The Chang Jiang is known in the West as the Yangtze (yang•see).

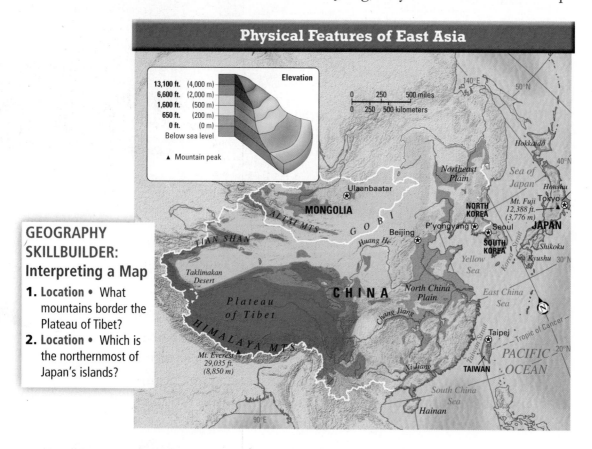

GEOGRAPHY SKILLBUILDER: Interpreting a Map

1. **Location** • What mountains border the Plateau of Tibet?
2. **Location** • Which is the northernmost of Japan's islands?

North of it, the Chang Jiang winds across China. At over 3,400 miles, this is China's longest river.

Vocabulary

silt:
windblown material similar to clay

The northernmost river is the Huang He, or Yellow River. Its name comes from the color of the fine silt that covers the plains along parts of the river. You can see that the Huang He begins in the Plateau of Tibet. On its course east through the North China Plain, it often overflows. Because of the thousands of lives lost in its floods, the Chinese often call the river "China's Sorrow."

China's Deserts Two large deserts span China's northern lands. You can see on the map that the Taklimakan (TAH·kluh·muh·KAHN) covers northwestern China. With an east-west length of about 600 miles, it is one of the world's largest sandy deserts. During the spring, dust storms with the strength of hurricanes occur frequently, lifting the desert's dust as high as 13,000 feet in the air.

East of the Taklimakan, in central northern China, sprawls the Gobi (GOH·bee). In Mongolian, *gobi* means "waterless place." The Gobi's dryness is harsh, and so are its temperatures. In the summer, the Gobi's temperature can rise to 113°F. In the winter, it may get down to -40°F.

Place •
Much of the Gobi is made of rock rather than sand. ▲

Japan

Japan is a country of islands that stretch for 1,500 miles across the Pacific Ocean. Look at the map on page 664 to see the four main islands—Hokkaido (hah·KY·doh), Honshu (HAHN·shoo), Shikoku (shee·KAW·koo), and Kyushu (kee·OO·shoo). Honshu is the largest, as well as the home of Japan's capital, Tokyo.

Japan sits atop two tectonic plates that often sink below a third plate. Because of this, Japan is more likely to have volcanic eruptions and earthquakes than are many places on Earth.

Reading
Social Studies

A. Drawing Conclusions Why do you think the Japanese built Tokyo where they did?

Mountains and Volcanoes Mountains cover more than 80 percent of Japan's land. Instead of forming ranges, these mountains are blocks separated by lowlands. This formation results from faults, or cracks in the rock, that cause the land either to lift up into a mountain or to drop down into lowlands. The largest stretch of lowlands is the Kanto Plain, where Tokyo lies.

East Asia, Australia, and the Pacific Islands: Land and History **677**

Human-Environment Interaction • More than 100,000 people a year climb Mount Fuji, which is considered sacred in Japan. ▲

Japan's tallest mountain, **Mount Fuji,** is an active volcano. Volcanic eruptions are common in Japan, which is part of the **Ring of Fire**—an area of volcanic activity along the borders of the Pacific Ocean. This is where most of the world's earthquakes and volcanoes occur.

Earthquakes Japan records as many as 1,500 minor earthquakes each year. In 1923, a major earthquake hit Tokyo and its surrounding regions, which you read about on page 675. After 1923, Japan became a world leader in constructing buildings able to withstand the shock of frequent earthquakes.

Climate Japan's climate is largely controlled by monsoons. In the winter, the monsoons bring cold rain and snow to Japan's western coast. In the summer, they bring warm rains to the south and east. During the summer and early fall, storms called typhoons also occur often. A **typhoon** is a hurricane that occurs in the western Pacific.

The Koreas

North and South Korea lie on the mountainous Korean Peninsula, which you can see on the map on page 676. North Korea is a land filled with mountains and valleys. Its major rivers, the Yalu and Tumen, mark the border with China. Its climate is temperate, with cold, dry winters and hot, humid summers.

BACKGROUND

Even with their top-notch construction, more than 100,000 buildings were destroyed in 1995 by another major earthquake in Kobe (KOH•BEE).

The Ring of Fire

GEOGRAPHY SKILLBUILDER: Interpreting a Map

1. **Location** • Which continents border the Ring of Fire?
2. **Place** • Is Mount Fuji the only volcano in Japan?

EUROPE ASIA NORTH AMERICA

Mt. St. Helens

ATLANTIC OCEAN

Mt. Fuji

AFRICA

PACIFIC OCEAN

ATLANTIC OCEAN

INDIAN OCEAN

SOUTH AMERICA

AUSTRALIA

ANTARCTICA

The Ring of Fire

▲ Ring of Fire volcano

Most of the rain each year falls between June and September, brought on by the monsoons of the Pacific. South Korea is a mix of rugged mountain ranges, coastal plains, and river valleys. Its main rivers are the Han, the Kum, and the Naktong.

Australia

Australia is one of the largest countries on Earth, though it is the smallest continent. Its landscape is unique in that it has not changed dramatically for more than 250 million years. In other continents, such as Europe and North America, major landscape changes have occurred even in just the past 25,000 years.

Flat and Dry Australia Look at the map below. Notice the Great Dividing Range that runs along Australia's eastern coast. This chain is the largest in Australia, but none of these mountains rise higher than 5,000 feet. To their west, vast plains extend across most of Australia. Australians call this huge stretch of interior land the **outback.**

Australia is the flattest continent on Earth, and it is also extremely dry. Deserts cover one-third of the country. The majority of people live along the northern and eastern coasts, where much of Australia's fresh water is found.

Reading
Social Studies

B. Contrasting
Contrast the influence of physical features on settlement patterns in Japan and Australia.

Place• Australia is home to many animals that are native only to that continent, such as the kangaroo. ▲

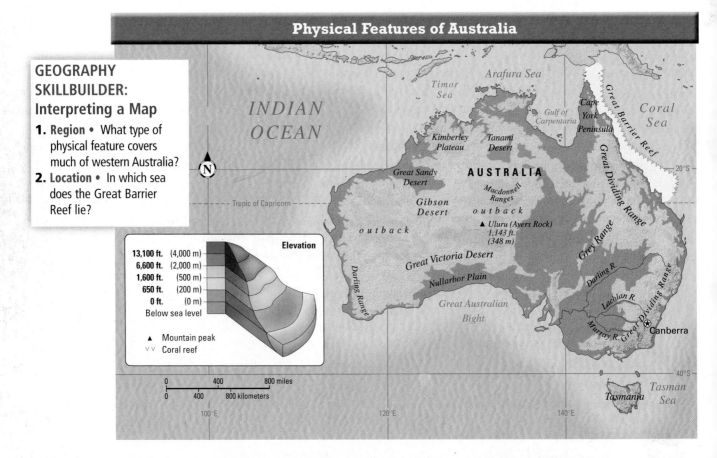

Physical Features of Australia

GEOGRAPHY SKILLBUILDER:
Interpreting a Map
1. **Region** • What type of physical feature covers much of western Australia?
2. **Location** • In which sea does the Great Barrier Reef lie?

INDIAN OCEAN

Arafura Sea

Timor Sea

Gulf of Carpentaria

Cape York Peninsula

Coral Sea

Great Barrier Reef

Kimberley Plateau

Tanami Desert

Great Sandy Desert

AUSTRALIA

Macdonnell Ranges

Gibson Desert

outback

▲ Uluru (Ayers Rock) 1,143 ft. (348 m)

outback

Great Dividing Range

Grey Range

Tropic of Capricorn

Great Victoria Desert

Darling R.

Nullarbor Plain

Darling Range

Lachlan R.

Great Australian Bight

Murray R. Great Dividing Range

⊛ Canberra

Elevation

13,100 ft.	(4,000 m)
6,600 ft.	(2,000 m)
1,600 ft.	(500 m)
650 ft.	(200 m)
0 ft.	(0 m)
Below sea level	

▲ Mountain peak
v v Coral reef

0   400   800 miles
0   400   800 kilometers

Tasman Sea

Tasmania

100°E   120°E   140°E

20°S

40°S

The Great Barrier Reef Off Australia's northeastern coast stretches the world's largest coral reef system, called the **Great Barrier Reef**. Made of more than 2,500 individual reefs and islands, the Great Barrier Reef extends 1,250 miles through the Pacific Ocean. Some of the reefs, called fringing reefs, run along coastlines. Others exist as far as 100 miles from shore. Over 400 species of coral and other ocean life call the reef home.

New Zealand and Other Pacific Islands

Thousands of islands dot the Pacific to the north and east of Australia. On the map on page 664 of the Unit Atlas, you can see that New Zealand's two main islands, which sit about 1,000 miles east of Australia, are among the largest. Most of the others are tiny in comparison.

The roughly 20,000 Pacific Islands are of three types: continental islands, high oceanic islands, and low oceanic islands. Continental islands, such as New Guinea (GIHN·ee) and New Zealand, are parts of Earth's crust that sit above the surface of the water. They often have active volcanoes, even though they were not formed by volcanic activity. High oceanic islands, such as Tahiti (tuh·HEE·tee), are mountainous islands formed by volcanic activity. Most of the Pacific Islands are low oceanic islands, which formed from coral reefs.

SECTION 1 ASSESSMENT

Terms & Names

1. Identify:
- (a) Mount Everest
- (b) Mount Fuji
- (c) Ring of Fire
- (d) typhoon
- (e) outback
- (f) Great Barrier Reef

Taking Notes

2. Make a chart like this one to note the physical features in each region. You can list more features than the ones shown here.

Region	Rivers	Deserts
China		
Japan		
The Koreas		
Australia		
The Pacific Islands		

Main Ideas

3. (a) How is Japan affected by the three tectonic plates on which its islands rest?

(b) Why are some regions of Australia much more suitable for living than others? Which regions are suitable?

(c) What three types of islands exist in the Pacific?

Critical Thinking

4. Drawing Conclusions

Considering China's geographic features, which areas do you think have large populations? Which have small populations?

Think About

- physical features that encourage population settlement
- physical features that would be hard to live in or near

ACTIVITY -OPTION- Make a **diagram** that shows how high oceanic islands and low oceanic islands form.

Ancient China

TERMS & NAMES

dynasty

Genghis Khan

Kublai Khan

Confucius

bureaucracy

Taoism

Lao Tzu

MAIN IDEA

The ancient Chinese developed a civilization that has lasted longer than any other on Earth.

WHY IT MATTERS NOW

China's very long and relatively stable existence has helped it to become one of the most powerful countries in the world.

DATELINE

THE IMPERIAL PALACE, CHINA, 2700 B.C.—Our 14-year-old Empress Si Ling-chi has made an amazing discovery. While walking in the palace gardens, she noticed that caterpillars, which just a few days before were eating mulberry tree leaves, had spun themselves into cocoons. These cocoons hung from branches, within easy reach of our empress, who plucked one and took it home to examine. When she dropped it into boiling water, it unraveled into a tangle of threads.

The empress immediately sent her maids to gather more cocoons. Soon she had enough thread for weaving, and she produced a shining fabric she called silk. Plans are now underway to begin manufacturing huge quantities of this wondrous fabric.

Human-Environment Interaction • Many Chinese women will work to twist the thin silk strands together to make thread thick enough for weaving. ▲

Foundations of Chinese Civilization

Silk is just one of the many inventions for which the ancient Chinese are known. Over the course of thousands of years, the Chinese have built the longest-lasting culture in the world.

As early as 5000 B.C., Chinese people lived in the fertile river valley of the Huang He. Sometime in the 1700s B.C., their lives changed drastically when invaders, called the Shang (shahng), entered their valley. These invaders established China's first permanent, organized civilization.

For most of China's history since the Shang takeover, the country was ruled by **dynasties,** or families of rulers. Dynasties rose and fell in succession—some lasting only 15 years, others continuing for hundreds of years. Look at the chart to the right to learn the names and dates of each dynasty.

The Dynasties of China	
Dynasty	**Dates**
Shang	1700s–1122 B.C.
Zhou	1122–221 B.C.
Qin	221–206 B.C.
Han	206 B.C.–A.D. 220
Sui	A.D. 581–618
Tang	A.D. 618–907
Song	A.D. 960–1279
Yuan	A.D. 1279–1368
Ming	A.D. 1368–1644
Qing	A.D. 1644–1911

SKILLBUILDER: Interpreting a Chart

1. Which dynasty ruled China in A.D. 1?
2. Which was the last dynasty to rule China?

Mongol Rule In the A.D. 1200s, China's greatest fear came to pass—foreign invaders conquered China. In 1211, the Mongols invaded China. They were led by **Genghis Khan** and later by his grandson **Kublai Khan.** In 1279, Kublai Khan conquered China's Song (sung) Dynasty. In its place, he founded the Yuan Dynasty. He also established a capital at Ta-tu.

The Ming Dynasty Warfare eventually broke out among the Mongol leaders, weakening the Yuan Dynasty significantly. The dynasty that took over was called the Ming. Because of his great military success, Ming founder Zhu Yuanzhang (joo yoo•ahn•jang) was called the Hongwu emperor—meaning "vast military power." In his battles, he won from the Mongols the Yunnan province. With this piece of land in his charge, he unified the region that is China today.

Reading
Social Studies

A. Making Inferences How might life in China have changed when foreigners took over?

Strange but TRUE

The Tomb of Shih Huang-ti In 1974, farmers near Xi'an (shee•ahn) made a spectacular discovery. While digging a new well, their shovels hit some broken bits of pottery. Digging deeper, they found not water but a headless clay body. What they had uncovered was the tomb of China's Qin emperor Shih Huang-ti (sheer•hwahng•dee)—filled with an army of about 8,000 life-sized clay soldiers and horses (shown at right).

The foot soldiers, charioteers, and archers were buried 22 centuries ago to guard the emperor in death just as his real soldiers had in life. Although the soldiers' heads and bodies are all similar, their eyes, ears, noses, lips, and hairstyles vary. Among the 8,000 soldiers, no two faces are the same.

When the Hongwu emperor died, one of his grandsons took power, naming himself the Yongle emperor—meaning "eternal contentment." He is famous for rebuilding the Yuan capital, which he renamed Beijing (bay·jihng). He ordered a huge palace complex to be constructed in the capital. This was called the Forbidden City because only the emperor, his family, and some of his officials could enter it.

Location •
The Forbidden City is the largest complex of buildings of its age in the world. ▲

The Ming Dynasty came to an end in 1644 at the hands of invaders from northeastern China, called the Manchu (MAN·choo). These attackers established China's last dynasty, the Qing (chihng), which ruled China until 1911.

Religion and Philosophy

China's dynasties are known for particular achievements—some military, some artistic, some technological, and some spiritual. Several of the world's most influential philosophies and religions arose during the thousands of years of Chinese history.

Confucianism Toward the end of the Zhou Dynasty, a man named Kongfuzi—later called **Confucius** (kuhn·FYOO·shuhs) by Europeans—developed a new philosophy. Confucius taught the importance of moral character and of individuals taking responsibility for the state of their society. He also taught that a ruler, like a good father, should take care of his people and be kind to them.

A VOICE FROM CHINA

If you are personally upright, things get done without any orders being given. If you are not personally upright, no one will obey even if you do give orders.

Confucius

Reading
Social Studies

B. Forming and Supporting Opinions What do you think of Confucius' opinion of how a successful ruler should behave?

The teachings of Confucius were not widely known during his lifetime. Only after his death did his students succeed in spreading his philosophy.

The Impact of Confucianism In 121 B.C., the Han emperor Wudi established Confucianism as the official philosophy guiding the Chinese bureaucracy. **Bureaucracy** is the administration of a government through departments, called bureaus. The appointed officials that staff the bureaus are called bureaucrats. The Han called their bureaucracy the civil service and staffed it with scholars of Confucianism. The civil service gave the government capable officials and contributed to the stability of the culture.

Vocabulary

scholar: specialist in a given subject

Taoism The Zhou period also gave rise to **Taoism** (DOW·IHZ·uhm). This philosophy was developed in the 500s B.C. by **Lao Tzu** (low dzuh), who wrote the main Taoist book—the *Tao-te Ching* (DOW· duh JIHNG). Lao Tzu described a force that guides the universe, though it cannot be seen or named. He called this force the *Tao*, which means "way of nature." The greatest achievement for any person, in Taoist belief, is to find harmony with the Tao and, therefore, with nature.

Buddhism in China During the A.D. 200s, while the Han Dynasty was beginning to collapse, Buddhism made its way to China through traders from India and other areas in Asia. During the Tang Dynasty, Buddhist teachings of how to escape suffering appealed to many Chinese. However, Buddhism did not replace Confucianism or Taoism in China. The Chinese belief system today includes elements of all three philosophies.

Culture •
This statue shows Taoism's founder, Lao Tzu. ▲

Achievements of the Dynasties

China has also given the world some important inventions. Around 2700 B.C., the Chinese invented silk cloth and a new system of writing. In the first two centuries A.D., the Chinese invented paper and a type of pottery called porcelain. In the A.D. 1200s, Chinese navigators began using the compass. These inventions helped shape the civilizations of Asia and, through trade, Europe.

Silk The ancient Chinese were able to keep the secret of how to manufacture silk from foreigners for centuries, although others did eventually learn the Chinese method.

Connections to Technology

Gunpowder One Chinese invention had an explosive impact on the world—gunpowder. The Chinese had invented the first gunpowder, called black powder, by A.D. 1000. They used it originally not in guns (which were invented in Southwest Asia in the 1300s), but in fireworks used in warfare.

By the 1300s, people in the West were using gunpowder to power weapons, such as guns and the medieval Belgian cannon shown below. By the 1600s, Europeans also began using it for more peaceful tasks like mining and road construction.

As long as no one else understood the process, however, China earned all the profits of the silk trade. Caravans carried the precious fabric for thousands of miles to cities in Europe and Southwest Asia, along a trade route named for the fabric—the Silk Road.

The Silk Road The first records of travel and trade along the Silk Road date to the Han Dynasty, around 114 B.C. On the map below, you can see the route of the 4,000-mile long Silk Road. Along it, the Chinese carried not only silk but also much-desired items such as porcelain, tea, incense, and spices. Travelers on the Silk Road faced many natural hazards— extreme heat, lack of water, sandstorms in the desert, and blizzards and altitude sickness in the mountains. Also, robbers lurked on the trade routes. Nevertheless, the Silk Road stayed in use until sea routes to Asia proved safer and until the Ming Dynasty decided to limit foreign trade.

Porcelain People often refer to fine pottery as china. The term actually refers to porcelain, a delicate but strong type of ceramic that the Chinese made from a kind of clay called kaolin (KAY·uh·lihn). When fired in a kiln, the clay changes into a hard, glassy substance. As with silk, the Chinese kept the method for producing porcelain secret for many years after its invention during the Tang Dynasty.

Reading
Social Studies

C. Clarifying If the Silk Road was so dangerous, why did the Chinese continue to use it?

Vocabulary

kiln: high-temperature oven used to bake clay until it hardens

Movement •
Porcelain was an important trade item that the Chinese carried along the Silk Road. ▼

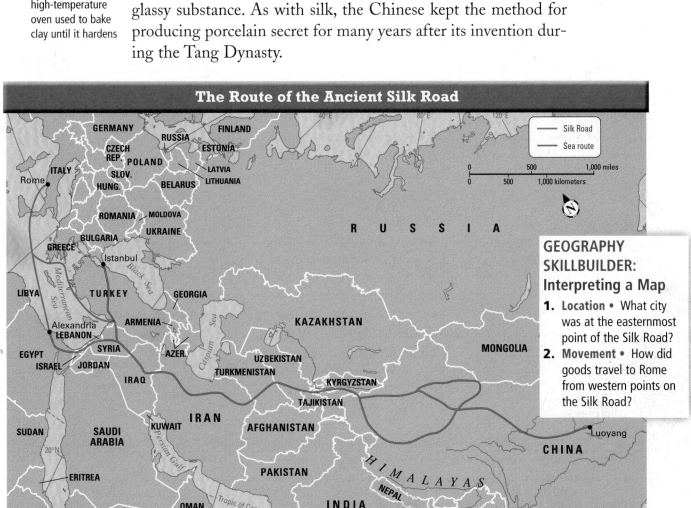

The Route of the Ancient Silk Road

Legend: Silk Road — Sea route

GEOGRAPHY SKILLBUILDER:
Interpreting a Map
1. **Location** • What city was at the easternmost point of the Silk Road?
2. **Movement** • How did goods travel to Rome from western points on the Silk Road?

Culture • Chinese characters like these are drawn with brushes dipped in ink. ▲

Writing During the Shang Dynasty, the Chinese developed a written language. As in cuneiform, the Chinese system at first used pictograms to represent objects or ideas. Later, they simplified the pictograms into symbols, called characters, that do not look exactly like what they represent. About 50,000 characters exist in the Chinese written language. Most words are made up of compound graphs—two or more characters used together. Both the Japanese and Koreans use Chinese characters in their writing systems.

The Great Builders The ancient Chinese built large construction projects like the Great Wall. Many emperors ordered the building of canals. The most important of these was the Grand Canal, which allowed grain from fertile river valleys to be carried more easily to the cities. Construction began on the first segment of the canal in the 600s B.C. Today, it extends for more than 1,000 miles to connect the northern city of Beijing with the southern city of Hangzhou (hahng·joh).

The Longest Wall Stretching for about 1,500 miles across northern China, the Great Wall is the world's longest structure. Construction began in the 600s B.C. with a number of fortified walls to keep out invaders. Later, a series of emperors ordered the walls to be connected. In the 1400s, damaged sections were rebuilt and new portions were added, giving the Great Wall its present form.

Building the Great Wall required the labor of thousands of workers using pounded earth, bricks, and stones. When the wall was finished, over a million soldiers stood guard in its watchtowers. Today, tourists from around the world come to see the Great Wall, which symbolizes China's long history. (See photograph on pages 662–663.)

SECTION 2 ASSESSMENT

Terms & Names
1. Identify:
   (a) dynasty
   (b) Genghis Khan
   (c) Kublai Khan
   (d) Confucius
   (e) bureaucracy
   (f) Taoism
   (g) Lao Tzu

Taking Notes
2. Make a time line like the one below to show the dates of Chinese inventions.

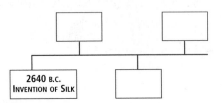

Main Ideas
3. (a) How did the Chinese incorporate Confucianism into their government?

   (b) Why did the Chinese try to keep their process for making silk secret?

   (c) In the Chinese writing system, what do characters stand for?

Critical Thinking
4. **Drawing Conclusions**

   More than just goods for trade traveled along the Silk Road. What else did the Silk Road bring to the people living along it?

Think About

• the different cultures that existed along the Silk Road

• the people and ideas that traveled along the Silk Road

ACTIVITY -OPTION- Imagine you lived in ancient China. Write a **journal entry** describing your experience with one of the religions that developed in China.

Creating a Database

▶▶ Defining the Skill

A database is a collection of information, or data, that is organized so that you can find and retrieve information on a certain topic quickly and easily. Once you set up a database on the computer, you can search for specific information without going through the entire database. Learning how to use a database will help you to create your own.

▶▶ Applying the Skill

The screen below shows a database for the history of settlement in Melanesia. Use the strategies listed below to help you understand and use the database.

How to Create a Database

Strategy ❶ Read the title to identify the topic of the database. In this title, the most important words, or keywords, are "history," "settlement," and "Melanesia." These keywords were used to begin the research for this database.

Strategy ❷ Identify the kind of data you need to enter in your database. These will become the column headings of your database. In this case, the key words "country," "settlement," "colonization," and "independence" were chosen to focus the research.

Strategy ❸ Identify the entries included under each heading.

Strategy ❹ Use the database to help you find information quickly. For example, if this database were on a computer, you could search for "United Kingdom" to find out which of these countries were colonized by the United Kingdom.

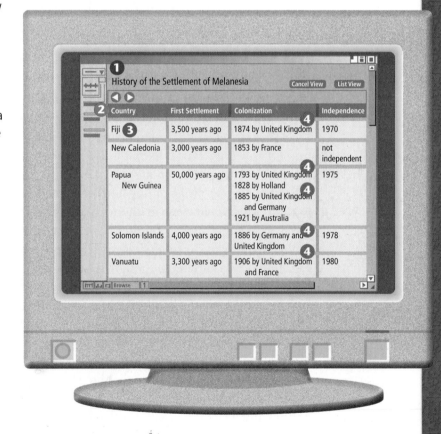

❶ History of the Settlement of Melanesia — Cancel View / List View

❷ Country	First Settlement	Colonization	Independence
Fiji ❸	3,500 years ago	1874 by United Kingdom ❹	1970
New Caledonia	3,000 years ago	1853 by France	not independent
Papua New Guinea	50,000 years ago	1793 by United Kingdom ❹ 1828 by Holland ❹ 1885 by United Kingdom and Germany 1921 by Australia	1975
Solomon Islands	4,000 years ago	1886 by Germany and ❹ United Kingdom	1978
Vanuatu	3,300 years ago	1906 by United Kingdom ❹ and France	1980

▶▶ Practicing the Skill

Turn to page 681 in Chapter 23, Section 2, "Foundations of Chinese Civilization." Create a database about the dynasties of China. Use the information in the section to provide the data. Use a format like the one above for your database.

WAR WOUNDS

BASED VERY CLOSELY on the life of its author, Sook Nyul Choi, *Echoes of the White Giraffe* is the story of a 15-year-old Korean girl, Sookan. As the war between North Korea and South Korea rages, Sookan, her mother, and her younger brother, Inchun, are forced to flee their home in Seoul. They become separated from Sookan's father and older brothers. Sookan, her mother, and Inchun find shelter at a settlement for war refugees in Pusan, a city in southern Korea. There, Sookan slowly begins to make friends, including Junho, a boy who sings with her in a church choir.

"**I**s that a picture of your dog?" Junho asked, looking at the pencil sketch of Luxy that rested on top of the bookcase. "You must miss it very much. . . ."

"Oh that," I said, flustered and surprised. "Yes, that's my boxer, Luxy." I missed my dog, but I hadn't talked about her with anyone since we left Seoul. . . . I frequently thought of how Luxy used to wait eagerly at the top of the stone steps in front of our house for me to come home from school. Then, at night, she would sleep at the foot of my bed. But I never talked of Luxy, for I was afraid that people might think I was childish and insensitive to mourn the loss of my dog when so many people were dead or missing. Junho was different, though . . . sharing my sadness. . . . I stared at Luxy's picture, and I imagined how scared she must have felt when we all abandoned her. Suddenly the acrid[1] smell of bombs and sweeping fires filled my lungs, and the sound of sirens and planes flying low overhead buzzed in my ears. My mind raced back to that horrible day in late June when the dark airplanes roared through the skies and dropped a shower of dark, egg-shaped bombs from their bellies. . . . I shook my head and swallowed hard. . . .

"What is it, Sookan? What are you thinking about?" Junho said, looking very concerned.

"Oh, Junho, I was remembering the first bombing of Seoul. It was horrible. . . . All I could do was stand by the window and watch the bombs explode. Hyunchun, my third brother,

1. Harsh; foul.

came rushing into my room, shouting, '. . . Come on. Those planes will be right on top of us next. Let's go.' "

"Did you all get out safely?" Junho asked anxiously. . . .

"Oh, yes. We put thick blankets over our heads and joined the throngs of people headed up Namsan Mountain. We stayed up on the mountain all night and watched the bombs erupt into flames in the city below. . . . As we were sitting there, I realized my brother Jaechun was holding a large bundle in his arms, which he rocked back and forth like a baby. I instantly realized it was Luxy wrapped in that bundle. . . . It was a good thing that Luxy was bundled up to look like an infant, for other people on the mountain would have been afraid if they knew a dog was with them. They would have panicked, fearing that a dog would go crazy with the noise and the crowds and might bite them. . . .

"The bombing finally stopped at dawn and we began making our way back home. We found our house half bombed and smoldering. We were hungry, and exhausted, and didn't know what we would do next. We . . . started to unwrap poor Luxy. When we uncovered her, she gave such a loud, joyous bark. . . . She made us laugh and forget that we were sitting in the middle of a bombed city."

Junho's face brightened. . . . "Luxy was lucky to be so well loved and cared for."

"Well, . . . Things got worse. About six months after that, we had to leave Seoul. I left her all alone. I don't know what happened to her. . . . There were more bombs, and we had to run and follow the retreating South Korean and U.N. soldiers going south. . . . Mother, Inchun and I were separated from my father and my three older brothers. The three of us, along with thousands of other refugees, walked the whole day in the bitter cold snow to Inchon harbor. I was terribly cold and scared. . . . It was only once we were on the ship that I even thought of my Luxy. . . . I felt so guilty and ashamed that I never mentioned Luxy to Mother or to Inchun. . . .

". . . Each time I see a dog or hear a dog bark, I feel guilty that I did not love Luxy enough to save her; she, my dog, who depended on me. I had thought only of myself. . . ."

Junho listened intently. . . . "You couldn't have walked with her in that cold snow. She may still be alive in Seoul. You shouldn't feel bad."

Reading
THE LITERATURE

How does the author show how much Sookan misses her pet? What are some of the reasons Sookan doesn't want to think or talk about her dog? Why does Sookan decide to share her feelings about her dog with Junho?

Thinking About
THE LITERATURE

How does the life of Sookan and her family change as a result of the war? Besides missing her pet, what other emotions does the loss of Luxy bring out in Sookan?

Writing About
THE LITERATURE

The title "War Wounds" has two meanings, one literal—the words mean exactly what they say—and the other figurative—the words have a symbolic meaning. What do you think are the literal and figurative meanings of the title of this selection?

About the Author

Sook Nyul Choi (b. 1937) was born in Pyongyang, Korea, and spent two and a half years as a refugee during the Korean War. She later emigrated to the United States, where she attended college and then taught school. She now lives in Cambridge, Massachusetts.

Further Reading The first book by Sook Nyul Choi was *Year of Impossible Goodbyes*. It is a moving fictionalized account of Choi's last months in Pyongyang under Japanese rule.

Ancient Japan

TERMS & NAMES
Shinto
clan
Heian Age
The Tale of Genji
Zen
samurai
shogun

MAIN IDEA	WHY IT MATTERS NOW
For hundreds of years, Japan developed its unique culture with influence from only its closest neighbors, China and Korea.	Japan continues to follow an independent path in world affairs.

DATELINE

THE COAST OF JAPAN, A.D. 1281

Fifty-three days ago, our people were horrified to see a fleet of ships carrying 140,000 Mongol invaders approaching our shores. The Mongol emperor of China, Kublai Khan, sent the ships to conquer our country. Our brave samurai fought valiantly, but the Mongols had powerful crossbows and catapults that hurled terrifying missiles. Our warriors were near defeat.

Then, out of nowhere, a typhoon arose on the water. Mongol ships were smashed and sunk by the furious storm. Our people will always remember this *kamikaze*—the "divine wind"—that saved our country.

Culture • Japanese samurai prepare to battle the Mongols. ▲

Early Japan

Long before the *kamikaze* (KAH·mih·KAH·zee) saved Japan from Mongol defeat, people inhabited its islands. From 10,000 to 300 B.C., hunters, gatherers, and skilled fishermen lived along Japan's eastern coast. Toward the end of this period, the Japanese began practicing a religion called **Shinto,** which means "the way of the gods." Shinto teaches that supernatural beings, called kami (KAH·mih), live in all objects and forces of nature.

The early Japanese lived in kingdoms organized around clans. A **clan** is a group of families who trace their descent from a common ancestor. Clans in Japan were each led by a chief who inherited the position. Around A.D. 250, the Yamato clan emerged as the most powerful, and it established a government that ruled Japan for hundreds of years.

Place • This gateway standing in the sea is the entrance to the Itsukushima Shrine, one of Japan's most famous places of Shinto worship. ▲

Outside Influences

Around the time that the Yamato clan took power, Japan began using new ideas and practices from its neighbors, Korea and China. From Korea, the Japanese gained knowledge of how to use bronze and iron technology to make tools and weapons, as well as how to grow an important crop—rice. Japanese religious life also changed significantly when the Koreans introduced Buddhism into Japan. This religion was one of many ideas and customs that originated in China and were brought to Japan by Koreans. In the A.D. 500s, China began to influence Japan's culture directly, as well.

Prince Shotoku At that time, Japanese rulers believed an understanding of Chinese civilization would help them gain political power in East Asia. Japan's Prince Shotoku Taishi (shoh·TOH·koo tay·EE·shee) became a Buddhist and a student of Chinese literature and culture. He established diplomatic relations with China and sent priests and students there to study its culture. Through this exchange, the Japanese adopted China's writing system, calendar, and system of centralized government.

The Heian Age In A.D. 794, the emperor Kammu built a new capital called Heian-kyo (HAY·ahn·KYOH). The period from that year to 1185 is called the **Heian Age** and is considered Japan's golden age. During this period, Japanese culture flourished. A bustling population of 100,000 made up of aristocrats, servants, and artisans lived in Heian-kyo.

Tokyo National Research Institute for Cultural Properties Keeping the rich cultural heritage of Japan alive is the mission of the Tokyo National Research Institute for Cultural Properties. The Institute's scientists, researchers, art historians, and other experts are dedicated to preserving Japan's art, artifacts, ancient monuments, and historic sites, such as Buddhist temples (see below).

In 1995, the Institute opened the Japan Center for International Cooperation in Conservation. The Japan Center works across national borders to help preserve ancient sites throughout the world.

Reading Social Studies

A. Recognizing Effects What does Japan's experience with learning from its neighbors tell you about the importance of cultural exchange?

Vocabulary

artisan: craftsperson

Members of the royal court lived in luxury and high style. Many aristocratic women wrote diaries, letters, and novels about life in the imperial court. Lady Murasaki Shikibu (MOO·rah·SAH·kee SHEE·kee·BOO) wrote the world's first novel, called *The Tale of Genji*. In the novel, Lady Murasaki described life at Heian-kyo's imperial court.

Zen Buddhism After first being established at the Heian-kyo court, Buddhism became a national religion. One branch of Buddhism, called **Zen,** was the most influential in Japan. Zen emphasizes that people can achieve enlightenment suddenly, rather than through many years of painful study. Zen teaches that to reach enlightenment, a person must focus intensely to understand certain concepts, called koans (KOH·AHNZ). Koans are statements or questions that seem to make little sense. However, if someone concentrates very hard to understand one of them, then he or she might reach enlightenment.

Culture • **In this illustration, Lady Murasaki sits under the moon, planning** *The Tale of Genji.* ▲

Vocabulary

imperial: relating to an empire or emperor

BACKGROUND

This is one of the most famous koans: "What is the sound of one hand clapping?"

Feudal Japan

By the 1100s, the Heian-kyo aristocracy lost control of the country to powerful lords. The strongest lords enlisted warriors to fight rival lords. Japan began to develop a feudal system similar to that of medieval Europe, with the country divided into huge estates.

The Samurai While the aristocracy at the Heian-kyo court lived lavishly, disorder and violence spread throughout the rest of the country. Lords needed protection against outlaws and bandits. They relied on warriors called **samurai** (SAM·uh·RY) to protect their estates.

Human-Environment Interaction • **Zen Buddhists take pride in creating peaceful gardens as settings for meditation.** ▼

B. Recognizing Important Details How did the use of samurai differ from the use of an army?

BACKGROUND

In a shogunate, the emperor and his court carried out merely ceremonial roles.

As with European knights, the samurai each pledged to serve a particular lord. They provided him with military and bureaucratic services. By law and privilege, samurai and their families became a distinct social class.

The Kamakura Shogunate During the 1100s, Japan was torn by a murderous war between two clans battling for power. After 30 years of fighting, the Minamoto clan claimed victory. In 1192 in Kamakura, the clan's leader, Yoritomo, established a new kind of warrior government called a shogunate (SHOH•guh•niht). He took on the role of **shogun**—or the emperor's chief general—and held most of the country's power.

In 1274 and again in 1281, the shoguns faced their greatest challenge—Kublai Khan attempted to invade and conquer Japan. On page 690, you read about the events of the second battle. The Kamakura shogunate defeated the Mongols, but at a great cost. The war drained the treasury, and the shogun was unable to pay the samurai. They turned back to individual lords for support, and many years of fighting among lords followed.

Tokugawa Shogunate

Finally, in the 1560s, the fighting began to settle down. The lord Tokugawa Ieyasu (TOH•koo•GAH•wah ee•yeh•YAH•soo) defeated his rivals and became shogun in 1603. In that year, he moved the capital to Edo.

Spotlight on CULTURE

Fine Protection Samurai, who fought hand to hand against their enemies, wore finely made suits of armor and helmets for protection. Low-ranking samurai wore lightweight armor made of small metal panels. The highest-ranking samurai sported much fancier armor, such as the suit shown here. Made of iron panels that were laced or pinned together, it could also include panels of thick leather or linked pieces of metal called chain mail.

The armor was often intricately decorated. The entire suit could weigh as much as 40 pounds. At celebrations, to add to the finery, a samurai wore over his armor a long, loose tunic made of brightly dyed silk and embroidered with his family symbol.

THINKING CRITICALLY

1. **Drawing Conclusions** What does this suit of armor tell you about the rank of the warrior who wore it?

2. **Clarifying** For what purpose did samurai wear beautiful tunics over their armor?

Place • Today, Edo is called Tokyo and is still Japan's capital. ▲

The First Europeans in Japan In 1543, just before the Tokugawa Shogunate began, the first Europeans arrived in Japan. They brought firearms and other goods to trade for gold and silver. In 1549, Catholic missionaries arrived in Japan and began converting many Japanese. By 1614, 300,000 Japanese had become Catholics, including many peasants.

The Closing Door By the 1630s, Tokugawa Ieyasu was worried about foreigners in Japan. He got word that the Spanish had established a settlement in the Philippines. To avoid such a situation in Japan, he ordered all Christians to leave the country. He also declared that any Japanese who left the country would be put to death upon their return. He banned most European trade, finalizing his decision to free Japan of European influences. This situation continued for 200 years, during which Japan isolated itself from most outside contact.

SECTION 3 ASSESSMENT

Terms & Names

1. **Identify:**
   (a) Shinto
   (b) clan
   (c) Heian Age
   (d) *The Tale of Genji*
   (e) Zen
   (f) samurai
   (g) shogun

Taking Notes

2. Use a spider map like this one to list important facts about the development of Japan's culture.

Main Ideas

3. (a) How did the Chinese and the Koreans influence Japan's culture?

   (b) What services did samurai provide, and to whom?

   (c) Under the shogunates, who held more power—the emperor or the shogun?

Critical Thinking

4. **Evaluating Decisions**

   Do you think Tokugawa Ieyasu was right to isolate Japan from European influence? Explain.

   Think About

   • the period before Tokugawa Ieyasu gained control of Japan

   • European influence elsewhere

   • effects of Japan's isolation

ACTIVITY -OPTION- Write a **short story** from the perspective of a samurai, a shogun, or a lord about life in feudal Japan.

Three Gorges Dam

Rising in the Kunlun Mountains of Tibet, the Chang Jiang winds for more than 3,400 miles. It flows through some of China's most fertile agricultural land before emptying into the East China Sea at Shanghai. A stretch of the Chang Jiang known as the Three Gorges includes some of the world's most beautiful scenery. It is also an area rich in archaeological treasures dating back thousands of years. At this site, the Chinese government is building the world's largest dam. With an estimated completion date of 2009, the dam will help control floods and generate much-needed electricity. At the same time, however, construction of the dam will destroy archaeological sites and much of the region's natural beauty while forcing between 1 and 2 million people to relocate.

Three Gorges Dam Facts

Height: 600 ft. (181 m)
Width: 1.5 mi. (2.415 km)
Reservoir: 370 mi. (595.7 km) long
Cost: $25 billion
Workers: 40,000
Years to Complete: 17

CHINA

Area to be flooded

Three Gorges Dam

Sandouping

Wuhan

Shanghai

Chang Jiang (Yangtze R.)

Jialing R.

Chongqing

Water-driven turbines will generate as much electricity as 18 nuclear reactors. This hydro-electric power, one of the cleanest forms of energy, will reduce air pollution. That is important in China because the Chinese burn so much coal.

A series of locks will enable ocean-going ships to travel as far as Chongqing, at the far end of the new reservoir. This is expected to greatly improve the economy of Chongqing.

The dam will control flooding. However, it may also affect fishing and create other environmental problems.

CHINA

When the Three Gorges reservoir is filled in 2009, it will be less than 1 mile wide but 370 miles long—about the distance from Los Angeles to San Francisco.

THINKING Critically

1. Analyzing Motives
How will the Three Gorges Dam benefit China? What are the drawbacks of the dam?

2. Recognizing Effects
The construction of the dam will cause the flooding of about 1,300 archaeological sites. How will this affect China's cultural heritage?

TERMS & NAMES

Explain the significance of each of the following:

1. Mount Everest
2. Ring of Fire
3. outback
4. dynasty
5. Confucius
6. bureaucracy
7. clan
8. *The Tale of Genji*
9. Zen
10. shogun

REVIEW QUESTIONS

Physical Geography *(pages 675–680)*

1. Why do the Chinese often call the Huang He "China's Sorrow"?
2. Where do most of the world's earthquakes and volcanic eruptions occur?
3. How does Australia's landscape differ from that of the world's other continents?

Ancient China *(pages 681–686)*

4. How did the Forbidden City get its name?
5. What are some important inventions from China?
6. Describe the three philosophies that were popular in ancient China.

Ancient Japan *(pages 690–694)*

7. How did Japanese culture show influences from both China and Korea?
8. What roles did the emperors, the lords, and the samurai play in feudal Japan?
9. How did the Japanese respond to Europeans arriving in Japan?

CRITICAL THINKING

Comparing and Contrasting

1. Using your completed chart from Reading Social Studies, p. 674, describe important similarities and differences between ancient China and ancient Japan.

Making Inferences

2. How do you think China's dynasties helped establish and maintain a stable government?

Drawing Conclusions

3. Why did the shogun Tokugawa Ieyasu feel that isolating Japan from Europe was a good idea?

Visual Summary

Physical Geography *1*

- The physical geography of East Asia, Australia, and the Pacific Islands affects how and where people live and how and where civilizations developed.
- Japan and the Pacific Islands are particularly vulnerable to earthquakes and volcanic eruptions.

2

Ancient China

- The ancient Chinese developed the longest-lasting civilization in history. It has existed for 4,000 years.
- Chinese civilization produced inventions and ideas that influenced both Asia and Europe.

Ancient Japan *3*

- Over hundreds of years, ancient Japan developed a unique culture that was influenced by only its nearest neighbors.
- Japan established a feudal system with lords and warriors. Eventually, the country established a central military government, which lasted into the 1800s.

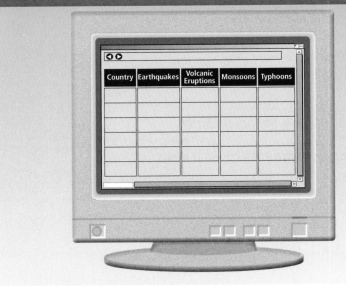

Country	Earthquakes	Volcanic Eruptions	Monsoons	Typhoons

SKILLBUILDER: Creating a Database

1. What is the topic of the database? What title would you give it?
2. Under which column heading would you list information to show which Pacific Islands experience seasonal winds?

FOCUS ON GEOGRAPHY

1. **Region** • What is the population density in most of Australia?
2. **Region** • In what regions are Australia's major cities located?

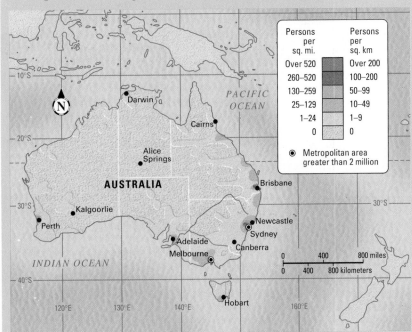

CHAPTER PROJECTS

Interdisciplinary Activity: Language Arts

Writing a Poem The ancient Japanese developed a type of poetry called tanka. A tanka is a 31-syllable poem with the theme of love, friendship, or nature. Research Japanese tanka. Then write your own tanka and illustrate it with images that reflect the poem's theme. You may also research Japanese art styles to use in your illustration.

Cooperative Learning Activity

Creating a Talk Show In a group of three to five classmates, create a talk show about travel on the Silk Road. Research the kinds of people and animals that traveled along the route, the terrain they passed through on the journey, the hazards they faced, and the cargo they carried.

- Take on the roles of talk-show host, travelers, and traders.
- Write a script for your roles.
- Conduct your talk show in front of the class.

INTERNET ACTIVITY

Use the Internet to do research about a recent earthquake or volcanic eruption that occurred in the Ring of Fire. Focus on the event itself and how it affected the people in the area.

Writing About Geography Write a report of your findings. Include pictures showing the event or its aftermath. List the Web sites you used to prepare your report.

For Internet links to support this activity, go to

RESEARCH LINKS
CLASSZONE.COM

CHAPTER 24

China and Its Neighbors

ATLANTIC

CHINA
AND ITS
NEIGHBORS

PACIFIC

PACIFIC

OCEAN

OCEAN

OCEAN

INDIAN
OCEAN

OCEAN

坚 持 四 项 基 本

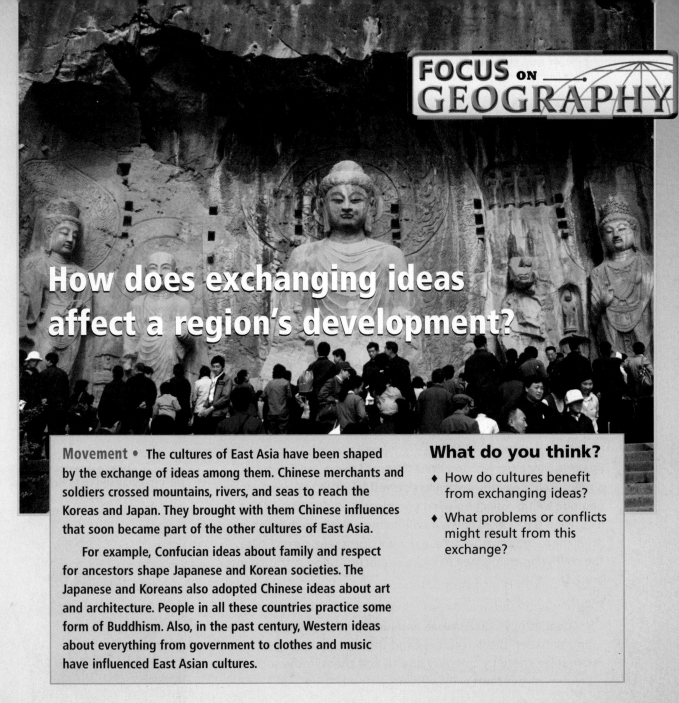

How does exchanging ideas affect a region's development?

Movement • The cultures of East Asia have been shaped by the exchange of ideas among them. Chinese merchants and soldiers crossed mountains, rivers, and seas to reach the Koreas and Japan. They brought with them Chinese influences that soon became part of the other cultures of East Asia.

For example, Confucian ideas about family and respect for ancestors shape Japanese and Korean societies. The Japanese and Koreans also adopted Chinese ideas about art and architecture. People in all these countries practice some form of Buddhism. Also, in the past century, Western ideas about everything from government to clothes and music have influenced East Asian cultures.

What do you think?

- ◆ How do cultures benefit from exchanging ideas?
- ◆ What problems or conflicts might result from this exchange?

Place Millions of people in China use bicycles as their main form of transportation. This bicycle parking lot in Shanghai is filled to capacity.

BEFORE YOU READ

▶▶ *What Do You Know?*

Before you read the chapter, consider what you already know about East Asia. Recall what you learned in Chapter 23 about ancient China and ancient Japan. Have you seen or tried the martial art tae kwon do? Do you know why sumo wrestlers are so honored in Japan? Reflect on what you have learned in other classes, what you have read in books or magazines, and what you have heard in the news about recent events in these countries.

▶▶ *What Do You Want to Know?*

Decide what else you want to know about East Asia. In your notebook, record what you hope to learn from this chapter.

Place • **Many children in China take part in activities led by the Chinese Communist Party.** ▲

READ AND TAKE NOTES

Reading Strategy: Making Predictions Making predictions is a helpful strategy for involving yourself in what you read. As you begin reading, reflect on what you already know about the subject. Then try to predict what will happen. After making your prediction, read further to see if your guess was correct. Use the following guidelines to make predictions about this chapter.

• Copy the chart into your notebook.

• Before you read, make predictions about what kinds of exchanges have taken place among the countries of East Asia and between those countries and the rest of the world. Organize these by category and record them in the second column of the chart.

• In the third column, list facts from the chapter that tell you whether your predictions were correct or incorrect.

Culture • **Chinese-American actor Bruce Lee brought kung fu to Hollywood.** ▼

Category	Predictions	Correct or Incorrect
Economy		
Religion		
Government		
Culture		

Establishing Modern China

SECTION 1

N W E S

TERMS & NAMES

Opium War

Taiping Rebellion

Boxer Rebellion

Sun Yat-sen

Chiang Kai-shek

Mao Zedong

Great Leap Forward

Cultural Revolution

MAIN IDEA

After the end of China's last dynasty and decades of conflict, a Communist government took control of China in 1949.

WHY IT MATTERS NOW

Because China is a large country with a huge population, its influence politically and economically is felt around the world.

DATELINE

EXTRA

THE FORBIDDEN CITY, BEIJING, CHINA, FEBRUARY 12, 1912

Word has just been received that Pu Yi, the six-year-old boy emperor, has given up China's throne. The Qing emperor, whose royal name is Xuantong, will probably be China's last emperor. Under a recent agreement, China will now be a republic led by a president. The age of dynasties has ended.

No one yet knows what will become of this last emperor, who once was called "The Son of Heaven." For the time being, he will be allowed to remain in the Imperial Palace of the Forbidden City. But his future, like China's, is uncertain.

Culture • Pu Yi is shown here, standing next to his father and brother. ▲

China's Last Dynasty

In 1644, the Manchus established the Qing Dynasty—China's last and largest empire. The Qing drew both the southwestern region of Tibet and the island of Taiwan into China. However, by the mid-1800s, China's population had more than tripled, straining the country's ability to produce enough food. Shortages, famines, and wars overwhelmed Qing rulers, helping to bring their empire to an end.

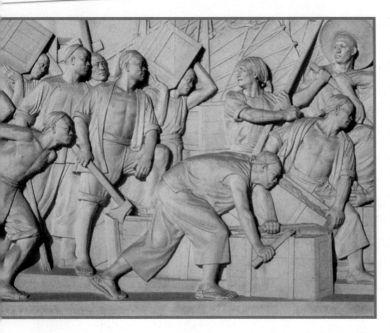

Place • **This monument in Tiananmen Square shows the Chinese seizing the British opium in Canton.** ▲

The Opium War The Qing rulers faced turmoil early on because of a drug called opium. They tried several times to prohibit the sale of opium in China but were not successful. In the late 1700s, the British began smuggling opium from India into China. They used opium, rather than money, to buy Chinese goods, which hurt China's economy.

In 1839, the Chinese government seized all the opium the British had stored in the Chinese port of Canton. The British responded with an attack, and the first **Opium War** began. Because Qing rule was weak, the British overpowered the Chinese. The Opium War ended in 1842 with the signing of the Treaty of Nanking. This treaty forced the Chinese to pay Great Britain money, hand over Hong Kong to British control, and allow British traders into more Chinese ports.

The Rise of Nationalism Angered by the Treaty of Nanking, peasants rebelled around China. The greatest revolt, the **Taiping Rebellion** (ty·PIHNG), raged for 14 years and took 20 million lives. Peasants demanded equality for women, the end of private property, and the division of surplus harvest among the neediest. The Chinese military, with help from other nations, finally crushed out the last of the rebellion in 1868.

In 1900, another rebel group, called the Boxers, rose up in the **Boxer Rebellion.** The Boxers hoped to defeat the Qing Dynasty and force all foreigners out of China. British, French, Russian, Japanese, and American troops joined together to defeat the Boxers, leaving China's government in turmoil.

A New Republic Many Western-educated Chinese wanted a new government. One ambitious leader, **Sun Yat-sen** (sun yaht·sehn), had long hoped China would become a democracy. He founded the Chinese Nationalist Party, which in 1911 toppled the Qing Dynasty. The next year, China became a republic. Sun Yat-sen was named the first provisional president. For political reasons, he gave up the first presidency to Yuan Shigai (yoo·AHN shee·ky).

Reading
Social Studies

A. Recognizing Important Details Why would the Treaty of Nanking have angered the Chinese?

BACKGROUND

The Boxers called themselves the "Righteous and Harmonious Fists." The British called this group the Boxers because they practiced a kind of boxing that they thought made them safe from bullets.

Over the next 16 years, China was in turmoil. Yuan struggled with rebels for power, and before and during World War I, China fought against Japan. During this time, the Nationalist Party gained more members. The Chinese Communist Party also formed. By the end of 1925, the Nationalist Party had about 200,000 members, and the Communist Party had about 10,000.

The Fight for Control In 1927, the two parties joined forces, and **Chiang Kai-shek** (chang ky·shehk), one of Sun Yat-sen's military commanders, became the leader of China. Soon, Chiang turned against the Communists, and the two parties began a long fight for power. In 1934, because the Nationalists seemed close to victory, the Communists retreated on what is known as the Long March. About 100,000 Communists marched more than 6,000 miles north to escape the Nationalist forces.

Chiang Kai-shek maintained control of China until 1949. During this time, the government improved transportation, provided education to more people, and encouraged industry. The lives of peasants and workers were not improved. Gradually many of these people turned to the Communist Party for help.

Communist Revolution

By the end of the Long March, a leader emerged in the Communist Party— **Mao Zedong** (mow dzuh·dahng). When World War II began and Japan invaded China, Chiang Kai-shek turned to Mao and the Communist Red Army for help. At the end of the war in 1945, China's two parties again turned on each other. In 1949, the Communists defeated the Nationalists, forcing Chiang Kai-shek to flee to Taiwan. On October 1, Mao declared China a Communist state called the People's Republic of China.

Sun Yat-sen (1866–1925) Sun Yat-sen grew up in a poor farmer's family in northern China. In 1879, his older brother, who had been working in Hawaii, brought Sun to Honolulu. Sun learned about Western ways and became interested in Christianity. This troubled his brother, who sent him back to China after four years.

Sun studied medicine and became a doctor, but he had bigger ideas. He thought that China needed to move ahead, to leave some of its traditional ways behind and overcome the past political humiliations. After many struggles, Sun helped China to become a republic. Today, he is known as the Father of Modern China.

Culture • Chiang Kai-shek waved his hat at a celebration of the founding of the Nationalist Party. ▼

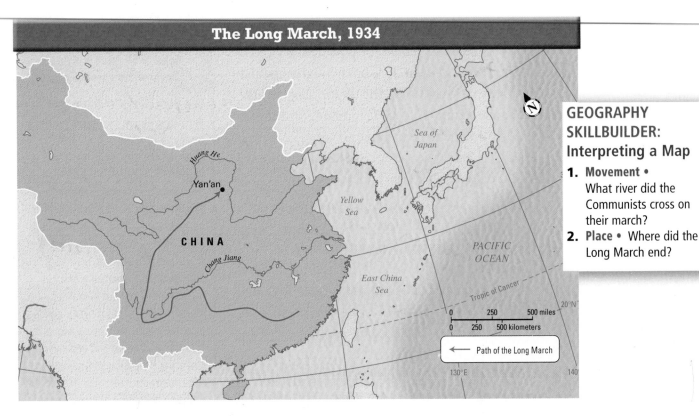

Yan'an

Huang He

CHINA

Chang Jiang

Sea of Japan

Yellow Sea

PACIFIC OCEAN

East China Sea

Tropic of Cancer

20°N

| 0 | 250 | 500 miles |
| 0 | 250 | 500 kilometers |

← Path of the Long March

130°E   140°

GEOGRAPHY SKILLBUILDER: Interpreting a Map

1. **Movement** • What river did the Communists cross on their march?
2. **Place** • Where did the Long March end?

Reform and Revolution

Mao Zedong became head of the Chinese Communist Party and China's government. The party set policy and the government carried it out, giving Chairman Mao nearly absolute power.

Chairman Mao's Reforms The Communists instituted many reforms. They seized land from the wealthy and gave it to the peasants. They also established a five-year plan that brought China's industry under government control. As in the Soviet Union, peasants combined their land into collective farms and worked together to grow food.

In 1958, Mao Zedong launched a program, called the **Great Leap Forward,** to speed up economic development. Collective farms became huge communes of 25,000 people. The communes grew crops, ran small industries, and provided education and health care for their members. In one year, this program shattered China's economy.

Reading Social Studies

B. Synthesizing How do you think Mao expected communes to help economic development?

Place • **This famous portrait of Mao Zedong hangs in Tiananmen Square.** ◄

Poor agricultural production, droughts, and floods caused one of the worst famines in history. From 1958 to 1960, as many as 20 million people starved, while millions more died of disease. China then abandoned the Great Leap Forward, and Mao's influence wavered.

The Cultural Revolution After the Great Leap Forward, many people in government called for reform. Mao feared that they wanted to make China a capitalist country. In 1966, Mao launched a movement called the **Cultural Revolution,** which aimed to remove opposition to the Communist Party. Mao's new supporters were called the Red Guards. They sought out and punished people who spoke against Mao's principles or who had contact with Western people or ideas. China fell into chaos once again.

During this time, the economy weakened, and the government was unable to carry out many of its duties. Goods and services, such as health care and transportation, were not made available to the people. Many Chinese began calling for reform.

Culture • These Red Guards at a rally waved copies of the "Little Red Book," a collection of Mao's sayings. ▼

SECTION 1 ASSESSMENT

Terms & Names

1. **Identify:** (a) Opium War (b) Taiping Rebellion (c) Boxer Rebellion (d) Sun Yat-sen (e) Chiang Kai-shek (f) Mao Zedong (g) Great Leap Forward (h) Cultural Revolution

Taking Notes

2. Use a sequence map like this one to list the events that led to the establishment of the People's Republic of China.

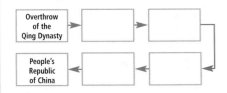

Main Ideas

3. (a) Who fought in the Opium War, and why?

   (b) What role did the Nationalist Party play in China?

   (c) What reforms did Mao Zedong make?

Critical Thinking

4. **Recognizing Effects**

   How do you think European actions in China contributed to feelings of discontent among China's peasants?

   Think About

   • European involvement in China during the 1900s

   • the different goals of Europeans and the Chinese

Imagine you are a journalist. Make a **list of questions** you would like to ask a person who lived during the Cultural Revolution.

Visit the Forbidden City

For centuries, only members of the emperor's household could pass through the gates of China's famous Forbidden City. Today, however, *you* are there to plan a TV feature about the palace complex. This collection of massive buildings with curving, golden-tiled roofs is actually a city within a city within a city. The Forbidden City is a square within the larger Imperial City, which is at the center of Beijing's Inner City district. The first things you see are huge buildings and broad, open squares. Stone carvings and fantastic animal figures decorate pillars and gateways.

COOPERATIVE LEARNING On these pages are challenges you will encounter as you visit the Forbidden City. Working with a small group, choose one of these challenges to meet. Divide the work among group members. You will find helpful information in the Data File. Keep in mind that you will present your solution to the class.

ARTS CHALLENGE

". . . China's greatest artists used all their skills."

China's Ming emperors built the Forbidden City as the heart of their vast empire. To please the Ming and later Qing (Ch'ing) emperors, China's greatest artists used all their skills. They decorated palaces with elaborate statues and paintings. Many are animal figures, which are important symbols in Chinese mythology. What aspects of art and architecture do you want to include? How will you present them? Choose one of these options. Look for information in the Data File.

ACTIVITIES

1. Design a home page for a museum exhibit and virtual tour, focusing on the arts of the Ming Dynasty and the Forbidden City.
2. Sketch one of the fantastic animals used in Chinese art and architecture, such as the dragon. Research what it symbolizes and write a short caption for your drawing.

- Completed in **1420** by the **Yung-lo** emperor of the Ming dynasty, who moved the capital to Beijing. Buildings have been enlarged and rebuilt.

- Major buildings in Beijing's Outer City and Inner City are built along a straight, north-south, 1.7-mile axis. The axis passes across **Tiananmen Square** through large parks to the gates of the Forbidden City. The city is surrounded by a moat and a wall, with watchtowers at each corner.

- The **entrance** to the Forbidden City is through the **Meridian Gate**, which leads to marble bridges over the moat. On the other side of the bridges is a great open square that leads to the **Gate of Supreme Harmony**. Through the Gate of Supreme Harmony lie the three state halls of the Forbidden City.

- **Outer Court:** three great halls of state—the **Hall of Supreme Harmony,** the **Hall of Complete Harmony,** and the **Hall of Preserving Harmony**—stand one behind another on a high marble platform.

- **Inner Court:** palaces, courtyards, and pavilions where the emperor, his family, and the palace staff lived.

MING DYNASTY (1368–1644)

- **Restored Chinese rule** after conquest and rule by Mongols.

- Extended China's empire into **Korea, Mongolia,** and **Vietnam.**

QING (CH'ING) DYNASTY (1644–1911)

- **Last emperors** of China; dynasty established by Manchus.

- Dynasty troubled by wars and rebellions; **overthrown by revolution.**

To learn more about the Forbidden City, go to

RESEARCH LINKS
CLASSZONE.COM

HISTORY CHALLENGE

". . . palaces and courtyards where the emperor's family . . . lived."

As you approach the Forbidden City, you pass through three great state halls, one behind another on a marble platform. Official receptions and banquets were held here. Behind the halls are palaces and courtyards where the emperor's family and the men and women who served them lived. How can you show the importance of what took place within these walls? Use one of these options to present information. Look in the Data File for help.

ACTIVITIES

1. Make an annotated map of the Forbidden City. Include captions to explain the events that took place in major palaces and halls.
2. Make a time line of the Ming and Qing (Ch'ing) rulers who built and occupied the Forbidden City.

Activity Wrap-Up

As a group, review your solution to the challenge you selected. Then present your solution to the class.

The Governments of East Asia

MAIN IDEA

The nations of China and North Korea have Communist governments. The other nations of East Asia are republics.

WHY IT MATTERS NOW

Many people in China and North Korea would like to see change in their governments and are turning to other nations for help.

DATELINE

SEOUL, SOUTH KOREA, DECEMBER 10, 2000— South Koreans are throwing a huge party today. President Kim Dae-jung has received the Nobel Peace Prize, a prize that is given annually to honor someone who has worked for peace.

Since 1947, when North and South Korea officially proclaimed themselves as separate nations, the relationship between the two countries has been tense. Just this year, for the first time, the presidents of North and South Korea met to discuss ways to reunite their divided countries. President Kim said that his goal was "to realize peace on the Korean peninsula, and to develop exchange [and] cooperation between both Koreas."

Culture • President Kim Dae-jung (on the right) received his Nobel Prize today in Oslo, Norway. ▲

Working Toward Change

North Korea and China are Communist nations, and both have seen war and conflict in the past 50 years. Through efforts from within and from organizations and nations around the world, both nations are working to improve the lives of their people. They are also gradually becoming a part of the world market.

China's Government Today

When Mao Zedong died in 1976, the Cultural Revolution ended. Moderates who wanted to restore order and economic growth took power in 1977. Their leader was **Deng Xiaoping** (duhng show·pihng).

Under Deng, the Chinese government established diplomatic relations with the United States and increased trade with other countries. It also made reforms, such as allowing farmers to own land. It released many political prisoners and reduced the police force's power. However, the government was not willing to give up any of its basic control.

Place • **The Chinese Communist Party sponsors activities for children, such as playing in a marching band.** ▲

The Chinese Communist Party Officially, China's highest government authority is the National People's Congress. In practice, the Chinese Communist Party holds the real power. It controls what happens locally. The government allows only churches and temples that are closely linked to this party to operate.

The Fight for Human Rights

Reading
Social Studies

A. Making Inferences What other rights would you include on a list of human rights?

China's Communist government has a history of repressing criticism of its policies. Such actions often lead to the violation of **human rights,** which are rights to which every person is entitled. They include the freedom to say or write what you think, to worship as you believe, to be safe from physical harm and political persecution, and to have enough to eat.

Tiananmen Square In 1989, the Chinese military denied citizens a basic human right—freedom of speech—when it attacked protesters calling for democracy in **Tiananmen Square** (tyahn·ahn·mehn). For weeks, protesters occupied this 100-acre square in Beijing. Demonstrations soon occurred in other Chinese cities. The military killed hundreds and wounded thousands in their attempts to end the protests. As the events of 1989 unfolded, people around the world spoke up against the Chinese government. Since then, efforts have been made to help the people of China in their struggle for human rights.

Culture • The protesters in Tiananmen Square included students, workers, and government employees. ▲

China's Neighbors

China's neighbors have different kinds of governments. Some are republics, while others are Communist.

Japan The United States occupied Japan after it was defeated in World War II. U.S. general Douglas MacArthur helped set up a constitutional monarchy with a parliamentary government and a separate judiciary. The parliament is called the **Diet,** and the House of Representatives holds most of the power. The Diet chooses the country's prime minister, who is then officially appointed by the emperor.

The constitution states that the emperor's position is symbolic. Thus the emperor has had limited power, though many people regard the emperor as partly divine. The constitution also gives the Japanese people rights and responsibilities similar to those of Americans.

North and South Korea Korea used to be one country, but it was divided after World War II. The Soviet Union helped set up a Communist dictatorship in the north, and the United States helped set up a democratic republic in the south. Each government thought it should govern the whole of the Korean Peninsula.

Reading
Social Studies

B. Hypothesizing
Why do you think Japan has an emperor, if the position is only symbolic?

GEOGRAPHY SKILLBUILDER:
Interpreting a Map

1. **Location** • Why do you think the capitals of North and South Korea are located on rivers?
2. **Movement** • Measure the distance between South Korea and Japan. What can you conclude about trade between these two nations?

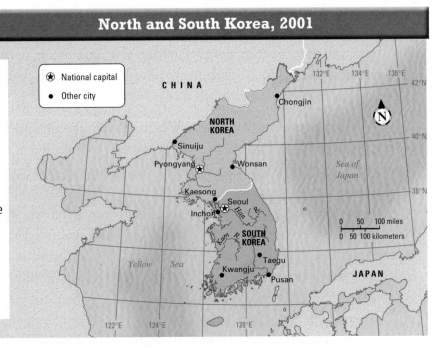

North and South Korea, 2001

In 1950, North Korea invaded South Korea. For three years the two fought the Korean War, but the borders did not change. In June of 2000, the two nations started talking about reuniting.

North Korea, or the Democratic People's Republic of Korea, is still a Communist state. Although there is a president and a cabinet, the Korean Workers' Party holds power. The people have little freedom, and the legislature—the Supreme People's Assembly—has little power.

South Korea, or the Republic of Korea, is a republic with a government similar to that of the United States. Power is divided among legislative, executive, and judiciary branches. People vote for the president as well as the legislature—the National Assembly. The government guarantees its citizens freedom of the press and of religion.

Mongolia One of the world's oldest countries, Mongolia was under either Chinese or Russian domination for years. It has been an independent republic since 1991 and has a constitution that guarantees its citizens certain basic rights. However, there is still a strong element of Communist party control in the government.

Taiwan Also a republic, Taiwan has a multiparty democratic system. For years it was a Chinese colony, but since 1949, the Chinese Nationalist government has been based there. The question of whether Taiwan and China will unify under one government has long caused conflict.

SECTION 2 ASSESSMENT

Terms & Names

1. Identify: (a) Deng Xiaoping   (b) human rights   (c) Tiananmen Square   (d) Diet

Taking Notes

2. Use a chart like this one to list and compare the major characteristics of East Asia's governments.

Country	Characteristics of Government
China	
Japan	
North Korea	
South Korea	
Mongolia	
Taiwan	

Main Ideas

3. (a) Who holds the power in China's government?

(b) Which East Asian countries have governments similar to China's?

(c) How do the governments of North Korea and South Korea differ?

Critical Thinking

4. **Hypothesizing**

Why do you think the Chinese government has taken actions that repress human rights?

Think About

♦ China's political stance

♦ the goals of China's dissidents

Write a **news story** that describes the events that helped establish the government of Japan, North Korea, or South Korea.

The Economies of East Asia

TERMS & NAMES
tungsten
antimony
textile
cooperative

MAIN IDEA

East Asian economies have changed, some drastically, since World War II.

WHY IT MATTERS NOW

As these economies grow stronger, they play a larger role in global markets and have a larger influence on the economies of other nations.

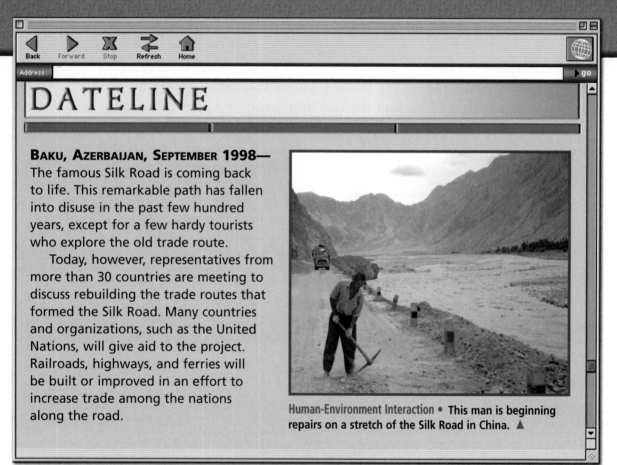

◁ Back ▷ Forward ✕ Stop ⇄ Refresh ⌂ Home

Address: ▶ go

DATELINE

BAKU, AZERBAIJAN, SEPTEMBER 1998—
The famous Silk Road is coming back to life. This remarkable path has fallen into disuse in the past few hundred years, except for a few hardy tourists who explore the old trade route.

Today, however, representatives from more than 30 countries are meeting to discuss rebuilding the trade routes that formed the Silk Road. Many countries and organizations, such as the United Nations, will give aid to the project. Railroads, highways, and ferries will be built or improved in an effort to increase trade among the nations along the road.

Human-Environment Interaction • This man is beginning repairs on a stretch of the Silk Road in China. ▲

Economies of the Region

Since World War II, East Asia's countries have grown more active in the world market. Today, Japan has one of the strongest economies in the world. Consumers in the United States regularly purchase goods made in China, Japan, Taiwan, and South Korea. However, wars, droughts, and internal conflicts have made economic growth difficult for some countries, such as North Korea.

China's Economy

Although this has begun to change, China's government controls most of its economy. It owns all financial institutions, such as banks, and the larger industrial firms. The government also sets the prices on goods and plans the quantity of goods each worker should produce.

Industry China has put a strong emphasis on improving its industry. It has become one of the world's largest producers of cotton cloth and of two metals—**tungsten** and **antimony**. The industries that have seen the most growth are machine building, metal production, and the making of chemical fertilizers and clothing.

Farming Many people in China live in the countryside and make a living by farming. They use traditional methods, such as plowing with oxen, rather than using farm machinery. Much of the land in China—in the deserts and mountainous regions—cannot be farmed. Nevertheless, China is the world's largest producer of rice. It is also a major source of wheat, corn, soybeans, peanuts, cotton, and tobacco.

Human-Environment Interaction • Much of China's rice is produced on terraced gardens like these. ▼

Human-Environment Interaction • Chinese villagers in Yunnan work in the rice terraces. ▲

Other East Asian Economies

Taiwan Taiwan has a growing market economy that relies heavily on manufacturing and foreign trade. Since 1988, Taiwanese businesses have invested billions of dollars in mainland China, significantly contributing to China's fast-growing economy.

North Korea Like China's, North Korea's government controls the economy. Also like China, North Korea has emphasized the growth of industry. Iron, steel, machinery, chemical, and textile production are the main industries in North Korea. A **textile** is a cloth manufactured by weaving or knitting.

Many people in North Korea are farmers. They work on large **cooperatives,** where some 300 families share the farming work. These farms have become more productive as improvements in irrigation, fertilizers, and equipment have been made.

Reading Social Studies

A. Evaluating Decisions Do you think it makes sense for so many farmers to share their work?

For most of the 20th century, North Korea traded with other Communist nations. Since the fall of the Soviet Union, North Korea has opened its borders to investment and trade with other countries.

South Korea The economy of South Korea has changed dramatically since the early 1960s. At that time, it was a poor nation of subsistence farmers. Since then, however, the government has supported the expansion of the textile industry and the building of factories that make electronics, small appliances, and equipment. The government also helped develop iron, steel, and chemical industries. Today, South Korea has one of the world's strongest economies. It is a major producer of automobiles and electronics and trades with many countries.

Place • **This is one of many new ships manufactured by South Korea's shipbuilding industry.** ▲

Japan The government of Japan does not control its economy in the way the governments of China and North Korea control theirs. However, it does oversee and advise all aspects of the economy, including trade, investment, banking, and production.

Like South Korea's, Japan's economy has grown significantly since the mid-20th century. Japan is a small nation with few natural resources and little farmland. Industry and a skilled, educated work force are vitally important to Japan's economy.

Reading Social Studies

B. Synthesizing What is the benefit of having the government control the economy?

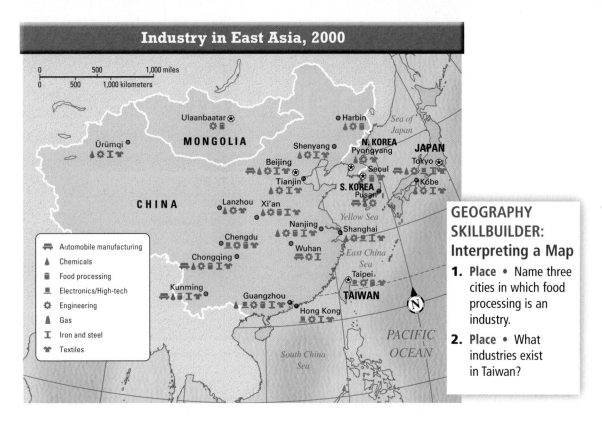

Industry in East Asia, 2000

GEOGRAPHY SKILLBUILDER: Interpreting a Map

1. **Place** • Name three cities in which food processing is an industry.
2. **Place** • What industries exist in Taiwan?

The country imports the raw materials it needs and transforms them into goods for export. Ships, automobiles, steel, plastics, machinery, cameras, and electronics are Japan's major exports. The United States is Japan's biggest customer, although Japan also exports goods around the world. It is currently one of the world's largest economic powers.

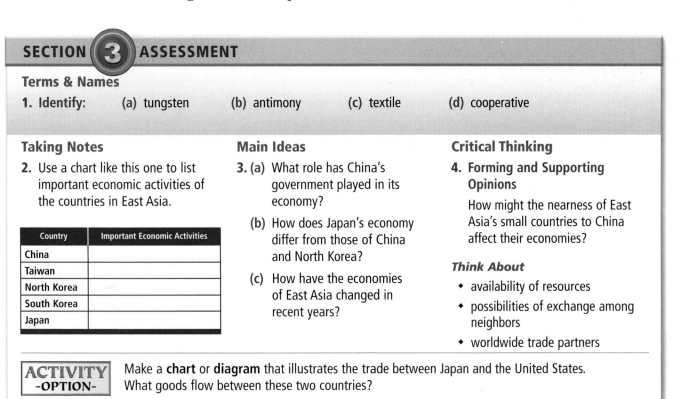

SECTION 3 ASSESSMENT

Terms & Names

1. **Identify:**   (a) tungsten   (b) antimony   (c) textile   (d) cooperative

Taking Notes

2. Use a chart like this one to list important economic activities of the countries in East Asia.

Country	Important Economic Activities
China	
Taiwan	
North Korea	
South Korea	
Japan	

Main Ideas

3. (a) What role has China's government played in its economy?

   (b) How does Japan's economy differ from those of China and North Korea?

   (c) How have the economies of East Asia changed in recent years?

Critical Thinking

4. **Forming and Supporting Opinions**

   How might the nearness of East Asia's small countries to China affect their economies?

   Think About

   ◆ availability of resources
   ◆ possibilities of exchange among neighbors
   ◆ worldwide trade partners

ACTIVITY -OPTION-   Make a **chart** or **diagram** that illustrates the trade between Japan and the United States. What goods flow between these two countries?

The Cultures of East Asia

TERMS & NAMES
zither
haiku
Han

MAIN IDEA

The cultures of the nations of East Asia share much in common because of years of cultural exchange.

WHY IT MATTERS NOW

As East Asians are introduced to Western culture, they are careful not to forget their own cultural heritage.

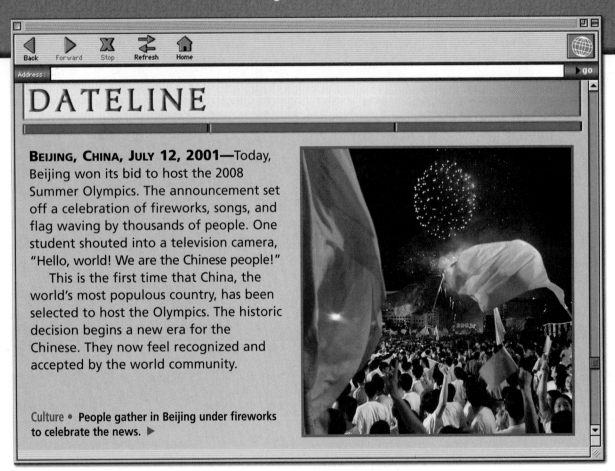

Back   Forward   Stop   Refresh   Home

Address: [   ] ▶ go

DATELINE

BEIJING, CHINA, JULY 12, 2001—Today, Beijing won its bid to host the 2008 Summer Olympics. The announcement set off a celebration of fireworks, songs, and flag waving by thousands of people. One student shouted into a television camera, "Hello, world! We are the Chinese people!"

This is the first time that China, the world's most populous country, has been selected to host the Olympics. The historic decision begins a new era for the Chinese. They now feel recognized and accepted by the world community.

Culture • **People gather in Beijing under fireworks to celebrate the news.** ▶

Cultural Exchange

Cultural exchange has occurred for centuries among the countries of East Asia. In recent decades, these countries have been influenced by Western culture as well. At the same time, aspects of East Asian cultures have spread outside the region. International events like the Olympics are sure to generate more awareness of the region around the world.

Exchange Within East Asia

East Asian cultures have much in common because of cultural exchange. Many of the shared aspects of culture originated in China, whose civilization has already existed for 4,000 years. For example, the Japanese and Koreans adapted the Chinese writing system to their own languages. The Japanese also adopted Chinese ideas about centralized government, urban planning, and painting techniques. Similarly, the Koreans picked up Chinese printing techniques and methods of government administration.

Place • This Buddhist temple in China stretches across a peaceful pond. ◄

Reading
Social Studies

A. Making Inferences By what means do you think the countries of East Asia passed their culture on to one another?

Religion The religions of East Asia are strong indicators of cultural exchange within the region. Buddhism, for example, originated in India. The Chinese learned about the religion around 1,700 years ago. They then passed on their understanding of it to the Koreans, who later transmitted their knowledge to the Japanese. Some of the elements of Buddhism that the Japanese adopted were incorporated into their native Shinto religion. The Koreans and Japanese also developed interest in Confucianism. It, too, spread from China to their countries.

Practices Today Throughout East Asia, many people still practice Buddhism and Confucianism. They also practice other religions, such as Christianity and Taoism. The Communist government of North Korea discourages religious freedom. South Koreans, however, practice Buddhism and Christianity. Mongolians practice Tibetan Buddhism. Taiwan's dominant religion is based on Buddhism, Confucianism, and Taoism. Japan's two major religions are Zen Buddhism and Shinto.

Culture • Many Taoists practice tai chi, a form of exercise meant to relieve the body of stress and worry. ▼

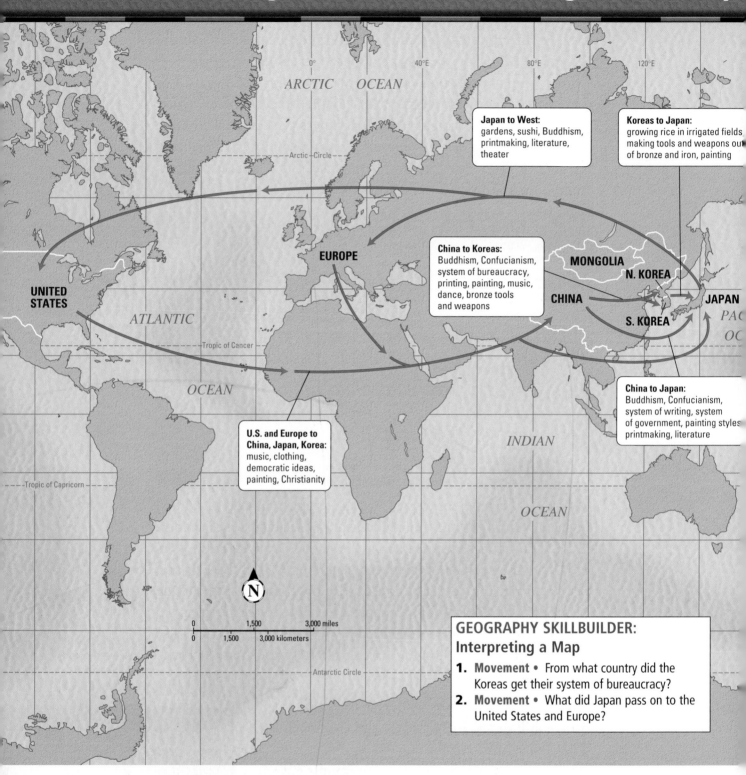

Japan to West: gardens, sushi, Buddhism, printmaking, literature, theater

Koreas to Japan: growing rice in irrigated fields, making tools and weapons out of bronze and iron, painting

China to Koreas: Buddhism, Confucianism, system of bureaucracy, printing, painting, music, dance, bronze tools and weapons

China to Japan: Buddhism, Confucianism, system of writing, system of government, painting styles, printmaking, literature

U.S. and Europe to China, Japan, Korea: music, clothing, democratic ideas, painting, Christianity

GEOGRAPHY SKILLBUILDER: Interpreting a Map

1. **Movement** • From what country did the Koreas get their system of bureaucracy?
2. **Movement** • What did Japan pass on to the United States and Europe?

Arts Past and Present

Like the religions, the art forms of East Asia's countries reflect cultural exchange. For example, similar methods of painting and making pottery are used throughout the region. However, each country also boasts unique artistic traditions.

Art in China Chinese art forms date back thousands of years. The art of bronze casting was developed around 1100 B.C. Music and dance are also ancient art forms in China. Many different kinds of instruments have been found in ancient tombs. Bells, flutes, drums, and a stringed instrument called a **zither** are all still played in China.

Fine porcelain dishes and vases are among China's greatest art treasures. The scenes, designs, and words that decorate them have also helped historians understand the cultural life of ancient China.

Today, theater is a popular art form in China. There are at least 300 forms of traditional opera in China. At the Beijing Opera, actors wear elaborate costumes to perform dramas based on Chinese stories, folklore, and history.

Art in Japan Buddhist ideas have influenced the arts in Japan. Artists consider simplicity, delicacy, and tradition to be important in their artwork. Painting, printing, dance, music, and theater all reflect these ideals. In literature, the **haiku** (HY·koo) is a world-famous form of Japanese poetry. Each haiku uses only 17 syllables. The goal of the form is to suggest, in a short description, much more than is stated. Many Japanese poets, such as Basho (1644–1694), have written haiku since the form was developed hundreds of years ago.

Reading
Social Studies

B. Clarifying
What importance does the Japanese government give to traditional arts?

Some artists in Japan are working to preserve traditional crafts. Potters and weavers, in particular, receive money from the Japanese government so that they can continue their work and teach others. These artists are considered living treasures.

Culture • *Bunraku* puppetry is a famous Japanese art form. The puppets are nearly life-size. Each one is manipulated by three puppeteers, who control different parts of it. ▼

Bunraku Puppetry

Omozukai
Chief manipulator
• holds puppet
• moves puppet's head, body, and right hand

Ningyo
Bunraku puppet

Ashizukai
Third manipulator
• moves puppet's legs

Hidarizukai
Second manipulator
• moves puppet's left hand

Culture and Communism

Communism has significantly affected some of East Asia's cultures. In North Korea and China, the Communists repressed artistic freedom. During the Cultural Revolution in China, artwork was frequently damaged or destroyed. Writers were forced to create propaganda instead of expressing their own ideas. Even Mao wrote poetry, but his poems only concerned Communist ideals. Playwrights and painters who created work that reflected Communist ideals were allowed to continue their work. Artists who used their art to criticize the government were punished.

In North Korea today, the government still controls the work of artists. The Chinese government has shown greater willingness to allow artists to pursue their own ideas.

Reading
Social Studies

C. Drawing Conclusions Why do you think the Communists worried about allowing artistic freedom?

The Chinese People

China contains about one-fifth of the world's population. Most people in China belong to an ethnic group called the **Han.** In addition, there are about 55 minority groups in China. Each has its own spoken language, and some also have their own written language. In school, students often speak their native language, and Mandarin Chinese is taught as the official language.

Spotlight on CULTURE

The Martial Arts The martial arts are a unique form of fighting. They originated in ancient East Asia but are now also practiced in other countries, such as the United States. Karate originated in Japan and involves striking and kicking with hands and feet. The Koreans practice a similar martial art called tae kwon do (ty kwahn doh). The Japanese also developed other forms, such as judo (JOO•doh) and aikido (EYE•kee•DOH), that involve throwing or blocking an attack.

The Chinese call their fighting style kung fu, and for centuries, they shared it only with other Chinese. In the mid-1800s, however, Chinese laborers introduced their martial arts to the United States. In the 1960s, a young Chinese American, Bruce Lee (shown at right), began teaching kung fu's fantastic flying leaps and spin-kicks to Hollywood stars. He soon became an international action-movie star. Today, 4 million people in the United States take martial arts classes to exercise, learn self-defense, and enjoy the sport. As one of the most popular forms, tae kwon do became an official Olympic sport in 2000.

Changes to the Family The Chinese have traditionally lived in large, extended families. To slow down population growth, the Chinese government decreed in the 1980s that each married couple in a city may have only one child. Rural families may be allowed to have a second child, and families in ethnic minorities may have more than one child. Most Chinese households today are made up of small family units that may include the grandparents.

Family members in China depend on one another and follow traditional patterns. In a family, elders are greatly respected. Children, because there are so few, are given lots of attention. In the past, marriages were arranged by the parents, but that is no longer common. In present-day China, most parents work outside the home, so grandparents often care for the children.

Place • **As is typical in China, this couple has only one child.** ▲

SECTION 4 ASSESSMENT

Terms & Names

1. Identify: **(a)** zither   **(b)** haiku   **(c)** Han

Taking Notes

2. Use a diagram like this one to list aspects of culture that East Asian countries have exchanged with each other.

The Koreas

China   Japan

Main Ideas

3. (a) What is the goal of Japan's living treasures?

(b) How has the government affected religion and art in China and North Korea?

(c) What led the Chinese government to place restrictions on family size?

Critical Thinking

4. Drawing Conclusions

What factors do you think encourage cultural exchange?

Think About

- migration patterns
- geographic features
- speaking related languages

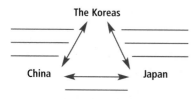

Make a **list** of five questions that you would like to ask a Chinese teenager about his or her life.

Establishing Modern Japan

TERMS & NAMES
Meiji Restoration
Hiroshima
Nagasaki
homogeneous
Ainu

MAIN IDEA

After World War II, the Japanese built a modern industrial economy that is one of the largest in the world.

WHY IT MATTERS NOW

One challenge for Japan is to protect its unique identity even as it welcomes influences from the rest of the world.

DATELINE

EXTRA

TOKYO, JAPAN, MAY 3, 1947

Today, Japan celebrated its rebirth as a new nation. Less than two years after its surrender at the end of World War II, Japan has a Western-style constitution.

Emperor Hirohito conducted a solemn ceremony to celebrate the occasion. The government issued a pocket-sized pamphlet to every Japanese family. The new constitution is printed inside. It expresses the hopes of the Japanese for a peaceful future.

Culture • Emperor Hirohito stands before a crowd of 20,000 people celebrating the new constitution. ▲

History

The people of Japan have seen remarkable changes in the past century, not just in their country's government, but also in its economy and its relations with the rest of the world. From the mid-1600s to the 1800s, Japan was a fairly isolated nation. It traded with China but was unaffected by the rest of the world.

The Meiji Restoration Japan's location made it a convenient place for ships sailing from the United States to stop and replenish supplies of food and fuel. In 1853, American naval vessels commanded by Commodore Matthew C. Perry landed in Japan. Perry used a show of force to open Japan to Western contact, ending nearly 200 years of Japanese isolation.

In 1867, a group of samurai overthrew the ruling Tokugawa Shogunate and restored the emperor as head of government. The period that followed, from 1868 through 1911, became known as the **Meiji Restoration,** because the new emperor was called Meiji (MAY·JEE). During this time, the Japanese people built modern industries and developed the economy. Japan became wealthy and powerful. Following a series of wars, Japan assumed control of Taiwan, Korea, and Manchuria.

Culture •
A Japanese artist painted this scene of Commodore Perry in Japan in 1853. ▲

Reading
Social Studies

A. Summarizing What factors contributed to instability in Japan in the early 1900s?

In the Early 1900s Japan, allied with the United States, Britain, and France, defeated Germany in World War I and thus was able to expand its holdings of ex-German colonies in the Pacific. The Great Kanto Earthquake in 1923 hurt Japan's economy, and like much of the world, Japan was affected by the Great Depression. During the 1930s, the military took control of Japan's government. In 1937, Japan invaded China and became involved in a long war there. Also at this time, Japan developed closer relations with Nazi Germany and Fascist Italy. As a result, the United States stopped selling oil to Japan. In 1941, Japan bombed the U.S. naval base at Pearl Harbor in Hawaii, bringing the United States into World War II.

World War II By 1942, the Japanese military had won many victories in East Asia and the South Pacific. But in June 1942, Japan lost the Battle of Midway; and in February 1943, it lost a battle on Guadalcanal Island. These defeats turned the tide of the war.

Place • This scene of Nagasaki after the bombing shows only a few buildings still standing. ▲

In 1945, the United States dropped atomic bombs on two Japanese cities—**Hiroshima** (HEER•uh•SHEE•muh) and **Nagasaki** (NAH•guh•SAH•kee). Emperor Hirohito then agreed to surrender, putting an end to the war.

Economy and Government

After World War II, Japan's economy and government were in shambles. Its cities had been bombed. Many Japanese were homeless and without jobs.

Economy The Japanese values of hard work and saving money helped to rebuild the economy. The United States also gave Japan help through loans and advice. By the mid-1950s, Japanese industrial production matched its prewar levels. Today, Japan has one of the most powerful economies in the world.

Like the United States, Japan encourages free enterprise. This type of system can motivate people to develop new ideas as well as to expand their businesses with little government interference.

Women and the Economy Women's participation in the work force has grown since World War II. However, discrimination exists, and long-held ideas about women's roles as mother and housekeeper are changing very slowly. Approximately two-fifths of Japanese women hold jobs, but many of these jobs are temporary or part-time. Few women hold management positions.

Culture • Many Japanese women, like this one, hold jobs in business and industry. ▼

Government After World War II, the United States occupied Japan until 1952. It helped set up a new government. Under the new constitution, the rights and responsibilities of the Japanese are similar to those of Americans.

Today, Japan has a constitutional monarchy with a parliamentary government. The Diet is the highest law-making body in the country. Before 1945, Japan's emperor was the head of the government. He is now a symbolic head of state.

Culture

Japan's population is **homogeneous,** or largely the same. Most of its people are descended from the Mongolian people who settled Japan thousands of years ago. The exception is the approximately 15,000 Ainu (EYE·noo) people. Scholars believe that the **Ainu** came to Japan from Europe well before the other settlers arrived.

Social Behavior In Western culture, especially in the United States, people think of themselves first as individuals. In Japan, as in most of Asia, people think of themselves first as part of a group. Social behavior in Japan is governed by an idea the Japanese call *on* (ohn). This value is based on Confucian principles about proper relationships. The Japanese take the relationship between children and their elders particularly seriously. People always display respectful behavior toward their parents and elders. They also put the needs of their parents and elders before their own needs. Japanese people also seriously consider an elder's judgment when making important decisions.

Urban Living More than 90 percent of Japanese families live in urban areas. Many people live in apartment buildings, in part because there is not much space for single-family homes; because of this, owning a home is very expensive.

Reading
Social Studies

B. Forming and Supporting Opinions What is your opinion of putting the group ahead of the individual? What are the pros and cons of it?

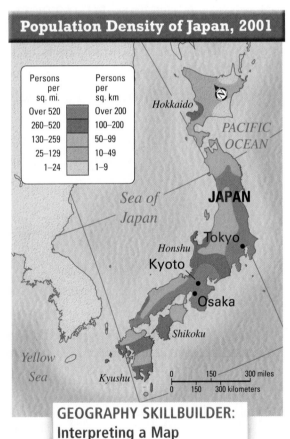

Population Density of Japan, 2001

Persons per sq. mi.	Persons per sq. km
Over 520	Over 200
260–520	100–200
130–259	50–99
25–129	10–49
1–24	1–9

Hokkaido

PACIFIC OCEAN

Sea of Japan

JAPAN

Tokyo

Honshu

Kyoto

Osaka

Shikoku

Yellow Sea

Kyushu

0   150   300 miles
0   150   300 kilometers

GEOGRAPHY SKILLBUILDER:
Interpreting a Map

1. **Place** • How many people per square mile live on the islands of Kyushu and Shikoku?
2. **Place** • Which large island has regions with only 1 to 24 people per square mile?

Many people commute to their jobs or to school. Most major cities have subway systems. During rush hour, these trains are packed with people traveling to and from work. High-speed commuter trains connect many of the big cities. The fastest trains reach speeds of 160 miles an hour. Railway tunnels also connect the islands. The world's first undersea railway tunnel was built to connect the islands of Kyushu and Honshu.

Culture • Excited fans release balloons before a baseball game at the Fukuoka Dome on the island of Kyushu. ▲

Cultural Exchange Some aspects of Japanese culture have gained popularity in the United States in recent years. These include the Japanese tea ceremony, sushi, and Japanese flower arranging. Japanese gardens, which stress simplicity in design, have been built in many parts of the world. Bonsai (bahn·SY)—the art of growing tiny, elegant plants and trees—has also gained popularity.

Two sports are wildly popular in Japan, both having come to Japan from other parts of the world. Baseball and soccer games draw enormous crowds. Today, several of Japan's top baseball players, such as Ichiro Suzuki, play on U.S. teams.

SECTION 5 ASSESSMENT

Terms & Names

1. Identify:
    (a) Meiji Restoration   (b) Hiroshima   (c) Nagasaki
    (d) homogeneous   (e) Ainu

Taking Notes

2. Use a sequence chart like this one to list the events leading to the growth of Japan's modern economy.

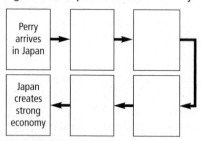

Main Ideas

3. (a) How did World War II affect Japan's economy?

(b) What effect has Confucianism had on the daily lives of the Japanese?

(c) How has Japan been influenced by other cultures?

Critical Thinking

4. **Analyzing Causes**

Why do you think Japan is such a densely populated country?

Think About

• Japan's land area and geographic features

• social and cultural beliefs

• standard of living

ACTIVITY -OPTION-   Plan the **schedule** of a Japanese Culture Day. Think about what activities you might have, what speakers you could invite, and what you would want participants to learn about Japan.

Reading a Population Density Map

▶▶ Defining the Skill

A population density map allows you to compare the population densities of different regions. It shows how many people live in each square mile or square kilometer.

▶▶ Applying the Skill

The map below shows the population density of North Korea, South Korea, and Japan. Use the strategies listed below to help you read the map.

How to Read a Population Density Map

Strategy ❶ Read the map key. This key uses color to show population density. Areas with very dense population are purple. Areas with sparse population are pale yellow.

Strategy ❷ Look at the map. Find the areas on the map that are most densely populated. Then locate areas that are less densely populated.

Strategy ❸ Read the labels on the map. Notice that the major cities of these countries are in very densely populated areas. Look at the islands of Japan and notice which ones are the least populated.

Strategy ❹ Summarize the information given in the map. Use the key to help you remember which areas are more densely populated than others.

Write a Summary

Write a summary that will help you understand the information given in the map. The paragraph below and to the right summarizes the information from the map.

▶▶ Practicing the Skill

Turn to page 725 in Chapter 24, Section 5, "Culture." Look at the map titled "Population Density of Japan, 2001" and write a paragraph summarizing what you learned from it.

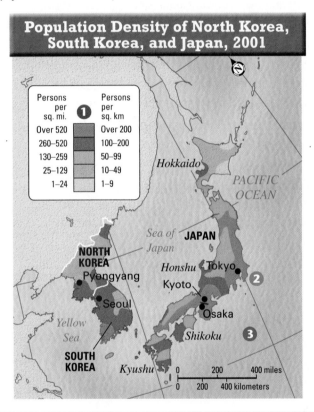

Population Density of North Korea, South Korea, and Japan, 2001

❹   All three of these East Asian countries are densely populated. Japan is the most densely populated of the three. The areas around Japan's cities are more densely populated than those around the cities of the Koreas. In all three countries, the cities are in very densely populated areas, as would be expected. Of the larger islands of Japan, Hokkaido is the least populated. North Korea is slightly less populated than South Korea.

ASSESSMENT

TERMS & NAMES

Explain the significance of each of the following:

1. Sun Yat-sen
2. Mao Zedong
3. Cultural Revolution
4. human rights
5. Diet
6. cooperative
7. haiku
8. Han
9. homogeneous
10. Ainu

REVIEW QUESTIONS

Establishing Modern China *(pages 701–705)*

1. Describe two rebellions under the Qing Dynasty.
2. What change did the Communists make in China in 1949?

The Governments of East Asia *(pages 708–711)*

3. What changes occurred in the Chinese government at the end of the Cultural Revolution?
4. How has the Chinese government repressed freedom?

The Economies of East Asia *(pages 712–715)*

5. Who controls China's economy?
6. What are some important East Asian products?

The Cultures of East Asia *(pages 716–721)*

7. Give two examples of cultural exchange in East Asia.
8. What changes did Communism bring to the arts in China?

Establishing Modern Japan *(pages 722–726)*

9. What changes occurred during the Meiji Restoration?
10. How do the Japanese regard their elders?

CRITICAL THINKING

Hypothesizing

1. Using your completed chart from Reading Social Studies, p. 700, explain which of your predictions proved correct.

Drawing Conclusions

2. Why do you think Mao Zedong was successful in winning the civil war against the Nationalists?

Forming and Supporting Opinions

3. What is your opinion of the dissidents who demonstrated in Tiananmen Square? Should they have been more obedient to their government?

Visual Summary

Establishing Modern China *1*

- The Nationalists toppled China's Qing Dynasty in 1911.
- Mao Zedong declared China Communist in 1949.

The Governments of East Asia *2*

- China and North Korea are the only Communist countries in East Asia.
- China's government continues to repress people's freedom, but less so than in the past.

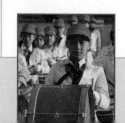

The Economies of East Asia

- Though they have faced challenges, East Asia's economies have grown strong.

3

The Cultures of East Asia *4*

- Over the years, much cultural exchange has occurred in East Asia.
- Communism has changed Chinese culture, but traditions such as the arts still thrive.

Establishing Modern Japan *5*

- After the devastating destruction of World War II, the Japanese rebuilt their economy to be one of the strongest in the world.

SOCIAL STUDIES SKILLBUILDER

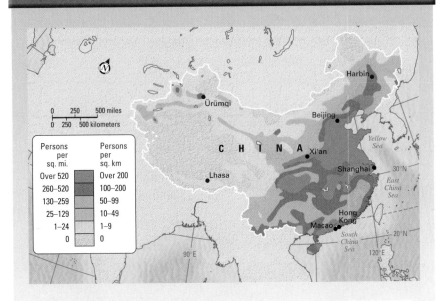

SKILLBUILDER: Reading a Population Density Map

1. Where are China's most densely populated areas?
2. Which areas are least populated? What might cause them to be so?

FOCUS ON GEOGRAPHY

1. Location • In what country did Buddhism originate?
2. Movement • From which countries did Buddhism spread to Japan?
3. Movement • When did Buddhism first spread to Korea?

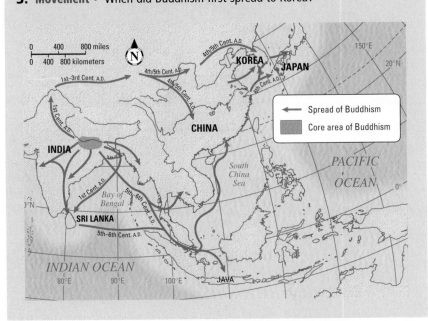

CHAPTER PROJECTS

Interdisciplinary Activity: Mathematics

Creating a Graph The countries of East Asia have widely different standards of living. Look at the Regional Data File on pages 668–671 to find the gross domestic products for China, North Korea, South Korea, Taiwan, and Japan. Then determine each country's per capita GDP—or GDP per person—by dividing its total GDP by its total population. Create a bar graph showing the GDP and per capita GDP for these countries.

Cooperative Learning Activity

Creating an Oral Presentation Work in a group of three to five classmates to create a visual presentation about Japan's living treasures. Each group member should research and prepare a report on one treasure. The reports should include pictures of the art being practiced. As a group, give a presentation to the class.

INTERNET ACTIVITY

Use the Internet to do research about the Long March. Find out details about the climate and terrain the marchers had to cross.

Writing About Geography Write a report of your findings, describing the climate and terrain along the route of the Long March. Explain what hardships the marchers probably faced due to these factors. List the Web sites you used to prepare your report.

For Internet links to support this activity, go to

RESEARCH LINKS
CLASSZONE.COM

CHAPTER
25

Australia, New Zealand, and the Pacific Islands

SECTION 1 History and Governments

SECTION 2 Economies and Cultures

Place Two main islands and several smaller islands make up New Zealand, whose capital, Wellington, encircles this harbor on North Island.

How can people affect a region's environment?

Human-Environment Interaction • When Europeans first came to Australia, New Zealand, and the Pacific Islands, the landscape had been largely unchanged for tens of thousands of years. In Australia and New Zealand, the settlers cleared the forests to provide land for farming and housing.

This human activity has had some unexpected consequences on the environment. In Australia, for example, more than 40 percent of the country's forests have been destroyed. Over-cultivation of this land has depleted the soil of valuable nutrients. Over-irrigation has resulted in too high a level of salt in the soil. As you can see above, very few plants are able to grow in salty soil.

What do you think?

♦ What do immigrants risk by changing an environment too quickly after settling in it?

♦ How might the people of Australia, New Zealand, and the Pacific Islands have benefited if the settlers had balanced development with environmental concerns?

BEFORE YOU READ

▶▶ *What Do You Know?*

Before you read the chapter, think about what you already know about Australia, New Zealand, and the Pacific Islands. What do you know about the history of these places? Have you read about the Aborigines or the Maori in other classes? Did you watch the 2000 Olympics when they were held in Australia? If you have been to this region, look back at your journal or photos and reflect on your experiences there.

▶▶ *What Do You Want to Know?*

Decide what else you want to know about this region. In your notebook, record what you hope to learn from this chapter.

Culture • Wood carvings like this are made by native people throughout New Zealand. ▲

READ AND TAKE NOTES

Reading Strategy: Making Inferences Making inferences means figuring out what a writer has suggested but not directly stated. It requires studying what is stated and using common sense and previous knowledge.

Use the chart below to gather facts about Australia, New Zealand, and the Pacific Islands. Then make inferences about Hawaii from them.

- Copy the chart in your notebook.
- As you read the chapter, record important facts about each place.
- After you read, review the facts and make inferences based on those facts.

Culture • Australian athlete Cathy Freeman lit the Olympic torch in the summer of 2000. ▲

	Place	Stated Facts	Inferences About Hawaii
Population	Australia		
	New Zealand		
	Pacific Islands		
Government	Australia		
	New Zealand		
	Pacific Islands		
Economy	Australia		
	New Zealand		
	Pacific Islands		
Culture	Australia		
	New Zealand		
	Pacific Islands		

History and Governments

TERMS & NAMES
Maori
Aborigine
Melanesia
Micronesia
Polynesia
Commonwealth of Nations

MAIN IDEA

The nations of this region were first settled by people from nearby and later colonized by European nations.

WHY IT MATTERS NOW

In many nations today, different groups struggle for their rights and for the opportunity to rule.

DATELINE

EXTRA

WAITANGI, NEW ZEALAND, 1940

One hundred years after it was signed, the Treaty of Waitangi can finally be seen by the public. On February 6, 1840, this historic treaty was signed by Lieutenant Governor William Hobson, several other Englishmen living in New Zealand, and about 45 Maori chiefs.

Long, heated arguments occurred between the English and the Maori chiefs about the treaty, which described how the British would rule New Zealand. The Maori chiefs were concerned that their people's rights would not be protected.

Many Maori today feel that the treaty has not been upheld and that their rights have not been protected. According to the treaty, lands, forests, and fisheries owned by Maori would remain theirs. Today, however, Maori citizens own only 5 percent of New Zealand's land.

Culture • **This painting shows William Hobson and a Maori chief signing the treaty in 1840.** ▲

History of the Region

Long before the British arrived in New Zealand, the country's first settlers—the **Maori** (MOW•ree)—lived there. In fact, people inhabited many of the islands in the Pacific and Indian oceans for thousands of years before any Europeans arrived. Today, we know this region as Australia, New Zealand, and the Pacific Islands.

Culture • **This Aborigine artist displays one of the paintings on tree bark for which his people are famous.** ▲

People of the Region

Australia's first inhabitants migrated there from Southeast Asia at least 40,000 years ago. Their descendants are called **Aborigines** (AB•uh•RIHJ•uh•neez). Settlers from Southeast Asia arrived in the Pacific Islands about 33,000 years ago. On the map on page 735, you can see the three regional groups of the Pacific— **Melanesia, Micronesia,** and **Polynesia.** Southeast Asians migrated first to Melanesia, then spread into Micronesia and finally Polynesia. About 1,000 years ago, Polynesians settled New Zealand. These settlers were the Maori.

Island Life Geography influenced which islands people settled. If an island had fresh water, wildlife, and vegetation, people settled there. If an island was too dry or too small, or lacked sources of food, it remained unpopulated.

Most of the early islanders fished or farmed. They also traded with nearby islanders. Because of the vast expanses of ocean, however, distinct languages and cultures developed over time.

Europeans in the Pacific In the 1500s, Europeans explored the Pacific for spices. In the 1600s and 1700s, missionaries and other settlers arrived. Some of them carried diseases, such as smallpox.

Reading
Social Studies

A. Using Maps
Look at the maps on pages 666 and 735. Why do you think Southeast Asians settled the islands in the order they did?

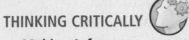

Spotlight on CULTURE

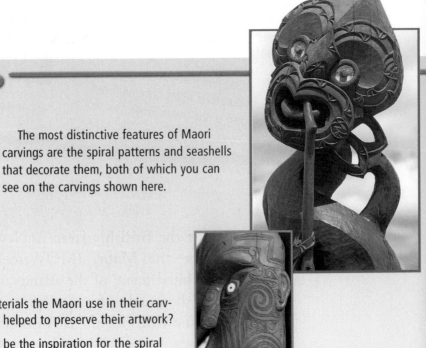

Maori Carvings The Maori have a long history of carving wood, stone, and bone. Many of the carvings are of human figures—either ancestors, gods, or characters from myths. Often, the carvings are found on items like canoes, weapons, and jewelry, though many also stand alone.

The most distinctive features of Maori carvings are the spiral patterns and seashells that decorate them, both of which you can see on the carvings shown here.

THINKING CRITICALLY

1. **Making Inferences** Think about the materials the Maori use in their carvings. How do you think these materials have helped to preserve their artwork?

2. **Hypothesizing** What do you think might be the inspiration for the spiral patterns that the Maori use on their carvings?

The Island Groups of the Pacific

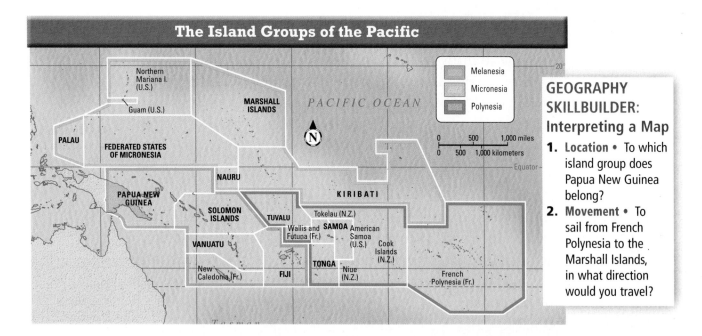

Northern Mariana I. (U.S.)

Guam (U.S.)

PALAU

FEDERATED STATES OF MICRONESIA

MARSHALL ISLANDS

PACIFIC OCEAN

Melanesia
Micronesia
Polynesia

NAURU

PAPUA NEW GUINEA

SOLOMON ISLANDS

TUVALU

KIRIBATI

Tokelau (N.Z.)

Wallis and Futuna (Fr.)

SAMOA

American Samoa (U.S.)

Cook Islands (N.Z.)

VANUATU

TONGA

Niue (N.Z.)

New Caledonia (Fr.)

FIJI

French Polynesia (Fr.)

Equator

0   500   1,000 miles
0   500   1,000 kilometers

GEOGRAPHY SKILLBUILDER: Interpreting a Map

1. **Location** • To which island group does Papua New Guinea belong?
2. **Movement** • To sail from French Polynesia to the Marshall Islands, in what direction would you travel?

Many of the native islanders died from these diseases. Some settlers also brought hardship upon the islanders by enslaving them.

Britain, France, Germany, Spain, the United States, and later Japan all established colonies in the Pacific. Since 1962, many islands have gained independence. Others are still colonies. For example, France governs New Caledonia, and the United States controls Guam.

Europeans in Australia and New Zealand In the 1700s, Great Britain sent many people to Australia. Some were convicts who labored on farms, and others were free colonists. By 1859, six British colonies made up Australia. In 1901, these colonies became states of the Commonwealth of Australia.

In the 1790s, New Zealand was settled by whale hunters and traders from Great Britain, the United States, and France, as well as European missionaries and colonists. In 1840, the Maori and the British signed the Treaty of Waitangi, which gave control of New Zealand to Britain. New Zealand did not become a self-governing country until 1907.

Mysterious Stone Statues Far out in the Pacific, along the slopes of Easter Island, stands a strange sight. Giant stone heads peer out across the landscape. Hundreds more lie knocked down all across the island.

The island's early inhabitants carved these statues (shown below), which weigh up to 90 tons, out of the side of a volcano. How they moved the statues many miles to their present locations, however, is a mystery that may never be solved.

Impact of European Settlement When Europeans first came to Australia, as many as 750,000 Aborigines populated the continent. As more settlers arrived, Aborigines were forced into the country's interior. Today, only 1 percent of Australia's population is of Aborigine descent. Similarly, in New Zealand, only about 14 percent of the population today is of Maori descent.

Governments

The governments of Australia, New Zealand, and the Pacific Island nations are quite varied. Some are democracies, some are monarchies, and some are ruled by other nations. Many countries have governments that resemble those of the nations that colonized them.

Australia and New Zealand Australia and New Zealand belong to the **Commonwealth of Nations.** This is a group of countries that were once British colonies and share a heritage of British law and government. Great Britain's monarch is their head of state but has no real power.

The Pacific Islands A few Pacific Islands still have official ties to various countries. For example, the United States is responsible for the defense of the Federated States of Micronesia, while the French Polynesians vote in French elections. Other islands rule themselves, such as Tonga, which is a constitutional monarchy.

Reading
Social Studies

B. Drawing Conclusions
What factors could explain why Aborigines are now such a small minority in Australia?

Region •
This photo shows a selection of flags from the Pacific Islands. ▼

SECTION ❶ ASSESSMENT

Terms & Names

1. Identify:
   (a) Maori
   (d) Micronesia
   (b) Aborigine
   (e) Polynesia
   (c) Melanesia
   (f) Commonwealth of Nations

Taking Notes

2. Use a chart like this one to list and compare important details of the history of Australia, New Zealand, and the Pacific Islands.

	Australia	New Zealand	Pacific Islands
Early Inhabitants			
European Settlement			
Government Today			

Main Ideas

3. (a) Where did the earliest settlers of Australia and the Pacific Islands come from?

   (b) List three reasons Europeans traveled to the region's islands.

   (c) What do the governments of Australia and New Zealand have in common?

Critical Thinking

4. **Summarizing**

   How did geography affect the region's settlement patterns?

   Think About
   • which islands the original settlers inhabited
   • how the arrival of Europeans affected native populations

ACTIVITY -OPTION- Imagine that you were a Maori inhabitant of New Zealand. Write a **dialogue** between you and one of the European settlers.

W N E S

Economies and Cultures

TERMS & NAMES
copra
matrilineal society
patrilineal society

MAIN IDEA

There is great diversity among the economies and cultures of the nations of the Pacific.

WHY IT MATTERS NOW

Modern communication and transportation have brought this once isolated region into closer contact with the rest of the world.

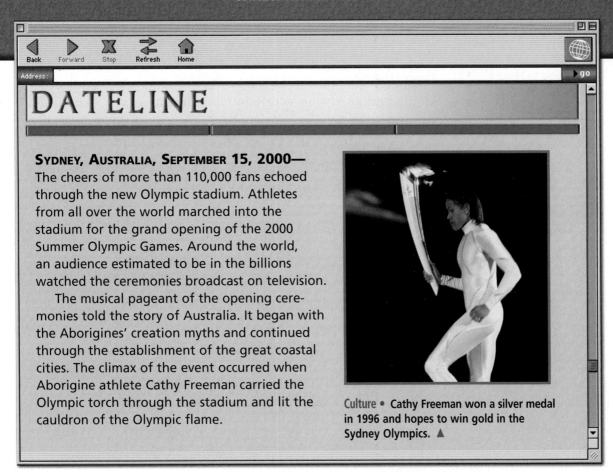

| ◁ Back | ▷ Forward | ✗ Stop | ⇄ Refresh | ⌂ Home | | 🌐 |

Address: [ ] ▶ go

DATELINE

SYDNEY, AUSTRALIA, SEPTEMBER 15, 2000— The cheers of more than 110,000 fans echoed through the new Olympic stadium. Athletes from all over the world marched into the stadium for the grand opening of the 2000 Summer Olympic Games. Around the world, an audience estimated to be in the billions watched the ceremonies broadcast on television.

The musical pageant of the opening ceremonies told the story of Australia. It began with the Aborigines' creation myths and continued through the establishment of the great coastal cities. The climax of the event occurred when Aborigine athlete Cathy Freeman carried the Olympic torch through the stadium and lit the cauldron of the Olympic flame.

Culture • Cathy Freeman won a silver medal in 1996 and hopes to win gold in the Sydney Olympics. ▲

Resources and Economies

The economies of Australia, New Zealand, and the Pacific Islands have various foundations. On the one hand, tourists travel to the region to enjoy its beaches, mountains, fjords, and unusual plant and animal life. Thousands also came to Australia for the 2000 Summer Olympic Games. On the other hand, agriculture is the traditional base of the region's economies. Australia and New Zealand still depend more on farming than do most other developed countries.

Australia, New Zealand, and the Pacific Islands **737**

Pacific Island Economies Most Pacific Islanders fish, grow their own food, and build their own homes. However, some commercial agriculture does exist on the islands. **Copra** (KOH•pruh)—dried coconut meat—and coconut oil are important agricultural exports. Tourism also contributes significantly to the economies of some Pacific Islands, such as Tahiti.

Australia's Economy Australia has a strong market economy and relatively free trade with other nations, especially Japan. Service industries—including health care, tourism, news media, and transportation—provide nearly three-fourths of the country's jobs.

Australia's strong economy also depends on mining and farming. Australia is the world's leading producer of bauxite, lead, and zinc. It has also developed vast fields of natural gas. Wheat is Australia's most important cash crop, and about 80 percent of the harvest is exported. Sugar cane is also an important cash crop.

Trade During colonial times, Australia and New Zealand mostly traded with Great Britain. Today, Australia's main trading partners are Japan and the United States, while New Zealand's main trading partner is Australia.

Reading
Social Studies

A. Synthesizing List some factors that might have allowed Australia to have a stronger economy than the Pacific Islands have.

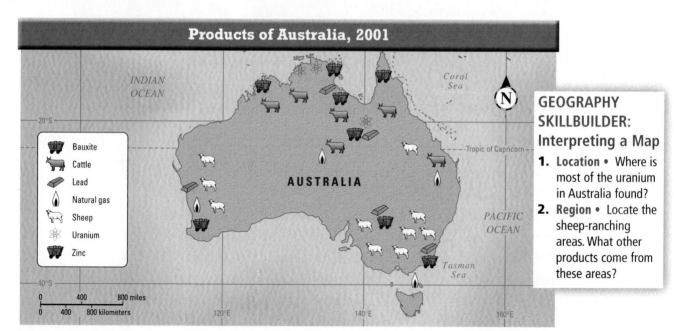

Products of Australia, 2001

Legend:
- Bauxite
- Cattle
- Lead
- Natural gas
- Sheep
- Uranium
- Zinc

GEOGRAPHY SKILLBUILDER: Interpreting a Map

1. **Location** • Where is most of the uranium in Australia found?
2. **Region** • Locate the sheep-ranching areas. What other products come from these areas?

Asian countries are also playing a bigger role in New Zealand's economy. In 1983, Australia and New Zealand signed a free-trade agreement to boost the trade between them.

Cultures and Change

Despite their remote locations, the islands of the region have attracted immigrants from around the world. Modernization and tradition both play strong roles in the region.

Reading
Social Studies

B. Hypothesizing
What else about Pacific Island life could modernization affect?

The Pacific Islands Modernization has affected life in some of the Pacific Islands. For example, modernization has clearly changed modes of transportation. For short trips, villagers take canoes just as they always have. However, for longer trips, they outfit canoes with modern outboard motors or travel by ship or airplane.

Tradition continues to be strong, especially in art forms and family structures. For example, matrilineal societies are less common than patrilineal societies, but they are still found in parts of the Pacific Islands, such as Papua New Guinea. In **matrilineal societies,** ancestry is traced through the mother's side of the family. In **patrilineal societies,** ancestry is traced through the father's side.

Place •
In Papua New Guinea, people still perform traditional dances. ▼

Biography

Charlie Perkins Charlie Perkins (shown above, center) grew up in Australia's outback near Alice Springs. Perkins was the first Aborigine in Australia to graduate from college. He also played professional soccer in England. However, he is best known for his struggle against discrimination.

In 1965, Perkins led "freedom rides" throughout Australia to teach people about equal rights for Aborigines. On these rides, he met with clubs and organizations to discuss discrimination. He also led activities such as taking Aborigine children swimming in pools where only white children were allowed to swim.

Perkins has been compared to Martin Luther King, Jr. When Perkins died in October 2000, Australia's prime minister said, "Charlie was a tireless fighter for the cause of his people."

Australia and New Zealand Australia has a diverse population. For example, people worship in mosques, churches, synagogues, and Buddhist temples. In the past 50 years, immigrants have come from many parts of the world, such as Cambodia, Laos, and Vietnam. Some of them came from places where there was war or other danger. In a memoir, writer Barbara Marie Brewster described her pleasant surprise at Australia's diversity.

A VOICE FROM AUSTRALIA

As we drove home, I was struck by the extraordinary mixture Australia represented. Here were two Americans, a German, a Hungarian, and a Malay girl from Brunei, and we'd been talking with an Englishman who was a Buddhist monk in a monastery in Australia, founded and funded by Thais and run by an Italian abbot. I liked it.

Barbara Marie Brewster

In New Zealand, over half a million people are Maori. Most others are descendants of Scottish, English, Irish, and Welsh settlers. Many Asians also live in the cities, such as the capital, Wellington, and the largest city, Auckland.

SECTION 2 ASSESSMENT

Terms & Names

1. Identify: (a) copra   (b) matrilineal society   (c) patrilineal society

Taking Notes

2. Use a diagram like this one to organize the important economic activities of Australia, New Zealand, and the Pacific Islands.

Economic Activities		
Australia	New Zealand	Pacific Islands

Main Ideas

3. (a) How do the economies of the Pacific Islands and Australia benefit from the region's physical geography?

   (b) How do Australia and New Zealand cooperate economically?

   (c) What is the relationship between modernization and tradition in the Pacific Islands?

Critical Thinking

4. **Drawing Conclusions**

   In what ways do you think Australia's ethnic diversity affects its culture and politics?

   Think About

   • the various ethnic groups in Australia and how long each has lived there

   • how different ethnic groups contribute to diversity in other countries

ACTIVITY -OPTION-   Make up an **advertising slogan** to promote tourism in Australia, the Pacific Islands, or New Zealand.

Using Primary Sources

▶▶ Defining the Skill

Primary sources are materials written by people who lived during historical events. They include letters, diaries, articles, videotapes, speeches, eyewitness accounts, and photographs. Secondary sources, such as social studies books, are materials designed to discuss or teach about an event. When you research a topic, look for useful primary sources. Include these in your writing if you want to illustrate or prove an important point.

▶▶ Applying the Skill

The passage to the right is an example of an essay about Captain James Cook's first voyage to the Pacific. Use the strategies listed below to help you determine when and how to use a primary source in your own writing.

How to Use Primary Sources

Strategy ❶ Choose a primary source that gives key information about your subject. Be sure that the material is from a primary source and not a secondary source.

Strategy ❷ Analyze the primary source and consider what the document was supposed to achieve and who would read it. Ask yourself how the primary source can help prove your point.

Strategy ❸ Quote the primary source exactly as it is written. Some primary sources, such as this letter, will have different language, spelling, capitalization, and punctuation than modern sources.

Make a Chart

Making a chart will help you determine when and how to use a primary source. The chart to the right explains the use of the primary source in the passage (above, right).

▶▶ Practicing the Skill

Turn to page 740 in Chapter 25, Section 2. Read the quotation from a primary source found there. Make a chart like the one above to determine how and why the primary source was used.

Captain James Cook made three trips from England to the South Pacific. The seeming purpose of his first trip in 1768 was to observe the movements of the planet Venus. ❶ As this letter from the king clearly shows, however, Britain's true purpose was to find and claim the southern continent:

❸ Whereas the making Discoverys of Countries hitherto unknown, and the Attaining a Knowledge of distant Parts … will redound greatly to the Honour of this Nation as a Maritime Power, as well as to the Dignity of the Crown of Great Britain, and may tend greatly to the advancement of the Trade and Navigation thereof; … You are therefore in Pursuance of His Majesty's Pleasure hereby requir'd and directed to put to Sea with the Bark you Command so soon as the Observation of the Transit of the Planet Venus shall be finished. …

Subject	Primary Source	Reason for Quoting the Primary Source
Captain Cook's first voyage to the South Pacific in 1768	The secret instructions given to Captain Cook	To prove that the true purpose of the voyage was different from the stated purpose

900 1910 1920 1930 1940 1950 1960 1970   1700 1710 1720 1730 1740 1750 1760 1780
990 2000   1800 1810 1820 1830 1840 1850 1860 1870
                                              1890 1900 1910 1920 1930 1940 1950 196
                                              1980 1990 2000

Linking Past and Present

The Legacy of East Asia, Australia, and the Pacific Islands

Australian Rock Art

There are thousands of sites in Australia where rocks are engraved and painted with silhouettes of humans and animals. Many of these rock-art sites have existed for almost 10,000 years. Every year, visitors tour these sites and learn about the early people of Australia.

Soybeans

Although the origin of the soybean plant is unknown, soybeans were being grown in China around 1200 B.C. They were intro-duced into the United States in 1804 and today are used as a vegetable and as a source of soymilk and tofu.

Martial Arts

Martial arts are forms of self-defense, many of them weapon-less. In ancient times, people developed martial arts in China, India, and Tibet in the belief that they allowed peaceful energy, called *chi,* to flow through one's body. Today, people around the world practice martial arts for self-defense, sport, exercise, and spiritual development and as a means of reducing stress and lowering blood pressure.

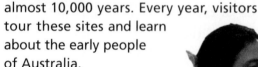

Find Out More About It!
Study the text and photos on these pages to learn about inventions, creations, and contributions that have come from East Asia, Australia, and the Pacific Islands. Then choose the item that interests you the most and do research in the library or on the Internet to learn more about it. Use the information you gather to write an article for your school or local newspaper that tells more about the contribution.

RESEARCH LINKS
CLASSZONE.COM

Origami

Origami, the art of folding paper into artistic objects, most likely originated from *gohei,* the art of folding cloth offerings in the Shinto religion of Japan. In origami, paper is folded to create figures of birds, animals, flowers, and people. Some origami figures actually have moving parts. Hundreds of books and courses on origami are available throughout the world.

Boomerangs

A boomerang is a curved, flat stick that is thrown either as a weapon or as a toy. Although boomerangs have been found in many parts of the world, they are most often associated with Australia and its native people, the Aborigines. Most Aboriginal boomerangs were "nonreturning"—that is, they did not return after they were thrown. A correctly thrown returning boomerang, on the other hand, will fly out, loop around, and return to the person who threw it. Returning boomerangs are used mainly for sport and as children's toys.

TERMS & NAMES

Explain the significance of each of the following:
1. Maori
2. Aborigine
3. Melanesia
4. Micronesia
5. Polynesia
6. Commonwealth of Nations
7. copra
8. matrilineal society
9. patrilineal society

REVIEW QUESTIONS

History and Governments *(pages 733–736)*
1. Which was populated first—Australia, New Zealand, or the Pacific Islands?
2. How did the isolation of the Pacific Islands from each other affect the languages and cultures that developed there?
3. Name two ways in which European settlers brought hardship to the Pacific Islands.
4. Do Aborigines and Maori represent large or small parts of their countries' populations?

Economies and Cultures *(pages 737–740)*
5. Name two crops that are beneficial to the economies of the Pacific Islands.
6. What type of industry provides the majority of jobs in Australia?
7. Which are there more of, matrilineal or patrilineal societies?
8. How has modern life transformed transportation in the Pacific Islands?

CRITICAL THINKING

Analyzing Motives
1. Using your completed chart from Reading Social Studies, p. 732, explain why you think Australia continues to attract immigrants from such a variety of cultures.

Drawing Conclusions
2. Why might the British have sent convicts to Australia to do labor?

Making Inferences
3. Why do you think Great Britain is no longer the main trading partner of Australia and New Zealand?

Visual Summary

1 History and Governments

- People from Southeast Asia settled Australia, New Zealand, and the Pacific Islands long before any Europeans arrived.
- Geographically isolated, these islands developed their own unique cultures.
- Europeans, Americans, and Japanese later colonized the region. The region now has many different forms of government.

2 Economies and Cultures

- Australia's economy is more developed than those of the Pacific Islands because it is richer in resources.
- Most Pacific Islands are self-sufficient, and traditional customs are practiced in some areas.
- The diverse populations of Australia and New Zealand are descended from early settlers, colonists, and immigrants.

Read the following quote by an Australian Aborigine who speaks only a little English. Then answer the questions that follow.

> *"First [white] people come to us, they started to run our life... quick.... First they should ask about fish, cave, Dreaming, but... they rush in. They make school... teach. Now Aborigine losing... everything."*

SKILLBUILDER: Using Primary Sources

1. How could you use this primary source in an essay about the effect of European settlement on Australia's Aborigines?
2. Why might you include this primary source instead of a secondary source that summarizes the same facts and ideas?
3. What would you want your readers to think or feel as they read the quote?

FOCUS ON GEOGRAPHY

1. **Region** • Human activities can cause desertification. Why is such a vast region of Australia not at risk for this?
2. **Human-Environment Interaction** • Is there a lot of or a little land in Australia at low risk of desertification?
3. **Location** • Locate the regions of high or very high risk. Why might these regions be particularly at risk?

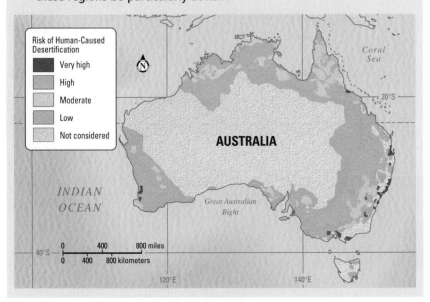

Risk of Human-Caused Desertification
- Very high
- High
- Moderate
- Low
- Not considered

AUSTRALIA

INDIAN OCEAN

Coral Sea

20°S

Great Australian Bight

40°S

| 0 | 400 | 800 miles |
| 0 | 400 | 800 kilometers |

120°E   140°E

CHAPTER PROJECTS

Interdisciplinary Activity: Ecology
Writing a Report The first Maori to arrive in New Zealand found an uninhabited land, with plants and animals they had never before encountered. Research these plants and animals, such as the moa. Then find out how the Maori changed the land. What new things did they bring? What animal faced extinction after their arrival? Write a report on your findings. Share your report with the class.

Cooperative Learning Activity
Creating an Illustrated Map The first settlers of Australia and the Pacific Islands came from Southeast Asia. In a group of three to five classmates, create an illustrated map with arrows showing the paths of migration. List the approximate dates of each migration. Illustrate the map with pictures or drawings of the people and items from their cultures. Divide the tasks of research, drawing, and writing among members of the group, assigning one or two members to each task.

 INTERNET ACTIVITY

Use the Internet to research Australia's Ayers Rock, which the Aborigines call Uluru. Focus on the appearance of the rock and its composition, and explain why it is so unusual.
Writing About Geography Write a report of your findings. If possible, include pictures of Ayers Rock. List the Web sites you used to prepare your report.

For Internet links to support this activity, go to

RESEARCH LINKS
CLASSZONE.COM

The War on Terrorism

Reporter's Notes

By Kevin McCoy

NEW YORK—First came a deep rumble. Then a roar like a giant speeding train. But the sound came crashing from the sky, not along steel tracks. In an instant, a warm, sunny September morning at the World Trade Center in Lower Manhattan became a darkened moonscape of choking cement dust and swirling paper, wailing sirens and screaming victims.

"I heard the rumbling and I looked up, and one of the towers was coming down," said Sergeant Moises Cruz, a New York City police officer who ran for his life with other survivors of the most horrible terrorist attack in U.S. history. Lower Broadway, normally a bustling checkerboard of financial traders, government officials, businessmen and tourists, lay silenced under a three-inch carpet of gritty gray dust.

"I can't even describe it, it was so awful," said Wilbert, a 50-year-old elevator maintenance worker. "All I could do was run."

News reporters who covered the attacks knew instinctively this was the most significant story of a lifetime.

The twin towers of the World Trade Center in New York City, before (inset) and after the terrorist attacks of September 11, 2001

The Attack on America

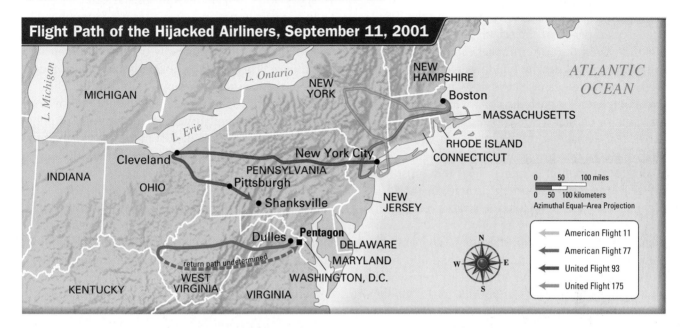

Flight Path of the Hijacked Airliners, September 11, 2001

Map labels: L. Michigan · L. Ontario · L. Erie · MICHIGAN · NEW YORK · NEW HAMPSHIRE · ATLANTIC OCEAN · Boston · MASSACHUSETTS · RHODE ISLAND · CONNECTICUT · Cleveland · New York City · INDIANA · PENNSYLVANIA · OHIO · Pittsburgh · Shanksville · NEW JERSEY · Dulles · Pentagon · DELAWARE · MARYLAND · WASHINGTON, D.C. · KENTUCKY · WEST VIRGINIA · VIRGINIA · return path undetermined

0   50   100 miles
0   50   100 kilometers
Azimuthal Equal–Area Projection

American Flight 11
American Flight 77
United Flight 93
United Flight 175

McCoy's reporter's instincts were right. Before the day was over, there would be more than 3,000 victims of the most destructive act of terrorism in modern history. **Terrorism** is the calculated use of, or threatened use of, violence against individuals or property for the purpose of intimidating or causing fear for political or social ends.

The terrorist attacks on September 11 were aimed at well-known symbols of the economic and military power of the United States. But what they mainly destroyed was something Americans value much more—the lives of thousands of individual citizens.

UNIMAGINABLE HORROR

On the morning of September 11, 2001, many New Yorkers were heading for work or school when 19 Arab terrorists hijacked four airliners from East Coast airports. The first plane crashed into the upper floors of the north tower of the World Trade Center and exploded into flames. About 20 minutes later, the second plane sliced into the south tower.

Desks, chairs, paper—and people—blew out of the windows of the twin towers. People on the streets below watched in horror as more than a dozen workers on the upper floors jumped from the blazing buildings to their deaths. Other workers poured out of the towers to escape the fire.

Less than an hour after the twin towers were hit, the third hijacked plane rammed into the west side of the Pentagon in Arlington, Virginia. It tore a 75-foot gash in the five-sided, five-story building. That crash

site, too, immediately became engulfed in flames. Meanwhile, passengers on the fourth hijacked plane had used their cell phones and had heard about the other plane crashes. Some of the passengers rushed the hijackers and prevented them from striking their intended target, thought to be either the White House or the Capitol.

Because of these heroic efforts, the plane crashed not into a crowded building but into an empty field in Pennsylvania. No one will ever know how many lives the passengers saved as they gave up their own.

Recovery efforts continue on the collapsed section of the Pentagon's southwest side two days after the attack.

The Destruction The planes were loaded with fuel. They became destructive missiles when they crashed into the World Trade Center and the Pentagon. As one investigator noted, the hijackers "couldn't carry anything—other than an atom bomb—that could be as bad as what they were flying."

The explosions and fires so weakened the damaged skyscrapers that they crumbled to the ground less than two hours after impact. The fire and raining debris caused nearby buildings to collapse as well. Nine buildings in New York City's financial district completely or partially collapsed. Six others suffered major damage. The disaster area covered 16 acres. The damage at the Pentagon, though extensive, was confined to one wing of the building.

But it was the toll in human lives that most grieved Americans and others around the world. About 3,000 people died in the attacks. All passengers on the four planes were killed, as well as workers and visitors in the World Trade Center and the Pentagon. The dead included more than 300 New York City firefighters and 40 police officers who rushed to the scene and were buried in the rubble when the skyscrapers collapsed.

Grieving Families and Companies "Please tell the children I love them," said a father of three from the World Trade Center before the phone line went dead. From the burning towers and the hijacked planes,

men and women used their last moments to call and to speak with their families for the last time.

In the first hours and days after the September 11 attacks, family members and friends of people in the World Trade Center frantically tried to find their loved ones. They checked hospitals and posted pictures of the missing on lampposts and walls. The thousands of people who escaped before the towers collapsed were reunited with their families. But only a few survivors were pulled from the wreckage of the buildings. For thousands of people, loved ones never returned home. Also, several businesses with offices in the towers lost large numbers of employees.

The horror of September 11 has haunted more than just the survivors and witnesses of the attacks, although they were the hardest hit. Millions of Americans watched the events on television shortly after they occurred. They, too, would have difficulty forgetting those horrifying images.

RESCUE EFFORTS

Amidst the brutal destruction at the World Trade Center, the courage, selflessness, and noble actions of New York City's firefighters, police officers, and rescue workers stood as a testament. Many of the first

Destruction in New York City

Destroyed
Severely Damaged

Millennium Hilton

TOWER 1   TOWER 2

WORLD TRADE CENTER

Bldg. 7   Bldg. 5

One Liberty Plaza

Bldg. 6

Bldg. 4   American Stock Exchange

WORLD FINANCIAL CENTER   Bldg. 3

3D model by Urban Data Solutions, Inc.

Bystanders view the twin towers of the World Trade Center shortly after impact (above). The destruction in New York City's financial district is illustrated in the infographic of "ground zero" to the right.

USA TODAY first appeared in print 9/25/2001

How the debris is removed

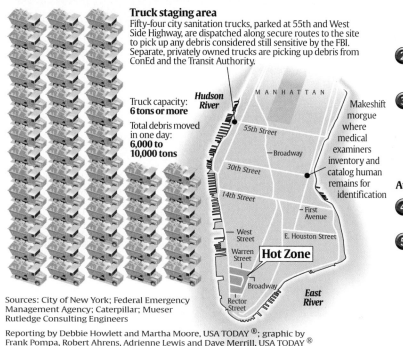

Truck staging area
Fifty-four city sanitation trucks, parked at 55th and West Side Highway, are dispatched along secure routes to the site to pick up any debris considered still sensitive by the FBI. Separate, privately owned trucks are picking up debris from ConEd and the Transit Authority.

Truck capacity: **6 tons or more**

Total debris moved in one day: **6,000 to 10,000 tons**

Hudson River

MANHATTAN

55th Street

Broadway

30th Street

14th Street

West Street

Warren Street

Hot Zone

Broadway

Rector Street

First Avenue

E. Houston Street

East River

Makeshift morgue where medical examiners inventory and catalog human remains for identification

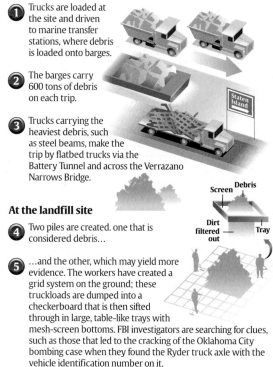

1 Trucks are loaded at the site and driven to marine transfer stations, where debris is loaded onto barges.

2 The barges carry 600 tons of debris on each trip.

Staten Island

3 Trucks carrying the heaviest debris, such as steel beams, make the trip by flatbed trucks via the Battery Tunnel and across the Verrazano Narrows Bridge.

At the landfill site

4 Two piles are created. one that is considered debris...

5 ...and the other, which may yield more evidence. The workers have created a grid system on the ground; these truckloads are dumped into a checkerboard that is then sifted through in large, table-like trays with mesh-screen bottoms. FBI investigators are searching for clues, such as those that led to the cracking of the Oklahoma City bombing case when they found the Ryder truck axle with the vehicle identification number on it.

Screen — Debris

Dirt filtered out

Tray

Sources: City of New York; Federal Emergency Management Agency; Caterpillar; Mueser Rutledge Consulting Engineers

Reporting by Debbie Howlett and Martha Moore, USA TODAY ®; graphic by Frank Pompa, Robert Ahrens, Adrienne Lewis and Dave Merrill, USA TODAY ®

---

firefighters at the scene disappeared into the burning buildings to help those inside and never came out again. Entire squads were lost. New York City Fire Department chaplain, Father Mychal Judge, was killed by falling debris just after giving the last rites of the Catholic Church to a firefighter at the scene.

Firefighters worked around the clock trying to find survivors in the wreckage. They had to contend with shifting rubble and smoky, ash-filled air. Medical workers from the area rushed to staff the city's trauma centers. But after the first wave of injured, there were few survivors to treat. One emergency medical technician said, "We were set up for any emergency. It was a great site, full of surgeons. But we were treating firemen and police who needed their eyes washed."

A flood of volunteers assisted rescue workers. Ironworkers helped cut through steel beams, while high school students helped provide water and food for the rescue workers. From around the country, people sent donations of blood, food, and money to New York City. The city kept functioning in the hours and days that followed the attack under the direction of its mayor, Rudy Giuliani.

The Cleanup After the first few days, the work at "ground zero," the World Trade Center disaster site, shifted to recovering bodies and removing the massive amount of debris. The twin towers alone contained more than 200,000 tons of steel, 425,000 cubic yards of concrete, and 14 acres of glass—an estimated 2 billion pounds.

SEARCH FOR TERRORISTS BEGINS
In the weeks that followed, the U.S. government organized a massive effort to identify those responsible for the attacks. Officials concluded that Osama bin Laden, a Saudi Arabian millionaire, directed the terrorists. He had been exiled from his native country because of suspected terrorist activities. Bin Laden was hiding in Afghanistan, protected there by the strict Islamic government known as the Taliban. The effort to bring him to justice would lead the United States to begin military action against Afghanistan in October, as the next section explains.

Thinking Critically

CURRENT EVENTS
CLASSZONE.COM

- Why were the specific targets of the September attacks selected by the terrorists?
- What might cause individuals to use terrorist tactics to attempt to change situations they think are a problem?

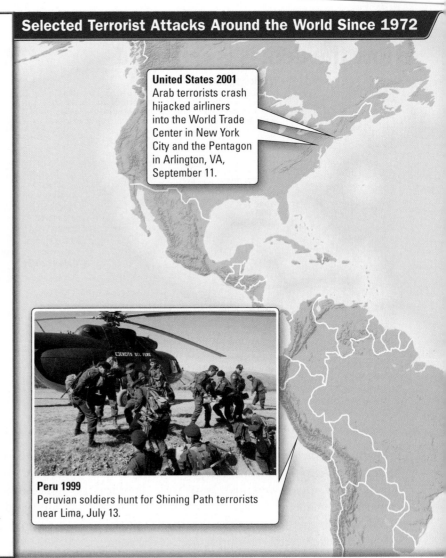

Selected Terrorist Attacks Around the World Since 1972

United States 2001
Arab terrorists crash hijacked airliners into the World Trade Center in New York City and the Pentagon in Arlington, VA, September 11.

Peru 1999
Peruvian soldiers hunt for Shining Path terrorists near Lima, July 13.

AFGHANISTAN— I entered Afghanistan from the north on an aging ferry boat at dusk on October 22. All I could see in the encroaching darkness were silhouettes of Northern Alliance fighters with Kalishnikov weapons slung loosely on their shoulders. My passport was stamped in a small mud hut under a dim lantern, then I was off to the village of Hoja Baddahuin, where the Northern Alliance had set up headquarters after the Taliban had taken over most of the country.

The United States had entered the war in Afghanistan after the terrorist attacks on September 11, 2001. Covering the war in Afghanistan has been the single most challenging experience of my career as a reporter at USA TODAY.

The most dangerous part of the experience was traveling through the front lines as I made my way to Kabul. My jeep had to cross minefields and the most narrow mountain roads imaginable. At Taloqan, the first city to be restored to the Northern Alliance, I wrote my stories while gunfire erupted outside my walled compound. I paid two men to stay inside with their machine guns and to answer the door should someone come knocking. Taliban fighters were still hiding out in houses just down the street. Through it all, I learned to stay calm by doing the best I could to ensure both my safety and the safety of my team, and to leave the rest to a healthy dose of faith.

Hunting for the Terrorists

Terrorism is not new. Reporters like Tim Friend have been covering terrorist attacks across the globe for the last three decades. Throughout history, individuals, small groups, and governments have used terror tactics to try to achieve political or social goals— whether it be to bring down a government, eliminate opponents, or promote a cause.

In recent times, however, terrorism has become an international problem. Since the late 1960s, more than 14,000 terrorist attacks have occurred worldwide. International terrorist groups have carried out increasingly destructive, high-profile attacks to attract global attention. Many countries also face domestic terrorists who oppose their governments' policies or have special interests to promote.

The reasons for modern terrorism are many. The traditional motives, such as gaining independence, expelling foreigners, or changing society, still drive various terrorist groups around the world. These terrorists use violence to force concessions from their enemies, usually the governments in power. But other kinds of terrorists, driven by radical religious motives, began to emerge in the late 20th century.

The goal of these terrorists is the destruction of what they consider the forces of evil. This evil might be located in their own countries or in other parts of the world. These terrorists often threaten to use weapons of mass destruction, such as chemical, biological, or nuclear weapons, to kill their enemies.

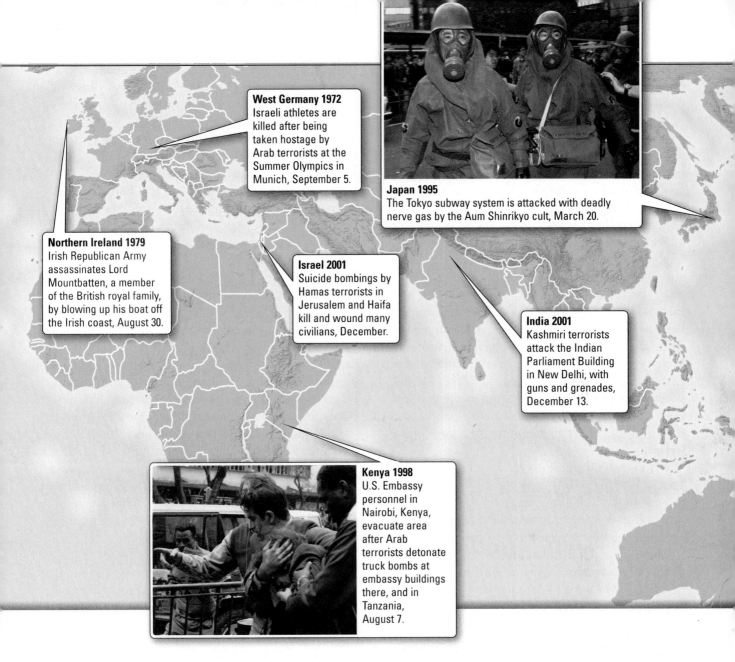

West Germany 1972
Israeli athletes are killed after being taken hostage by Arab terrorists at the Summer Olympics in Munich, September 5.

Japan 1995
The Tokyo subway system is attacked with deadly nerve gas by the Aum Shinrikyo cult, March 20.

Northern Ireland 1979
Irish Republican Army assassinates Lord Mountbatten, a member of the British royal family, by blowing up his boat off the Irish coast, August 30.

Israel 2001
Suicide bombings by Hamas terrorists in Jerusalem and Haifa kill and wound many civilians, December.

India 2001
Kashmiri terrorists attack the Indian Parliament Building in New Delhi, with guns and grenades, December 13.

Kenya 1998
U.S. Embassy personnel in Nairobi, Kenya, evacuate area after Arab terrorists detonate truck bombs at embassy buildings there, and in Tanzania, August 7.

TERRORISM AROUND THE WORLD

The problem of international terrorism first came to world attention in a shocking way during the 1972 Summer Olympic Games in Munich, Germany (then West Germany). Eight members of a Palestinian terrorist group called Black September killed two Israeli athletes and took nine others hostage. Five of the terrorists, all the hostages, and a police officer were later killed in a bloody gun battle. The attack became known as the Munich Massacre. Since then, few regions of the world have been spared from terrorist attacks.

The Middle East Like Black September, many terrorist organizations have their roots in the Israeli-Palestinian conflict over land in the Middle East.

(*Middle East* is the political term for the geographic region of Southwest Asia.) Arab terrorist groups such as the Palestine Islamic Jihad, Hamas, and Hizballah have sought to prevent a peace settlement between Israel and the Palestinians. They want a homeland for the Palestinians on their own terms, with the most extreme among them denying Israel's right to exist. In a continual cycle of violence, the Israelis retaliate after each terrorist attack, and the terrorists attack again.

Among Muslims in the Middle East, the Israeli-Palestinian violence has bred widespread Arab anger at Israel—and at the United States for supporting Israel. For example, the Lebanese-based group Hizballah seeks to eliminate all non-Islamic influences in Muslim countries. It is thought to have been responsible for bombing the U.S. embassy and marine barracks in Beirut in 1983 and the U.S. embassy annex in Beirut in 1984.

In December 2001, terrorist attacks on Israeli civilians in Jerusalem and Haifa killed 27 people and wounded more than 200. Hamas claimed responsibility, and the Israelis responded with military strikes against Palestinian targets.

Israel then declared a "war on terrorism," patterned after the U.S. response to the September 11 attacks. Moderates in the region believe that the only long-term solution is a compromise between Israel and the Palestinians over the issue of land.

Europe Many countries in Europe—including Great Britain, Germany, and Italy—have been targets of domestic terrorists who oppose government policies. For example, for decades the Irish Republican Army engaged in terrorist attacks against Britain because it opposed British control of Northern Ireland. By 2001, however, the British and the IRA were peacefully negotiating for greater autonomy for Northern Ireland.

Both Germany and Italy have suffered terrorist attacks by extreme left-wing and right-wing domestic groups. In general, left-wing groups oppose capitalism, and right-wing groups support capitalism and oppose government regulation.

These groups sometimes join forces with other terrorist organizations when it suits their purposes. In 1975, for example, West Germany's Red Army Faction and Italy's Red Brigades cooperated with the Palestine Liberation Organization to kidnap officials at a meeting of the Organization of Petroleum Exporting Countries (OPEC) in Vienna, Austria.

South Asia and East Asia South Asia has become another hotbed of terrorism in recent years. Afghanistan became a haven for international terrorists after the extremist Muslim Taliban came to power in 1996. In that year, Osama bin Laden moved to Afghanistan and began using mountain hideouts in that country as a base of operations for his global network of Muslim terrorists known as al-Qaeda.

Muslim extremists from all over the world came to al-Qaeda training camps. Bin Laden and these other extremists were opposed to American influence in Muslim lands. Bin Laden called for terrorist attacks against Americans and U.S. allies.

Terrorist groups have arisen in East Asia, as well. Japanese terrorist groups include the Aum Shinrikyo (Supreme Truth Sect) and the Japanese Red Army. The Aum Shinrikyo (called Aleph since 2000) is a religious cult that wants to control Japan. In 1995, it released sarin, a deadly nerve gas, in subway stations in Tokyo. Twelve people were killed and more than 5,700 injured. This attack brought global attention to the threat of biological and chemical agents as terrorist weapons.

Africa Civil unrest and regional wars were the root causes of most terrorist activity in Africa at the end of the 20th century. But al-Qaeda cells operated in

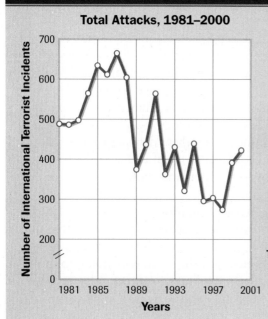

International Terrorist Attacks

Total Attacks, 1981–2000

International Casualties of Terrorism, 1995–2000

	Africa	Asia	Euroasia	Latin America	Middle East	North America	Western Europe
1995	8	5369	29	46	445	0	287
1996	80	1507	20	18	1097	0	503
1997	28	344	27	11	480	7	17
1998	5379	635	12	195	68	0	405
1999	185	690	8	9	31	0	16
2000	102	898	103	20	69	0	4
Totals	5782	9713	199	299	2190	7	1232

Source: U.S. Department of State

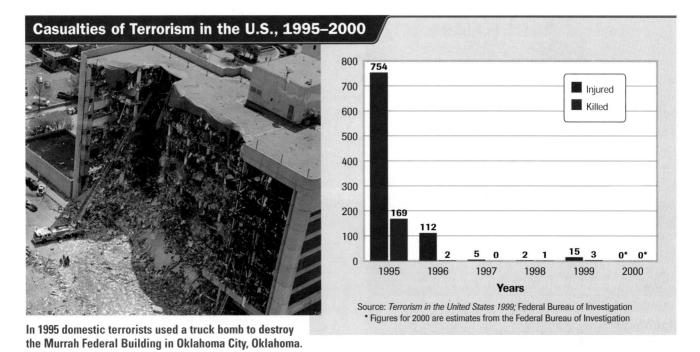

Injured
Killed

800
754
700
600
500
400
300
200
169
112
100
2 5 0 2 1 15 3 0* 0*
0
1995 1996 1997 1998 1999 2000
Years

Source: *Terrorism in the United States 1999;* Federal Bureau of Investigation
* Figures for 2000 are estimates from the Federal Bureau of Investigation

In 1995 domestic terrorists used a truck bomb to destroy the Murrah Federal Building in Oklahoma City, Oklahoma.

many African countries, and several major attacks against U.S. personnel and facilities in Africa were linked to al-Qaeda.

For example, a 1993 attack on U.S. soldiers in Somalia killed 18. In 1998, bombings at the U.S. embassies in Kenya and Tanzania left 301 dead and more than 5,000 people injured. The United States responded to these attacks with missile strikes on suspected terrorist facilities in Afghanistan, and in Sudan where bin Laden was based from 1991 to 1996.

Latin America In 2000, more terrorist attacks occurred in Latin America than in any other region of the world. Terrorist activity was particularly heavy in Colombia, a country where powerful narcotics organizations have frequently turned to violence. The Revolutionary Armed Forces of Colombia (FARC) is a left-wing guerrilla group responsible for numerous bombings, hijackings, and kidnappings of Colombians and foreign citizens. It has attacked Colombian political, military, and economic targets, as well as those with American ties. FARC is linked to narcotics traffickers.

The region where the borders of Argentina, Brazil, and Paraguay meet has become a center of Islamic extremism and terrorist financing. The Israeli embassy in Buenos Aires, Argentina, was bombed in 1992, and another Israeli target was hit in 1994.

The United States Before September 11, the most destructive act of terrorism on American soil had been the 1995 truck bombing of the Murrah Federal

Building in Oklahoma City, Oklahoma. That attack killed 168 people, but it was an act of domestic terrorism. It was carried out by an antigovernment extremist named Timothy McVeigh. Such domestic terrorists are motivated by the belief that the government has too much power to regulate people's lives.

The longest-lasting terrorist campaign by an individual in U.S. history was conducted by Theodore Kaczynski, who was known as the Unabomber. From 1978 to 1995, Kaczynski mailed bombs to business executives and scientists because he opposed the effects of modern technology on society. He killed 3 people and injured 23 others.

The attack on the World Trade Center on September 11 was not the first to have occurred there. A previous attack took place in 1993, when a van filled with explosives was detonated in the center's parking garage. Six people died and more than 1,000 were injured. The person responsible, Ramzi Yousef, was captured and imprisoned, but Osama bin Laden was suspected of being part of the plot. Another bin Laden-linked attack was the bombing of the destroyer USS *Cole* in Yemen in October 2000.

FINDING THOSE RESPONSIBLE

Immediately after the September 11 attacks, the Bush administration launched the largest criminal investigation in U.S. history. The FBI searched across the country—and the world—for clues to the identities of the suicide hijackers and those who aided them.

In an address to Congress and the nation, President George W. Bush pledged, "Whether we bring our enemies to justice or bring justice to our enemies, justice will be done." He called the terrorist attacks "acts of war" and declared that the United States would wage a war to end global terrorism. He vowed that as a part of that war, "We will pursue nations that provide aid or safe haven to terrorism. Every nation in every region now has a decision to make. Either you are with us, or you are with the terrorists."

Seven nations were on a U.S. government list of state sponsors of terrorism in 2001—Iran, Iraq, Syria, Libya, Cuba, North Korea, and Sudan. In addition, Afghanistan, Pakistan, Lebanon, and Yemen were considered major centers of terrorist activity. After the September 11 attacks, however, some of these countries, including Pakistan and Sudan, began to cooperate with the United States in hunting down those responsible.

The investigation into the September 11 attacks soon showed that top leaders in the al-Qaeda network were responsible for planning the attacks. The U.S. government then undertook a worldwide hunt for terrorists linked to al-Qaeda.

The United States built an international coalition, or alliance, to fight the war on terrorism. Canada, China, Great Britain, Pakistan, Russia, and many other nations joined the coalition. They agreed to share intelligence information, to arrest terrorists operating within their borders, and to seize the financial assets of terrorist groups. The coalition also gave support to U.S. military action in Afghanistan.

Great Britain took an especially active role in the coalition. One Londoner left a card at the U.S. embassy that reflected the surge of support that the United States received immediately after the devastating attacks: "Dear America, You supported us in two world wars. We stand with you now."

The War in Afghanistan

The U.S. government first focused its military response on Afghanistan, because that country was the home base of Osama bin Laden's al-Qaeda network. The strict Islamic regime that controlled most of Afghanistan—the Taliban—had harbored bin Laden and al-Qaeda since 1996. In return, bin Laden helped keep the Taliban in power by providing fighters in their civil war against the Northern Alliance, a coalition of anti-Taliban Afghan groups.

The United States demanded that the Taliban turn over bin Laden. After they refused, the United States began military action. The U.S. goals were to find bin Laden, to destroy al-Qaeda, and to end Taliban rule.

USA TODAY — first appeared in print 10/16/2001

The corporate structure of Terror Inc.

Osama bin Laden's terrorist organization, al-Qaeda, is organized like a business. Here is a flow chart of its structure, as of the terrorist attacks on September 11, 2001:

A key member of the military committee is Muhammad Atef, also known as Abu Hafs el Masry. The second-ranking person in al-Qaeda, he was indicted in the U.S. embassy bombings in Kenya and Tanzania in 1998. Atef was killed during the bombing of Afghanistan.

Emir
Osama bin Laden

Shura council
A policymaking council of about 30 top aides, business associates and religious scholars.
Ayman al-Zawahri

A key member of the shura council is Ayman al-Zawahri, bin Laden's top aide. The Egyptian-born surgeon, sentenced to death for terrorism in his native country, reportedly slipped into the United States in 1995 as Abdel Moez for a fundraising tour. He supplied $250,000 in 1991 for the purchase of a farm for al-Qaeda in Sudan.

Military committee — **Atef**
Responsible for training, weapons acquisition and planning attacks.

Money/business committee
Runs al-Qaeda business operations. Key members include Abu Fadhl al Makkee and Abu Hammam al Saudi.

Media committee
Ran now-defunct al-Qaeda newspaper, *Newscast*, and did public relations.

Islamic study/ fatwah committee
Issues *fatwahs*, or religious edicts, such as an edict in 1998 telling Muslims to kill Americans.

Travel office
Provides plane tickets and fake passports.

Payroll office
Pays al-Qaeda members.

Management office
Oversees money-making businesses (banks, farms).

Abu Fadhl and Abu Hammam managed the business operations and deployed assets and al-Qaeda members. Abu Fadhl was identified in court papers as "the man who bought bin Laden a salt farm in Sudan." Abu Hammam did advance work on the move to Sudan.

Source: Reported by Dennis Cauchon, USA TODAY®

By Dave Merrill, USA TODAY®

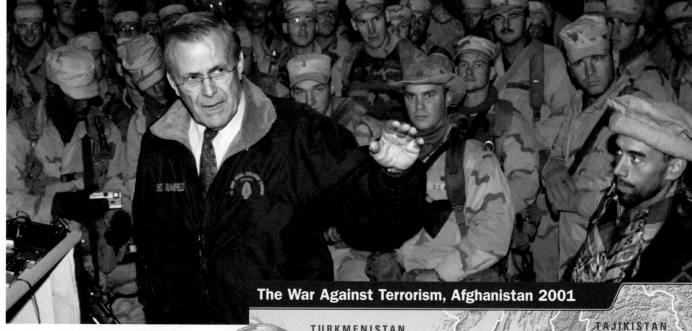

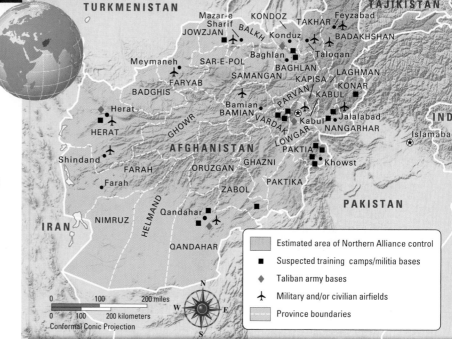

The War Against Terrorism, Afghanistan 2001

Estimated area of Northern Alliance control
■ Suspected training camps/militia bases
◆ Taliban army bases
✈ Military and/or civilian airfields
Province boundaries

Secretary of Defense Donald Rumsfeld addresses U.S. troops in Afghanistan.

In October 2001, the United States began bombing Taliban air defenses, airfields, and command centers, as well as al-Qaeda training camps. On the ground, the United States relied on anti-Taliban groups—first, the Northern Alliance and later, the Eastern Alliance—to do most of the fighting against the Taliban. These Afghan groups were assisted by U.S. air strikes against Taliban military positions and by a small number of U.S. special-forces troops and marines.

In December, the Taliban were driven from power, but the fight to destroy al-Qaeda continued. Meanwhile, the United Nations worked with the Northern Alliance and other Afghan groups to establish an interim government to replace the Taliban.

A number of nations in the antiterrorism coalition actively assisted the United States in Afghanistan, including Pakistan. The Pakistanis shared intelligence information and allowed the United States to stage military operations from their country.

Pakistan, a Muslim country, took a political risk by giving support to the United States. The Pakistani government's actions were opposed by groups within Pakistan who believed the antiterrorism campaign to be anti-Islamic.

The United States tried to make it clear to Muslim nations that the antiterrorism campaign was *not* anti-Islamic and that Americans respected the religion of Islam. For the United States, maintaining the support of moderate Muslim leaders was important to the long-term success of the war against terrorism—a war that in its next phase would target other nations that supported international terrorism.

Thinking Critically

CURRENT EVENTS
CLASSZONE.COM

• How will the graph on page US 8 change when the statistics for the year 2001 are added?

• What are some of the reasons for domestic terrorism in the various regions of the world?

WASHINGTON, D.C.—A month after the September 11 terrorist hijackings, the pilot of US Airways Flight 62 stepped from the cockpit just before takeoff, an ax in his hand. "These are extraordinary times," he told passengers over the jet's public address system. The cabin quieted. Then he rattled off three scenarios in the event of a terrorist attack aboard the San Francisco-to-Charlotte flight.

"One, someone stands up and says 'bomb,' " the pilot said. "If they tell you that, it's a lie." Second, someone pretends to be an air marshal. "We don't have an armed marshal on this flight," he said, still holding the ax. Third, someone might threaten to release some sort of biological agent. Don't be afraid, he told passengers. Pilots would land the plane before any lasting harm could be done.

In any case, the pilot advised, passengers should not back down. "Throw your shoes at them. A couple of you get up and tackle him. Beat him. I don't care." As for the ax he was holding, standard on jets in case of emergency? It's kept in the cockpit, he said. "It's very sharp. I can shave with it. For anyone to try to break into this cockpit would be a very bad idea." Then the pilot paused. "Having said all this, I'd like you all to sit back, relax, and enjoy the trip." Some passengers chuckled. Almost everyone clapped.

The stunning announcement illustrates just how much flying changed in the wake of the September 11 terrorist attacks—and how quickly Americans have grown to accept the new reality.

The Impact on American Life

 first appeared in print 9/18/2001

Airport security tightens up

As the nation's 400 airports get back to business, passengers around the country are finding tighter security. Since the Sept. 11 hijacking of four U.S. airliners, the procedures from ticket counter to gate are stiffer. Airlines are recommending that passengers arrive between two and four hours early for flights. Security measures and wait times varied widely, according to USA TODAY® reporters.

Before the Sept. 11 attack

After the attack

Security
Passengers, and their families and friends, could all go to the gate. Keys, cell phones and change could be dropped into plastic dishes or cups to one side of the metal detectors. Hand-held sensors were used if metal still detected, or sometimes a manual pat-down.

Check in
Photo ID required. Ticket agent asks "Have your bags been in your possession since you packed them?"

Curb-side luggage check-in permitted

No curb-side luggage check permitted.

Carry-on
Bags are placed on a conveyor belt and contents displayed on a screen. Security employees are trained to spot suspicious objects.

Increased use of bomb-sniffing dogs. Dogs and police officers were highly visible at Newark International.

Security
Only passengers beyond this point. Cell phones, keys, pagers and other loose objects have to be put on the conveyor belts, where they are screened, according to passengers at San Francisco and Chicago airports Monday. Knives and cutting tools prohibited. Overhead metal detectors are being used in addition to hand-held units. In Baltimore, some bags were checked for bomb dust.

Before security checkpoint
Passengers asked to show tickets and photo IDs again.

Check in
Baggage checked randomly. Photo ID required. In some cases, passengers had to exchange e-tickets for paper tickets. Passengers still asked if they have had their bags in their possession since packing.

Sources: FAA; reporting by Jack Gruber, Debbie Howlett, Martin Kasindorf, USA TODAY®; and Reed Stacey

By Frank Pompa, USA TODAY®

After the September 11 attacks, many Americans reported feeling that everything had changed—that life would never be the same. Before, Americans had viewed war as something that happened in other countries. Now they felt vulnerable, and the threat of terrorism began to affect many aspects of American life—as the experience of those on Flight 62 showed.

THE AIRLINES AND THE ECONOMY

In the wake of the terrorist attacks, the Federal Aviation Administration (FAA) shut down all airports in the United States for the first time in the nation's history. They did so to prevent any other hijackings. When the airports reopened and flights resumed a few days later, the airlines had few passengers. Some people did not feel safe flying, and others did not want to face the delays caused by tighter airport security.

The number of passengers dropped 43 percent in the days after flights resumed. The airline industry lost an estimated $5 billion in September and cut more than 100,000 jobs to reduce their costs. Congress quickly passed a $15-billion-aid package to help the industry get through the crisis. After September, airline business partially recovered. But even months later, the passenger airfleet was still flying well below capacity.

Industries related to the airlines also suffered. Travel agents, hotels, resorts, and theme parks all lost business. Also hard hit was the insurance industry, which would have to pay billions in death and property loss claims due to the attacks.

The New York Stock Exchange and other stock markets closed after the attacks and did not reopen until the following Monday. The last time the New York exchange had shut down for more than three days was in 1914, at the start of World War I. After the stock markets reopened, the Dow Jones Industrial Average suffered its biggest weekly drop since the Great Depression—14.3 percent.

Over the next few weeks, the markets began to rebound, but the economy continued to decline. Consumers spent less, and unemployment rose. Experts believed that the attacks had only worsened an economic slowdown that had begun early in 2001. They agreed that the nation was in a recession.

THE ANTHRAX THREAT

Not long after September 11th, terrorism struck America again, but in a different form. Letters containing spores of a bacterium that causes the disease anthrax were sent to persons in the news media and to members of Congress in Washington, D.C.

Anthrax bacteria can cause illness when they come in contact with skin or when inhaled. The skin form of anthrax is usually not fatal. But if anthrax bacteria are inhaled, the poisons they produce can damage body tissues. If not treated quickly, inhalation anthrax can cause death.

The threat of biological warfare became real when letters containing the anthrax bacterium (right) were sent to some members of the U.S. Congress in Washington D.C. (below) and persons in the news media after the September 11 attacks.

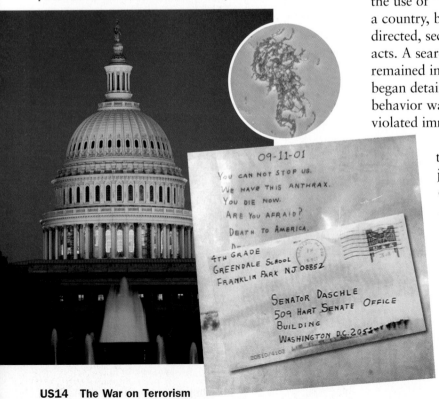

Five people who came in contact with spores from the tainted letters died of inhalation anthrax. Two were postal workers. Many others contracted the skin form of the disease. Thousands who were exposed to anthrax were treated with antibiotics.

The anthrax scare frightened many Americans. The U.S. Postal Service warned Americans to be suspicious of mail without return addresses or in strange packages and to wash their hands after handling mail. Many businesses began taking precautions.

Investigators did not immediately find a link between the anthrax letters and the September 11 attacks. Some experts believed that the anthrax letters might be the work of a lone terrorist rather than an organized group. The anthrax scare not only made Americans fearful of the mail but also of the threat of other biological or chemical weapons, such as the smallpox virus or the nerve gas sarin.

ANTITERRORISM MEASURES

The federal government warned Americans that additional terrorist attacks were likely. It then took actions to prevent such attacks. The Office of Homeland Security was created to coordinate national efforts against terrorism. Antiterrorism measures included a search for terrorists in the United States, the passage of an antiterrorism law, and the adoption of new aviation security regulations.

Searching for Terrorists The al-Qaeda network was able to carry out its terrorist attacks partly through the use of "sleepers." These are agents who move to a country, blend into a community, and then, when directed, secretly prepare for and carry out terrorist acts. A search to find any al-Qaeda terrorists who remained in the United States was started. Officials began detaining and questioning Arabs whose behavior was considered suspicious or who had violated immigration regulations.

Because the hijackers had been Arabs, the government held that the actions were justified. But some critics charged that detaining these men was unfair to the innocent and violated their civil rights. In one incident, Mohammed Irshaid, a Jordanian-born civil engineer who had lived in the United States for more than 20 years, was jailed for three weeks without being charged. His three children were American citizens. Although the incident humiliated him, he said that it "doesn't change my love of America."

President George W. Bush discusses the war against terrorism with advisers, including Vice President Dick Cheney (left) and Secretary of State Colin Powell (right).

More than three million Arab Americans live in the United States, and many were viewed with distrust by other Americans after the September 11 attacks. In one incident, three Arab Americans were taken off a plane when other passengers refused to fly with them. After questioning the men, officials allowed them to take a later flight.

Such incidents sparked debate about the need to respect civil rights while conducting searches for terrorists. The government argued that it was not unusual to curtail civil liberties during wartime in order to protect national security. This argument was also used to justify a proposal to try some terrorist suspects in military tribunals rather than in criminal courts.

Antiterrorism Law On October 26, 2001, President Bush signed into law an antiterrorism bill. The law allowed the government to
- detain foreigners suspected of terrorism for seven days without charging them with a crime
- tap all phones used by suspects and monitor their e-mail and Internet use
- make search warrants valid across states
- order U.S. banks to investigate sources of large foreign accounts
- prosecute terrorist crimes without any time restrictions or limitations

Again, critics warned that these measures would let the government infringe on people's civil rights.

Aviation Security The federal government also increased its involvement in aviation security. The Federal Aviation Administration ordered airlines to install bars on cockpit doors to prevent passengers from gaining control of planes, as the hijackers had done. Sky marshals were assigned to fly on planes; National Guard troops began patrolling airports.

In November 2001, a new aviation-security law made airport security the responsibility of the federal government. Previously, individual airports had been responsible. The law provided for a federal security force that would inspect passengers and carryon bags. It also required the screening of checked baggage.

Airline and government officials debated these and other measures for making air travel more secure. Major concerns were long delays at airports and respect for passengers' privacy. It also became clear that public debate over security measures would continue as long as the United States fights terrorism and tries to balance national security with civil rights.

Thinking Critically

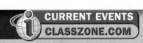
CURRENT EVENTS CLASSZONE.COM

- Is it important for the U.S. government to respect people's civil rights as it wages a war against terrorism? Why or why not?
- What has been the greatest impact of terrorism on American life, aside from the tragic deaths caused by the September 11 attacks?

Glossary

A

Aborigine (AB•uh•RIHJ•uh•nee) *n.* one of Australia's first inhabitants or their descendants. (p. 734)

absolute location *n.* the exact spot on Earth where a place is found. (p. 36)

acid rain *n.* rain or snow that carries air pollutants to Earth. (p. 386)

Aegean (ih•JEE•uhn) **Sea** *n.* a branch of the Mediterranean Sea that is located between Greece and Turkey. (p. 279)

African National Congress (ANC) *n.* a group of black Africans opposed to apartheid. (p. 562)

Afrikaner *n.* a descendant of the Dutch settlers of South Africa. (p. 561)

Ainu (EYE•noo) *n.* the descendants of Japan's early settlers from Europe. (p. 725)

alliance (uh•LY•uhns) *n.* an agreement among people or nations to unite for a common cause and to help any alliance member that is attacked. (p. 334)

Anasazi *n.* a group of Native Americans who developed a complex civilization in the U.S. Southwest. (p. 88)

Angkor Wat *n.* a Hindu temple in Cambodia, built by the Khmer people. (p. 602)

antimony *n.* a type of metal. (p. 713)

apartheid (uh•PAHRT•HYT) *n.* an official policy of racial separation formerly practiced in South Africa. (p. 516)

Arab-Israeli Wars *n.* a series of wars between 1948 and 1973 that were fought between Israel and the Arab countries of Iraq, Syria, Egypt, Jordan, and Lebanon. (p. 450)

archipelago (AHR•kuh•PEHL•uh•GOH) *n.* a group of islands. (p. 587)

armed neutrality *n.* a policy by which a country maintains military forces but does not take sides in the conflicts of other nations. (p. 385)

Aryan (AIR•ee•uhn) *n.* a member of an ethnic group that migrated from what is now southern Russia through central Asia, settling in India. (p. 592)

Aswan High Dam *n.* a dam built in 1956 by the Egyptian leader Gamal Abdel Nasser to control the flooding of the Nile River. (p. 463)

Athens *n.* the capital of Greece and once one of the most important ancient Greek city-states. (p. 280)

Austria-Hungary *n.* in the 1900s, a dual monarchy in which the Hapsburg emperor ruled both Austria and Hungary. (p. 332)

B

Bahasa (bah•HAH•suh) **Indonesian** *n.* the national language of Indonesia. (p. 651)

Bantu migration *n.* the gradual spreading of the Bantu across Africa over 2,000 years. (p. 503)

batik (buh•TEEK) *n.* a method of dyeing fabric in which any parts of the fabric not intended to be dyed are covered with wax that is later removed. (p. 653)

Berlin Wall *n.* a wire-and-concrete wall that divided Germany's East Berlin and West Berlin from 1961 to 1989. (p. 395)

bilingual *adj.* able to speak two languages. (p. 133)

Bill of Rights *n.* ten amendments to the U.S. Constitution that list specific freedoms guaranteed to every U.S. citizen. (p. 96)

Boer *n.* one of a group of Dutch colonists in South Africa or one of their descendants. (p. 561)

Boxer Rebellion *n.* a rebellion led by a group called the Boxers in China in 1900. (p. 702)

Brasília *n.* the capital of Brazil. (p. 246)

Buddhism *n.* a religion founded by Siddhartha Gautama in India in the 500s B.C. (p. 600)

bureaucracy *n.* the administration of a government through departments called bureaus. (p. 684)

C

caliph (KAY•lihf) *n.* the title used by rulers of the Muslim community from 632 until 1924. (p. 441)

capitalism *n.* an economic system in which the factories and businesses that make and sell goods are privately owned and the owners make the decisions about what goods to produce. (p. 315)

Carnival *n.* a Cuban holiday that celebrates the end of the harvest each year in July. (p. 220); *n.* a Brazilian holiday that occurs during the four days before Lent. (p. 247)

cartographer *n.* a person who makes maps. (p. 45)

cash crop *n.* a crop grown for sale. (p. 531)

caste *n.* an inherited social class of traditional Hindu society that separates people from other classes by birth, occupation, or wealth. (p. 594)

censorship *n.* the outlawing of materials that contain certain information. (p. 403)

chinampa (chee•NAHM•pah) *n.* a floating garden on which the Aztec grew crops. (p. 162)

Christianity *n.* a religion that developed out of Judaism and that is based on the life and teachings of Jesus. (p. 437)

circumnavigate *v.* to sail completely around. (p. 310)

citizen *n.* a legal member of a country. (p. 20)

citizenship *n.* the status of a citizen, which includes certain duties and rights. (p. 91)

city-state *n.* a central city and its surrounding villages, which together follow the same law, have one form of government, and share language, religious beliefs, and ways of life. (p. 279)

clan *n.* a group of families who trace their descent from a common ancestor. (p. 691)

class system *n.* a system in which society is divided into different social groups. (p. 425)

climate *n.* the typical weather of a region over a long period. (p. 75)

coalition government *n.* a government formed by political parties joining together. (p. 362)

Cold War *n.* after World War II, a period of political noncooperation between the members of NATO and the Warsaw Pact nations, during which these countries refused to trade or cooperate with each other. (p. 347)

collective farm *n.* a government-owned farm that employs large numbers of workers, often in Communist countries. (p. 345)

colonialism *n.* a system by which a country maintains colonies outside its borders. (p. 331)

Columbian Exchange *n.* the exchange of goods between Europe and its colonies in North and South America. (p. 166)

Commonwealth of Nations *n.* a group of countries, including Australia and New Zealand, that were once British colonies and that share a heritage of British law and government. (p. 736)

Communism *n.* an economic and political system in which property is owned collectively and labor is organized in a way that is supposed to benefit all people. (p. 217)

competition *n.* the rivalry among businesses to sell the most goods to consumers and make the greatest profit. (p. 106)

Constantinople *n.* the capital of the Ottoman Empire, now called Istanbul. (p. 442)

constitutional amendment *n.* a formal change or addition to the U.S. Constitution. (p. 96)

constitutional monarchy *n.* a government ruled by a king or queen whose power is determined by the nation's constitution and laws. (p. 125)

consumer *n.* a person who uses goods or services. (p. 105)

continent *n.* a landmass above water on earth. (p. 35)

cooperative *n.* a large farm on which hundreds of families work. (p. 714)

copra (KOH•pruh) *n.* dried coconut meat. (p. 738)

coup d'état (KOO day•TAH) *n.* an overthrow of a government by force. (p. 525)

Court of Human Rights *n.* the Council of Europe's court that protects the rights of all citizens in whichever of its member countries they live. (p. 370)

criollo (kree•AW•yaw) *n.* a person born in Mexico whose parents were born in Spain. (p. 175)

Crusades *n.* a series of military expeditions led by Western European Christians in the 11th, 12th, and 13th centuries to reclaim control of the Holy Lands from the Muslims. (p. 301)

Cultural Revolution *n.* a movement that Mao Zedong began in China in 1966 in an attempt to remove opposition to the Communist Party. (p. 705)

culture *n.* the beliefs, customs, laws, art, and ways of living that a group of people share. (p. 21)

culture region *n.* an area of the world in which many people share similar beliefs, history, and languages. (p. 24)

culture trait *n.* the food, clothing, technology, beliefs, language, and tools that the people of a culture share. (p. 21)

cuneiform (KYOO•nee•uh•FAWRM) *n.* a Sumerian system of writing, in which wedge-shaped symbols were used. (p. 426)

currency *n.* money used as a form of exchange. (p. 369)

czar (zahr) *n.* in Russia, an emperor. (p. 319)

D

Dalit *n.* a member of a group of people in India, formerly known as untouchables, who were outside the caste system, were considered lower than the lowest caste, and have gained some rights under India's new constitution. (p. 618)

Day of the Dead *n.* a Mexican holiday, on November 1 and 2, for honoring loved ones who have died. (p. 194)

Deccan Plateau *n.* a plateau that makes up most of southern India. (p. 586)

deforestation *n.* the process of cutting and clearing away trees from a forest. (p. 157)

delta *n.* a triangular deposit of soil at the mouth of a river. (p. 585)

democracy *n.* a government that receives its power from the people. (p. 91)

departamento (deh•pahr•tah•MEHN•taw) *n.* a Guatemalan state. (p. 223)

dependency *n.* a place governed by or closely connected with a country that it is not officially part of. (p. 203)

deposed *v.* removed from power. (p. 356)

desertification *n.* the process by which land that can be farmed or lived on turns into desert. (p. 500)

détente (day•TAHNT) *n.* a relaxing of tensions between nations. (p. 357)

developing nation *n.* a newly industrialized nation. (p. 650)

dialect *n.* a regional variety of a language. (p. 627)

dictator *n.* a person who has complete control over a country's government. (p. 207)

Diet *n.* Japan's parliament. (p. 710)

dissident *n.* a person who openly disagrees with a government's policies. (p. 403)

distribution *n.* the process of moving products to their markets. (p. 187)

diversify *v.* to conduct business activities in a variety of industries. (p. 209)

diversity *n.* variety of cultures and viewpoints. (p. 515)

doi moi (doy moy) *n.* the name of a Vietnamese policy, meaning "change for the new." (p. 658)

dowry *n.* money or property given by a bride's family to her new husband and his family. (p. 629)

Dravidian *n.* an Indian language. (p. 628)

drought *n.* a long period of time without rain. (p. 500)

dual monarchy *n.* a form of government in which one ruler governs two nations. (p. 332)

Duma (DOO•muh) *n.* one of the two houses of the Russian legislature. (p. 364)

dynasty *n.* a family of rulers. (p. 682)

E

East Timor *n.* an island nation in Southeast Asia. (p. 647)

economic indicator *n.* a measure that shows how a country's economy is doing. (p. 241)

economics *n.* the study of how resources are managed in the production, exchange, and use of goods and services. (p. 20)

economy *n.* the system by which business owners in a region use productive resources to provide goods and services that satisfy people's wants. (p. 79)

ECOWAS *n.* the Economic Community of West African States, formed in 1975 to improve trade within Western Africa and with countries outside the region. (p. 527)

Eightfold Path *n.* in Buddhism, a set of guidelines for how to escape suffering. (p. 601)

ejido (eh•HEE•daw) *n.* in Mexico, a community farm owned by the people of a village together. (p. 182)

El Niño (ehl NEE•nyaw) *n.* a current in the Pacific Ocean that results from changes in air pressure and that causes changes in weather patterns. (p. 159)

empire *n.* a nation or group of territories ruled by an emperor. (p. 287)

encomienda (ehn•kaw•MYEHN•dah) *n.* a system that the rulers of Spain established in Mexico, under which Spanish men received a Native American village to oversee and gain tribute from. (p. 176)

equal opportunity *n.* a guarantee that government and private institutions will not discriminate against people on the basis of factors such as race, religion, age, gender, or disability. (p. 90)

erosion *n.* the process by which environmental factors, such as wind, rivers, and rain, wear away soil and stone. (p. 74)

ethnic cleansing *n.* the organized killing of members of an ethnic group or groups. (p. 363)

euro *n.* the common unit of currency used by European Union countries. (p. 369)

European Community *n.* an association developed after World War II to promote economic unity among the countries of Western Europe. (p. 392)

European Union (EU) *n.* an economic and political grouping of countries in Western Europe. (p. 368)

export *n.* a product traded with or sold to another country. (p. 129)

F

factor of production *n.* one of the elements needed for production of goods or services to occur. (p. 103)

fascism (FASH•IHZ•uhm) *n.* a political philosophy that promotes a strong, central government controlled by the military and led by a powerful dictator. (p. 336)

federal government *n.* a national government. (p. 96)

fellahin (FEHL•uh•HEEN) *n.* peasant farmers in Egypt. (p. 465)

fertile *adj.* rich in resources and nutrients. (p. 419)

Fertile Crescent *n.* a region consisting of what is now Iraq, northeast Syria, and part of southeast Turkey, shaped like a crescent and having fertile soil. (p. 423)

feudalism *n.* in medieval Europe, a political and economic system in which lords gave land to less powerful nobles, called vassals, in return for which the vassals agreed to provide various services to the lords. (p. 292)

fiesta *n.* a holiday celebrated by a village or town, with events such as parades, games, and feasts. (p. 194)

First Nations *n.* in Canada, a group of descendants of the first settlers of North America, who came from Asia. (p. 120)

Five Pillars of Islam *n.* in Islam, the most important teachings of Muhammad. (p. 440)

fjord (fyawrd) *n.* a long, narrow, deep inlet of the sea located between steep cliffs. (p. 274)

Florence *n.* a city in Italy that was a bustling center of banking, trade, and manufacturing during the 14th century. (p. 302)

Four Noble Truths *n.* the central teachings of Buddhism. (p. 601)

Francophone *n.* a French-speaking person. (p. 133)

free enterprise/market economy *n.* an economy that allows business owners to compete in the market with little government interference. (p. 105)

free-trade zone *n.* an area in which goods can move across borders without being taxed. (p. 241)

French Resistance *n.* an anti-German movement in France during World War II. (p. 390)

French Revolution *n.* a revolution that began on July 14, 1789, and that led to France's becoming a republic. (p. 316)

G

Gadsden Purchase *n.* the 1853 purchase by the United States of a piece of land from northern Mexico. (p. 178)

GDP *n.* gross domestic product, or the total value of the goods and services produced in a country during a given time period. (p. 104)

geography *n.* the study of people, places, and the environment. (p. 18)

glacier *n.* a thick sheet of ice that moves slowly across land. (p. 73)

globalization *n.* the spreading of an idea, product, or technology around the world. (p. 111)

Good Friday Accord *n.* an agreement signed in 1998 by Ireland's Protestants and Catholics that established the Northern Ireland Assembly to represent voters from both groups. (p. 381)

government *n.* the people and groups within a society that have the authority to make laws, to make sure they are carried out, and to settle disagreements about them. (p. 19)

Grand National Assembly *n.* Turkey's legislature. (p. 477)

Great Barrier Reef *n.* world's largest coral reef system, located off Australia's northeastern coast. (p. 680)

Great Leap Forward *n.* a program that Mao Zedong began in China in 1958 to speed up economic development. (p. 704)

Great Rift Valley *n.* a series of broad, steep-walled valleys that stretch from the Red Sea to Mozambique. (p. 499)

Great Zimbabwe *n.* a stone city built by the Shona people, beginning in the A.D. 900s, in the area that is today Zimbabwe. (p. 547)

Green Revolution *n.* a movement that began in the late 1960s, through which genetically improved grains, pesticides, and new farming methods were introduced to farmers in developing nations. (p. 625)

guerrilla warfare *n.* nontraditional military tactics by small groups involving surprise attacks. (p. 253)

guild *n.* a business association created by people working in the same industry to protect their common interests and maintain standards within the industry. (p. 294)

H

hacienda *n.* in Spanish-speaking countries, a big farm or ranch. (p. 181)

haiku (HY•koo) *n.* a Japanese form of poetry that contains only 17 syllables. (p. 719)

haj *n.* a pilgrimage to Mecca that most Muslims try to make at least once in a lifetime (p. 457)

Han *n.* the majority ethnic group in China. (p. 720)

harambee *adj.* a Swahili term that means "pulling together" and that is used in reference to Kenyan schools built by Kenyan people rather than by the government. (p. 566)

Hausa (HOW•suh) *n.* the largest ethnic group in Nigeria. (p. 537)

Heian Age *n.* the golden age of Japanese culture, from 794 to 1185. (p. 691)

hieroglyph *n.* a picture or symbol used in hieroglyphics. (p. 161)

hieroglyphics *n.* a writing system in which pictures and symbols are used to represent words and sounds. (p. 431)

Himalayas *n.* a mountain range that stretches about 1,500 miles across south-central Asia. (p. 584)

Hinduism *n.* a religion developed in ancient India. (p. 593)

Hiroshima (HEER•uh•SHEE•muh) *n.* a Japanese city on which the United States dropped an atomic bomb in 1945. (p. 724)

history *n.* a record of the past. (p. 18)

Holocaust *n.* the organized killing of European Jews and others by the Nazis during World War II. (p. 336)

homogeneous *adj.* mostly the same. (p. 725)

human right *n.* a right to which every person is entitled. (p. 709)

hunter-gatherer *n.* a person who finds food by hunting, fishing, and gathering wild grains, fruits, and nuts. (p. 420)

Hutu *n.* the ethnic majority of Rwanda-Burundi. (p. 511)

hydroelectricity *n.* electrical power generated by water. (p. 386)

I

Igbo *n.* an ethnic group in southeastern Nigeria. (p. 537)

immigrant *n.* a person who comes to a country to take up residence. (p. 88)

imperialism *n.* the practice of one country's controlling the government and economy of another country or territory. (p. 310)

import *n.* a product brought into a country through trade or sale. (p. 130)

impressionism *n.* a style of art that creates an impression of a scene rather than a strictly realistic picture. (p. 393)

Indian National Congress *n.* in India, a congress formed in 1885 to provide a forum for Indians to discuss their problems. (p. 612)

Indo-Aryan *adj.* related to the family of languages that includes almost all European and many Indian languages. (p. 628)

Industrial Revolution *n.* a period of change beginning in the late 18th century, during which goods began to be manufactured by power-driven machines. (p. 314)

industry *n.* any area of economic activity. (p. 129)

inflation *n.* a continuing increase in the price of goods and services, or a continuing decrease in the capability of money to buy goods and services. (p. 245)

information technology *n.* technology, including computers, software, and the Internet, that helps us process and use information. (p. 624)

Institutional Revolutionary Party *n.* the most powerful political party in Mexico from the 1920s to 2000, which won every presidential election during that time. (p. 183)

interdependence *n.* the economic, political, and social dependence of culture regions on one another. (p. 26)

Iron Curtain *n.* a political barrier that isolated the peoples of Eastern Europe after World War II, restricting their ability to travel outside the region. (p. 342)

irrigation *n.* the process of bringing water to dry land. (p. 421)

Islam *n.* a religion that teaches that there is one god and that Muhammad is his prophet. (p. 438)

J

Janissary *n.* one of a group of soldiers loyal to the sultan of the Ottoman Empire. (p. 443)

Judaism *n.* the monotheistic religion founded by Abraham and whose followers are called Jews. (p. 436)

jute *n.* a fibrous plant used to make twine, bags, sacks, and burlap. (p. 623)

K

Khmer (KMAIR) *n.* an ancient ethnic group in Cambodia. (p. 602)

kibbutz (ki•Bo͞oTS) *n.* a Jewish farming village in Palestine (or present-day Israel) whose members own everything in common, sharing labor, income, and expenses. (p. 471)

kinship *n.* family relationships. (p. 555)

Kurd *n.* a member of a group of mountain people who live in Armenia, Georgia, Iran, Iraq, Lebanon, Syria, and Turkey. (p. 452)

L

labor force *n.* a pool of available workers. (p. 315)

ladino (lah•DEE•noh) *n.* a person of mixed European and Native American ancestry. (p. 205)

landform *n.* a feature of Earth's surface, such as a mountain, valley, or plateau. (p. 73)

latitude *n.* a measure of distance north or south of the equator. (p. 36)

Law of Return *n.* a law enacted in 1950 in Israel, granting Jews anywhere in the world permission to move to Israel and become citizens. (p. 472)

limited government *n.* government in which the powers of the leaders are limited. (p. 95)

London *n.* the capital of England. (p. 379)

longitude *n.* a measure of distance east or west of a line called the prime meridian. (p. 36)

M

Machu Picchu (MAH•choo PEEK•choo) *n.* an ancient stone city built by the Inca. (p. 165)

Magna Carta (MAG•nuh KAHR•tuh) *n.* a document signed by England's King John in 1215 that guaranteed English people basic rights. (p. 295)

Mahabharata (MAH•huh•BAH•ruh•tuh) *n.* an epic poem about the growth of Hinduism. (p. 627)

malnutrition *n.* poor nutrition, usually from not eating the right foods, which can result in poor health. (p. 220)

mandala (MUHN•duh•luh) *n.* in Southeast Asia, a political system in which a central ruler worked to gain support from others and used trade and business to influence others and maintain power. (p. 644)

mandate *n.* a country placed under the control of another power by international agreement. (p. 450)

Mangla Dam *n.* a dam built on the Jhelum River in northeast Pakistan to control floodwaters and to provide hydroelectricity. (p. 634)

manorialism *n.* a social system in which peasants worked on a lord's land and supplied him with food in exchange for his protection of them. (p. 293)

Maori (MOW•ree) *n.* the first inhabitants of New Zealand. (p. 733)

map projection *n.* one of the different ways of showing Earth's curved surface on a flat map. (p. 47)

maquiladora (mah•kee•lah•DAW•rah) *n.* in Mexico, a factory that imports duty-free parts from the United States to make products that it then exports back across the border. (p. 187)

market economy See **free enterprise/market economy.**

martial law *n.* temporary military rule during a time of war or a time when the normal government has broken down. (p. 617)

Masai (mah•SY) *n.* a nomadic ethnic group in Africa. (p. 547)

matrilineal society *n.* a society in which ancestry is traced through the mother's side of the family. (p. 739)

mediate *v.* to help find a peaceful solution. (p. 527)

medieval (MEE•dee•EE•vuhl) *adj.* relating to the period of history between the fall of the Roman Empire and the beginning of the modern world, often dated from 476 to 1453. (p. 291)

Mediterranean Sea *n.* an inland sea that borders Europe, Southwest Asia, and Africa. (p. 274)

Meiji Restoration *n.* in Japan, the period from 1868 to 1911, during which the country was again ruled by an emperor after hundreds of years of military rule. (p. 723)

Melanesia *n.* one of three regional island groups into which the Pacific Islands are divided. (p. 734)

mestizo (mehs•TEE•saw) *n.* a person of mixed European and Native American ancestry. (p. 175)

Micronesia *n.* one of three regional island groups into which the Pacific Islands are divided. (p. 734)

migrate *v.* to move from one area in order to settle in another. (p. 38)

military dictatorship *n.* a government ruled by a person in the military. (p. 647)

missionary *n.* a person who goes to another country to do religious and social work. (p. 509)

Mohenjo-Daro (moh•HEHN•joh•DAHR•oh) *n.* a large ancient city in the Indus River valley. (p. 592)

monsoon *n.* a seasonal wind that brings great amounts of rain. (p. 588)

Mount Everest *n.* the highest mountain peak in the world, located in the Himalayas on the border of China and Nepal. (p. 676)

Mount Fuji *n.* the tallest mountain and an active volcano in Japan. (p. 678)

Mughal Empire *n.* an empire, lasting from 1526 to 1707, that covered most of the subcontinent of India. (p. 610)

mulatto (mu•LAT•oh) *n.* a person of mixed African and European ancestry. (p. 204)

multiculturalism *n.* an acceptance of many cultures instead of just one. (p. 121)

multiparty system *n.* a political system in which two or more parties exist. (p. 565)

Muslim *n.* a follower of the religion Islam. (p. 438)

Muslim Brotherhood *n.* a fundamentalist Muslim group that believes that Egypt should be governed solely by Islamic law in order to be true to the principles of Islam. (p. 464)

Muslim League *n.* a group formed by Muslims in India in 1906 to protect their rights. (p. 612)

N

Nagasaki (NAH•guh•SAH•kee) *n.* a Japanese city on which the United States dropped an atomic bomb in 1945. (p. 724)

national identity *n.* a sense of belonging to a nation. (p. 132)

nationalism *n.* strong pride in one's nation or ethnic group. (p. 329)

nationalize *v.* to establish government control of a service or industry. (p. 188)

NATO (NAY•toh) *n.* the North Atlantic Treaty Organization, a defense alliance formed in 1949, with the countries of Western Europe, Canada, and the United States agreeing to defend one another if attacked. (p. 337)

nonrenewable resource *n.* a resource that cannot be replaced or that can be replaced only over millions of years. (p. 501)

Northern Plains *n.* plains that lie between the Himalaya Mountains and southern India. (p. 585)

O

oasis *n.* a region in a desert that is fertile because it is near a river or spring. (p. 251)

OAU *n.* the Organization of African Unity, an organization formed in 1963 to promote unity among all Africans. (p. 527)

oligarchy (AHL•ih•GAHR•kee) *n.* a government in which a few powerful individuals rule. (p. 280)

ombudsman *n.* a Swedish official who protects citizens' rights and ensures that the courts and civil service follow the law. (p. 385)

one-party system *n.* a system in which there is only one political party and only one candidate to choose from for each government position. (p. 343)

OPEC *n.* the Organization of Petroleum Exporting Countries, which decides the price and amount of oil produced each year in Iraq, Iran, Saudi Arabia, Kuwait, Venezuela, and other countries. (p. 456)

Opium War *n.* a war over the trade of the drug opium, which was fought between the Chinese and the British from 1839 to 1842. (p. 702)

Organization of American States (OAS) *n.* an organization of the nations of the Americas that encourages democracy and promotes economic cooperation, social justice, and the equality of all people. (p. 234)

Orthodox Jew *n.* a Jew who strictly follows Jewish law. (p. 473)

Ottoman Empire *n.* a Muslim empire that lasted from the early 1400s until after World War I. (p. 442)

Outback *n.* the vast, flat plain that extends across most of central Australia. (p. 679)

overgrazing *n.* a process in which animals graze grass faster than it can grow back. (p. 553)

P

pagoda *n.* a Buddhist tower built in many levels, with sculptures or carvings of Buddha on each level. (p. 652)

paleontologist *n.* a scientist who studies fossils. (p. 502)

Palestine *n.* a Southwest Asian region often called the Holy Land. (p. 450)

Pan-American *adj.* relating to all of the Americas. (p. 234)

panchayat *n.* a village council in India. (p. 618)

papyrus (puh•PY•ruhs) *n.* a paperlike material made from a reed. (p. 430)

Parliament *n.* Canada's national lawmaking body. (p. 125)

parliamentary republic *n.* a republic whose head of government, usually a prime minister, is the leader of the political party that has the most members in the parliament. (p. 361)

pastoralism *n.* a way of life in which people raise cattle, sheep, or goats as their primary economic activity. (p. 553)

patrician (puh•TRIHSH•uhn) *n.* in ancient Rome, a member of a wealthy, landowning family that claimed to be able to trace its roots back to the founding of Rome. (p. 285)

patrilineal society *n.* a society in which ancestry is traced through the father's side of the family. (p. 739)

patriotism *n.* love for one's country. (p. 91)

PEMEX *n.* *Petróleos Mexicanos,* or "Mexican Petroleum," a government agency that runs the oil industry in Mexico. (p. 188)

peninsula *n.* a body of land surrounded by water on three sides. (p. 274)

peninsular (peh•neen•soo•LAHR) *n.* a person who was born in Spain but who lived in Mexico after the Spanish took control. (p. 175)

Persian Gulf War *n.* a 1991 war between the United States and Iraq. (p. 453)

petrochemical *n.* a product made from petroleum or natural gas. (p. 457)

pharaoh (FAIR•oh) *n.* a king of ancient Egypt. (p. 431)

philosopher *n.* a person who studies and thinks about why the world is the way it is. (p. 281)

plain *n.* a large flat area of land that usually does not have many trees. (p. 275)

plateau *n.* a raised area of relatively level land. (p. 498)

plebeian (plih•BEE•uhn) *n.* a common citizen of ancient Rome. (p. 285)

polis *n.* the central city of a city-state. (p. 279)

Politburo (PAHL•iht•BYUR•oh) *n.* the group that heads a Communist party. (p. 658)

political process *n.* legal activities through which a citizen influences public policy. (p. 91)

Polynesia *n.* one of three island groups into which the Pacific Islands are divided. (p. 734)

precipitation *n.* moisture that falls to Earth, such as rain or snow. (p. 75)

primary product *n.* a raw material used to manufacture other products. (p. 456)

prime minister *n.* in a parliamentary democracy, the leader of the cabinet and often also of the executive branch. (p. 125)

private property rights *n.* the right of individuals to own land or industry. (p. 355)

privatization *n.* the process of replacing community ownership with individual, or private, ownership. (p. 186)

profit *n.* the money that remains after the costs of producing a product are paid. (p. 105)

propaganda (PRAHP•uh•GAN•duh) *n.* material designed to spread certain beliefs. (p. 354)

Protestant *n.* a member of a Christian church based on the principles of the Reformation. (p. 306)

Punjabi *n.* one of two most commonly spoken languages in Pakistan. (p. 634)

puppet government *n.* a government that is controlled by an outside force. (p. 343)

pyramid *n.* a structure with four triangular sides that rise from a rectangular base to meet at a point on top. (p. 431)

Q

Quechua (KEHCH•wuh) *n.* people who live in the Andes highlands and speak the Inca language Quechua. (p. 253)

Qur'an (kuh•RAN) *n.* the sacred text of Islam. (p. 438)

R

racism *n.* the belief that one race is inferior to another. (p. 514)

Ramadan (RAM•uh•DAHN) *n.* the ninth month of the Islamic year. (p. 457)

Reformation *n.* a 16th-century movement to change practices within the Roman Catholic Church. (p. 305)

refugee *n.* a person who flees a country because of war, disaster, or persecution. (p. 122)

Reign of Terror *n.* the period between 1793 and 1794 during which France's new leaders executed thousands of its citizens. (p. 317)

relative location *n.* the location of one place in relation to other places. (p. 37)

Renaissance *n.* an era of creativity and learning in Western Europe from the 14th century to the 16th century. (p. 302)

renewable resource *n.* a resource that can be used and replaced over a relatively short time period. (p. 501)

republic *n.* a form of government in which people rule through elected representatives. (p. 285)

reunification *n.* the uniting again of parts. (p. 396)

Riksdag (RIHKS•DAHG) *n.* Sweden's parliament. (p. 384)

Ring of Fire *n.* an area of volcanic activity along the borders of the Pacific Ocean. (p. 678)

Rio de Janeiro *n.* a city in Brazil. (p. 246)

rite of passage *n.* a special ceremony that marks the transition from one stage of life to another. (p. 534)

river system *n.* a network that includes a major river and its tributaries. (p. 74)

Rosh Hashanah (RAWSH huh•SHAW•nuh) *n.* the Jewish New Year. (p. 473)

rural *adj.* of the countryside. (p. 193)

Russian Revolution *n.* the 1917 revolution that removed the Russian monarchy from power after it had ruled for 400 years. (p. 322)

S

Sahel (suh•HAYL) *n.* a semiarid region south of the Sahara Desert. (p. 500)

samurai (SAM•uh•RY) *n.* a Japanese warrior who pledged to serve a particular lord and protect his estate. (p. 692)

sanction *n.* a penalty imposed upon a nation that is violating international law. (p. 562)

Sanskrit *n.* the classical language of India and Hinduism. (p. 592)

São Paulo *n.* a city in Brazil. (p. 246)

savanna *n.* a flat grassland in a tropical or subtropical region with scattered trees and shrubs. (p. 500)

scarcity *n.* a word economists use to describe the conflict between people's desires and limited resources. (p. 20)

Scientific Revolution *n.* a period of great scientific change and discovery during the 16th and 17th centuries. (p. 314)

scribe *n.* a professional record keeper or copier of documents. (p. 426)

secede *v.* to withdraw from a political union, such as a nation. (p. 381)

secondary product *n.* a product manufactured from raw materials. (p. 456)

secular *adj.* not specifically relating to religion. (p. 473)

sediment *n.* small fragments of rock or other materials that can be moved around by wind, water, or ice. (p. 585)

Senate *n.* the assembly of elected representatives that was the most powerful ruling body of the Roman Republic. (p. 285)

separatist *n.* a person who wants to separate from a body to which he or she belongs, such as a church or nation. (p. 127)

Shinto *n.* a Japanese religion that developed around 300 B.C. (p. 690)

shogun *n.* in feudal Japan, the emperor's chief general, who held most of the country's power. (p. 693)

Sindhi *n.* a language spoken in Pakistan. (p. 634)

single-product economy *n.* an economy that depends on just one product for the majority of its income. (p. 209)

skerry *n.* a small island. (p. 387)

socialism *n.* an economic system in which businesses and industries are owned collectively or by the government. (p. 392)

Solidarity *n.* a trade union in Poland that originally aimed to increase pay and improve working conditions and that later opposed Communism. (p. 400)

standard of living *n.* a measure of quality of life. (p. 369)

subcontinent *n.* a large landmass that is part of a continent but that has its own geographic identity. (p. 584)

subsistence farming *n.* a method of farming in which people grow food mainly to feed their households rather than to sell. (p. 531)

sugar cane *n.* a plant from which sugar is made. (p. 209)

Sumerian *n.* one of the first inhabitants of Mesopotamia. (p. 424)

supply and demand *n.* an economic concept that states that the price of a good rises or falls depending on how many people want it (demand) and depending on how much of the good is available (supply). (p. 658)

Swahili (swah•HEE•lee) *n.* a Bantu language spoken in Africa. (p. 566)

T

Taiping (ty•PIHNG) **Rebellion** *n.* the greatest of the peasant revolts that occurred in China in response to the signing of the Treaty of Nanking. (p. 702)

Taj Mahal *n.* the most famous building in India, built by the Mughal emperor Shah Jahan in the A.D. 1640s. (p. 626)

Tale of Genji, The n. the world's first novel, written by Lady Murasaki Shikibu of Japan in the 11th century. (p. 692)

Taliban *n.* a group of fundamentalist Muslims who took control of Afghanistan's government in 1996. (p. 616)

Taoism (DOW•ihz•uhm) *n.* a Chinese philosophy founded in the 200s B.C. by Lao Tzu. (p. 684)

Tarbela Dam *n.* a dam built on the Indus River to improve irrigation and flood control. (p. 634)

tariff *n.* a fee imposed by a government on imported or exported goods. (p. 369)

technology *n.* tools and equipment made through scientific discoveries. (p. 112)

Tet *n.* the Vietnamese New Year. (p. 659)

textile *n.* cloth manufactured by weaving or knitting. (p. 714)

thatch *n.* woven palm fronds, reeds, or straw used to build roofs. (p. 652)

thematic map *n.* a map that focuses on a specific idea or theme. (p. 46)

theocracy (thee•AHK•ruh•see) *n.* a government ruled by a religious leader. (p. 441)

Tiananmen (tyahn•ahn•mehn) **Square** *n.* a square in Beijing, China, where thousands of protesters gathered in demonstration and were injured or killed by the military in 1989. (p. 709)

tourism *n.* the business of helping people travel on vacations. (p. 189)

tradeoff *n.* an exchange of one benefit for another. (p. 464)

transportation barrier *n.* a geographic feature that prevents or slows transportation. (p. 131)

transportation corridor *n.* a path that makes transportation easier. (p. 131)

Treaty of Guadalupe Hidalgo *n.* a treaty that the United States forced Mexico to sign in 1848, giving Mexico's northern lands to the United States. (p. 177)

tributary *n.* a stream or river that flows into a larger river. (p. 157)

Tropical Zone *n.* the region of the world that lies between the latitudes 23°27' north and 23°27' south. (p. 158)

tungsten *n.* a type of metal. (p. 713)

Tutsi *n.* the ethnic minority of Rwanda-Burundi. (p. 511)

typhoon *n.* a hurricane that occurs in the western Pacific Ocean. (p. 678)

U

United States Constitution *n.* the document that is the foundation for all U.S. laws and the framework for the U.S. government. (p. 94)

unlimited government *n.* a government in which the leaders have almost absolute power. (p. 95)

Ural (YUR•uhl) **Mountains** *n.* a mountain range that divides Europe from Asia. (p. 275)

urban *adj.* of the city. (p. 193)

urbanization *n.* the movement of people from the countryside to cities. (p. 241)

Urdu *n.* the official language of Pakistan. (p. 634)

V

value *n.* a principle or ideal by which people live. (p. 110)

Vedas (VAY•duhz) *n.* the Books of Knowledge of the ancient Aryans, which were the basis of Hinduism. (p. 593)

vegetation *n.* plant life, such as trees, plants, and grasses. (p. 75)

veldt (vehlt) *n.* the flat grassland of Southern Africa. (p. 560)

W

Warsaw Pact *n.* a treaty signed in 1955 that established an alliance among the Soviet Union, Albania, Bulgaria, Czechoslovakia, East Germany, Hungary, Poland, and Romania. (p. 347)

weather *n.* the state of Earth's atmosphere at a given time and place. (p. 75)

West Indies *n.* the Caribbean Islands. (p. 203)

World War I *n.* a war fought from 1914 to 1918 between the Allies (Russia, France, the United Kingdom, Italy, and the United States) and the Central Powers (Austria-Hungary, Germany, Turkey, and Bulgaria). (p. 333)

World War II *n.* a war fought from 1939 to 1945 between the Axis powers (Germany Italy, and Japan) and the Allies (the United Kingdom, France, the Soviet Union, and the United States). (p. 336)

Y

Yom Kippur (YAWM KIHP•uhr) *n.* in Judaism, the Day of Atonement. (p. 473)

Yoruba (YAWR•uh•buh) *n.* an ethnic group in southwestern Nigeria. (p. 537)

Z

Zen *n.* a branch of Buddhism practiced in Japan, which emphasizes that people can achieve enlightenment suddenly. (p. 692)

ziggurat *n.* a Mesopotamian terraced pyramid in which each terrace is smaller than the one below it. (p. 424)

Zionism *n.* a movement that encouraged Jews to return to Palestine, the Jewish homeland, which many Jews call Zion. (p. 470)

zither *n.* a type of stringed instrument. (p. 719)

Zulu (ZOO•loo) *n.* an ethnic group in Africa. (p. 548)

Spanish Glossary

A

Aborigine (AB•uh•RIHJ•uh•nee) [aborigen australiano] *s.* los primeros pobladores de Australia o uno de sus descendientes. (pág. 734)

absolute location [ubicación absoluta] *s.* lugar exacto donde se halla un lugar en la Tierra. (pág. 36)

acid rain [lluvia ácida] *s.* lluvia o nieve que lleva sustancias contaminantes a la Tierra. (pág. 386)

Aegean (ih•JEE•uhn) **Sea** [mar Egeo] *s.* parte del Mar Mediterráneo ubicada entre Grecia y Turquía. (pág. 279)

African National Congress [Congreso Nacional Africano] *s.* grupo de africanos negros que se oponen al apartheid. (pág. 562)

Afrikaner [afrikander] *s.* descendiente de los primeros colonos holandeses en Sudáfrica. (pág. 561)

Ainu [ainu] *s.* descendientes de los primeros pobladores de Japón provenientes de Europa. (pág. 725)

alliance (uh•LY•uhns) [alianza] *s.* acuerdo de unión entre pueblos o naciones por una causa común y de ayuda mutua en caso de que uno sea atacado. (pág. 334)

Anasazi [anasazi] *s.* grupo de indígenas que desarrollaron una cultura compleja en el sudoeste de Estados Unidos. (pág. 88)

Angkor Wat [Angkor Wat] *s.* templo hindú en Camboya construido por el pueblo khemer. (pág. 602)

antimony [antimonio] *s.* tipo de metal. (pág. 713)

apartheid (uh•PAHRT•HYT) [apartheid] *s.* política oficial de segregación racial que se llevó a cabo anteriormente en Sudáfrica. (pág. 516)

Arab-Israeli Wars [guerras árabe-israelíes] *s.* guerras del período comprendido entre 1948 y 1973, entre Israel y los países árabes de Irak, Siria, Egipto, Jordania y el Líbano. (pág. 450)

archipelago (AHR•kuh•PEHL•uh•GOH) [archipiélago] *s.* grupo de islas. (pág. 587)

armed neutrality [neutralidad armada] *s.* política mediante la cual un país mantiene fuerzas armadas pero no participa en conflictos de otras naciones. (pág. 385)

Aryan [ario] *s.* miembro de un grupo étnico que emigró de lo que hoy es el sur de Rusia y se estableció en la India, pasando por Asia central. (pág. 592)

Aswan High Dam [presa de Aswán] *s.* dique construido en 1956 por el líder egipcio Gamal Abdel Nasser con el fin de controlar las inundaciones del río Nilo. (pág. 463)

Athens [Atenas] *s.* capital de Grecia y una de las ciudades-estado más importantes de la antigua Grecia. (pág. 280)

Austria-Hungary [Austria-Hungría] *s.* monarquía dual mediante la cual a comienzos del siglo XX el emperador de la dinastía de los Hasburgo gobernó Austria y Hungría. (pág. 332)

B

Bahasa (bah•HAH•suh) **Indonesian** [bahasa indonesia] *s.* lengua nacional de Indonesia. (pág. 651)

Bantu migration [emigración bantú] *s.* difusión gradual de los bantú por África durante más de 2000 años. (pág. 503)

batik (buh•TEEK) [batik] *s.* método de teñido mediante el cual las partes de la tela que no se deben teñir son cubiertas con cera que luego se remueve. (pág. 653)

Berlin Wall [Muro de Berlín] *s.* pared de cemento y alambre que desde 1961 a 1989 dividía la parte este de Berlín de la parte oeste. (pág. 395)

bilingual [bilingüe] *adj.* que puede hablar dos idiomas. (pág. 133)

Bill of Rights [Declaración de Derechos] *s.* las diez enmiendas a la Constitución de los Estados Unidos que enumeran libertades específicas garantizadas a todos los ciudadanos estadounidenses. (pág. 96)

Boer [boer] *s.* miembro de un grupo de colonos holandeses o sus descendientes establecidos en Sudáfrica. (pág. 561)

Boxer Rebellion [Rebelión Bóxer] *s.* rebelión llevada a cabo en 1900 por un grupo denominado Bóxer en la China. (pág. 702)

Brasília [Brasilia] *s.* capital de Brasil. (pág. 246)

Buddhism [budismo] *s.* religión fundada por Siddhartha Gautama en la India en el siglo VI a. de C. (pág. 600)

bureaucracy [burocracia] *s.* administración de un gobierno que se divide en departamentos o ministerios. (pág. 684)

C

caliph (KAY•lihf) [califa] *s.* título que recibían los gobernantes de las sociedades musulmanas desde el año 632 hasta 1924. (pág. 441)

capitalism [capitalismo] *s.* sistema económico en el cual las empresas y comercios que fabrican y venden productos y mercancías son de propiedad privada; los dueños de dichas empresas y comercios deciden lo que desean producir y vender. (pág. 315)

Carnival [carnaval] *s.* feriado cubano que celebra cada año el fin de la cosecha en el mes de julio. (pág. 220); *s.* feriado brasileño de cuatro días anterior al comienzo de la cuaresma. (pág. 247)

cartographer [cartógrafo] *s.* persona que hace mapas. (pág. 45)

cash crop [cultivo industrial] *s.* cultivo que se produce para la venta. (pág. 531)

caste [casta] *s.* clase social heredada que separa a las personas de otras clases por motivos de nacimiento, ocupación o riqueza. (pág. 594)

censorship [censura] *s.* prohibición de materiales que contienen cierta información. (pág. 403)

chinampa (chee•NAHM•pah) *s.* huerta flotante en la que los aztecas sembraban sus cultivos. (pág. 162)

Christianity [cristianaismo] *s.* religión derivada del judaísmo, basada en la vida y las enseñanzas de Jesús. (pág. 437)

circumnavigate [circunnavegar] *v.* dar la vuelta alrededor de algo en una nave. (pág. 310)

citizen [ciudadano] *s.* habitante legal de un país. (pág. 20)

citizenship [ciudadanía] *s.* estado de un ciudadano que incluye derechos y obligaciones. (pág. 91)

city-state [ciudad estado] *s.* ciudad central y sus aldeas aledañas que acatan las mismas leyes, tienen una sola forma de gobierno y comparten una lengua, creencias religiosas y estilos de vida. (pág. 279)

clan [clan] *s.* grupo de personas con lazos familiares que tienen en común los mismos ancestros. (pág. 691)

class system [sistema de clases] *s.* sistema mediante el cual se divide la sociedad en diferentes grupos sociales. (pág. 425)

climate [clima] *s.* condición típica de la atmósfera en determinada región. (pág. 75)

coalition government [gobierno de coalición] *s.* gobierno formado por la unión de partidos políticos. (pág. 362)

Cold War [Guerra Fría] *s.* período político posterior a la Segunda Guerra Mundial, caracterizado por la falta de cooperación y relaciones comerciales entre los países miembros de la OTAN y las naciones del Pacto de Varsovia. (pág. 347)

collective farm [granja colectiva] *s.* granja que pertenece al gobierno, que emplea a gran número de trabajadores generalmente en países comunistas. (pág. 345)

colonialism [colonialismo] *s.* sistema mediante el cual un país mantiene colonias en otras partes del mundo. (pág. 331)

Columbian Exchange [intercambio colombino] *s.* intercambio de mercancías entre Europa y sus colonias en América. (pág. 166)

Commonwealth of Nations [Mancomunidad Británica de Naciones] *s.* grupo de países, que incluye Australia y Nueva Zelandia, que fueron colonias británicas y que en la actualidad comparten la herencia británica en el campo jurídico y de gobierno. (pág. 736)

Communism [comunismo] *s.* sistema político y económico en el cual la propiedad es colectiva y la actividad laboral es organizada de manera de beneficiar a todos los individuos. (pág. 217)

competition [competencia] *s.* rivalidad entre empresas por vender la mayor cantidad de productos y mercaderías a los consumidores y por obtener el mayor beneficio. (pág. 106)

Constantinople [Constantinopla] *s.* capital de Turquía durante Del Imperio otomano, ahora llamada Estambul. (pág. 442)

constitutional amendment [enmienda constitucional] *s.* cambio formal a la constitución de los Estados Unidos. (pág. 96)

constitutional monarchy [monarquía constitucional] *s.* gobierno encabezado por un rey o reina, cuyo poder está determinado por la constitución y leyes de la nación. (pág. 125)

consumer [consumidor] *s.* persona que usa productos o servicios. (pág. 105)

continent [continente] *s.* masa continental sobre agua en la Tierra. (pág. 35)

cooperative [cooperativa] *s.* grande establecimiento agrícola donde trabajan centenares de familias. (pág. 714)

copra (KOH•pruh) [medula de coco] *s.* substancia seca que forma parte del coco de la palma. (pág. 738)

coup d'état (KOO day•TAH) [golpe de estado] *s.* acción de derrocar o hacer caer un gobierno por la fuerza. (pág. 525)

Court of Human Rights [Corte de Derechos Humanos] *s.* corte que protege los derechos de ciudadanos que habitan en países miembros (pág. 370)

criollo (kree•AW•yaw) *s.* persona nacida en México cuyos padres provienen de España. (pág. 175)

Crusades [las cruzadas] *s.* serie de expediciones militares dirigidas por cristianos de Europa occidental en los siglos XI, XII y XIII, para apoderarse de nuevo de las Tierras Santas, en poder de los musulmanes. (pág. 301)

Cultural Revolution [Revolución Cultural proletaria] *s.* movimiento iniciado en 1966 por Mao Tse Tung en China, en un intento de eliminar la oposición del Partido Comunista. (pág. 705)

culture [cultura] *s.* conjunto de creencias, costumbres, leyes, formas artísticas y de vida compartidas por un grupo de personas. (pág. 21)

culture region [región cultural] *s.* territorio donde muchas personas comparten creencias, historia y lenguas similares. (pág. 24)

culture trait [característica culturale] *s.* alimento, vestimenta, tecnología, creencia, lengua u otro elemento compartido por un pueblo o cultura. (pág. 21)

cuneiform (KYOO•nee•uh•FAWRM) [escritura cuneiforme] *s.* sistema sumerio de escritura que usa símbolos con forma de cuña. (pág. 426)

currency [moneda] *s.* sistema que sirve para medir el valor de las cosas que se intercambian. (pág. 369)

czar (zahr) [zar] *s.* emperador ruso. (pág. 319)

D

Dalit [dalit] *s.* miembro de un grupo de personas en la India, también conocidas como los "intocables", fuera del sistema de castas y considerados por debajo de la casta inferior, que adquirieron algunos derechos bajo la nueva constitución de la India. (pág. 618)

Day of the Dead [Día de los Muertos] *s.* feriado mexicano del 1 al 2 de noviembre en honor a los seres queridos que han muerto. (pág. 194)

Deccan Plateau [meseta de Dekán] *s.* meseta que ocupa casi todo el sur de la India. (pág. 586)

deforestation [deforestación] *s.* proceso mediante el cual se cortan árboles y se van eliminando bosques. (pág. 157)

delta [delta] *s.* depósito de tierra de forma triangular en la boca de un río. (pág. 585)

democracy [democracia] *s.* sistema de gobierno mediante el cual los gobernantes reciben el poder del pueblo. (pág. 91)

departamento (deh•pahr•tah•MEHN•taw) *s.* nombre que reciben los estados en Guatemala. (pág. 223)

dependency [territorio dependiente] *s.* lugar gobernado o que está estrechamente conectado con un país del cual no forma parte. (pág. 203)

deposed [depuesto] *v.* removido del poder. (pág. 356)

desertification [desertificación] *s.* proceso mediante el cual la tierra que antes podía cultivarse o era habitable se convierte en un desierto. (pág. 500)

détente (day•TAHNT) [distensión] *s.* disminución de la tensión entre países. (pág. 357)

developing nation [nación en vías de desarrollo] *s.* nación recién industrializada. (pág. 650)

dialect [dialecto] *s.* forma regional de una lengua. (pág. 627)

dictator [dictador] *s.* persona que tiene el control absoluto del gobierno de un país. (pág. 207)

Diet [Dieta] *s.* nombre que recibe el parlamento de Japón. (pág. 710)

dissident [disidente] *s.* persona que abiertamente muestra desacuerdo con la política de un gobierno. (pág. 403)

distribution [distribución] *s.* proceso mediante el cual se transporta la mercancía a los mercados. (pág. 187)

diversify [diversificar] *v.* llevar a cabo actividades comerciales en una variedad de industrias. (pág. 209)

diversity [diversidad] *s.* variedad de culturas y puntos de vista. (pág. 515)

doi moi (doy moy) [doi moi] *s.* nombre que recibe una política de renovación y reforma llevada a cabo en Vietnam. (pág. 658)

dowry [dote] *s.* dinero o propiedad que entrega la familia de la novia a su futuro esposo y su familia. (pág. 629)

Dravidian [lengua drávida] *s.* lengua india. (pág. 628)

drought [sequía] *s.* período largo de falta de lluvia. (pág. 500)

dual monarchy [monarquía dual] *s.* gobierno en que un solo jefe gobierna dos naciones. (pág. 332)

Duma (DOO•muh) [Duma] *s.* una de las dos cámaras de la legislatura rusa. (pág. 364)

dynasty [dinastía] *s.* familia de soberanos. (pág. 682)

E

East Timor [Timor Oriental] *s.* nación situada en una isla en el sudeste asiático. (pág. 647)

economic indicator [indicador económico] *s.* medida que muestra el estado de la economía de un país. (pág. 241)

economics [economía] *s.* estudio del uso de los recursos naturales y del modo de producción, intercambio y utilización de los productos, mercaderías y servicios. (pág. 20)

economy [economía] *s.* sistema de administrar recursos de producción en una región con el fin de proveer productos y servicios que satisfagan las necesidades humanas. (pág. 79)

ECOWAS [CEDEAO, Comunidad Económica de los Estados de África Occidental] *s.* comunidad económica formada por los estados de África occidental en 1975 para mejorar el comercio en la región del África occidental y con países fuera de la región. (pág. 527)

Eightfold Path [Óctuple Sendero] *s.* conjunto de reglas en la religión budista que enseñan cómo escapar del sufrimiento. (pág. 601)

ejido s. granja comunitaria en México que pertenece colectivamente a los habitantes de un pueblo o localidad. (pág. 182)

El Niño s. corriente del océano Pacífico que surge de los cambios en la presión atmosférica y que causa cambios meteorológicos. (pág. 159)

empire [imperio] *s.* nación o conjunto de territorios gobernados por un emperador. (pág. 287)

encomienda s. sistema establecido en México por los gobernantes españoles mediante el cual los españoles controlaban comunidades indígenas y recaudaban tributo. (pág. 176)

equal opportunity [igualdad de oportunidades] *s.* garantía de que el gobierno e instituciones privadas no discriminarán en contra de ciertas personas por motivos de raza, religión, edad o sexo. (pág. 90)

erosion [erosión] *s.* desgaste del terreno y suelo producido por factores ambientales tales como el viento, la lluvia y los ríos. (pág. 74)

ethnic cleansing [limpieza étnica] *s.* matanza sistemática (genocidio) de uno o varios grupos étnicos que conforman una minoría. (pág. 363)

euro [euro] *s.* unidad monetaria de los países miembros de la Unión Europea. (pág. 369)

European Community [Comunidad Europea] *s.* asociación creada después de la Segunda Guerra Mundial para promover la unidad económica entre los países de Europa occidental. (pág. 392)

European Union [Unión Europea] *s.* asociación económica y política de países de Europa occidental. (pág. 368)

export [exportación] *s.* mercadería que se vende a otro país. (pág. 129)

F

factor of production [factor de producción] *s.* elemento necesario para producir mercaderías y ofrecer servicios. (pág. 103)

fascism (FASH•IHZ•uhm) [fascismo] *s.* filosofía que promueve un gobierno centralista fuerte, controlado por el ejército y dirigido por un dictador poderoso. (pág. 336)

federal government [gobierno federal] *s.* gobierno nacional. (pág. 96)

fellahin (FEHL•uh•HEEN) [fellahín] *s.* nombre que recibe un agricultor en Egipto. (pág. 465)

fertile [fértil] *adj.* abundante en recursos y nutrientes. (pág. 419)

Fertile Crescent [Media Luna Fértil] *s.* región comprendida entre lo que hoy es Irak, el nordeste de Siria y parte del sudeste de Turquía, que tiene la forma de un creciente o medialuna y que posee tierras fértiles. (pág. 423)

feudalism [feudalismo] *s.* sistema político y económico de la Europa medieval en el que los señores feudales repartían tierras a miembros de la nobleza menos poderosos, llamados vasallos, quienes, a cambio de éstas, se comprometían a brindar varios servicios a los señores feudales. (pág. 292)

fiesta *s.* feriado celebrado por una comunidad o pueblo, con desfiles, juegos y banquetes. (pág. 194)

First Nation [Primera Nación] *s.* nombre que reciben en Canadá los descendientes de los primeros pobladores en Norteamérica que provenían de Asia. (pág. 120)

Five Pillars of Islam [los cinco pilares del Islam] *s.* las enseñanzas más importantes de Mahoma en la religión musulmana. (pág. 440)

fjord (fyawrd) [fiordo] *s.* entrada larga y estrecha del mar formada entre acantilados abruptos. (pág. 274)

Florence [Florencia] *s.* ciudad italiana que durante el siglo XIV mantuvo una dinámica actividad bancaria, comercial y manufacturera. (pág. 302)

Four Noble Truths [las cuatro nobles verdades] *s.* las enseñanzas más importantes del budismo. (pág. 601)

Francophone [francófono] *s.* persona que habla francés. (pág. 133)

free enterprise/market economy [librecambismo/economía de libre mercado] *s.* economía que permite a empresarios y comerciantes competir en el mercado con poca interferencia del gobierno. (pág. 105)

free-trade zone [zona de libre comercio] *s.* área en la que tanto personas como mercaderías pueden circular más allá de las fronteras sin que esta actividad sea gravada con impuestos. (pág. 241)

French Resistance [Resistencia francesa] *s.* en Francia, un movimiento antialemán durante la Segunda Guerra Mundial. (pág. 390)

French Revolution [Revolución francesa] *s.* revolución que comenzó el 14 de julio de 1789 y tuvo como resultado la conversión de Francia en una república. (pág. 316)

G

Gadsden Purchase [Compra de Gadsden] *s.* compra mediante la cual los Estados Unidos adquirieron en 1853 parte del territorio del norte de México. (pág. 178)

GDP [PIB, Producto Interno Bruto] *s.* valor total de los productos y servicios producidos en un país durante un período determinado. (pág. 104)

geography [geografía] *s.* estudio de los pueblos, lugares y el medio ambiente. (pág. 18)

glacier [glaciar] *s.* espesas formaciones de hielo que se mueven lentamente por la tierra. (pág. 73)

globalization [globalización] *s.* difusión de una idea, producto o tecnología por todo el mundo. (pág. 111)

Good Friday Accord [Acuerdo del Viernes Santo] *s.* acuerdo firmado por los protestantes y católicos de Irlanda del Norte que estableció la Asamblea de Irlanda del Norte, asamblea esta que representa a los votantes de ambos grupos. (pág. 381)

government [gobierno] *s.* los individuos y grupos en una sociedad que tienen la autoridad de crear leyes y hacerlas cumplir, y de resolver desacuerdos que puedan surgir con respecto a ellas. (pág. 19)

Grand National Assembly [Gran Asamblea Nacional] *s.* poder legislativo de Turquía. (pág. 477)

Great Barrier Reef [Gran Barrera de Arrecife/Coral] *s.* arrecife de coral más grande del mundo, ubicado al noreste de la costa australiana. (pág. 680)

Great Leap Forward [Gran Salto Adelante] *s.* programa llevado a cabo por Mao Zedong en China en 1958 para acelerar el desarrollo económico. (pág. 704)

Great Rift Valley [Valle de la Gran Depresión] *s.* sucesión de extensos valles profundos que se extienden desde el Mar Rojo hasta Mozambique. (pág. 499)

Great Zimbabwe [Gran Zimbabue] *s.* ciudad en Zimbabue construida por los shona a principios del siglo X a. de C. y hecha de piedra. (pág. 547)

Green Revolution [revolución verde] *s.* movimiento que empezó a fines de la década de los 60 y que introdujo granos mejorados con ingeniería genética en la agricultura de naciones en vías de desarrollo. (pág. 625)

guerrilla warfare [guerrilla] *s.* tácticas militares no tradicionales llevadas a cabo por grupos pequeños que realizan ataques sorpresivos. (pág. 253)

guild [gremio] *s.* asociación creada por personas que trabajan en una misma industria, con el fin de proteger sus intereses comunes y mantener ciertos criterios y principios aplicables a la industria. (pág. 294)

H

hacienda s. en países hispanos, finca o granja de gran tamaño. (pág. 181)

haiku (HY•koo) [haiku] s. forma de poesía japonesa que tiene sólo 17 sílabas. (pág. 719)

haj [haj] s. peregrinación a la Meca que la mayoría de los musulmanes intenta hacer por lo menos una vez en su vida. (pág. 457)

Han [han] s. etnia principal en China. (pág. 720)

harambee [harambee] *adj.* término en swahili que significa cooperar, que se usa para referirse a las escuelas construidas por los kenianos y no por el gobierno de Kenia. (pág. 566)

Hausa (HOW•suh) [hausa] s. etnia más numerosa en Nigeria. (pág. 537)

Heian Age [Período de Heian] s. época de oro de la cultura japonesa, desde 794 hasta 1185. (pág. 691)

hieroglyph [jeroglífico] s. dibujo y símbolo de la escritura jeroglífica. (pág. 161)

hieroglyphics [jeroglíficos] s. sistema de escritura que utiliza dibujos y símbolos para representar palabras y sonidos. (pág. 431)

Himalayas [El Himalaya] s. cadena montañosa cuya extensión es de aproximadamente 1500 millas en el sur de Asia. (pág. 584)

Hinduism [hinduismo] s. religión desarrollada en la antigua India. (pág. 593)

Hiroshima (HEER•uh•SHEE•muh) [Hiroshima] s. ciudad japonesa en donde Estados Unidos arrojó una bomba atómica en 1945. (pág. 724)

history [historia] s. un registro de los acontecimientos del pasado. (pág. 18)

Holocuast [Holocausto] s. matanza sistemática (genocidio) de los judíos europeos y otros por el partido nazi durante la Segunda Guerra Mundial. (pág. 336)

homogeneous [homogéneo] *adj.* sin diferencias en la mayor parte. (pág. 725)

human right [derecho humano] s. derecho que pertenece a toda persona. (pág. 709)

hunter gatherer [cazador y recolector] s. persona que procura alimentos mediante la caza y la recolección de granos y frutas salvajes. (pág. 420)

Hutu [hutu] s. mayoría étnica de Rwanda-Burundi. (pág. 511)

hydroelectricity [electricidad hidráulica] s. energía eléctrica producida por el agua. (pág. 386)

I

Igbo [igbo] s. grupo étnico del sudeste de Nigeria. (pág. 537)

immigrant [inmigrante] s. persona que llega a un país y allí se establece. (pág. 88)

imperialism [imperialismo] s. práctica mediante la cual un país controla el gobierno y la economía de otro país o territorio. (pág. 310)

import [importación] s. mercadería y producto que se compra del extranjero. (pág. 130)

impressionism [impresionismo] s. estilo de arte que crea una impresión de algo en lugar de una obra con características concretas. (pág. 393)

Indian National Congress [Congreso Nacional Indio] s. congreso formado en 1885 en la India, donde los habitantes podían debatir sus problemas. (pág. 612)

Indo-Aryan [indoario] *adj.* que pertenece a la familia de lenguas que incluye a todas las lenguas europeas y muchas lenguas indias. (pág. 628)

Industrial Revolution [Revolución industrial] s. período de cambio en el siglo XVIII que dio lugar a la fabricación de productos por máquinas. (pág. 314)

industry [industria] s. sector o rama de actividad económica. (pág. 129)

inflation [inflación] *s.* aumento continuo del precio de mercaderías y servicios, o disminución continua de la capacidad de la moneda de comprar mercaderías y servicios. (pág. 245)

information technology [tecnología informática] *s.* tecnología como computadoras, software y la Internet, que sirve para procesar y usar la información. (pág. 624)

Institutional Revolutionary Party [PRI, Partido Revolucionario Institucional] *s.* partido político mexicano más poderoso desde 1920 hasta 2000, período en que ganó todas las elecciones presidenciales. (pág. 183)

interdependence [interdependencia] *s.* dependencia económica, política y social que mantienen las sociedades de diversas regiones culturales. (pág. 26)

Iron Curtain [Cortina de Hierro] *s.* barrera política que aisló los países de Europa del Este luego de la Segunda Guerra Mundial, limitando la capacidad de movimiento y tránsito fuera de esta región. (pág. 342)

irrigation [irrigación] *s.* proceso mediante el cual se riega el terreno seco. (pág. 421)

Islam [Islam] *s.* religión que enseña que hay un dios y que Mahoma es su profeta. (pág. 438)

J

Janissary [jenízaro] *s.* miembro del grupo de soldados leales al sultán del Imperio otomano. (pág. 443)

Judaism [judaísmo] *s.* primera religión monoteísta fundada por Abraham y cuyos seguidores se denominan judíos. (pág. 436)

jute [yute] *s.* planta fibrosa que se usa para hacer cordel, bolsas, sacos y arpillera. (pág. 623)

K

Khmer (KMAIR) [khmer] *s.* antigua etnia en Camboya. (pág. 602)

kibbutz (ki•BŏoTS) [kibutz] *s.* pueblo o comunidad judía de agricultores en Palestina (o lo que hoy es Israel), cuyos miembros poseen todo en forma colectiva y comparten la labor agrícola, el ingreso y los gastos. (pág. 471)

kinship [parentesco] *s.* relación entre miembros de una familia. (pág. 555)

Kurd [kurdo] *s.* habitante que vive en las montañas de Armenia, Georgia, Irán, Irak, Líbano, Siria y Turquía. (pág. 452)

L

labor force [fuerza laboral] *s.* trabajadores disponibles. (pág. 315)

ladino s. persona de descendencia mixta, con sangre europea e indígena. (pág. 205)

landform [accidente geográfico] *s.* característica del suelo o terreno, como montañas, valles y mesetas. (pág. 73)

latitude [latitud] *s.* distancia norte-sur con relación al ecuador, de la superficie terrestre. (pág. 36)

Law of Return [Ley de Retorno] *s.* ley sancionada en 1950 mediante la cual se otorga permiso a los judíos de cualquier parte del mundo para inmigrar a Israel y convertirse en ciudadanos. (pág. 472)

limited government [gobierno limitado] *s.* gobierno en que los gobernantes tienen poderes limitados. (pág. 95)

London [Londres] *s.* capital de Inglaterra. (pág. 379)

longitude [longitud] *s.* distancia este-oeste de un punto de la Tierra, a partir de la línea inicial llamada primer meridiano (meridiano de Greenwich). (pág. 36)

M

Machu Picchu (MAH•choo PEEK•choo) *s.* antigua ciudad de piedra construida por los incas. (pág. 165)

Magna Carta (MAG•nuh KAHR•tuh) [Carta Magna] *s.* documento firmado por el rey Juan de Inglaterra en 1215 que garantizó los derechos básicos de las personas en ese país. (pág. 295)

Mahabharata (MAH•huh•BAH•ruh•tuh) [*Mahabharata*] *s.* poema épico sobre la expansión del hinduismo. (pág. 627)

malnutrition [desnutrición] *s.* mala nutrición debida a la falta de alimentos nutritivos que puede causar mala salud. (pág. 220)

mandala (MUHN•duh•luh) [mandala] *s.* sistema político en el sudeste de Asia en el que el gobernante con poder central intentó obtener apoyo de otros y recurrío al comercio para ejercer influencia y mantener el poder. (pág. 644)

mandate [protectorado] *s.* país puesto bajo el control de otro por medio de un acuerdo internacional. (pág. 450)

Mangla Dam [presa Mangla] *s.* dique construido en el río Jhelum en el nordeste de Pakistán con el fin de controlar las aguas y proveer energía hidroeléctrica. (pág. 634)

manorialism [régimen señorial] *s.* sistema social en el que campesinos trabajan las tierras de un señor, a cambio de protección y seguridad. (pág. 293)

Maori (MOW•ree) [maorí] *s.* los primeros pobladores de Nueva Zelandia. (pág. 733)

map projection [proyección cartografía] *s.* una de las diversas maneras de mostrar la curvatura de la Tierra en una superficie plana. (pág. 47)

maquiladora *s.* fábrica en México que importa partes sin arancel aduanero de los Estados Unidos para fabricar productos que luego envía de vuelta a través de la frontera. (pág. 187)

market economy Ver **free enterprise.**

martial law [ley marcial] *s.* sistema temporal de gobierno militar durante tiempos de guerra o cuando el gobierno está en crisis. (pág. 617)

Masai (mah•SY) [masai] *s.* grupo étnico en África. (pág. 547)

matrilineal society [sociedad matrilineal] *s.* sociedad en la que sólo la línea materna se tiene en cuenta para determinar el árbol genealógico. (pág. 739)

mediate [mediar] *v.* ayudar en un conflicto para encontrar soluciones de paz. (pág. 527)

medieval (MEE•dee•EE•vuhl) [medieval] *adj.* que pertenece al período de la historia comprendido entre la caída del Imperio romano y el comienzo del mundo moderno, aproximadamente desde 476 a 1453. (pág. 291)

Mediterranean Sea [mar Mediterráneo] *s.* mar interno que bordea Europa, el sudoeste de Asia y África. (pág. 274)

Meiji Restoration [Restauración Meiji] *s.* período japonés comprendido entre 1868 y 1911 durante el cual Japón fue gobernado nuevamente por un emperador después de siglos de gobierno militar. (pág. 723)

Melanesia [Melanesia] *s.* uno de los tres grupos regionales de islas en el océano Pacífico. (pág. 734)

mestizo *s.* persona de descendencia mixta, con sangre europea e indígena. (pág. 175)

Micronesia [Micronesia] *s.* uno de los tres grupos regionales de islas en el océano Pacífico. (pág. 734)

migrate [migrar] *v.* irse de un área para establecerse en otra. (pág. 38)

military dictatorship [dictadura militar] *s.* gobierno de una persona militar. (pág. 647)

missionary [misionero] *s.* persona que va a otro país para transmitir enseñanzas religiosas y realizar obras de bien. (pág. 509)

Mohenjo-Daro (moh•HEHN•joh•DAHR•oh) [Mohenjo-Daro] *s.* ciudad antigua de gran tamaño ubicada en el valle del río Indo. (pág. 592)

monsoon [monzón] *s.* viento de estación que trae gran cantidad de lluvias. (pág. 588)

Mount Everest [monte Everest] *s.* pico más alto del Himalaya y en el mundo, ubicado en las fronteras de China y Nepal. (pág. 676)

Mount Fuji [monte Fuji] *s.* montaña más alta en Japón. (pág. 678)

Mughal Empire [Imperio mogol] *s.* imperio que duró de 1526 hasta 1707 y que comprendió la mayor parte del subcontinente de la India. (pág. 610)

mulatto [mulato] *s.* persona con descendencia mixta, de sangre europea y africana. (pág. 204)

multiculturalism [multiculturalismo] *s.* la aceptación de muchas culturas en vez de una solamente. (pág. 121)

multiparty system [sistema pluripartidista] *s.* sistema político en donde existe dos o más partidos. (pág. 565)

Muslim [musulmán] *s.* seguidor de la religión islámica. (pág. 438)

Muslim Brotherhood [Hermandad Musulmana] *s.* grupo musulmán fundamentalista que cree que Egipto debe ser gobernado solamente por la ley islámica para cumplir con los principios del Islam. (pág. 464)

Muslim League [Liga Musulmana] *s.* grupo formado por musulmanes en la India en 1906, establecido para proteger sus derechos. (pág. 612)

N

Nagasaki (NAH•guh•SAH•kee) [Nagasaki] *s.* ciudad japonesa en donde Estados Unidos arrojó una bomba atómica en 1945. (pág. 724)

national identity [identidad nacional] *s.* sentimiento de pertenencia a una nación. (pág. 132)

nationalism [nacionalismo] *s.* intenso orgullo por el país o grupo étnico propio. (pág. 329)

nationalize [nacionalizar] *v.* pasar al control gubernamental un servicio o industria. (pág. 188)

NATO (NAY•toh) [OTAN, Organización del Tratado del Atlántico Norte] *s.* alianza de defensa que agrupa a los países de Europa occidental, Canadá y Estados Unidos, que acuerdan la defensa común en caso de ataque. (pág. 337)

nonrenewable resource [recurso no renovables] *s.* recurso que no se puede sustituir o que se puede sustituir sólo tras miles o millones de años. (pág. 501)

Northern Plains [llanuras del a norte] *s.* llanuras que se extienden entre el sistema montañoso del Himalaya y el sur de la India. (pág. 585)

O

oasis [oasis] *s.* región fértil en un desierto que se formó alrededor de un río o manantial. (pág. 251)

OAU [OUA, Organización de la Unidad Africana] *s.* organización formada en 1963 para promover la unidad entre todos los africanos. (pág. 527)

oligarchy (AHL•ih•GAHR•kee) [oligarquía] *s.* gobierno de sólo unos pocos individuos poderosos. (pág. 280)

ombudsman [defensor del pueblo] *s.* funcionario del gobierno sueco que protege los derechos de los ciudadanos y asegura que los tribunales y la administración pública cumplan con la ley. (pág. 385)

one-party system [sistema monopartidista] *s.* sistema donde sólo se puede votar por un partido político y por un candidato para cada puesto de gobierno. (pág. 343)

OPEC [OPEP, Organización de Países Exportadores de Petróleo] *s.* organización que determina el precio y la cantidad de petróleo que se deberá producir cada año en Irak, Irán, Arabia Saudita, Kuwait y Venezuela. (pág. 456)

Opium War [Guerra del Opio] *s.* guerra por el control del comercio del opio entre China y Gran Bretaña desde 1839 a 1842. (pág. 702)

Organization of American States (OAS) [OEA, Organización de los Estados Americanos] *s.* organización de todas las naciones americanas, que promueve la democracia y la cooperación económica, la justicia social y la igualdad entre los pueblos. (pág. 234)

Orthodox Jew [judío ortodoxo] *s.* judío que cumple estrictamente con la ley judía. (pág. 473)

Ottoman Empire [Imperio otomano] *s.* imperio musulmán, desde comienzos del siglo XV hasta la década de 1920. (pág. 442)

outback [llanura desértica] *s.* vasta superficie plana que se extiende por casi toda la zona central de Australia. (pág. 679)

overgrazing [pastoreo excesivo] *s.* proceso mediante el cual se lleva a pastar demasiado ganado sin permitir que la tierra recupere su vegetación. (pág. 553)

P

pagoda [pagoda] *s.* torre budista de muchos niveles, con esculturas o imágenes del Buda talladas en cada nivel. (pág. 652)

paleontologist [paleontólogo] *s.* científico que estudia los fósiles. (pág. 502)

Palestine [Palestina] *s.* región en el sudoeste de Asia, comúnmente llamada Tierra Santa. (pág. 450)

Pan-American [panamericano] *adj.* relativo a todas las Américas. (pág. 234)

panchayat [panchayati] *s.* consejo rural en India. (pág. 618)

papyrus (puh•PY•ruhs) [papiro] *s.* material semejante al papel, hecho de un junco. (pág. 430)

Parliament [Parlamento] *s.* cuerpo legislativo nacional de Canadá. (pág. 125)

parliamentary republic [república parlamentaria] *s.* república cuyo jefe de estado, en general un primer ministro, es el líder del partido político que tiene la mayoría de representantes en el parlamento. (pág. 361)

pastoralism [pastoreo] *s.* forma de subsistencia mediante la cría de ganado, ovejas o cabras. (pág. 553)

patrician (puh•TRIHSH•uhn) [patricio] *s.* miembro de familia adinerada y hacendada en la antigua Roma, que afirmaba que sus orígenes se remontan a la época de la fundación de Roma. (pág. 285)

patrilineal society [sociedad patrilineal] *s.* sociedad en las que sólo la línea paterna se tiene en cuenta para determinar el árbol genealógico. (pág. 739)

patriotism [patriotismo] *s.* amor por el país propio. (pág. 91)

PEMEX *s.* Petróleos Mexicanos, agencia gubernamental que administra la industria petrolera en México. (pág. 188)

peninsula [península] *s.* territorio rodeado de agua en tres de sus lados. (pág. 274)

peninsular s. persona que nació en España pero vivió en México luego de la conquista de los españoles. (pág. 175)

Persian Gulf War [Guerra del Golfo Pérsico] *s.* guerra entre Estados Unidos e Irak, en 1991. (pág. 453)

petrochemical [producto petroquímico] *s.* producto derivado del petróleo crudo y gas natural. (pág. 457)

pharaoh (FAIR•oh) [faraón] *s.* antiguo rey egipcio. (pág. 431)

philosopher [filósofo] *s.* persona que estudia y piensa sobre el mundo y su naturaleza. (pág. 281)

plain [llanura] *s.* superficie extensa y plana que suele no tener muchos árboles. (pág. 275)

plateau [meseta] *s.* área plana situada a cierta altura sobre el nivel del mar. (pág. 498)

plebeian (plih•BEE•uhn) [plebeyo] *s.* ciudadano corriente (sin título de nobleza) en la antigua Roma. (pág. 285)

polis [polis] *s.* ciudad central de una ciudad estado. (pág. 279)

Politburo (PAHL•iht•BYUR•oh) [Politburo] *s.* grupo que encabeza un partido comunista. (pág. 658)

political process [proceso político] *s.* actividades permitidas por la ley mediante las cuales el ciudadano influye en las políticas públicas. (pág. 91)

Polynesia [Polinesia] *s.* uno de los tres grupos regionales de islas en océano Pacífico. (pág. 734)

precipitation [precipitación] *s.* humedad como la lluvia o la nieve que cae a la Tierra. (pág. 75)

primary product [producto primario] *s.* materia prima. (pág. 456)

prime minister [primer ministro] *s.* en una democracia parlamentaria, líder del gabinete y frecuentemente de la administración ejecutiva. (pág. 125)

private property rights [derechos de propiedad privada] *s.* derechos individuales de ser propietario de bienes raíces, campos o industrias. (pág. 355)

privatization [privatización] *s.* proceso mediante el cual la propiedad que pertenece a la comunidad se convierte en propiedad privada o individual. (pág. 186)

profit [ganancia] *s.* dinero que sobra luego de pagar el costo de producir un producto. (pág. 105)

propaganda (PRAHP•uh•GAN•duh) [propaganda] *s.* material cuyo objetivo es difundir ciertas creencias. (pág. 354)

Protestant [protestante] *s.* miembro de una iglesia cristiana fundada de acuerdo a los principis de la Reforma. (pág. 306)

Punjabi [punjabí] *s.* lengua hablada en Pakistán. (pág. 634)

puppet government [gobierno títere] *s.* gobierno que hace lo que le indica un poder exterior. (pág. 343)

pyramid [pirámide] *s.* estructura con cuatro lados triangulares que se erige de una base rectangular y se junta con un vértice común en la parte superior. (pág. 431)

Q

Quechua (KEHCH•wuh) *s.* habitante de los Andes que habla una lengua inca del mismo nombre. (pág. 253)

Qur'an (kuh•RAN) [Corán] *s.* texto sagrado del Islam. (pág. 438)

R

racism [racismo] *s.* creencia de que una raza es inferior a otra. (pág. 514)

Ramadan (RAM•uh•DAHN) [Ramadán] *s.* noveno mes del año islámico. (pág. 457)

Reformation [Reforma] *s.* movimiento del siglo XVI que se propuso cambiar las prácticas de la Iglesia Católica. (pág. 305)

refugee [refugiado] *s.* persona que huye de un país a raíz de una guerra, catástrofe, o porque es objeto de persecuciones. (pág. 122)

Reign of Terror [reino del Terror] *s.* período comprendido entre 1793 y 1794 durante el cual las nuevas autoridades en Francia ejecutaron miles de ciudadanos. (pág. 317)

relative location [ubicación relativa] *s.* ubicación de un lugar en relación con otros. (pág. 37)

Renaissance *s.* período de creatividad y de aprendizaje en Europa occidental entre los siglos XIV y XVI. (pág. 302)

renewable resource [recurso renovable] *s.* recurso que puede usarse y reemplazarse luego de un relativamente corto período. (pág. 501)

republic [república] *s.* forma de gobierno controlado por sus cuidadanos a través de representantes elegidos por los cuidadanos. (pág. 285)

reunification [reunificación] *s.* acción de unificar nuevamente las partes. (pág. 396)

Riksdag (RIHKS•DAHG) *s.* parlamento sueco. (pág. 384)

Ring of Fire [Cinturón de Fuego del Pacífico] *s.* área de actividad volcánica en el océano Pacífico. (pág. 678)

Rio de Janeiro *s.* ciudad brasileña. (pág. 246)

rite of passage [rito de paso] *s.* ceremonia especial que marca la transición de una etapa de la vida a otra. (pág. 534)

river system [sistema fluvial] *s.* red que incluye ríos principales y sus tributarios. (pág. 74)

Rosh Hashanah (RAWSH huh•SHAW•nuh) [Rosh Hashana] *s.* año nuevo judío. (pág. 473)

rural [rural] *adj.* que pertenece al campo. (pág. 193)

Russian Revolution [Revolución rusa] *s.* revolución de 1917 que eliminó la monarquía rusa del poder luego de 400 años de vigencia. (pág. 322)

S

Sahel (suh•HAYL) [Sahel] *s.* región semiárida en el sur del Sahara. (pág. 500)

samurai (SAM•uh•RY) [samurai] *s.* guerrero japonés que mediante juramento presta servicio a un señor particular, protegiendo su propiedad. (pág. 692)

sanction [sanción] *s.* multas impuestas en un país que viola la ley internacional. (pág. 562)

Sanskrit [sánscrito] *s.* lengua clásica de la India y del hinduismo. (pág. 592)

São Paulo [San Pablo] *s.* ciudad brasileña. (pág. 246)

savanna [sabana] *s.* llanura de regiones tropicales y subtropicales con escasos árboles y vegetación. (pág. 500)

scarcity [escasez] *s.* palabra usada por los economistas para describir el conflicto que existe entre el deseo de los seres humanos y los recursos limitados para satisfacerlo. (pág. 20)

Scientific Revolution [Revolución científica] *s.* período de grandes cambios científicos y descubrimientos durante los siglos XVI y XVII. (pág. 314)

scribe [escriba] *s.* profesional que se encarga de archivar o copiar documentos. (pág. 426)

secede [separarse] *v.* independizarse de una unidad política, como una nación. (pág. 381)

secondary product [producto secundario] *s.* producto manufacturado con materias primas. (pág. 456)

secular [secular] *adj.* no relacionado con ninguna religión. (pág. 473)

sediment [sedimento] *s.* pequeños fragmentos de roca que son movidos por el viento, el agua o el hielo. (pág. 585)

Senate [Senado] *s.* asamblea más poderosa de la República romana, cuyos representantes eran elegidos. (pág. 285)

separatist [separatista] *s.* persona que desea separarse del cuerpo al que pertenece, como la iglesia o la nación. (pág. 127)

Shinto [shinto] *s.* religión japonesa que se desarrolló alrededor de 300 a. de C. (pág. 690)

shogun [shogun] *s.* jefe militar del emperador japonés, en la época feudal, que ejercía el mayor poder. (pág. 693)

Sindhi [sindhi] *s.* lengua que se habla en Pakistán. (pág. 634)

single-product economy [economía de un solo producto] *s.* economía cuya mayor parte de los ingresos depende de un solo producto. (pág. 209)

skerry [arrecife] *s.* islote. (pág. 387)

socialism [socialismo] *s.* sistema económico en donde algunos negocios e industrias le pertenecen a una cooperativa o al gobierno. (pág. 392)

Solidarity [Solidaridad] *s.* sindicato polaco cuya finalidad inicial fue aumentar el salario, mejorar las condiciones laborales de los trabajadores y luego oponerse al Comunismo. (pág. 400)

standard of living [nivel de vida] *s.* forma de medir la calidad de vida. (pág. 369)

subcontinent [subcontinente] *s.* gran masa territorial que es parte de un continente pero que posee su propia identidad geográfica. (pág. 584)

subsistence farming [agricultura de subsistencia] *s.* método de agricultura mediante el cual los agricultores cultivan alimentos principalmente para alimentar a sus familias en vez de venderlos. (pág. 531)

sugar cane [caña de azúcar] *s.* planta de la que se extrae el azúcar. (pág. 209)

Sumerian [sumerio] *s.* uno de los primeros pobladores de la Mesopotamia. (pág. 424)

supply and demand [oferta y demanda] *s.* concepto económico que establece que el precio de un producto sube o baja según la cantidad de personas que lo deseen (demanda) y según la disponibilidad del mismo (oferta). (pág. 658)

Swahili (swah•HEE•lee) [swahili] *s.* lengua bantú africana. (pág. 566)

T

Taiping (ty•PIHNG) **Rebellion** [rebelión Taiping] *s.* la mayor insurrección campesina que ocurrió en China a raíz de la firma del Tratado de Nanking. (pág. 702)

Taj Mahal [Taj Majal] *s.* la construcción más famosa de la India, construida por el emperador mogol Sha Jahan, en la década de 1640. (pág. 626)

Tale of Genji, The [*Cuento de Genji*] *s.* primera novela de la literatura universal, escrita por la japonesa Murasaki Shikibu en el siglo XI. (pág. 692)

Taliban [talibán] *s.* grupo musulmán fundamentalista que tomó el poder en Afganistán en 1996. (pág. 616)

Taoism (DOW•IHZ•uhm) [taoísmo] *s.* filosofía china fundada en el siglo III a. de C. por Lao Tzu. (pág. 684)

Tarbela Dam [presa de Tarbela] *s.* dique construido en el río Indo para el control de aguas e irrigación. (pág. 634)

tariff [arancel aduanero] *s.* tarifa o suma de dinero impuesto por el gobierno en productos que se importan o exportan. (pág. 369)

technology [tecnología] *s.* herramientas o equipos que se crean a partir de ciertos descubrimientos. (pág. 112)

Tet [Tet] *s.* año nuevo vietnamita. (pág. 659)

textile [textil] *s.* material que se produce mediante el tejido de fibras. (pág. 714)

thatch [techo de paja] *s.* hojas de palmeras, cañas o paja que se usan para construir techos. (pág. 652)

thematic map [mapa temático] *s.* mapa que se centra en una idea o tema particular. (pág. 46)

theocracy (thee•AHK•ruh•see) [teocracia] *s.* gobierno encabezado por una autoridad religiosa. (pág. 441)

Tiananmen (tyahn•ahn•mehn) **Square** [Plaza de Tiananmen] *s.* plaza en Beijing, China, donde miles de manifestantes fueron heridos o matados por el ejército en 1989. (pág. 709)

tourism [turismo] *s.* industria que estimula a la gente a viajar por placer. (pág. 189)

tradeoff [contrapartida] *s.* la renuncia de ciertos beneficios a cambio de otros. (pág. 464)

transportation barrier [barrera al transporte] *s.* obstáculo que impide el transporte o lo disminuye. (pág. 131)

transportation corridor [vía de transporte] *s.* camino que facilita el transporte. (pág. 131)

Treaty of Guadalupe Hidalgo [Tratado de Guadalupe Hidalgo] *s.* tratado que Estados Unidos exigió a México que firmara en 1848, mediante el cual México cedió a Estados Unidos su territorio en el norte. (pág. 177)

tributary [tributario] *s.* arroyo o río que confluye en otro río de mayor caudal. (pág. 157)

Tropical Zone [Zona Tropical] *s.* región del mundo comprendida entre las latitudes 23°27' al norte y 23°27' al sur. (pág. 158)

tungsten [tungsteno] *s.* un metal. (pág. 713)

Tutsi [tutsi] *s.* etnia minoritaria en Rwanda-Burundi. (pág. 511)

typhoon [tifón] *s.* huracán muy frecuente del océano Pacífico occidental. (pág. 678)

U

United States Constitution [Constitución de Estados Unidos] *s.* documento que fundamenta todas las leyes del gobierno de Estados Unidos y constituye su marco jurídico. (pág. 94)

unlimited government [gobierno ilimitado] *s.* gobierno en el que las autoridades ejercen la mayor parte del poder. (pág. 95)

Ural (YUR•uhl) **Mountains** [Montes Urales] *s.* cadena montañosa que divide Europa de Asia. (pág. 275)

urban [urbano] *adj.* que pertenece a la ciudad. (pág. 193)

urbanization [urbanización] *s.* movimiento de personas del campo a la ciudad. (pág. 241)

Urdu [urdu] *s.* lengua oficial en Pakistán. (pág. 634)

V

value [valor] *s.* principio e ideal básico de las personas. (pág. 110)

Vedas (VAY•duhz) [Vedas] *s.* libros sagrados que contienen el conocimiento de los antiguos arios y en los cuales se basa el hinduismo. (pág. 593)

vegetation [vegetación] *s.* conjunto de plantas, arbustos, árboles y hierbas. (pág. 75)

veldt (vehlt) [estepa meridional africana] *s.* pradera del sur de África. (pág. 560)

W

Warsaw Pact [Pacto de Varsovia] *s.* tratado firmado en 1955 que estableció una alianza entre la Unión Soviética, Albania, Bulgaria, Checoslovaquia, Alemania Oriental, Hungría, Polonia y Rumania. (pág. 347)

weather [tiempo] *s.* estado atmosférico cercano a la Tierra en un momento y lugar determinados. (pág. 75)

West Indies [Indias Occidentales/las Antillas] *s.* islas del Caribe. (pág. 203)

World War I [Primera Guerra Mundial] *s.* guerra de 1914 a 1918 entre los aliados (Rusia, Francia, el Reino Unido, Italia y los Estados Unidos) y las potencias centrales (Imperio autro-húngaro, Alemania, Turquía y Bulgaria). (pág. 333)

World War II [Segunda Guerra Mundial] *s.* guerra de 1939 a 1945 entre las potencias del Eje (Alemania, Italia y Japón) y los aliados (el Reino Unido, Francia, la Unión Soviética y los Estados Unidos). (pág. 336)

Y

Yom Kippur (YAWM KIHP•uhr) [Yom Kippur] *s.* Día de la Expiación (purificación) en la religión judía. (pág. 473)

Yoruba (YAWR•uh•buh) [yoruba] *s.* grupo étnico en el sudoeste de Nigeria. (pág. 537)

Z

Zen [zen] *s.* rama del budismo que se practica en Japón, que hace hincapié en el hecho de que el ser humano puede alcanzar el iluminismo repentinamente. (pág. 692)

ziggurat [zigurat] *s.* pirámide de la región mesopotámica, formada por terrazas, cada una de las cuales es más pequeña que la de abajo. (pág. 424)

Zionism [sionismo] *s.* movimiento que fomenta el deseo de los judíos de volver a Palestina, la tierra natal judía, que muchos judíos llaman Sión. (pág. 470)

zither [cítara] *s.* instrumento de cuerda. (pág. 719)

Zulu (ZOO•loo) [zulú] *s.* grupo étnico africano. (pág. 548)

Index

An *i* preceding a page reference in italics indicates that there is an illustration, and usually text information as well, on that page. An *m* or a *c* preceding an italic page reference indicates a map or a chart, as well as text information on that page.

C

freedom rides, *i739*
free enterprise, 105
Freeman, Cathy, *i732, i737*
free trade, 107, 739
Free-Trade Zone of the Americas, 241
French and Indian War, 120–121
French-Canadian culture, 127
French Polynesians, 736
French Resistance, 390
French Revolution, 232, 233, 316–317
fringing reefs, 680
fruit, *m240*
Fuji, Mount, *i678*
Fujimori, Alberto, *i253*
Fukuoka Dome, *i726*
fundamentalism, 458, 616
fur trading, 128

G

Gadsden Purchase, 178, *m178*
Gagarin, Yuri, *i353, i354*
Galápagos Islands, *i36*, 39
Galbraith, John Kenneth, 637
Galilee, 436
Galilei, Galileo, *i314*
Gama, Vasco da, 309
Gambia River, *i524*
Gandhi, Indira, 618
Gandhi, Mohandas, 96, *i612, i613*,
    618, 630
Ganges River, *i37, i581, i585, m593*,
    i606–607, i609
ganuwar Amina, i536
Garcia, Andy, 85
García Márquez, Gabriel, 242
Gaul, 286
Gaulle, Charles de, 390, *i390*, 391
Gdańsk, Poland, *i399*
generalization, making, *c283*, 297
Genghis Khan, 682
geography, 18–19, 35–40
geometry, *i46*
geosynchronous satellites, *i93*
Germany, *i35*, 394–397
    as member of EU, *c368*
Ghana, 505, *c512*, 533
ghats, *i606–607*
Ghats, 586, *i606–607*
Gilgamesh, i427
Giuliani, Rudy, US5
glaciers, 37, 73, *m80*
gladiators, *i258–259*

globalization, 111
Global Positioning System, *i43*, 45
global warming, 158, 586
globe, *i46*
Globe Theater, *i382*
glyphs. *See* hieroglyphs.
Gobi Desert, *i677*
gold, *i128, m365*, 505, *i560*, 599
Good Friday Accord, 381
Good Hope, Cape of, 309
Gorbachev, Mikhail, 360, *i360*
gorilla, *c541*
Gospels, 436
government, 19, 103
    of Brazil, 244
    of Guatemala, 221–223
    limited, 95
    of Mexico, 183–184
    of South America, 234
    of United States, 95–98
    unlimited, 95, 234
grain, *m240*
Gran Colombia, *c233*
Grand Banks, 129
Grand Canal, 686
Grand Canyon, 39, *i72*, 74
Grand National Assembly, 477
granite, 461
graphs
    interpreting, *i244*
    reading, *i49, i176, i195, i199*
Grass, Günter, 397
grassland, *c38*, 67, *m76, m365*
Great Barrier Reef, 680
Great Britain, 379–383
    antiterrorism coalition and, US10
Great Depression, 723
Great Enclosure, 547
Great European Plain, 275, 277
Great Kanto Earthquake, 723
Great Lakes, 122
Great Leap Forward, 704–705
Great Plains, 72
Great Rift Valley, 499
Great Seal of the U.S., *i88*
Great Sphinx, *i466*
Great Wall of China, *i662–663*, 686
Great Zimbabwe, 547
Greece
    ancient, 278–282
    as member of EU, *c368*
Greenland, 70, 73

Green Revolution, 625, 651
Greenwich, England, 27, 41
Grenada, *i201*
Grenadines, *c148–149*
Grito de Dolores, 176, 177
gross domestic product (GDP), *c104*,
    223, *c244, c554*
"ground zero." *See* September 11
    terrorist attack.
Guadalajara, Mexico, 190
Guadalcanal Island, 723
Guadalupe Hidalgo, Treaty of,
    177, *m178*
Guam, 735
guano, *i250*
Guantanamo Bay, 216
Guatemala, *i160*, 161, 162, *i200–201*,
    c214, i221
guerrilla warfare, 252–253
guilds, 294
guillotine, 317
Gujarati, *m627*
Gulf Stream, *m297*
gunpowder, 611, *i684*
Gupta Dynasty, 581, 595, *m596*
Gutenberg, Johannes, *i305, i372*
Guyana, *c148–149, c241*
Guzmán, Abimael, 253

H

haciendas, i181, 182
Hadar, Ethiopia, *i545*
Haida, 120
Haifa, Israel, 457
haiku, 719
Haiti, *c148–149*, 203, 205
haj, i457
half-timber architecture, *i397*
Hammurabi, *i423*
Han, 679, 720
Han Dynasty, *c682*, 685
Hangzhou, China, 686
harambee schools, 566
Harappan civilization, 591
Harrison, George (Australian
    prospector), *i560*
Harrison, John, 43
Hatshepsut, *i432*
Hausa, *i536, m537*
Havana, *i216*
Hawaiian Creole, 25
health care, 219, 366, 704

Acknowledgments

Text Credits

Chapter 4, page 100: "Coney" from *Subway Swinger* by Virginia Schonborg, copyright © 1970 by Virginia Schonborg. Used by permission of HarperCollins Publishers.

Chapter 4, page 100: "Knoxville, Tennessee" from *Black Feeling, Black Talk, Black Judgment* by Nikki Giovanni. Copyright 1968, 1970 by Nikki Giovanni. Reprinted by permission of HarperCollins Publishers Inc.

page 101: "Scenic" from *Collected Poems, 1953–1993* by John Updike, copyright © 1993 by John Updike. Used by permission of Alfred A. Knopf, a division of Random House, Inc.

Chapter 9, page 239: "Chilean Earth" from *A Gabriela Mistral Reader,* translation copyright 1993 by Maria Giachetti. Reprinted by permission of White Pine Press.

page 249: Copyright © 2000 by Houghton Mifflin Company, Reproduced by permission from *The American Heritage Dictionary of the English Language, Fourth Edition.*

Chapter 10, page 281: Quote by Herakleitos, translated by Guy Davenport, from *7 Greeks,* copyright © 1995 by Guy Davenport. Reprinted by Sales Territory: U.S./Canadian rights only.

Chapter 12, page 340: "The Giant's Causeway" from *Irish Fairy Tales and Legends* retold by Una Leavy. Copyright © 1996 by The Watts Publishing Group Ltd.

Chapter 15, page 427: Quote from *Everyday Life in Babylonia and Assyria* by H. W. F. Saggs. Copyright © 1965 by B. T. Batsford.

Chapter 16, page 468: "Thread by Thread" by Bracha Serri, translated by Shlomit Yaacobi and Nava Mizrahi, from *The Space Between Our Footsteps: Poems and Paintings from the Middle East,* selected by Naomi Shihab Nye. Copyright © 1998.

Chapter 19, page 558: "My Father's Farm" text copyright © 1995 by Isaac Olaleye from *The Distant Talking Drum: Poems from Nigeria* by Isaac Olaleye. Published by Wordsong/Boyds Mills Press, Inc. Reprinted by permission.

Chapter 23, page 683: Quote from "Analects," page 57 from *The Essential Confucius,* translated by Thomas Cleary. Copyright © 1992 by Thomas Cleary. Reprinted by permission of HarperCollins Publishers Inc.

page 688: From *Echoes of the White Giraffe* by Sook Nyul Choi. Copyright © 1993 by Sook Nyul Choi. Reprinted by permission of Houghton Mifflin Company. All rights reserved.

Art Credits

Beverly Doyle 28; John Edwards Studio 81; Ken Goldammer 12; Nenad Jakesevic 163, 164, 168, 381, 404, 434, 614; Rich McMahon 44, 323; Gary Overacre 340–341; Matthew Pippin xiv, 236–237, 420, 431, 460–461, 517, 550–551, 592, 706–707, 719. All other artwork created by Publicom, Inc.

Map Credits

This product contains proprietary property of **MAPQUEST.COM** Unauthorized use, including copying, of this product is expressly prohibited.

Photography Credits

Cover *left* Joe McDonald/Corbis; *center* Copyright © R. Richardson/H. Armstrong Roberts; *right* Marc Chamberlain/Stone/GettyImages; *bottom* K. Horgan/NASA/Stone/GettyImages; **ii–iii** NASA/K. Horgan/Stone/GettyImages; **ii** *top left* Joe McDonald/Corbis; *top right* R. Richardson/H. Armstrong Roberts; **iii** *top* Marc Chamberlain/Stone/GettyImages; **vi** *bottom* NASA; *children* (See page 14 for full credits); **vii** *left* Terry Wild Studio; *bottom* Copyright © Panoramic Images; *top* D. Robert and Lorri Franz/Corbis; *right* Copyright © SuperStock; **viii** *top* Michel Zabe/Art Resource, New York; *center* AFP/Corbis; *bottom* Staffan Widstrand/Corbis; **ix** *top left* Erich Lessing/Art Resource, New York; *bottom left* Dave Bartruff/Corbis; *bottom right* Hulton|Archive/Getty Images; *top* Erich Lessing/Art Resource, New York; *top right* Reunion des Musées Nationaux/Art Resource, New York; *center right* Scott Gilchrist/Archivision.com; **x** *top left* S. Bavister/Robert Harding Picture Library; *bottom left* John Noble/Corbis; *bottom* John Launois/Black Star Publishing/PictureQuest; *bottom right* AFP/Corbis; *top* Copyright © Brannhage/Premium/Panoramic Images; **xi** *bottom left* Archivo Iconografico, S. A./Corbis; *bottom* Copyright © IFA/Bruce Coleman; *top center* Carmen Redondo/Corbis; *top right* Ashmolean Museum, Oxford, England/The Bridgeman Art Library; **xii** *top left* John Noble/Corbis; *center left* Charles and Josette Lenars/Corbis; *bottom left* Copyright © Boyd Norton/The Image Works; *top right* Giraudon/Art Resource, New York; **xiii** *center left* Brian A. Vikander/Corbis; *bottom* Wolfgang Kaehler/Corbis; *center right* Caroline Penn/Corbis; *top right* Paul Almasy/Corbis; **xiv** *top* Reunion des Musées Nationaux/Art Resource, New York; *bottom* N. Blythe/Robert Harding Picture Library; **xv** *top* Quadrillion/Corbis; *center* James L. Amos/Corbis; *bottom* Eric Crichton/Bruce Coleman/PictureQuest; *bottom right* Michael S. Yamashita/Corbis; **S12** Reprinted with the permission of the *St. Louis Post Dispatch,* 2002; **S13** Copyright © Tribune Media Services, Inc. All rights reserved. Reprinted with permission; **S26** Hulton|Archive/Getty Images; **S29** The Granger Collection, New York; **S30** Victoria & Albert Museum, London/Art Resource, New York; **S32** Mary Evans Picture Library.

UNIT ONE

2–3 NASA; **4** *bottom right* NOAA; *left* Copyright © Owen Franken/Stock Boston/PictureQuest; *top right* Science Museum/Science and Society Picture Library, London.

Chapter 1

14 *top left* Brian A. Vikander/Corbis; *top center* Owen Franken/Corbis; *bottom left* Tim Thompson/Corbis; *center left* Kevin Schafer/Corbis; *bottom center* Maria Taglienti/The Image Bank/GettyImages; *center right* James A. Sugar/Corbis; *bottom right* Nicholas deVore III/Photographers Aspen/PictureQuest; *top right* Dean Conger/Corbis; **15** *top* John Callahan/Stone/GettyImages; *bottom left* The Purcell Team/Corbis; *center left* Helen Norman/Corbis; *center* Nik Wheeler/Corbis; *bottom center* Dennis Degnan/Corbis; *center right* Neil Rabinowitz/Corbis; *bottom right* Martin Rogers/Corbis; **16** *top* Copyright © Jim West; *bottom* K. Gilham/Robert Harding Picture Library; **17** *top* Picture Finders/eStock Photography/PictureQuest; *bottom* The Military Picture Library/Corbis; **18** *bottom* Thomas Hoepker/Magnum/PictureQuest; *top* Copyright © Ellen Senisi/The Image Works; **19** *left* Oliver Benn/Stone/GettyImages; *right* Copyright © Alon Reininger/Contact Press Images; *center* Copyright © Alex Farnsworth/The Image Works; **20** *top right* Copyright © Jim West; *bottom left* Richard Drew/AP/ Wide World Photos; **21** NASA/ Roger Ressmeyer/Corbis; **22** Joseph Sohm/Visions of America, LLC/PictureQuest; **23** *bottom* Joe Sohm, Chromosohm/Stock Connection/PictureQuest; *top* Scott Teven/Stock Connection/ PictureQuest; **24** *right* Hulton|Archive/Getty Images; *left* Lindsay Hebberd/Corbis; **26** *left* Dean Conger/Corbis; *right* K. Gilham/Robert Harding Picture Library; *center* Chris Andrews Publications/Corbis; **30** *bottom left* Picture Finders/eStock Photography/PictureQuest.

Chapter 2

32–33 Copyright © SuperStock; **33** *top* NASA; **34** *top* Christopher Morris/Black Star Publishing/PictureQuest; *bottom* David Muench/Stone/GettyImages; **35** *left* The Granger Collection, New York; **36** Schafer and Hill/Stone/GettyImages; **37** *top* Christopher Morris/Black Star Publishing/PictureQuest; *bottom* World Perspectives/Stone/GettyImages; **38** Copyright © Eastcott-Momatiuk/The Image Works; **39** David Muench/Stone/GettyImages; **42** *top left* Ethnic Art Institute of Micronesia; *top right* National Maritime Museum Picture Library, London; *bottom right* Royalty Free/Corbis; **43** *bottom* Austrian Archives/Corbis; *center right, top* National Maritime Museum Picture Library, London; *center left* Reproduced with permission of Garmin Corporation; **45** *right* The Granger Collection, New York; **47** The Newberry Library/The Granger Collection, New York; **50** David Muench/ Stone/GettyImages; **51** NASA.

UNIT TWO

52–53 Copyright © Panoramic Images.

Chapter 3

66–67 Paul A. Souders/Corbis; **67** *top* James Randklev/Corbis; **68** *bottom* Michael Melford/The Image Bank/ GettyImages; *top* Raymond Gehman/Corbis; **69** *right* Corbis; *left* Pat O'Hara/Corbis; **70** Michael Melford/ The Image Bank/GettyImages; **71** *top* D. Robert and Lorri Franz/Corbis; *center* Bettmann/Corbis; *bottom* Bettmann/Corbis; **72** *right* Paul A. Souders/Corbis; *left* Copyright © Didier Dorval/Masterfile; **73** M. L. Fuller and the U.S. Geological Society; **74** Paul A. Souders/Corbis; **75** Copyright © F. Hoffman/The Image Works; **76** Bettmann/Corbis; **78** *top* Raymond Gehman/Corbis; *bottom* Phillip Gould/Corbis; **79** David Reed/AP/ Wide World Photos; **82** *right* David Reed/AP/Wide World Photos; *left* Corbis.

Chapter 4

84–85 Copyright © Tom Jelen/Panoramic Images; **85** *bottom right* Dennis Brack/Black Star Publishing/ PictureQuest; *top left* Reuters NewMedia Inc./Corbis; *bottom left* Ed Kashi/Corbis; *top center* Copyright © Marianne Barcellona/TimePix; *center* Reuters NewMedia Inc./Corbis; *bottom center* Copyright © David Lassman/The Image Works; *top right* AFP/Corbis; **86** *top* The Granger Collection, New York; *bottom* Reuters NewMedia Inc./Corbis; **87** The Granger Collection, New York; **88** *bottom* Copyright © Nancy Richmond/The Image Works; *top* The Granger Collection, New York; **89** The Granger Collection, New York; **90** Reuters NewMedia Inc./Corbis; **92** *top left* NASA; *bottom right* European Space Agency; **93** *bottom right* European Space Agency; **93–94** NASA The Everett Collection; **94** The Everett Collection; **95** Art Resource, New York; **96** *bottom* Copyright © Topham/The Image Works; *top* The Granger Collection, New York; **100** *top* Tony Freeman; *bottom* Copyright © Rafael Macia/Photo Researchers; **101** *bottom* Copyright © Jim Corwin/Photo Researchers; **102** Copyright © Norbert Schwerine/The Image Works; **103** Teri Bloom; **104** *bottom* U.S. Treasury Department; **105** Kevin R. Morris/Bohemian Nomad PictureMakers/Corbis; **106** Copyright © Monika Graff/The Image Works; **108** *top* Corbis; *center* Spencer Grant III/Stock Boston/ PictureQuest; *bottom* Paul A. Souders/Corbis; **109** *bottom right* Culver Pictures; *top* Archive Photos/PictureQuest; *bottom left* Farrell Greham/Corbis; *center* Michael S. Yamashita/Corbis; **110** Tom Vano/Index Stock Imagery/PictureQuest; **111** *right* Terry Wild Studio; *left* William Folsom/Words and Pictures/PictureQuest; **114** *left* The Granger Collection, New York; *right* Terry Wild Studio; *center* The Everett Collection.

Chapter 5

116–117 Copyright © First Light/Panoramic Images; **117** *top* Canadian Museum of Civilization, image number S93-2826; **118** *top* Kevin R. Morris/Corbis; *bottom* Hockey Hall of Fame; **119** *all* The Granger Collection, New York; **120** Kevin R. Morris/Corbis; **121** Private Collection/Phillips, Fine Art Auctioneers, New York/The Bridgeman Art Library; **123** *top* Copyright © James Schwabel/Panoramic Images; **124** Copyright © SuperStock; **125** Copyright ©

Chapter 10

270–271 Copyright © James L. Stanfield/National Geographic Society Image Collection; 271 *top* Robert Harding Picture Library; 272 *top* Sef/Art Resource, New York; *bottom left, bottom right* Erich Lessing/Art Resource, New York; 273 Bill Ross/Corbis; 274 Arnulf Husmo/Stone/GettyImages; 275 Walter Bibikow/Index Stock Imagery/PictureQuest; 276 *top left* Jonathan Blair/Corbis; *top right* Eye Ubiquitous/Corbis; *bottom* Johan Elzenga/Stone/GettyImages; 278 *all* Greek Culture Ministry/AP/Wide World Photos; 279 HorreeZirkzee Produk/Corbis; 280 Foto Marburg/ Art Resource, New York; 281 Sef/Art Resource, New York; 282 *left* Nimatallah/Art Resource, New York; *right* Scala/ Art Resource, New York; 284 Copyright © Macduff Everton/The Image Works; 285 Erich Lessing/Art Resource, New York; 286 Giraudon/Art Resource, New York; 287 Erich Lessing/Art Resource, New York; 288 *top left* Jeff Rotman; *center* Scala/Art Resource, New York; *bottom right* O. Alamany and E. Vicens/Corbis; *bottom center* Bettmann/Corbis; 289 Erich Lessing/Art Resource, New York; 290 Art Resource, New York; 291 Reunion des Musées Nationaux/Art Resource, New York; 292 Catherine Karnow/Corbis; *spread* Musée de la Tapisserre, Bayoux, France/The Bridgeman Art Library; 293 *top* Jose Fuste Raga/eStockPhotography/PictureQuest; 294 Erich Lessing/Art Resource, New York; 295 *right* Dept. of the Environment, London/The Bridgeman Art Library; *left* The Granger Collection, New York; 296 *top left* Sef/Art Resource, New York; *bottom* Erich Lessing/Art Resource, New York; *top right* Jose Fuste Raga/eStockPhotography/PictureQuest.

Chapter 11

298–299 Bruno Barbey/Magnum/PictureQuest; 299 *top* The Granger Collection, New York; *center* Leonard L. T. Phodes/Animals Animals; 300 *center* Mary Evans Picture Library; *top* Reunion des Musées Nationaux/Art Resource, New York; *bottom* The Pierpont Morgan Library/Art Resource, New York; 301 The Granger Collection, New York; 302 Alinari/Art Resource, New York; 303 *top* Scott Gilchrist/Archivision.com; *bottom* Palazzo Medici-Riccardi, Florence, Italy/The Bridgeman Art Library; 304 *bottom* Scala/Art Resource, New York; *top* Reunion des Musées Nationaux/Art Resource, New York; 305 The Pierpont Morgan Library/Art Resource, New York; 306 Corbis; 307 Giraudon/Art Resource, New York; 309 North Wind Pictures; 310 Reunion des Musées Nationaux/Art Resource, New York; 313 AKG London; 314 *center* Scala/Art Resource, New York; *top* NASA; *bottom* Copyright © Will & Deni McIntyre/Photo Researchers; 315 The Granger Collection, New York; 316 Hulton-Deutsch Collection/Corbis; 317 Victoria & Albert Museum, London/Art Resource, New York; 318 *right* © Courtesy of the Estate of Ruskin Spear/Private Collection/Phillips, Fine Art Auctioneers, New York/The Bridgeman Art Library; *left* Giraudon/Art Resource, New York; 319 *top* Scala/Art Resource, New York; *bottom* Roger Tidman/Corbis; 320 Erich Lessing/Art Resource, New York; 321 Chuck Nacke/Woodfin Camp/PictureQuest; 322 Hulton-Deutsch Collection/Corbis; 324 *top left* North Wind Pictures; *bottom left* Alinari/Art Resource, New York; *bottom right* Hulton-Deutsch Collection/Corbis; *top right* © Courtesy of the Estate of Ruskin Spear/Private Collection/Phillips, Fine Art Auctioneers, New York/The Bridgeman Art Library; 325 The Library of Congress Website.

Chapter 12

326–327 Michael S. Yamashita/Corbis; 327 *top* Owen Franken/Corbis; 328 *top* Ralph White/Corbis; *bottom* Hulton|Archive/Getty Images; 329 Hulton|Archive/Getty Images; 331 *bottom* Hulton|Archive/Getty Images; *center* Gianni Dagli Orti/Corbis; *top* Mark Rykoff/Rykoff Collection/Corbis; 333 *right* Bettmann/Corbis; *left* Hulton|Archive/Getty Images; 334 *top* Hulton|Archive/Getty Images; *bottom* Art Young; 335 Hulton|Archive/Getty Images; 337 *bottom* Hulton|Archive/Getty Images; *top* Hulton-Deutsch Collection/Corbis; 339 Reprinted with the permission of the *St. Louis Post Dispatch*, 2002; 342 Paul Almasy/Corbis; 343 *bottom* Sovfoto/Eastfoto/PictureQuest; *top* Ralph White/ Corbis; 344 *bottom* Hulton|Archive/Getty Images; *top* Sovfoto/Eastfoto/PictureQuest; 345 Culver Pictures; 346 *bottom* Hulton|Archive/Getty Images; *center* The Kobal Collection; 347 Dave Bartruff/Corbis; 348 *right* Sovfoto/Eastfoto/PictureQuest; *left* Hulton|Archive/Getty Images; *center* Hulton-Deutsch Collection/Corbis; 349 Mandeville Special Collections at UCSD.

Chapter 13

350–351 Copyright © Brannhage/Premium/Panoramic Images; 351 *top* Sovfoto/Eastfoto; 352 *top* Premium Stock/Corbis; *bottom* Craig Aurness/Corbis; 353 Mark Rykoff/Corbis; 354 *left* NASA/AP/Wide World Photos; *right* Sovfoto/Eastfoto; 355 Copyright © Giuliano Bevilacqua/TimePix; 356 Bryn Colton/Corbis; 357 *top* Bettmann/Corbis; *bottom* AP/Wide World Photos; 358 Bojan Brecelj/Corbis; 360 David and Peter Turnley/Corbis; 362 Craig Aurness/Corbis; 363 Copyright © Bios (F. Gilson)/Peter Arnold; 364 Scala/Art Resource, New York; 366 Sovfoto/Eastfoto/PictureQuest; 367 *bottom* Hoa Qui/Index Stock Imagery/PictureQuest; *top* Premium Stock/Corbis; 368 AFP/Corbis; 369 Mike Mazzaschi/Stock Boston/PictureQuest; 370 S. Bavister/Robert Harding Picture Library; 371 Copyright © Malcolm S. Kirk/Peter Arnold; 372 *bottom* John Neubauer/Photo Edit/PictureQuest; *top right* Underwood & Underwood/Corbis; *top left* Bettmann/Corbis; 373 *top* Wolfgang Kaehler/Corbis; *left* Paul A. Souders/Corbis; *center* Roger Ressmeyer/Corbis; *bottom right* Academy of Natural Sciences of Philadelphia/Corbis; 374 *left* Bettmann/Corbis; *right* Premium Stock/Corbis; *center* David and Peter Turnley/Corbis.

Chapter 14

376–377 Alan Thornton/Stone/GettyImages; 377 *top* Mark A. Leman/Stone/GettyImages; 378 *top* Ted Spiegel/Corbis; *bottom* www.carpix.net; 379 *bottom right* Michael Neveux/Corbis; *center* AFP/Corbis; 382 *bottom* John Launois/Black Star Publishing/PictureQuest; *top* Copyright © Julian Nieman/Collections; 383 AFP/Corbis; 384 *right* Nik Wheeler/Corbis; *left* Ted Spiegel/Corbis; 385 Hans T. Dahlskog/Pressens Bild; 386 *bottom* AFP/Corbis; *top* Alex Farnsworth/The Image Works; 387 John Noble/Corbis; 388–389 Museo de Firenze Com'era, Florence, Italy/The Bridgeman Art Library; 390 *right* Bettmann/Corbis; *left* Corbis; 391 Bettmann/Corbis; 392 Robert Estall/Corbis;

© Bob Burch/Index Stock; *top center* Adam Woolfitt/Corbis; *bottom right* Copyright © Marc and Evelyne Bernheim/Woodfin Camp.

Chapter 18

520–521 Jason Lauré; **521** *top* Copyright © Robert Caputo/Aurora; **522** *top* Reuters NewMedia Inc./Corbis; *bottom* Owen Franken/Corbis; **523** *bottom* Bettmann/Corbis; *top* The Granger Collection, New York; **524** Hulton| Archive/Getty Images; **525** *bottom* Copyright © Griffith J. Davis/TimePix; **526** *top* Copyright © Kwaku Sakyi-Addo/Reuters/TimePix; *bottom* Jason Lauré; **527** AFP/Corbis; **528** *right* Edward R. Degginger/Bruce Coleman/ PictureQuest; *left* Tony Wilson-Bligh/Papilio/Corbis; **529** *top left* Kennan Ward/Corbis; *top center* Julian Calder/ Corbis; *bottom right* Werner Forman Archive/Art Resource, New York; **530** *right* Reuters NewMedia Inc./ Corbis; *left* AFP/Corbis; **531** *left* Owen Franken/Corbis; *right* Steve Jackson/Black Star Publishing/PictureQuest; **533** *bottom* Bonhams, London/The Bridgeman Art Library; *top* Jose Azel/Aurora/PictureQuest; **534** Chris Barton; **536** Werner Forman Archive/Art Resource, New York; **537** *right* Margaret Courtney-Clarke/Corbis; *left* AFP/Corbis; **538** *bottom* AFP/Corbis; *top* Wolfgang Kaehler/Corbis; *center* Richard A. Cooke/Corbis; **539** Werner Forman Archive/Art Resource, New York; **540** *left* Copyright © Kwaku Sakyi-Addo/Reuters/TimePix; *center* Jose Azel/Aurora/ PictureQuest; *right* AFP/Corbis.

Chapter 19

542–543 Jim Zuckerman/Corbis; **543** *top* The Durcell Team/Corbis; **544** *top* David and Peter Turnley/Corbis; *bottom* Thierry Geenen/Liaison/GettyImages; **545** Copyright © John Reader/Science Photo Library/Photo Researchers; **546** Courtesy, Kathy Schick & Nicholas Toth. Artwork by R. Freyman & N. Toth based on a drawing by Mary Leakey; **547** *right* Wolfgang Kaehler/Corbis; *left* Yann Arthus-Bertrand/Corbis; **548** *top* Bettmann/Corbis; *bottom* David and Peter Turnley/Corbis; **549** Copyright © Betty Press/Woodfin Camp/PictureQuest; **552** AFP/Corbis; **553** *left* Copyright © Grant Heilman/Grant Heilman Photography; *top center* Frank Lane Picture Agency/Corbis; *bottom right* Yann Arthus-Bertrand/Corbis; **554** David Samuel Robbins/Corbis; **555** Nubar Alexanian/Corbis; **556** Carmen Redondo/Corbis; **557** NASA; **558–559** Betty Press/Woodfin Camp/PictureQuest; **560** *bottom right* Lee Foster/Words and Pictures/PictureQuest; *top* *Photographs of South Africa* (Cape Town, 1894). Reprinted from Photo Publishing Co.; **561** *bottom* AFP/Corbis; *top* The Granger Collection, New York; **563** Pictor International/ PictureQuest; **564** Michele Burgess/Index Stock Imagery/PictureQuest; **565** *right* Corbis; *left* Copyright © William F. Campbell/TimePix; **566** *top* Yann Arthus-Bertrand/Corbis; *bottom* Charles and Josette Lenars/Corbis; **567** Thierry Geenen/Liaison/GettyImages; **568** *top left* Courtesy, Kathy Schick & Nicholas Toth. Artwork by R. Freyman & N. Toth based on a drawing by Mary Leakey; *top right* AFP/Corbis; *bottom left* Nubar Alexanian/Corbis; *bottom right* Charles and Josette Lenars/Corbis; **569** NASA.

UNIT SEVEN

570–571 John Lamb/Stone/GettyImages; **578** *left* Ann and Carl Purcell/PictureQuest; *center* Bettmann/Corbis; *right* Alison Wright/Corbis; **579** *center* James Strachan/Stone/GettyImages; *left* Lindsay Hebberd/Corbis; *right* AFP/Corbis.

Chapter 20

580–581 John Elk/Stone/GettyImages; **581** *top* Ann and Carl Purcell/PictureQuest; **582** *top* Reunion des Musées Nationaux/Art Resource, New York; *bottom* Corbis; **583** Hulton-Deutsch Collection/Corbis; **585** Copyright © RafiQur Rahman/Reuters/TimePix; **586** *bottom* James Strachan/Stone/GettyImages; *top* Ted Wood/Black Star Publishing/PictureQuest; **587** Paul Almasy/Corbis; **588** Charles O'Rear/Corbis; **589** Lindsay Hebberd/Corbis; **591** Sarnath, Uttar Pradesh, India/The Bridgeman Art Library; **592** *top center* Archivo Iconografico, S. A./Corbis; *top right* Paul Almasy/Corbis; *bottom center* Charles and Josette Lenars/Corbis; *bottom right* Corbis; **594** *all* Reunion des Musées Nationaux/Art Resource, New York; **595** *bottom* The Granger Collection, New York; *top* Chris Lisle/Corbis; **598** The Granger Collection, New York; **600** Jeremy Homer/Corbis; **603** *top right* Eye Ubiquitous/ Corbis; *all others* Charles and Josette Lenars/Corbis; **604** *center* The Granger Collection, New York; *right* Jeremy Homer/Corbis; *left* James Strachan/Stone/GettyImages.

Chapter 21

606–607 David Sutherland/Stone/GettyImages; **607** *top* Catherine Karnow/Corbis; **608** *top* Caroline Penn/Corbis; *bottom* Amma Clopet/Corbis; **609** Christie's Images, London/The Bridgeman Art Library; **610** *top* Ric Ergenbright/ Corbis; *bottom* Victoria & Albert Museum, London/The Bridgeman Art Library; **611** Hulton-Deutsch Collection/ Corbis; **612–613** Bettmann/Corbis; **615** Hulton|Archive/Getty Images; **616** Copyright © Robert Nickelsberg/ TimePix; **617** *bottom* Corbis; *top* Sena Vidanagama/AFP/Corbis; **618** *top* Sebastian D'Souza/AFP/Corbis; *bottom* Bettmann/Corbis; **619** Copyright © D. Banerjee/Dinodia Picture Agency; **620** *center* Lindsay Hebberd/Corbis; *top left* Baron/Hulton-Deutsch Collection/Corbis; *top right* Chris Lisle/Corbis; *bottom right* Richard Bickel/Corbis; **621** *center* Jeremy Homer/Corbis; *top* Diego Lezama Orezzoli/Corbis; *bottom* Victoria & Albert Museum, London/The Bridgeman Art Library; **622** Courtesy of AID; **623** Caroline Penn/Corbis; **624** *top* Adam Woolfitt/Corbis; *bottom* Lindsay Hebberd/Corbis; **626** Cris Haigh/Stone/GettyImages; **627** Amma Clopet/Corbis; **628** Surya Temple, Somnath, Bombay, India/Dinodia Picture Agency, Bombay India/Bridgeman Art Library; **629** Earl & Nazima Kowall/Corbis; **631** Bettmann/Corbis; **632** Paul Almasy/Corbis; **634** *left* Bettmann/Corbis; *right* Nik Wheeler/Corbis; **635** *left* Saeed Khan/AFP/Corbis; **636** *bottom left* Bettmann/Corbis; *top left* Sebastian D'Souza/AFP/ Corbis; *top right* Earl & Nazima Kowall/Corbis; *center* Lindsay Hebberd/Corbis; *bottom right* Nik Wheeler/Corbis; **638** Ric Ergenbright/Corbis; **639** Dave Bartruff/Corbis.

Chapter 22

640–641 Wolfgang Kaehler/Corbis; **641** *top* Alison Wright/Corbis; **642** *bottom* Ted Streshinsky/Photo 20-20/PictureQuest; *top* Copyright © Walter H. Hodge/Peter Arnold; **643** The British Library, London/The Bridgeman Art Library; **644** *left* Nik Wheeler/Corbis; *right* Copyright © TomPix/Peter Arnold; **645** *left* AFP/Corbis; *right* Copyright © Jose Azel/Woodfin Camp; **646** Hulton|Archive/Getty Images; **647** AFP/Corbis; **648** *bottom left* Brian A. Vikander/Corbis; *bottom right* David Samuel Robbins/Corbis; **649** Brian A. Vikander/Corbis; **650** Hulton|Archive/Getty Images; **651** Ted Streshinsky/Photo 20-20/PictureQuest; **652** *top* Pictor International/PictureQuest; *bottom* Copyright © Walter H. Hodge/Peter Arnold; **653** *right* Kevin R. Morris/Corbis; *left* Chris Rainier/Corbis; **655** Bettmann/Corbis; **656** Charles Bonnay/Black Star Publishing/PictureQuest; **657** *left* Bettmann/Corbis; *right* Dennis Brack/Black Star Publishing/PictureQuest; **658** Copyright © Dan Gair/Index Stock; **659** Hulton|Archive/Getty Images; **660** *left* Hulton|Archive/Getty Images; *center* Chris Rainier/Corbis; *right* Hulton|Archive/Getty Images.

UNIT EIGHT

662–663 Copyright © Panoramic Images; **670** *left* Penny Tweedie/Corbis; *center* James L. Amos/Corbis; *right* Reuters NewMedia Inc./Corbis; **671** *left* Keren Su/Stone/GettyImages; *center* Copyright © Bill Lai/The Image Works; *right* Christopher Arnesen/Stone/GettyImages.

Chapter 23

672–673 Copyright © Eric Crichton/Bruce Coleman/PictureQuest; **673** *top* Liu Liqun/Corbis; **674** *bottom* Scala/Art Resource, New York; *top* Dallas and John Heaton/Corbis; **675** Bettmann/Corbis; **676** David Samuel Robbins/Corbis; **677** Dean Conger/Corbis; **678** Charles Rotkin/Corbis; **679** Michael S. Yamashita/Corbis; **681** Giraudon/Art Resource, New York; **682** Erich Lessing/Art Resource, New York; **683** Dallas and John Heaton/Corbis; **684** *right* Reunion des Musées Nationaux/Art Resource, New York; *left* North Wind Pictures; **685** Reunion des Musées Nationaux/Art Resource, New York; **686** Reunion des Musées Nationaux/Art Resource, New York; **688–689** Corbis; **688** *bottom* Robert Pearcy/Animals Animals; *spread* Corbis; **690** Culver Pictures; **691** *top* Copyright © Bill Lai/The Image Works; *bottom* Craig Lovell/Corbis; **692** *top* Tsukioka Yoshitoshi/ Asian Art and Archaeology, Inc./*bottom* Michael S. Yamashita/Corbis; **693** Scala/Art Resource, New York; **694** N. Blythe/Robert Harding Picture Library; **696** *left* Charles Rotkin/Corbis; *center* Reunion des Musées Nationaux/Art Resource, New York; *right* Copyright © Bill Lai/The Image Works.

Chapter 24

698–699 Paul W. Liebhardt/Corbis; **699** *top* Wolfgang Kaehler/Corbis; **700** *bottom* Bettmann/Corbis; *top* Jay Dickman/Corbis; **701** Bettmann/Corbis; **702** Wolfgang Kaehler/Corbis; **703** *all* Bettmann/Corbis; **704** Roger Ressmeyer/Corbis; **705** Sovfoto/Eastfoto/PictureQuest; **706** John Wang/PhotoDisc/GettyImages; **708** AFP/Corbis; **709** Jay Dickman/Corbis; **710** David and Peter Turnley/Corbis; **712** David Samuel Robbins/Corbis; **713** *bottom left* Keren Su/Stone/GettyImages; *top* Travelpix/FPG/GettyImages; *bottom right* Yann Layma/Stone/GettyImages; **714** Vito Palmisano/Stone/GettyImages; **716** Reuters NewMedia Inc./Corbis; **717** *top* Brian A. Vikander/Corbis; *bottom* Vince Streano/Corbis; **720** Bettmann/Corbis; **721** Christopher Arnesen/Stone/GettyImages; **722** Bettmann/Corbis; **723** Courtesy of the U.S. Naval Academy Museum; **724** *top* Corbis; *bottom* Jed & Kaoru Share/Corbis; **726** Michael S. Yamashita/Corbis; **728** *bottom left* Roger Ressmeyer/Corbis; *bottom center* Jay Dickman/Corbis; *center* Keren Su/Stone/GettyImages; *top* Christopher Arnesen/Stone/GettyImages; *bottom right* Michael S. Yamashita/Corbis.

Chapter 25

730–731 Copyright © John Eastcott/YVA Momatiuk/The Image Works; **731** *top* Penny Tweedie/Corbis; **732** *top* Daniel Aubry; *bottom* Reuters NewMedia Inc./Corbis; **733** Alexander Turnbull Library, Wellington, N. Z./The Bridgeman Art Library; **734** *center* Daniel Aubry; *top* Penny Tweedie/Corbis; *bottom* Werner Forman/Corbis; **735** James L. Amos/Corbis; **736** Royalty Free/Corbis; **737** Reuters NewMedia Inc./Corbis; **739** *top* Penny Tweedie/Corbis; *bottom* Quadrillion/Corbis; **742** *bottom left* Galen Rowell/Corbis; *top right* Richard Hamilton Smith/Corbis; *top left* Penny Tweedie/Corbis; **743** *top* Walter Hodges/Corbis; *bottom* Scott Faulker/Corbis; *top center* Felicia Martinez/PhotoEdit/PictureQuest; **744** *left* James L. Amos/Corbis; *right* Quadrillion/Corbis.

The War on Terrorism

US2 Copyright © AFP/Corbis; *inset* Copyright © John Annerino/TimePix; **US3** *top* MapQuest.com; *bottom* Susan Walsh/AP/Wide World Photos; **US4** *left* AP/Wide World Photos; *right* MapQuest.com; **US5** USA TODAY®; **US6–US7** MapQuest.com; **US6** *inset* Copyright © Reuters NewMedia Inc./Corbis; **US7** *top inset* Katsumi Ksashara/AP/Wide World Photos; *bottom inset* Sayyid Azim/AP/Wide World Photos; **US9** *left* AP/Wide World Photos; **US10** USA TODAY®; *top inset* AP/Wide World Photos; *middle inset* Al-Jazeera/AP/Wide World Photos; *bottom inset* AP/Wide World Photos; **US11** *top* Copyright © David Hume Kennerly/Corbis Sygma; *bottom* MapQuest.com; **US12** Copyright © Jeff Christensen/Reuters/TimePix; *inset* Copyright © Greg Mathieson/MAI/TimePix; **US13** USA TODAY®; **US14** *left* Copyright © Digital Stock/Corbis; *top inset* Copyright © Kent Wood/Photo Researchers; *bottom* FBI/AP/Wide World Photos; *bottom inset* Justice Department/AP/Wide World Photos; **US15** Copyright © Eric Draper/The White House/TimePix.

McDougal Littell Inc. has made every effort to locate the copyright holders for the images used in this book and to make full acknowledgment for their use. Omissions brought to our attention will be corrected in subsequent editions.